KU-141-277

Contents

568932

302.234 HOW

ONE WEEK LOAN

0096021323

Understanding
COMMUNITY
MEDIA

EEN WERKDAG

For Debora

Understanding
COMMUNITY
MEDIA

Edited by
Kevin Howley

Los Angeles | London | New Delhi
Singapore | Washington DC

Copyright © 2010 by SAGE Publications, Inc.

All rights reserved. No part of this book may be reproduced or utilized in any form or by any means, electronic or mechanical, including photocopying, recording, or by any information storage and retrieval system, without permission in writing from the publisher.

For information:

SAGE Publications, Inc.
2455 Teller Road
Thousand Oaks,
   California 91320
E-mail: order@sagepub.com

SAGE Publications Ltd.
1 Oliver's Yard
55 City Road
London EC1Y 1SP
United Kingdom

SAGE Publications India Pvt. Ltd.
B 1/I 1 Mohan Cooperative
   Industrial Area
Mathura Road, New Delhi 110 044
India

SAGE Publications Asia-Pacific Pte. Ltd.
33 Pekin Street #02-01
Far East Square
Singapore 048763

Printed in the United States of America

Library of Congress Cataloging-in-Publication Data

Understanding community media / editor, Kevin Howley.
     p. cm.
Includes bibliographical references and index.
ISBN 978-1-4129-5904-9 (cloth)
ISBN 978-1-4129-5905-6 (pbk.)
   1. Local mass media. I. Howley, Kevin.

P96.L62U63 2010
302.23—dc22   2009014358

Printed on acid-free paper.

09   10   11   12   13   10 9 8 7 6 5 4 3 2 1

Acquiring Editor:	Todd R. Armstrong
Editorial Assistant:	Aja Baker
Production Editor:	Sarah K. Quesenberry
Copy Editor:	QuADS Prepress (P) Ltd.
Proofreader:	Wendy Jo Dymond
Indexer:	Sheila Bodell
Typesetter:	C&M Digitals (P) Ltd.
Cover Designer:	Bryan Fishman
Marketing Manager:	Jennifer Reed Banando

SOUTHAMPTON SOLENT
UNIVERSITY LIBRARY

SUPPLIER   DAWSON

ORDER No

DATE   04 / 12 / 09

List of Tables, Figures, and Photos

Tables

Figures

Photos

Preface

When I first met Kevin Howley at a 2004 Symposium on Media Studies and the liberal arts, I was struck by the originality and significance of his research on community media. Howley had just completed his book *Community Media: People, Places, and Communications Technologies,* and as he spoke of his broader research agenda, I was reminded of some of the big questions that initially drew me to media studies two decades earlier, questions about media, representation, power, participation, and identity.

On its publication, *Community Media* quickly jumped to the top of my reading list, and it has been required reading for my advanced media studies students ever since. Howley has a rare capacity to make connections between theory and practice: He can both see how particular cases illuminate broader processes and how social theory helps identify productive questions about specific media objects. At the same time, Howley has experience working with various community media projects, which gives him valuable practical knowledge that enhances his scholarly work on community media.

All this makes Howley an ideal person to conceptualize and assemble a much-needed collection on the current state of community media. So I was not surprised by the richness and depth of this new reader, *Understanding Community Media.* As you will see, this edited collection is a rare gem, one that will stand out among bookshelves of edited volumes in media studies for its clarity and coherence, the depth of the questions it explores, and the range of the cases it considers.

Perhaps most important, though, is the sheer significance of the subject matter this collection treats; *Understanding Community Media* shines a light on nagging issues that we, in media studies, have neglected far too long.

We've known for a very long time that mainstream, commercial media, while relentlessly visible, are only part of media culture. A whole range of media objects, practices, and experiences exist alongside, often in critical relation to, commercial media. While media studies scholarship has long nodded in the direction of these alternative media forms—with some outstanding studies that have helped nurture the field, including Ron Jacobs's *Race, Media, and the Crisis of Civil Society,* Deirdre Boyle's *Subject to Change,* and Howley's *Community Media*—the study of community media (or alternative, independent, underground, radical media—our inability to name these media is a sign of our general inattention) has remained marginal. This persistent marginality has real costs. With new forms of digital media emerging— media that may have some capacity to challenge, if not replace, traditional forms of media—the lack of a well-developed body of critical research and theory has the unfortunate consequence of limiting our collective understanding of what's at stake and what's possible.

The agenda for media studies is quite clear at this point: We need to move beyond the simple platitudes that appear in so much of the buzz about new media and look carefully and critically at the structure and forms of community media, how people create and use such media, and how community media interact with major corporate media. In other words, we need a theoretically informed and empirically rich media studies of community media. Anything less, at this historical moment, would be more than simply a missed opportunity but would challenge the fundamental relevance of media studies in the 21st century.

Understanding Community Media is more than a productive starting point. It is an investment in our field's commitment to the study of the wide range of objects and practices, experiences and identities that are part of the community media landscape. Throughout this volume, Howley and the contributors take seriously the complexity of what it means to *understand* their object of study. As a result, there are no simple narratives or easy answers here; instead, the contributors challenge us to think with them about how and why community media might matter, and what it means to put community media at the center of our scholarly inquiry.

It is also worth noting that several specific strengths of this collection set it apart from many other edited collections. The thematic organization of *Understanding Community Media* is, itself, an important contribution, as it helpfully articulates key dimensions of the field. Even more important, Howley has written a series of substantive introductions to the seven parts, identifying the key questions and how each specific contribution fits in to the broader picture. I found the introductory essays for the parts most closely aligned with my own work—"Civil Society and the Public Sphere" and "Community Media and Social Movements"—to be refreshingly clear and challenging. These part introductions will provide a treasure trove of ideas and questions for seasoned scholars and graduate students alike. In addition, this collection is genuinely global, with chapters that focus on media in a stunning range of settings. This diverse collection of case studies is organized so effectively that each part remains coherent, with each set of chapters reflecting on a core set of questions. As a result, the global dimension on display here help open up a productive cross-national dialogue about the meanings and possibilities of community media.

The variety of community media out there— some long standing, others still emerging— should be a central focus for media studies. *Understanding Community Media* moves us a significant step forward by giving us a series of valuable theoretical frameworks and rich case studies that help map the contours of a field that will only become more significant in the years ahead. This collection deserves our attention and Howley our gratitude, both for the work contained here and for the new questions and projects it will undoubtedly inspire.

—William Hoynes
Vassar College
March 2009

Acknowledgments

I want to express my sincere gratitude to all the contributors for their efforts. It has been a rare privilege to work with such a talented and committed group of scholars and writers. And at the risk of being presumptuous, I believe we are all indebted to the community media workers and organizations who inspired and supported our research efforts. On behalf of myself and my contributors, I'd also like to thank the following reviewers for their helpful comments and suggestions: Rosemary Day, Mary Immaculate College, University of Limerick; Carlos Fontes, Worcester State College; Eric Freedman, Florida Atlantic University; Josh Greenberg, Carleton University; William Hoynes, Vassar College; Robert Huesca, Trinity University; Fred Johnson, University of Massachusetts, Boston; Peter M. Lewis, London School of Economics & Political Science; Rashmi Luthre, University of Michigan, Dearborn; Vicki Mayer, Tulane University; Clemencia Rodriguez, The University of Oklahoma; and Susan Ryan, The College of New Jersey. Finally, to my editor, Todd Armstrong; his assistants, Aja Baker and Katie Grim; production manager, Sarah Quesenberry; and all their colleagues at SAGE, I offer my heartfelt thanks for your encouragement, professionalism, and skill in bringing this work to fruition.

Introduction

Kevin Howley

On August 29, 2005, WQRZ-LP, a non-profit, low-power FM radio station located in Bay St. Louis, Mississippi, was one of only four radio stations between Mobile, Alabama, and New Orleans, Louisiana, operating in the immediate aftermath of Hurricane Katrina. WQRZ-LP provided vital emergency communication—including information related to evacuation procedures, search and rescue operations, and distribution points for food and water—for area residents when other local media outlets had gone silent. Nine months after the storm, WQRZ-LP was still the only broadcaster serving Bay St. Louis, Waveland, Diamondhead, and other devastated communities in Hancock County, Mississippi.

Between 1999 and 2002, hundreds of children, fourth-generation Palestinians living in refugee camps in Lebanon and the Occupied Territories, took part in a participatory media project sponsored by Save the Children UK called Eye to Eye. The program offered photography workshops to Palestinian children and encouraged them to tell their stories and share their perspectives through words and pictures. Photographs and accompanying text documenting the children's lives, their surroundings, and their daily experiences were exhibited locally and shared with students in the United Kingdom and elsewhere, via an interactive Web site.

Since 2002, media activists have appropriated broadcast television technology and unused portions of the electromagnetic spectrum to create microbroadcast stations in neighborhoods throughout Italy. By combining "old technologies," such as analog video cameras and TV antennas, with "new technologies," such as computer servers and broadband Internet connections, microbroadcasters have fashioned a nationwide network of street television stations. Building on a rich tradition of radical media in Italy, the so-called telestreet movement attempts to reconfigure the relationship between the Italian people, local neighborhoods, and the medium of television.

These brief cases illustrate different facets of the fundamental relationship between communication and community. For instance, WQRZ-LP was instrumental in helping the residents of Hancock County sustain and rebuild their community in a time of crisis. The Eye to Eye project raised public awareness of the thoughts, feelings, and experience of Palestinian children—a marginalized group among a marginalized people—within their own communities as well as for far-flung audiences across the globe. Finally, the telestreet movement reveals that the institutional structures and technological apparatus of television are rather flexible and can be reoriented to serve the distinctive needs and interests of local communities. Thus, despite the geographic, cultural, and technological diversity of these initiatives—and the varied motives and aspirations behind them—each can be said to represent a form of community media.

Understanding Community Media examines how, why, and to what ends communities make use of communication and information technologies. The term *understanding* is used in the title to indicate that community media is a complex and dynamic object of study—one that demands critical scrutiny to fully comprehend the range of structures and practices, experiences and meanings, associated with community media. The word "understanding" is also used to signal the fact that, until quite recently, community media have been somewhat misunderstood and undervalued within academic circles and among the general populace.

The phrase "community media" encompasses a range of community-based activities intended to supplement, challenge, or change the operating principles, structures, financing, and cultural forms and practices associated with dominant media. This rather generic definition is purposeful insofar as it accommodates a diverse set of initiatives—community radio, participatory video, independent publishing, and online communication, to name but a few—operating in a variety of social, political, and geocultural settings. Indeed, the *context* in which community media operate plays a decisive role in shaping and informing these disparate efforts (Tacchi, Slater, & Lewis, 2003).

For example, in the United States, where commercial interests have long dominated the media system, community media oftentimes operate as a noncommercial alternative to profit-oriented media industries (Halleck, 2002). Conversely, in Western Europe, Canada, and Australia—where public service broadcasters enjoyed monopoly status throughout much of the 20th century—community media challenge the public broadcaster's construction of a unified, homogeneous national identity by addressing the diverse tastes and interests of ethnic, racial, and cultural minorities that are often ignored, silenced, or otherwise misrepresented by national broadcasters (Berrigan, 1977).

Community media are also common in postcolonial societies across Latin America and Africa. In this context, participatory communication strategies and techniques are used to help stimulate social, political, and economic development (Berrigan, 1979). And in societies where state-run media was commonplace, community media emerged in direct opposition to repressive

regimes and the propaganda associated with "official" media (Ibrahim, 2000; O'Connor, 1990). Of course, these motives are not mutually exclusive; for instance, even in societies with constitutional protections of freedom of speech and expression, oppositional and radical media are quite common (Downing, 2001).

All this is to suggest that community media assumes many forms, and takes on different meanings, depending on the "felt need" of the community and the resources and opportunities available to local populations at a particular time and place. With this in mind, *Understanding Community Media* aims to reveal the value and importance of community media in an era of global communication. In doing so, this volume seeks to promote greater comprehension of, and appreciation for, community media's significance in the social, economic, political, and cultural lives of people around the world.

This introductory chapter proceeds with a succinct discussion of community media's relevance to the issues and concerns taken up by media studies. The implicit assumption here is that community media is a significant, if largely overlooked, feature of contemporary media culture; as such, it warrants scholarly attention. In addition to providing a rationale for the academic study of community media, we briefly consider broader intellectual concerns and social-political issues raised by the growth and development of a global community media sector. As we shall see, community media hold enormous potential for interrogating the forces and conditions associated with globalization. For instance, the relationship between the struggle for communication rights and the emergence of global civil society is especially germane to community media studies. Furthermore, community media provide an exceptional site of analysis to consider the changing dynamics of *place* in an era marked by transnational flows of people, culture, capital, and technology.

Taken together, these insights help situate this collection of original articles in relation to previous work on "participatory," "alternative," "citizens," and, of course, "community media." As a number of critics have observed, the proliferation of terms and analytic categories has complicated the study of community media (Fuller, 2007; Howley, 2005; Rennie, 2006). Nevertheless, rather than attempt to make hard-and-fast distinctions between these categories, contributors to this volume recognize the explanatory value of each of these terms insofar as they yield distinct yet related insights into different facets of community-based media. Put differently, this collection attempts to capture the *multidimensional* character of community media through an examination of a geographically diverse field of countervailing structures, practices, and orientations to dominant media.

Why Study Community Media?

The global dimensions of community media reveal that the struggle to create media systems that are at once relevant and accountable to local communities resonates with disparate peoples and across different cultures. This realization has stimulated considerable interest in the theory and practice of community media. Before addressing this growing body of literature directly, we should briefly consider community media's relevance to the key issues and debates taken up by communication and media studies. Only then can we productively engage with the insights, perspectives, and developments of the emergent field of community media studies.

As a field of inquiry, media studies examine the influence and impact of media and communication on human culture and society. In this vein, media studies consider how communication technologies and communicative forms and practices affect community structures, social and economic relations, and political processes. The study of community media likewise interrogates these issues. Significantly, the study of community media also provides an opportunity to turn this formulation on its head. That is to say, community media studies examine how, through community organizing and collective action, local communities affect media structures, behaviors, and performance. To borrow media scholar Roger Silverstone's (1999) useful phrase, community media represent a fertile site to examine "what media do as well as what we do with media" (p. 2). As an object of study, then, community media serve as an exceptional vehicle to explore the way local populations create media texts, practices, and institutions to serve their distinctive needs and interests.

Political Economy and Cultural Studies

The study of community media foregrounds one of the central concerns of contemporary media studies: namely, the issue of media ownership and control. Working under the rubric of political economy, scholars have demonstrated how methods of financing, organizational structures, and the regulatory environment in which media institutions operate have important and far-reaching consequences on media behaviors and performance (Golding & Murdock, 1991; Herman & Chomsky, 1994). Political economists are particularly interested in documenting the detrimental impact privately owned, advertising-supported, and profit-oriented media systems have on cultural production and democratic processes. Indeed, in an era marked by the decline of public service broadcasting on the one hand and the ascendancy of corporate-controlled media on the other, the political economy of media has enormous implications for the character and conduct of public discourse on the local, national, and, given the scale and scope of transnational media corporations, global levels (Croteau & Hoynes, 2006).

Community media operate in sharp contrast to their corporate counterparts. For instance, in terms of financing, community media rely on donations, underwriting and limited advertising, grant funding, in-kind contributions, and other noncommercial forms of support. In this way, community media are insulated from the direct and indirect influence advertisers exert over media form and content. Likewise, the organizational structure of community media is far less hierarchical than either corporate or public service media (Carpentier, Lie, & Servaes, 2003). More often than not, community media operate with relatively small paid staffs, relying instead on volunteers to perform the tasks and functions associated with media production and distribution. And, like other voluntary associations, community media encourage participatory decision-making structures and practices of the sort that are antithetical to either commercial or public service media outlets.

From a political economic perspective, then, community media represent a significant intervention into the structural inequalities and power imbalances of contemporary media systems. By providing local populations with access to the means of communication, community media offer a modest, but vitally important corrective to the unprecedented concentration of media ownership that undermines local cultural expression, privatizes the channels of public communication, and otherwise threatens the prospects for democratic self-governance.

Informed by political economic perspectives, ideological criticism examines the role media plays in reinforcing and legitimating systems of domination and control. For scholars interested in ideological critique, media take center stage in the process of legitimating and naturalizing structural inequalities and hierarchies of power and prestige. From this perspective, media form and content do the important ideological work of supporting the status quo, glossing over the contradictions of the prevailing socioeconomic order, and otherwise taming or neutralizing dissent (Gitlin, 1982).

In contrast to corporate and public service media, community media organizations often align themselves with, and emerge from, counterhegemonic struggles. In terms of ideological critique, then, community media represent a field to examine hegemonic processes at work at the local level. Indeed, by providing a vehicle for individuals and groups routinely marginalized by dominant media to express their hopes and fears, their aspirations and frustrations, community media can serve as a forum for oppositional politics and ideological perspectives that are inconsistent and incompatible with the interests of dominant media.

For scholars working from a cultural studies perspective, then, community media provide ample opportunity to examine how media are embedded in the everyday lived experience of so-called ordinary people. Likewise, cultural studies' emphasis on "active audiences," negotiated readings of media texts, and the innovative and creative ways audiences resist ideological manipulation is especially suitable to academic analyses of community media (Howley, 2002).

Keen to complicate earlier assumptions regarding media effects, including the ideological force and influence of media texts, cultural scholars have focused attention on individual and collective agency in light of structural constraints and power imbalances (e.g., Ang, 1985). Insofar as community media undermine notions of the passive audience by providing community members with the technical skills and infrastructure to become media makers, community media represent palpable expressions of organized, local resistance to ideological manipulation and repressive regimes of state and corporate power. In short, community media embody what cultural theorists describe as the "emancipatory potential" (Enzensberger, 2000) of media technologies and techniques.

Media Power

The operation of media power figures prominently in the study of alternative, citizens,' and community media (Couldry & Curran, 2003; Langlois & Dubois, 2005; Lewis & Jones, 2006). For instance, dominant media habitually misrepresent or underrepresent individuals and groups based on distinctions of race, class, gender, ethnicity, and lifestyle. For those with little or no access to mainstream media outlets, community media provide resources and opportunities for marginalized groups to tell their own stories, in their own voices, and using their own distinctive idioms (Rodriguez, 2001). In doing so, community media are instrumental in protecting and defending cultural identity while simultaneously challenging inaccurate, prejudicial, and otherwise unflattering media representations. Thus, through the production and dissemination of media texts that assert and affirm cultural identities, and otherwise challenge the ghettoization (Downing & Husband, 2005) of marginalized groups, community media make visible cultural differences in discursive as well as social space.

Media power is also exercised in terms of relaying and representing formal as well as informal political processes. Nowhere is this more evident than in the realm of news and public affairs reporting. In highly mediated societies, news organizations play a decisive role in setting the political agenda, framing the terms of public debate, and shaping public opinion. News, therefore, is not a simple reflection of historical reality; rather, it is a complex system through which we attempt to understand and make sense of the world. More to the point, as Philip Schlesinger (quoted in Gitlin, 1980) observes, "News is the exercise of power over the *interpretation of reality* [italics added]" (p. 251). All too often, commercial and public service media unproblematically relay elite consensus in the interpretation of reality, thereby narrowing the range of debate and limiting public participation in deliberative processes (Hall, Critcher, Jefferson, Clarke, & Roberts, 1978).

Embracing innovative practices variously described as "alternative," "participatory," and "citizens'" journalism, community media disrupt the codes and conventions associated with contemporary journalistic practice (Harcup, 2003; Huesca, 1996). For example, community journalism eschews objective journalism's uncritical reliance on official sources. Instead, community journalism features the voices, opinions, and perspectives of ordinary people, not just those in positions of power and authority. In its more radical formulation, community journalism challenges the category of "professional" journalism altogether by adopting the philosophy associated with the Indymedia movement: "Everyone is a witness, everyone is a journalist" (Independent Media Center, 2004).

Equally important, community journalism addresses the shortcomings of contemporary journalistic practice. In an effort to reduce costs and increase profit margins, mainstream news outlets have "downsized" newsroom staffs and all but abandoned local newsgathering and investigative reporting. In the process, news organizations have grown dependent on tabloid journalism, celebrity gossip, and prepackaged news items. Not surprisingly, as journalistic standards and values deteriorate so too does public confidence in news workers and institutions. In contrast, community journalists, often working on shoestring budgets, draw on the talents and inclinations of concerned citizens in an effort to provide local communities with useful, relevant information of the sort that enhances and expands community communication (Forde, Foxwell, & Meadows, 2003). Doing so, community journalism revitalizes the public sphere and counteracts the apathy, disenfranchisement, and depoliticization cultivated by lackluster press performance. In short, community media provide opportunities and resources for local publics to reassert journalism's place in the conversation of democracy.

The History of the Future

As the preceding discussion illustrates, the study of community media corresponds with the core concerns of media studies. Adopting media studies' familiar tripartite analysis (e.g., Devereux, 2007), community media studies examine the production, content, and reception of media texts—albeit within a setting that has received surprisingly little academic attention. By the same token, community media offer new points of entry into other aspects of media studies.

For instance, community media represent a blind spot in media historiography. As Rodger Streitmatter (2001) argues, historians frequently overlook the contributions of newspapers operating outside the mainstream of American social and political thought. Furthermore, media scholars seldom acknowledge the contributions of alternative, citizens' and community media in the realms of cultural production, oppositional politics, and public policy. With a few notable exceptions—Jeff Land's (1999) analysis of the Pacifica radio network, Chris Atton and James Hamilton's (2008) history of alternative journalism, and Ralph Engelman's (1990, 1996) work on the development of public access television in the United States readily come to mind—alternative and community media are underdeveloped areas of media history.

Just as the study of community media can complicate and inform our understanding of the past, community media studies are likewise an effective, if underappreciated vehicle to evaluate current and future developments in the technologies and techniques of media production, distribution, and reception. For instance, popular and academic interest in the interactive, collaborative, and participatory potential of social networking technologies and related developments associated with Web 2.0 can be enhanced with insights gleaned from the study of community media. After all, notions of "access" and "participation," so thoroughly embedded in the discourse of "new media," are long-standing concepts in the literature on community media (Berrigan, 1979).

Furthermore, as Ellie Rennie (2006) has argued, community media prefigures what has been described as "participatory culture" (Jenkins, 1992) not only in terms of peoples' use of media technologies but also, significantly, in relation to the policy issues raised by new media and the potential these technologies hold for enhancing public participation in political processes and cultural production. In this light, the marginalization of community media in policy studies has enormous implications for the current state and future prospects of a sustainable independent media sector at the local, national, regional, and international

levels. Indeed, inattention and neglect of community media within policy-making circles effectively bars elements of civil society (volunteer associations, clubs, religious organizations, advocacy groups, trade unions, etc.) from fully participating in "legitimate" or "sanctioned" media production and distribution—hence the emergence of "pirate" broadcasting and other forms of "illegal" or "clandestine" media (e.g., Sakolsky & Dunifer, 1998; Soley & Nichols, 1986).

Typically, communication policy debates revolve around a false dichotomy between state-sponsored media systems on one hand and market-based approaches to communication policy on the other (McChesney, 2004). For media activists, community organizers, and others interested in structural reform of existing media systems, community media represent a "third way" for regulators and policy analysts to consider mechanisms that promote the public interest while accommodating commercial and profit-oriented approaches to media and cultural production (Girard, 1992).

As we have seen, community media provide scholars with an opportunity to examine a dynamic if somewhat uncharted aspect of contemporary media culture. Insofar as it represents an object of study, then, community media not only invite but also demand critical inquiry of the sort associated with the finest traditions of media and communication studies (Day, 2009). And as a social practice that is at once local, cross-cultural, and transnational, community media encourage us to consider broader issues and concerns related to globalization and the struggle for communicative democracy in the 21st century.

Communication Rights and Global Civil Society

The advent of satellite communication in the 1960s ushered in an era of unprecedented global communication between distant people and places. For some observers, most notably those representing the scientific, military, and corporate interests of the English-speaking world, these developments signaled the beginning of a new era of international cooperation, security, and prosperity. Others, particularly people from "the global South," were far less sanguine. These critics expressed concerns over the imposition of Western and, more specifically, Anglo-American values and ideologies—individualism, modernity, and consumerism—on non-Western societies that threatened traditional ways of life and undermined the sovereignty of newly independent nations.

In the absence of legal and structural arrangements that would ensure equal access to satellite communication technologies, address the imbalance in news flows between the North and South, and otherwise work to democratize communication within and between nation-states, representatives from so-called developing societies feared a new form of domination described as "cultural imperialism" (Schiller, 1976). In this context, the struggle to define, secure, and preserve "communication rights" became an issue of global proportions.

Throughout the 1970s, governments debated the question of communication rights in the United Nations and other international bodies. Although Cold War politics confounded these deliberations, an emerging consensus supported democratic-minded reform of global communication systems Eventually, these deliberations produced the McBride Report: the United Nations Educational, Scientific and Cultural Organization (UNESCO) sponsored study that recommended structural reform of the global communication infrastructure (UNESCO, 1980). Predictably, perhaps, both the United States and the United Kingdom withdrew from UNESCO in protest over the reports findings and conclusions. This development set the stage, throughout the 1980s and 1990s, for the ascendancy of neoliberalism—a regulatory philosophy that advocates market-based approaches to economic, social, and cultural policy—and all but ensured that the debate over communication rights at the inter-governmental level would put the interests of multinational corporations above those of individuals, communities, and societies.

In the intervening years, nongovernmental organizations (NGOs), community organizers, academics, media workers, and other civil society groups have taken up the cause of communication rights in a number of international venues, most recently the World Summit on the Information Society (WSIS). Addressing a range of issues, civil society groups amplified and expanded popular understandings of communication rights (Civil Society Declaration to the World Summit on the Information Society, 2004). According to one such group, the World Association of Christian Communicators (WACC, 2006), communication rights

> go beyond mere freedom of opinion and expression, to include areas such as democratic media governance, participation in one's own culture, linguistic rights, rights to enjoy the fruits of human creativity, to education, to privacy, peaceful assembly, and self-determination. These are questions of inclusion and exclusion, of quality and accessibility. In short, they are questions of human dignity. (p. 67)

Thus, civil society groups positioned communication rights within a broader framework of human rights articulated in various international agreements and conventions such as the Universal Declaration of Human Rights (UDHR). This strategy has been instrumental in garnering broad-based support for an emerging global media reform movement and encouraging unprecedented popular participation in global communication policy debates (Calabrese, 2004). Nevertheless, as media activist Sean O'Siochrú (2003) observes, the codification of communication rights in international agreements—let alone widespread recognition that communication is a basic human need as well as a fundamental human right—is no guarantee that these rights are respected or upheld within and between nation-states.

> In theory, many of the key aspects of communication rights are included in legally binding Treaties . . . to which virtually every government is a signatory. The practice on the

ground, however, is very different. All of these Treaties are virtually unenforceable, lacking the instruments to compel compliance by signatory states. They provide little more than moral and political guidance, too often ignored. (p. 23)

In the post-9/11 environment, the struggle to secure and maintain communication rights takes on an even greater sense of urgency. Indeed, the crackdown on political dissent coupled with illegal wiretapping and other forms of electronic surveillance represent an ominous form of collusion between state and corporate interests. In this light, civil society assumes a tremendous responsibility for ensuring that communication rights are upheld at a moment when these rights, and a host of civil liberties, are under assault across the globe.

Place Matters

As the previous discussion illustrates, developments in communication and information technologies are deeply implicated in the process of globalization. To be sure, modern communication systems enable geographically dispersed people to interact with a sense of intimacy and immediacy as never before. In an era of instantaneous worldwide communication, it is easy to see why some people might think place is losing its significance in human experience.

For instance, media theorist Joshua Meyrowitz (1986) makes a compelling argument that modern communication systems create new realms of social interaction that render place inconsequential, if not irrelevant. There is, of course, an element of truth to such claims. Consider, for example, the "placeless" interaction of telephone conversations or online chat sessions between two people living in different parts of the world. Likewise, satellite technologies allow us to witness events—football matches, political rallies, and, in the case of the Iraq War, a full-scale military invasion—in "real time" as they unfold in far-off places. Furthermore, cultural forms such as hip-hop, telenovelas, and zines are easily adapted and reconfigured to suit the tastes and preferences of (trans)local audiences. In

many respects, then, proximity and copresence are no longer prerequisites for myriad forms of cultural production and social interaction in the era of global communication.

That said, the disappearance of place, or to be more precise, the diminishing importance of place to our understanding and experience of community that typifies much of the discourse on globalization, is overstated. As economist Michael Shuman (2000) reminds us, the relationship between place and community remains an essential feature of everyday lived experience: "Parcels of real estate are where consumers live, farmers grow food, producers operate factories, and workers clock-in their time. And around these stationary islands emerge the networks of people, arts, music, crafts, religion, and politics we call *community*" (p. 8). Without putting too fine a point on it, even in the era of cell phones, satellite broadcasting, and the Internet, place matters. In fact, place may have even greater significance in our daily lives in the wake of the social disruptions, economic reorganizations, and cultural encounters associated with globalization.

For example, cultural geographer David Harvey (1989) suggests that the forces of globalization—worldwide flows of people and capital, goods and services, technology and culture—upset or challenge popular conceptions of place as being a stable, coherent, or bounded social space. Thus, when immigrants alter the demographic makeup and cultural character of local neighborhoods or when factories close and employers relocate, our sense of place is upset. In light of these social, economic, and cultural disruptions, Harvey argues, we reassert collective feelings of safety and security, solidarity and belonging, associated with a particular place. On the one hand, this impulse may manifest itself innocently enough, in nostalgic and idealized longings for a sense of place. On the other hand, these same feelings may have far more sinister consequences, as evidenced by recent instances of ethnic cleansing.

Place, it turns out, has long been, and continues to be, subject to claims from rival groups and factions. That is to say, in the era of globalization, place—and the meanings we attach to and derive from place—remains a site of intense struggle. Consider ongoing disputes over place in the Holy Land, the Darfur region of Sudan, or at World Trade Center site in New York City, for that matter.

The point is that place still has enormous relevance to human experience. Indeed, far from making place less relevant to our everyday lives, globalization intensifies the significance of place. As the world's population increases, so too will the competition for scarce resources. By some accounts, the 21st century will be marked by "resource wars"—economic, political, and military conflicts over access to natural resources such as oil and natural gas, potable water, and arable land (Klare, 2002). As a result, place will become the site of enormous contest over access and control of these dwindling resources.

Place also has a less tangible, if not a more fundamental relationship to human experience. As anthropologists have long observed, place provides a basis for individual and collective identity formation. Indeed, our sense of self, and of others, is shaped in large part by our identification with, and our affinity for, a particular place. What's more, we articulate a shared sense of place through custom and tradition, dress and food, sound and imagery: in a word, through "culture." In short, the relationship between place and identity is intimately tied to cultural forms, practices, and traditions. By way of illustrating this point, consider the use of flags, anthems, intellectual and aesthetic traditions, and founding narratives that are part of "the calculated constructions of national identity" (Massey & Jess, 1995, p. 2). All this is to suggest that our sense of place—neighborhood, city, region, or nation-state—is not only a matter of individual subjectivity but also a social construction mediated within and through communication and culture.

Knowable Communities

Beyond issues of personal and place-based identity, cultural theorist Raymond Williams (1973) alerts us to the crucial role communication plays in shaping individual and collective consciousness of the relations of "significance and solidarity" that we call community. Williams captures this dynamic with his notion of "knowable communities," a phrase he used in relation to the historical development of the English novel: a cultural form that registered and articulated the dramatic social, economic, and cultural changes associated with the Industrial Revolution. Briefly stated, Williams argued that the scale and complexity of modern industrial societies made it increasingly difficult for people to discern the connections, dependencies, and relationships that give structure and meaning to human communities. By articulating the significance of these relationships within and between disparate characters and settings—relationships that are often hidden or obscured—the novel presents a set of social relations that are manifest, accessible, and comprehensible: a knowable community.

Here, we can begin to appreciate the utility of Williams's (1973) notion of "knowable communities" to community media studies. That is, while dominant media tend to conceal the interconnected and mutually dependent character of social relations, community media work to reveal this fundamental aspect of human communities. Elsewhere I have argued that the democratic structures and participatory ethos associated with community media enable local communities to articulate relations of solidarity and significance through a variety of communicative forms and practices (Howley, 2005). In a similar vein, media anthropologist Alan O'Connor (2006) employs Williams's concept of the knowable community in his analysis of "mountain community radio." Despite their apparent isolation and seclusion, O'Connor observes, the lives of indigenous people in Ecuador and the miners of Bolivia are determined by forces and conditions that are, at once, close at hand and at a distance.

No village or community exists apart from these underlying global systems. Every village is internally shaped by the demand for its commodities and work, by the national government that seldom leaves the village alone and by wars that call its people to serve in the army. There is therefore, Williams argues, an urgent need to have a sense of this larger system. (p. x)

At a time when our lives are intertwined with people and places far removed from our local communities, there is, as O'Connor (2006) argues, "an urgent need" for a much more sophisticated understanding of our mutual dependencies. Furthermore, we need to recognize that the process of globalization is complex and contradictory, uneven and unequal, and bound up in relations of power and domination. The irony here is that despite all our technological sophistication, we often fail to comprehend what Williams described as the "crucial and decisive" relationships we have with people across town and around the world. Simply put, the concept of the knowable community has enormous relevance in an era of globalization.

None of this is to suggest that there is anything new in all this. The process of globalization—understood in terms of mass migration, colonialism, international trade, and global communication—has long been a part of human history. Rather, the current era is marked by an *intensification* of these historical processes. More so than ever, then, our experience of a place called home is shaped by circumstances from within and without. As we shall see, in an increasingly interconnected and interdependent world, community media provide a modest but by no means inconsequential mechanism to promote "a global sense of place" (Massey, 1994).

Thematic Overview

Acknowledging the disparities of material and symbolic relations of power in an increasingly interconnected and interdependent world, *Understanding Community Media* aims to identify and analyze the role community media play in the global struggle for communicative democracy. Drawing on insights and perspectives gleaned from a growing body of literature on alternative, citizens,' and community-based media, this volume represents a comprehensive, but by no means definitive account of community media in the early 21st century. That is to say, despite the scope and variety of cases contained herein, this collection has its limitations.

First, this collection features contemporary case studies or historical assessments of community media of a recent vintage. Missing from this collection are historical analyses of alternative and community-based media prior to the 1970s—arguably a watershed moment in the global movement for communicative democracy. Second, many of the cases discussed throughout are affiliated with progressive politics if not the "political left." This is not to suggest, however, that community media do not align themselves with conservative, "right-wing" or even reactionary political projects. Rather, it is to acknowledge that this collection falls short of capturing the experience of alternative and community-based media from across the political spectrum. All this is to say that choosing illustrative and representative studies for inclusion in this volume proved a daunting task.

Ultimately, four factors informed my decision-making process. First, I was eager to include theoretically informed empirical analyses of community media alongside perspectives from community organizers, media activists, and others engaged in the day-to-day operation of community media initiatives. Second, because community media is common the world over, the collection needed to reflect the geographic and cultural diversity of these efforts. Third, because local populations must make use of resources that are not only available to but also appropriate for a specific geocultural setting, this collection includes discussions of "old" and "new" technologies, as well as innovative examples of "converged" media. Finally, I sought contemporary research from an international team of well-known experts, media activists, and promising young scholars who together could bring fresh insights to the study of community media.

Organized thematically, *Understanding Community Media* explores the relationship between community media and democratic theory; cultural politics and social movements; media activism and neoliberal communication policy; as well as grassroots organizing and international solidarity building The volume is structured to accommodate sequential reading as well as a more selective approach to the specific issues addressed in each of the book's seven sections. Introductory remarks preceding each section are designed to orient the reader to the terms, concepts, and debates taken up in each of these thematic sections. Specifically, *Understanding Community Media* is organized into seven overlapping sections described below.

Part I: Theoretical Issues and Perspectives

In this section, contributors offer a variety of theoretical perspectives that account for the multifaceted character of community media. For some, community media are equivalent to oppositional, radical, and so-called alternative media. Others note the correspondence between emerging forms of participatory culture and community media. Taken together, these chapters examine the relationship between community media and local constituencies—a line of inquiry that emphasizes community building and maintenance. Throughout, contributors wrestle with questions of "citizenship," "publics," and "community" raised by community-based media.

Part II: Civil Society and the Public Sphere

Chapters in this section explore the relationship between media institutions, public discourse, and civil society. Each chapter illustrates the significance of neighborhood associations, advocacy groups, NGOs and other elements of civil society to specific community media initiatives. Likewise, contributors draw on Jurgen Habermas's influential work on the role communicative forms and practices play in the constitution of the public sphere. In doing so, these case studies demonstrate community media's potential to democratize media structures and practices. Throughout, contributors underscore community media's role in creating discursive spaces for individuals and groups marginalized by state-run and commercial media organizations.

Part III: Cultural Geographies

This section explores the relationship between place, culture, and collective identity in an era of global communication. Several case studies consider indigenous peoples' media in relation to dominant media structures, forms, and practices. Others use community media as a site to explore the dynamic interplay between local and global cultures. These chapters examine community media in terms of strategies of resistance and accommodation to cultural globalization. Throughout, contributors emphasize community media's role in articulating cultural identities, and the sociocultural specificity of place, in a global media landscape.

Part IV: Community Development

In this section, contributors consider the relationship between participatory communication and community building and development. Significantly, community development projects, long associated with the Third World, are increasingly common in postindustrialized societies as well. Chapters move from theoretical and pedagogical issues related to training "illiterate" and "nonprofessional" media makers to case studies of community media initiatives that promote economic development and social inclusion. Throughout, contributors explore community media's capacity to promote collaborative efforts aimed at addressing common problems within the local community.

Part V: Community Media and Social Movements

This section features historical and contemporary analyses of the role of local and grassroots media in popular movements for political change and social justice. Drawing on social movement theory, contributors examine the importance of media to political organizing and mobilization. Chapters consider the strategies and tactics employed by community activists to use media for purposes of advancing progressive causes and garnering popular support for their efforts. Throughout, contributors highlight the decisive role community media play in facilitating cultural expression that gives shape to and informs social movements

Part VI: Communication Politics

The chapters in this section examine the extent to which communication policies enable or constrain democratic communication. The specter of neoliberalism figures prominently in debates over the creation of a viable community media sector in various national settings. Foregrounding the social, political, and economic forces and conditions that shape communication policy, contributors highlight the efficacy of reform efforts in creating more equitable media systems. Case studies and policy analyses reveal the significance of independent and community-based media in promoting structural reform of existing media systems.

Part VII: Local Media, Global Struggles

The final section examines community media's role in constructing a critical communication infrastructure through which civil society groups around the world address common concerns, forge alliances, and develop solutions to (g)local problems. Contributors examine a variety of initiatives and communication strategies, including the rise of Independent Media Centers and their relationship to an emerging global justice movement. Not surprisingly, new technologies figure prominently in these chapters as does the potential these technologies hold for galvanizing global civil society.

After years of neglect, community media has begun to attract scholarly attention. The recent surge in community media studies parallels the explosive growth of locally oriented, participatory, and noncommercial media around the world. Incorporating theoretical, empirical, and practitioner perspectives, *Understanding Community Media* represents the "state of the art" in this emerging field of study. As scholarly interest in this field intensifies, there is growing demand for a comprehensive text—one suitable for advanced undergraduate- and graduate-level coursework—that examines community media in a global context. In short, *Understanding Community Media* provides instructors and students with a single, authoritative text on an intriguing aspect of contemporary media culture.

Furthermore, the book's thematic organization allows instructors to integrate this material into a variety of courses in communication and media studies. Demonstrating the relevance of alternative, citizens,' and community media in an era of global communication, *Understanding Community Media* offers an incisive and timely analysis of the relationship between media and society, technology and culture, and communication and community.

Finally, *Understanding Community Media* seeks to contribute to ongoing debates within activist and policy-making circles regarding communication rights on the local, national, and international level. In addition to providing models for community access and participation in existing media systems, this volume aims to enhance public participation in policy deliberations surrounding the development of new and emerging communication and information technologies.

References

Ang, I. (1985). *Watching* Dallas: *Soap opera and the melodramatic imagination.* London: Methuen.

Atton, C., & Hamilton, J. F. (2008). *Alternative journalism.* London: Sage.

Berrigan, F. (Ed.). (1977). *Access: some western models of community media.* Paris: UNESCO.

Berrigan, F. (1979). *Community communications: The role of community media in development.* Paris: UNESCO.

Calabrese, A. (2004). The promise of civil society: A global movement for communication rights. *Continuum: Journal of Media & Cultural Studies, 18*(3), 317–329.

Carpentier, N., Lie, R., & Servaes, J. (2003). Community media: Muting the democratic discourse? *Continuum: Journal of Media & Cultural Studies, 17*(1), 51–68.

Civil Society Declaration to the World Summit on the Information Society. (2004). Shaping information societies for human needs: Civil society declaration to the World Summit on the Information Society. *International Communication Gazette, 66*(3/4), 323–346.

Couldry, N., & Curran, J. (Eds.). (2003). *Contesting media power: Alternative media in a networked world.* Lanham, MD: Rowman & Littlefield.

Croteau, D., & Hoynes, W. (2006). *The business of media: Corporate media and the public interest* (2nd ed.). Thousand Oaks, CA: Pine Forge Press.

Day, R. (2009). *Community radio in Ireland: Participation and multiflows of communication.* Cresskill, NJ: Hampton Press.

Devereux, E. (2007). *Media studies: Key issues and debates.* London: Sage.

Downing, J. (2001). *Radical media: Rebellious communication and social movements.* Thousand Oaks, CA: Sage.

Downing, J., & Husband, C. (2005). *Representing "race": Racisms, ethnicities and media.* London: Sage.

Engelman, R. (1990). The origins of public access cable television: 1966–1972. *Journalism Monographs, 123*, 1–47.

Engelman, R. (1996). *Public radio and television in America: A political history.* Thousand Oaks, CA: Sage.

Enzensberger, H. M. (2000). Constituents of a theory of the media. In P. Marris & S. Thornham (Eds.), *Media studies: A reader* (2nd ed., pp. 68–91). New York: New York University Press. (Original work published 1970)

Forde, S., Foxwell, K., & Meadows, M. (2003). Through the lens of the local: Public arena journalism in the Australian community broadcasting sector. *Journalism, 4*(3), 314–335.

Fuller, L. K. (2007). *Community media: International perspectives.* New York: Palgrave Macmillan.

Girard, B. (Ed.). (1992). *A passion for radio.* Montreal, Quebec, Canada: Black Rose Books.

Gitlin, T. (1980). *The whole world is watching: Mass media and the making and unmaking of the new left.* Berkeley: University of California Press.

Gitlin, T. (1982). Prime time ideology: the hegemonic process in television entertainment. In H. Newcomb (Ed.), *Television: the critical view* (3rd ed., pp. 426–454). New York: Oxford University Press.

Golding, P., & Murdock, G. (1991). Culture, communications and political economy. In J. Curran & M. Gurevitch (Eds.), *Mass media and society* (pp. 70–92). New York: Oxford University Press.

Hall, S., Critcher, C., Jefferson, T., Clarke, J., & Roberts, B. (1978). *Policing the crisis: Mugging, the state, law and order.* London: Macmillan.

Halleck, D. (2002). *Hand-held visions: The impossible possibilities of community media.* New York: Fordham University Press.

Harcup, T. (2003). "The unspoken—said": The journalism of alternative media. *Journalism, 4*(3), 356–376.

Harvey, D. (1989). *The condition of postmodernity: An enquiry into the origins of cultural change.* Oxford, UK: Basil Blackwell.

Herman, E., & Chomsky, N. (1994). *Manufacturing consent: The political economy of media.* London: Vintage Books.

Howley, K. (2002). Communication, culture, and community: Towards a cultural analysis of community media. *Qualitative Report, 7*(3). Retrieved March 28, 2008, from www.nova.edu/ssss/QR/QR7–3/howley.html

Howley, K. (2005). *Community media: People, places and communication technologies.* Cambridge, UK: Cambridge University Press.

Huesca, R. (1996). Participation for development in radio: An ethnography of the reporteros populares of Bolivia. *International Communication Gazette, 57*(1), 29–52.

Ibrahim, Z. (2000). Tarzan doesn't live here any more: Musings on being donor-sponsored in Africa. *International Journal of Cultural Studies, 3*(2), 199–205.

Independent Media Center. (2004). *The IMC: A new model.* Retrieved November 3, 2007, from www.ucimc.org

Jenkins, H. (1992). *Textual poachers: Television fans and participatory culture.* London: Routledge.

Klare, M. T. (2002). *Resource wars: The new landscape in global conflict.* New York: Holt.

Land, J. (1999). *Active radio: Pacifica's brash experiment.* Minneapolis: University of Minnesota Press.

Langlois, A., & Dubois, F. (Eds.). (2005). *Autonomous media: Activating resistance and dissent.* Montreal, Quebec, Canada: Cumulus Press.

Lewis, P., & Jones, S. (2006). *From the margins to the cutting edge: Community media and empowerment.* Cresskill, NJ: Hampton Press.

Massey, D. (1994). A global sense of place. Retrieved December 3, 2007, from www.unc.edu/courses/2006spring/geog/021/001/massey.pdf

Massey, D., & Jess, P. (Eds.). (1995). *A place in the world?* New York: Oxford University Press.

McChesney, R. W. (2004). *The problem of the media: US communication politics in the 21st century.* New York: Monthly Review Press.

Meyrowitz, J. (1986). *No sense of place: The impact of electronic media on social behavior.* New York: Oxford University Press.

O'Connor, A. (1990). The miners' radio in Bolivia: A culture of resistance. *Journal of Communication, 40*(1), 102–110.

O'Connor, A. (2006). *The voice of the mountains: Radio and anthropology.* Lanham, MD: University Press of America.

O'Siochrú, S. (2003). Communication rights create spaces for democratic discussion. *Media Development, 51*(3), 23–26.

Rennie, E. (2006). *Community media: A global introduction.* Lanham, MD: Rowman & Littlefield.

Rodriguez, C. (2001). *Fissures in the mediascape: An international study of citizens' media.* Creeskill, NJ: Hampton Press.

Sakolsky, R., & Dunifer, S. (1998) *Seizing the airwaves: A free radio handbook.* San Francisco: AK Press.

Schiller, H. I. (1976). *Communication and cultural domination.* New York: International Arts and Sciences Press.

Shuman, M. H. (2000). *Going local: Creating self-reliant communities in a global age.* New York: Routledge.

Silverstone, R. (1999). *Why study the media?* London: Sage.

Soley, L. C., & Nichols, J. C. (1986). *Clandestine radio broadcasting: A study of revolutionary and counterrevolutionary electronic communication.* Westport, CT: Praeger.

Streitmatter, R. (2001). *Voices of revolution: The dissident press in America.* New York: Columbia University Press.

Tacchi, J., Slater, D., & Lewis, P. (2003). *Evaluating community-based media initiatives: An ethnographic action research approach.* Retrieved March 18, 2008, from pcmlp.socleg.ox.ac.uk/it4d/think-pieces/tacchi.pdf

UNESCO. (1980). *Many voices, one world.* (Report by the International Commission for the Study of Communication Problems). Paris: UNESCO.

World Association of Christian Communicators. (2006). The no-nonsense guide to communication rights. *Media Development, 53*(1), 67–72.

Williams, R. (1973). *The city and the country.* New York: Oxford University Press.

PART I

Theoretical Issues and Perspectives

Writing in a theme issue of the journal *Javnost—The Public* dedicated to community media, Nicholas Jankowski (2003) celebrates the "renaissance of interest" in community media studies. Jankowski's enthusiasm for this growing body of literature is tempered, however, by his observation that "the main deficiency in community media research is the paucity of theoretical grounding and model building" (p. 11). Other scholars have expressed similar concerns. For instance, Nico Carpentier, Rico Lie, and Jan Servaes (2003) note that "the concept of 'community media' has proven to be, in its long theoretical and empirical tradition, highly elusive" (p. 51). Elsewhere, I have suggested that community media is a "notoriously vague construct" (Howley, 2002, ¶ 12).

Two factors contribute to the conceptual ambiguity and theoretical underdevelopment common to community media studies. First and foremost is a lack of definitional precision; the phrase "community media" is but one of a number of terms, including "participatory," "alternative," and "citizens' media," used to describe media produced by, for, and about local communities (Carpentier, 2007; Rodriguez, 2001).

Second, the sheer variety of formats—free radio, participatory video, street newspapers, computer networking—associated with alternative and community-based media further complicate theoretical development (Downing, 2001; Rennie, 2006). In short, theory building in community media studies is confounded, in part, by the particular and distinctive use of various technologies in disparate geographic and cultural settings.

Rather than adhere to a single theoretical perspective, let alone attempt a grand synthesis of theoretical approaches, contributors in this volume embrace an ensemble of conceptual frameworks borrowed from social, political, and cultural theory. In this way, this volume acknowledges community media's innate heterogeneity while simultaneously developing a comprehensive analysis of community media. Together, these theoretical perspectives provide a robust yet flexible framework to examine community media's multifaceted nature. With this in mind, then, we proceed with a concise review of some of the leading perspectives that have informed community media studies over the past 30 years. Throughout, we highlight the conceptual affinities and crosscurrents operating across these perspectives.

Access and Participation

In a series of influential studies sponsored by the United Nations Educational, Scientific and Cultural Organization (UNESCO), Frances Berrigan (1977, 1979) identifies two concepts vital to any understanding of community media: *access* and *participation*. Briefly stated, access refers to the availability of communication tools and resources for members of the local community. In practical terms, this means that community members have a platform for all manner of individual and collective self-expression, from news and opinion to entertainment and education. Participation refers to community involvement in production processes, as well as the day-to-day operations and oversight of media organizations. Here, participation is closely aligned with the idea of self-management. Accordingly, Berrigan (1979) defines community media as "adaptations of media for use by the community, for whatever purposes the community decides" (p. 8).

Berrigan's (1979) theoretical perspective draws on social-political thought concerned with questions of citizenship, governance, and deliberative democracy. Thus, the concepts of access and participation "have wide implication, beyond reform of media organizations, and media production techniques" (p. 8). That is to say, community media is not "simply" a matter of opening up the channels of communication to nonprofessional media makers. Rather, community media's raison d'être is to facilitate two-way communication within the local community. In doing so, Berrigan contends, community media enable groups and individuals to enter into public discourse, thereby supporting popular participation in decision-making processes and promoting a greater sense of individual and collective agency in directing the community's growth and development.

Berrigan's (1979) analysis reveals a common desire to reorient communication systems away from top-down models of message production/distribution in favor of a decentralized approach to communication that supports dialogue and exchange.

The demand for a more participative use of communications media has its origins in the industrialized nations, where it has been seen as one way of evolving more responsive political and institutional structures. Application in developing countries is based upon an understanding of development as a participative process. In both there is a rejection of a one-way communications flow, of centralized decision-making, of a view of the community as passive and non-contributory. (p. 17)

We can illustrate the theoretical importance, as well as the practical application, of these insights with a brief discussion of the work of the American filmmaker and activist George Stoney, "the father of public access television."

Stoney first made his mark directing documentaries for the Depression-era Farm Security Administration (FSA). Working in the segregated South of the 1930s, Stoney came to appreciate the value of incorporating into his films the voices, experiences, and perspectives of "ordinary people." This approach proved to be an effective mechanism for overcoming differences in race and class, facilitating community organizing, and enhancing communication between local constituencies, elected officials, and outside authorities. However, not until he teamed up with Bonnie Sherr Klein and Dorothy Hénaut, during his tenure as executive producer for the National Film Board of Canada's Challenge for Change program (1968–1970), did Stoney fully realize the social and political value of participatory production techniques (Boyle, 1999).

Briefly, Challenge for Change (CC) drew on a tradition of social documentary filmmaking associated with Robert Flaherty and John Grierson that sought to involve the subjects of films in the production process. CC elaborated on these methods in a series of innovative films produced on Canada's Fogo Island. The "Fogo Island Process," as it came to be known, brought the residents of the island into almost every phase of the filmmaking process, from story selection and editing to coordinating community screenings and group discussions (Williamson, 1991).

Here, we can detect the importance of participation in creating a communicative and cultural environment that promotes dialogue, facilitates problem solving, and enhances community solidarity. In his history of public access television, Ralph Engelman (1990) notes that "Group viewings organized all over the island fostered dialogue within an isolated, divided population. The films and discussions heightened the awareness of the people that they shared common problems and strengthened their collective identity as Fogo Islanders" (p. 9). The success of the Fogo experiments, coupled with the introduction of portable video production equipment and the expansion of cable television across Canada, led Stoney and his colleagues to explore the possibilities of community-oriented television.

On his return from Canada in 1970, Stoney cofounded the Alternative Media Center (AMC) in New York City. The AMC quickly emerged as the focal point for the nascent public access television movement in the United States. In contrast to the adversarial approach taken by so-called guerrilla video collectives that emerged at this time, Stoney took the more conciliatory tack of using video as an organizing tool, as advocated by his Canadian colleagues. As media historian Deirdre Boyle (1999) puts it, "Klein and Hénaut weren't interested in the prevalent style of organizing that depends on creating antagonisms. . . . Instead, they stressed the building of coalitions and the empowerment that comes when people learn they can speak for themselves" (p. 16).

This approach paid handsome dividends for the AMC's "initiatives in both production and policy-making" (Engelman, 1990, p. 19). The AMC developed a pedagogy of access television that stressed social responsibility and community service. Equally important, the AMC forged an alliance between disparate constituencies— community organizers, video artists, cable television operators, and state and federal regulators— that established the legal and regulatory framework for U.S. public access television. In short, the AMC developed an influential model for community communication, predicated on the principles of access and participation, that continues to inform community media initiatives around the world.

Radical and Alternative Media

Like "community media," "alternative media" is a rather slippery concept that has proved difficult to define and equally challenging to theorize. Chris Atton (2001) puts it plainly: "To decide what alternative media are and how they may be considered alternative are tasks not easily achieved" (p. 1). Indeed, according to John Downing, one of the field's leading scholars, the phrase "alternative media" is an oxymoron: In common usage, the label describes all sorts of media, from underground newspapers and pirate radio to niche publications and commercial entertainments that stray from established aesthetic conventions. For his part, Downing (2001) uses the "extra designation" *radical* to capture the overt political orientation and emancipatory potential of alternative media (p. ix).

Downing (2001) draws on insights gleaned from critical theory and media and cultural studies, as well as social movement theory, to explain radical alternative media. At the risk of oversimplifying Downing's model, his work identifies two principal functions of radical alternative media. First, these media are vehicles to "express opposition vertically from subordinate quarters" toward concentrations of economic and political power. Here, radical alternative media are a resource for production and dissemination of "counter-information" that challenges the veracity and legitimacy of dominant media representations of social or historical reality. Second, Downing argues that radical alternative media play a pivotal role in building "support, solidarity, and networking laterally" within and between disparate constituencies working toward social transformation (p. xi). Thus, radical alternative media provide audiences with "mobilizing information" that animates political activism, nurtures collective forms of resistance, and brings social change agendas to wider publics (e.g., Streitmatter, 2001).

Here, we can appreciate the applicability of Jurgen Habermas's (1989) notion of the public sphere to the alternative media theory. According to Habermas, the public sphere is a discursive space between civil society and the state, wherein citizens debate matters of common concern. Habermas's initial formulation of the concept of the public sphere has since been challenged on normative, empirical, and historical grounds. As a result, the concept has been revised to acknowledge the existence of multiple, overlapping, and competing public spheres (Butsch, 2007). Using this theoretical framework, scholars consider alternative media's capacity to open up discursive spaces for voices and perspectives that are marginalized by or otherwise excluded from public discourse (e.g., Harcup, 2003; Herbst, 1994). Work in this vein highlights alternative media's role in constituting alternative public spheres that operate in "explicit opposition to the 'official' public sphere of mainstream media with their intimate ties to political and economic elites" (Haas, 2004, p. 117).

While this line of thinking has gone a long way toward illuminating the synergies between nonmainstream media, alternative public spheres, and social movements, the emphasis on alternative media's oppositional stance toward dominant media has two shortcomings. First, privileging the oppositional character of alternative media suggests a reactive formation against existing structures and practices. But, as Alfonso Gumucio-Dagron (2001) observes, this perspective fails to account for projects in communities with little or no access to electronic media. "Participatory communication experiences are 'alternative' in a different perspective. Most of them were originated not so much to oppose an existing pervasive media, but just because there was no media around and a community voice needed to be heard" (p. 16).

Second, pitting alternative media against dominant media leads some critics to evaluate alternative media using inappropriate criteria. For instance, critics contend that alternative media's inability to attract large audiences, develop sustainable funding mechanisms, and compete head-to-head with mainstream media constitutes a failure (e.g., Comedia, 1984). But as Hamilton and Atton (2001) have argued, applying professional standards to alternative media misses the point. In other words, evaluating alternative media in terms of production values, audience size, and profit-making acumen fails to appreciate alternative media in terms of their ability to transform social relations and encourage innovative forms of cultural expression through new ways of organizing media production.

In this line of thinking, we can detect an interest in alternative media beyond the realm of oppositional politics per se. This approach shifts the analytical focus away from an overriding concern with the *content* produced by alternative media projects and turns our attention to "the *processes and relations* [italics added] that form around alternative media production" (Atton, 2001, p. 3). Broadening the range of cultural forms included under the rubric of "alternative media" to include Do-It-Yourself (DIY) publications such as zines and personal Web sites that may have little overt political content, Atton examines the organizational structures and cultures of production associated with alternative media practice. Atton's analysis reveals the significance of nonhierarchical, nonprofessional, and noncommercial modes of cultural production. These communicative practices, Atton contends, blur the line between media producers and media audiences: a critical step toward democratizing communication.

Thus, Atton's reconceptualization of alternative media is concerned with a "realignment" of communication and cultural production that corresponds with the principles of participatory communication outlined above. Moreover, Atton's emphasis on the cultivation of social relationships within and through cultural production anticipates the line of thinking taken up by community media studies. All this is to suggest that there is considerable common ground in the theory and practice of participatory, alternative, and community media. As Mark Schulman (1992) reminds us,

> The agenda of questions and social practices that a study of alternative communication proposes, it is clear, overlaps with the agenda of community communication. In access, participation, and self-management, for example, are both the seeds of an alternative system and the foundation of the communications system of the healthy community. (p. 35)

Citizens' and Community Media

Clemencia Rodriguez (2001) makes a compelling case for reframing alternative and participatory media in terms of "citizens' media." Rodriguez's formulation grew out of dissatisfaction with analyses of alternative media that conceptualize media power as a zero-sum game wherein media corporations are viewed as all-powerful while so-called ordinary people are powerless. For Rodriguez, this "David versus Goliath" framework fails to capture the complex and contradictory ways in which power is exercised within and through media. Synthesizing insights from development communication, social-movement studies, and radical democratic theory, Rodriguez links access to communication media with collective efforts to support indigenous forms of expression, defend cultural identities, and otherwise empower subordinate groups.

Examining citizens' media through the lens of radical democracy, Rodriguez argues that participatory media projects encourage individuals and groups to recognize their capacity to intervene in and redefine power relations within (and sometimes beyond) the local community. Thus, by demonstrating peoples' ability to alter the community's symbolic environment, citizens' media promotes a sense of self-esteem and empowerment—attributes that are rarely acknowledged, let alone cultivated, by dominant media forms and practices. Rodriguez (2001) further contends that despite their ephemeral character, participatory

media projects often activate citizen action in other realms of civic life. As such, citizens' media provide a unique setting for articulating "a more fluid notion of citizenship as a social dynamic that moves and fluctuates from one social site to another" (p. 160).

Rodriguez's emphasis on enacting citizenship within and through media production recalls the philosophy of community communication advanced by Berrigan and Stoney. Significantly, the connection between media production, collective empowerment, and civic engagement is supported by recent empirical analyses of community media (e.g., Johnson & Menichelli, 2007). For example, in an assessment of Australian community broadcasting, researchers found that the "community media sector is a cultural resource that facilitates cultural citizenship in ways that differentiate it from other media" (Forde, Foxwell, & Meadows, 2003, p. 316).

Working along similar lines, Ellie Rennie (2006) locates community media squarely within the realm of civil society. Drawing on political theories of community and citizenship, Rennie argues that community media provide a resource for local communities to develop civic competencies outside of and in addition to formal political structures and practices. Rennie sums up her project this way:

> At the core of the book is the notion of civil society and its revival. Civil society is sometimes referred to as the "third sector." It is the sphere of formal and informal networks and groups, such as associations, clubs, and cultural allegiances, and the social bonds that tie communities together. . . . The practical and ideological obstacles that community broadcasting has had to deal with are a reflection of the status and treatment of civil society. (p. 7)

Taking this tack, Rennie surveys community media initiatives with an eye toward developing a fuller appreciation of new forms of citizenship and civic engagement enacted through community media. Against the backdrop of theoretical debates between supporters of liberalism, with their emphasis on individual rights, and advocates of communitarianism, who emphasize the importance of collective responsibility, Rennie explores the tension between regulatory structures and public policy (especially communication policy), on one hand, and community values and practices, on the other. Throughout, Rennie returns to a central question: What is the place of community in contemporary politics?

Implicit in all this is an interest in understanding what Rodriguez (2001) calls *quotidian politics:* the everyday practices, forces, and conditions that shape daily life in ways both subtle and profound. Significantly, Rodriguez identifies the realm of the symbolic—the cultural codes of representation, identity formation, and public expression—as a decisive site of quotidian politics. As Rodriguez observes, a "community can be oppressed not only by exploiting its labor force, but also through the imposition of symbolic systems" (p. 20). Accordingly, symbolic relations of power constitute a critical site for democratic struggle.

This focus on the realm of the symbolic demonstrates the utility of community media studies in efforts to "explore and specify the relationship between communication and community" (Jankowski, 1991, p. 163). Briefly stated, this approach draws on work in political science, communication, and cultural studies that examine the *symbolic construction of community* (e.g., Anderson, 1991; Cohen, 1985). Foregrounding the fundamental role communication and culture play in reproducing and maintaining community relations, this perspective informs contemporary theories of community that conceptualize these ubiquitous yet enigmatic social formations in terms of "processes of social solidarity, material processes of production and consumption, law making and symbolic processes of collective experience and cultural meaning" (Fernback, 2007, p. 50). This process-oriented view has not entirely supplanted place-based theories of community; nevertheless, it serves to highlight the constructed, contested, and contingent character of community—a theme I have explored elsewhere (Howley, 2005) and to

which I return in Chapter 5 through the lens of articulation theory.

In sum, despite the conceptual difficulties associated with defining community media as a discrete object of study, theory development in the field depends on our ability to identify and analyze, as Couldry and Curran (2003) suggest, "the specific factors that enable or constrain challenges to media power *in specific local conditions* [italics added] within the increasingly global frame of Internet-enhanced communication space" (p. 14). In the chapters that follow, contributors follow this line of thought with an eye toward refining our theoretical understanding of participatory, alternative, and community-based media.

Chapter 1 underscores the importance of social and cultural context in understanding the dynamics of cultural production in the community media sector. Specifically, Charles Fairchild draws on theoretically informed empirical analysis in an effort to discern the social functions of Australian community radio. Fairchild's emphasis on the "formal and informal" relations between radio stations, listening publics, and governmental institutions reveals the ongoing process of negotiation that community media enter into with various elements of the state, the market, and civil society. Significantly, Fairchild's theorizing is set against the background of recent debates regarding the future of the Australian community broadcasting sector in light of the ascendancy of neoliberal approaches to social, economic, and communication policy.

In Chapter 2, Pantelis Vatikiotis locates a discussion of "citizens' media practices" in relation to three key concepts in democratic theory: public sphere, civil society, and citizenship. Calling attention to the interventions in political discourse, public culture, and representational politics enacted within and through citizens' media, Vatikiotis draws on the concepts of participatory communication and alternative media to illuminate the significance of local/activist media in creating discursive spaces that support individual and group identity formation, the rise of social movements, and the enactment of radical democracy. Throughout, Vatikiotis highlights the value and importance of grassroots and alternative media to the everyday lived experience of so-called ordinary people.

Chapter 3 takes up the relationship between community and communication through a critical analysis of community arts, music, and media in Britain. Specifically, George McKay traces the definition and deployment of the idea of "community" by cultural workers in political and social justice movements since the 1960s. The "question of community"—its varied, diffused, and often diluted meanings as well as its strategic value for realizing progressive social change—figures prominently in McKay's evaluation of contemporary cultural politics in Britain. McKay's analysis is less concerned with community media per se than with uncovering the relationship between community media and other forms of cultural production, principally music and arts, in the context of community communication.

Chapter 4 considers the emancipatory potential of new media technologies in relation to community-based media and participatory culture. Drawing on leftist media theory, Otto Tremetzberger examines the tension between the economic/commercial and social/political potential of interactive digital technologies. The foundational concepts of access and participation inform Tremetzberger's review of innovative approaches to community communication realized within and through new media. By foregrounding these notions in relation to new developments in participatory media—from well-known Web resources such as Wikipedia and YouTube to less familiar experiments such as Van Gogh TV—Tremetzberger underscores the creative and collaborative potential of digital technologies. Notwithstanding this upbeat assessment of digital culture, Tremetzberger sounds a note of caution when he reminds us of the role these same technologies play in facilitating the growth and expansion of transnational "media empires."

We conclude this section by returning to the subject of community radio (Chapter 5). Specifically, I discuss the utility of articulation theory for enhancing our understanding of community radio. Throughout, I note the strategic value of the theory and method of articulation for community radio practitioners. Comparing three instances of community radio in the United States, I emphasize how the social, cultural, and political specificities of place shape and inform community radio form and practice.

References

Anderson, B. (1991). *Imagined communities: Reflections on the origin and spread of nationalism.* London: Verso.

Atton, C. (2001). *Alternative media.* London: Sage.

Berrigan, F. (1977). *Access: Some western models of community media.* Paris: UNESCO.

Berrigan, F. (1979). *Community communications: The role of community media in development.* Paris: UNESCO.

Boyle, D. (1999). O lucky man! George Stoney's lasting legacy. *Wide Angle, 21*(2), 10–18.

Butsch, R. (Ed.). (2007). *Media and public spheres.* New York: Palgrave Macmillan.

Carpentier, N. (2007). The on-line community media database RadioSwap as a translocal tool to broaden the communicative rhizome. *Observatorio Journal, 1,* 1–26.

Carpentier, N., Lie, R., & Servaes, J. (2003). Community media: Muting the democratic media discourse? *Continuum: Journal of Media & Cultural Studies, 17*(1), 51–68.

Cohen, A. (1985). *The symbolic construction of community.* Cambridge, UK: Tavistock.

Comedia. (1984). The alternative press: The development of underdevelopment. *Media, Culture & Society, 6,* 95–102.

Couldry, N., & Curran, J. (Eds.) (2003). *Contesting media power: Alternative media in a networked world.* Lanham, MD: Rowman & Littlefield.

Downing, J. (2001). *Radical media: Rebellious communication and social movements.* Thousand Oaks, CA: Sage.

Engelman, R. (1990). The origins of public access cable television 1966–1972. *Journalism Monographs, 123,* 1–47.

Fernback, J. (2007). Beyond the diluted community concept: A symbolic interactionist perspective on online social relations. *New Media & Society, 9*(1), 49–69.

Forde, S., Foxwell, K., & Meadows, M. (2003). Through the lens of the local: Public arena journalism in the Australian community broadcasting sector. *Journalism, 4*(3), 314–335.

Gumucio-Dagron, A. (2001, May). *Call me impure: Myths and paradigms of participatory communication.* Paper presented at the ICA Pre-Conference on Alternative Media, Washington, DC.

Haas, T. (2004). Alternative media, public journalism and the pursuit of democratization. *Journalism Studies, 5*(1), 115–121.

Habermas, J. (1989). *The structural transformation of the public sphere: An inquiry into a category of bourgeois society.* Cambridge: MIT Press.

Hamilton, J., & Atton, C. (2001). Theorizing Anglo-American alternative media: Toward a contextual history and analysis of US and UK scholarship. *Media History, 7*(2), 119–135.

Harcup, T. (2003). "The unspoken—said": The journalism of alternative media. *Journalism, 4*(3), 356–376.

Herbst, S. (1994). *Politics at the margin: Historical studies of public expression outside of the mainstream.* New York: Cambridge University Press.

Howley, K. (2002). Communication, culture, and community: Towards a cultural analysis of community media. *Qualitative Report, 7*(3). Retrieved March 28, 2008, from www.nova.edu/ssss/QR/QR7–3/howley.html

Howley, K. (2005). *Community media: People, places, and communication technologies.* New York: Cambridge University Press.

Jankowski, N. W. (1991). Media contexts: Qualitative research and community media. In K. B. Jensen & N. W. Jankowski (Eds.), *A handbook of qualitative methodologies for mass communication research* (pp. 163–174). London: Routledge.

Jankowski, N. W. (2003). Community media research: A quest for theoretically-grounded models. *Javnost—The Public, 10*(1), 5–14.

Johnson, F., & Menichelli, K. (2007). *What's going on in community media?* Washington, DC: Benton Foundation.

Rennie, E. (2006). *Community media: A global introduction.* Lanham, MD: Rowman & Littlefield.

Rodriguez, C. (2001). *Fissures in the mediascape: An international study of citizens' media.* Cresskill, NJ: Hampton Press.

Schulman, M. (1992). Communications in the community: Critical scholarship in an emerging field. In J. Wasko & V. Mosco (Eds.), *Democratic communication in the information age* (pp. 28–41). Toronto, Ontario, Canada: Garamond Press.

Streitmatter, R. (2001). *Voices of revolution: The dissident press in America.* New York: Columbia University Press.

Williamson, A. H. (1991). The Fogo Process: Development support communications in Canada and the developing world. In F. Casmir (Ed.), *Communication in development* (pp. 270–287). Norwood, NJ: Ablex.

CHAPTER 1

Social Solidarity and Constituency Relationships in Community Radio

Charles Fairchild

The Central Ambiguity of Community Radio

Community radio stations are, by their very nature, compelled to deal with numerous institutions of governance, be they arms of the state or the market. Given its marginality to mainstream politics and economics, this "third sector" of broadcasting often faces crises that are both the intended and unintended consequences of larger systems of power. These can only be successfully navigated if the character of the relationships between community radio stations and the main actors in the governing infrastructure of the state, the public sphere, and civil society are thoroughly understood. For decades, the ideology governing most areas of political and economic

power has been defined by a specific brand of "economic fundamentalism" called neoliberalism (Kelsey, 1995). One primary consequence of neoliberalism has been the socializiation of cost and risk and the privatization profit and power (Chomsky, 2000, pp. 188–189). The mechanisms used to turn over public assets for private profit have had varied and dramatic impacts. Yet, while the logics of neoliberal governance are pristine, they have long had consequences that are paradoxically unintended and yet perfectly in keeping with their animating intent (Pollin, 2003).

Many community radio stations in Australia have been forced to face down crises caused by strict adherence to neoliberal ideology by the state and corporations. They have done so by clarifying the major issue lurking behind these crises:

Author's Notes: This is a significantly altered version of an article that appeared in *Southern Review* (Adelaide, Australia) in 2006.

This research work for this article was made possible by the Sesquicentennial Research Fund at the University of Sydney. I conducted research at five radio stations: 2SER and FBi in Sydney, and 2XX, ArtSound FM, and 1WayFM in Canberra in January 2004, September 2005, and from August to November 2007. I am very grateful for the support and participation of the staff and volunteers of each radio station.

Why do we need community radio? Is it merely a safety valve for dissent or a form of general public expression? Does it mimic the function of a public sphere but without the binding influence of publicly formed opinion on power? Is it a pressure point whose power is limited but can occasionally be brought to bear in a consequential way? Or is it a lever that ordinary people can use to empower themselves? The precise character of community radio's social functions are the central ambiguity of the form. Given its multifarious nature, making any crisp and brittle distinctions between these social functions is neither necessary nor useful. Whether we call it "radical," "alternative," or "citizen's" media, community radio is all of these, sometimes simultaneously (Atton, 2002; Downing, 2001; Rodriguez, 2003). But these descriptors have stark limits, only describing ideal functions, not actual ones. Each is heavily dependent on constantly evolving social contexts in which the very meaning of terms such as *alternative, radical,* and *citizenship* are being constantly redefined. Instead, to answer these questions, we have to understand how the social organization of the kinds of cultural production facilitated by community radio stations is shaped by ways in which participants at these radio stations make sense out of their practices and experiences. If we can understand these processes of making meaning in relation to the contexts in which they exist, contexts that can often be unfriendly, then we can understand how to make this often-misunderstood media sphere stronger and more resilient.

My primary goal here is to re-imagine community radio as the means through which ordinary people organize themselves by creating a series of what I call "constituency relationships." Community media organizations are unusually complex ways of constructing "social solidarity," a uniquely democratic form of social organization that is largely the consequence of a series of acts of mutual choice. "Social solidarity" is a particular way of organizing people through the mutual construction of a series of broadly recognizable worldviews to both produce and maintain a series of lived social relationships (Calhoun,

2002, pp. 161–162). Most forms of community media must inevitably make deals with their participants based on some form of social solidarity if they are to have any hope of survival. Crafting and maintaining the constituency relationships that make this solidarity possible is what I call the "problem of the public."

This article is based on fieldwork in Canberra and Sydney from 2004 to 2005. While the evidence offered here comes from the study of the relationship between community radio and local music scenes in Australia, the arguments I have drawn from this evidence are more widely applicable. The radio stations I've studied create a space for local cultural production that is substantially outside the mainstream. The practices and experiences of this sphere's participants consistently demonstrate values that contrast dramatically with the supposedly dominant values of Australian society. However, this cultural sphere can only exist if these institutions can successfully negotiate and maintain an officially recognized role in a larger system of economic and cultural power that is fundamentally contrary to their interests. The practices participants use to respond to these contrary forces help define and clarify the practical limits of their efforts. Any understanding of the roles community radio plays in fostering local cultural production has to take into account both the formal and informal relations between radio stations and larger institutions of governance, public or private, ideological or material.

Social Networks Created Through Constituency Relationships

To understand how community radio is "embedded" (see Bromell, 2001) in the world, we have to understand what distinguishes this form of cultural production from the multitude of other forms of cultural production that surround and contextualize it. This is not as easy as one might think, in large part because the form is so intimidating in its diversity. As many can attest, community radio stations are as varied as the localities that produce and sustain them (see Girard, 1992). As a result, much scholarship on the form gets caught between the necessary goal of showing how specific practices are drawn from equally specific contexts and the demonstrable need for a general explanation of the form's social importance and sustainability. Recent work on Australian community radio is broad and often comprehensive (Forde, Meadows, & Foxwell, 2002; Marcato, 2005; Spurgeon & McCarthy, 2005; van Vuuren, 2002). Yet almost all of this work seeks to find the cure for what ails the sector without much agreement on what that sector actually is. Conversely, a recent spate of work on alternative media more generally have proceeded precisely by trying to forge specific definitions of the term (Atton, 2002, pp. 28–30; Downing, 2001, pp. 69–72; Rodriguez, 2003, p. 190). While these works have produced valuable conceptual frameworks, I am not convinced that community media can or should be defined in normative terms. Normative definitions of community media run the risk of imagining institutions founded on exclusions based on political affiliation, ideology, geography, or specific models of what counts as citizenship and civic participation. Instead, focusing on the type, character, and quality of the relationships organizations have with their various publics can help us to craft a clearer understanding of the character of community media. Community radio stations in particular often succeed very well when they act as what Liora Salter presciently called a "fulcrum," balanced, perhaps precariously, between the multiple interests, issues, participants, listeners, and publics they exist to animate. No one is implicitly excluded, as the boundaries of community or participation are not cordoned off in advance. Instead, boundaries are established only as a consequence of the actual practices of specific participants in particular institutions. These boundaries cannot be established by fiat but must evolve through practice (Fairchild, 2001, pp. 98–106; Salter, 1980, p. 114).

Community radio is a stubborn medium that does not lend itself to easy description or prescription. So I want to build on existing studies by focusing on the irreducible aspects of community

radio that can help define its often ambiguous social functions. First, community radio is unavoidably part of civil society. It exists through the kinds of voluntary participation in community institutions that define this often misunderstood social arena. Community radio stations are exactly the type of institutions that define the contours of civil society. They are self-governing, nonstate actors that exist as non-profit-seeking expressions of the mutual and collaborative intent of ordinary people to effect social change through discursive means (Deakin, 2001, pp. 4–10). This alone is enough to make it an "alternative" expression of citizenship and, given recent attacks on the institutions of civil society in Australia, on occasion even a "radical" one (Maddison, Denniss, & Hamilton, 2004).

Second, community radio exists to create social networks through means that are not market based. Access is not based on one's ability to pay for it, either directly, as a fee-paying subscriber whose money guarantees access, or indirectly as the specifically conjured and desirable demographic object sold to advertisers. The value placed on community radio's participants and audiences is not based on a commercial contract but on a civil one. Despite the fact that the civil character of community radio has often proved far more controversial than one might expect, it is not simply a matter of ideological convenience; it is a matter of definition (El-Guhl, 2005; Fairchild, 2001, pp. 106–114). Importantly, this is not a determination internal to these organizations. For example, in Australia, the extent to which community radio can reproduce the values of commercial radio is severely hampered, not just by ideological objections from those who govern the community media sector but also by the practical measures taken by regulators and commercial media to make sure the sector doesn't compete with them too successfully (Farouque, 2002b). While some community stations are more defined by market relationships than others, it is doubtful that these values will ever be allowed to constitute the social basis of the sector, as the Australian Broadcasting Authority (ABA) has repeatedly ruled against licensing community radio aspirants that appear to be profit-making enterprises (Javes, 2003; Marcato, 2005). This is one of the few paradoxes of neoliberalism from which community radio can claim some measure of benefit, if only for the rare burst of regulatory clarity it provides.

Finally, community radio is distinct not only because of the type and character of the social networks it helps create or facilitate but also because of the ways in which these networks are constructed. Community radio stations do not exist simply as sets of ideals or regulations or even as unique and dynamic relationships between organizations and their participants, mediated and linked by particular kinds of content produced in particular ways. They exist as a series of overlapping social networks based on the material, literal connections, and relationships embodied in a range of creative cultural practices shaped and governed both by regulations and the larger dynamics of power in which they exist. These networks stretch well beyond the stations themselves, shaped by a wide variety of institutions of governance, formal and informal, practical and ideological, actual and conceptual. As I have argued elsewhere, community radio stations are constituted by a constantly evolving range of affiliations that defines the contours and limits of the expressive practices that go on air. As such, the lived experience of these institutions is unalterably multidimensional. They look different to everybody who comes into contact with them. They reflect the experience of those who populate them but cannot be conflated with those experiences. They exist as actual places through which lived experience is funneled and produced, embodied in a wide range of creative cultural practices (Fairchild, 2005, pp. 308–309; see also Carpentier, Lie, & Servaes, 2003; van Vuuren, 2002).

But we still have to make a qualitative leap from ideals to reality by asking the kinds of research questions that can help us trace the lines of practice and experience that lead people to participate in this distinct branch of civil society. If we invert the widely held notion in media studies that audiences are constructed by media institutions, we can then ask to what extent are these institutions constructed by their constituents? Of all forms of media, surely this question is most relevant to community radio. The character of the relationships formed within this particular type of civil institution are not formed by audiences or listeners, but by participants, defined by relationships in which all listeners are assumed to be potential contributors. In the broadest and most literal terms, we are talking about political participants, or more exactly, constituents. Constituency relationships are defined by a mutual recognition of the rights of constituents to participate in formal institutions, institutions that are statutorily required to recognize the agency of their participants in mutually agreed on ways. Commercial and even many public institutions are simply not held to the same standard. They are free from having to recognize the agency of the public in terms of operations and programming and are rarely subjected to the interventions of the public in forums they do not control or dominate (see Fairchild, 1999).

Australians have been increasingly constituted as consumers with choices, not citizens with rights. They are economic units, not political participants, living in a consumer society, not a civil one. The relationships through which community radio is constituted stand in plain contrast with these dominant values expressed by most institutions of the state and the private sector. I have found this to be true even of the most politically conservative or market-oriented stations I've studied. In fact, this is the only unifying principle I've found in my research to link the participants at the five stations where I've carried out fieldwork. Each station is run by people who seem to have little in common with those at other radio stations, except for the character and quality of the social networks in which they participate and the practices that define their participation. In the normal course of events, people from the stations I've studied don't even so much as compare notes with those at other stations, much less work together. Yet, regardless of their specific goals, ideological proclivities, and the programming that results, each station I've observed survives on the back of a remarkable amount of often passionate, mostly unrecompensed, voluntary work undertaken in a context in which such work has a history of being treated at best with patronizing neglect if not outright hostility. What I will do with the balance of this work is to give two brief, illustrative examples of the depredations of neoliberalism on two community radio stations and how both used their ability to construct and maintain constituency relationships to survive.

The Constant Work of Survival

When doing my research, I am routinely confronted with the glaring contrasts of values between the ways in which community radio stations work in relation to the larger forces that surround them. The nonmarket dynamics of the social networks through which these stations are constituted contrast dramatically with the larger political and economic contexts in which these networks exist. These contrasting sets of social facts clearly demonstrate the points at which these social networks bump up against the limits of their material expression. The people I have been talking with in Sydney and Canberra exhibit several important similarities. They work long hours mostly without pay to produce their radio shows; they labor endlessly to help open and publicize new venues for musicians; they do much of the heavy lifting required to make their radio stations work without much in the way of obvious material benefit. Community radio stations are not formed from isolated atoms of cultural production but are often pivotal centers of gravity for the actual and potential productive activity of numerous and particular groups of people and organizations to come together and strengthen the networks that enable them to produce their music or their radio programs, to spread information, and to organize activities that often have no other form of public expression and acknowledgment.

The vast majority of people I spoke with told me they became involved in community radio through previous social and political affiliations that existed independently of the radio station. In fact, most presenters I interviewed did not simply walk into a radio station and apply to present their own program. Instead, most had been approached by someone at the station for an interview or advice. Originally interested in seeking publicity and support for other activities, most gradually increased their involvement in the radio station as a means to that end. This kind of relationship reflects a more widespread dynamic in these stations, a dynamic defined both by formal monetary agreements and, just as often, by informal barter relationships. Importantly, these relationships are the central way of inciting the varied forms of public participation in these organizations on which their existence depends. It is these defining aspects of public participation in community radio that tie these stations and their constituencies together.

These relationships have distinct dynamics in each city in which I've done research and each radio station at which I've conducted fieldwork. One such station is 2XX, one of Australia's oldest community radio stations. Located in Canberra, the contextual dynamic in which this station operates is defined by the fact that the city is, in essence, both a large regional centre and something of a company town, being the seat of the federal government. The life of the city is defined by the unusually high socioeconomic status of its residents, provided by their reliance on the steadying economic influence of a generally expanding federal government bureaucracy. The music scene in Canberra is defined by a small number of formal, high-profile venues and a larger number of smaller, less formal ones. At the time I was doing research, only community radio stations allowed local musicians to sell their CDs through their offices or have their music played on their broadcasts. Also, given the transience inherent in Canberran social life, the pull of Sydney, just a few hours down the road, is particularly strong on young ambitious musicians. This means that Canberra's community radio stations tend to be very solicitous of local musicians of whatever stripe, offering an extensive and public commitment of airtime to locally produced music. This odd fact often has interesting consequences. For example, after watching several interviews on a few weekday afternoon slots, I had the opportunity to speak to some of the musicians, few of whom appeared to have any intention of making the work they had just presented on air commercially available. Making music was simply one more interesting thing they did, but they were not necessarily going on the radio in the hopes of brisker sales of what was usually a nonexistent commercial product. One particular byproduct of this circumstance is that several local music programs were dominated by conversations simply about the personal meaning of the wide array of local music on offer, as opposed to the all-too-familiar tales of the life of a working musician.

The situation for music presenters in Sydney is, not surprisingly, quite different. FBi radio is a prominent organization within the city's large and diverse collection of music cultures. It is inundated with local music and rarely has trouble in filling the programming time devoted to local music. The question for FBi is the comparatively luxurious question of how to shape and use that programming time for the greatest mutual benefit of the station and local musicians. This means that this station implements far more formal, specific, and strategic procedures for dealing with a wider range of musician inquiries as well as more developed policies detailing exactly which kinds of local music to promote than their counterparts in Canberra. While the context and circumstance of Sydney community radio stations inevitably shapes the type and character of the relationships it has with musicians, these relationships often have a similar dynamic to those found in Canberra. Similar forms of informal barter and formal commercial exchange exist at stations in both cities, distinguished primarily by their specificity in Sydney and their generality in Canberra. The manner in which the social relationships that animate each of the stations I have studied are constructed differ markedly due to the context in which the participants work. However, there are underlying similarities that define the dynamics of these relationships that can often be surprisingly

hard to see, obscured as they sometimes are by particularities of the kinds of programming that result from these relationships. This fact is often most evident during a crisis.

The contemporary Australian public sphere plays host to numerous circumstances that can cripple a community institution, especially one that depends on such complex networks of mutuality for survival. Two specific threats to 2XX and FBi came from the push to privatize a broad range of public infrastructure and the introduction of so-called market values into the public sector. Each effort has had significant consequences for community radio in Australia, consequences that were not planned and have only recently been publicly acknowledged.

In 2004, 2XX found itself teetering on the brink of insolvency and dissolution, a situation brought on by an arrangement uniquely exploited in the Australian Capital Territory (ACT). 2XX had accumulated substantial debts to an organization called Broadcast Australia, a private entity and subsidiary of Macquarie Bank, one of the world's richest purveyors of formerly public infrastructure. 2XX was taken off air and not allowed to broadcast until they could demonstrate that the debts would be paid. Macquarie had acquired a monopoly on broadcast transmissions in the ACT when it bought the assets of NTL Australia from a struggling U.S. company in 2002 (Hughes, 2002). Broadcast Australia (BA), the entity through which Macquarie managed its monopoly, began to charge all radio stations in the ACT the same substantial fee to use the Black Mountain Broadcast Tower, the only radio tower capable of reaching any substantial portion of the local population. There are few other places a radio station could go to send out a comparable signal, hemmed in as they are by the extensive regulatory system surrounding placement and use of broadcast towers. Macquarie had knowingly bought what economists euphemistically call a practical monopoly. BA's strengths included a predictable revenue base, potential for high revenue growth, predictable operating costs, costs that are largely fixed (none of which Macquarie incurred when Black Mountain

Tower was built). In fact, at the time of purchase almost all the forecast revenue was "locked in with long term contracts" with several public broadcasting organizations. This is a textbook operation in the annals of privatization: The risks and costs of constructing the facility were socialized and the profits and power that resulted were privatized (Hughes, 2002; Macquarie Bank, n.d.). The public sector built the transmission tower, assumed all the associated costs, serving the public good by providing comparatively equitable access to a common resource. When the government sold the tower, the resulting situation saw community groups across the territory sending their donations to 2XX, the only station that gives these groups a public voice, to a bank whose record-breaking profits have come largely from squeezing every last cent out of what used to be important pieces of public infrastructure.

Privatization has had many unanticipated consequences that have been every bit as consequential as the aforementioned example. One of these has been the institution of market-values tests in the public sector (Spurgeon & McCarthy, 2005). Simply confining ourselves to the bureaucracy that deals with broadcast regulation, the institution of market-values tests means that all decisions made by the public sector have to be analyzed for their potential harm or benefit to the Australian economy. With the advent of a regime of "self-regulation" for broadcasters and the auctioning off of commercial radio services through the de facto purchase of frequencies, important changes have been made to the ways in which radio is regulated and, more importantly, the ways in which broadcast policy is crafted and implemented (Farouque, 2002a). When FBi applied for its license in the late 1990s, they won a license that covered the entire Sydney region. The fight for this license was a difficult contest against numerous other aspirants that lasted nearly a decade. One of these aspirants, adjudged by the ABA to be a barely disguised commercial operation, took its failure very badly (ABA, 2001; Davies, 2001). Given the shape of the Sydney radio market, it was unlikely that any further community licenses would be offered. Realizing this, the spurned applicant gathered together supporters and made a mass application of memberships to FBi in a transparent bid to stack the membership, elect a new board, and take over the license. An extensive, expensive, and precedent-setting court action ensued, which FBi eventually won (Molitorisz, 2003). However, the case significantly taxed the financial and operational foundations of the fledgling organization, setting back the launch of the station significantly; the delay even "raised concerns the station would never get off the ground" (Javes, 2003).

This fight was unusual in large part because it was an indirect consequence of the "marketization" of the public sector. The length and intensity of this battle was exacerbated by the fact that the spurned applicant had no other options to gain a license. Their proposed service was not necessarily projected to be a huge revenue-generating operation. Commercial radio licenses in Australia are extremely valuable commodities, with metropolitan properties often fetching over one hundred million dollars on the open market. This has the effect of pricing out almost all applicants who don't already have significant investment capital at the time of application, regardless of the potential value of their future services. In essence, the licensing process has been privatized, with market values trumping any public goods test in the licensing process. As a result, even those applying for noncommercial licenses are finding it that much harder to make their claims to the ostensibly public airwaves stick. These claims are increasingly being tested in unexpected ways with demonstrable effects on community broadcasters, forcing them to defend their claims to "free" spectrum access beyond the formal terrain of licensing procedures.

In both cases, the existential crises faced by the stations were overcome through a variety of means, all of which were based on the existing relationships each had with a variety of social networks to which each was bound in relationships of mutual benefit. In each case, individuals and organizations contributed the means for survival. Staff at 2XX noted with satisfaction and gratitude that, after a series of urgent appeals for support went out through Canberra, they were inundated with offers of support, helping them to raise over $10,000 in a matter of days ("An Antidote on Air," 2004; "Community Radio Back on Air," 2004). FBi, which had not yet begun to broadcast when facing the legal challenge to their membership, was still able to survive through similar means, including donated services and extensive volunteer efforts to maintain the subscriber base and sponsorship relationships in the unusually long run-up to their official launch. Both stations used a clever mix of social organizing, solicitation of donations, expanding sponsorship arrangements, and fully exploiting the few market mechanisms open to each organization. Each station triangulated between political organizing, volunteer support, and commercial solicitation through the unique array of relationships that constituted each organization.

Conclusion

What we might call the problem of democracy rests in the freedom it needs to breath in the mundane and ordinary acts it often takes to exercise those freedoms, freedoms that grow out of the contradictions, contests, and negotiations that exist between the world in which we live and the world we imagine. Community radio exists because of these kinds of contests and contradictions, as the deal community radio stations make with their constituents is essentially a protracted sort of public negotiation. The public participation and organizational openness on which community radio is founded inevitably bring a tenuous hold on the future. They must recognize their audiences not just as consumers or listeners but as political constituents who exist within complex webs of power. In order to survive, these stations must balance themselves carefully within the full range of their constituents and recognize them as the people who give them purpose.

I've found in a wide variety of circumstances that community radio stations most often accept the inherent tensions produced by the housing of an immense variety of interests within the same cultural space, a space at odds with almost all the larger systems of which it is a part. Community radio exists in a sphere in which the difficulties encountered in trying to construct a community organization based on openness and participation are not simply organizational distractions but are their animating purpose. A broad and contradictory set of social facts define the range of practices for most of these radio stations and sustain them on the very thin and volatile margins of a public culture that is constantly evolving through rules and forces larger than all of us. Many of the community radio stations I have studied in Canada, the United States, and Australia face similar problems. The kind of cultural production on which they base their existence becomes more and more necessary even as the conditions needed to produce it become harder to maintain. It should not be surprising that neoliberalism, a thoroughgoing ideology whose practitioners declare themselves uniquely able to explain and remedy all social ills, has severe consequences even for those who, by their actions if not their sentiments, so completely reject their prescriptions.

References

An antidote on air. (2004). *Communicado*. Canberra, Australia: ACT Office of Multicultural Affairs.

Atton, C. (2002). *Alternative media*. London: Sage.

Australian Broadcasting Authority. (2001). *Report of the Australian Broadcasting Authority on the allocation of three community radio broadcasting licences to serve the Sydney licence area*. Sydney, New South Wales, Australia: Author.

Bromell, N. (2001). Music, experience, history. *American Quarterly, 53*(1), 165–177.

Calhoun, C. (2002) Imagining solidarity: Cosmopolitanism, constitutional patriotism and the public sphere. *Public Culture, 14*(1), 147–171.

Carpentier, N., Lie, R., & Servaes, J. (2003). Community media: Muting the democratic media discourse? *Continuum: Journal of Media & Cultural Studies, 17*(1), 51–68.

Chomsky, N. (2000). *Rogue states: The rule of force in world affairs.* Cambridge, MA: South End Press.

Community radio back on air. (2004, May 11). *Canberra Times,* p. 6.

Davies, A. (2001, April 20). ABA likely to find wild FM selling itself short of a licence. *Sydney Morning Herald,* p. 29.

Deakin, N. (2001). *In search of civil society.* Basingstoke, UK: Palgrave.

Downing, J. (2001). *Radical media: Rebellious communication and social movements.* Thousand Oaks, CA: Sage.

El-Guhl, S. (2005). A balancing act: Entrepreneurship in community radio. *3CMedia: A Journal of Community, Citizen's and Third Sector Media,* 1(1), 37–49.

Fairchild, C. (1999). Deterritorializing radio: Deregulation and the continuing triumph of the corporatist perspective. *Media, Culture & Society,* 21(4), 549–562.

Fairchild, C. (2001). *Community radio and public culture, being an examination of media access and equity in the nations of North America.* Cresskill, NJ: Hampton Press.

Fairchild, C. (2005). The currency of collusion: The circulation and embrace of the ethic of authenticity in mediated musical communities. *Journal of Popular Music Studies,* 17(3), 301–323.

Farouque, F. (2002a, May 21). ABA snarls at community radio. *The Age* (Green Guide), p. 6.

Farouque, F. (2002b, May 16). Community radio calls for ratings. *The Age* (Green Guide), p. 4.

Forde, S., Meadows, M., & Foxwell, K. (2002). *Culture, commitment, community: The Australian community radio sector.* Brisbane, Queensland, Australia: Griffith University.

Girard, B. (Ed.). (1992). *A passion for radio: Radio waves and community.* Montreal, Quebec, Canada: Black Rose Books.

Hughes, A. (2002). Macquarie gets set for $350 million broadcast float. *Sydney Morning Herald Online.*

Retrieved February 15, 2006, from www.smh.com.au/articles/2002/06/13/ 1023864303438.html

Javes, S. (2003). Better late than never. *Sydney Morning Herald Online.* Retrieved February 24, 2006, from www.smh.com.au/articles/2003/06/11/ 1055220640167.html

Kelsey, J. (1995). *Economic fundamentalism: The New Zealand experiment. A world model for structural adjustment?* London: Pluto Press.

Macquarie Bank. (n.d.). *Broadcast Australia.* Retrieved September 19, 2005, from www.macquarie.com.au/au/mcg/assets/broadcast.htm

Maddison, S., Denniss, R., & Hamilton, C. (2004). *Silencing dissent: Non-government organizations and Australian democracy* (Discussion paper 65). Canberra, Australia: Australia Institute.

Marcato, P. (2005). Different values for changing times? The Melbourne 2001 community radio licence grants. *3CMedia: A Journal of Community, Citizen's and Third Sector Media,* 1(1), 50–57.

Molitorisz, S. (2003). Licence to thrill. *CBOnline.* Retrieved February 21, 2006, from www.cbonline.org.au

Pollin, R. (2003). *Contours of descent: U.S. economic fractures and the landscape of global austerity.* New York: Verso.

Rodriguez, C. (2003). The bishop and his star: Citizen's communication in southern Chile. In N. Couldry & J. Curran (Eds.), *Contesting media power: Alternative media in a networked world* (pp. 177–194). Lanham, MD: Rowman & Littlefield.

Salter, L. (1980). Two directions on a one-way street: Old and new approaches in media analysis in two decades. *Studies in Communication,* 1, 85–117.

Spurgeon, C., & McCarthy, J. (2005). Mobilising the community radio audience. *3CMedia: A Journal of Community, Citizen's and Third Sector Media,* 1(1), 1–12.

van Vuuren, K. (2002). Beyond the studio: A case study of community radio and social capital. *Media International Australia,* 103, 94–108.

CHAPTER 2

Democratic Potentials of Citizens' Media Practices

Pantelis Vatikiotis

Theoretical Interplays

The concept of *public space* plays a central role in political theory regarding the realization of the democratic process. It has been principally evaluated on the lines of the dichotomy between the state and the household/economy as well as of the public—private polarity. On the one hand, in the republican tradition, public space has been assessed in reference to the participatory model of the Athenian *polis*. On the other hand, in the liberal tradition, it has been addressed in representative terms, as a public forum, in relation to diverse interests expressed in modern large-scale societies. However, the constitution of public space in both approaches is grounded, though from different positions, within the formal political domain exclusively.

From a procedural-deliberative view of democratic politics, the concept of public space has been drawn in Habermas's (1962/1989) category of the *public sphere*. A certain form of publicness (the bourgeois public sphere) is acknowledged here on the principles of rational-critical discourse and popular participation. Both "publicity" and "public opinion" are formed within the

context set by privileged private citizens; issues of public concern are discussed in a free, rational way through personal interaction that takes place in public settings (coffeehouses, literary clubs) and is mediated by the press, forming a critical public.

However, according to Habermas (1969/1989), the refeudalization of society resulted in the "transformation of the public sphere." In the first place, the state penetrated the private realm; the interlocking of state and society transformed the political space of the exercise and equilibration of power toward the *direct negotiation between private bureaucracies, special-interest associations, parties, and public administration, without involving any rational-critical political debate on the part of private people* (p. 176). Moreover, the assumption of public power by private organizations undermined the equation of the intimate sphere and private life, promoting in contrast the division between family and economic society; then, the reciprocal character of public discourse was displaced by a passive culture of consumption (Calhoun, 1996). Central to the transition from a "culture-debating" public to a "culture-consuming" public has been the function of mass media—the prioritization of their economic role to produce audiences for advertisers over their civic one to provide information for public debate (Peters, 1993).

The critique of Habermas's scheme—drawn historically in the bourgeois context, excluding other discourses from being modes of formation of different "publics," and omitting the discursive nature of the space between state and economy (Eley, 1996)—has contributed to the expanding of the concept of the public sphere. The work of Negt and Kluge (1993) questions the singularity and homogeneity of the model of the bourgeois public sphere and sheds light on the wider realm of public sphere activity that encompasses divergent social sites of production and reproduction, pointing out accordingly the possibility of the constitution of a counter, proletarian public sphere, based on accounts of "experience." From another standpoint, that of recognizing "difference" in general, Fraser (1996) adopts a pluralistic approach that accommodates the contest between competing publics within society: Subordinate social groups respond to their exclusion from dominant publics by constituting alternative ones. The public sphere is thus viewed as the setting for the articulation of a variety of ideological and cultural differences.

Habermas's concept of the public sphere has provided, alongside the critique of its historical and normative foundations, a framework for the reconsideration of the concept of civil society and of the dialectic relationship between the two notions.

In Marxist tradition, civil society is conceived in a negative form through the prism of economic reductionism: that of class structure. The Hegelian conception of civil society—systems of needs, rights, and associations—has been subjected here to the "anatomy of political economy" (Arato, 1989). Since civil society forms the economic base of modern capitalist state, it potentially provides the battling ground for the "withering away of the state." In contrast, in liberal political theory, civil society has been constituted in plural, yet individualistic, terms. The institutionalization of aspects of civil society echoes the legitimization of formal rights (speech, assembly, and association). Alternatively, Gramsci (1929–1935/1971) introduces a functionalistic tripartite model, differentiating civil society from both the economy and the state. By sketching civil society in terms of this twofold "declaration of independence," Gramsci identifies the associational and cultural dimension of civil society (Adamson, 1987/1988). Yet, this approach, being exclusively articulated in terms of the functional role of civil society in the production of hegemony and counter hegemony (which could question and replace the bourgeois one), does not take into account another parameter, the fact that elements of civil society constitute forms of self-government that have value in and of themselves. Following Gramsci's model, the work of Cohen and Arato (1992) considers the interplay and the structural interrelations among civil society, the economy, and the state. Especially, it elaborates on Habermas's (1987) distinction between *system* and *lifeworld* and the relevant differentiation between strategic (instrumental) and communicative (intersubjective) rationality, expanding the internal realm of each category and classifying a more complex set of relations between them (stressing both their public and private dimensions).

Social movements have been prominently considered to feature strongly in the discursive space between lifeworld and system. On the one hand, the role of social movements in forming and organizing collective action in the pursuit of common interests is strategic ("resource mobilization paradigm"). On the other hand, the discursive struggles into which new forms of collective identity and action are engaged, contesting established social norms and cultural codes, are politically significant ("new social movements paradigm") (Cohen, 1985; Melucci, 1989). Both of these paradigms are compatible with Cohen and Arato's (1992) scheme of the institutionalized dimension of lifeworld as civil society, acknowledging a double political task of social movements: "the acquisition of influence by publics, associations, and organizations on political society, and the institutionalization of their gains (new identities, autonomous egalitarian associational forms, democratised institutions) within the lifeworld" (pp. 555–556). However, the evaluation of life-world is literally done here within the realm of political society—"somehow tied by definition to . . . the zone of social life narrowly wedged between the world of power and money (state/economy) and the prepolitical group associations of civil society" (Keane, 1998, p. 182).

From a different perspective, Melucci (1989) addresses both aspects of mobilization and identity in terms of grading social movements as public spaces themselves, transcending the lifeworld–system duality.

> Inasmuch public spaces are situated between the levels of political power and decision-making and the networks of everyday life, they are structurally ambivalent: they express the double meaning of the terms representation and participation. Representation means the possibility of presenting interests and demands; but it is also means remaining different and never being heard entirely. Participation also has a double meaning. It means both taking part, that is, acting so as to promote the interests and the needs of an actor as well as belonging to a system, identifying with the "general interests" of the community. (pp. 173–174)

The terrain of social movements, encompassing a variety of small groups, organizations, networks, citizens' initiatives, local contacts, and friendships submerged in the everyday life patterns of civil society, constitutes a fertile environment for the articulation of social claims and the formation of social identities, wherein the subjects of these positions are "nomads of the present."

In an all-encompassing account of the parameters sketched above, Dahlgren (1995), drawing on Held's (1989) "double democratization" of state and civil society, addresses the interplay between the public sphere and civil society as a discursive space for the realization of the democratic process, each one constituting the conditions for the other's democratization: "A 'favorable organization of civil society,' the site of

everyday interaction, in other words, is an essential prerequisite for a viable public sphere. At the same time, a democratically functioning public sphere can give shape to civil society" (p. 131).

In the inseparable relationship between the public sphere and civil society, another fundamental aspect of democratic process, that of *citizenship,* has been reevaluated. Diverse applications of the ideal of citizenship have been proposed in liberal and civic republican traditions. In the liberal context, it is the free, impartial pursuing of individuals' diverse self-interests that citizenship presupposes and promotes. Marshall (1950) points out three dimensions of citizenship, which incorporate a range of rights needed for individuals to be represented and participate in society: "civil citizenship" (legal rights that protect the individual's freedom), "political citizenship" (rights of individuals to participate in politics), and "social citizenship" (rights related to minimal economic security and welfare). In the civic republican framework, it is the sense of community, the notion of the public/common good, prior to, and independent of, individual desires and interests, that citizenship encompasses and privileges. From a communitarian perspective that declares social pluralism, the concept of citizenship is constituted in terms of agency rather than of belonging, in accordance to the multiple facets of civil and political community (Benhabib, 1992).

The parameters of *difference, agency,* and *identity* have provided the basis for challenging the realm of citizenry further. From a postmodern position, Young (1990) argues for the "unassimilated others" to be recognized and enabled to participate in a democratic public. In this way, Young problematizes the prospect of a homogeneous citizenship, introducing instead that of "differentiated citizenship as the best way to realize the inclusion and participation of everyone in full citizenship (p. 118). Likewise, Phillips (1996) points out the need for the representation of differences in the actual field of "political presence," taking into consideration the experience of "social groups who by virtue of their race or ethnicity or gender have felt themselves excluded from the democratic process" (p. 141).

From the point of view of radical democracy, Mouffe (1992, 1993) reviews citizenship as an articulating principle in terms of the multidimensional subjectivity of social agents. Social agents' different subject positions and their interrelations reflect different identities of citizens, which are performed within a culture of democratic values (*res publica*) that "provides the grammar of citizen's conduct" (Mouffe, 1993, p. 72). Through this prism, "citizenship is not just one identity among others, . . . nor is it the dominant identity that overrides all the others" (Mouffe, 1992, p. 378), but it is a form of identification constituted in actual terms, echoing different and antagonistic interpretations of the res publica.

Finally, feminist theory views citizenship as a form of identity. By probing into Arendt's (1958/1989) work, different approaches promote the idea of active citizenship, meaning the civic engagement and collective deliberation about all matters that affect the political community. "The practice of citizenship is valued because it enables each citizen to exercise his or her powers of agency, to develop the capacities for judgment, and to attain by concerted action some measure of political efficacy" (d'Entreves, 1992, p. 146). Prominent here is the performative character of citizenship production; it is the agents who create their identities, including that of citizen.

> The key idea here is that citizenship must be conceived of as a continuous activity and a good in itself, not as a momentary engagement (or a socialist revolution) with an eye to a final goal or a societal engagement. (Dietz, 1992, pp. 76–77)

Moreover, although Arendt addresses the "processes of becoming" exclusively within the public realm, feminist theories evaluate the private realm as another social context for identity formation. Such a perspective does not suggest the total eradication but the redefinition of the boundaries between the public and private spheres.

On the whole, further issues are raised on the grounds of citizenship concerning the interplay between the public sphere and civil society. By evaluating difference instead of unity as the ground for the realization of citizenry, the postmodern strand questions the notion of a universal public space that promotes a homogeneous polity. The radical democratic position, taking into account the multiplicity of subject positions, points out the individual and collective identity-formation processes that run through the terrain of civil society. And the feminist perspective places both the *private* and the *public* in the discursive terms of identity formation, expanding the realm of sociocultural interaction, which is the common denominator of the public sphere and civil society. Thus, citizenship expands to include the realm of civic life, as another social terrain where the principles of belonging and participation have to be justified. In this view, the realization of citizenship has not only political but also civil, social, and even cultural manifestations.

Media: Conveyors of Public Sphere(s)

Any consideration of public/democratic communication convincingly incorporates the interplay between the public sphere, civil society, and citizenship. First, the category of the public sphere has provided an ideal type for sketching the role of the media in contemporary societies. The media could facilitate one of the strengths of the concept of the public sphere, that of universalism, in terms of the principles of general accessibility to information and the full representation of different interests of the society.

Garnham (1990) critically assesses the profound change in the structure of public communication as it is reflected in the "reinforcement of the market and the progressive destruction of public service as the preferred mode of the allocation of cultural recourses" (p. 104). From this point of view, Garnham calls for the consideration of public service broadcasting as the arena for the realization, though imperfect, of the ideal of the public sphere. In addition, the embodiment of the principle of universalism of the public sphere within public service broadcasting—being committed to "properly public, social values" and facilitating a free, open, reasoned public dialogue—is consistent with the formation of the polity of a nation-state (Scannell, 1989). Yet, a number of questions are raised concerning the public service model and its role as conveyor of the very public sphere. At the macrolevel, the territorially structured mode of public communication has been questioned by the development of media networks beyond the nation-state framework (Garnham, 1993). At the microlevel, the public service model fails to satisfy the multiplicity of discourses articulated in the "nooks and crannies" of civil society (Keane, 1998). In general, the universal character of public service broadcasting is addressed from above, and as a result, it is not linked in its very constitution to the sociocultural realm. Aspects of representation and participation are articulated here in relation to different publics, but less on the grounds of these publics themselves.

From a radical democratic approach, Curran (1991, 2000) sketches the democratic purposes of a pluralistic media system with reference to the representation of different social groups both within and through the media. Accordingly, a *democratic media system* should consist of "specialist" and "general" sectors—diverse functions, structures, and services for different media. The specialist sector accounts for minority media that enable various social groups to communicate their discourses, grievances, and concerns to a wider public, strengthening the intervening role of civil society. The general media sector, composed of public service channels, provides the arena where divergent groups of society are engaged in a reciprocal debate of competing definitions of the common good. This perspective attempts to establish a functional relation between the "particular" and the "universal," between "fragmentation" and "unity." Although the proposal puts emphasis on the collective, self-organized tradition of civil society, this has been done from above, in terms of structurally acknowledging its role in any organization of a democratic media system, rather than from below, in terms of civil society's own practices.

However, the reconsideration of the concept of the public sphere on the basis of issues of "difference" has evaluated its multiple dimensions, drawing attention to the development of a "complex mosaic of differently sized, overlapping and interconnected public spheres" (Keane, 1998, p. 169). In particular, Keane distinguishes between "macro public spheres," developed in spatial (global, regional) terms: "meso public spheres," constituted at the level of the territorial nation-state, and "micro public spheres," set at the substate level (pp. 170–181). This approach significantly sets a dynamic understanding of the public sphere on the grounds of practices realized in the arena of civil society. Such an evaluation of the concept of the public sphere, in terms of its context and functioning, has advanced arguments for a diverse and plural media system, as being part of the "intermediary structures" of modern democracy.

On the basis of the interaction between the public sphere and civil society, Dahlgren (1995) conceptualizes the public sphere in dynamic terms, making an analytical distinction between the "common" and "advocacy" domains. On the one hand, the common domain accounts for universalism; the dominant mass media that ideally provide information, debate, and opinion for all members of society, figure prominently here. On the other hand, the advocacy domain (civic media) promotes the representation and development of special interests and alternative and oppositional discourses, and it supplements the common domain. In that order, the association between the two domains is conceptualized in dialectic terms as a "continual and dynamic interface" facilitated by the "dialogic and contesting voices" that elements of the advocacy domain provide for the common one (pp. 155–157).

On the whole, it is in their own terms of reference that the segments of civil society renegotiate identities, values, and proposals. Keane evaluates the variety of bottom-up, small-scale locales in which citizens forge their identities and define their place in public life. What is more, Dahlgren incorporates this aspect in his concern for a two-way implementation of the process of sociocultural interaction, acknowledging the expression of "identity work" in mediated terms, too.

Citizens' Media Practices

In empirical terms, a polymorphic ensemble of small-scale, grassroots media implemented in diverse contextual circumstances has revealed various aspects of their intervention in the public and political spheres.

The rebellious character of relevant media practices features distinctly in their radical standing as locales for shaping political consciousness, either as conveyors of counterinformation to the oppressing reality, or, widely, as agents of developmental power, forming in any case a popular oppositional culture (Downing, 1984, 2001). Moreover, the two-way communication process of participatory media projects provides a strong basis for counterbalancing the unequal distribution of communication resources, as well as for the development and empowerment of the cultures of the publics they serve (Dowmunt, 1993; Servaes, 1999). In addition, the calls for representation and participation of diverse interest groups in the communication process made by community media point out another terrain of public communication beyond the dominant ones defined by the state and the market (Jankowski, Prehn, & Stappers, 1992; Lewis & Booth, 1989). Finally, decentralized methods of media production and distribution, experimental cultural forms of communication, and marginal practices of disrupting media power, which run through different alternative media projects, evaluate significant instances of empowerment for their agents along the very process of their practice (Atton, 2002; Couldry, 2001).

In an overall consideration of a range of relevant practices, Rodriguez (2001) sets a nonessentialist context for their role as citizens' media. First and foremost, Rodriguez reviews citizens' media in terms of diverse processes of civic engagement, molded in the actual field of their lived experience across the fields of both reception and production. From a radical perspective that conceives the constitution of the political in the realm of everyday life as another terrain of social and political struggle, citizens' media practices are more than relevant. Accordingly, Rodriguez evaluates citizens' media as significant sites for the enactment of citizenship, where the social subjects negotiate and renegotiate social definitions, their identities, cultures, and lifestyles, on the personal as well as on the collective level. "Citizens have to enact their citizenship on a day-to-day basis, through their participation in everyday political practices" (p. 19). Hence, the relation between civil society and the public sphere is addressed here from below. The evaluation of the very field of civil society, of its various inputs and their particular interests, as well as their need for representation and expression in a public form, grounds the ideal of citizenship in active terms.

This liberated framework of understanding citizenship acknowledges the role of citizens' media in constituting a discursive arena for political action at the local, national, and global level. No matter what the foundation of these practices is, in spatial and/or activist terms, prominent in any case is a claim for societal progress articulated through citizens' engagement in the process. Attempts to reestablish and advance localities, initiatives of self-development, and configurations of transnational social networking run through diverse citizens' media projects. First, their process, based on participatory experience, incorporates instances of social change, locally and culturally (Gumucio, 2001). Second, their practice, anchored within the very field of civil society, allows alternative conceptions and interpretations of social reality to flourish (Dahlgren, 1995). In addition, the twofold nature of activism, technical (new information technologies) and social, creates a "politics of connections" in uncharted spaces (Carroll & Hackett, 2006).

Yet, citizens' media prospects are not set quite apart from their interrelation to currently transforming public spaces, discursively constituted with local, national, and global forces. The social and cultural implications of globalization processes have triggered changes in the field of social conflict, moving from class struggles to "lifestyle politics" (Bennett, 2003), while the terrain of the exercise and contestation of symbolic power moves away from nation-state borders to transnational and global applications and institutions. The "anti-globalization movement" (Della Porta & Tarrow, 2005) and the "global movement for communication rights" (Calabrese, 2004), as well as the "World Social Forum" (Patomäki & Teivainen, 2004) and the "World Summit on the Information Society" (Sreberny, 2004), are a few manifestations of global social justice media activism "contributing to the setting of new standards to define the meaning of multi- and inter-cultural civic competence in this age of expanding global communication" (Calabrese, 2005, p. 311). Besides, processes of global communication networking (re)address relevant issues in the national and local contexts, developing hybrid forms of politics and power. These dynamics run mostly through places characterized by intensive diversity of peoples and media flows. "Importantly, global cities are sites for the localization of globalization, opening up possibilities for 'place-specific politics with a global span'" (Sassen, 2002, quoted in Couldry & Dreher, 2007, p. 81).

In general, citizens' media involve considerable occurrences of representation and participation of the "ordinary" (people, issues, and activities) in social and political reality, mediating complex power relations and configurations across space and time; they are bottom-up locales "in which citizens enter into disputes about who does and who ought to get what, when and how" (Keane, 1998, p. 170). Every instance of these practices involves *self-expression*—"representing oneself, ideas, creativity, or politics is an act of participation" (Rennie, 2006, p. 187)—having profound consequences for democracy.

Conclusion

A radical understanding of representation and participation in public and political life has been advanced in theory. The relevant communication space expands to include practices and processes that are not realized within formal political society but across the nooks and crannies of civil society and along different public spheres formed on multiple scales. As such, the terrain of the realization of citizenship incorporates realms of the quotidian field, too, where social agents claim and occupy a public space to make politics in their own way. When it comes down to it, citizens' media facilitate issues of access, self-representation, participation, and the democratization of mediated communication at the same time as they advance the principles of societal diversity, discursive multiplicity, and pluralistic democracy in significant ways.

In fact, citizens' media are intrinsically part of what Dahlgren (2002) calls *civic culture*—"civic culture points to these features of the socio-cultural world—dispositions, practices, processes—that constitute pre-conditions for people's actual participation in the public sphere, in the civil and political society" (p. 2). In this way, people's engagement in relevant practices produces reflexively—learning to intervene in public affairs in dialogic ways—respective accounts of their further representation and participation in public space by and large. From this perspective, citizenship is conceived as a lived multidimensional source of empowerment. "For true political power involves not only acting so as to effect decisive changes; it also means the capacity to receive power, to be acted upon, to change and to be changed" (Wolin, 1992, quoted in Rodriguez, 2001, p. 19).

Furthermore, the broad realm of practices and networks through which people intervene in social and political reality at the everyday level entails the reiteration of the "presence" of alternative voices. At the microlevel, the appropriation of means of communication within specific socio-cultural environments, though fluid enough, having short life cycles, becomes tradition, conveying valuable experience for relevant practices to follow. At the macrolevel, the interrelation of activities and the intersection of processes running through citizens' media practices in the evolving discursive terrain of global sociocultural interaction set further and advance representative forms of *being political*, respectively. Although a global civil society is not fully formed in a compelling way, the transformative potential it envisages is responsive enough.

Last, but not least, *contingency* and *mobility* in citizens' media occurs not only internally, across organizations, movements, and associations of civil society at the local and trans-local levels, but also externally, on the grounds of an antagonistic relationship with mainstream media. In the first place, citizens' media are the "meeting point" for diverse social groups/movements and relevant grassroots activities, bringing together different forms of struggle. At the same time, citizens' media are intrinsically connected with the market and the state in critical ways. On the one hand, their practice and function "question and destabilize the certainties and rigidities of public and commercial media organization"; on the other hand, "these deterritorializing effects can open (discursive) spaces for the more fluid aspects of mainstream media identities," creating room for strategic alliances between alternative and mainstream media (Bailey, Cammaerts, & Carpentier, 2008, pp. 29–33).

On the whole, citizens' media practices are dynamic agents in the strengthening of public communication and open out another agonistic public space for the democratic process. As Dahlgren (2002) convincingly puts it, "there are many ways of being a citizen and of *doing* democracy" (p. 4).

References

Adamson, W. (1987/1988). Gramsci and the politics of civil society. *Praxis International, 7*(3/4), 320–339.

Arato, A. (1989). Civil society, history and socialism: Reply to John Keane. *Praxis International, 9*(1/2), 133–151.

Arendt, H. (1998). *The human condition* (2nd ed.). Chicago: University of Chicago Press. (Original work published 1958)

Atton, C. (2002). *Alternative media.* London: Sage.

Bailey, G. O., Cammaerts, B., & Carpentier, N. (2008). *Understanding alternative media.* Maidenhead, UK: Open University Press.

Benhabib, S. (1992). *Situating the self.* Cambridge, UK: Polity Press.

Bennett, W. L. (2003). New media power: The Internet and global activism. In N. Couldry & J. Curran (Eds.), *Contesting media power: Alternative media in a networked world* (pp. 13–37). Oxford, UK: Rowman & Littlefield.

Calabrese, A. (2004). The promise of civil society: A global movement for communication rights. *Continuum: Journal of Media & Cultural Studies, 18*(3), 317–329.

Calabrese, A. (2005). Communication, global justice and the moral economy. *Global Media and Communication, 1*(3), 301–315.

Calhoun, C. (1996). Introduction. In C. Calhoun (Ed.), *Habermas and the public sphere* (pp. 1–48). Cambridge: MIT Press.

Carroll, K. W., & Hackett, R. A. (2006). Democratic media activism through the lens of social movement theory. *Media, Culture & Society, 28*(1), 83–104.

Cohen, J. L. (1985). Strategy or identity: New theoretical paradigms and contemporary social movements. *Social Research, 52*(4), 663–716.

Cohen, J. L., & Arato, A. (1992). *Civil society and political theory.* Cambridge: MIT Press.

Couldry, N. (2001, May). *Mediation and alternative media, or, reimagining the centre: Media and communication studies.* Paper presented at the ICA preconference, Our Media, Not Theirs, Washington, DC. Retrieved March 16, 2009, from www.ourmedianetwork.org/files/papers/2001/Couldry.om2001.pdf

Couldry, N., & Dreher, T. (2007). Globalization and the public sphere: Exploring the space of community media in Sydney. *Global Media and Communication, 3*(1), 79–100.

Curran, J. (1991). Mass media and democracy: A reappraisal. In J. Curran & M. Guveritch (Eds.), *Mass media and society* (pp. 82–117). London: Arnold.

Curran, J. (2000). Rethinking media and democracy. In J. Curran & M. Guveritch (Eds.), *Mass media and society* (pp. 120–154). London: Arnold.

Dahlgren, P. (1995). *Television and the public sphere: Citizenship, democracy and the media.* London: Routledge.

Dahlgren, P. (2002, August). *Reconfiguring civic culture in the evolving media milieu.* Paper presented at the European Summer School: Public Access—Public Service Broadcasting (ECCR) conference, Westminster, UK.

Della Porta, D., & Tarrow, S. (2005). *Transnational protest and global activism: People, passions and power.* Oxford, UK: Rowman & Littlefield.

d'Entreves, P. M. (1992). Hannah Arendt and the idea of citizenship. In C. Mouffe (Ed.), *Dimensions of radical democracy: Pluralism, citizenship, community* (pp. 145–168). London: Verso.

Dietz, M. (1992). Context is all: Feminism and theories of citizenship. In C. Mouffe (Ed.), *Dimensions of radical democracy: Pluralism, citizenship, community* (pp. 63–85). London: Verso.

Downing, J. (1984). *Radical media: The political experience of alternative communication.* Boston: South End Press.

Dowmunt, T. (Ed.). (1993). *Channels of resistance: Global television and local empowerment.* London: British Film Institute, in association with Channel 4.

Downing, J. (2001). *Radical media: Rebellious communication and social movements.* Thousand Oaks, CA: Sage.

Eley, G. (1996). Nations, publics, and political cultures: Placing Habermas in the nineteenth century. In C. Calhoun, (Ed.), *Habermas and the public sphere* (pp. 289–399). Cambridge: MIT Press.

Fraser, N. (1996). Rethinking the public sphere: A contribution to the critique of actually existing democracy. In C. Calhoun (Ed.), *Habermas and the public sphere* (pp. 109–142). Cambridge: MIT Press.

Garnham, N. (1990). *Capitalism and communication: Global culture and the economics of information.* London: Sage.

Garnham, N. (1993). The mass media, cultural identity, and the public sphere in the modern world. *Public Culture, 5* (2), 251–265.

Gramsci, A. (1971). *Selections from the prison notebooks of Antonio Gramsci* (Q. Hoare & G.-N. Smith, Trans.). New York: International. (Original work published 1929–1935)

Gumucio, D. A. (2001). *Stories of participatory communication for social change.* New York: Rockfeller Foundation.

Habermas, J. (1987). *The theory of communicative action.* Vol. 2: *Lifeworld and system: A critique of functionalist reason* (T. McCarthy, Trans.). Boston: Beacon Press.

Habermas, J. (1989). *The structural transformation of the public sphere: An inquiry into a category of bourgeois society* (T. Burger with F. Lawrence, Trans.). Cambridge, UK: Polity Press. (Original work published 1962)

Held, D. (1989). *Political theory and modern state.* Cambridge, UK: Polity Press.

Jankowski, N., Prehn, O., & Stappers, J. (Eds.). (1992). *The people's voice: Local radio and television in Europe.* London: John Libbey.

Keane, J. (1998). *Civil society: Old images, new visions.* Cambridge, UK: Polity Press.

Lewis, P., & Booth, J. (1989). *The invisible medium: Public, commercial and community radio.* Basingstoke, UK: Macmillan Education.

Marshall, T. (1950). *Citizenship and social class.* Cambridge, UK: Cambridge University Press.

Melucci, A. (1989). *Nomads of the present: Social movements and individual needs in contemporary society.* Philadelphia: Temple University Press.

Mouffe, C. (1992). Feminism, citizenship and radical democratic politics. In J. Butler & J. Scott (Eds.), *Feminists theorizing the political* (pp. 369–384). New York: Routledge.

Mouffe, C. (1993). *The return of the political.* London: Verso.

Negt, O., & Kluge, A. (1993). *Public sphere and experience: Toward an analysis of the bourgeois and proletarian public sphere.* Minneapolis: University of Minnesota Press.

Patomäki, H., & Teivainen, H. (2004). The World Social Forum: An open space or a movement of movements? *Theory, Culture & Society, 21*(6), 145–154.

Peters, J. (1993). Distrust of representation: Habermas on the public sphere. *Media, Culture & Society, 15*(4), 541–571.

Phillips, A. (1996). Dealing with difference: A politics of ideas, or a politics of presence? In S. Benhabib (Ed.), *Democracy and difference: Contesting the boundaries of the political* (pp. 139–152). Princeton, NJ: Princeton University Press.

Rennie, E. (2006). *Community media: A global introduction.* Oxford, UK: Rowman & Littlefield.

Rodriguez, C. (2001). *Fissures in the mediascape: An international study of citizens' media.* Cresskill, NJ: Hampton Press.

Scannell, P. (1989). Public service broadcasting and modern public life. *Media, Culture & Society, 11,* 135–166.

Servaes, J. (1999). *Communication for development: One world, multiple cultures.* Cresskill, NJ: Hampton Press.

Sreberny, A. (2004). WSIS: Articulating information at the summit. *Gazette, 66*(3/4), 193–201.

Young, I. M. (1990). Polity and group difference: A critique of the ideal of universal citizenship. In C. R. Sunstein (Ed.), *Feminism and political theory* (pp. 117–142). Chicago: University of Chicago Press.

CHAPTER 3

Community Arts and Music, Community Media

Cultural Politics and Policy in Britain Since the 1960s

George McKay

> The process of communication is in fact the process of community.
>
> —Raymond Williams
> (quoted in Everitt, 1997, p. 80)

This chapter considers ways in which "community" has been understood and constructed in arts and media movements concerned with a progressive social change agenda in Britain since the counterculture of the 1960s and early 1970s. This will help us understand what the meanings of the term *community* are in today's cultural economy. Kevin Howley (2005) writes of having once "disappeared down . . . [a] rabbit hole" in his efforts at definition, pointing out that "the difficulties associated with adequately defining the term 'community' have confounded the study of community media" (p. 5). This is not, though, unique to community media—as Anthony Everitt (1997) has pointed out, in the arts world from the 1970s on, "the word 'community' became increasingly

problematic" (p. 85). By the mid-1990s, even the specific constituency of *community* musicians, at a conference hosted by Community Music East, and titled The Voice in Community Music Seminar, could come to

> no consensus on the definition of "the community," or indeed, who should define it. . . . Boundaries are contestable and difficult to set. . . . Generally, people thought it better to resist such definitions as they could become straitjackets. (p. 85)

The introductory sentences to Petra Kuppers and Gwen Robertson's (2007) *The Community Performance Reader* confess, "A sentence that starts 'Community performance is . . . ' should, arguably, begin this book. Trying to finish that sentence, however, is no easy matter" (p. 1). For other community artists, the term's definitional looseness has been viewed less as a constriction and more as a strategic opportunity—so Anne Cahill (1998) in the context of community music in Australia has sought to uncover and exploit any "advantage in the fuzziness" of definitions of "community" (p. 6).

Let us revisit the question of "community"—and to make it less complex, my view is taken from those working in the fields of community arts, music, and media over the decades, that is, from the ways in which workers and participants in these movements, primarily in Britain, have themselves understood and employed, and possibly strategically redefined, the term. This, I think, will be useful— not least as, a couple of pages after his lagomorphic experience, Howley (2005) writes of community media as "efforts to *re*claim [italics added] the media" (p. 20), while Everitt (1997) has described community music as a sociocultural project aimed at "the *re*-creation [italics added] of community" (chap. 4). Such "re-"s as these may suggest a golden age, or a nostalgia, but they also signal for us the essential requirement to look back, to historicize.

The chapter originates with a concern that the contemporary use of "community" masks a depoliticization of once radical projects or a dilution of their legacy. In exploring connections between community media and social change, I have been interested in ways in which the alternative media movement from the 1960s on has maintained a presence within—or been erased from—the rise of community media. Many community media organizations do articulate their roles in ways that might have sounded familiar to some of their alternative media antecedents. For instance, the director of the Hereford-based Rural Media Company, Nic Millington, explains the rationale of its activities as being "personal empowerment [of its users] *and social change* [italics added]" (quoted in Waltz, 2005, p. 33). The adequacy of the critical position—or suspicion—of depoliticization

is interrogated by looking at issues including the following: community arts and music, community media post-1997 in Britain, and interrogating "community" in the context of soft capital. It should be clear that my approach to this media topic is not via media history, policy, or institutions, but instead springs from an interest in the cultural politics and history of community arts and music. From this perspective, I hope to identify and explore what I think of with only some awkwardness as the *nonmedia side* of community media. I am not so concerned with community media as a contemporary practice and form of organization of media production and consumption; rather, I am interested in viewing it in relation to other forms of cultural and countercultural work that have been (or claimed to be) located in the community.

Community Arts and Media From the 1960s On

Primarily, I am concerned with the community arts movement of the 1960s on, the rise of community music in the 1980s and its continued presence in the 21st century, and the extraordinary explosion of what can legitimately be termed the community media *movement* from the 1990s on. The most obvious thread connecting these, of course, is the term, the claim, the desired object, the problem of "community" itself, and I aim to historicize "community" within the cultural production and participation of these movements. Also, though it needs contextualizing for each cultural practice as well as for each period, "community" is constructed differently through music than it is through media (of course), but, furthermore, it carries different meanings in the 1960s than it does in the 2000s. Both cultural and social contexts signify. In his influential book *The Politics of Performance*, Baz Kershaw (1992) has traced what he acknowledges as a "somewhat circuitous route" of influence across the decades and across community cultural formations alike, by creating "models for cultural action" within the counter-cultures, which then spread through their networks to influence cultural practices in other spheres, alternative theatre made significant contributions to the changing patterns of cultural production generally. Thus, mid-1970s experiments in participatory community theatre in part provided models for the community activist movement which in the 1980s influenced many local authorities to adopt culturally democratic policies. (p. 254)

Notwithstanding the qualifications and occasional hesitancies in this provisional chart of influence—perhaps, textual symptoms of the uncertainty of the community arts movement during the "mean hard times" of the early 1990s in which Kershaw was writing—my argument is that it is possible to extend the trajectory into the later 1990s and beyond, within the different cultural contexts of community music and media. As a specific example to illustrate this from Britain, consider an organization such as the London Musicians' Collective (LMC), founded in 1976 in a late gasp of the counter-cultural enthusiasm for improvised and experimental sonicities and performances, the anarchopolitics of mutual aid, and cultural activism—another strand of which was contemporaneously giving rise to a significant sector of the community music movement. The LMC grabbed the opportunity to move into community media as it developed in the late 1990s, to form Resonance FM, a groundbreaking Restricted Service License radio and Internet station playing and commissioning experimental music, sound art, and left-field documentaries (see Atton, 2004; McKay, 2005). A cultural curiosity and openness to collaboration characterized many who worked in community arts and experimentation, which also meant that, on a pragmatic level, when new opportunities or technologies became available—in performance, music, or media, as well as in arts and education funding—these could be explored and exploited. Clive Bell (quoted in McKay, 2005) describes the

cross-cultural mid-1970s context that saw the establishment of the LMC:

> Improvisers were dipping their fingers into many of the pies of mixed media, dance, film, and performance art. And in fact at this time, just before punk and its DIY ethic erupted, there was a remarkable burst of energy in the underground arts scene. Dancers founded the X6 Dance Collective and the New Dance magazine at Butlers Wharf, while film makers the London Film Makers Co-op[erative]. (p. 233)

In fact, the LMC could trace its provenance back to

> the alternative culture of London in the latter part of the 1960s, intrinsic to a wider cultural explosion in the arts which was characterised by the music and happenings of the UFO club, and the diversity of theatre, performance and poetry readings. (Reynolds, 2007, p. 158)

That is, the counterculture included important innovations within the organization and production of media more widely than simply the generally acknowledged significance of the underground press of the time. In due course, the LMC's in-house magazine, *Resonance,* gave its title in turn to Resonance FM—a media development made possible not only by funding and policy shifts but also by the digital expertise of some of the experimental musicians as well as the flexibility of such cultural workers to adapt. Here we need to acknowledge the savviness or survival instinct of the cultural worker at the margins when sensing a new funding pot. It is just such diachronic (sometimes micro-)narratives of cultural and social radicalism that matter, for they speak to us of ways in which notions and practices such as political idealism, the operation of culture for social change, subcultural contumacy not only survive but also adapt and, perhaps, even thrive across decades and generations (Figure 3.1).

There are many precedents for the idea of community arts, but, as with other postwar areas of experimentation in life and culture, the events

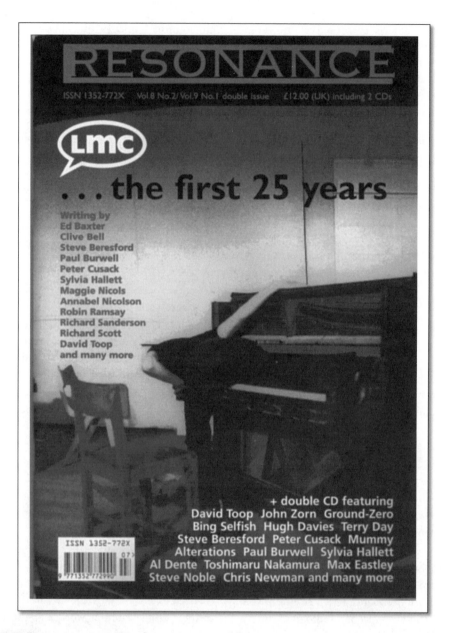

Figure 3.1 London Musicians' Collective's Magazine, *Resonance,* Anniversary Edition, 2000: Bridging Radical Music (1970s), Print Media (1980s), Community Radio (2000s)

Source: © London Musicians' Collective, 2000. Used with permission.

of one recent decade in particular do have to be acknowledged. According to Vicky White (quoted in Moser & McKay, 2005):

> The 1960s could be regarded as the true beginning of the community arts movement and it sought to challenge the prevalent standards and assumptions about the value of art but found itself judged against them anyway. . . . These pioneers wanted participation and relevance for the people as a whole. But they found themselves having to be judged within the standards set by larger organisations and funders within the dominant. . . . The participants and instigators saw [the community arts movement] as *giving people a*

voice as it was used not only for social means but also for political demonstrations. It saw itself as anti-institutional and it used arts to effect social change. (p. 63)

What this new generation of socially committed community artists viewed as more traditional questions of cultural value were "sidestepped by an emphasis on process rather than product. To offer a 'product' was to enter the capitalist world of production and to accept the very notion of professionalism which it was the community artist's task to subvert" (Everitt, 1997, p. 83) (Figure 3.2). In part because of such a critical stance toward

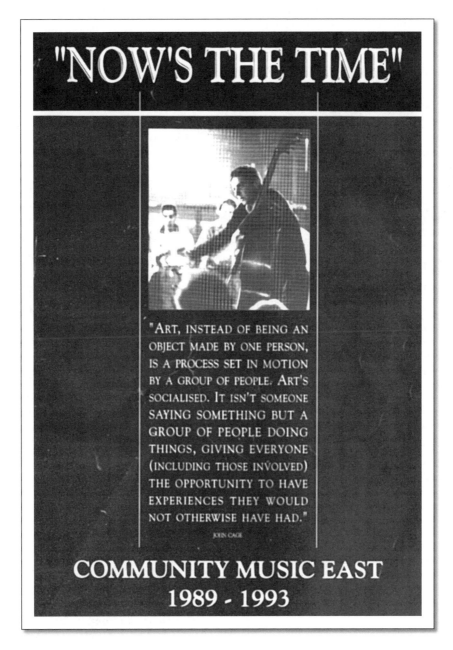

Figure 3.2   Community Music East 1989 to 1993 Report, Showing George McKay on Bass, Running a Workshop

Source: © Community Music East, 1993. Used with permission.

established arts organizations, as well as strands of elitism and self-interest from the latter, there was a certain amount of mutual distrust, even antagonism, between cultural or countercultural workers and some funding bodies. Despite this, in Kershaw's (1992) view,

> By 1970 the key ideological, organisational and aesthetic features of the . . . community theatre movement were relatively easy to detect. Whether organised for touring or resident projects, the groups worked outside the existing theatre system in venues where their counter-cultural message would be welcomed. Relationships between performers and audience, and between companies and communities, were characterised by a new directness. This aimed to both de-mystify the art form, especially to strip it of its mystique of professionalism, and to promote greater equality between the stage and the auditorium. (p. 103)

Yet, for all their radicalism from the 1970s on, community arts generally relied on local and national government or arts organizations and sympathetic charities for funding. In the 1980s, for example, a national scheme called the Community Programme was a government initiative aimed at reducing (many said massaging) registered unemployment figures by establishing projects across the community. (This could include anything from teaching water safety in schools, to improvised music in youth centers, to providing gardening and landscape services in neglected parks or for families on benefit.) Like me, Dave Price was a community musician then:

> In 1989, community music often defined itself in oppositional terms. We didn't quite know what we were, but we were sure that we were *not* formalized education, nor were we anything to do with the dominant ideology. Indeed some of us (somewhat grandiosely, it must be admitted) saw ourselves as acting in open defiance of the [right wing, conservative] Thatcher administration. . . . How things have

changed. . . . It is a remarkable transformation . . . [caused significantly by] the willingness of the 1997-elected Labour Government to establish a dialogue with artists, educators and social scientists in addressing . . . "social exclusion." (quoted in Moser & McKay, 2005, p. 67)

The centrality of arts within the community was then recognized by the 1997 and subsequent Labour administrations as part of the equation seeking to address issues of social exclusion and urban regeneration, as a report to the Social Exclusion Unit for the Department of Culture, Media and Sport articulated in 1999: "Arts . . . are not just an 'add-on' to regeneration work. They are fundamental to community involvement and ownership of any regeneration initiative when they offer means of positive engagement in tune with local interests" (quoted in Moser & McKay, 2005, p. 67). Of course, there are more negative readings of such arts-oriented regeneration policies, whereby "cultural strategies work as a 'carnival mask,' . . . and conceal— and even increase—the growing social inequality, polarization, and conflict within cities" (Stanziola, 1999, p. 6). Nonetheless, in Britain, this new language of community arts has indeed translated into concrete action so that in the past few years, the quantity of community music and community media activity across the country has developed impressively, with significant investment and support, and the recognition of the need for a network and infrastructure. It is in this context that Everitt (1997) speaks of "the subsidy revolution" (chap. 8).

The Congregationist Imperative

Most community arts define "community" by their very act of constructing it in the moment of performance: the community comes together, is invented or strengthened temporarily, as a special group event, in the form of the performers (choir, big band, theatre ensemble) and (usually) of the audience. Kuppers and Robertson's (2007) definition has a very simple starting point: "the audience—the community" (p. 2). The spectated performance (rather than, say, a studio-based music recording) takes place in a particular group location: a village hall, a town square, a procession along a promenade, an ad hoc theater. The artistic project itself—song cycle, play, or other event—combines with the performance in a bringing and coming together of people in a local space, often within a narrative of site specificity. This is the *congregationist imperative* of community arts as opposed to the more mediated "non-social form[s] of participation" (Everitt, 1997, p. 24). (I am conscious here of trying to avoid reaffirming what Shirley A. White [1994] has memorably called "participatory euphoria" [p. 18].) The sense of locality is often emphasized in the narrative or subject materials of the event being centered on the local environment itself—so a community play set in a particular village will tell the story of that village. Kershaw (1992) outlines some of the other "interactive techniques" employed in the congregationist imperative, including those

> drawn from popular historical genres such as pantomime and music hall; through techniques derived from the popular media of comic-strips, film animation, cinema and television which encouraged more active approaches to the reading of performance; through the adaptation of environmental forms such as fun-fairs and festivals to produce the sensory, wrap-around effects of psychedelic spectacles; through the physical participation of the audience in the action of the show, reminiscent of the techniques of "primitive" rituals. (p. 103)

The desire for community through culture and congregation is also evident in Britain in the phenomenal success and expansion of festival culture in recent years: Commonly understood as a sociocultural practice of the transatlantic 1960s, pop festivals have absolutely thrived as a seasonal experience of British youth and weekend counterculturalists to the extent that in the 2000s festival culture is debatably more widespread (if by and large less edgy and socially radical) than at any previous time in its half-century history (see McKay, 2000, 2004). Instances of congregationalism such as community arts and pop festival culture are partly about place but in their contemporary manifestations are also sociocultural responses to the perceived atomizing effects of the technologies of the digital era. They work in part by blurring the distinction between participant and observer—communities performing themselves (rather than sitting watching professional actors playing their life roles or histories), musicians playing and learning with and from each other (the workshop as social music making), festivalgoers being their own story (the crowd and temporary community of audience rather than bands on stage as the pivotal festival experience).

Other cultural workers view the notion of locating cultural practice within a specific community as itself inherently restricting, as one closing down as many options as it may open up. Working from an elite music education institution in London, and in the context of orchestral music, Peter Renshaw (quoted in Everitt, 1997) warns against fetishing place:

> Community music is much too rooted in locality, to place in a narrow sense.... This means that it doesn't really "empower," for it locks people into their cultural relativity, even if it does politically "empower." There is little sense of wider standards. (p. 85)

Such critiques can be extended from debates about cultural values into a social or world view—where the privileged "local" or community orientation is from another, more critical perspective parochial or even functionally exclusive. (Social phenomena such as xenophobia and nationalism are often cited in debates about the reactionary potential of "community"; see

Delanty, 2007) As Chris Atton (2004) has noted in another countercultural context (following John Downing), there can be the danger of "the 'locked circuit' of alternative-media participation, in which activists 'colonise' the alternative media, closing off access to both non-activist sources and non-activist audiences" (p. 52). This is more than the familiar accusation of the "alternative ghetto" (see Atton, 2002, pp. 33–35), or of niche interest groups preaching to the converted, since it suggests an active exclusivity and silence on the part of the countercultural sector that so often claims to be precisely giving voice.

To what extent is the congregationist imperative central to community *media*, though? By extension, are we looking at a different understanding in the context of media, rather than theater or music, of what "community" means and how it is constructed? Even—Do community media in some formal ways actually work *against* the congregationist imperative and undermine the (potentially, whether problematically or radically) nostalgic reclamation of community that earlier (or other) community movements may be predicated on? Of course, media scholars have explored widely ways in which dispersed or apparently individuating media forms, such as broadcasting or the Internet, have successfully constructed or reformatted community in their audiences—the viewing public, local radio, the chat room, or social networking, for instance. Other work has focused on communities of interest, rather than ones spatially defined. Furthermore, community media, too, can claim a similar sociocultural tactic as community arts and festivals—a certain blurring of categories between production and consumption. Indeed, Howley (2005) argues that this is central to community media's political impact: "By collapsing the distinction between media producers and media consumers . . . community media provide empirical evidence that local populations do indeed exercise considerable power at precisely the lasting and organizational levels" (p. 3). But

what I have argued here is that there is an important initial distinction around the social act of congregation to be made within this specific context of community arts in relation to community media, even if it is a distinction made to be subsequently problematized. Where the production and dissemination of community arts and music are compellingly congregationist, community media and their various technologies do not rely on that same simple tactic. This matters precisely because of that same primary word, *community,* and what it might be claiming—that is, how the secondary words (community *arts,* community *music,* community *media*) change the meaning and the experience of community.

Yet today, it is in the localizing impulse, at the local level of organization and reportage, that community media practice is identifiable and efficacious. One of the shifts in our understanding of community has been as a result of globalization discourse, in which community is often presented as under threat, to the extent that, in Howley's (2005) view, community media are "a dynamic response to the forces of globalization" (p. 33). Here, the developments of the media industries in recent decades have had an impact on notions of community that distinguish community media from community arts more generally in two important ways. First, the intense concentration of global media technologies into a relatively small number of very powerful transnational corporations is an altogether more radical economic and cultural shift than has been seen across the music (some aspects of the pop industry notwithstanding) and arts worlds generally. Second, the media plays a more pivotal role in directly disseminating and shaping political discourse on a daily basis: With some exceptions, even at their most engaged, music and arts (community or otherwise) make interventions into agendas that are set elsewhere—sometimes *by* the media and always *through* it. I would argue that community arts and music can also be read as dynamic responses to globalization, of course—aspects of the sociocultural desire to (re)inscribe the local—though, perhaps, they were a little earlier than community media to the debating chamber or barricade, and perhaps, too, they were less complicit than media in causing the problem (if such it is) of globalization in the first place.

Other "Communities," Other "Community Media"

There is something irresistible about "community," for it can function as an ideologically blank template to be shaped from above as well as below, from right and left (and any "postideological" or third-way destabilization of such positions). It is a zone of contestation—never more apparent in a British political context than in the startling alternative use of "community" by the Conservative government of Margaret Thatcher in the late 1980s. Here "community" entered the political lexicon and produced a heated (and sometimes hated) response from left-wing activists and citizens alike. The introduction of new arrangements for collecting local council rates was formally termed by the government the "community charge." Because of links between a new register for tax collection and the electoral register, and also drawing on British radical history—the uprising against a previous tax in 1381, activists called it the "poll tax." Oppositional tactics to it included mass civil disobedience and boycott campaigns around the slogan "Can't pay won't pay" as well as a high-visibility public riot in London in 1990. The abolition of the tax was announced the following year (a few months after Mrs. Thatcher had resigned her premiership). Such use of "community" was widely understood at the time as an instance of political doublespeak and has remained in the activist memory—like the Peasants' Revolt of 600 years earlier, which was referenced by anti–poll tax campaigners. Also, though, activists themselves sought to reclaim the term from the right: In Scotland, the primary

anarchist-influenced organization against the tax named itself Community Resistance (Burns, 1992, pp. 32–33), while in Trafalgar Square, London, one banner's slogan instructed simply, "COMMUNITIES . . . CHARGE!" (Anonymous, 1990, p. 33). In this profound moment, the very notion of "community," and indeed the actual term itself, was at the heart of the political struggle.

Other, less dramatic manifestations of community—now in the specific context of media—can further complicate the social activist impulse that we have identified as a core feature of the community arts movement historically and that is often claimed in the community media field, too. From the apparent soft sell of big business's charity donations to the discourse of corporate social responsibility, we should ask questions about what might be termed *community capitalism* and the complicity of certain forms of media in it. This can be seen equally in local and global contexts. Locally, for example, a key Web site address—www.communitymedia.co.uk—is registered to, and is also the business place of, a British company called Community Media, which produces and sells marketing materials. These marketing "media" range from traditional ones such as bookmarks, beer mats, and coffee mugs to more contemporary versions such as mobile phone screensavers and packets of garden seeds. Boldly promising "a new marketing ethos," the company's original expertise was in working with public and voluntary sector organizations and campaigns, from literacy to health or policing and safety. A short company profile articulates its blend of idealism and commerce:

> Community Media was first established in 1995, as a one-man operation, run from home. . . . Community Media has a talented, innovative and highly skilled design team that bring together all elements of design to create thought-provoking and visual designs. We also specialise in providing advertising, graphic design and print management for voluntary and private sector organisations and have built up a reputation for providing a

quality, flexible and value for money service. (www.communitymedia.co.uk; accessed June 25, 2007)

A progressive agenda is acknowledged by the company through drawing attention to its work with the voluntary sector and local authorities, which functions also to distinguish its business activity from the more purely capitalistic end of the public relations and advertising industries. The purpose of the word "community" in the company title is to strengthen that difference and to further signal its general worthiness and ethical awareness. Community Media, the business, offers an illuminatingly ambivalent small-scale case study of ways in which "community" is employed in the negotiation of political positioning, in the context of both the social community itself (in this instance voluntary, local authority, implicitly socialist) and the commercial environment (deliberately *not* part of the cutthroat world of advertising executives).

There are also global perspectives to something as apparently rooted as community media. In Britain, a dedicated mainstream television facility was made available in 2000, initially as a rather modest opportunity to air material produced by voluntary, charity, and burgeoning community media organizations, "mainly showing charity advertisements and selling charity merchandise." Largely funded by the government, the Community Channel was quite rapidly capitalized on as a means by which the television industry could display its credentials for widening participation and for social inclusion. By 2004, all major British broadcasters had pledged to support it—including BBC and ITV and Channels Four and Five as well as Sky and Discovery. The joint declaration signed by these terrestrial and satellite broadcasters aimed "to make the Community Channel a key external TV partner in our efforts to bring news, information and enthusiasm about the work of the voluntary, charitable and community sectors to our viewers" (www.communitychannel.org). They were

joined 2 years later by transnational media organizations, including MTV and Disney. The channel's Web site explains to viewers that

> Community Channel is TV that gives a damn. It makes you think again about the world around you, and inspires you to take action on the causes and issues that matter to you. Broadcasting original shows, the best of terrestrial TV and showcasing the work of new directors and community programme makers, Community Channel is the place for real-life stories. . . .
>
> We receive free airtime from Sky, NTL, Telewest, and Freeview, and we thank them for their support. (www.communitychannel.org/content/view/814/12/; accessed June 25, 2007)

Fred Powell and Martin Geoghegan (2004) have identified the key responses to globalization available to organizations involved in community development as

> first, a rejectionist stance, based on critical alternative models of development that seek to reclaim civil society for democracy; [and] second, a co-operative stance, following an integrationist model based on co-operation in the "New Economy" that draws community development into a partnership with government and capital. (p. 4)

The Community Channel effectively tries to take both these stances at the same time. There is, if not an outright rejection, then certainly a critical alternative on offer, both in the claim that the channel broadcasts "TV that gives a damn" (note, too, the perhaps more powerful implication that programming on the other channels from its sponsoring broadcasters might well *not* "give a damn"), as well as its claim to transform its viewers into activist citizens focused on social "causes and issues." At the same time, incorporating the discourse and practice of community media in a national and transnational media context, there is a clearly cooperative and integrationist model on offer. Placing community media directly and even critically in a global media context, as the Community Channel does, surely dramatizes for us the continuing stark yet crucial questions of power and access within the industry. It should also remind us of ways in which the notion of "community," as understood by activists for social engagement and change, can be surprisingly easily co-opted and deconstructed. Readers will and must evaluate for themselves the extent to which such a pact is worth making, and what may be lost, in the chase for wider dissemination of community television programs.

Conclusion

I have suggested in this chapter the extent to which, historically, community arts and music and, more recently, community media, have existed in an ambivalent political space. We might simply term that awkward and energetic space of politics and culture "community" itself. By cultural and media community workers, it is constructed pragmatically, if precariously—following funding opportunities and in response to changes in governments and their policies—and idealistically, from alternative media and radical arts for social change projects and interventions. We have seen that it has also been constructed in a spirit of compromise, or indeed imposed as a label to mask ideologically contradictory positions. My fundamental point is that it is essential for media scholars to recognize in the term *community media* not only media issues, however important (or inflated) these may be. We must also critically acknowledge the full weight of "community" as a cluster of shorthand definitions, as a set of problems, yes, but as part of the wider and longer-lasting movement for liberation and radical social change manifested in much community arts and community music practice over the decades. Community media is part of this trajectory, even if it also has its own

specificities, not least of which may be a more complex set of negotiations around questions of globalization in the media industry generally. However, as Gay Hawkins (quoted in Cahill, 1998) has written (of the experience of the community arts movement in Australia):

> Community is not something to be magically recovered but a goal to be struggled for. It is not something to be manufactured by outside professionals but emerges out of collaboration and shared commitment and expression. Cultural work is an effective tool in the formation of community, it is a tool for activism. (p. 109)

As we have seen, the post-1997 "subsidy revolution"—a New Labor government committed to more socially inclusive arts funding, urban regeneration via the engine of culture, and the funds from the then new National Lottery to support such a "seismic" shift (Everitt, 1997, p. 157)—in community arts in Britain saw specific cultural forms benefit significantly. These included community music and community media.

References

Anonymous. (1990). *Poll tax riot: 10 hours that shook Trafalgar Square.* London: Acab Press.

Atton, C. (2002). *Alternative media.* London: Sage.

Atton, C. (2004). *An alternative Internet: Radical media, politics and creativity.* Edinburgh, UK: Edinburgh University Press.

Burns, D. (1992). *Poll tax rebellion.* Stirling, UK: AK Press.

Cahill, A. (1998). *The community music handbook: A practical guide to developing music projects and organisations.* Strawberry Hills, New South Wales, Australia: Currency Press.

Delanty, G. (2007). Critiques of community: Habermas, Touraine and Bauman. In P. Kuppers & G. Robertson (Eds.), *The community performance reader* (pp. 28–33). London: Routledge. (Original work published 2002)

Everitt, A. (1997). *Joining in: An investigation into participatory music.* London: Calouste Gulbenkian Foundation.

Howley, K. (2005). *Community media: People, places, and communication technologies.* Cambridge, UK: Cambridge University Press.

Kershaw, B. (1992). *The politics of performance: Radical theatre as cultural intervention.* London: Routledge.

Kuppers, P., & Robertson, G. (Eds.). (2007). *The community performance reader.* London: Routledge.

McKay, G. (2000). *Glastonbury: A very English fair.* London: Gollancz.

McKay, G. (2004). "Unsafe things like youth and jazz": Beaulieu Jazz Festivals (1956–61) and the origins of pop festival culture in Britain. In A. Bennett (Ed.), *Remembering Woodstock* (pp. 90–110). Aldershot, UK: Ashgate.

McKay, G. (2005). *Circular breathing: The cultural politics of jazz in Britain.* Durham, NC: Duke University Press.

Moser, P., & McKay, G. (Eds.). (2005). *Community music: A handbook.* Lyme Regis, UK: Russell House.

Powell, F., & Geoghegan, M. (2004). *The politics of community development: Reclaiming civil society or reinventing governance?* Dublin, Ireland: Farmar.

Reynolds, L. (2007). Filmaktion: New directions in film art. In C. Grunenberg & R. Knifton (Eds.), *Centre of the creative universe: Liverpool and the Avant-Garde* (pp. 156–167). Liverpool, UK: Liverpool University Press.

Stanziola, J. (1999). *Arts, government and community revitalization.* Aldershot, UK: Ashgate.

Waltz, M. (2005). *Alternative and activist media.* Edinburgh, UK: Edinburgh University Press.

White, S. A. (1994). The concept of participation: Transforming rhetoric into reality. In S. A. White, K. S. Nair, & J. Ashcroft (Eds.), *Participatory communication: Working for change and development* (pp. 15–32). London: Sage.

CHAPTER 4

Collaborative Pipelines

Otto Leopold Tremetzberger

Living in an Age of Access

In the late sixties, George Gerbner (1969) defined mass media as technologies used by industrial organizations for the production and distribution of messages in dimensions only reachable with mass production and high-speed distribution methods.

Considering the *normative power of the factual,* technology significantly defines and affects the form and content of today's communication and communication processes. According to Bert Brecht's (1932/1967) utopian audience input, interaction and the rise of two-way media experiences are simply "natural consequences of technological development" (p. 134). In the past decades, technology has evolved to the point that everyone can at least theoretically communicate with everyone else, anytime and anywhere, using a computer, cell phone, or any other kind of information and communication system or network that allows us to interact—assuming that everybody is "plugged in" correctly (Schöpf & Stocker, 2002). But still, many of the emancipatory expectations, democratic visions, and hopes that have been invested above all in the Internet and new media remain unfulfilled; their broad-based democratic, participative potential has hardly been exploited. Experience shows that technological potential alone does not lead to a democratization of information and knowledge; quite the contrary—completely in the interest of globalized markets, the "command/control" structure of technologies leads to increasing social homogenization (Becker, 2002).

> The great experiment of an unfettered communication space that the Internet as a public medium seemed to provide now seems more like a historical and temporary window of opportunity. If we still care about a common space of knowledge, ideas and information mediated world-wide by networked digital media, we can no longer accept that principle as a given; i.e. as "naturally" embodied in the Internet. (Kluitenberg, 2003)

According to Eric Kluitenberg (2003), the creation of independent "open zones" is now not only a matter of safe havens for data and a sort of "hygienic (off) cyberspace" but also of the formulation of strategies and tools for use in actual practice. After all, "the common space is defined and constructed through us. It is not given."

In the past, technology was often seen as the basic requirement of globalization itself and a neoliberalism that deeply believes in the ability of markets to solve even social problems. In times of Bertelsmann, AOL-Time Warner, and the News Corporation, radical improvements in communication technology make global media empires "feasible and lucrative in a manner unthinkable in the past" (McChesney, 2001). But according to Robert W. McChesney (2001), there is nothing inherent in the technology that required neoliberalism. The new communication technology could also have been used "to simply enhance public service media had a society elected to do so."

> This leads to the question of political strategies and tools to enhance the emancipatory and democratic potentials of new communication technologies and a pluralistic media landscape. In an "age of access" (Rifkin, 2002), what a democratic society requires above all is access to information and knowledge, but also corresponding open forums and spaces in which this knowledge can be produced, distributed, discussed and published. (Tremetzberger, 2003, p. 53)

Community media have always seen themselves as "communication platforms," noting public access simultaneously as the precondition and the most important tool for bringing about communication. Thanks to the development and adaptation of technologies that transcend the boundaries of individual media, independent media initiatives are creating expanded possibilities for communication, particularly in socially and geographically marginal zones. They are setting up "creative patchworks of technologies and communication systems" that are especially well adapted to each respective social, political, and spatial context and that open up additional future prospects and expanded scope for action (Tremetzberger & Leiner, 2004, p. 201). In recent years, debates centering on technological developments have taken on an increasing relevance to opening up new and challenging media spaces. As we may see, facing the ongoing process of transformation and development in the field of information and communication technology (ICT), in fact, the changes have always been in the instruments and not in the general objectives.

But in spite of the decreasing costs of ICT and a growing variety of open source and free software offers, the question arises, How can these "chronically under-resourced and otherwise marginalized" (Raboy, 2003) media organizations develop and continuously provide appropriate systems and applications? The production situation is definitely not that of commercially oriented developers and broadcasters with a lot more financial means.

Czech and Austria-based media artist Karel Dudesek explained the difference between artistic and politically motivated interactive TV projects such as Van Gogh TV and "Piazza virtuale" (shown at Documenta IX in 1992) and so-called professional products, "Artistic motives serve as the basis for conception, and not the creation of a product that presupposes user passivity; instead, the user is challenged to participate in these new media" (Dudesek, 2005). Community media projects challenge people to participate, interact, and change from consumer passivity to producer activity. One of the guiding principles and artistic strengths of the Austrian arts and media initiative Linzer Stadtwerkstatt, which has been hosting a community radio station for more than 10 years, is "incitement of initiative" (www.stwst.at). People actually have to be challenged in a specific way to join a community and to contribute to a community. The way in which these projects deal with technical innovation and adaptation functions like a "self-designed modular construction system" (Tremetzberger & Leiner, 2004, p. 202). The individual technological elements are frequently obsolete and—like FM broadcasting technology—still even rather traditional, for the most part. In actual practice, what is called for is often by no means technical mastery but rather the capability of assembling combinations, selecting serviceable components for immediate objectives, and creating "intelligent patchworks" and versatile systems out of them (Tremetzberger & Leiner, 2004, p. 202). It is the creative hybridity of those information and communication systems—usually underestimated and sniggered at by commercial competitors—that is in fact the successful source of their artistic and community-relevant potential.

More than ever, the question about the emancipatory potential of media is being raised. Every discussion about new media on the basis of technical development, especially new forms of participation and interaction, has been accompanied by Bert Brecht's rudimentary reflections on a leftist media theory based on the beginnings of a (primarily) still analog media age. "Every receiver is a transmitter" is still a paradigm of today's media culture and a credo for political media activists such as Indymedia (www.indymedia.org). As a result of digitalization, economic and technological development, and a spread of broadband technologies, along with a dynamic change of user behavior (Gerhards & Ringler, 2004), in fact, it has also become a business model, either for commercial reasons or for nonprofit or social-profit reasons. More than 35 years ago, when the German media philosopher Hans Magnus Enzensberger (1970) presented his "Baukasten zur Theorie der Medien" for German TV viewers, the decision-making process was quite limited: Channel 1, Channel 2, and switching off as abstaining from voting (p. 161). In 1986, artists and technicians from Germany and Austria worked together as Van Gogh TV, proposing visions about how to use mass media technology to approach the viewer in artistic ways, heading off into "uncharted tele-VISIONARY territory" (Dudesek, 2004, p. 178). This was actually seen as the first project in TV history with interactive features and multiuser systems. The aim of the project was to transform the mass medium of television into an interactive medium that reverses the relationship of one broadcaster and many receivers (Ponton/Van Gogh TV, 1992).

In the 1980s and 1990s, projects such as Van Gogh TV or Checkpoint95, a live TV show involving artists and TV channels from Moscow and New York at the Ars Electronica Festival 1995, were far ahead of developments in the television market at the time (www.servus.at/stwst/kunst/checkpointneu/checkpoint.htm).

The primary aims were not only to practice art in television but to work with the medium itself live, directly, interactively, and experimentally (Prokhorov, 1995). The Austrian artists Georg Ritter and Zelko Wiener later propagated the term "television of the third kind" for this (Reck, 1994).

We Want to Be Part of It!

Today's average TV viewer is confronted with various opportunities for feedback and interaction. But, referring to Brecht again, Germany's quiz channel 9-Live—which calls itself "Mitfachfernsehen" (take part TV)—probably has nothing to do with an emancipatory use of media at all (www.9live.de). In adopting the same interactive formats as Van Gogh TV, "Piazza virtuale," and Checkpoint95, it demonstrates how a principle such as interactivity, developed in the media arts context, is co-opted and commercialized by mainstream media and turned toward the opposite of its originally intended goals (Daniels, 2004, p. 152). "Capitalism immediately and continuously transforms the poison injected against it into a narcotic drug and enjoys it," as Bert Brecht (1932/1967, p. 593) wrote.

Will 9-Live be the future of television? It will not replace traditional TV, says German media professor Jo Gröbel, but it tells us, like *American Idol* or *Yamster,* that people noticeably appreciate interactivity: "We want to be part of it" (Groebel, 2003). Unlike in Brecht's time and the beginning of audio broadcasting, we can now provide the means and the technology to actually let people take part and involve themselves in mindless interactive quiz games as well as in the creative process of producing, editing, and repurposing content.

Clash of Culture and Commerce

According to Jeremy Rifkin, the market economy as "indisputably the most venerable institution of the modern age and a "pillar of contemporary social life" is beginning to crumble. Software, telecommunications, and the Internet are creating a rival new economic system that Rifkin (2002) describes as the "age of access." "The exchange of property between sellers and buyers—the most important feature of the modern market system—gives way to short term access between servers and clients operating in network relationships" (p. 43).

The shift from a propertied regime to an access regime will lead to massive changes, dangers, and dislocations, and to great benefits. The changes are part of an even larger transformation process, the long-term shift from industrial production to cultural production (Rifkin, 2002, p. 44). Along with the metamorphosis from industrial production to cultural capitalism, transnational media companies with global communication networks begin "mining local resources in every part of the world and repackaging them in the form of paid-for cultural commodities and entertainment" (Rifkin, 2002, p. 45). Rifkin mentions various kinds of cultural activities and resources—rituals, community events, arts, sports, games, and social gatherings—all being encroached on by the commercial sphere. But within what economists call "experience economy," each person's life becomes a commercial market and everybody's experiences are going to be exploited and turned into profit (Rifkin, 2002, p. 45). We all know that this already happens. The mining and distribution of user-generated content (UGC), as is well proved by artistic projects, independent media initiatives, community radios, open access TV stations, and temporarily interactive telepresence shows such as the already-mentioned

Checkpoint95, has turned into a widely accepted business model. Again, it is the cultural and artistic sector leading the way as well as proceeding and improving general tendencies. Web sites such as ThisIsHowYouDoIt.com tried to jump on the bandwagon by providing a streaming video on "How to teach your kids to use the potty" for $10. The idea: All of us are experts in our own right. If you want to know about "becoming a great public speaker," there is already somebody with the proper experience who may have already created an instructional video on this topic. An amazing idea? Probably not. The site went off-line in April 2006. It is probably not a coincidence that this was about the same time as YouTube entered the Internet on a rapidly ascending path. In fact, there are countless offers in the style of ThisIsHowYouDoIt.com to be found on YouTube. Nevertheless, ThisIsHowYouDoIt.com is one of countless (unsuccessful) examples of a general tendency: Media companies increasingly discover their *consumers* as content suppliers and provide affordable, advanced tools to a growing contingent of active *users* (IBM Business Consulting Services, 2004).

The commercial sphere is increasingly absorbing the entire cultural sphere, with troubling consequences. "You've made a great video. Now who will watch it? Your work deserves to be seen." This might not be the real reason why what started in 1998 as a simple search engine is now asking *you* to sign up for "Google Video" (http://video.google.com). Apart from Wikipedia, YouTube (though commercially oriented) might currently be the most spectacular and dynamic model of *participatory and open media*. Like no other online platform, within less than two years, YouTube had succeeded in developing into a kind of user-generated mass medium of the next generation. The takeover by Google in 2006 was only the next logical step. Google itself did not succeed in dynamizing its own video platform as broadly or as successfully.

But looking at the future of video.google, YouTube, or Joost raises the question, Will I have to download a video that is reviewed and approved by Google and pay a fee and "a small revenue share" to cover some of Google's costs to get access to even local cultural resources and products that are digitalized, formatted, and commercialized for cyberspace? Google's smart mission is "to organize the world's information and make it universally accessible and useful" (www.google.com/intl/en/corporate/index.html). But in view of the increasing deregulation of government functions and services, shall we really think of Google as *the* common independent public sphere, a communication and information platform that unselfishly serves democracy, integration, freedom of speech, and information? Which kind of information will Google declare "useful"? What does "universally accessible" mean against the background of the digital divide?

When Telecom Industry Reinvents Community Television

Thanks to new ubiquitous tools and the so-called broadband revolution, which makes it possible for anyone to publish and distribute anything, allegedly "pioneering projects" such as Buntes Fernsehen (Colorful TV)—a net-based TV station run by at least some of the 8,000 residents of Engerwitzdorf—are drawing even the BBC's attention to a local village in Upper Austria (www.buntesfernsehen.tv). The channel covers local politics, sports, and events and even features local businesses—anything that residents want to film and upload on a portal for others to watch on their PCs.

What Rudolf Fischer, head of Telekom Austria's fixed line division, called the "democratization of local TV" (BBC News, 2005) requires AON TV membership and AON Speed ADSL broadband Internet access provided by Telekom Austria. This is the only way to have access to videos created "by citizens—for citizens." The project is an outgrowth of Telekom Austria's pay-for-download online TV Channel, aonTV, which lets people watch programs on their PCs and has

been in existence since 2003 (www.aon.tv). The pilot in Engerwitzdorf was started in October, 2004, and is "growing unbelievably fast," says Rudolf Fischer (BBC News, 2005). By May 10, 2005, there were 46 features ready for download on the portal.

But what Telekom Austria presents as a unique success is just a trickle as compared with what Free Radio Freistadt—a local community radio station 20 km from Engerwitzdorf and covering a population of about 40,000 people in the Austrian countryside—has been broadcasting more than 1,200 different radio shows done by local citizens each year since 2005 (www.frf.at).

Nevertheless, *Buntes Fernsehen* is widely seen as a prototype representing the future of television. While working with ideas, concepts, and even well-known terms from the community media sector, Telekom Austria's aim is simply to develop a prototype that can be sold to other Austrian villages (OÖ Nachrichten, 2005). The project attracts international attention and big media coverage. Asked about his opinion on *Buntes Fernsehen,* Austrian media artist Georg Ritter, who has been working on the topic of community media for more than 20 years now, hits the mark: "When the industry is doing it, it's cool and exciting. When we do it, it's dingy and the public authorities disavow it" (personal communication, February 15, 2005). There is no question but that grassroots community media have to be aware of competitive commercial projects such as Buntes Fernsehen—facing similar needs for information and communication in rural areas and even tapping the same public funds. In view of the financial and especially the marketing capacities of Telekom Austria, it seems to be a fight of David against Goliath. But what happens if the big media lose their interest in *Buntes Fernsehen* as the unique pilot is followed by similar projects in other regions? And what happens if people don't get the attention, the service, and the support they need to go on filming, producing, and editing on a voluntary basis?

The Rise of New Voices: Every Citizen Is a Journalist

In the past decade, there has been a wide range of commercial community-related Internet, broadcasting, and print media projects. Many of them have already disappeared. Building audiences by delivering local news and information is a well-used strategy in the growing field of "citizens' journalism." The idea is that citizen-generated content on the one hand lowers costs—or doesn't even cost anything for journalistic work—and on the other hand creates more loyal audiences. Hyperlocal citizen media sites on the Internet are springing up with a bottom-up, open-source approach, written and photographed by citizens and—like voluntary programs from community radios—usually overlooked and underestimated by "real" journalists (Glaser, 2004). Internet-based projects such as OhMyNews or Northwest Voice have often been cited as successful, and some of them are even profitable. Cheap online tools have given anyone with an Internet connection the chance to start a publication, a blog (Weblog), a chat room, or a bulletin board. Citizen media sites have a focus on tiny communities, giving journalists a new role as "content shepherds, whipping the chaos of reader-generated content into a manageable morass" (Glaser, 2004).

The Northwest Voice's approach is similar to the editorial model of community radios, where usually a trained journalist or experienced project manager as "program shepherd" coordinates the radio shows created by volunteers within a specific program schedule, subdivided according to language, topic, or target groups. The major difference, of course, is that Northwest Voice's raison d'être is simply to be profitable. Although "still unproven," the "business strategy or hope" is to attract, with a "critical mass of very local content," a "critical mass of local audience," says Jeff Jarvis, noted as a "big believer in hyperlocal citizen content" (Glaser, 2004).

Lack of content and community involvement is a constant threat to Northwest Voice, *Buntes Fernsehen,* and the aforementioned Free Radio Freistadt All projects that are community based mostly rely on voluntary labor, on easy participation on every level, and on an editorial concept that ensures at least a sufficient level of quality and local attraction of the material that is published by print or Internet or broadcast media. All the projects try to attract small businesses at a local level and present themselves as unique advertising and communication media. All the projects presuppose that, in a sense of civic involvement for people, there is a booming need to interact and participate, sharing and contributing local citizen content from those who a desire to write, publish, broadcast, film, or photograph.

From Collaborative News to Collaborative Broadcasting

The concept of citizen journalism or participatory journalism is of great interest for community radios and public access TV stations. The objectives are similar: It is the act of citizens playing an active role in the process of collecting, reporting, analyzing, and disseminating news and information. According to the seminal report, *We Media: How Audiences are Shaping the Future of News and Information,* by Shayne Bowman and Chris Willis (2003), the intent of this participation is "to provide independent, reliable, accurate, wide-ranging and relevant information that a democracy requires" (p. 9).

The hard part is populating these media sites and media initiatives with content. In the past, community radios have always been confronted with the question of whether people are really interested in and are actually ready for broadcasting their shows and features on a regular basis with consistent quality. In light of the currently more than 1,200 different shows broadcast by Free Radio Freistadt, the prognosticated "lack of content" should no longer be a topic.

One positive effect of *Buntes Fernsehen* definitely could be a more positive image of participatory media. But one should not forget that what Telekom Austria is willing to define as the future of television is already the past of quite a lot of artistic media projects and has been successfully realized by community media for decades now.

How to Recruit a Guerrilla Army of Activists?

One of the most prominent examples for—in some sense—participatory media is Current TV, an independent cable and satellite TV network in the United States (www.current.tv). Current TV is under the patronage of former U.S. vice president Al Gore and broadcasts to almost 20 million homes. The mission is convincing:

> There's plenty to watch on TV, but as a viewer, you don't have much chance to influence or contribute to what you see. This medium— the most powerful, riveting one we have—is still a narrow vision of reality rolled out in predictable 30-minute chunks. It's still a fortress of an old-school, one-way world. We want to bust it open. (http://www.current.tv)

Like Buntes Fernsehen, Current TV wants to create a "pipeline of your production" offering access, a worldwide distribution via Google, a studio, and a participatory production program open to everyone.

With regard to the notion of "critical mass" in terms of content and audience, "What makes Current TV relevant for a community radio?" According to Greg Lindsay, Al Gore and Current TV offer, above all, credibility and legitimacy: "Not only is it TV, but it's Al Gore's channel! . . . Just having Gore's name attached will make it must-see TV in Mediaville" (Lindsay, 2005).

What actually motivates people to submit their productions? With Al Gore as chairman, Current TV has more than just a usual mission statement (it is perceived as "Gore's channel"), but contributing to the program even becomes a political statement in itself. Recruiting a guerrilla army of young activists certainly requires more than just a common platform for everybody to publish everything— maybe least of all for somebody else's financial

profit. By comparison with Indymedia, a "network of collectively run media outlets for the creation of radical, accurate, and passionate tellings of the truth," a guerrilla activist clearly needs to know what to fight for: "We work out of a love and inspiration for people who continue to work for a better world, despite corporate media's distortions and unwillingness to cover the efforts to free humanity" (www.indymedia.org/en/static/about.shtml). Above all, "credibility" and "legitimacy" are not achieved by appealing to people's vanity alone but by a strong thread that links together the diversity of UGC and that also links together the users themselves as a strong community. The crucial point is, What does the organization stand for in the eyes of its users, consumers, or contributors? According to Marshall McLuhan's prophetic proposal, stated in the sixties of the last century, "The media is the message" (McLuhan, 1994).

Hunter-Gatherers: Collecting, Mining, and Distribution

Together with blogs, global trends such as wikis and podcasting show that more and more people are changing from consumer passivity to producer activity. This leads not only to a highly unmanageable mess of trivial information lost in cyberspace but, in fact, also to an increasing offer of high-quality content comparable with established media. To paraphrase Rifkin again, today's challenge is not so much about motivating people to participate and interact within the sphere of media and ICT—they already want to be part of it.

The role of a media organization is definitely changing. Media consumers, to varying degrees, will be increasingly involved in the creative process of creating, editing, and repurposing content. Global corporations such as IBM align their strategies to assume "a . . . shift from capturing attention to managing attention" as the strategic focus of media businesses. This management of attention is driven by the increased involvement of the media experiencer with content creation via digital media. According to IBM, a "pervasive media environment" as the future direction of media is characterized by increased consumer content creation and feedback and individualized customization of content. The media users of the future vary from a passive consumer using interactive TV programming guides, a contributor bringing in active feedback and suggestions, a producer programming content and devices from various sources—such as digital playlists—all the way to authors using Web tools "to tailor content to business or personal interests, seeking self-expression or control" (IBM Business Consulting Services, 2004). IBM provides a truly convincing scenario of how (mass) media will develop in the next 5 years. Under the motto "don't hate the media—be the media," Indymedia has already been successfully improving IBM's thesis since 1999.

> The mission of communication platforms like free radio stations is to make available opportunities for the expression of opinions and self-representation, to actively involve listeners in the work with the medium and, in contrast to the role of pure consumers, to integrate them into the production process. Anyone can advance directly to the status of producer in this media endeavor and establish a relationship with others via the medium. (Tremetzberger & Leiner, 2004, p. 201)

After all, the models of citizen journalism and participatory journalism in recent years not only led to new (commercial or noncommercial) grassroots-oriented, open-media projects but also have been increasingly becoming an integral part of commercial media production itself. From the print industry up to iReports on CNN, media companies are paying more and more attention to citizen journalism and amateur reporting tools. But this development has its dark side, often overseen or neglected by enthusiastic comments on a sudden and apparent accessibility of media. In fact, only a fraction of UGC finds its way to be broadcast or printed in professional media. And if someone's amateur picture is actually published, maybe the picture of people dying in a tsunami, seen from the balcony of a hotel at

the coast of Thailand, it is not a symbol of the democratization of media but a result of the exploitation of cheap or free labor for the usual commercial purposes.

The Rise of the Digital Media

It is not only the Internet that has revolutionized the way people inform themselves. In fact, the development of the technological environment, along with changing user behavior, brought new challenges for so-called old media. Traditional newspapers are confronted with decreasing circulation, and digital offers are attracting more and more advertisers. The media business is shifting from old print to new digital media. People gather up-to-the-second information from Google or Yahoo. The Internet as a current and specific news and information medium will strengthen its position within the market (Gerhards & Ringler, 2004, p. 476).

But still, new media have actually not replaced old media. Established media are not displaced by their follow-up media but have been changed and extended. Nevertheless, a complete fusion of old and new media into comprehensive multimedia offerings will still take time (Gleich, 2003, p. 515). Experts see the situation of traditional broadcasting media different from print media. While daily circulation of print media tends to decrease, the total viewing and listening time of TV and radio remains constant. TV and radio can still be seen as "everyday media" for the average person. But, especially with young people, the use of traditional TV is decreasing (Gerhards & Ringler, 2007, p. 301), and we must also take into account changes at the supply side, for example, the growing variety of programs (Gerhards & Ringler, 2007, p. 298). Without a doubt, the tie will loosen to traditional media (Gerhards & Ringler, 2004, p. 472). The traditional media will still be able to assert and make their mark with their genre-specific qualities (Gleich, 2003, p. 515). However, the concept of a dominant, "stand-alone" medium will increasingly become obsolete. The consequences are not a multimedial fusion, but combined media, where attempts are made to combine intrinsic strengths. The way in which the media landscape will change is in this sense "evolutionary" and not "revolutionary" (Gerhards & Ringler, 2004, p. 472). The development of new information and communication technologies facilitates the convergence between analog and digital media and leads to a fundamental transformation of the broadcasting model. Terrestrial radio is still the most widespread medium in our time, with availability far beyond the Internet—especially in rural areas. But the next-generation radio station is a hybrid and convergent cross-media communication platform. It combines the potential and advantages of analog radio with the Internet and digital broadcasting technologies.

> The strategies and practices have had to transcend the purview of individual media. The analog medium of radio was expanded by digital (network) options (audio streaming, radio-on-demand, database based program exchange, etc.) since the—in many cases initially experimental—process of taking advantage of all available possibilities of establishing means of communication functions above all through the permanent expansion and adaptation of the offerings. (Tremetzberger & Leiner, 2004, p. 201)

Linking new ICT with broadcast technologies to create more powerful and ubiquitous media offers, in the sense of a two-way relationship with their users and customers, will be a big challenge for community media in the years to come.

References

BBC News. (2005, March 25). *Local net TV takes off in Austria.* Retrieved November 20, 2007, from http://news.bbc.co.uk/1/hi/technology/4378945.stm

Becker, K. (2002). *Tactical reality dictionary.* Vienna: Edition Selene.

Bowman S., & Willis, C. (2003). *We media: How audiences are shaping the future of news and information* (J. D. Lasica, Ed.). New York: Media Center at the American Press Institute. Retrieved November 20, 2007, from www.hypergene.net/wemedia/download/we_media .pdf

Brecht, B. (1967). Radiotheorie. In *Gesammelte Werke* (Vol. 7, pp. 117–134). Frankfurt am Main, Germany: Suhrkamp. (Original work published 1932)

Daniels, D. (2004). Interaction versus consumption: Mass media and art from 1920 to today. In C. Schöpf & G. Stocker (Eds.), *Timeshift: The world in 25 years* (pp. 146–152). Wien, NY: Springer.

Dudesek, K. (2004). Hotel Pomino: VGTV—A reactor for new media. In C. Schöpf & G. Stocker (Eds), *Timeshift: The world in 25 years* (pp. 178–180). Wien, NY: Springer.

Dudesek, K. (2005). About VGTV: Experience with the new media since 1986. Retrieved November 28, 2007, from http://web.archive.org/web/20050204152749/www.vgtv.com/n,150004,1.html

Enzensberger, H. M. (1970). Baukasten zu einer Theorie der Medien. *Kursbuch, 20,* 159–186.

Gerbner, G. (1969). Institutional pressures upon mass communications. In P. Halmos (Ed.), *The sociology of mass media communicators* (pp. 205–248). Keele, UK: University of Keele.

Gerhards, M., & Ringler, W. (2004). Mediennutzung in der Zukunft—Konstanz und Wandel: Trends und Perspektiven bis zum Jahr 2010. *Media Perspektiven, 10,* 472–482. Retrieved November 20, 2007, from www.media-perspektiven.de/uploads/tx_mppublications/10–2004_Gerhards.pdf

Gerhards, M., & Ringler, W. (2007). Mediennutzung in der Zukunft: Eine Trendanalyse auf der Basis heutiger Datenquellen. *Media Perspektiven, 6,* 295–309. Retrieved November 11, 2008, from www.media-perspektiven.de/uploads/tx_mp publications/06–2007_Gerhards.pdf

Glaser, M. (2004, November 17). The new voices: Hyperlocal citizen media sites want you (to write)! *Online Journalism Review.* Retrieved November 20, 2007, from ojr.org/ojr/glaser/1098833871.php

Gleich, U. (2003). Crossmedia—Schlüssel zum Erfolg: Verknüpfung von Medien in der Werbekommunikation. *Mediaperspektiven, 11,* 510–516.

Groebel, J. (2003, March). *Massenmedien in der Informationsgesellschaft—Tendenzen, Chancen und Risken.* Paper presented at the Medien in der Informationsgesellschaft: Status Quo und Perspektiven in Österreich conference, Vienna, Austria. Retrieved on November 28,

2006, from http://www.bka.gv.at/2004/7/6/Gesamtdokumentation.pdf

IBM Business Consulting Services. (2004). *Media and entertainment 2010: Open on the inside, open on the outside: The media company of the future.* Available at www-935.ibm.com/services/us/index.wss/ibvstudy/imc/a1001755?cntxtId=a1000062

Kluitenberg, E. (2003). *Constructing the digital commons: A venture into hybridisation.* Retrieved November 20, 2007, from www.n5m4.0rg/journa16f5c.html?118+575+3411

Lindsay, G. (2005, April 25). *The smart money behind video blogging: The history of exploiting film on the Web hasn't been good. Do Google and Gore have the formula?* Retrieved May, 20, 2006, from www.business2.com/b2/web/articles/0,17863,1054099,00.html

McChesney, R. W. (2001, March). Global media, neoliberalism, and imperialism. *Monthly Review, 52*(10). Retrieved November 20, 2007, from http://www.monthlyreview.org/301rwm.htm

McLuhan, M. (1994). *Understanding media: The extensions of man.* Cambridge, MA: McGraw-Hill.

OÖ Nachrichten. (2005, May 15). *BBC-Kameraauge im Mühlviertel.* Retrieved April 5, 2009, from www.nachrichten.at

Ponton/Van Gogh TV. (1992). *Piazza virtuale.* Retrieved November 27, 2007, from www.medienkunstnetz.de/works/piazza-virtuale

Prokhorov, A. (1995). Checkpoint 95. In K. Gerbel & P. Weibel (Eds.), *Mythos information: Welcome to the wired world.* Retrieved November 20, 2007, from http://90.146.8.18/de/archives/festival_archive/festival_catalogs/festival_artikel.asp?iProjectID=8656

Raboy, M. (2003). Media and democratization in the information society. In S. O'Siochru & B. Girard (Eds.), *Communicating in the information society* (pp. 101–119). Geneva, Switzerland: United Nations Research Institute for Social Development.

Reck, H. U. (Ed.). (1994). *Fernsehen der 3. Art.* Lehrkanzel für Kommunikationstheorie anläßlich des Symposions Fernsehen der Dritten Art. Vienna: Hochschule für Angewandte Kunst.

Rifkin, J. (2002). The age of access. In C. Schöpf & G. Stocker (Eds.), *Unplugged: Art as the scene of global conflicts* (pp. 43–49) (Ars electronica 2002). Ostfildern, Germany: Hatje Cantz.

Schöpf, C., & Stocker, G. (Eds.). (2002). *Unplugged: Art as the scene of global conflicts* (Ars electronica 2002). Ostfildern, Germany: Hatje Cantz.

Tremetzberger, O. (2003). Towards a society of control: New digital standards and theirimpact on freedom of information, current consequences and strategies for an independent public sphere. In C. Schöpf & G. Stocker (Eds.), *Code: The language of our time* (pp. 51–54). Ostfildern, Germany: Hatje Cantz.

Tremetzberger, O., & Leiner, V. (2004). Collaborative broadcasting: Models of technological innovation for tactical media. In C. Schöpf & G. Stocker (Eds.), *Timeshift: The world in 25 years* (pp. 201–203). Ostfildern, Germany: Hatje Cantz.

CHAPTER 5

Notes on a Theory of Community Radio

Kevin Howley

In this chapter, I want to share a few thoughts on community media in general and community radio in particular. Specifically, I offer some notes on a theory of community radio. Having said this, I want to make it clear that my work does not privilege theory over practice. Like many academics with an interest in community media studies, I have worked in the community media sector for most of my adult life. Thus, my theoretical perspective developed over time through an inductive method of observation and analysis that considers the historical development as well as the day-to-day practice of community media. By the same token, I do not want to forsake the theoretical in the name of the concrete, the empirical, and the practical. Simply put, my analysis foregrounds the *unity* of theory and practice.

I begin with a concise discussion of what cultural theorists refer to as "articulation." In doing so, I want to suggest that the theory of articulation holds enormous potential for the field of community media studies. My principle aim here is to recommend articulation as a descriptive and analytical tool for revealing the varied (and sometimes competing) forces and conditions that shape community radio initiatives. Moreover, I want to highlight the utility of articulation as a resource for community organizing and activism. Here, I observe the importance of cultivating strategic partnerships within and among state, civic, and private actors and institutions.

Following this, I move on to consider a handful of cases that, I hope, will illuminate these theoretical insights. For the bulk of this discussion, I draw on two cases that I have discussed elsewhere: WFHB, community radio in Bloomington, Indiana (Howley, 2001), and Allston-Brighton Free Radio, in Boston, Massachusetts (Howley, 2004). I also briefly consider one additional case that has only recently come to my attention—Allegheny Mountain Radio (Reed & Hanson, 2006), serving several counties on the border between Virginia and West Virginia— and that likewise helps illustrate some of the salient features of articulation that I would like to highlight. Each of these cases underscores the theoretical relevance and practical utility of articulation as a means not only for exploring but also for promoting and developing community radio.

In short, I want to suggest that, viewed through the lens of articulation theory, community radio might be understood as a set of institutional, technical, political, and economic arrangements; a range of social and cultural practices; and an ongoing process of community building and maintenance. As such, articulation offers scholars a powerful analytical tool to examine community radio and practitioners an invaluable resource to guide their actions and inform their practice.

What Do We Mean by Articulation?

Articulation, as I am using it here, is associated primarily with the work of cultural theorist Stuart Hall (1986). By way of explaining the concept of articulation, Hall notes two distinct but related definitions of the word. In the first instance, articulation refers to speaking or enunciating. The second meaning, common in the United Kingdom but less so in the United States, refers to the act of joining or combining separate elements. Hall's example is that of the connection between a truck and trailer; the relationship between these two discrete vehicles is said to be articulated.

While its usage in cultural theory tends to focus on the notion of a combination of elements or the connection between various groups, ideas, and practices, I have found both definitions—speaking and connection—to be enormously useful in thinking about community media. In saying this, I am acknowledging my debt to a line of thinking that foregrounds the relationship between communication and community. Specifically, I am thinking of the work of Benedict Anderson (1991), James Carey (1989), and Anthony Cohen (1985), among others, whose work focuses on what might best be described as the "symbolic construction of community."

Briefly stated, this line of inquiry emphasizes the role of communication—language, print and broadcast media, and other symbolic practices—in creating a sense of shared identity and collective solidarity between disparate groups and individuals. Significantly, these symbolic practices serve not only to create a common identity among different people but also to differentiate one community from another. To paraphrase Anthony Cohen (1985), communities are expressions of commonality as well as difference. This notion of a "unity in difference" is, to my mind, an elegant way of thinking about community. That is, while commonsense understandings of community highlight the similarities within and between community members and their everyday lived experience, community life is far more diverse and our experience of community far more heterogeneous than we tend to acknowledge at first blush.

From the standpoint of cultural theory, then, articulation foregrounds the connection between disparate elements and groups, as in a multicultural neighborhood or, to borrow Benedict Anderson's poetic phrase, the "imagined community" of the nation-state. That is to say, the feelings of affinity, belonging, "we-ness" that we share for our local neighborhoods, ethnic communities, or nationality are, in large measure, articulated within and through communication—broadly conceived—as in literature, performance, ritual, dress, and other symbolic forms and practices.

Three particularly salient insights emerge from this perspective. First, articulation emphasizes the act of joining or combining disparate elements rather than the linkage in and of itself. That is, how things are joined together—the *process* of articulation—is of paramount importance here. As Jennifer Daryl Slack (1996) observes, "Articulation is, then, not just a thing (not just a connection) but a process of creating connections" (p. 114). And, as a number of scholars interested in independent, alternative, citizens,' and participatory media have argued, this emphasis on process, on practice, on the "doing" of community-based media underscores the relationship between communication and community building (e.g., Atton, 2001; Gumucio Dagron, 2001; Rodriguez, 2001).

Second, articulation suggests that the connections, linkages, or alliances within any social formation, be it a nation-state, a neighborhood, or a media system, for that matter, are neither natural nor inevitable. Put another way, articulation highlights the dynamic and contingent character of any articulated relationship. The way in which a particular set of interests, groups, individuals, or practices are articulated is but one of many possible arrangements. Other arrangements, alliances, and articulations are also possible.

A third insight that follows from this is that of the pivotal role human action plays in articulating, and potentially *rearticulating,* any social formation. That is to say, if there is nothing inevitable or irreversible about any given set of arrangements or articulated relationships and, furthermore, these arrangements are not static, immobile, or fixed, then this articulated relationship is subject to change. In other words, articulation foregrounds what social theorists refer to as *agency*—the ability of human action to alter, remake, or re-create any social formation.

These insights have enormous consequences for the theory and practice of community radio. For analysts, articulation provides a framework to examine the various players, interests, and practices that make up community radio. By attending to the *specificity* of these practices, to the varied and sometimes competing forces and interests at play, and to the disparate stakeholders involved in organizing and operating a community radio station, scholars can develop a far more nuanced understanding of community media in any particular setting.

Articulation is equally useful for practitioners. With its focus on the contingent nature of any given set of arrangements and its emphasis on the process of forming alliances within and between disparate groups and interests, articulation serves an important strategic function. That is, articulation helps shape and inform the community-organizing efforts that are so critical to the establishment, viability, and long-term sustainability of a community radio station.

Theory Into Practice, Practice Into Theory

As noted earlier, my thinking on community radio has evolved over time. Nevertheless, it bears repeating that the theoretical perspectives I bring to the study of community radio developed from an ongoing engagement with the practice of community radio. With this in mind, I hope the following examples will serve to illustrate some of the insights I've discussed above.

WFHB

The initial effort to establish a community radio station for Bloomington, Indiana, began in 1975, soon after a handful of local residents attended the first National Alternative Radio Konference (NARK) in Madison, Wisconsin. WFHB first signed on the air in January 1993. The 18-year struggle to establish community radio for Bloomington is noteworthy and, as I have written elsewhere, indicative of the political economy of radio broadcasting in the United States (Howley, 1999). For our present purposes, I want to call attention to the specificity of *place* in shaping WFHB. In particular, I want to emphasize the importance of strategic alliances within and between various groups, and the subsequent arrangement of economic, institutional, and sociopolitical forces, in creating and sustaining community radio in Bloomington, Indiana.

The struggle to create a noncommercial and participatory community broadcasting service involved a host of players, including a handful of radio enthusiasts, area artists, musicians and recording engineers, members of the local business community, and Herman B Wells, the influential, highly respected, and well-connected chancellor of Indiana University (IU). Each of these "stakeholders" had different, sometimes divergent motives for and interests in establishing a community station.

The core group of community radio organizers, Jim Manion, Jeffery Morris, Richard Fish, and Brian Kearney, were eager to create a local broadcast service that reflected their eclectic sonic sensibilities. Like many community radio enthusiasts, the principle architects of WFHB have what Bruce Girard (1992) refers to as a "passion for radio." Prior to WFHB's arrival, commercial stations and a rather staid public service broadcaster located on the IU campus dominated the local airwaves in Bloomington and south-central Indiana—community radio would provide a "sound alternative" to these existing services.

Members of the artists' community, including musicians, recording engineers, and local club owners saw in the station an opportunity to cultivate the local music scene and leverage Bloomington's growing reputation as a hotbed of musical experimentation and expression. The significance of music and the music industry to Bloomington's identity cannot be overstated in this regard.

On the other hand, local business owners were less enthusiastic. That is, until Brian Kearney managed to persuade Herman Wells to support the station. Wells legitimized the community radio project for skeptical business and civic leaders in and around Bloomington. While Wells's motives are less clear, his desire to promote a community service outside of and in addition to the campus public broadcaster seems to have led him to support the establishment of a noncommercial station unaffiliated with Indiana University.

Brian Kearney's work in securing the support of various constituencies was pivotal—and demonstrated a formidable strategic intelligence, at that. His task was to articulate a vision of community radio that would appeal to various stakeholders whose cultural tastes and political orientations were quite distinct.

For business leaders, Kearney highlighted the economic development opportunities that a community station represented. For artists and musicians, the community station provided an outlet for their creative work. Indeed, following protracted negotiations, it was determined that the station would be housed in the newly established Bloomington Arts Center. And finally, for local radio enthusiasts, whose creativity and adventurism were cultivated by a cable TVFM service, various student-run outlets, as well as a handful of "pirate" operations, the station would at long last provide an alternative to the uninspired broadcasting of commercial and public radio in and around Bloomington.

In articulating this vision of community radio, however, community radio enthusiasts in Bloomington chose to depoliticize community radio. That is to say, the dominant model of community radio in the United States owed a great deal to the philosophical orientation and programming strategies associated with Lew Hill, founder of KPFA, and the Pacifica stations, known in broadcasting circles for their progressive (some might say radical) politics and their decidedly and unapologetically unconventional approach to radio (e.g., Milam, 1988).

Thus, while WFHB is listener supported and largely volunteer run, as is common in the community broadcasting sector, the station's organizers made a conscious and deliberate decision to avoid the progressive orientation that had come to characterize U.S. community radio. In doing so, the founders of WFHB rearticulated an established tradition of community radio to accommodate those interests whose support was crucial to getting the station on the air and making the operation sustainable over time.

To this day, WFHB continues to negotiate the tensions between sometimes competing visions of community broadcasting. Suffice it to say, then, that WFHB articulates a community broadcasting service that accommodates diverse stakeholders, including the local business community, social service organizations, university students, faculty, and staff, artists and musicians, as well as labor, housing, environmental groups, and other members of Bloomington's activist community.

Allston-Brighton Free Radio

In contrast to the depoliticized approach that WFHB took to community broadcasting, Allston-Brighton Free Radio (A-B Free) is predicated on addressing the dramatic imbalance between those with access to the airwaves—and the enormous material and symbolic power that broadcasting represents—and those whose opinions, interests, and perspectives are rarely heard on either commercial or public service radio (Howley, 2004).

A-B Free had its origins in a so-called free radio station, Radio Free Allston (RFA), that operated in direct opposition to the Federal Communication Commission's (FCC) prohibition against low-power FM (LPFM) transmissions. Whereas WFHB sought to distance itself from a tradition of community broadcasting that embraced an oppositional political culture, RFA articulated its operation with an emerging microbroadcasting movement that coalesced in the United States in the late 1990s: a movement that sought to "reclaim the airwaves" through direct action and other forms of electronic civil disobedience (Howley, 2000).

Unlike the clandestine operations of so-called pirate radio common in the United States and much of Western Europe during the 1970s, the free radio movement operated "in plain sight" of federal regulators. Accordingly, RFA set up its broadcasting and transmission gear in a local ice cream parlor frequented by the residents of the densely populated, multicultural neighborhood of Allston-Brighton in Boston, Massachusetts.

RFA's initial success was impressive by any standard. Despite its limited transmitting power and abbreviated broadcast schedule, RFA quickly established a participating listenership that represented a broad crosssection of the neighborhood. Given the illegal character of the operation, it is all the more remarkable that local business owners, area civic and religious leaders, and even the Boston City Council supported RFA and its mission to provide a community broadcasting service to the residents of Allston-Brighton.

The station also had considerable appeal for immigrant groups recently settled in the neighborhood. For instance, both the Irish and Brazilian Immigration Centers were early supporters of and contributors to the station. Indeed, a good deal of RFA's program schedule featured news, cultural, and public affairs programming produced in Spanish, Portuguese, and Haitian Creole. This programming, in some instances the only programming of its kind in the entire city of Boston, was instrumental in helping recent immigrants make a home in their newly adopted land. In this modest but significant fashion, RFA was instrumental in articulating a sense of community within and between various ethnic groups—recent arrivals and longtime residents alike.

RFA's success was short lived, however. Although one of the tactics of the free radio movement was to precipitate an enforcement crisis for the FCC, thereby putting LPFM on the regulatory agenda, the FCC forced RFA off the air after only a few months of operation. Rather than give up, however, RFA founder Stephen Provizer and his "staff" decided to take their operation to the expanded AM band. The newly christened A-B Free, part of a larger organization called the Citizen's Media Corps (CMC), began the ambitious task of conducting public information campaigns regarding proposed legislation to legalize LPFM, conducted media-literacy programs in local schools, and continued to work with local residents on community-oriented broadcasting.

Here, then, A-B Free articulated its community broadcasting service with the larger sociopolitical issues related to communication policy at the national level. In addition to working alongside members of the Prometheus Radio Project, an organization committed to establishing LPFM and other community radio outlets across the country, the CMC also worked with Boston Neighborhood Network and local public access television as well as the national organization People for Better Television (PBTV) to discuss the public service implications of the transition from analog to digital television.

However, A-B Free faced even greater odds against reaching local audiences than its predecessor. Operating at only one tenth of a watt (100 milliwatts), A-B Free had an extremely limited broadcast range. Indeed, for some observers, A-B Free was an exercise in futility. And yet, community residents continued to make use of the facilities and produce a range of programs covering local environmental, education, and social justice issues as well as music and cultural programming that reflected the neighborhood's ethnic and cultural diversity. Despite the logistical problems involved, A-B Free sought a number of technical "work-arounds" to get beyond its diminutive broadcast range. To that end, A-B Free explored retransmission of its Web streaming in and around Allston-Brighton. These technological arrangements were coupled with institutional alignments with a number of local stations, including WMBR-FM, originating from the Massachusetts Institute of Technology (MIT), and WJIB-AM in Quincy, Massachusetts. By articulating the station's operations, especially its impressive news and public affairs programming, with other public service and commercial radio stations in and around Boston, A-B Free managed to keep its programming relevant to local listeners and, in certain instances, reach even wider publics.

Allegheny Mountain Radio

In contrast to WFHB and A-B Free, my working knowledge of Allegheny Mountain Radio (AMR) is limited. Nevertheless, I want to discuss a few salient features about AMR that help illustrate

some of the points I've been making. Specifically, I want to highlight how community radio on the border of Virginia and West Virginia is articulated with the social, cultural, and geographic dimensions of the remote and isolated communities of this region. Here, then, I'll emphasize how the specificity of place—in this case, the geographic and cultural dimensions of a community—shapes and informs the institutional mission and programming philosophy of these stations.

AMR is a network of community stations: WVMR, 1370 AM, Frost, West Virginia; WCHG, 107.1 FM, Hot Springs, Virginia; WVLS, 89.7 FM, Monterey, Virginia; and Radio Durbin, W278AL, 103.5 FM, Durbin, West Virginia. The stations are owned and operated by the Pocahontas Communication Cooperative Corporation. One of the distinguishing features of AMR is the fact that these stations are "first service providers" in their respective communities. There are no commercial or public radio stations serving the Highland and Bath counties of Virginia or the Pocahontas County of West Virginia.

Whereas both WFHB and A-B Free grew out of a profound dissatisfaction with existing broadcast outlets, the stations of AMR were organized to provide a broadcast service where none had existed before (Reed & Hanson, 2006). In a rather dramatic fashion, then, AMR vividly demonstrates that community radio is an expression of the *felt need* of a community to use broadcasting for purposes of community communication.

Indeed, in this isolated part of the country, broadcasting takes on a level of significance that is perhaps difficult for many of us to comprehend but which is nevertheless undeniable. That is to say, for those of us who live in communities served by any number of radio stations, the lack of even a single broadcast service is difficult to imagine. And yet, this condition is revealing, inasmuch as it demonstrates just how remote and inaccessible these communities are.

Recognizing the need for a broadcast service that was responsive to the very particular needs of these communities, then, a handful of community organizers launched WVLS (Virginia's Little Switzerland) in the early 1980s. WVLS provides programming to the other stations of the network on an as-needed basis.

Like other community stations across the United States, AMR operates with a small staff and dozens of volunteer programmers. Listener support helps supplement federal grant and foundation monies that go toward equipment purchases and otherwise help sustain the station. Equally important, community support, in the forms of in-kind contributions and sweat equity, has enabled AMR to expand its operation over the course of the past 10 years. For instance, carpentry students at Highland High School constructed the studios of WVLS.

Despite some important similarities, AMR is quite distinct from other community radio stations across the country. For example, whereas other community stations consciously eschew a single program format or musical genre, AMR's program schedule is dedicated primarily to bluegrass and gospel music. Likewise, the news and public affairs programming reflects the social and political conservatism of this region. Rather than run programming produced by Pacifica or even National Public Radio (NPR), AMR broadcasts conservative talk shows, such as Rush Limbaugh's, that are more commonly associated with commercial AM stations. Furthermore, given the rugged terrain and extreme weather conditions that have a profound influence on day-to-day life and social interaction among local residents, weather-related information, including crisis management activities, are a central feature of AMR's operation.

All this is to suggest that, while the impulse behind all these initiatives is to enhance and improve community communication through radio broadcasting, these services are articulated within and through existing structures, practices, and values. AMR is unique in the U.S. community radio sector precisely because it operates in a distinctive geographic, social, and cultural milieu. In other words, the dynamics of place

articulate a particular organizational culture and program philosophy for the stations of AMR.

Conclusion

Of course, a more thorough discussion of each of these organizations would reveal the finer points of the argument that I have been making. Nevertheless, I trust that these brief case studies illuminate some insights that I have regarding community radio theory and practice. In conclusion, then, let me restate in general terms the utility of the concept of articulation for both community radio scholars and practitioners.

Articulation foregrounds several aspects of community radio that are especially germane to communication and media studies. By offering a broadcast service by, for, and about a specific locality, community radio provides what Roger Silverstone (1999) calls "the symbolic raw materials" for community building and maintenance. Through music and cultural programming, news, opinion, and public affairs, as well by the ritual of the daily program schedule, community radio constructs a shared experience and a collective sense of identity. Put another way, community radio highlights the fundamental yet enigmatic relationship between communication and community.

Of course, commercial and public service broadcasting accomplish much the same thing. What distinguishes community radio, then, is precisely the way in which the institutional and technological arrangements of broadcasting are *rearticulated* to suit the particular and distinctive needs of local communities. Here, we can detect the relevance of articulation in understanding the process by which local populations come to make use of communication technologies for purposes of community communication.

From a theoretical perspective, then, articulation highlights the contingent and indeterminate character of media systems that appear to be somehow natural or inevitable. In other words, community radio highlights people's ability to alter and rearrange existing media structures to better suit their needs. In doing so, community radio vividly demonstrates the possibility for alternative broadcasting structures, forms, routines, and practices.

For practitioners, articulation offers important insights into the process of establishing and sustaining a community radio station. As we have seen, while the impulses behind the community radio initiatives described above are rather similar, the strategies and tactics used to realize these projects are unique to each particular community.

With this in mind, then, community radio organizers and advocates are best served by identifying those groups and individuals, including social service organizations, civic associations, and racial, ethnic, and religious groups as well as business owners and government agencies, that might share an interest in community broadcasting. Strategic thinking that leverages the human, technical, institutional, cultural, and economic capital within a particular place is crucial to the establishment, viability, and long-term success of community radio.

In sum, one size does not fit all. Practitioners are, therefore, confronted with the daunting task of articulating a vision of community that resonates with diverse constituencies and encourages broad-based participation in the community station's mission, management, and day-to-day operations. The experiences of community radio that I have outlined above indicate how a sensitivity to the particular and distinctive assets and attributes of any given place might be articulated to create a media system that respects, as well as reflects, the lives and experiences of local communities.

References

Anderson, B. (1991). *Imagined communities: Reflections on the origins and spread of nationalism.* London: Verso.

Atton, C. (2001). *Alternative media.* London: Sage.

Carey, J. (1989). *Communication as culture: Essays on media and society.* Cambridge, UK: Unwin.

Cohen, A. (1985). *The symbolic construction of community.* Cambridge, UK: Tavistock.

Girard, B. (1992). *A passion for radio.* Montreal, Ontario, Canada: Black Rose Books.

Gumucio Dagron, A. (2001). *Making waves: Stories of participatory communication for social change.* New York: Rockefeller Foundation.

Hall, S. (1986). On postmodernism and articulation: An interview with Stuart Hall. *Journal of Communication Inquiry, 10*(2), 45–60.

Howley, K. (1999). Finding a spot on the dial: The struggle for community radio in Bloomington, Indiana. *Journal of Radio Studies, 6*(1), 41–55.

Howley, K. (2000). Radiocracy rulz! Microradio as electronic activism. *International Journal of Cultural Studies, 3*(2), 256–267.

Howley, K. (2001). Talking about public affairs programming: WFHB and the legacy of listener-sponsored radio. *Historical Journal of Film, Radio and Television, 21*(4), 399–415.

Howley, K. (2004). Remaking public service broadcasting: Lessons from Allston-Brighton Free Radio. *Social Movement Studies, 3*(2), 221–240.

Milam, L. W. (1988). *The original sex and broadcasting: A handbook on starting a radio station for the community* (4th ed.). San Diego, CA: Mho & Mho Works.

Reed, M., & Hanson, R. (2006). Back to the future: Allegheny Mountain Radio and localism in West Virginia community radio. *Journal of Radio Studies, 13*(2), 214–231.

Rodriguez, C. (2001). *Fissures in the mediascape: An international study of citizens' media.* Cresskill, NJ: Hampton Press.

Silverstone, R. (1999). *Why study the media?* Thousand Oaks, CA: Sage.

Slack, J. D. (1996). The theory and method of articulation in cultural studies. In D. Morley & K. Chen (Eds.), *Stuart Hall: Critical dialogues in cultural studies* (pp. 112–127). New York: Routledge.

PART II

Civil Society and the Public Sphere

The chapters included in this section draw on two distinct but related concepts that are central to contemporary democratic theory: *civil society* and the *public sphere*. Civil society is by far the older of the two ideas—one with a "distinguished pedigree" in Western social and political thought (Hodgkinson & Foley, 2000). Conversely, the public sphere is a relatively new concept associated with the work of the German social theorist Jurgen Habermas (1989). Together, these two ideas have informed a great deal of thinking about the character, conduct, and constitution of democratic societies in the post–Cold War era. Indeed, debates surrounding civil society and the public sphere are common across a variety of disciplines, from political science and international relations to anthropology and social psychology. As we shall see, the two concepts have enormous relevance for community media studies.

Civil Society

Briefly tracing the concept from its roots in Ancient Greece, through the rise of the modern nation-state in the 18th and early 19th centuries,

to the present era, we find discrete, sometimes competing if not contradictory visions of what civil society is and what its relationship is to the social order and political organization. For instance, the Greek term *polis,* roughly translated as an "association of associations," emphasizes the development of civic virtue through the art and practice of self-governance. Accordingly, shared decision making would not only ensure a just and ordered society but also create a loyal, engaged, and virtuous citizenry.

Until the middle of the 18th century, civil society was considered synonymous with the state. In the modern formulation, civil society is separate and distinct from the state. This perspective, first articulated by the Scottish philosopher Adam Ferguson, suggests that civil society exists independently from, sometimes in tension with, state authority and institutions. Herein lies the origin of the notion, common to liberal democratic theories of the state, that while the state is the guarantor and defender of individual rights, civil society is responsible for ensuring good governance.

Viewed from this perspective, one aim of civil society is to legitimize and reinforce state authority.

In contrast, during the 1930s, the Italian political theorist Antonio Gramsci (1971) elaborated a Marxist interpretation of the concept that viewed civil society as a site of hegemonic struggle between dominant and subordinate social groups and interests. Thus, civil society is not a mechanism to support the status quo but is, potentially at least, an arena for social transformation. This perspective informed the transition from authoritarian regimes to more representative forms of government in Eastern Europe and across Latin America in the late 1980s and 1990s.

Current usage of the phrase *civil society* builds on and extends some of these ideas. For instance, the cultivation of civic virtue through association and everyday relations is still deemed essential to civil society. Likewise, contemporary understandings of civil society retain a healthy skepticism toward state power and authority. In recent years, the concentration of political power and social influence within the market economy pits elements of civil society against corporate as well as state excess and abuse. Finally, the transformative potential of civil society continues to serve as a wellspring for popular movements and remains a source of inspiration for resistance to repressive regimes of state and corporate power.

With this in mind, we can offer the following as a general working definition of the term: *civil society* refers to *voluntary associations,* distinct from both the state and the market, that enable and encourage widespread participation in public life. Thus, civil society comprises those nongovernmental or nonprofit organizations whose members are neither compelled nor coerced to participate. Examples of civil society groups include advocacy and citizens' action groups, neighborhood and tenant associations, social movements, nongovernment organizations (NGOs), athletic clubs, trade unions, professional societies, and the like. In short, civil society consists of a diverse set of actors operating in a variety of formal and informal settings who share common values, interests, and pursuits.

Of course, not all voluntary associations are egalitarian, let alone progressive. Consider, for instance, gangs, paramilitary organizations, or white supremacist groups that endorse intolerance, hostility, or violence toward racial, ethnic, lifestyle, or religious groups. However, because there is a strong normative dimension to the concept, civil society is commonly understood as a vehicle for defending human, civil, and political rights against institutional or systematic abuse. Here, then, we can detect the importance of "citizenship," "pluralism," "the rule of law," and "the common good" to the theory and practice of civil society.

For our purposes, we can tease out a few salient themes from the extensive literature on civil society to help us better understand the value and importance of community media. The problem of defining "the common good," for example, is a perennial concern in the civil society tradition. Here, the tension between private matters and public life, between the individual and the community, take center stage. Civil society emerges as a mechanism for negotiating competing interests in a way that defends individual autonomy on the one hand, while promoting public service and community mindedness on the other. Thus, civil society serves as an intermediary between the private individual and the wider community—a realm in which cultural values and social norms are articulated, reinforced, and renegotiated.

Berger and Neuhaus (2000) coined the phrase "mediating structures" to describe the role civil society plays in promoting active and engaged citizenship in increasingly complex, impersonal, bureaucratic societies. Mediating structures—the neighborhood, the church, and voluntary associations—they argue, counteract the alienating effects of government bureaucracies, business conglomerates, and other so-called megastructures that have eroded public confidence in social institutions and democratic practices. While their neoconservative approach minimizes the role of the market in exacerbating economic disparities and social injustice, their concept of mediating structures is useful insofar as it captures some of the essential features of community media.

According to Berger and Neuhaus (2000), mediating structures are "those institutions standing between the individual and his [*sic*] public life and the large institutions of public life" (p. 214). Community media fulfill this role in a significant and distinctive fashion. Through information, news, opinion, and cultural fare, community media outlets such as newspapers and magazines, radio and television broadcasts, electronic bulletin boards, and social networking sites connect us to people and institutions outside of and apart from the domestic sphere of the home and family.

For example, in so-called developing societies, community media (typically community radio) are a primary source of news and information. Especially in rural areas where commercial, public service, or state-run media are unavailable, community media represent the only link between the local population and the wider world. Conversely, in highly mediated societies, where the economic logic of media consolidation has effectively hollowed out local media markets and replaced locally produced content with canned news and cultural programming, community media "fill in the gap" left by national chains and transnational media organizations. In this respect, community media are significant inasmuch as they are "alternative mechanisms" (Berger & Neuhaus, 2000, p. 213) for the provision of social services that neither the state nor the market offer to local communities.

What makes community media distinctive is the opportunity that they offer various elements of civil society to "talk back" to the large institutions of public life. That is to say, by providing civil society groups—such as environmental activists, cultural associations, peace and social justice advocates, and youth groups—with the technical infrastructure and training to use communication technologies to communicate with wider publics, community media represent a unique intermediary institution that emerges from, supports, and regenerates civil society. This last point is critical, inasmuch as it indicates that mediating structures have value for local populations precisely because they reflect the community's desire to create institutions and cultivate practices that are relevant and accountable to the local community. Like other mediating structures, then, community media are "expressions of the real values and the real needs of people in society" (Berger & Neuhaus, 2000, p. 217).

Another prominent theme in the literature on civil society, one that is especially pertinent to community media studies, is the relationship between voluntary associations and the cultivation of democratic values and practices. For instance, the French political theorist Alexis de Tocqueville famously celebrated the voluntary associations he encountered during his travels across the United States in the early 19th century. For de Tocqueville, voluntary associations were "schools for democracy" insofar as they encouraged participants to gain civic competencies at the local level. In other words, voluntary associations provide private individuals with the opportunity to develop skills and attitudes—speaking and listening, cooperation and equanimity—required of a self-governing people: skills and attitudes that are transferable to a variety of contexts and that are essential for securing a democratic society.

Like other voluntary associations, community media consciously adopt participatory decision-making structures and practices that promote a sense of belonging to, and responsibility toward, the organization, its mission, and its relationship to the wider community. Equally important, community media encourage private individuals to work collaboratively in meaningful activities that not only promote sociability among individual participants but also serve a variety of local needs and interests. In doing so, community media cultivate a more deliberate approach to participation in public life, nurture social networks within and between communities, and, potentially at least, encourage innovative ways to think about the practice of democracy.

Finally, this focus on voluntary association underscores the importance of local groups and structures in reviving a sense of belonging and community solidarity at a time when these affective relations are losing ground in an increasingly complex, often alienating modern world. Voluntary associations remind us of just how important a shared sense of place is for overcoming the feelings of apathy and disenfranchisement that undermine democratic values, practices, and institutions.

Public Sphere

In his seminal analysis of modern political discourse *The Structural Transformation of the Public Sphere,* Jurgen Habermas (1989) contends that the public sphere emerged in Western Europe during the 17th and 18th centuries as a means for bourgeois society to articulate its economic interests and assert its political autonomy from the state. In Habermas's formulation, the public sphere is a discursive realm between civil society and the state in which private individuals engage in *rational-critical debate* to discuss matters of common concern. Within this discursive space, the rank and status of individual speakers is overlooked, participants are treated as equals, and decision making is based on logic and reason. Accordingly, the public sphere is a deliberative space in which a self-organizing public debates matters of common interest in a rational and civil fashion.

Significantly, Habermas extols the virtues of local institutions—coffeehouses, salons, and other public meeting places—as egalitarian spaces in which private citizens could temporarily suspend their individual interests and deliberate as equals in pursuit of "the common good." Although his account privileges face-to-face communication among individual participants, Habermas recognizes the value of an independent press for encouraging public discourse and otherwise publicizing matters of common concern. In short, Habermas argues that the free exchange of ideas among equals constituted a public sphere that served to keep state power in check, promoted an active and engaged citizenry, and supported the development of modern liberal democracies.

Habermas's history proceeds to chart the erosion of the public sphere throughout the 19th and early 20th centuries. The advent of systems of mass communication, Habermas asserts, undermined the foundation of civil society. Like other critical theorists associated with the Frankfurt School, Habermas argues that large-scale, commercial media displace civic culture and promote consumer culture: a whole way of life predicated on the pursuit of individual self-interest rather than the cultivation of community-minded values and attitudes. From this perspective, the "culture industries" serve as a form of ideological domination that depoliticizes and isolates private individuals, substituting entertainment and spectacle for rational debate and civic virtue. For Habermas, then, the institutions and technologies of modern media—film, radio, and television—have a degenerative effect on the public sphere that threatens the viability of a vigorous civil society.

Habermas's work has generated considerable and often contentious debate. For some critics, Habermas's history neglects "alternative public spheres" developed over time by women, racial and cultural minorities, the working class, and other groups deliberately excluded from participation in the bourgeois public sphere (Herbst, 1994; Negt & Kluge, 1993). Likewise, critics contend that the normative model of public discourse that Habermas develops avoids the complexities and contradictions inherent in pluralistic societies.

For instance, philosopher Nancy Fraser's (1992) critique calls into question a number of Habermas's assumptions regarding the possibilities of equitable deliberation and debate in heterogeneous and socioeconomically stratified societies. For Fraser and others, Habermas's formulation ignores power differentials between various members of society. What's more, Habermas's insistence on rational-critical debate excludes expressive and affective forms of communication, publicity, and persuasion. Fraser's main contribution to this debate is the notion of *subaltern counter publics* (i.e., oppressed, subordinate, or marginalized groups who organize themselves in efforts to challenge their subordinate status) a concept that foregrounds unequal distribution of political, economic, and social capital in nominally democratic cultures. As we shall see, this notion of "counter publics" figures prominently in discussions of community media.

Despite these criticisms, Habermas's work continues to inform debates about the relationship between public discourse and democratic theory and practice. Not surprisingly, media occupy contested terrain in these debates. Summing up this condition, sociologist Richard Butsch (2007) observes, "Issues of the media and public sphere revolve around the central axis of *whether media enable or undermine a healthy public sphere with widespread participation* [italics added]" (p. 3). For analysts taking a political economic perspective, popular participation in the public sphere is seriously compromised by the concentration of media ownership and control (McChesney, 1997). From a culturalist perspective, the situation is not so clear-cut (McKee, 2005).

For instance, some observers contend that despite unequal access to the technologies of media production and distribution, audiences are endlessly creative in using commercial, public, and state-run media to participate, even if in a limited and tenuous fashion, in the public sphere. Moreover, media audiences participate in the public sphere through a variety of forms and genres—not just "deliberative" formats such as news reports and current affairs programming. From this perspective, then, daytime talk shows, popular music, and reality television are legitimate resources for public deliberation and debate (Kramer, 2007; Lunt & Pantti, 2007).

Given the complexities and contradictions of contemporary media culture, it is unlikely that debates regarding the deliberative possibilities afforded by our current media system will be resolved anytime soon, especially if we adhere to Habermas's normative formulation. Rather than dispense with the concept altogether, then, we would do well to adopt "a relaxed set of criteria" for evaluating actually existing public spheres (Butsch, 2007). After all, few public spheres meet the standards of participation and rational-critical

debate associated with Habermas's model. What's more, the proliferation of media forms and outlets—print, radio, and television broadcasting, cable and satellite distribution, and all manner of online communication—challenges the idea(l) of a singular or unified public sphere.

Theorizing along these lines indicates that we can better appreciate the character of public discourse in an era of modern communication by thinking in terms of multiple, overlapping, and competing public spheres (Calhoun, 1992; Fraser, 1992). This move has proved beneficial for legitimizing the study of alternative and community media within academic circles (Atton, 2002; Downing, 2001). For years, grassroots and other so-called small media were deemed too esoteric or inconsequential for serious academic inquiry. In light of their "amateur" production values, "inferior" aesthetics, and "small" audiences vis-à-vis dominant media, analysts rarely subjected these media outlets to sustained critical inquiry. However, as recent scholarship vividly demonstrates, community-based media are significant precisely because they provide an opportunity for those whose perspectives, opinions, and interests are marginalized within dominant media discourse to participate in the public sphere (Howley, 2007; Rodriguez, 2001).

Furthermore, by providing the institutional resources for individuals and groups to produce their own media form and content, community-based media play a significant, if somewhat overlooked, role in the construction and maintenance of public sphere(s). Thus, community media represent a fertile site for empirical analyses of the structure, sustainability, inclusiveness, and deliberative potential of actually existing public spheres. With this in mind, we can begin to appreciate the contribution that community media studies can make to ongoing debates surrounding the public sphere(s).

Contributors in this section wrestle with the theoretical and practical questions raised by these issues. Specifically, the following chapters interrogate the relationship between civil society and community-based media. As a number of our contributions demonstrate, "community media originates, circulates and resonates from the sphere of civil society" (IAMCR, quoted in Rennie, 2006, p. 4). Throughout, contributors consider how community-based media enable or constrain the formation of more egalitarian and diversified public sphere(s) in a variety of geographic settings.

The first chapter in this section (Chapter 6) examines the role that community radio has played in the reconstruction of civil society in the former Yugoslavia. Mojca Planšak and Zala Volčič call our attention to community radio's significance in the process of building community and reestablishing the public sphere following an intense period of ethnic conflict, political turmoil, and civil war. In doing so, they challenge radio's "invisible status" in both the popular imagination and academic circles. Planšak and Volčič's contribution alerts us to the medium's capacity to promote reconciliation and renewal in the aftermath of national crisis.

Nkosi Ndlela's contribution (Chapter 7) highlights alternative media's significance in a landscape dominated by state-run media. Ndlela demonstrates the extent to which Zimbabwe's communication policies have limited the ability of individuals and groups to access news and information from perspectives that are critical of the government. In this situation, communities make use of a variety of communication technologies and practices in the construction of an alternative public sphere for the production and distribution of oppositional discourse.

Vanessa Parlette (Chapter 8) follows with a case study of *Toronto Street News* (*TSN*)—a weekly alternative newspaper established to address the crisis of homelessness in one of Canada's major cities. Combining ethnographic analysis with close readings of *TSN*, Parlette contends that street newspapers amplify the voices of the homeless: a group that is typically excluded from participation in civic life, demonized in the press, and otherwise marginalized within the wider community.

Shifting our focus from print to computer-mediated communication, Ian Goodwin (Chapter 9) describes efforts to use community informatics to reinvigorate the public sphere in suburban Birmingham, the United Kingdom. Drawing on contemporary theories of civic engagement and the public sphere, Goodwin's analysis of the Moseley Egroup finds that the ability of communication and information technologies to revitalize local democracy "from the ground up" is constrained by perennial difficulties associated with deliberative democracy.

This sobering assessment of community in cyberspace is not unique. The situation confronting the Roma people of the Republic of Macedonia presents an equally vexing set of problems related to community communication. In this section's final chapter (Chapter 10), Shayna Plaut describes an information impasse between two key constituents of Macedonian civil society: Romani media and Romani NGOs. According to Plaut, the lack of communication between these two segments of civil society not only confounds the ability of Roma people to integrate into wider national culture but also inhibits the social, economic, and political development of this ethnic minority community.

References

Atton, C. (2002). *Alternative media*. Thousand Oaks, CA: Sage.

Berger, P., & Neuhaus, R. J. (2000). To empower people. In V. A. Hodgkinson & M. W. Foley (Eds.), *The civil society reader* (pp. 213–233). Lebanon, NH: University Press of New England. (Original work published 1977)

Butsch, R. (Ed.). (2007). *Media and public spheres*. New York: Palgrave Macmillan.

Calhoun, C. (Ed.). (1992). *Habermas and the public sphere*. Cambridge: MIT Press.

Downing, J. (2001). *Radical media: Rebellious communication and social movements*. Thousand Oaks, CA: Sage.

Fraser, N. (1992). Rethinking the public sphere: A contribution to the critique of actually existing democracy.

In C. Calhoun (Ed.), *Habermas and the public sphere* (pp. 109–142). Cambridge: MIT Press.

Gramsci, A. (1971). *Selections from the prison notebooks of Antonio Gramsci* (Q. Hoare & G. N. Smith, Eds. & Trans.). New York: International.

Habermas, J. (1989). *The structural transformation of the public sphere: An inquiry into a category of bourgeois society.* Cambridge: MIT Press.

Herbst, S. (1994). *Politics at the margin: Historical studies of public expression outside of the mainstream.* Cambridge, UK: Cambridge University Press.

Hodgkinson, V. A., & Foley, M. W. (Eds.). (2000). *The civil society reader.* Lebanon, NH: University Press of New England.

Howley, K. (2007). Community media and the public sphere. In E. Devereux (Ed.), *Media studies: Key issues and debates* (pp. 342–360). London: Sage.

Kramer, M. (2007). The psychedelic public and its problems: Rock music festivals and civil society in the sixties counterculture. In R. Butsch (Ed.), *Media and public spheres* (pp. 149–161). New York: Palgrave Macmillan.

Lunt, P., & Pantti, M. (2007). Popular culture and the public sphere: Currents of feeling and social control in talk shows and reality TV. In R. Butsch (Ed.), *Media and public spheres* (pp. 162–174). New York: Palgrave Macmillan.

McChesney, R. (1997). *Corporate media and the threat to democracy.* Boston: Seven Stories Press.

McKee, A. (2005). *The public sphere: An introduction.* Cambridge, UK: Cambridge University Press.

Negt, O., & Kluge, A. (1993). *Public sphere and experience: Toward an analysis of the bourgeois and proletarian public sphere.* Minneapolis: University of Minnesota Press.

Rennie, E. (2006). *Community media: A global introduction.* Lanham, MD: Rowman & Littlefield.

Rodriguez, C. (2001). *Fissures in the mediascape.* Cresskill, NJ: Hampton Press.

CHAPTER 6

Reimagining National Belonging With Community Radio

Mojca Planšak

Zala Volčič

In the past decade, there has been much interest among scholars from a variety of disciplines in the question of how countries and communities recover from episodes of social change, political collapse, or violence and of how, precisely, the media should help in this process (Fletcher & Weinstein, 2002). The role of the media in re-creating a sense of belonging and reconciliation occupies a special place in globally circulating social change literature (Servaes, 2003; Wilson, 2003). The media are seen as a crucial player in the formation of identities, based on their role in providing space for (community) discussion and in helping sustain, suppress, or simply deal with cultural memories, myths, and collective fears, hopes, and desires for the future (Billig, 1995; Morley, 2000; Williams, 1977, 1980). Furthermore, mass media, as the area for public representation of ideas, interests, and free discussion, are an essential and basic condition for the constitution of civil society. In particular,

community media (media produced for and by different community groups) have often been viewed as offering alternative (nonnationalistic and noncommercial) spaces of belonging.

The break up of Yugoslavia into seven independent nation-states is usually associated with wars that started in the summer of 1991.[1] However, it is less often recognized that the collapse of the Yugoslav state had been preceded by almost a decade of protests, demonstrations, (nationalistic) media propaganda, and other types of political mobilization in the 1980s and 1990s. In that, the role of community radio was understood and continues to be crucial in providing an alternative means of communication about local and global cultures, politics, and identity during the 1980s (a period of nationalistic mobilizations), 1990s (a period of wars and media propaganda), and today (a period of commercialization and privatization of media). Most of the scholars point to the mainstream media and analyze how media have played an important role in spreading nationalistic propaganda (Skopljanac Brunner, 2000; Thompson, 1995) and continue to play a role in the reproduction of nationalisms (Erjavec & Volčič, 2006). Thompson (1995) argues how the media were and are used as a homogenizing medium in all former Yugoslav states. He shows how, for example, national(istic) television, as a profitable ground for unequivocal representations, served the creation of a unified sense of national identity in Slovenia, Croatia, and Serbia alike.

However, the invisible status of *radio* in the general research agenda of media studies warrants an attempt to reestablish the significance of such a taken-for-granted medium and salvage it from the cultural neglect it has been subjected to. Particularly in the former Yugoslav region (community), radio continues to play a significant role not only in the dissemination of information but also in the community-building and development programs, providing various minorities and remote and disenfranchised communities with a low-cost public domain. However, the field of community radio and media activism in the former Yugoslav context is relatively unexplored (see more in Richardson, 2006). Magazine, newspaper, and Internet articles briefly discuss the existence of community radio channels; yet, to date, there are no scholarly analyses of this topic.

Generally speaking, community radio is a "nonprofit" organization, serving communities in which they are located, or to which they broadcast, while promoting the participation of this community in the radio. Or, as Johnson and Menichelli (2007) put it, the community media "are media created to allow individuals to tell the stories and have the conversations necessary for their own self-directed development as citizens" (p. 34). Community radio was founded in the middle of the 1960s and early 1970s and, among other characteristics, started to challenge the idea of a nation as the most important container or identification marker for people. Community radio, from its beginning, believed that there are other scales of senses of belonging—other connections and identities, such as class, gender, ethnicity, or different

"taste" communities—that are of special importance in the former Yugoslav region, where community radio continues to offer a space to reflect back on belonging to a community and to further question nationalistic politics. In Bosnia, Croatia, and Serbia, it is a community radio that encourages different ethnic communities to face the violent past in an open radio forum (see more in Föllmer & Thiermann, 2006; Skopljanac Brunner, 2000; Steinert, Peissl, & Weiss, 2006).

The aim of this chapter is to investigate rearrangements in the ways that community radio and a sense of belonging are connected in countries affected by the violent collapse of Yugoslav state socialism. Critically reflecting on academic research and the political role of community media, Rennie (2006) claims that community media "have received surprisingly little scholarly attention, even within the field of media studies itself" (p. 6). The same is true in the former Yugoslavia, where no concrete studies on community media have been produced since Slovenia and Macedonia gained their independence in the 1990s. However, the main question that the recent media literature starts to explore is the role of community media in the after-socialist and/or after-wars period (for Latin America, see Huesca, 1995; Osandon, 1992; for Africa, see Kasoma, 2002; for Eastern Europe, see Jankowski, Prehn, & Stappers, 1992).

This chapter focuses on two examples of community radio in the region of the former Yugoslavia that function as a space of multicultural belonging, debate, exchange of opinion, and grounded community decision making. First, we establish some necessary historical and theoretical frameworks for understanding these case studies. Later, we introduce Radio Mars, in Slovenia, and Cross-Radio, in the former Yugoslav region. We present a current political-economic context for their existence and argue that while mainstream media are preoccupied with commercial and national(istic) topics, Radio Mars and Cross-Radio do not rely on this discourse as a framework of reference. Radio Mars and Cross-Radio consciously provide a space *for* and *of* community—and in that they offer a particular space for an alternative belonging in nationalist(ic) spaces and for dealing with the past and with Yugoslav memories. Our intention here is to achieve some understanding of how community radio stations help determine and sustain the consciousness of a community and its belonging.

The Former Yugoslavia, National(istic) Belongings, and the Rise of Commercial Mediascapes

Yugoslavia collapsed in 1990, and most scholars agree that the factors that triggered the violent dissolution were a part of the international changes (collapse of socialism and communism, the rise of neoliberalism) and the internal transformations (such as Slovene and Croatian independence and the rise of Milosevic in Serbia) that followed (Banac, 1992; Hayden, 1996). After the wars that resulted in an estimated 300,000 deaths and millions of refugees (Skjelsbaek & Smith, 2001) ended, in 2000, the crucial question remained of how to create a sense of ending when the (nationalistic) past continued to live in the present in the form of objective conditions (Popov, 2000).

Mainstream Commercial Media Landscapes

A number of scholars engaged in the critique of mass media (e.g., see Garnham, 1990) explore the processes of commercialization and commodification of the media and focus on, for example, how historically the commercial, popular press undermined the ability of citizens to act as rational actors engaged in public debate. Calabrese (2004) argues that the commercial media fail to provide for informed citizenship.

After the collapse of communism and the former Yugoslav wars, the media came under attack by (re)nationalization and commercialization. Political elites in all former Yugoslav countries are trying to use the media for political purposes, but at the same time, both the media and elites are oriented toward the maximization of profit, because a capitalist market economy is seen as the only way to legitimize political changes (Trpevska, 2005).

The neoliberal rhetoric of deregulated media is celebrated on the ground that the media are paralleled with parliamentary democracy and that democratic requirements for more communication channels and media can be met only under market conditions. Media debates reflect the key controversies of the general project of (political) democratization of different countries. Briefly, what we now have in the former Yugoslav republics are significant transformations of the media systems themselves in accordance with the processes of deregulation, commercialization, and privatization, combined with those processes that are reshaping nationalisms (Volčič, 2009).

In a society that relies on the (nationalistic) commercial media for forming a sense of belonging, public life and re-creation of identities become even more inhibited. *The citizens* are being increasingly addressed as consumers and (ethnic) nationals at the same time by the mainstream media. Some regional scholars have already pointed out how discourse and a process of forming a sense of belonging, creation of public opinion, social change, and reconciliation have been replaced by discourse about economics (Bieber, 2005). The sharing of past memories and the expression and any formation of identities are all to be realized in the commercial (media) spheres only. This is a particularly dangerous situation, and we argue that in the viewers and consumers within such a space, a schizophrenic feeling is created.

In all former Yugoslav countries, no doubt, community media and community radio in particular played and continue to play one of the most important civic roles—because they offer a place where, on the one hand, one can escape "the nationalistic and patriotic insanities of nationalistic governments, and on the other hand, one could hide from commercial colonization of the media" (personal communication, Cross-Radio's activist, December 2005). In the global society, everyone should have free access to information. Community media, as part of the free media, are not only representing civil society and minorities but also the right and possibility to communicate. What that means in practice is that diverse communities have to have the possibility of free access to information—to that produced by the global media networks and also to that produced by free and community media. To apply a very broad definition here, free media "are produced within a ludic and generation-specific frame, where social transgression has so far been accepted" (Glevarec, 2005, p. 338), while community media "are mission-driven, in service to the broader community. They insist on the inclusion of diverse voices within the community, and their production and distribution processes emphasize community participation" (Johnson & Menichelli, 2007, p. 3). The need for the latter seems to be extremely important.

Mapping Community Radio in the Former Yugoslavia

Community radio in Eastern Europe and the Balkans continues to have many forms and employ many approaches. First, community radio *serves a community,* where community is not defined by advertisers and is not imposed from the top down but is an entity shaped by its members, who dialectically frame its identity. Second, community radio offers an *alternative to mainstream media,* where community radio is defined as an alternative to mainstream media at both the organizational and content levels. Representing the "third sector" then is also an option—there is a particular level and extent of access that community radio provides for minority voices.

A precise definition of free and community media does not exist in any of the former Yugoslav countries. For example, the 2006 Slovene Mass Media Act defines and differentiates radio and television programs with "special purpose and meaning" (in Articles 76 to 82). Radio or television owners can request support for their local, regional, student, or nonprofit radio or television programming. Examples of such community media in the Slovene media space are Radio Student in Ljubljana (www.radiostudent.si/), Radio Mars in Maribor

(www.radiomars.si), and Radio Romic in Murska Sobota (www.romic.si/radio_romic.html, broadcasting for/with/about the Roma community in both Slovene and Roma languages).

Also in Serbia, there is no formal definition and acknowledgment of a role for community radio. However, there exist a couple of community radios. During the 1990s wars, Radio B92 played the crucial role of a community radio station in challenging and resisting the Milosevic regime. It served as a political space where an anti-Milosevic community had an opportunity to organize itself within radio spheres, first, and later on the streets. For example, in the winter of 1996 to 1997, B92 helped organize the demonstrations on the streets of Belgrade, where for five cold months, the protesters marched the city, organized forums, and occupied buildings and streets. B92 began broadcasting in 1989 as part of a Socialist Party vision

> to appear hip by sponsoring a two-week youth radio, but it stayed on the air, challenging the weakening power of the regime. It became an important part of the alternative scene in Belgrade, a kind of an umbrella for NGOs, anti-war activists, feminists and minority groups, and a force behind many street demonstrations. (Richardson, 2006, p. 4; see www.b92.net)[2]

Similarly, Kanal 103 (accessible at www.kanal103.com.mk/) in Skopje, Macedonia, was established by the students in 1991. It represents a unique radio station, in that its diverse community radio programming can be heard in the multiethnic capital city Skopje. It is a so-called low-power radio station, which functions within Macedonian public service (MKRTV). This represents a very specific example of a community radio scene in the former Yugoslav territory because most community radio stations in the former Yugoslavia (or Europe) do not operate under the patronage of public broadcasting services.

Radio Mars[3]

Slovenia mostly escaped the wars of the 1990s but has equally witnessed the rise of nationalism and commercialization of media alike during the last decade. In September 2006, a new Mass Media Act was adopted but the special purpose declaration remained the same as in the previous 2001 Media Act (local, regional, student, and nonprofit radio or television stations have to daily contain, e.g., at least 30% of informative, artistic, educational, and cultural-amusing contents by its own production).

Radio Mars came into existence in 1984 and has presented an active community voice within Slovene civil society throughout the 1980s and 1990s.[4] It continues to be a part of civil society—in a political sense. Community radio in Slovenia is called "the third voice" between state and commercial media. According to many authors (e.g., Mastnak, 1992), the Slovene "third voice of a civil society" was created by new social movements and community media, which have played the most important role in the creation of civil society. The beginnings of these processes go back to the 1970s, for example, Radio Student, the Punk movement, and different citizens' groups that were concerned with peace and ecology, feminist and gay issues, and new age spirituality.

Today, Mars can be heard on 95.9 MHz, providing radio fusion broadcasting, and, additionally, on www.radiomars.si/. Mars attempts to offer diversity, freedom, and an innovative approach. Mars is based on the notion of participatory communication, a form of communication that aims at empowering different (ethnic, class) local communities to determine their objectives and facilitate people's expression of their needs. It is used for these purposes to give voice to those groups of society neglected by the mostly commercial and nationalistically oriented mainstream media.

Mars was, from its beginning, revolutionary in its content and form: It promised to be a nonprofit station, serving community and *involving* community. Community in its model is not passive but gets invited to participate. For example, every year, Radio Mars has an open call for members of the community who would like to participate and create different media contents dealing with the issues of "belonging" and "identities." No matter from which field or perspective the ideas come from, no matter the age, gender, class, or ethnicity

of the participants—what gets supported are ideas, creativity, passion, and enthusiasm. Importantly, at the same time, the community is a receiver and a producer of the program. In the words of one of the Mars activists,

> Community is a part of a journalistic/media production process as well—and in that sense, is a part of a radio work/labor, if you want. Community feels and experiences *the journalism at work.* . . . It transcends, and goes beyond the "ordinary" one-way communication, where topics are chosen in the same way, by professional communicators . . . who usually belong to the economic and political elites anyhow . . . and are, for the most part indeed, detached and alienated from the problems and everyday belongings of *the people.* Mars attempts to transcend this and go beyond the usual *we-them* dichotomy. (personal communication, September 2005)

Mars stands for different subcultural, ethnic, social, and other marginal groups that cannot find communication space in the mainstream media space. In its functioning, Radio Mars offers an open, interactive channel for passing the information, sharing the feelings about belonging, confrontation of opinions, and disseminating the views of different groups to a wider range of communities in the region. Moreover, it offers a direct response to the community. As a Serbian Mars activist claimed,

> In an "ethnically" pure Slovenia, that looks down upon anyone who comes from "the South" or from any other former Yugoslav state, I want to offer a program for all the "Southerners" in Slovenia. I want to create a "Southern" place, a place where the Serbs and Bosnians . . . can also feel a part of a community. (personal communication)

Different radio creators who are young students and ethnic (Roma people) or minority groups (Bosnian, Serb, Macedonian, etc.) receive basic knowledge, including the use of infrastructure needed for independent radio creativity.

In its political program, Mars is socially critical and informative and encourages debates about belonging. In the words of one of the journalists, "reopening the painful questions of the past and present might in some way show us how to heal them more effectively." Many of the shows are actually a part of a vision of rebuilding a nation's identity not around contestation with one's neighbors but rather around a transparent political system focusing on the importance of cohabitation with and respect for difference in a long-term process. For example, the author of the Roma show *Romano Krlo* claimed,

> Our main task is to inform our Roma people living in Maribor and the region around. But this is not the only purpose. As you know, in Slovenia there are many different Roma groups, which do not even understand each other. One of the main tasks is connection and linking between Roma people. The listeners have the possibility to call live in the studio and share with us the information, they want. Even, if they only want to wish a friend a happy birthday. (personal communication, September 2005)

Mars's primal tasks are to be informative and to encourage a plurality of voices.[5] As a community, Mars tries to create a program whose purpose is to reach widely into the space in which it functions and depends on. Its program content offers to the city community a plurality of opinions, a space for expression, and a sphere of production and consumption of different identities. In the words of a Radio Mars activist, "the core of our community radio practice is activist work. Our agenda is formulated through the people with whom we work, in alignment with their efforts, and with a shared sense of purpose."

The general orientation of the music choices of Mars is mostly noncommercial, with an emphasis on presenting interesting new bands, creative production, and playing music from former (e.g., Yugoslav/socialist) spaces and times. The goal of Radio Mars is also to encourage and promote quality and creative domestic and foreign musical development. Mars encourages creative, original, and innovative artistic activities.[6] The development and strengthening of the contribution of Radio Mars in a pluralistic media landscape should be widely supported, but Radio Mars must continue to struggle with different authorities—the University of Maribor, the State and its Mass Media Act, and the board of the institution—to survive.

Cross-Radio: "Reestablishing Cultural Connections"

One of the questions that Cross-Radio poses is how to find the necessary common ground on which to create a more promising vision of a shared, multicultural future. Cross-Radio as a community radio supports the idea of multiculturalism—of belonging not *only* and *exclusively* to the nation-state but to different multicultures.

This is the role and importance of Cross-Radio in the former Yugoslav region—not only to offer multicultural perspectives but also to encourage the articulation of common multi-identities that used to be vivacious, powerful, and respectful of the cultural diversity of the former Yugoslavia. During the 1990s, communication and interchange among cultural and arts scenes of former Yugoslav republics became the victims of armed conflicts in the Balkans. As Mancek, a Cross-Radio activist, claimed in a personal interview, "the connections were broken, information blocked, and production was being obstructed. What once seemed to be a homogenous cultural and multilingual scene of Yugoslavian regions was broken to pieces."[7]

Cross-Radio project was one of the first initiatives for rebuilding bridges of multilingual and multiethnic communication and cooperation, especially in radio spaces. In February 2001, a group of radio activists from Radio B92, Belgrade, Serbia, Radio Student, Zagreb, Croatia, and Radio Student, Ljubljana, Slovenia, came up with the idea of various radio program exchanges to promote the expression of ideas, hopes, fears, memories, and reconciliation. Each radio produced a 20-minute-long feature about current activities and happenings in local political/cultural scenes. Each radio station then broadcast all three productions in an hour of Cross-Radio program time. The importance of this common idea was that stories are produced in the native language, which gives the audiences and radio producers the possibility to work on a multilingual task. This has an importance in peacetime conflict resolution. One of the first Cross-Radio participants claimed that

> especially the first shows were creative, challenging, and very important, because their contents were not politically and hostile loaded. On the contrary, they were informative and incorporated in terms of language, culture and music, which we have played. And this is the same attitude that today Cross-Radio employs in its practice. (personal communication, December, 2005)

Cross-Radio media programs are not created by the so-called professional journalists but by the community itself, comprising enthusiastic individuals driven by their concern for cultural, musical, artistic, and linguistic roots. The Cross-Radio project covers a geographical-cultural area that was not only aggressively destroyed but still faces more and more problems in cross-border activities due to a different geographical-political situation in the new countries that were formed in the area.[8] The danger of further disintegration and the alienation of some cultural scenes make Cross-Radio activities extremely important, as they are not limited to simply informing the audience. Instead, they also move forward in actively preserving and renewing links, contacts, and mediation between interested individuals and institutions, and they organize events that bring together artists from different former Yugoslav areas.[9]

Cross-Radio functions within a very loose, informal framework, without any solid institutional and financial basis. The major linking force that has kept the project going for such a long time is the enthusiasm of the individuals involved. But every team or radio station has to come up with their own funds to produce their part of the project, so a lot of voluntary work is also invested in it. Mancek (personal communication, September 2005) claims,

> One of the most important things around Cross Radio is its multi-lingual principle. Namely,

each radio crew produces their part in their own language . . . so the listeners are challenged to renew or learn anew their knowledge of similarities and differences among Serbian, Croatian, Macedonian, and Slovenian language. In some parts this is still quite a problematic issue. In Kosovo for example, Serbian language is practically banned from everyday life. Even though this practice faces some problems regarding understanding of certain parts of radio shows in certain areas, we think that the multilingual principle is of an extreme importance for promoting the cultural and linguistic diversity of ex-Yugoslav regions— especially among younger listeners. Currently, Cross-Radio project integrates action of twelve radio stations—five from Serbia, two from Bosnia and Herzegovina, two from Slovenia, one from Kosovo, one from Macedonia and one from Switzerland (produced by Bosnian radio activists living and working in Zürich). More than 300 shows were produced and broadcasted so far and can be accessed at www.crossradio.org.

Conclusion

The Slovene Mass Media Act states that

> one of the objectives of the Mass Media Act is to create "the possibility of putting into practice the principles of freedom of information and of the right of local and minority communities to be kept informed; ensuring that information is spread in minority languages and upholding the principles of cultural diversity and gender equality; and implementing a policy of tolerance." (*Zakon o medijih—Zmed—A*, 2006, Article 4.a, para 11)

So far, given the neoliberal agenda, with its economic pressures, the unprecedented transborder global growth of the new technologies, and unresolved psychocultural issues in the former Yugoslav region, a regressive pattern of pseudo-political issues has emerged. Specifically, by accepting the discourse of privatization, deregulation, and commercialization, the regional elites not only (financially and metaphorically) help reinforce the dominance of Western mainstream perspectives of privatization driven by neoliberal principles, but they help conceal the further relations of domination that privatization and deregulation propagate. Demystifying the promises and results of commercialization and privatization means considering them not in isolation but in relation to other processes. What one recognizes, then, while analyzing the media systems in the former Yugoslavia, is another substitution of commercial entertainment for democracy. Free market demands, with their falsely assumed principles of equality, choice, and freedom, on the one hand, and their inherent contradictions, on the other hand, are replacing the demands for political inquiry into issues of, for example, public memory. We need to be critical not only of nationalisms but also of (global) capitalism in this region, which draws on the depoliticized language of the free market.

We argue here that community radio has strong roots and importance in the region and has proved itself able to stay as a part of the media landscape. Community radio actions, practices, and demands should be taken seriously, and the respect for their work should be maintained. Attention should be paid to the effect of media concentration on diversity of media content, and news programs should be promoted that foster public debate, intercultural dialogue, and efforts to deal with the past.[10] That's why it is of special importance to ensure the *policy* and *regulatory regimes* that will create discursive spaces for civil society on a local level and global media levels.

Notes

1. These six nation-states are Slovenia, Croatia, Bosnia and Herzegovina, Serbia, Montenegro, and Macedonia.

2. The radio had many struggles with the Milosevic regime and was actually closed in 1991 because it criticized the official regime regarding the Serbian military involvements in Bosnia and Croatia. It was closed again in December 1996 for supporting street protestors against Milosevic. With the help of Progressive Networks and XS4ALL, an Internet Service Provider in Amsterdam, it continued over the Internet in Real Audio format; its programs were then rebroadcast by local Serbian stations and the BBC.

3. More details of the radio MARS history and current program scheme can be found at www.radiomars.si/.

4. From 1990 to 1994, Mars expanded its original program to 12 hours daily. Sunday's weekly program, *Thank God the Weekend's Over,* has become a cult show. Importantly, many young people are involved in all the fields and get vital experience in media broadcasting.

5. The program itself is meant to follow the interests of students and also of a wider community that is interested in the diverse cultures in which they live, work, and function. By that, we mean that program content dictates trends instead of just following or even copying them.

6. In the history of Radio Mars, the music emphasis has always been on alternative rock and its subgenres, folk, acoustic singer-songwriters, chanson performers, jazz musicians, roots reggae, ethnic musicians, and so on. That is, Mars creates an alternative music sphere of belonging, where the music from past Yugoslav times and spaces can be heard and shared. Mars still tries to serve this ideal today, and it incorporates more of the nonpopular styles from ethno to progressive jazz, funk, quality and experimental electronic music, and so on. In the specialized shows, there is also a place for classical and contemporary improvisational music.

7. Matjaz Mancek, Cross-Radio network, Radio Student, Ljubljana, September 2005.

8. As has Slovenia already joined the European Union and the other former Yugoslav countries find themselves at different stages in the European Union application process, new obstacles to cultural cooperation and interchange have emerged.

9. So far, Cross-Radio festivals have been organized in Ljubljana, Zagreb, Belgrade, Sarajevo, Zrenjanin, and Novi Sad.

10. See more suggestions about support for community media at https://wcd.coe.int/ViewDoc.jsp?id=1089699&BackColorInternet=9999CC&Back, created by the Committee of Ministers on January 31, 2007, at the 85th meeting of the Ministers' Deputies.

References

Banac, I. (1992). Historiography of the Countries of Eastern Europe: Yugoslavia. *American Historical Review, 97*(1), 1084–1104.

Bieber, F. (2005). *Post War Bosnia: Ethnic structure, inequality and governance of the public sector.* London: Palgrave.

Billig, M. (1995). *Banal nationalism.* London: Sage.

Calabrese, A. (2004). Toward a political economy of culture. In A. Calabrese & C. Sparks (Eds.), *Toward a political economy of culture: Capitalism and communication in the twenty-first century* (pp. 99–105). Lanham, MD: Rowman & Littlefield.

Erjavec, K., & Volčič, Z. (2006). Mapping the notion of "terrorism" in Serbian and Croatian newspapers. *Journal of Communication Inquiry, 30*(4), 298–318.

Fletcher, L., & Weinstein, H. M. (2002). Violence and social repair: Rethinking the contribution of justice to reconciliation. *Human Rights Quarterly, 24*(3), 573–639.

Föllmer, G., & Thiermann, S. (Eds.). (2006). *Beiträge zur Zukunft des Radios* [Relating radio. Communities, aesthetics, access]. Leipzig, Germany: Spector Books.

Garnham, N. (1990). *Capitalism and communication: Global culture and the economics of information.* London: Sage.

Glevarec, H. (2005). Youth radio as "social object": The social meaning of "free radio" shows for young people in France. *Media, Culture & Society, 27*(3), 333–351.

Hayden, R. M. (1996). Imagined communities and real victims: Self-determination and ethnic cleansing in Yugoslavia. *American Ethnologist, 23*(4), 783–784.

Huesca, R. (1995). A procedural view of participatory communication: Lessons from Bolivian tin miners' radio. *Media, Culture & Society, 17*(1), 101–119.

Jankowski, P., Prehn, O., & Stappers, J. (Eds.). (1992). *The people's voice: Local radio and television in Europe.* London: John Libbey.

Johnson, F., & Menichelli, K. (2007). *What's going on in community media.* Washington, DC: Benton Foundation.

Kasoma, F. P. (2002). *Community radio: Its management and organisation in Zambia.* Lusaka, Zambia: ZIMA.

Mastnak, T. (1992). *Vzhodno od Raja* [Easterly from the paradise]. Ljubljana, Slovenia: Drzavna zalozba Slovenije.

Morley, D. (2000). *Home territories: Media, mobility and identity.* London: Routledge.

Osandon, F. (1992). Fighting for community radio in Chile. *Media Development, 39*(3), 55–56.

Popov, N. (2000). *The road to war in Serbia.* Budapest, Hungary: CEU Press.

Rennie, E. (2006). *Community media: A global introduction.* Lanham, MD: Rowman & Littlefield.

Richardson, J. (2006). Beyond the spectrum: Net.radio experiments in Eastern Europe. In G. Föllmer & S. Thiermann (Eds.), *Beiträge zur Zukunft des Radios* [Relating radio. Communities, aesthetics, access] (pp. 276–284). Leipzig, Germany: Spector Books.

Servaes, J. (Ed.). (2003). *Approaches to development. Studies on communication for development.* Paris: UNESCO.

Skjelsbaek, I., & Smith, D. (Eds.). (2001). *Gender, peace and conflict.* London: Sage.

Skopljanac Brunner, S. (2000). An analysis of media presentation of reality. In N. Skopljanac Brunner, S. Gredelj, A. Hodzic, & B. Kristofic (Eds.), *Media & war* (pp. 223–259). Belgrade, Serbia: Agency Argument.

Steinert, F., Peissl, H., & Weiss, K. (Eds.). (2006). *Wer spricht. Interkurturele Arbeit und Mehrsprachigkeit in Kontext Freier Medien* [Who is talking. Intercultural work and multilinguisticizm in the context of free media]. Celovec, Austria: Drava Verlag.

Thompson, M. (1995). *Proizvodnja rata: Mediji u Srbiji, Hrvatskoj i Bosni i Hercegovini* [War production: Media in Serbia, Croatia and Bosnia and Herzegovina]. Beograd, Serbia: Medija centar Radio B-92.

Trpevska, S. (2005). Macedonia. In M. Preoteasa (Ed.), *Media: The business of ethics, the ethics of business* (pp. 285–320). Bucharest, Romania: Centre for Independent Journalism.

Volčič, Z. (2009). Television in the Balkans: Reinforcing the National and Regional. In G. Turner & J. Tay (Eds.), *Television studies after TV* (pp. 44–56). London: Routledge.

Williams, R. (1977). *Marxism and literature.* Oxford, UK: Oxford University Press.

Williams, R. (1980). *Problems in materialism and culture.* London: Verso.

Wilson, R. (2003). Justice and retribution in postconflict settings. *Public Culture, 15*(1), 187–190.

Zakon o medijih—Zmed—A [The Slovene Mass Media Act]. (2006). Uradni list RS, št. 60/06 z dne 9. 6. 2006. Ljubljana, Slovenia: Drzavna zalozba Slovenije.

CHAPTER 7

Alternative Media and the Public Sphere in Zimbabwe

Nkosi Martin Ndlela

The advent of democratic transitions in Africa in the early 1990s saw some countries experiencing a boom in media pluralism, an introduction of multi-channel broadcasting systems, independent media, and even experimentation with community media. However, there are many exceptions to this trend, and Zimbabwe is one of those unfortunate cases where there has been a dramatic reversal to the democratization process. Since 2000, the country has been engulfed in a multifaceted sociopolitical crisis. Since the existing media are strongly influenced by the ruling party elites, they are heavily tilted toward the mainstream voices and official interpretations of the events unfolding in the country. The relentlessly critical civil society, opposition parties, and other prodemocracy movements, not happy with the suppression of their voices and the restricted access to the public sphere, are increasingly turning to the alternative communicative spaces. They have emerged as active contributors of news and information disseminated via alternative media—be it "illegal" radio stations broadcasting into Zimbabwe from foreign countries or communication spaces offered by the Internet.

Some theorists have argued that there can be no meaningful definition of the term *alternative media* (Abel, 1997). *Alternative media* is used here to denote any media which fall outside the formal corporate mainstream media, and for media to be considered "alternative," they must embody the Gramscian notion of the counterhegemonic. Alternative media can be expressed in different forms, both printed and electronic, creative writing, art, music, and video. Alternative media can also be expressed in terms of perspectives that hardly appear in dominant media. Access to alternative media is open to ordinary actors. In recent years, the term *alternative media* has taken on a new dimension as a result of dynamism in the information and communication technologies.

In this chapter, alternative media are analyzed in terms of their contribution to the political public sphere in Zimbabwe. The public sphere is defined by Keane (1995) as an extensive physical and symbolic space for the formation of public opinion and is composed of a society's communication structure. In a situation where a society's communication structures are heavily tilted toward mainstream discourses, oppositional forces and reformists often resort to alternative media, hence creating an alternative public sphere. As Woo-Young (2005) has argued, an alternative public sphere is a space in which counterdiscourse is produced and consumed by counterpublics, who had their expression or voices suppressed by the existing social order. Since the alternative media are not controlled by government, they arguably revitalize the political public sphere by giving access to oppositional and social movements that could not easily access the formal public sphere.

The Media and Democratization

The wave of democratization that swept across sub-Saharan Africa in the late 1980s and early 1990s is one of the consequences of globalization. The end of the Cold War marked the beginning of a new global political order and open demands for democracy—fundamental human rights, multipartism, and greater representation. The confluence of internal and external pressures led to unprecedented political transformations in Africa, and these have been described by Huntington (1991) as a "third wave of democratisation." The basic tenets of this liberal dispensation emphasize an introduction of extensive competition among individuals and organized groups (especially political parties) for political power. The media have been identified as crucial elements in the process of building, consolidating, and nurturing a democratic society. Democratization thus envisages an expansion of communicative democratic spaces.

A study of democratization processes is inevitable a study of access to communicative spaces. The media's role in the democratization process resolves around their relation to wider structures and systems of power contestation. The linkage invites a reconsideration of the relative power of media in relation to organized interests. Individuals and institutions vying for power also contend to influence the media in terms of representation, access, and participation. Political entities compete for media space and strategically mobilize forms of communicative power. The media in a democracy constitute prime areas for contending interests, values, and viewpoints—in pursuits of public recognition, legitimacy, and strategic aims. As McNair (2000) argues, any study of democracy in contemporary conditions is a study of how the media report and interpret political events and issues (p. x).

While modern politics in Western countries has been largely mediated through the mainstream media and more recently through the Internet, in the sub-Saharan countries, the situation is different. Many critics would dispute the existence in Africa of a Habermasian public sphere—that communicative space in which private people come together as a public. Nonetheless, African media are central to political processes in Africa even though they are not as widespread as in Western countries. The media in Africa provide mediating mechanisms for political representation, despite their being limited to urban areas. In countries still in democratic transition, given greater political freedom and a responsive public, the role of the media is crucial in educating the people about the different political parties and candidates available for choice (Randall, 1999).

The role of the media has to be assessed in relation to freedom of expression, that is, the ability for citizens to participate in political discussions and safely express their political convictions by voting for a party of their choice without fear of reprisals. Ideally, the media should provide communicative spaces where people can openly participate in discussion and debates. The metaphor of space defines the social, political, and physical configurations in which positions of power, domination, and marginality are negotiated and reproduced (Barnett, 2003). However, in authoritarian societies, or during periods of conflict, there is an inclination by the powerful sectors toward controlling the communicative spaces. Therefore, from a Gramscian perspective, the media have to be interpreted as instruments for disseminating and reinforcing the hegemonic perspective.

Contested Communicative Spaces

The political landscape in Zimbabwe has, since independence in 1980, been dominated by one political party, ZANU-PF, led by President Robert Mugabe. Through the years, the party has extended its hegemony into the economic, social, and cultural spheres, including the mass media, where the government controls the only broadcasting institution and the nominally public-owned Zimbabwe Newspapers Group. However, toward the end of the 1990s, there has been a growing discontent over limited political participation, human rights violations, the declining economy, and limited communication platforms. This discontent against the ruling party saw the formation of a new opposition party, the Movement for Democratic Change (MDC), backed by important groups in the civil society and supported by Western countries. Another development was the formation of an independent daily newspaper, *The Daily News*, to give voice to oppositional discourses. The *Daily News* made an enormous contribution by opening up political communication spaces in the country and provided access to alternative interpretations of unfolding events. Within a short space of time, its readership became the largest in the country, thus challenging the ruling party's hegemony in the national political public sphere.

The controversial land reforms in which the government violently confiscated white-owned commercial farms in the late 1990s, the disputed Parliamentary elections in 2000, and the presidential elections in 2002 are all events that ignited a multifaceted crisis and have been centers of contestation in the communicative spaces. The deepening conflict in Zimbabwe dichotomized the political public sphere, with contending groups adopting polarized views on the

political crisis unfolding in the country. The crisis affected the communicative spaces in several ways. Firstly, the increasingly authoritarian government responded to domestic and international pressure by protecting its own information spaces and, secondly, by also attempting to influence the media impact outside its own borders. The response can also be interpreted in light of government's efforts to reinforce sovereignty in the face of what has been defined as unwarranted interference in the national affairs by the former colonial power, the United Kingdom, the European Union, and the United States. Control of media space within the national boundaries can be seen as competition to dominate national consciousness and reinforce patriotism.

Faced by multifaceted problems, the government fundamentally shifted the communication spaces. It did so by emasculating the mainstream national media, attempting to influence public opinion in its own favor by directing the state-owned newspaper oligopoly to serve out government propaganda; by regulating the reception of international media in the country; and by restricting external communication channels. The government also developed media policies that undermine the growth of the media and their possible extension to new areas, creating an environment of insecurity that scares away local investors, and put up stringent conditions that effectively discourage foreign investment and limit access to the media.

Control of the media extends through ownership structure and by means of legal and extralegal measures. The ownership structure of the media gives the government dual control over the country's largest print media and only broadcasting institution. In the broadcasting media, the government has, since 1980, kept the broadcasting sector firmly under control with a stringent monopoly situation, notwithstanding pressures for liberalization in the 1990s. Even though broadcasting reforms saw the enactment of a new broadcasting law that theoretically promoted a three-tier broadcasting system, in practice a status quo of monopoly prevailed. In the print media sector, the government through a public trust has, since independence, controlled a large stake in the print media, controlling the main daily and weekly newspapers, with only a few independent weeklies working on the fringes, targeting mainly the urban elite. The dual control of the print and broadcasting media has ensured that access to the mainstream media is mainly given to the dominant discourses, while alternative discourses are subdued.

Legal measures have been used to close down at least five independent newspapers, including the country's main independent daily newspaper *The Daily News.* The laws have been roundly condemned by the international community. The legislative environment that gives the authorities unlimited powers to license newspapers and to subsequently close them has been used to curtail freedom of expression in the country, so that only the dominant voices are heard in the official media. On the pretext of protecting individual dignity, privacy, reputation, national security, and public order, laws that have been promulgated cumulatively limit access to the political public sphere and limit the voices that can be heard, by limiting the channels that can be used.

Extralegal activities, such as arrests and harassment by security forces, have also been applied to instill fear, compliance, and self-censorship among journalists. Consequently, a number of journalists have since left the country. It has also been alleged that the Central Intelligence Organisation (CIO) has taken over some independent newspapers. The newspapers in question include the Zimbabwe Mirror Newspapers Group, which publishes the *Daily Mirror,* the *Daily Mirror on Saturday,* and the *Sunday Mirror.* The chief executive officer of the group was ousted through a boardroom coup. Another independent weekly newspaper, the *Financial Gazette,* has also been linked to the CIO takeover. The owner of two other independent weeklies, *The Zimbabwe Independent* and *The Zimbabwe Standard,* has repeatedly been harassed by the authorities, who at one point questioned his citizenship status.

The government policies and actions have also sought to suppress the development of community media. Attempts have also been made by the government to delink the rural areas from the urban areas through the use of "coerced" traditional leaders who have monitoring powers over their communities and have powers to expel noncompliant residents. Residents supporting other political parties, other than the ruling party, have been denied access to basic materials such as food aid, fertilizers, and farming equipment.[1] It is also illegal to say something that undermines the authority of the president. A number of people have been hauled into court for uttering "subversive" comments on the president. People in small communities are therefore not free to express their political opinions. Fear of repercussions undoubtedly undermines "word-of-mouth" communication, one of the most important channels of communication in rural areas.

Developments in grassroots communication have also been hampered by the repressive contexts within which the media in the whole country operate and the cumulative self-censorship that prevails in the country. Not only has the government dominated the media landscape, it has also tried to control and manipulate indigenous communication systems such as music, theater, and religious performances. Artists, especially musicians considered too critical of the government, have had their music banned on the airwaves, and some have been forced into self-censorship or exile. These include Thomas Mapfumo, who is currently living in exile in the United States. Theater groups such as Amakhosi Theatre Productions and Rooftop Productions have had their plays banned due to their critical political content. Police have banned the performance of three satirical plays from Amakhosi—*The Good President, Everyday Soldier,* and *Overthrown*— citing political incorrectness. They have also banned Rooftop's play *Super Patriots and Morons.* This shows the government's determination to control both the written and the oral public sphere. There are other artists who have dedicated their works toward challenging the status quo. As one radical musician, Sam Farai Monro has vowed that "the government is manipulating the arts and culture for propaganda to brainwash the nation, and we are coming in to challenge that and liberate our people's mental perceptions of reality" (Shumba, 2007). Some artists have even formed a protest arts movement to challenge the government's restrictions on artistic expressions (see, e.g., www.voicesfromzimbabwe.com).

The cumulative effects of the legal and extralegal measures of control have turned the media into both crucial settings and tools for power struggles. Freedom of expression is curtailed with impunity, and communicative spaces have shrunk as a result of the government's concerted policy of shutting down all avenues of access to the political public sphere. Alternative discourses are silenced, marginalized, and isolated.

Alternative Media as Communicative Spaces

As would be expected in any environment where there is little or no access to mainstream media, social movements and local communities turn to alternative communicative spaces independent of government control. As Nyamnjoh (2005) has argued,

> However repressive a government is and however profound the spiral of silence induced by standardized global media menus, few people are ever completely mystified or wholly duped. In other words, there is always room—sometimes through radical or alternative media. (p. 204)

The restricted communicative space in Zimbabwe has generated an array of alternative media and alternative public spheres. Political reformists are turning to the ICTs (information and communication technologies), especially the Internet and radio stations hosted in foreign countries for remedies, while some communities are riveted to indigenous communication systems,

especially the word of mouth, oral literature, theater, festivals, and metaphysical forms in their endeavor to air their views—not without risks, though, as already pointed out above.

Alternative Radio Stations

Radio is the most-used medium in Zimbabwe, as access to other media, such as newspapers, is limited by factors such as illiteracy, costs, and distribution and access patterns. Radio can thus be described as the most powerful and strategic mass medium in the country, and this explains why the government has been reluctant to liberalize the radio sector. People in the villages have access only to government-owned radio stations. This gives the incumbent ruling party unlimited access to the majority of the population, hence a competitive advantage over other political parties also seeking rural votes.

Disgruntled by the lack of access to mainstream radio, prodemocracy movements have turned to alternative radio stations, mostly with the support of Western governments advocating for regime change in Zimbabwe. Alternative radio stations, referred to as clandestine radio by Nichols and Soley (1987), are defined as "unlicensed radio stations designed to create political change within countries targeted by their transmission" (Zeller, n.d.). These stations often appear in countries experiencing political crisis and where opposition forces have limited access to mainstream broadcasting media. Prodemocracy movements, aware of the strategic importance of the medium in reaching the masses, have thus turned to alternative radio stations. The primary goal is advocating for political change and offering alternative explanations to the crisis in the country.

There are today three alternative radio stations relying on foreign transmission facilities and the Internet, and these are SW Radio Africa, Voice of the People (Radio VOP), and Voice of America's Studio 7. The stated objective for starting these radio stations is the endeavor to provide

Zimbabweans with alternative radio channels and provide news and perspectives that are silent in the government-owned radio programming. These radio stations target the grassroots population in Zimbabwe, using all the three main languages, English, Shona, and Ndebele.

SW Radio Africa is based in the United Kingdom, and its stated objective is to be the voice of the voiceless, giving its audience opportunities to call in and air their firsthand experiences of the situation in Zimbabwe. It also allows readers of its Web site opportunities to participate through discussion forums. SW Radio Africa's Web site includes links to major prodemocracy groups in Zimbabwe. SW Radio Africa has broadcast every day via shortwave and Web radio, and in December, 2006, it introduced an SMS service where it sends news headlines to mobile telephone subscribers in the country. The initiative followed reports that the security agents were confiscating shortwave radios from listeners in an effort to prevent people from accessing alternative radio broadcasts. Several NGOs have also been distributing solar-powered radio receivers in remote rural areas so as to enable people to access shortwave broadcasts from alternative radio stations. The government has, on several occasions jammed shortwave broadcasts from SW Radio Africa and other alternative broadcasters.

Radio VOP was established in 2000 as an alternative voice for Zimbabweans in the run-up to that year's parliamentary elections and is broadcast in shortwave 1 hour everyday. Its stated objectives are "to cover issues that would not make it to the state controlled electronic media" and to give Zimbabweans an opportunity to look at issues critically. Programs are produced by journalists based in the country and then shipped or e-mailed to the Netherlands for transmission via Radio Netherlands' relay transmission in Madagascar. Radio VOP promotes the works of prodemocracy organizations such as Zimbabwe Lawyers for Human Rights, National Constitutional Assembly, Zimbabwe Electoral Support Network, and many others. For this,

Radio VOP has been a target of harassment by government through raids, arrests, jamming, and seizure of equipment and office files. In August 2002, the offices of Radio VOP in Harare were destroyed in a bomb blasts, and the assailants have never been caught. But the motives for bombing the offices were clear—to silence and intimidate journalists working for the station. Its directors were, between December 2005 and January 2006, arrested and charged with operating a radio station without a license, but the case against them failed, since they operate a "communication trust" rather than a radio station.

Voice of America Studio 7 is another radio initiative based in foreign countries. Studio 7 is a radio news channel launched by the Voice of America in 2003, and it is manned by exiled Zimbabwean journalists based in the United States. It features interviews and commentary on social, political, and economic matters. The government has repeatedly accused the U.S. government of sponsoring a hostile radio station.

Another ingenious alternative radio is the Radio Dialogue project. Radio Dialogue is a community radio program whose original aim was to have a community broadcasting license for Bulawayo and its surrounding. As the name implies, it intended to create a forum for debate and information on economic, political, social, cultural, and developmental issues. Radio Dialogue has embarked on a project of diffusing community views by other methods, which do not rely on radio transmission technology. These methods include road shows in which the communities, local artists, and musicians participate in artistic works such as dancing, singing, talk shows, workshops, and meetings to plan advocacy issues around democracy, the rule of law and human rights, and discussion forums in schools. These programs are recorded in audio and video cassettes and then distributed to the community. Radio Dialogue's stated aims are that it should be available, accessible, and affordable to the community it serves. It is the community's own means of communication and a platform for everyone to express themselves.

The alternative radio stations are clearly an endeavor to democratize the political public sphere in Zimbabwe, and they provide alternative discursive spaces for marginalized voices.

The Internet and New Media Spaces

The repressive media environment in Zimbabwe has ignited the rapid growth of political news Web sites hosted in foreign domains, mainly South Africa, the United States, and the United Kingdom. The aim of these news sites is to provide access to those who otherwise would not have such access in the Zimbabwean media. These include protests groups, "dissidents," trade unions, and opposition parties. The Web sites are driven by a focused political agenda aimed at democratic reforms in Zimbabwe. Today, there are more than 12 Zimbabwe-focused news sites.[2] Almost all the news sites describe and perceive themselves as alternative spaces of communication and information for Zimbabweans. Their intention is thus to expand the shrinking communicative space.

For example, New Zimbabwe.com describes itself as "a vehicle for mass participation" motivated by a belief that "every Zimbabwean and every African with a voice deserves to be heard—including those who have forfeited the freedoms of the majority" (www.newzimbabwe.com/pages/us1.html). The Web site claims to be driven by freedom of expression, hence its being open to those suppressing freedom of expression in Zimbabwe. Another news site, ZWNews.com, is also concerned with social issues such as politics, human rights, and the economy. ZimOnline describes itself as an alternative medium seeking to expand the democratic space being shrunk by repressive media laws in Zimbabwe. It further describes itself as being independent of any political party, neither civic organization nor any lobby group. Zimdaily.com describes itself in almost the same language as other news sites. Some of these news sites are linked to radio stations described above.

The popularity of these Web sites is evidenced through the ratings they get. In 2005, New Zimbabwe.com was rated by the U.S.-based Alexa Web Search as the most popular Web site in Zimbabwe, scoring higher than the country's largest daily newspaper, *The Herald*. Johwa (2007) has noted that "with draconian media laws continuing to throttle the life of publishing and broadcasting in Zimbabwe, these online agencies have become an increasingly important source of alternative information for many Zimbabweans who can access them." The popularity of the news sites is also due to the fact that a quarter of Zimbabwe's 12 million people live in foreign countries, where access to the Internet is better than in Zimbabwe. The news sites are linked and sometimes financed by various social movements and NGOs, have other priorities than making money, and are sympathetic to certain factions in Zimbabwe's fragmented politics. Sometimes there is animosity between news sites.

The government's reaction to these online publications has been milder than its reaction to other publications. This might be due to the fact that these news sites target groups other than the ruling party's grassroots supporters, that they are hosted outside the reach of its draconian national media laws, and that most of the articles are published under pseudonyms. The regime is, however, eager to control the news sites, which it claims are sponsored by foreign interests bent on effecting regime change in the country. Journalists and individuals have also been warned against contributing stories to foreign-hosted news sites. A new law, the Interception of Communications Bill, will allow the government to monitor e-mails and other communications through Internet service providers.

The prevalence of online newspapers actively engaged in political commentary is indicative of the liberating function played by new technologies for prodemocracy movements contesting established structural constraints. The new technologies, especially the Internet, stand today as mobilizing tools both socially and politically in

Zimbabwe, and they offer linkages to fragmented and dispersed dissenting voices.

An Alternative Public Sphere

The Gramscian notion of counterhegemony is discernable in these alternative media. The absence of an accessible public sphere, as a space where the people can come together and participate in inclusive political discussions, gave rise to an alternative realm of political debate. With the mainstream media controlled and dominated by government, the alternative media constitute alternative communicative spaces independent of the cohesive apparatus of the state and are thus positioned to challenge the dominant sociopolitical order. The alternative media offer platforms for political advocacy to democracy activists and the transnationally integrated prodemocracy social movements.

The democratic potential of alternative media is, however, not without shortcomings. Alternative media are so often hailed as having the potential to enhance democracy and citizenship (Bolton, 2006). They provide platforms for the marginalized groups who do not see their interests and concerns reflected in the mainstream media. New communication technologies, especially the Internet, have created opportunities for the establishment of a counterpublic sphere, revitalizing citizen-based democracy on the basis of access, participation, and pluralism. The potential of the Internet arises in its capability to host new spaces for distribution of content and discussion. Characteristics of interactivity and anonymity enable many to be heard without fear of victimization or reprisals.

However, the optimism generated by the upsurge of new political communicative spaces ought not to ignore other factors militating against this view. Bolton (2006) argues that while the Internet does provide a space for more participation, the social distribution of cultural capital or know-how discriminates against full participation online. There are a number of social, political, and cultural factors that limit the effectiveness of alternative media as communicative spaces in Zimbabwe.

First, the alternative media movement is created mostly by self-exiled journalists, refugees, expatriates, academics, students, and experts based outside Zimbabwe, mostly in South Africa, the United Kingdom, and the United States. This group effectively uses news sites to catch up with the latest news from home and seeks to influence political discourse. The ruling elites perceive this group as comprising potential supporters of the opposition movement. Therefore, despite their capacity to generate political discussion, the government has made sure that little of these discussions reach the grass roots in Zimbabwe by, for example, jamming the radio frequencies, confiscating radio receivers, criminalizing comments critical of the president— primarily to dissuade rumor mongering and word of mouth. In that way, there is a disjuncture between a highly engaged political movement based abroad and a less-informed majority residing within the country. The state machinery has drastically disempowered the diaspora through disenfranchisement.

Second, the prevailing economic situation shapes the spread of the Internet in the country. The International Telecommunication Union figures of 2005 show that the Internet penetration rate is 6.7%. While a significant number of Zimbabweans can access the Internet from Internet cafés, prices are beyond the reach of many. This implies that the Internet public sphere is an exclusionary and elitist public sphere. The promise of the Internet as a domain for an alternative public sphere fostering debate and information exchange is lost when conversations are limited to the few who can afford the costs. This lack of access to alternative media hampers the advocacy work and mobilization by social movements whose target group is the majority within the country.

Third, the alternative media with reformist agendas often tend to be elitist. Studies of the U.K. activists' newspaper *SchNews* have shown that while at first glance the paper appears to privilege "ordinary" voices, closer examination reveals a "counter-elite" (Bolton, 2006). While no systematic study has been carried out on Zimbabwe-focused news sites, the journalistic sourcing practices used in the sites reveal hegemonic tendencies. These sourcing practices determine which news actors are included and excluded. This practice can eventually work to silence the very voices that the alternative public sphere claims to amplify. The pluralism expected from these alternative media can also be reduced by the presence of active participants who tend to dominate the discourses.

Nevertheless, it can be argued that alternative media such as online news sites, radio stations, and other communication media are promoting communicative democracy by recovering the spaces for political participation. The alternative media are aiding social movements in their relentless pursuit of democratic change in Zimbabwe.

Notes

1. See *The Politics of Food Assistance in Zimbabwe* on the Human Rights Watch Web site: www.hrw.org/backgrounder/africa/zimbabwe/2004/5.htm

2. www.newzimbabwe.com, www.zimdaily.com, www.zwnews.com, www.zimonline.co.za, www.thezimbabwean.co.uk, www.zimbabwesituation.com, www.thezimbabwetimes.com, www.zimobserver.com, www.zimbabwepost.com, www.changezimbabwe.com, www.zimbabwejournalists.com, w.studi07news.com (accessible at http://www.voanews.com/english/africa/zimbabwe/), www.swradioafrica.com, and www.vopradio.co.zw

References

Abel, R. (1997). An alternative press. Why? *Publishing Research Quarterly, 12*(4), 78–84.

Barnett, C. (2003). *Culture and democracy: Media, space and representation.* Edinburgh, UK: Edinburgh University Press.

Bolton, T. (2006). News on the net: A critical analysis of the potential of online alternative journalism to challenge the dominance of mainstream news media. *Journal of Media Arts and Culture, 3*(1). Retrieved April 3, 2009, from www.scan.net.au/scan/journal/print.php?j_id=34&journal_id=71

Huntington, S. P. (1991). *The third wave: Democratisation in the late twentieth century.* Norman: University of Oklahoma Press.

Johwa, W. (2007, January 23). Media-Zimbabwe: From turning pages to downloading them. *IPS Inter Press Service News Agency.* Retrieved February 6, 2007, from http://ipsnews.net/print.asp?idnews=36273

Keane, J. (1995). Structural transformation of the public sphere. *Communication Review, 1*(1), 1–22.

McNair, B. (2000). *Journalism and democracy: An evaluation of the political public sphere.* London: Routledge.

Nichols, J., & Soley, L. (1987). *Clandestine radio broadcasting: A study of revolutionary and counterrevolutionary electronic communication.* New York: Praeger.

Nyamnjoh, F. (2005). *Africa's media: Democracy and the politics of belonging.* London: Zed Books.

Randall, V. (1999). The media and democratisation in the Third World. *Third World Quarterly, 14*(3), 624–646.

Shumba, T. (2007, November 22). *Young Zimbabwe rebel artists take on Mugabe.* Retrieved November 29, 2007, from the ZimOnline Web site: www.zimonline.co.za/Article.aspx?ArticleId=2358

Woo-Young, C. (2005). The Internet, alternative public sphere and political dynamism: Korea's non-gaek (polemist) websites. *The Pacific Review, 18*(3), 393–415.

Zeller, G. (n.d.). *The Ace "clandestine profile": Clandestine radio stations.* The Association of Clandestine Radio Enthusiasts. Retrieved November 4, 2007, from www.frn.net/ace/clandpro.htm

CHAPTER 8

Toronto Street News as a Counterpublic Sphere

Vanessa Parlette

The past two decades have seen an explosive growth of street newspapers emerging in major cities on a transnational scale in attempts to combat rising levels of homelessness and poverty (Dodge, 1999). These papers are characterized by their formation of entrepreneurial opportunities for homeless and economically marginalized individuals to sell the papers for income. Although there are more than 100 known street papers in existence, in more than 37 countries across 6 continents,[1] individual papers can be seen to follow autonomous mandates with unique goals and structures. Consequently, the ownership, content, control, and mission vary strikingly from one street paper to the next. *Toronto Street News* (*TSN*) is one such paper that has developed locally to address and contribute solutions to the crisis of homelessness in one particular city.[2]

The following case study provides an analysis of the goals, operational structure, and practice as well as the content of *TSN*. *TSN* is a weekly alternative newspaper that is sold on the streets of Toronto by homeless people and the underemployed. The publicized purpose of this publication to serve as a "homeless newspaper" suggests that the paper may offer an alternative set of discourses surrounding homelessness, class, labor, and economic oppression while offering the potential for self-advocacy and representation to publicly marginalized groups. Hence, *TSN* will be approached as a potential "counterpublic sphere" to give voice and visibility to homeless people, who are typically marginalized, excluded, or degraded in mainstream civic culture and news discourse. While this study is primarily focused on the organizational structure and distribution

Author's Note: I wish to acknowledge the generous support of SSHRC (the Social Science and Humanities Research Council) throughout the writing process. I also wish to thank Patricia Mazepa and Anne MacLennan for encouraging this project and for their invaluable comments. I'm also grateful for the input of Kevin Howley, Deb Cowen, and Alan Walks along with the input from the anonymous reviewers.

of *TSN*, it is necessary to consider the social, political, and economic conditions that underlie the constitution of mainstream and counterpublics (Downing, 2001, pp. 27–33).

Publics and Counterpublics

The contentious notion of what in fact constitutes a public is at the root of the distinction between public and private as well as publics and counterpublics. In Habermas's (1962/1989) original formulation, the public sphere is composed of private individuals coming together to rationally discuss public matters of collective concern. While this model may be useful for its aim toward an alternative democratic space for public debate, this theory has been widely criticized for its idealization of an exclusive zone composed primarily by and in the interests of educated, propertied, and white male elites (Downing, 2001; Fraser, 1993; Thompson, 1993). The public sphere is idealized to be distinct from the state as well as the market. Yet, in popular understandings, the term *private* refers not only to intimate, personal or "domestic" life but, more significantly, also to any form of nonstate activity, namely corporate and business relations (Mosco, 1996). The conflation between business and domesticity indicates the high degree of extension that the commodity form has assumed in personal life, yet the domestic has not been adopted as a newsworthy topic in the mainstream media. The conceptual separation of the assumed public, economic realm from the private realm of domesticity severely limits the boundaries of permissible discussion (Garnham, 1986; Mosco, 1996).

The homeless are double hit by this exclusion, as individuals who must conduct private life in public yet who for this reason are typically not accepted as members of "the public" (Mitchell, 1995). In relation to the concept of class in capitalist society, homelessness is commonly perpetuated as an area of public disdain. Even modern

scholarly conceptions of the public still implicitly exclude the "homeless" through the assumption of the citizen's right to vote as resting on private property rights (Garnham, 1986, p. 52), while in practice, homeless people are categorized as pathological outcasts. This concept of citizenship has become more acute due to the process of commodification, whereby citizenship rights and public participation have become conflated with the right to consume. Mainstream consumer hegemony has inculcated widespread commonsensical adoption of neoliberal free market ideology. The resulting manifestation of these assumptions has materialized as a general hostile "public" attitude toward homeless and underemployed persons, who are often actively feared, denigrated, or ignored; they are not seen to possess the social qualities necessary for success and participation in the capitalist system (Zygmunt, 1998). The mainstream press reinforce such (mis)perceptions through depictions of homeless people as social deviants, substance abusers, and criminals (Mitchell, 1995).

The force of the media in constituting the public sphere (Hartley, 1992) is complicated by the fact that, although allegedly serving a public purpose, the mainstream media hardly make up a public institution; indeed, they are highly corporatized and driven by bottom-line profit making. The commercial model necessarily promotes capitalist interests, assuming that each individual can enter the market "as if" all were equal; however, it does not focus on production or labor, only on consumption. This is reflected in the structure of mainstream newspapers, which contain business, lifestyle, and entertainment sections, but little or no reference to labor or unemployment issues. The implicit assumption that class can be "bracketed" obscures and exacerbates the reality of class division and inequalities endemic to capitalist society (Fraser, 1993). With the public good determined by consumer demand, the needs and interests of social groups who are not considered potential or worthwhile customers are not given space for expression. The exclusion of social disparities in the mainstream media is seen to favor the interests of the politically and economically powerful, as the conflicts associated with poverty, labor, racism, gender, and ethnicity are beyond the realm of "public" debate despite their enduring effects on society at large (Fraser, 1993; Garnham, 1986).

The contentious notion of what constitutes the public provides a further limitation through the assumption that one unified public is better than diversified and competing publics (Fraser, 1993). Thompson (1993) notes that the existence and operation of alternative publics distinct from and often in conflict with the bourgeoisie inevitably shapes the "formation and development" of the bourgeois sphere (p. 180). These subaltern or counterpublics are defined by Nancy Fraser (1993) as "parallel discursive arenas where members of subordinated social groups invent and circulate counter discourses, which in turn permit them to formulate oppositional interpretations of their identities, interests and needs" (p. 14). Independent publications made locally by and for the people can be seen as a greater reflection of public interests than those of the official public media (Downing, 2001; Magder, 1989, p. 291). Rather than glossing over competing publics as "special interests," conflicting accounts are brought to the fore so that the many needs and realities that constitute "the public" are afforded voice and recognition (Downey & Fenton, 2003; Fraser, 1993). Although counterpublics may at times tend toward exclusivity, their value is in promoting a space for commonly marginalized voices and issues (Fraser, 1993), although, ideally, linkages should be pursued to broaden discourse, debate, and connection with wider publics.

Counterstreet

The counterpublic potential of street newspapers grows out of concern that common representations of homelessness tend to reduce homeless individuals to static categories that reinforce

the assumptions of negative stereotypes based on superficial observation (Madden, 2003). To move beyond categorical prejudice, it is vital to account for the active formation and experience of homeless identities via conflict and relations with structures, capital, and other social classes (Christian & Abrams, 2003; Clapham, 2003; Evans & Forsyth, 2004; Mosco, 1996, pp. 223–227). In the present case study, the theory of structuration is useful to understand the structural factors that constrain homeless individuals while acknowledging that *TSN* may be an enabling resource for impoverished social actors to work within and upon these constraints to change existing societal structures (Mosco, 1996, pp. 212–230).

As *TSN* promotes itself as a paper for and by the homeless, it can be seen as an attempt to rupture the presiding hegemonic and oppressive view of homelessness as a "culture of poverty" (Mosco, 1996, p. 244), while providing a critique of social and political power relations. This chapter presents an analysis of the material content and operational policies of the newspaper to assess the extent to which it permits a democratic alternative for homeless people to participate in decision making and contribute to social discussion (Downey & Fenton, 2003; Tonkiss, 2005, p. 68). While homeless people sell the paper, the money to support production comes from external advertising; also, the purchasers and hence primary readership of the paper are not homeless or underemployed but rather have discretionary income to aid support for the sellers. This presents an interesting entry point to explore the extent to which a voluntary production structure dependent on advertising and purchase revenue, yet dedicated to socialist distribution, affects the content and purpose of the newspaper.

The empirical portion of this study applies the theoretical concepts outlined above to an examination of the internal and external relations of *TSN* in terms of its effect on the seller (or potential sellers) of the paper. The purpose is to assess the extent to which the newspaper, whether through structure or sale, provides a means for public participation and empowerment through self-representation for homeless or underemployed individuals. This has involved a combination of textual analysis and ethnographic field work to study both the material production of the paper and the views and practices of participants.

The present structural analysis of the publication rests on investigation into its financial resources and constraints on production and distribution as well as its organizational logic, goals, and achievements as indicated through e-mail correspondence and four hours of personal interviews with the publisher and editor. Assessment of the overall mission of the paper to provide a means for the homeless to help themselves has been informed through personal, semistructured interviews with two current *Street News* vendors, "Walter," who frequently sells in front of No Frills in the Bloor West Market area of Toronto, and "Vincent," who sells near the Victoria Park subway station.

TSN Content and Mission

TSN describes itself as a homeless newspaper, helping "homeless, handicapped and underemployed" people help themselves. Furthermore, the Web site claims that the paper is owned and produced by homeless people who have worked their way off the streets: "The Toronto Street News is owned and operated by ex-Street People and sold on The Streets of Toronto by the homeless so they can make money to live on and have the Pride of owning the newspaper they sell."

This identification with ex-street life may be intended to effect a sense of solidarity with the public they claim to serve and legitimate their authority to assume this role. The Web site announces,

> We at the *Toronto Street News* work very hard to help our community, especially the homeless, abused and impoverished. We support any and all services that actually help our people and when posable [*sic*] all others as well. Our goal

is to STOP ABUSE! (http://debramoon-ivil .tripod.com/thetorontostreetnews)[3]

On the surface, the content and political orientation of *TSN* appears to provide a more democratic alternative to the silenced oppression and marginalization of homelessness. Referring to the homeless as "our people" suggests the potential for the paper to provide a space for the voices of the homeless to gain recognition and legitimacy by both alerting homeless individuals to critical information and also instilling readers with a sense of awareness of the homeless reality. Given that those who purchase the paper are typically from another social background than that of the vendor, the publication may also have the potential to alter general public perceptions by calling attention to class structure and dominance (Downing, 2001; Howley, 2003; Mailloux-Beique, 2005; Mosco, 1996).

However, this function would necessitate a significant proportion of homeless-oriented and -authored articles in the paper. While these types of articles may have a greater likelihood of support from *TSN* than from the mainstream press, they do not in fact occupy a consistent presence or focus in regular editions. For example, the November 1 to 7, 2004, *TSN* features two headlines directly related to the circumstances of homeless individuals in Toronto. One is written by a regular contributor, Joseph Couture (2004): "Letting the Bedbugs Bite: Toronto's Shelters Just Got a Whole Lot Nastier" (p. 5). The other is a report from a former homeless woman describing her experience of abuse, neglect, and dehumanization through a series of stays at various Toronto shelters. The direct personal account particularly emphasizes the human element behind the stigma of homelessness while stressing the structural and social barriers to (re)gaining secure housing, a process that seems to be further derailed rather than facilitated by city shelters where basic needs are misunderstood and unfulfilled. The woman says,

> I think staff who work at those places should be required to spend a week in an abandoned car, or sleep under a bridge and panhandle to

make ends meet. Then they would discover for themselves what the homeless really need. ("Some of My Experiences," 2004, p. 5)

The need for understanding and social change is articulated to the reader through the voice of direct experience from a former homeless person who has personally been able to overcome structural impediments to get off the streets and recount her struggles.

Both articles address the lives of homeless people in general, focusing on the lack of security, sanitation, respect, and services in the city shelters. All these factors have forced people to sleep on the streets rather than in shelters and have contributed to long-term health risks, illness, abuse, and increased stress levels. This alternative form of reporting suggests a potential mechanism to shatter categorical assumptions about homelessness as a wholly individual problem and misconceptions that shelters are safe havens from the street (Madden, 2003). Awareness and public dialogue surrounding the causes and factors contributing to and intensifying homeless struggles could provide a vital public sphere where the multiple-class publics formed between readers, vendors, and contributors could consolidate strategies to influence change at the political level. In principle, homeless or underemployed social actors could then exercise greater agency to challenge structures toward promotion of a more equitable and democratic society (Fraser, 1993; Mosco 1996). This is of course an ideal; the pending question that this study seeks to explore is whether or not *TSN* does provide a democratic forum, and if so, how and to what extent and effect?

While the content of the articles discussed above is clearly of significant social value, this is perhaps undermined by the fact that these are merely 2 out of 45 articles in the November 1 to 7, 2004, edition of the paper. Moreover, such articles are not a consistent weekly feature, which is further evidenced by the fact that two of the papers published in October had no homeless articles at all (*TSN* October 4–10 and 18–24). The week of October 11 to 17 only had two articles written *about* the homeless, and the week of October 25 to 31 had three.

Furthermore, the only regular features that may be seen as related to homelessness are contributed by LoveCry, a charity for street youth and also a partner with *TSN*. Each edition has 12 pages, of which the fifth and eighth are run by LoveCry; these are the only spaces where the homeless articles appear, if at all. On the eighth page of each edition is a write-in advice column, "Spring Eagle," which is characterized by issues traditionally associated with homelessness and poverty, such as substance and sexual abuse, addiction, and mental illness. The LoveCry director also contributes poetry, philosophy, and a personal column, all of which have a religious self-help theme, as seen in the piece titled, "Love Is The True Healer: Truth, Responsibility, Forgiveness" ("Love," 2004, p. 5). The emphasis is on finding God to take self-responsibility for forgiveness and healing from abuse. These pages do appear to be in sync with the mandate stipulated on the Web site to stop abuse, and it is possible that the advice and self-help columns may provide an otherwise unavailable support resource for homeless, impoverished, or similarly abused readers, though at the same time, it is valid to question the way that these pages position the reader as passive and helpless.

The advice column is the only section of the paper that actually prints letters from abused or impoverished people, which notably structures them as victims seeking help, with LoveCry providing the answers. The short question and answer format mirrors the advice columns in the mainstream press and does not permit the underlying conditions of substance abuse or poverty to be addressed, which oversimplifies these highly complex issues. The focus on religion and Christ as the savior is also highly suggestive, connoting that these are misguided people who need direction to make more appropriate life choices. The emphasis on Christianity may also exclude a significant number of people who do not hold these beliefs, as the construction of faith as "the answer" constructs non-Christians as "lost" individuals who must rediscover faith in worship rather than accepting alternative forms of spirituality that may not be based on a central figure. This overall focus on need and self-help connects poverty with the same negative stereotypes that circulate in the mainstream press such as drugs and mental illness (Fitzgerald, 2004). It is therefore doubtful that this section provides a means of self-empowerment for homeless people to "re"present themselves and that it may rather reinforce pathological stereotypes held by mainstream readers.

The fact that personal representations by, and the presence of, homeless, underemployed, and impoverished people is virtually absent in the paper is cause for concern. In fact, the one article discussed above is a rarity, as is any divergence from the general structure and weekly features. This may be due to the decisions made by the sole editor and owner, who designs the layout and makes all organizational decisions independently as well as producing the vast majority of the content in each edition, amounting to approximately 80% of each paper. The remainder of the content is also largely managed by the owner-editor, which includes Lovecry's section and columns from regular contributors, whom the owner-editor actively pursues via the Internet, and none of whom are homeless, underemployed, or impoverished.

Not only is the overwhelming majority of the newspaper content produced solely by one writer-editor, but even the submission pieces are pursued and filtered by him prior to publication. In our interview, he did mention that there are things in the paper that he does not agree with but prints anyway, though at the same time, when he was asked if anyone can submit, the reply was that "Yes, they can, but it does not mean the work will be published." The owner also added, however, that many people say that they will submit an essay or story but are unreliable because they never follow thorough. When questioned about the absence of homeless articles in most editions, he pointed out that the homeless are "not really up to producing something once a week," indicating a variety of material constraints such as lack of time, resources, undeveloped literacy skills, and preoccupation with mere survival. These are real and enduring limitations that create unique barriers against such

a publication attempting a democratic structure; however, one may also note that very few outreach efforts have been made to overcome these constraints. The homeless are not actively pursued for submissions nor are there educational training sessions or other kinds of forums available to include the homeless in decision making, as can be seen at some other street papers (see Dodge, 1999; Howley, 2003; Mailloux-Beique, 2005; Mewburn & Harris, n.d.).

Organizational Structure

The material publication of *TSN* may be seen as a primarily independent and self-enclosed venture rather than a democratically organized collective, yet it would be preemptive to dismiss the social purpose of the paper. Although the content provides a type of "personal therapy" for the editor, he writes to expose what he sees as corruption emanating from government and corporate organizations to oppress and marginalize the citizenry. The amount of content that appears to be specifically by or for the homeless is questionable, since continuance of the paper is dependent on an affluent market of buyers. Yet, one might consider that adherence to the owners' rigid production structure may be seen as a necessary strategy to ensure a consistent publication in fulfillment of a larger social purpose to expose social injustice and provide income and employment opportunities for impoverished people. This is the model taken by some other street papers such as *The Big Issue* in the United Kingdom (see www.bigissue.com), which seeks to provide quality content to ensure high sales and maximum income for vendors.

The financial structure of *TSN* is telling of this purpose. The owner-editor does repairs and maintenance at a community center in exchange for office space, while donating a lot of his own money to cover printing costs; any help with the production process is based purely on volunteer labor. The paper does accept advertisements, but only a few businesses come forward, amounting to approximately five advertisements per edition, none of which have any influence on content. On the rare occasion that the paper secures surplus revenue, the funds are directed back into the paper to maintain a fair price for the vendors. Vendors may purchase the paper from anywhere between 10 and 25 cents, depending on their personal circumstances, though in many cases, the owner will give the papers away for free if an individual vendor cannot afford to pay. The sale of the papers is intended to create an entrepreneurial income opportunity for the vendors, who then sell each issue for a dollar and keep the profits above cost.

The sale of the paper can have a direct benefit for the vendor and may be a vital tool for meeting basic survival needs. The decision on how the money is to be used is left entirely up to the discretion of the vendor, although the owner-editor provides the caveat that at times the money is used for coping substances such as alcohol, cigarettes, or drugs. For some, it may just be a means of subsisting from one day to the next, but for others, it can provide an opportunity to save money for housing and to integrate with society. The owner-editor provides an example of a young former seller, "Gerard," who had struggled with periods of homelessness but has since worked his way off the street while selling the paper and has also been able to attend 2 years of college. Gerard is now running an independent masonry business that he advertises on Page 3 of every edition of *TSN*. Another example was given by "Walter," a current vendor who lives in a rental unit but finds that housing costs more than swallow the meager income supplied by his disability check. "If I could work, I would," he says, adding that his back injury was caused by factory work for which he was never compensated. The paper provides a means for Walter to supplement a fixed income and for others with no income to attain one legally.

What seemed more important to some of the vendors are the social relationships that can be formed over the course of long-term vending. Sitting daily at the same location in the Bloor West Village for years, Walter has gotten to know other community members and has routine conversations with many familiar buyers. Vincent sees himself as a temporary vendor and has only recently become homeless due to the end of a common-law relationship, though he has expressed a similar liking for selling the newspaper: "It's better than panhandling; the people are nicer. . . . They listen to what I have to say." These interactions may provide a vital link between the homeless or underemployed public and that of the mainstream (Downey & Fenton, 2003; Fraser, 1993). There is no guarantee that buyers will become "readers" of the paper, but the interaction at the point of exchange is unavoidable (once a decision has been made to purchase). While vendors may not necessarily have the opportunity or the means to publish their words for greater distribution, this spatialized constitution of a discursive "'public sphere'" at least ensures that they will be heard. This form of dialogue presents the opportunity for vendors to increase awareness of their struggles and opinions through self-representation while foregrounding issues, problems, and concerns defined according to their own experience (Downing, 2001; Fraser, 1993; Howell, 1993).

Moreover, the relations across class divisions extend the public reach of *TSN* so that it is not merely a microcosm among the homeless community. Identity is both relational and formational in this case, where discussion can lead to mutual negotiation of class and identity experience (Mosco, 1996). In seeing the responsible agency of the vendors, buyers may observe information that runs counter to existing stereotypes; a hopeful case would be that this would mobilize action across multiple classes to challenge policies, unfair laws, and socioeconomic configurations that contribute to and perpetuate poverty ("Bread not Circuses", 2001).

"Counter" Dictions

However, it might also be argued that *TSN* may not challenge the existing structure in either production or distribution. First of all, although the content of the newspaper is against corporate and government systems of oppression, the top-down structure and lack of diversity do not provide an alternative means of self-advocacy and empowerment through participation and decision making. Second, even though selling the paper is self-directed and permits a means of social mobility and public participation, this is not always the case. Some street vendors report abuse and opposition to their presence on the street from police officers for selling without a license as well as sometimes from people walking by. Although the paper involves a sale in which the buyer receives something, the exchange still resembles that of panhandling, as some buyers purchase precisely because they feel sorry for the vendor (Torck, 2001). Many exchanges do involve dialogue, as discussed above; however, even so, it is still questionable as to how often this leads to social change or even increased awareness. It is quite possible that the sale process may substantiate the individualist approach to a social problem and hence perpetuate unequal structuration of social resources and relationships (Mosco, 1996). It is individual vendors with whom buyers interact, and the maxim, "helping the homeless help themselves," proposes that buying the paper may be a sufficient amount of action toward the citywide (and international) crisis,[4] which further obscures the need for political change and funding for social services, welfare, and affordable housing (Wellesley Institute, 2006). Similarly, the individualist approach that pushes the vendors into a neoliberal entrepreneurialism also maintains divisions between homeless and underemployed people, which is perhaps further entrenched by the failure of the printed publication to function as a homeless "sphere." The effect is that there is no formation of class consciousness and consequently no collective action taken to challenge oppressors and reclaim social rights to housing, a decent income, and adequate living standards.

Curiously, *TSN* as an organization does not attempt to gain political influence through collaboration with groups struggling for the same cause. A case in point is seen in relationship to Ontario Coalition Against Poverty (OCAP). Although the owner-editor does occasionally print press releases sent from OCAP, overall, he feels that the anarchist group is merely a "bunch of thugs . . . (and) . . . not a political unit." He perceives that the direct action approach against social structures merely "gives everybody a bad name." The contrast is significant: OCAP's commitment to collective action is a direct subversion of structures seen as unequal and oppressive, whereas, although *TSN* may rhetorically revile neoliberal political economic arrangements, the production process mirrors the same closed structure at the same time that the vendors only engage an *individual* opportunity to (re)integrate productively into the existing social formation. Effectually, the individual as well as the group agency of homeless persons is at once confined by the structure of society as well as by that of *TSN*, which itself is organized in replication of its own oppressors, to perhaps unwittingly limit the agency of homeless people to challenge and reconstitute the greater inequalities of neoliberal socioeconomic structures (Downey & Fenton, 2003).

Conclusion

It may be argued that direct collective action and independent initiative need not, and in fact should not, be mutually exclusive, in view of the fact that homelessness affects and is affected by both individuals and society. *TSN* is an independent venture with progressive goals that could be better served through outreach and collaboration with similar agencies. A more inclusive structure could combine a material publication with direct social activism through democratic initiatives to provide training opportunities, resources, and community forums to encourage and enable participation of homeless and nonhomeless individuals to contribute to production procedures, decision making, and collective movements (Howley, 2003; Mailloux-Beique, 2005). An internally democratic structure based on open expression and dialogue can permit both material and discursive space for lateral communication, thereby enabling individual and collective action to challenge the wider sociopolitical structure.

Having pointed out the contradictions and constraints of *TSN*, it becomes that much more important to highlight the critical functions of the newspaper. I certainly do not intend to disparage the progressive intent of the paper, merely to emphasize the very real material constraints and limitations that affect the potential democratization of "actually existing" counterpublics (Downey & Fenton, 2003; Fraser, 1993). Although direct poverty and homeless articles are minimal, the fact that when they do appear, issues are expressed empathetically and at times originate from direct experience is certainly an improvement over the mainstream press, which in most cases excludes the severity of the issue altogether while explicitly expounding negative and unfounded assumptions about homeless individuals. As well, even if the individualist approach to selling the paper may not mobilize social actors to challenge the status quo, the exchange does improve the quality of life for vendors in both material and symbolic terms. As major changes to social policy and structures may take considerable time to take effect, the paper provides a valuable resource for personal survival and the attainment of a more satisfying social position.

Notes

1. For street paper facts and background, see International Network of Street Papers, www.streetpapers.org/ and the North American Street Newspapers Association, www.NASNA.org.

2. For comparative studies of street papers, see Dodge (1999) and Howley (2003).

3. The information on the *Toronto Street News* Web site is dated and not actively maintained but provides a useful description of the goals and background of the paper: http://debramoon-ivil.tripod.com/thetoronto streetnews

4. Toronto has been designated a "homeless disaster zone" since 1998; for reports on homelessness in Canada, including the United Nations' recent findings, see http://wellesleyinstitute.com/blog/michael-shapcott.

References

Bread Not Circuses. (2001). *Housing: Plenty of promises in the homeless disaster zone*. Toronto, Ontario, Canada: Author.

Christian, J., & Abrams, D. (2003). The effects of social identification, norms and attitudes on use of outreach services by homeless people. *Journal of Community & Applied Social Psychology, 13*, 138–157.

Clapham, D. (2003). Pathways approaches to homelessness research. *Journal of Community & Applied Social Psychology, 13*, 119–127.

Couture, J. (2004, November 1–7). Letting the bedbugs bite: Toronto's shelters just got a whole lot nastier. *Toronto Street News*, p. 5.

Dodge, C. (1999). Words of the street: Homeless people's newspapers. *American Libraries, 30*(7), 60–62.

Downing, J. (2001). *Radical media: Rebellious communication and social movements*. Thousand Oaks: Sage.

Downey, J., & Fenton, N. (2003). New media, counter publicity and the public sphere. *New Media and Society 5*, 185–202.

Evans, R., & Forsyth, C. (2004). Risk factors, endurance of victimization, and survival strategies: The impact of the structural location of men and women on their experiences within homeless milieus. *Sociological Spectrum, 24*, 479–505.

Fitzgerald, J. (2004, September 11). Marseille' rich new cultural brew: The French city is shrugging off its gritty reputation and drawing visitors with its museums, lively port and famous fish stew (travel). *Globe & Mail*, p. T2.

Fraser, N. (1993). *The phantom public sphere*. Minneapolis: University of Minnesota Press.

Garnham, N. (1986). The media and the public sphere. In M. Golding & P. Schlesinger (Eds.), *Communicating politics* (pp. 45–53). Leicester, UK: Leicester University Press.

Habermas, J. (1989). *The structural transformations of the public sphere: An inquiry into a category of Bourgeois society* (T. Burger & F. Lawrence, Trans.). Cambridge: MIT Press. (Original work published 1962)

Hartley, J. (1992). *The politics of pictures: The creation of the public in the age of popular media*. London: Routledge.

Howell, P. (1993). Public space and the public sphere: Political theory. *Environment and Planning D, 11,* 303–322.

Howley, K. (2003). A poverty of voices: Street papers as communicative democracy. *Journalism, 4*(3), 273–292.

Love is the true healer: Truth, responsibility, forgiveness. (2004, November 1–7). *Toronto Street News,* p. 5.

Madden, M. (2003). Braving homelessness on the ethnographic street with Irene Glasser and Rae Bridgman. *Critique of Anthropology, 23*(3), 289–304.

Magder, T. (1989). Taking culture seriously: A political economy of communications. In W. Clement & G. Williams (Eds.), *The new Canadian political economy* (pp. 278–296). Kingston, Ontario, Canada: McGill-Queen's University Press.

Mailloux-Beique, I. (2005). Echoes from the curb: Street newspapers and empowerment. In A. Langlois & F. Dubois (Eds.), *Autonomous media: Activating resistance and dissent* (pp. 89–102.) Montreal, Ontario, Canada: Cumulus Press.

Mewburn, L., & Harris, T. (n.d.). *Street papers: A guide to getting started.* Available from the International Network of Street Papers and North American Street Newspaper Association Web sites, at www.street-papers.org/start-a-street-paper and www.nasna.org/startapaper.html

Mitchell, D. (1995). The end of public space? People's park, definitions of public and Democracy. *Annals of the Association of American Geographers, 85,* 108–133.

Mosco, V. (1996). *The political economy of communication rethinking and renewal.* Thousand Oaks, CA: Sage.

Some of my experiences at Mary's Home and Elisa's Place. (2004, November 1–7). *Toronto Street News,* p. 5.

Thompson, J. (1993). The theory of the public sphere. In M. Featherstone (Ed.), *Theory, culture and society* (pp. 170–187). London: Sage.

Tonkiss, F. (2005). *Space, the city and social theory: Social relations and urban forms.* Cambridge, UK: Polity Press.

Torck, D. (2001). Voices of homeless people in street newspapers: A cross-cultural exploration. *Discourse & Society, 12*(3), 371–392.

Toronto Street News. (n.d.). Homepage. Retrieved April 23, 2009, from http://debramoon-ivil.tripod.com/thetorontostreetnews

Wellesley Institute. (2006). *The blueprint to end homelessness in Toronto: A two-part action plan.* Retrieved April 23, 2009, from http://wellesleyinstitute.com/theblueprint

Zygmunt, B. (1998). *Work, consumerism and the new poor.* Philadelphia: Open University Press.

CHAPTER 9

Evaluating Community Informatics as a Means for Local Democratic Renewal

Ian Goodwin

ommunity informatics (CI), as an emerging field of academic study, aims to evaluate uses of information and communications technology (ICT) for community development. It is diverse in its origins and is influenced by a variety of preexisting disciplines. These include computer science, management, sociology, education, development studies, and social policy studies (Taylor, 2004). It is also linked to the practice of citizens using ICTs for progressive community change and empowerment, which both precedes and informs the study of CI (Gurstein, 2000, 2004, 2006). As opposed to examining "virtual" communities, CI research studies the appropriation of ICTs by "physical" communities within specific localities or territories (Gurstein, 2000; Keeble & Loader, 2001; O'Neil, 2002; Taylor, 2004). This geographical orientation translates into a focus on analyzing specific uses of ICTs by local community groups as a means for meeting their self-defined social, cultural, economic, and political goals (Gurstein, 2000; Loader, Hague, & Eagle, 2000; Taylor, 2004).

Given its diversity and dynamism, the study of CI examines a "wide range of ICT activities and applications" (Gurstein, 2000, p. 14). For the purposes of the current chapter, however, I focus specifically on links between CI and the (re)development of local democracy. It could be validly argued that the centrality of notions of empowerment to CI, which is related to reintegrating into society those who have been traditionally disenfranchised by advances in ICTs (Gurstein, 2000; Keeble & Loader, 2001; Taylor, 2004), makes the revitalization of local democracy central to the broader CI agenda. By providing citizens with better access to information and lower-cost publishing, as well as creating a means for local communication, the development of CI certainly holds a democratizing potential (Williams, 2006). Thus, Gurstein (2006) notes that efforts to develop citizen participation in local decision making inform the broader CI research perspective, while O'Neil (2002) more forcefully argues that the development of "strong local democracy" (p. 79) has become one of the key goals of CI initiatives. Horning (2007) even goes so far as to argue that community ICT projects interested in long-term sustainability should concentrate on, alongside efforts to develop social capital, "fostering strong democracy" (p. 417).

Democracy itself is, however, a concept and an ideal that is both "complex and contested, as are its justifications and practical implications" (Gutmann, 1993, p. 411). Indeed, several disparate theoretical models of democracy are potentially applicable to analyzing CI. O'Neil's (2002) and Horning's (2007) references to "strong democracy" are an explicit acknowledgment of Barber's (1984) stress on participatory democracy. However, the emphasis CI initiatives often place on inclusive, informed local debate suggests that theories of deliberative democracy are equally relevant. Deliberative democracy is itself closely related to notions of the public sphere (Habermas, 1989), which is particularly pertinent for CI in terms of theoretical developments that stress the need for "micro-public spheres" that operate in small-scale locales and yet remain connected to the higher level, national "meso-public sphere" (Keane, 1995). In this sense, CI could be tied to broader calls for the creation of a more responsive civil society (see Habermas, 2006, pp. 415–418) capable of engaging with elite, mainstream political discourses. Alternatively, insofar as CI sets itself against state and corporate media control by stressing the need for citizens to appropriate ICTs, it shares some elements with the version of radical democracy (see Laclau & Mouffe, 1985; Lummis, 1996) espoused by theorists of indymedia (e.g., Pickard, 2006). However, although such diverse models of democracy could inform the study of CI, it is clear that they are not entirely compatible with one another. This fact, in conjunction with the status of CI as an emerging field lacking clear definition (Stoecker, 2005), makes analyzing the claims surrounding CI and democracy a difficult affair.

Given its emphasis on the grounded *practices* of citizens (Gurstein, 2006), it is not surprising

that the vision of local democratic renewal CI espouses does not map neatly onto established theoretical models. In any case, the version of local democracy that CI advocates has yet to gain full coherence and often varies from project to project. Against this decidedly fluid background, this chapter develops our understanding of CI and local democracy by presenting a case study of Moseley Egroup, a CI initiative developed in Moseley, a suburb of Birmingham, United Kingdom. Perceiving his community as "in decline" and being failed by unresponsive local democratic processes, the founder of Moseley Egroup set out to use the Internet to disseminate community information more broadly, to generate greater knowledge of and involvement in local decision making, and to create more diverse debate over local affairs. As with the broader CI agenda, these goals are based in a pragmatic attempt to change complex social and political relations and could be assessed against varied theoretical models of democracy. Thus, rather than arguing that any particular theoretical model is best suited to drive the analysis, this chapter produces an exploratory, yet theoretically informed, grounded evaluation to investigate the actual practices of egroup members.

This case study is based on insights derived from a period of online participant observation (February 2001 to September 2001), semistructured interviewing of 10 egroup members, and a documentary analysis that included a review of local histories (Fairn, 1973; Morris-Jones, 1981), the community magazine titled *B13* (a title derived from Moseley's postal code), local press articles focused on Moseley (from the *Evening Mail* and the *Birmingham Post*), and documents posted to the egroup. In what follows, a brief contextual overview of Moseley and Moseley Egroup is offered, and then the extent to which Moseley Egroup has renewed local democracy is considered in reference to three issues: increased information provision, the generation of local political knowledge, and new forms of local deliberation. These gains are then set against three limiting factors: unrepresentative egroup membership, aspects of e-mail posting and reading patterns, and the fragmentation of the egroup. The issue of "fragmentation" is explored in reference to a period of conflict that resulted in the creation of a rival local egroup: Moseley Free.

Introducing Moseley and Moseley Egroup

Moseley is a suburb of Birmingham City, the United Kingdom. Located 4 km south of the city center, Moseley is thoroughly urbanized. Yet, up until the latter half of the 19th century, Moseley was in fact a village bordering Birmingham but detached from it. Many local historians date habitation in Moseley back much further in time. The *Doomsday Book,* published in 1086, cites "Muselei" as a berewick (colony) established in the area (Morris-Jones, 1981). Many residents still refer to Moseley as "Moseley Village." Moreover, many of Moseley's public spaces are shaped by this history. For example, the Village Green, established in 1801 (Fairn, 1973), is still considered the center of Moseley and hosts events such as the monthly Farmers' Market and the yearly celebration of Easter by local churches.

This sense of history, and its legacy in terms of aspects of Moseley's physical layout, inflects modern understandings of Moseley as a community. However, Moseley has been thoroughly changed in the process of urbanization. Although some streets have retained their original middle-class Victorian character, they now sit directly beside those that contain more modern, and more modest, accommodation. Thus, Moseley is now characterized by extremes of poverty and wealth. A wave of immigration into the area from the 1960s onward has also altered Moseley's character. This primarily involved people from Indian, Pakistani, Bangladeshi, Black Caribbean, and Black African ethnic backgrounds. As of the 2001 census, these ethnic minorities accounted for 31.2% of Moseley's population. Thus, modern Moseley is profoundly influenced by its past and yet has been transformed by a process of urbanization (the major referents of which relate to changes in residential space, socioeconomic differentiation, and immigration).

The founder of Moseley Egroup is an individual with a history of local activism; for example, since moving into Moseley in 1993, he had become a committee member of the Moseley Society as well as a trustee of the Community Development Trust. This involvement in local activities motivated him to create Moseley Egroup. Well aware of the locale's history, he had become convinced that the Moseley community was in slow decline. Moreover, he considered that existing institutions and democratic processes no longer adequately represented Moseley but were "dominated by a few individuals who make all the decisions" (interview, October 18, 2001). Such concerns contributed to setting the agenda for Moseley Egroup. First, he hoped to use the egroup to "undermine" (interview, October 18, 2001) the existing ways of conducting community affairs by disseminating local information more broadly (in particular, information on decisions made in civic forums). Second, he hoped that this would stimulate greater community involvement and generate more diverse debate over local affairs.

The founder therefore proceeded to create the egroup in January 2000 using the "Yahoo! Egroups" system (originally "Onelist"), which involves the use of a standardized Web site package hosted from Yahoo's server. Interested Internet users are then required to sign up on the Web site to join the egroup, which hosts an e-mail discussion list and a searchable e-mail archive. It also allows users to post documents online. All users can also nominate hyperlinks to other Web sites on a separate "links" page. The founder assigned himself the role of moderator and then actively promoted Moseley

Egroup to a set of key social actors. These included members of the police and local councilors, the editor of the *B13* magazine, as well as members of the Neighbourhood Forum and the Moseley Society. Via this method, a critical mass of people, estimated to be around 30 (interview, October 18, 2001), joined. Subsequently, the egroup was advertised more broadly via leafleting in public spaces. By the time the study commenced in February 2001, the number of e-mail accounts registered had reached 136. The growth of the egroup is also reflected in the growth of e-mails posted, which averaged 381 per month during the study period.

Moseley Egroup: Rebuilding Local Democracy?

Increased Information Provision

The requirement for citizens to have access to a wide array of information is vital to the functioning of a democratic system of government, regardless of the particular model of democracy considered. For example, quality political information helps citizens form stable opinions and enables them to translate their opinions into political participation (Delli Carpini & Keeter, 1996). Similarly, Morrisett (2003) notes that "a vital part of any deliberative discussion is the provision of relevant information" (p. 28). Yet, decades of research suggests the presence of a "permanent information underclass" (Jerit, Barabas, & Bolsen, 2006, p. 266) in advanced Western democracies, which is related to aspects of the "information environment" (p. 279)—the extent and quality of the coverage of political issues across various media. Indeed, CI's agenda is set against these broader concerns and is premised on an acknowledgment that state- and corporate-controlled media often fail to provide communities with the information needed for effective local democracy.

It is therefore salient to note the extent to which Moseley Egroup became highly valued as a device for disseminating local information, which was one of the most consistent themes to emerge in interviews with members. Indeed, accessing information was consistently reported by all interviewees as a motivating factor for membership. For example,

I mean the kind of things that I originally joined the egroup for were finding out about . . . well people putting reports on from the various bodies. There's the Moseley Forum, and the Ward Committee. . . . [They are] quite significant bodies which are concerned with what's going on in Moseley, and then there's the planning applications. . . . [O]ccasionally when there's some kind of commercial development going on it's quite interesting to find out just where it is and what they're doing, what they're proposing, and that kind of thing. (interview, September 6, 2001)

Civic information related to formal local democratic processes, as in this interviewee's reference to the "Ward Committee," was routinely posted to the egroup. Not only did this provide political information that members might not otherwise have accessed, it was also provided in a timely fashion. For example, local planning applications, a formal aspect of Birmingham City Council's planning procedures also referred to by this interviewee, were posted ahead of deadlines for citizen submissions to be made.

However, the egroup was equally valued as a source of broader information than a strict focus on formal civic affairs would suggest. Information regarding local community events, local bands, and local comedy gigs were routinely posted to the egroup. Although not directly related to formal political processes, such information is still essential to community life and community politics. The "links" function on the home page was also used by members to create an easily accessible database of virtual activity going on in the area in the form of a list of hyperlinked WWW sites (e.g., to the satirical local site, Eye on Moseley, or to the local online news magazine, *Birmingham 101*). Some interviewees noted that they often shared these various sources of information with networks of friends who were not subscribed. This suggests that the egroup may act to disseminate information more broadly than its limited membership base would suggest.

Moseley Egroup, Local Discussion, and Local Political Knowledge

As Schudson (2003) notes, "Information is necessary for democracy, but information by itself is inert" (p. 59). For information to feed effectively into forms of democratic political action, it needs to be transformed into relevant forms of political knowledge. Yet, while it seems clear that the Internet provides access to a broad range of information, it is far from clear that users have "the necessary skills to interpret the information" (Polat, 2005, p. 442) in ways that can lead to meaningful political participation. In this section, I argue that two aspects of the day-to-day discussions in Moseley Egroup help embed "raw" information on the locality and its politics into the lives of participants in ways that help develop local democracy.

First, the provision of formal information on political processes was often provided alongside discussion that helped citizens make sense of it. For example, after the posting of a planning application, the following online exchange took place:

From: [name withheld]

Date: Tue Apr 10, 2001 4:02 pm

Subject: RE: West Brom Building Society re-development

So how do I find out what is planned? Who would I contact? Is it usual to have such a short amount of time to comment or is the development being steam-rollered onto us?

From: [name withheld]

Date: Wed Apr 11, 2001 10:03 pm

Subject: Help with planning / developments

[name withheld]—If you want local people with experience on planning issues try [name withheld], or anyone from Friends of the Earth.

For more info on how the planning system works, try West Midlands Planning Aid—their raison d'etre is to provide planning help and advice to local communities. They're based at the Custard Factory, and their number is 0121 766 8044.

These types of exchanges reveal a process of ongoing civic education that reflects the ideals of participatory democracy by increasing knowledge of, as well as interest in, formal civic processes. Despite the reference in this particular exchange to the "short notice" provided, by increasing citizens' ability to keep track of issues as they arise, such discussions also enhance democratic accountability.

Second, rather than relying on the sporadic spotlight of established media, such as the *Birmingham Post*, to raise awareness of the issues facing Moseley, day-to-day discussions in Moseley Egroup also act as a means for the membership to contribute to setting the agenda of community politics. That is, the egroup does not simply generate and disseminate more locally relevant information, but it develops discussions that work on it to produce an intelligible agenda for debate that is based on the concerns of egroup members themselves. In this way, the generation of political knowledge becomes rooted in a form of autonomy that extends and enhances the work of traditional community media forms such as the local community magazine *B13*.

New Forms of Local Deliberation

Aside from stimulating local discussion, there is some evidence to suggest that Moseley Egroup provides a new space for deliberation over local affairs. Several e-mail exchanges stand out in this regard, for example, threads relating to debate over community services such as the Citizens

Advice Bureau, debate over community events such as the Farmers' Market and the Moseley Festival, and discussions of the use of the Village Green. An e-mail exchange sparked off by an incident involving the vandalism of a Christian cross erected at Easter on the Green (by the local churches) illustrates this process. Discussion quickly moved on from reports of the event to a debate over who has the right to use public space. The following contribution illustrates the nature of this process:

From: [name withheld]
Date: Tue Apr 17, 2001 10:43 pm
Subject: Re: [moseley] Re: Cross on Green
Although there is no way that I would condone the smashing of this cross I must say I was somewhat surprised at its appearance. For myself, as an atheist, I considered it an imposition, almost a threat. It is best down. Public spaces must be secular—to be enjoyed by all irrespective of race or creed! In any case: Who erected it? Who is responsible for repairing the paving which was damaged by its erection (not rate-payers I trust)? Was planning permission obtained? If so why in such a multi-ethnic, multi-religious community such as Moseley was it given to erect in a public space on public land an icon to one particular faith that is probably a minority faith within the community, especially if non-believers are included in the figures.

This particular thread attracted 25 e-mails from 13 different individuals over the course of 2 days, including 2 posts from a local councillor. Many of these e-mails articulated a variety of views by drawing on reasoned argument, often taking account of the views of others. To this extent, such exchanges approximate deliberative processes. However, within the egroup, such processes are not formalized or bounded by clear rules. For example, deliberative discussion is often interspersed with e-mails that make no attempt at rational argumentation, as evident in the debate discussed above that included the following contribution:

From: [name withheld]
Date: Wed Apr 18, 2001 9:53 am
Subject: Re: [moseley] Re: Cross on Green
In a message dated 18–04–01 09:02:53 GMT Daylight Time, [name withheld] writes: << I think that is a sign of the sad state our society has got to in that people are more concerned with self-interest and less concerned with the interests of others. >>   What, like you?

Nevertheless, in interview, the value of the egroup as a new space for members to articulate their own views, as well as learn about the views of others and engage in debate with them, was raised as a benefit of membership. For example,

I think the discussion there's been about the Festival this year has been quite interesting. . . . Because at the end of the day this list is the only medium I've got for communicating what I think. . . . You know it's provided a useful function for that. (interview, August 30, 2001)

Thus, for some members, at least, Moseley Egroup enables new forms of deliberation over local affairs.

Moseley Egroup and Democratic Renewal: Limiting Factors

Egroup Membership

As of 2004, the population of Moseley ward was estimated to be 24,273 (Birmingham City Council, 2005). In this light, the membership of the egroup, at approximately 130 people during the period of study, is highly unrepresentative of the community. Even given that the egroup is embedded into the off-line social networks of those joined in ways that enhance, for example, its ability to disseminate information in the locality, this is obviously problematic. Furthermore, several interviewees commented that the egroup was dominated by the white middle classes. The following reference to people "who always do stuff in Moseley" is telling in this respect:

> Um but I mean I don't know how much it [the egroup] really draws people in who would never otherwise have been involved.... You know in Moseley for example the Asian communities, Asian women in particular, all of these people I mean they're still not there.... I don't see how ... it brings those people in and I think that problems still exist... about getting more people involved from non traditional backgrounds and away from ... the kind of white, middle class, middle aged liberals who always do stuff in Moseley. (interview, September 26, 2001).

Thus the egroup, rather than reflecting Moseley's growing ethnic and socioeconomic diversity, has in large part added an additional means for "the kind of white, middle-class, middle-aged liberals" within Moseley already dominating community activity to get even more involved. As the above extract demonstrates, egroup members are often aware of, and concerned about, this problem. However, during the study period, there was a lack of resources available to effectively address it. On a more positive note, however, the reference to "middle-aged" people in the quoted extract may overstate the situation, as four of those interviewed were aged 32 or younger. Moreover, three of these interviewees stated that they had never been heavily involved in Moseley's community life or community politics before. Thus, in this respect, the egroup does seem to be encouraging a more diverse involvement in community affairs.

Patterns of E-mail Posting and E-mail Reading

While particular e-mail threads stimulate broad participation, the overall pattern of e-mail posting reveals a more limiting picture of social interaction in the egroup. Table 9.1 provides a quantitative analysis of e-mails posted during three separate months in the study period. This breakdown demonstrates that in any given month there are a significant number of users who do not post at all, as indicated by the figures for "lurkers" that show as many as 73% of e-mail accounts registered fail to send a single e-mail to the egroup. Moreover, a significant percentage of

Table 9.1 Analysis of E-mails Posted to Moseley Egroup

	March 2001	June 2001	September 2001
Total e-mail accounts registered	119	124	132
E-mail accounts that posted	73 (61%)	45 (36%)	35 (27%)
"Lurkers"	46 (39%)	79 (64%)	97 (73%)
E-mail accounts with 5 or fewer posts	41 (56%)[a]	25 (56%)[a]	25 (71%)[a]
Total number of e-mails posted	891	555	175
Total number of e-mails posted by top 5 e-mail accounts	449 (50%)	296 (53%)	92 (53%)

a. Percentage given is against total number of users *who posted*.

those who do post (from 56% to 71%) only do so five times or less in a given month. At the other end of the scale, the top five posters account for half of all the e-mails posted. These posting patterns raise questions about the nature of the egroup as a means for encouraging political participation and as a means for developing inclusive deliberation.

The problematic aspects of these posting patterns are accentuated by reading patterns. That is, six of those interviewed reported highly selective e-mail reading patterns. For example,

> When I'm going through a backlog of messages I just keep the mouse over the delete area and I just press it, and they just go [laughs]. You know next one, delete, next one, delete. It only takes a few minutes. (interview, September 6, 2001)

Such patterns suggest that the "social" space created by the egroup is, in important respects, individuated. This raises further questions as to whether or not a truly "public" debate, even within the limited confines of egroup membership, is going on at all.

The Egroup(s) and the Fragmentation of Online Space: "Moseley Free"

Social tension was an integral part of the functioning of Moseley Egroup from the beginning. The founder's construction of Moseley as a community in decline, ill-served by failing civic institutions, was central to motivating the egroup's development. However, these views were challenged by a range of community members, including some who chose to join: "He [the founder] said Moseley is a horrible rubbish place, all going down the drains. . . . I thought it was weird. I've been here 30 years. I mean it's never been better" (interview, October 9, 2001).

However these tensions came to a head with the founder's announcement, in late February, 2001, of his intention to run for local office as a Liberal Democrat councillor. This immediately generated a protracted online argument that ultimately resulted in the creation of a rival local egroup, Moseley Free, set up by members dissatisfied with the founder's actions. Their main concerns were that his posts were becoming increasingly tainted with political bias and that his new role as a local electoral candidate compromised his position as moderator of the egroup, a position he refused to vacate. His decision to ban an egroup member during this period exacerbated these tensions. This conflict, and the subsequent creation of Moseley Free, has complex roots and multiple effects. I have written in detail about these elsewhere (Goodwin, 2008). However, for the purposes of the current chapter, I want to highlight the most salient aspect of this situation in respect of Moseley Egroup's goal of renewing local democracy.

Moseley Egroup did not collapse as a result of this conflict. As of November 2008, it continues to operate, now in its 9th year, with 190 e-mail accounts registered (as does Moseley Free, which has now been operating for 8 years and has grown to 360 e-mail accounts registered). However, democracy, chiefly in terms of deliberative practices, relies on citizens' sustained engagement with one another, particularly in relation to issues that—at least initially—divide them. The fracturing of online space heralded by the creation of Moseley Free ultimately raises questions about the Internet's overall suitability for this purpose. At the time the study was conducted, 7 out of 10 interviewees did remain members of both egroups, suggesting that these spaces do remain closely interconnected in the social practice of cross-membership. However, the disparate growth rates of the two egroups since then would seem to suggest that this is not the case for the majority of those who subsequently chose to join Moseley Free.

Rebuilding Democracy From the Ground Up?

Moseley Egroup, and its offshoot Moseley Free, are a significant new means for disseminating information throughout the locality and—at times—act to enhance their members' discussion of local affairs and deliberation over local issues. This has led to the generation of new forms of situated, relevant political knowledge and debate that may not have happened in the egroups' absence. In this respect, they have demonstrated a democratizing potential, but this does not yet amount to a rebuilding of local democracy. There are aspects of the egroups that currently limit their democratic potential, and many members of Moseley community are at present unrepresented in online discussions. Entrenched problems that preexisted their creation, for example, in terms of the lack of diverse participation in Moseley's politics, still remain. However, this certainly does not mean that the egroups are valueless. They are often highly valued by those who are members and to this date retain a dynamic capacity for growth and development that renders any attempt to reach a definitive conclusion here erroneous. Perhaps, then, they will eventually help rebuild local democracy in more substantive ways than are documented here. However, given their unrepresentative demographics, there is also a possibility, should this pattern of membership continue, that they may act to reinforce forms of social exclusion that, somewhat ironically, prompted Moseley Egroup's creation in the first place.

In sum, this exploratory case study suggests that CI's potential for rebuilding democracy, while currently unfulfilled, merits closer analysis. In particular, in an age where there are growing fears over the development of an "information underclass," the potential CI holds for disseminating relevant information and helping foster political knowledge deserves further scrutiny. Yet, in pursuing the study of these positive potentialities of ICTs, we should not lose sight of the limitations described here. As the study of CI progresses, there will also be a need to further theorize and explore CI's broader role in the community media movement as a whole.

References

Barber, B. (1984). *Strong democracy: Participatory politics for a new age.* Berkeley: University of California Press.

Birmingham City Council. (2005). *Moseley and Kings Heath electoral ward information.* Retrieved December 5, 2005, from www.birmingham.gov.uk/community

Delli Carpini, M., & Keeter, S. (1996). *What Americans know about politics and why it matters.* New Haven, CT: Yale University Press.

Fairn, A. (1973). *A history of Moseley.* Halesowen, UK: Sunderland Print.

Goodwin, I. (2008). Community informatics, local community and conflict: Investigating under-researched elements of a developing field of study. *Convergence: The International Journal of Research into New Media Technologies, 14*(4), 419–437.

Gurstein, M. (2000). Community informatics: Enabling community uses of information and communications technology. In M. Gurstein (Ed.), *Community informatics: Enabling communities with information technologies* (pp. 1–31). London: Idea Group.

Gurstein, M. (2004). Editorial: Welcome to the *Journal of Community Informatics. Journal of Community Informatics, 1*(1), 2–4.

Gurstein, M. (2006, February). *Notes towards an integrative research agenda and community informatics theory* (CRACIN Working Paper No. 14). Toronto, Ontario, Canada: Canadian Alliance for Community Innovation and Networking.

Gutmann, A. (1993). Democracy. In R. E. Goodin & P. Pettit (Eds.), *A companion to contemporary political philosophy* (pp. 411–421). Oxford, UK: Blackwell.

Habermas, J. (1989). *The structural transformation of the public sphere: An inquiry into a category of bourgeois society* (Trans. T. Burger with F. Lawrence). Cambridge: MIT Press.

Habermas, J. (2006). Political communication in media society: Does democracy still enjoy an epistemic dimension? The impact of normative theory on empirical research. *Communication Theory, 16*(4), 411–426.

Horning, M. A. (2007). Putting the community back into community networks: A content analysis. *Bulletin of Science, Technology and Society, 27*(5), 417–426.

Jerit, J., Barabas, J., & Bolsen, T. (2006). Citizens, knowledge, and the information environment. *American Journal of Political Science, 50*(2), 266–282.

Keane, J. (1995). Structural transformations of the public sphere. *Communication Review, 1*(1), 1–22.

Keeble, L., & Loader, B. D. (2001). Community informatics: Themes and issues. In L. Keeble & B. D. Loader (Eds.), *Community informatics: Shaping computer mediated social relations* (pp. 1–10). London: Routledge.

Laclau, E., & Mouffe, C. (1985). *Hegemony and socialist strategy: Towards radical democratic politics.* London: Verso.

Loader, B. D., Hague, B. N., & Eagle, D. (2000). Embedding the net: Community development in the age of information. In M. Gurstein (Ed.), *Community informatics: Enabling communities with information and communication technologies* (pp. 81–103). London: Idea Group.

Lummis, C. D. (1996). *Radical democracy.* Ithaca, NY: Cornell University Press.

Morris-Jones, J. (1981). *Moseley.* Unpublished manuscript.

Morrisett, L. (2003). Technologies of freedom? In H. Jenkins & D. Thorburn (Eds.), *Democracy and new media* (pp. 21–32). Cambridge: MIT Press.

O'Neil, D. (2002). Assessing community informatics: A review of methodological approaches for evaluating community networks and community

centres. *Internet Research: Electronic Networking Applications and Policy, 12*(1), 76–102.

Pickard, V. W. (2006). Assessing the radical democracy of Indymedia: Discursive, technical, and institutional constructions. *Critical Studies in Media Communication, 23*(1), 19–38.

Polat, R. K. (2005). The Internet and political communication: Exploring the explanatory links. *European Journal of Communication, 20*(4), 435–459.

Schudson, M. (2003). Click here for democracy: A history and critique of an information-based model of citizenship. In H. Jenkins & D. Thorburn (Eds.), *Democracy and new media* (pp. 49–60). Cambridge: MIT Press.

Stoecker, R. (2005). Is community informatics good for communities? Questions confronting an emerging field. *Journal of Community Informatics, 1*(3), 13–26.

Taylor, W. (2004). Community informatics in perspective. In S. Marshall, W. Taylor, & X. Yu (Eds.), *Using community informatics to transform regions* (pp. 1–17). London: Idea Group.

Williams, A. (2006, October 7–11). *Disruptive spaces and transformative praxis: Reclaiming community voices through electronic democracy.* Paper presented at the Community Informatics Research Network Conference, Prato, Italy.

CHAPTER 10

Mapping Communication Patterns Between Romani Media and Romani NGOs in the Republic of Macedonia

Shayna Plaut

Since its independence in 1991, the Republic of Macedonia, like many former socialist countries, has seen a proliferation of nongovernmental organizations (NGOs) and nongovernmentally regulated media.[1] Due to the cultural and linguistic diversity of Macedonia and its history of state-supported multicultural identity, many of these organizations and media were founded to, and purport to, serve specific ethnic groups. According to existing literature and the experience of other former Yugoslavian states (notably Serbia and Bosnia), one would expect cooperation between the NGOs and independent media that target these specific ethnic groups (Brunnbauer & Grandits, 1999; Downing, 1996). We might also expect the growth of viable and critical civil institutions to enable the proliferation of "radical media" (Downing, 2001). However, by comparison with the forms and practices of independent media that flourish and provide public space for agitation in other "countries in transition," it becomes apparent that such a space has failed to take root in Macedonia (Batiwala & Titus, 2007; Cooley & Ron, 2002).

This chapter offers an analysis of the effects of international funding organizations on the

Author's Note: This research would not have been possible without the support of the U.S. Department of State's Fulbright Program, the University of Chicago's Human Rights Internship Program, and Open Society Institute–Macedonia (particularly Neda Zdraveva and Violeta Gligoroska). I would also like to thank Biljana Bejkova, Roberto Belichanec, Vesna Shopar, Eben Friedman, Hall Smeltzer, Johanna Schoss, and Ivan Dihoff. All interviews were conducted in either the Macedonian or Romani language based on the preference of the person interviewed. I am indebted to Denis Durmis for his assistance in linguistic and cultural translation, consistent support and keen sense of analysis.

agendas set by both NGOs and independent media in Macedonia. I argue that in addition to fueling competition for this funding, these international donor agencies actually help produce a context in which Macedonian NGO and independent media groups take on more conservative and less socially active roles in their relationship to each other and their audiences. This conservatism manifests itself in a lack of shared goals and communication between NGOs and independent media, resulting in a growing distinction between the NGOs constituency and the media's audience. This chapter looks particularly at NGOs and media targeting Romani constituencies.

Background

The Republic of Macedonia, with a population of 2.2 million, is a multiethnic country and "home" to six officially recognized "nationalities" living together in varying degrees of harmony.[2] It declared its independence in 1991 and avoided most of the bloodshed suffered in other former Yugoslav Republics. Despite an average unemployment rate of 40% (European Centre for Minority Issues [ECMI] & Minority Rights Group [MRG], 2004, citing Najcevska, 2002), Macedonia has comparatively high primary education and literacy rates (84% and 92%, respectively) (ECMI & MRG, 2004, citing the Statistical Office of Macedonia, 1997). It is also heavily reliant on state-centered policies, including health, employment, and education.

Macedonia is the only country recognizing its Romani citizens in its original constitution (Government of Macedonia, 2001). However, official recognition does not always translate into positive reality (Project on Ethnic Relations [PER], 2001). With the majority of Roma (with an official population of 53,879, based on the 2002 census, and an unofficial population estimate of 80,000 to 135,000) surviving below recognized standards of health, economic viability,

and education, Roma are universally regarded as the most marginalized population within Macedonia (Amnesty International, 2007; Barany, 2002; European Roma Rights Center, 2006; UNDP, 2005).[3]

According to the 2005 CEDAW Shadow Report submitted by the Roma Center of Skopje, European Roma Rights Center, and Roma Women's Initiative (OSI-Network Women's Program), although the state has the responsibility to ensure equal, adequate education through primary school, more than 50% of Romani women leave school before completing the eighth grade, thus prohibiting them from obtaining regular social protection and benefits later in life. According to the report,

> Despite alarming data about the educational status of the Romani community—and especially Romani girls—in Macedonia, during 13 years of independence, state institutions have not proposed or implemented any specific programs for the advancement of the education level of this population group. (p. 19)

Many of these concerns are covered by the media, including the Romani media, yet much of the responsibility for "fixing" the "problem" has fallen to NGOs often backed by international donors. According to Fisher (1997), this reliance on NGOs to fulfill what is traditionally the state's responsibilities results in hollowing out the state's power. It also pulls NGOs from their role as watchdogs and advocacy organizations and instead shapes them into service providers often tailoring and shifting their projects to external donors' agendas (Fisher, 1997; Smillie, 1995).

According to the 2002 census, more than 90% of Roma identify as Muslim and nearly 95% of ethnic Albanians also identify as Muslim. There is a fear that Roma in Skopje and in the western part of the state might identify as ethnic Albanians (V. Friedman, 1996). Such "identity switching" based on language and religion has historical grounding and is perceived to threaten the majority status enjoyed by ethnic Macedonians. The government is aware of this "identity switching," and some scholars cite this "fear" as one of the motives for the Macedonian government's relatively "benign" treatment of Roma as compared with other European countries (E. Friedman, 2002a, 2002b).

This official support of Romani identity has pacified accusations of discrimination on the part of the state. In fact, when state officials are questioned regarding disproportionate poverty, unemployment, or health concerns facing the Romani population, the response is often to reference the Constitution and late President Trajkovski's public statements as evidence that there is no discrimination in Macedonia (Plaut, 2006).

The 1999 war between ethnic Albanian insurgents and the predominantly ethnically Serbian Yugoslav army resulting in the subsequent NATO-led bombing in Kosovo created dramatic demographic reshuffling in the region. Although small, Macedonia was often referenced as the last bastion of stability in the former Yugoslavia. After 1999, many members of the international community who previously focused on Bosnia and Kosovo turned their focus (and funding) to Macedonia. The Organization for Security and Cooperation in Europe (OSCE) and other international organizations established "spill over missions" (from Kosovo) to ensure that Macedonia remain intact and multiethnic.

Much of their funding focused on the creation of independent media and civil society organizations, including those established to serve specific ethnic populations. In fact, Macedonia's "treatment" of its ethnic minorities is often directly promoted as a positive example to other governments in the region (Radio Free Europe/Radio Liberty [RFE/RL], 2006).[4] The Macedonian government is aware of its international reputation and is eager for acceptance within the EU and NATO. Thus the government works hard to cultivate a multiethnic and tolerant presentation.

The Struggle of (Ethnically Targeted) Civil Society Within Macedonia

Healthy media following their mission should serve as a reflection of the society, both in content (entertaining, informing, educating) and structure (staffing, coverage, funding). Ethnically specific media are usually established to respond to the specific needs and interests of a given community in the most accessible format (Downing, 1996; OSCE, 2003). Therefore, ethnically specific media have a higher responsibility to know and address the needs of their audience. As this article demonstrates, Romani media in Macedonia do not fulfill this responsibility because they are not working with Romani NGOs to function as an effective element of civil society.

New NGOs, as well as radio and television stations, proliferated rapidly in Macedonia in the mid-1990s. Mirroring increasingly fragmented ethnic communities, many chose to focus on specific demographics. Roma were no exception. According to the Macedonian Center for International Cooperation, 150 to 200 NGOs focused their attention on Macedonian Roma (though the registered, formally recognized number is smaller). As of January 2008, 271 legal electronic media outlets operated in Macedonia. Five catered to the Romani population. Nearly all Romani NGOs and media relied on international donors for more than 75% of their funding.

International funders assume that ethnically targeted media advocate for their particular sectors of civil society (Angheli et al., 2003). For Macedonian Roma, this assumption proves problematic. A clear lack of communication (defined in this article as "information sharing for a common goal") between Romani NGOs and Romani media results in a shell of Romani civil society. According to the organizations' annual reports, it is the NGOs that serve as a foundation for Romani civil society. Yet according to Batliwala and Titus's (2007) findings, as well as my (Plaut, 2006) own research, "there is no evidence of a grassroots movement of Roma people. . . . [Further,] NGO activities focus on service delivery rather than on organizing or political mobilization."

Missing Strategic Partners: Romani NGOs and Romani Media

Romani NGOs and Romani media share considerable potential for collaboration: They are often founded within 1 year of each other, they were created to address similar issues and often share donors. More important, they share an audience hungry for more information. To access this information, most turn to Romani media in their area. They are invariably disappointed.

In April 2003, a Romani NGO active in Skopje organized a series of events for that year's International Romani Day. Speakers were invited, posters made, space rented, and a press release drafted. Two days before the event, the press release was faxed and/or e-mailed to every media outlet in Skopje: Roma and non-Roma, national and local. With 1,000 people in attendance, only one journalist showed up.

In 2003, I conducted in-person interviews with all legal Romani media in Macedonia, 10 Romani NGOs (based on thematic and geographic distribution), and 15 "nonaffiliated Roma" in the sampled cities.[5] ("Nonaffiliated Roma" here means people identifying as Roma and consuming media but working for neither an NGO nor a media outlet.) What this research revealed was a constellation of attitudes enabling the type of disappointment described above.

Romani NGOs

Romani NGOs are found throughout Macedonia, with the bulk of active NGOs based in the capital, Skopje. Romani NGOs often provide the first, if only, connection that Roma people have to social services guaranteed by the state. However, few of the NGOs can supply reliable data regarding the size of their client base. On average, they served 245 people annually (the exception, Romani Shukaripe, claims to serve 6,000 to 7,000 people). More than 32 donors were supporting the 10 NGOs interviewed, the majority receiving funding from both international and national donors. Only one NGO, Luludi, received governmental support, which it has since been unable to renew. All Romani NGOs supplied project proposals, including annual reports, to me. Most were willing to make them public.

Romani NGOs were often founded with very general goals but specified and changed focus depending on project-specific funding. These projects were often conceptualized and monitored by the international donors. Change in project often means a change in focus. Often one NGO worked in three or four divergent fields—simultaneously viewing and presenting itself as a social service provider, an advocate, and a watchdog. There was often a sharp discrepancy between the image projected by the NGO and the projects they were engaged in.

NGOs within the same geographic location communicate with each other regardless of their organization's focus, and NGOs working on similarly themed projects also communicate with each other across the country. The most common sources of information for Roma NGOs are personal contacts and "walk-ins" (80%). When asked how people know where to go for services or information, Dilbera Kamberovska, president of DAJA (Kumanovo), stated it best: "We are consistent; we've been here for 10 years. We are always at conferences. People know us" (interview, September 19, 2003). Word of mouth publicity is common, whereas collaborating with Romani media to create the more deliberate outreach strategies most often associated with social movements is quite rare. Of the seven NGOs, all invite local/national media to events, but only four regularly invite Romani media. Although all NGOs reported consuming Romani media, only 50% use them as sources of information regarding the Romani public.

Romani NGOs are well aware of the power of the media; that is demonstrated by their requests for increased media attention. However, nearly all Romani NGOs complain that media are only interested in contacting them when a story is "hot." Only Mesecina and ARKA included specific strategies in their work plans to make one of their stories "hot" (Figure 10.1).

Romani Media

Romani media, excepting e-media and the state television station, are all local, serving a listener/viewer base of 15,000 to 200,000 people. Legal Roma media are found throughout Macedonia, concentrated in the western part of the country and Skopje. Pirate Romani media, while notable for their abundance, receive no official funding and are thus out of the purview of this study.

According to their mission statements, all Romani media were founded with the goals of informing and educating "the Romani population." They all have programming schemes (schedules) that include news, education, and call-in shows. Romani media, excepting MRTV and Radio Roma, are supported primarily through international donors, and all but Radio Roma hold weekly meetings to determine content and "programming schemes."[6]

Roma media typically broadcast in Romani and Macedonian (MRTV/BTR broadcasts almost exclusively in Romani, whereas Roma Radio and Radio Cherenja broadcast nearly exclusively in Macedonian).[7] According to information presented during interviews and a review of programming schemes, it is evident that all Romani media *seek* to cover human rights, legal issues, activism, and culture, thus mirroring issues addressed by Romani NGOs.

That said, severe gaps exist between Romani media's goals and actual programming. According

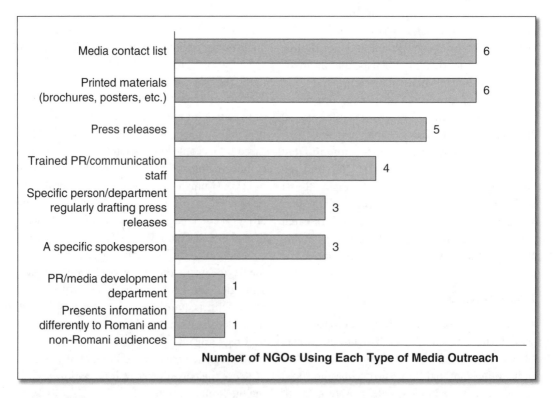

Number of NGOs Using Each Type of Media Outreach

Media contact list	6
Printed materials (brochures, posters, etc.)	6
Press releases	5
Trained PR/communication staff	4
Specific person/department regularly drafting press releases	3
A specific spokesperson	3
PR/media development department	1
Presents information differently to Romani and non-Romani audiences	1

Figure 10.1   Media Outreach Techniques Used by Romani NGOs. Of the 10 NGOs interviewed, only ARKA reported general satisfaction with the media attention it receives, yet they still had specific complaints about Romani media's apparent "indifference" to their activities.

to BTR station founder and president Zoran Dimov, BTR's mission was to "educate our Romani people." However, excepting 85 minutes of news, the station's daily schedule consists entirely of dedicated music videos (baxtalina) and pirated films.[8] Although this may be an extreme example, two thirds of Romani media fill two thirds of their broadcasts with music and baxtalina. This neither fulfills the goals nor their audience's needs.

This schism between mission and reality is often explained by a prevalence of "lack." There is a lack of funding, equipment, and training, all of which, when budgets and logistics were analyzed, are true. There also appears to be a lack of vision. Romani media do not have reliable information on their listeners/watchers (nor do they see its importance), and Roma media do not use the potential of working with Romani NGOs to obtain information regarding the Romani community that they were founded to serve. Nor, as evidenced previously, do the Romani NGOs reach out to the Romani media. These deficiencies point to a lack of responsiveness and accountability to their targeted audience.

BTR and Shutel do conduct monthly surveys, but only to count viewers—they ignore ethnic, educational, economic, age, and gender composition. On the other hand, Radio Roma, Radio Ternipe, Radio Cherenja, and MRTV don't even have those data.[9] When asked how programming decisions are made and successes measured without such information, all media outlets responded based on assumptions about their audiences' wants and needs. As Enise Demirova, Founder and Director of Radio Cherenja (Shtip) stated,

> We know their needs because I'm from here; I live here and I follow the issues. I am directly involved in the mahaala (neighborhood) and have been for 10 years; my husband (who is a journalist at Cherenja) has been working with Roma issues for 22 years. (interview, September 29, 2003)

However, it is evident that Roma media are not responding to their audiences' desires. When asked what he would like to see/hear on Romani media, Sushica Ajdin, a Rom working in Skopje's hospitality industry, explained,

> They should have documentaries. It needs to be more educational, especially for the children. It should include international news—information about the rest of the world. This will help promote and inspire our children to continue their education. This is not just me saying this. . . . I would tell them this myself, but it'll have no affect. (interview, October 2, 2003)

As Nori Rusanovski, a 54-year-old Romani pensioner of Prilep, explained, "We live in a greater society and we need to know about it . . . but they also need to know about us." In fact, when nonaffiliated Roma were asked what three issues should be covered on Romani media stations, "Wider Society" earned the largest response (Figure 10.2).

Romani media envision themselves as service providers to their targeted population and recognize their potential as educational and activist tools. However, their sources are disproportionately informal networks, personal contacts, and governmental rather than other sectors of civil society. When one examines the mission statements and programming of NGOs and media, it becomes apparent that partnership is not only possible but also essential if either is to truly reach its oft-cited but rarely explained goal of "Romani emancipation."[10]

Incomplete Communication Network

"Communication breakdown" is cited as a cause of failure within any segment of civil society but is often diagnosed in the wrong place (Keck & Sikkink, 1998). Internal communication structures within Romani media and NGOs are well-established. The communication breakdown is not *within* the respective spheres but rather *between* the NGO and media sectors. This results in a lack of mutual recognition regarding place and importance within civil society. The research, therefore, points not to a *lack* of communication but to an *incomplete* communication network.

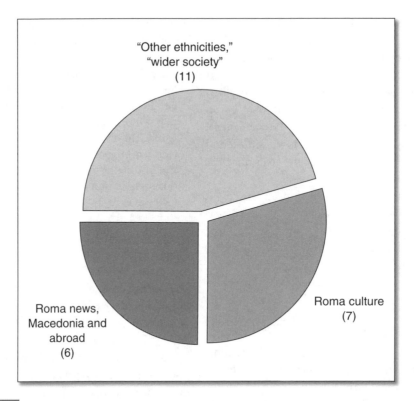

Figure 10.2   Media Coverage Desired by Romani Respondents

Romani NGO members consistently communicate with one another: exchanging information in often overlapping circles, participating in conferences/seminars, and at times cooperating on projects. Ahmet Jasharevski, president of DROM (Kumanovo) explains, "We are an activist-based NGO and information is meant to be acted upon . . . therefore we must share the information" (interview, September 18, 2003). While not all Romani NGOs define themselves as "activist," all interviewed belong to a formal NGO network. Seven out of 10 use the formal NGO network(s) to present activities.

Romani media also organize into informal networks: Staff often exchange information, lend equipment, and share files/programs. All Romani media, excepting Roma Radio, have at least one strategic media partner outside their city.[11] All Roma media (again except Roma Radio) are in contact with national and international information networks, a clear example of which was presented by Omar and Enise Demirova of Radio Cherenja

(Shtip). Based on its strategic location, Radio Cherenja was the first media outlet to cover the tragic death by severe child abuse of a young Roma child on March 2003. Information was then sent to national and regional Roma and non-Roma media alike, with Radio Cherenja credited as the source.

As seen from this episode, Romani media are often in contact with non-Romani news sources. Radio Cherenja, BTR, and Shutel all receive information daily from the Macedonia Information Agency (MIA) and Roma-specific news sources. Radio Ternipe suspended its MIA subscription due to lack of funds but continues receiving *Roma Times* (Skopje) and often exchanges information about local and national events via its partnership with a local non-Romani radio station in Prilep.

The communication breakdown between Romani media and NGOs lies not in a lack of organization or structure but in disregard for the other's importance. Although Romani NGOs invite local and national media to 60% to 70% of their events, Romani media are invited only 40%

of the time. When asked why, the NGOs most often cited "lack of professionalism," "lack of consistency," and "must often pay for time on the air." The underlying reasons appear to be perceived worth and market. Rather than recognizing their community or "target group" as their audience, NGOs focus media attention as a tool for publicity and legitimization before the greater society."[12]

In other words, for NGOs, media serve the outside world. In that context, Roma media have little strategic importance, no matter their symbolic value. This perception stems from a vision of media as publicity tool rather than information source. This perception was not shared by Romani audiences. All nonaffiliated Roma interviewed (aged 16–55) were familiar with Romani media in their area and viewed them with a sense of pride, yet more than three fourths felt compelled to consume non-Romani media to feel informed about Romani issues.

Romani media mirror this blindness. Although all Romani media have run at least one story on Romani NGOs, they rarely reach out to them for quotes, expert opinions, or surveys of current Romani community issues.[13] None of the Romani media stations have current Romani NGO directories, but nearly all have current lists of governmental ministries and their spokespeople. When asked who Romani media turn to for information/collaboration on a story, NGOs were consistently rated below personal contacts and governmental sources.

The parallel networks phenomenon constitutes the basis of communicative and collaborative breakdown between Romani media and NGOs, pointing to a faulty framework in which (Roma) media are not seen as an important part of civil society. They tend instead to be relegated to the domain of ethnic pride rather than one with power to challenge and change societal structures. As Feat Kamberovski from ARKA (Kumanovo) stated, "We want to work with MRTV 1, 2, and 3 (state run national media outlets)—especially MRTV 1; it's national—everyone watches" (interview, September 19, 2003). Kamberovski's opinion reflects that of most NGOs interviewed. While all expressed a desire to work more closely with media, only three expressed a desire to more closely

collaborate with Romani media. Kamberovski also echoes the attitude among NGOs that Romani media value the work of governmental or personal sources more than NGOs:

> It is pretty sad when these other . . . [non-Romani] television stations are interested in our work and Shutel can't even pick up the phone. . . . Roma media is not doing their job. They are too selective and this runs counter to their purpose as a public service. (interview, September 19, 2003)

Ljatif Demir from DARHIA (Skopje) feels that his organization's work is also ignored by Romani media. "In Skopje, we never use Roma media because we send faxes and they never send a reporter." He explains his perception of why: "Because they (Romani media) don't want to inform their viewers about our activities" (interview, September 8, 2003).

This attitude of perceived disinterest is recognized by Roma Radio, Radio Ternipe, and BTR journalists who bemoan the fact that they are contacted by NGOs only as a means of free publicity, rather than as vital information outlets. Selman Bajram, director of and journalist for Radio Ternipe (Prilep), recounts many instances when he was given 2 hours' notice to cover an event for local Romani NGOs, if he was invited at all. Most of the time, his requests for collaboration with NGOs, like other Romani media outlets, were ignored.

Conclusion

This cycle of distrust and disregard between NGOs and media damages both sectors of what potentially could be a vibrant and unique civil society within Macedonia. A healthy, supported dialogue between Romani NGOs and Romani media would expose the fact that neither actually engage the people they claim to represent. Despite their founding principles, Romani NGOs' activities often follow agendas given to them by international donors. Romani media's programming reflects neither their own mission statements nor the interests of their audience. Neither segment brings its constituency into designing agendas or activities, instead operating in silos and wondering why the other doesn't take it seriously, while the international community perpetuates the notion that Roma just "can't agree on anything."

The Romani population is well aware of this and responds by employing a sophisticated approach of picking and choosing services and information: Romani NGOs provide services, Romani media provide pride, and the national media provide information. This reinforces existing hegemonic power structures and keeps civil society from becoming a vital alternative. The state is not held accountable for its lack of responsibility to Romani citizens, and the Roma population remains passive consumers (or dependent grant recipients) rather than active agents in advocating for systemic and structural change within Macedonia.

This is not inevitable. Romani civil society could be quite strong and offer a means of strengthening Macedonian civil society as a whole. Romani media can be uniquely positioned to influence non-Roma populations, as they are often the only "ethnic media" regularly consumed by all ethnic groups in the country. This potential for creating larger social change cannot be underestimated. Yet, Romani media and NGOs' oft-touted goal of fighting the marginalization of Roma and increasing their "emancipation" cannot happen without their greater cooperation with each other. Such cooperation, and thus the strengthening of civil society and state accountability, can and should be encouraged by international donors.

Notes

1. Recognizing the controversy surrounding the name of the Republic of Macedonia and the Greek state of Macedonia, I am choosing to refer to the Republic of Macedonia, as this is how the country refers to itself in all official and unofficial documents.

2. Drzhavnost = citizenship, nationality = narodnost; in this article, I will use the term *ethnicity*.

3. More than 90% of Macedonian Roma live in urban communities, a unique phenomenon among Roma in Europe.

4. Although there are six recognized nationalities, the majority of the domestic attention and political capital addressing multiethnic issues is focused on the large (25.7%, according to the 2002 census) ethnic Albanian population. This was true even before the 2001 conflict but has only intensified since then. Prior to 2004, there was minimal official attention paid to Roma by either the government or academe (ECMI & MRG, 2004). There were programs designed for the Romani population, but they were primarily focused on language and culture and most often designed and funded with (primarily international) nongovernment money (Plaut, 2006).

5. As of January 2007, seven media exist: Skopje (BTR, Shutel, and MRTV-Roma program), Gostivar (Roma Radio), Shtip (Radio Cherenja), Prilep (Radio Ternipe), and Kumanovo (e-media sent to romnews.org). The existence of such media determined the areas visited (see Plaut, 2006).

6. In 2004, the majority of Romani media received funding support from Swedish Helsinki Committee, FOSIM, and Medienhilfe.

7. By statute, MRTV is only allowed to broadcast in Romani with other languages in subtitles.

8. Since the original research was conducted, BTR has received licensing rights to broadcast throughout Europe via satellite. Based on this provision, and in upholding copyright laws, BTR is legally prohibited from screening movies.

9. The lack of demographic surveying is not unique to Romani media; it is found throughout media outlets. However, it is worth noting that international donors funding Romani media find its acquisition no more important than the media themselves.

10. This phrase was used in 85% of Romani NGOs and media interviewed.

11. At this time, there is no consistent Roma news agency in Macedonia, but the regionwide, informal Roma Media Network was established with help from donor Medienhilfe. The MIA also participates in mentoring one Romani journalist per year. More time is needed to assess this endeavor's viability.

12. Romani NGO "Mesechina" stands as a marked exception to this rule; its information/coordination department is split evenly between using media to reach its target group and sharing information with the NGO sector. It is the only NGO interviewed that uses the media as a strategic activism tool.

13. In 2003, Shutel began a Roma NGO interview/talking head show, hosted by Asmet Elezovski, titled *Amen E Roma*. Elezovski is the point person for much of

the e-media/news on romnews.org and is a radio journalist for a local Kumanovo station. He is also the director of Roma National Centrum (Kumanovo); he attempts to keep his journalism and activism rolls separate.

References

Amnesty International. (2007). *Little by little we women have learned our rights: The Macedonian government's failure to uphold the rights of Romani women and girls* (AI Index: EUR 65/003/2007). Retrieved January 3, 2008, from www.amnesty.org/en/library/info/EUR65/003/2007/en

Angheli, N., Karlsreiter, N., Blum, R., Duve, F., Skopljanac, N., & Popovic, T. (2003). *Media in multilingual societies: Freedom and responsibility.* Vienna: OSCE.

Barany, Z. (2002). *The East European gypsies: Regime change, marginality and ethnopolitics.* New York: Cambridge University Press.

Batliwala, S., & Titus, S. (2007). *Making and breaking social movements: The case of the European Roma.* Unpublished manuscript.

Brunnbauer, U., & Kaser, K. (1999). *How to construct civil societies? Education, human rights and media in southeast Europe: A critical guide.* Graz, Austria: The Center for the Study of Balkan Studies and Culture, University of Graz. Retrieved March 30, 2009, from www-gewi.kfunigraz.ac.at/csbsc/guide/Introduction.htm

Cooley, A., & Ron, J. (2002). The NGO scramble: Organizational insecurity and the political economy of transnational action. *International Security, 27*(1), 5–39.

Downing, J. (1996). *Internationalizing media theory: Transition, power, culture.* Thousand Oaks, CA: Sage.

Downing, J. (2001). *Radical media: Rebellious communication and social movements.* Thousand Oaks, CA: Sage.

Elezovski, A. (2003). *Pomegju fikcijata I realnosta/Between the fiction and reality/Maskar I fikcija thaj o realitoteto.* Kumanovo, Macedonia: DROM.

European Centre for Minority Issues & Minority Rights Group. (2004). *Shadow report on minority issues.* Skopje, Macedonia: ECMI. Retrieved March 30, 2009, from www.ecmimacedonia.org/publications.htm

European Roma Rights Center, Network Women's Program, Roma Centre of Skopje. (2006). *CEDAW Shadow Report on the status of Romani women.* Retrieved March 30, 2009, from www.soros.org/initiatives/women/articles_publications/publications/macedonia_20051101/nwp_20060303.pdf

Fisher, W. (1997). DOING GOOD? The politics and antipolitics of NGO practices. *Annual Review of Anthropology, 26,* 439–464.

Friedman, E. (2002a). *Explaining the political integration of minorities: Roms as a hard case.* PhD dissertation, University of California, San Diego.

Friedman, E. (2002b, November). Political integration of the Roma minority in post-communistic Macedonia. *Southeast European Politics, 3*(2/3), 107–126.

Friedman, V. (1996). Observing the observers: Language, ethnicity, and power in the 1994 Macedonian census and beyond. In B. Rubin (Ed.), *Toward comprehensive peace in Southeastern Europe: Conflict prevention in the South Balkans* (pp. 81–105, 119–126). New York: Council on Foreign Relations/Twentieth Century Fund.

Government of Macedonia. (2001, November). *Constitution of the Republic of Macedonia* (Macedonian ed.). Skopje, Macedonia: Author.

Keck, M., & Sikkink, K. (1998). *Activists beyond borders: Advocacy networks in international politics.* Ithaca, NY: Cornell University Press.

Organization for Security and Co-Operation in Europe. (2003). *Media in multilingual societies.* Vienna: Office of the Representative on Freedom of the Media, OSCE.

Plaut, S. (2006, March). *Absent Roma, imported interest: The case of Macedonia.* Paper presented at the annual meeting of the International Studies Association, Town & Country Resort and Convention Center, San Diego, CA. Retrieved October 5, 2006, from www.allacademic.com/meta/p99074_index.html

Project on Ethnic Relations. (2001). *State policies towards the Roma in Macedonia.* Retrieved March 30, 2009, www.per-usa.org/reports/MacedoniaRoma.pdf

Radio Free Europe/Radio Liberty. (2006, February 20). Retrieved March 30, 2009, from www.rferl.org/content/article/1065978.html

Smillie, I. (1995). *The alms bazaar: Altruism under fire—non-profit organizations and international development.* London: Intermediate Technology.

UNDP. (2005). *Dimensions of vulnerability: At risks Roma and the displaced in South East Europe.* Retrieved March 30, 2009, from http://europeandcis.undp.org/home/show/A3C29ADB-F203–1EE9-BB0A 277C80C5F9F2

PART III

Cultural Geographies

This section explores the relationship between place, collective identity, and cultural production. We begin with a brief discussion of the complex and contradictory effects of globalization on local communities. On the one hand, globalization threatens much that is unique or distinctive about a particular place. The forces associated with globalization—the ebb and flow of people and capital, technology, and culture—challenge the values, reorient the social relations, and alter the practices and traditions associated with community life. In short, globalization disrupts our individual and collective sense of place. On the other hand, globalization restructures, accelerates, and deepens connections between disparate people, cultures, and places. In this way, globalization opens up new spaces and creates unique opportunities for communities to articulate shared identities, concerns, and experience. As we shall see, community media constitute just such a space and offer local populations an opportunity to reassert their political and cultural autonomy in light of the shifting geographies of power that mark the current era.

A Sense of Place

One of the most telling consequences of globalization has been a renewed interest in place within popular and academic discourse. This should come as no surprise, however, given how fundamental a sense of place is to human experience (Basso, 1996; Casey, 1993). In recent years, the field of human geography has made significant contributions to debates over the relationship between place, culture, and identity in an era of globalization. A concise review of a number of salient themes that emerge from this literature can help us better understand and appreciate the social and cultural significance of community media.

Briefly stated, human geography examines human interaction with the physical environment. Significantly, human geography considers the *material* as well as the *cultural* dimensions of place. The material dimension of place includes the natural as well as the "built" environment. Thus, the material dimension of place is constituted by human activity within a physical landscape (e.g., for purposes of farming), as well as the construction of private and public spaces, such as buildings, parks, plazas, monuments, and the like. Conversely, the cultural dimensions of place emphasize the role of myth, narrative, poetry, song, and other forms of human expression in creating a sense of place.

Human geographers are especially attentive to the interplay between the material or physical character of place on the one hand and the symbolic or communicative dimension of place on the other. Accordingly, human geography considers the varied ways in which human societies inscribe place with meaning through social practices and cultural forms and traditions (Rose, 1995). No doubt, it is the dynamic interaction between these material and cultural dimensions that accounts for the ancient and enduring relevance of place to human experience.

These insights highlight an important facet of our sense of place; that is, *representations of place* (e.g., literature, painting, music, advertising, film and television) are not at all inconsequential. Rather, representations of place tell us who is, and who is not, of a particular place. Furthermore, representations of place are important for constructing the boundaries that differentiate one place from another. Indeed, the boundaries that mark off one place from another are, for the most part, symbolic: a product of what Doreen Massey (1995b) describes as the "geographic imagination." Thus, this collective act of imagination is crucial to cultivating an individual sense of self as well as a collective sense of identity and belonging.

Because our sense of place is socially constructed, the meanings assigned to place are open to interpretation and, therefore, contested and subject to change. This line of thought underscores what has been described as the "cultural politics of place" (Rose, 1994) and suggests how thoroughly our sense of place is structured by unequal relations of power within and between places. Put another way, representations of place are embedded in power relations and constitute a site of political struggle. Indeed, a close reading of representations of place can reveal the competing social, political, and economic interests at work in creating a sense of place. Moreover, as Gillian Rose (1995) suggests, we can discern the way power relations shape and inform a sense of

place "in cases where one sense of place becomes so dominant that it obscures the other" (p. 100).

Consider, for example, the exercise of power in representing place during the European colonization of Australia in the 18th century. When European colonizers came to Australia, they described the land as *terra nullius* (an empty space devoid of people). This perspective was instrumental in legitimating, in the minds of the colonizers, at any rate, inhumane treatment of indigenous peoples and the ruthless acquisition of their land. The European colonizers' representation of the land as "uninhabited" and "unclaimed" has had, and continues to have, enormous implications for Aboriginal people whose relationship to place—in their view a repository of collective memories and local knowledge for millennia—is intimately bound up in the people's sense of identity, culture, and sovereignty.

In our time, the cultural politics of place has intensified in response to the process of economic restructuring that is occurring across the globe. In postindustrial societies, for instance, the demands of capital to remake urban spaces so that they might be more appealing to investors and upscale clients has led to pitched battles between working-class residents, city planners, and real estate developers. Those in favor of redevelopment represent place as an engine for economic growth and urban renewal. Opponents of gentrification depict neighborhoods as containers of collective memories, social networks, and cultural traditions that are threatened by redevelopment schemes. Significantly, the struggle to define these neighborhoods is played out in a variety of communicative forms and practices, from multimillion-dollar advertising campaigns produced by development corporations to protest literature and imagery produced on shoestring budgets by community organizers.

In short, our sense of place—of the boundaries that mark one place from another; of defining the differences between "insiders" and "outsiders"—is inextricably bound up in relations of power. Moreover, the diverse, competing, and often contradictory meanings attached to place exert a profound, if sometimes unacknowledged, influence on our everyday lives.

These insights have enormous implications for community media studies. Indeed, Doreen Massey's (1995b) observation that representations of place "provide an insight into how people who produced them imagine the world in which they live and how they place themselves within it" is certainly applicable to community media (p. 26). As the chapters in this section demonstrate, regardless of the medium being used, cultural expression produced and distributed by community media provide a distinctive lens to explore how local populations understand and make sense of place in the era of globalization.

The Local/Global Nexus

Globalization is a bewildering, sometimes threatening process that is difficult to grasp, let alone come to terms with. Phrases such as "the local" and "the global" only go so far in explaining the effects of globalization on social, political, and economic relations within and between communities. Cultural theory avoids the abstractions associated with notions of the local and the global through description, analysis, and interpretation of everyday lived experience. This approach has been extremely helpful insofar as it highlights the dynamic and relational character of place. For instance, by taking a historical perspective to the process of globalization, cultural analysts remind us that there is nothing new in all this. Rather, it is the frequency, intensity, and direction of daily interactions between the local and global that mark this latest round of globalization.

Consider the following. For people living in industrial societies, recent waves of immigration from so-called undeveloped countries are tangible (and for some distressing) signs that it really is a small world after all. But for indigenous peoples in the Americas, Africa, Asia, and the Pacific Rim, their world was shrinking hundreds of years ago—during the age of European expansion and conquest that lasted from the late 15th to the early 20th century. Taking a long view of the process of globalization reveals that this process has in fact been an ongoing one: a process that is open to multiple interpretations depending on whose sense of place is being ruptured at the time (Massey, 1995a).

Likewise, by focusing our attention on the ordinary and everyday character of the interplay between local, regional, national, and global forces, cultural theory steers clear of essentialist notions of place that lament the loss of "pure" or "authentic" places. Instead, this approach illuminates the various ways in which place is, and has long been, embedded in and produced through, wider social relations. Put another way, contemporary cultural theory views place as a *hybrid* entity—a site for the meeting, intersection, and mingling of "local" and "nonlocal" forces and actors.

None of which is to suggest, however, that places are becoming indistinct or that they are in danger of losing their unique attributes. Rather, it is to say that it is the manner in which the local and the nonlocal meet in a particular place, at a particular moment, that gives place its specificity.

These insights provide a basis for a nuanced understanding of place that not only helps us make sense of community media but also enhances our appreciation of the progressive possibilities of "a global sense of place" (Massey, 1994). Indeed, if we think about globalization in terms of the interconnected and interdependent character of social, political, and economic relations spread out around the world, then it follows that the local makes up the global, just as the global makes up the local.

For our purposes, then, community media constitute but one instance of the local/global nexus—a site in which the local, regional, national, and global intersect, coalesce, and reconfigure (Howley, 2005). As we shall see, community media provide an exceptional vehicle to examine the process of globalization from the perspective of local communities. Indeed, as expressions of local knowledge and experience, community media are particularly well suited to articulate a local community's response to the changes, both dramatic and mundane, associated with globalization.

Local Media Cultures

Globalization has had a profound influence on the conceptual issues and analytical frameworks taken up by media studies. Whereas the nation-state once provided a stable frame of reference for exploring the influence of regulatory systems, funding mechanisms, and technological infrastructures on the cultural output of national media systems, an emerging transnational media system constitutes a new realm of analysis. The changing dynamics of cultural production associated with satellite broadcasting, digitization, and Internet communication have prompted scholars to concentrate their efforts on media flows that transcend national borders and reach far-flung audiences across the globe.

Insofar as the prevalence of transnational media flows represents a challenge to decades of Anglo-American dominance of global communication, these developments have eased some of the anxieties associated with cultural imperialism. However, it is important to keep in mind that the global mediascape is still marked by deeply uneven cultural exchanges. What's more, the twin motivations of profit accumulation and market dominance continue to govern the logic of the global cultural economy.

Nevertheless, by shifting the emphasis away from the nation-state and toward local media centers, scholars signal the need to examine the forces and conditions that shape global media culture: new sites and modes of production and distribution, the emergence of innovative textual forms and strategies, and the dramatic restructuring of media reception contexts. One of these new sites of global cultural production is what media scholar Michael Curtin (2004) refers to as "media capitals." According to Curtin, cities such as Hong Kong, Cairo, and Mumbai (formerly Bombay) are increasingly influential hubs of media financing, production, and distribution that compete alongside more established players such as New York, Los Angeles, and London in the global media market.

Drawing on Jesus Martin-Barbero's concept of *mediation,* Curtin (2004) calls our attention to the social and cultural forces that inform and influence media institutions, production environments, and textual practices. Curtin observes that Martin-Barbero's analysis is particularly sensitive to the "complex ways in which quotidian experiences of human migration, social change, and popular memory in Latin America have found expression in the cultural output of media institutions during the twentieth century" (p. 273). In short, the concept of mediation not only acknowledges the political and economic determinants of cultural production but also recognizes the influence social and cultural factors play in shaping media form and content.

Applying the concept of mediation to the cultural output of media capitals, Curtin (2004) argues that these institutional forms and practices are successful insofar as they "register and articulate the social experience of their audiences" (p. 273). This insight helps refine our analysis of the changing dynamics of the culture industries in the early 21st century. Indeed, the concept of mediation focuses our attention not on the sameness of global communication, but rather so as to appreciate the importance, and persistence, of *cultural difference* expressed within and through the global media system.

Accordingly, scholars analyze media capitals across a number of dimensions: the locale's social history and physical environment, demographics and migration patterns, economic and regulatory conditions, and communication and transportation infrastructures, as well as local traditions, practices, and sensibilities. This focus on the influence of local actors, conditions, and resources on cultural production in media capitals yields important insights into the process of globalization. For instance, by emphasizing the interplay between local, regional, national, and global forces, this approach captures the cross-cultural dynamics that shape and give rise to transnational media flows. Moreover, this perspective's attentiveness to the issue of cultural relevance as an indication of the popular appeal of media texts for geographically dispersed audiences enhances our understanding of the relationship between communication, culture, and community.

Most of the scholarship that follows this line of inquiry retains a focus on powerful groups—advertising agencies and public relations firms as well as the film, television, music, and publishing industries—working in so-called global cities. But what of cultural production from elsewhere, produced by nonprofessionals or marginalized groups and without much concern for market share or profit making? As the following chapters demonstrate, community media are a significant, if somewhat neglected, element in the "resurgence of local content and strategies across a range of media channels" that constitutes global media culture (Brennan, 2007, p. 434). In this light, community media studies are extremely well suited to chart the cultural geography of media production and distribution in an era of global communication.

Furthermore, the insights gleaned from analyses of "media capitals" can help us better understand and appreciate the social and cultural significance of community media. For instance, in her study of television production in Vancouver, British Columbia, Canada, Serra Tinic (2006) observes how the city and provincial governments attempted to portray Vancouver as a media capital that would appeal to regional, national, and international production companies. These efforts were part and parcel of a broader scheme to attract foreign investment to the province and cement Vancouver's reputation as a global city. Tinic's study uncovers a glaring contradiction of media capitals: Despite the extensive use of local actors, resources, and talent by so-called runaway productions from Hollywood and elsewhere, the bulk of television programming produced in Vancouver tends to obscure, rather than illuminate, the distinctive social, cultural, and political characteristics of the place.

Significantly, Tinic (2006) finds that

for those producers who seek to develop ideas that draw on the experiences of life in the place of Vancouver, community television does offer a structure and level of access that is particularly suited to the representation of the sociocultural specificity of the city. (p. 173)

In other words, despite their "amateur status" and lack of big-budget "production values," community television organizations throughout the city produced culturally relevant content that

was more effective than its commercial and transnational counterparts at provoking a sense of place that resonated with the disparate people who call Vancouver home.

In short, our comprehension of the complex cultural dynamics at work in the global media system is limited and incomplete if we fail to recognize community media's contribution to contemporary media culture. As contributors in this section demonstrate, community media are fertile sites for empirically grounded analysis of the interplay between local cultures of production and global media culture.

The chapters in this section demonstrate the creative and innovative ways in which communities negotiate the homogenizing effects of cultural globalization by (re)asserting place-based and cultural identities. Throughout this section, contributors call our attention to the social, economic, and political factors that enable as well as constrain community media in a variety of geocultural contexts. In doing so, these chapters foreground the pivotal, but often overlooked, ways in which community media contribute to the enormous variation of cultural production around the world.

Chapter 11 considers the use of information and communication technologies (ICT) by Aboriginal peoples in Canada. María Victoria Guglietti calls our attention to the role of collective imagination, and especially artistic expression, in creating a sense of community in cyberspace. Exploring the limits and possibilities of the Internet as a medium for Aboriginal cultural expression, Guglietti highlights interaction between Aboriginal peoples' sense of place, new media technologies, and emerging aesthetic practices in creating autonomous spaces for (re)presenting an imagined Aboriginal community.

In Chapter 12, Tanja Dreher examines a range of interventionist media strategies employed by Arab and Muslim communities in Sydney, Australia. According to Dreher, in the wake of the so-called war on terror, media outlets across Sydney adopted a racialized news frame that dominated media representations of Arab and Muslim communities. In response, these communities took up a variety of initiatives, including a news-monitoring project and a youth radio program designed to counter this racialized discourse. Dreher uses the concept of interventions to emphasize the common objective of these disparate projects: to alter mainstream media's coverage of, and relationship with, Sydney's Arab and Muslim communities.

Chapter 13, coauthored by members of the Edmonton Small Press Association (ESPA), focuses our attention on the role of arts activism in facilitating and promoting local cultural production. Written from a practitioner perspective, this chapter provides an overview of the organizational structure, financial support mechanisms, and creative work produced under the auspices of ESPA. Despite a hostile political climate and intense competition for limited grant funding, ESPA nurtures collaborative, community arts projects that encourage local development initiatives and support progressive social causes.

In Chapter 14, Rita Rahoi-Gilchrest examines the role of broadcast television in overcoming the disenfranchisement of New Zealand's indigenous Māori people. As Rahoi-Gilchrest observes, however, Māori Television's mission, to become a "world-class indigenous broadcaster," is not without contradiction and controversy. Rahio-Gilchrest's analysis of Māori Television underscores the success, as well as the challenges and shortcomings, of this indigenous broadcasting service in the context of an increasingly transnational television marketplace.

We conclude this section with another look at online community communication. In this chapter, Matt Sienkiewicz (Chapter 15) explores the contradictory impulses behind an Orthodox Jewish community's use of new media technologies to uphold and maintain traditional values, beliefs, and practices. Sienkiewicz's chapter examines the intersection of religious and secular culture as well as the interpenetrations between local and global forces, inscribed in a children's cartoon program, *The Itche Kadoozy Show*, distributed through the Internet. In presenting this

unusual and distinctive case study, Sienkiewicz reminds us of the fundamental relationship between communication, culture, and community.

References

Basso, K. (1996). *Wisdom sits in places: Landscape and language among the Western Apache.* Albuquerque: University of New Mexico Press.

Brennan, M. (2007). This place rocks! The Brisbane street press, local culture, identity and economy. *Continuum: Journal of Media & Cultural Studies, 21*(3), 433–444.

Casey, E. S. (1993). *Getting back into place: Toward a renewed understanding of the place-world.* Bloomington: Indiana University Press.

Curtin, M. (2004). Media capitals: Cultural geographies of global TV. In L. Spigel & J. Olsson (Eds.), *Television after TV: Essays on a medium in transition* (pp. 270–302). Durham, NC: Duke University Press.

Howley, K. (2005). *Community media: People, places, and communication technologies.* Cambridge, UK: Cambridge University Press.

Massey, D. (1994). *A global sense of place.* Retrieved December 3, 2007, from www.unc.edu/courses/2006spring/geog/021/001/massey.pdf

Massey, D. (1995a). The conceptualization of place. In D. Massey & P. Jess (Eds.), *A place in the world? Places, cultures and globalization* (pp. 45–77). Oxford, UK: Oxford University Press.

Massey, D. (1995b). Imagining the world. In J. Allen & D. Massey (Eds.), *Geographical worlds* (pp. 6–42). Oxford, UK: Oxford University Press.

Rose, G. (1994). The cultural politics of place: Local representation and oppositional discourse in two films. *Transactions of the Institute of British Geographers* (New Series), *19*(1), 46–60.

Rose, G. (1995). Place and identity: A sense of place. In D. Massey & P. Jess (Eds.), *A place in the world? Places, cultures and globalization* (pp. 87–132). Oxford, UK: Oxford University Press.

Tinic, S. (2006). Global vistas and local reflections: Negotiating place and identity in Vancouver television. *Television and New Media, 7*(2), 154–183.

CHAPTER 11

Aboriginal Internet Art and the Imagination of Community

María Victoria Guglietti

In this chapter, I trace the way Canadian-based Aboriginal Internet art has imagined community online. This ongoing work of imagination, which began with the popularization of the Internet in the mid-1990s, has been affected not just by the specific networking needs of an artistic community geographically dispersed and systematically marginalized from mainstream artistic institutions but also by the Internet's technological and cultural characteristics.

Aboriginal Internet art is a network of artistic and institutional practices engaged in the production of electronic and digital artworks. A quick tour round some well-known Aboriginal Internet art projects reveals a tightly knitted and multifaceted web, constituted by individual and collective online galleries, blogs, chat spaces, and artist Web sites. Outside cyberspace, Canadian-based Aboriginal Internet artists are slowly gaining recognition from mainstream artistic institutions (e.g., the Banff Centre for the Arts, the Royal Ontario Museum, the Vancouver Art Gallery), media festivals, and different provincial and federal government institutions. The complexity of the Aboriginal Internet art field

is remarkable considering Aboriginal people's actual difficulties in accessing technology and know-how in Canada. Low income and education levels together with geographical isolation are major obstacles to Aboriginal people's engagement with technology (Crompton, 2004).

Aboriginal Internet art is a field where community happens. Indeed, the association between Aboriginal Internet art, networking, and community dates from the early 1990s, when the Aboriginal Film and Video Art Alliance began a series of attempts at setting up a computer-based communication network in partnership with the Banff Centre for the Arts (Aboriginal Arts Program, n.d.). The Alliance was created in 1991 with the mandate of encouraging interdisciplinary video and film production and promoting new cultural storytelling forms within self-government principles. In March 1994, after a year of negotiations with funding partners such as the Banff Centre, the Canada Council, and the Department of Canadian Heritage, the Alliance gathered a group of Canadian- and U.S.-based Aboriginal filmmakers, video artists, and cultural producers at the Banff Centre to discuss the possibilities of developing a nation-wide computer-based multimedia telecommunications network. The meeting was called "Drum Beats to Drum Bytes" and targeted a growing community of Aboriginal artists, filmmakers, and researchers to evaluate the possibilities and shortcomings of the Internet as a "medium of Aboriginal expression" (L'Hirondelle, 2004). The agenda of the group was intellectually fuelled by a widespread corporate, governmental, and academic fascination with the Internet's potential to not only strengthen connections but also supersede the flaws of offline communities.[1] Even the most cautionary voices within the Aboriginal arts community attributed to the Internet the power to alter the way humans relate to each other and to the environment (Todd, 1996).

This early link between community media and art complicates the labeling of Aboriginal Internet art as "just" art. In fact, Aboriginal Internet artists have been using their art to network with peers and to build up a presence in a medium perceived as, paradoxically, full of possibilities and foreign.

Internet Art and the Popularization of the Internet

Internet art is an umbrella term that refers to various Web-based art practices whose forms range from alternative browsers and hypertext projects to online communities and software activism. Greene (2004) views Internet art as interlaced as much with issues of access to technology and political decentralization as with artistic strategies of appropriation, dematerialization, and participation (p. 8). Unlike other forms of non-Web-based digital art, Internet art focuses on the communicative and collaborative aspects of the medium. In fact, some genres of Internet art overtly explore the medium's potential for collective and communal activism (e.g., open source artworks, tactical media, social networks, collaborative art blogs).

The development of Internet art is closely connected to the Internet's evolution. Since the privatization of the Internet in the early 1990s, which occurred as a response to a series of challenges such as service distribution, technological maintenance, and regulation, the medium was quickly transformed from a tool of academic communication and research to a medium of communication, publishing, and, most important, commerce (Abbate, 1999). Nevertheless, it was only on the creation of the Web interface in 1994 that the medium became truly popular.

The popularization of the Internet and the invention of Web browsers facilitated the development of an Internet art movement beyond the restricted field of artistic experimentation with computers that had been taking place since the early 1960s in research centers across the developed world. The avant-garde of artists exploring e-mail and bulletin board systems welcomed the Web as a sign of a new area of artistic exploration. The development of graphic interfaces also attracted artists from more traditional disciplines, who began exploring the Web because they were drawn by the communication potential of the new medium and by the possibilities of working with images and sound online. Recognition from artistic institutions quickly followed the popularization of the medium when, in 1997, Internet art was first shown in Documenta X in Kassel, Germany (Tribe & Jana, 2006, p. 9). In Canada, in the mid-1990s, the Banff New Media Institute and the Daniel Langlois foundation (Montreal) became two of the most important centers for research and development of Internet art. The Canada Council for the Arts contributed to this quick institutionalization of Internet art by establishing funding for new media art and audio works in the late 1990s.

Aboriginal Internet Art and the Imagination of Community Online

While Aboriginal Internet art shares some of the traces of the larger Internet art movement such as the exploratory nature of works and the search for new modes of accessing audiences, its development presents a distinct communal orientation. This orientation is manifested in the fact that Aboriginal Internet art projects seek to facilitate the communication and exchange of information among Aboriginal artists, to preserve and disseminate Aboriginal languages and culture, and to create online venues of exhibition open to the Aboriginal arts community. This communal orientation is articulated at the discursive level in different representations of community in images and words, what in these pages I call the imagination of community.

The ephemeral nature of many Aboriginal Internet art projects and the difficulty of access to documentation that describe the actual practices of networking have transformed these representations of community into an important source of information about Aboriginal Internet art's community media practices. Moreover, the analysis of Aboriginal Internet art's discursive articulations of community also shows how the Aboriginal arts community has negotiated the Internet's political and cultural characteristics.

In this chapter, I focus on two projects that are now part of the canon of Aboriginal Internet art in Canada: CyberPowWow and Drumbytes.org. These projects are representative of a period of expansion and incipient institutionalization of Aboriginal Internet art that occurred in the late 1990s. They are also symptomatic of the difficult engagement of Aboriginal Internet artists with a technology whose politics and culture are still problematic, and largely foreign, to the Aboriginal arts community.

CyberPowWow

In 1997, First Nations artists Skawennati Tricia Fragnito, Ryan Rice, and Eric Robertson launched CyberPowWow, an online gallery and chat room dedicated to the exhibition and discussion of Aboriginal contemporary art. The trio had formed the collective Nation to Nation only 3 years before, with the specific goal of creating new venues of exhibition for young Aboriginal artists, who were in the fringes of artistic mainstream venues and the established Aboriginal arts community. Fragnito, exposed to new media technology as a result of her work at Oboro, a new media center in Montreal, introduced the idea of CyberPowWow to the group as a logical continuation of the community events that the group had been organizing since 1994.

The first version of CyberPowWow, presented in two chat events at both Galerie Oboro in Montreal and Circle Vision Arts Corporation in Saskatoon, depended on the free chat application called *palace*. A second version issued 2 years later, CyberPowWow 2, sought further independence by presenting its own *palace*. In 2001, a third development of the project, CPW 2K: CyberPowWow, centered on issues of Aboriginal digital aesthetics and encouraged the participation of Aboriginal artists from Australia and the United States as well as non-Native artists in the design of avatars and Web-based works. A last version, released in 2004, CPW04: Unnatural Resources, discusses the meaning—and feasibility—of an Aboriginal territory online.

CyberPowWow's palace, a series of interconnected chat rooms, was designed to not only serve as a gathering place—the actual powwow—but as a gallery where online works would be exhibited and discussed. Participants could access the palace by downloading the free chat application, logging in, and customizing their avatar. Once in the gallery, participants would meet other viewers and—in theory—follow the moderator who would act as a tour guide.

Besides its online existence, CyberPowWow consisted in a series of offline events that sought to connect Aboriginal artists and audiences across Canada and the United States. Each event coincided with the release of a new version and, thus, functioned as openings celebrated in art galleries. During the openings, participants were invited to view new digital work showcased in the Web site and to communicate with other Native and non-Native artists online. Rather than operating as a simple "extension" of the Web site, the openings facilitated the recognition of the projects as art. They also intended to make visible and to extend the ongoing work of online networking. The last of these performance events took place in May 2004, and since then, CyberPowWow has remained inactive. Technical difficulties, lack of funding, and the enormous time and effort that the project required from its main operator, Fragnito, are all factors that, ultimately, brought it to an end.

By 1997, the Internet had become a popular medium, a paradigm of the new global economy, and the center of a digital utopianism that had quickly spread in the media. This technological utopian vision, fuelled by programmers, cultural gurus, and lobbyists of Silicon Valley, presented the Internet as a technology that could fulfill both the dreams of the old new communalists and the needs of the global economy.[2] This vision, popularized in books such as *The Virtual Community: Homesteading at the Electronic Frontier* (Rheingold, 1993) and magazines such as *Wired* and *Mondo 2000*, proposed the Internet as a space—a "cyberspace"—where a communion of minds could finally be realized.

The image of the Internet as a space was particularly useful to the artists behind CyberPowWow. Nation to Nation did not have an institutional space where work could be permanently displayed or artists could gather and discuss the concerns of the community. Until 1997, the group had had a nomadic life, moving from event to event. The arrival of CyberPowPow would slowly change these dynamics and provide the group with an "Aboriginally determined territory in cyberspace," as the Web site claimed.

The representation of the Internet as a space (i.e., cyberspace), typical of the early 1990s, is due to a widespread fascination with the new medium's virtuality. First introduced in William Gibson's (1984) science fiction novel *Neuromancer*, cyberspace, a parallel virtual reality universe, became a popular metaphor among programmers, journalists, technological entrepreneurs, and scholars (Benedikt, 1991; Jones, 1997; Turkle, 1995). However, it is in the writings of cyberlibertarians[3] where cyberspace adopts a unique politics:

> In its present condition, cyberspace is a frontier region, populated by the few hardy technologists who can tolerate the austerity of its savage computer interfaces, incompatible communication protocols, proprietary barricades, cultural and legal ambiguities, and general lack of useful maps or metaphors. (Kapor & Barlow, as cited in Silver, 2006, p. 63)

The metaphor of the frontier would frequently reappear in cyberlibertarian manifestos and journalistic accounts of the new medium during the first half of the 1990s (Dyson, Gilder, Keyworth, & Toffler, 1996; Rheingold, 1993; Whittle, 1997). In each incarnation, it would associate the development and popularization of cyberspace with the American "conquest" of the West. Cyberspace's representation as frontier land facilitates the legitimization of online uses and behavior that celebrate a radical laissez-faire and sanitize difference. It also promises the end of history, politics, and distance by making available a space where material differences are eliminated and "individual achievement and genuine community" are finally possible (Mosco, 2004, p. 15).

In his curatorial introduction to CPW2K: CyberPowWow, Internet artist Archer Pechawis explained that the Native artists involved in CyberPowWow "saw the Internet not just as a new technology but a new territory, one that we could help shape from its inception" (Pechawis, 2001, ¶ 1). The idea of building up an Aboriginal space online where artists could meet and show their work was a new take on an issue that had troubled the Aboriginal artistic community since the first Society of Canadian Artists of Native Ancestry (SCANA) meetings: the lack of Aboriginal artistic venues. It is not surprising then that the territory proposed by CyberPowWow was the palace, the online gallery where Aboriginal artists could control the terms in which their works were exhibited and interpreted.

The return to a definition of community rooted in a territory came also at a time when reflection on the meaning of "home" was taking place within the Aboriginal artistic community. The search for educational and artistic venues has often forced contemporary Aboriginal artists to move out from reserves and to relocate in big urban centers, where contact with the cultural community is restricted to friendship centers and to the local arts community.

A discursive analysis of the curatorial writings that accompany the online exhibitions reveals, however, a complicated appropriation of the image of cyberspace. This appropriation reveals, at times, CyberPowWow's awareness that cyberspace is a territory with a politics of its own, as when Jolene Rickard (1999) states, in her article that accompanies the launch of CyberPowWow 2, "'CyberPowWow 2' does not represent a shift in the intellectual paradigm of the west. It is a very direct application of the palace software but somehow when you exit this site you definitely know you were in Indian territory" (¶ 2).

The complex nature of CyberPowWow's appropriation of the cyberspace image is most evident in the theme of the last online exhibition, "Unnatural Resources," where the curatorial team proposes that artists explore ways in which online resources are being used and what can be learned from the experience of colonization to avoid excesses online:

> CyberPowWow 04 continues that expansion of Indian Territory beyond the reservation. By involving itself with fundamental questions about the nature and direction of cyberspace as a whole, the exhibition places itself—and Natives—into direct exchange with the wider virtual world. By reflecting on the past and seeking to understand how that history shares similar dynamics with the New World, the exhibition helps ensure that there are no reservations in cyberspace. (Lewis, 2004, ¶ 13)

As part of this ambiguous appropriation, the project also challenges the elimination of difference implicit in the image of the electronic frontier:

> CyberPowWow 2 is a place where anyone can drop in, pick up an Indian persona or avatar or chat with one. It was described by all the artists in the formation of this site as a new "community." Edward Poitras sees this application of the Palace as a "pow-wow" as an intervention on a de-racialized space. He observed that the internet and graphical chat rooms are void of cultural reference. This site clearly makes its position known. (Rickard, 1999, ¶ 8)

Once again, CyberPowWow presents a complex engagement with cyberlibertarian imagery by alluding to both the formation of a "new community" online and the deracialized nature of cyberspace. This oscillation reveals the community's long-term skepticism, manifested in the early days of the Drum Beats to Drum Bytes gathering, toward a technology that is perceived as both revolutionary and foreign.

This ambiguous appropriation of cyberlibertarian imagery is also observed in CyberPowWow's engagement with the "virtual community" metaphor as observed in its call for a "new community." The metaphor, popularized by Rheingold in his 1993 bestseller *The Virtual Community: Homesteading at the Electronic Frontier,* defines virtual communities as "social aggregations that emerge from the Net when enough people carry on those public discussions long enough, with sufficient human feeling, to form webs of personal relationships in cyberspace" (p. 5).

Rheingold's definition is based on his experiences as a member of the WELL, a computer conferencing system that emerged in 1985 and was frequented by the cyberlibertarian movement (e.g., Kevin Kelly, Esther Dyson, and John Perry Barlow, among others). Rheingold imagines community as a spontaneous gathering of people who share common interests. The virtual community is presented as a new—and ultimate—development in human interaction, praised for its equality and convenience in times of globalization and apparent disintegration of traditional social institutions (e.g., nuclear family, territorially based communities) (Putnam, 2000; Turner, 2006).

The metaphor of the virtual community was the perfect fit for the electronic frontier. In the virtual community, individual expression and interests take precedence over obligations (Winner, 1997). The metaphor also dissociates community from any historical reference by proposing spontaneous contact without any mention of "material" differences such as race or class: "[In cyberspace] we do everything people do when people get together, but we do it with words on computer screens, leaving our bodies behind" (Rheingold, 1993, p. 58).

The new community proposed by CyberPow-Wow shares many of the characteristics of the virtual community. It is a community of interest, constituted primarily by contemporary Aboriginal artists interested in new media. It is also a community of equals, where free expression is nurtured. Finally, it is a community where individuals choose to remain anonymous behind their avatars. However, this imagined new community also challenges the virtual community metaphor by proposing off-line interaction as necessary to the community's growth and development. In fact, CyberPowWow never fully developed as "just" a chat room or online gallery but depended on the off-line openings and gatherings to maintain the online community alive. As Fragnito (2001) explains,

> The idea that only being on the Internet wasn't good enough. When I first started it I knew that not everybody would know how to use the Palace and not everybody would know how to use the World Wide Web or browser. So what I wanted to do is to make sure that people did come together in groups, at real places which have since come to be called "gathering sites," where they could help each other access the internet; help each other to learn how to use the Palace, talk to one another and of course eat food. (Skawennati section, ¶ 4)

As in the case of the "frontier" metaphor, the "virtual community" metaphor becomes insufficient to address the needs of CyberPowWow's community. This misfit between the cyberlibertarian imagery and the needs of the Aboriginal Internet art community results in an imagery undermined by tensions and contradictions.

Drumbytes.org

Drumbytes.org is an Aboriginal Internet art project that seeks to provide the Native artistic community in Canada with a space and tool for the development, presentation, and promotion of Internet artworks. Its producer and developer, Ahasiw Maskegon-Iskwew, was a Cree/French Métis multimedia artist, performer, and curator, who presented Drumbytes.org as an example of online community in the group exhibition Language of Intercession, curated by Steve Loft for the Art Gallery of Hamilton, Ontario, Canada, in June 2003. Conceived as both Internet art and a cultural network, Drumbytes.org is inspired by the network imagined in the Drum Beats to Drum Bytes gathering. In fact, in 2004, Maskegon-Iskwew got permission from the then Head of the Aboriginal Arts Department at the Banff Centre, Marrie Mumford, to use the name Drumbytes.org for his new project. Unfortunately, its development was brought to a halt by the sudden death of Maskegon-Iskwew in September 2006.

Both tool and space, Drumbytes.org was divided into three sections: "Tipiwiki members-Camp," a customized platform for the development of a free Web-hosting community; a section dedicated to new media art news published by the members of the community; and a homepage with the project's general information. It is in the Tipiwiki camp that most of the networking happened. It is there that members posted news, discussed topics related to Aboriginal art, and asked for advice from other members. The tipiwiki application was free, and it only required a username and password to join the community.

Drumbytes.org was conceived as an open source project modeled after Wikipedia—the famous self-generating online encyclopedia—and in consonance with the principles of a free Web-hosting community. These principles serve the long-term goal of self-government in the arts pursued by the Aboriginal Film and Video Art Alliance since 1991 and adopted by Maskegon-Iskwew since his participation in the Drum Beats to Drum Bytes gathering. The abrupt end of Drumbytes.org complicates any assessment of the project's success. The platform was beginning to be adopted by Aboriginal organizations such as the Aboriginal Curatorial Collective (ACC) and by a few Aboriginal artists when Maskegon-Iskwew died. Since then, the project has not been updated, and there is no indication that it will be managed by anybody else.

Unlike CyberPowWow, Drumbytes.org does not imagine a "new community" whose members engage in role playing to discuss art-related matters online but a community that takes part in the construction of its own space through the process of "open communal information aggregation" (Maskegon-Iskwew, 2004, ¶ 1). *Open communal information aggregation* refers to collaborative and communally regulated processes of knowledge construction, which often benefit from free Web-hosting services. In the case of Drumbytes.org, the network relied on the use of a wiki-based content management system (CMS) called Tikiwiki. Tikiwiki is a free software and open source CMS that allows data management online via a Web browser. In Maskegon-Iskwew's hands, the tikiwiki application became the "*tipi-wiki*," the actual "membersCamp" where the community gathered, which reveals that, like CyberPowWow, Drumbytes.org still imagines community as linked to an online Native territory. In this sense, it is a project that imagines the Internet as a social space prone to the development of online communities, and it is therefore to be expected that the project engages with metaphors such as the "electronic frontier" and the "virtual community." However, conceived in

2004, Drumbytes.org was faced with a different discursive scenario that preserved and reformulated some of the early tenets associated with "cyberspace." This new scenario is characterized by growing concerns about cyberspace's commercialization and its potential effect on users' freedom of expression (Mosco, 2004; Zittrain 2008). A symptom of this changing online scenario is the open source movement's popularity.

Despite discursive differences and strategic tensions within the open source movement, the general trend is to resist any corporate attempt to control cyberspace by appealing to horizontal—and often anarchic—forms of online organization. This trend connects the open source movement with an early anarcho-utopian trend, popular among cyberlibertarians and hackers.

Bradley (2005) traces back cyberspace's anarcho-utopian discourse to Barlow's pronouncement against the Communications Decency Act (CDA) of 1996, a component of the Telecommunications Reform Act introduced by the U.S. government in an attempt to regulate online content. In "A Declaration of the Independence of Cyberspace," Barlow (1996), a founding member of the Electronic Frontier Foundation (EFF), imagines cyberspace as a self-regulated world, located outside the sphere of influence of nation-states. The world that Barlow colorfully depicts is rooted in cyberlibertarian principles of radical laissez-faire, individualism, and gregariousness, and in a hacker ethics that celebrates freedom of speech, decentralization, unlimited access to information, and a profound mistrust of authority (Bradley, 2005; Coleman, 2004; Ross, 2000). Barlow's anarcho-utopian image of cyberspace is reformulated in the open source movement's mistrust of authority and support of nonhierarchical forms of organization.

The open source movement proposes a model of community that is loose and whose common thread is the sharing of values such as free software and collaboration (Ljungberg, 2000). Unlike the model of virtual community proposed by Rheingold, the open source movement imagines community as a "great babbling bazaar," where members drop by and exchange information at their own convenience (Raymond, 1999). In this sense, the bazaar model lacks the sharing of feelings and warmth mentioned by Rheingold as one of the characteristics of virtual communities (Rheingold, 1993). Status within open source networks is dependent on the quality of the contribution (Ljunberg, 2000).

The ideology of collaboration and spontaneous sharing has traveled well beyond the technological sectors, and it is now adopted in different fields such as journalism, art, and science (Coleman, 2004). In all incarnations, collaboration and sharing are based on the constitution of a "creative commons," that is, an informal community based on free exchange of information and knowledge.

The image of a "creative commons" is present in the imagination of cyberspace since the Internet's heyday. A popular and fully articulated version of it is found in Pierre Lévy's (1997) notion of "collective intelligence," defined as "networks of knowledge production, transaction, and exchange" (p. 2). For Lévy, the development of this collective intelligence is crucial for the successful realization of the "knowledge age." Collective intelligence depends on unrestricted mobility and individual ethos. It is in this emphasis on "freedom" and "openness" that Lévy's words foresee the ideology of the open source movement. If collective intelligence requires a commons, this commons is regarded as an instrument to achieve the full realization of the individual's potentialities in a world where history and difference have been wiped out.

In Drumbytes.org, the contrasting discourses of the open source movement meet an Aboriginal agenda whose priority is the control of knowledge production: "In contemporary media saturated culture, the necessity of making creative statements that incorporate the essential definitions of animist cultures is essential to Aboriginal cultural survival," writes Maskesgon-Iskwew in Drumbytes.org (Maskegon-Iskwew, 2004, ¶ 4). Drumbytes.org adopts the open source model of collaboration and sharing by proposing an "open communal information aggregation" model. However, this adoption is not without tensions, particularly in the way the project defines the role and practices of the online community:

> The key relationship between the wiki model and Aboriginal media arts is the self-generating, self-determining process of collaboration by communities of interest on building bodies of knowledge that, by their fragmentation and isolation, have been previously indistinct and unavailable. . . . The communal and self-regulating nature of the Aboriginal arts community also nurtures a commitment to self-determination and innovation. (Maskegon-Iskwew, 2004, ¶ 2)

This appeal to the "communal and self-regulating nature" of the Aboriginal arts community reinforces and complicates the "bazaar" rhythm of most open source projects. The objective is not just collaboration and sharing for the sake of individual expression but the development of a body of knowledge that facilitates the self-government in arts proposed by the Alliance since 1991. If Maskegon-Iskwew finds the wiki model useful as a means to gather knowledge that is fragmentary and dispersed, this collaboration is expected to be regulated by the community itself, which is responsible for the production of its own image. While individual expression is encouraged, the ultimate goal is the construction of a coherent image, a unique voice, and not a "great babbling bazaar."

Unlike the commons evoked by the open source movement, the community imagined by Drumbytes.org preexists the project. The imagined network is constituted by members who already form a community of Aboriginal artists who meet each other at conferences, exhibitions, and artist-run centers. This community is described as "broadly distributed, nomadic, yet intimately connected" (Maskegon-Iskwew, 2004, ¶ 1). This reference to intimacy challenges the informal, sporadic, and often anonymous interventions of members of the "creative commons," while it associates the project with more traditional definitions of virtual commonality. In practice, participation was seldom anonymous and members often recognized each other at least by name.

It is possible to conclude, then, that the appropriation of the open source model is a strategic choice meant to meet the communication needs of an already established community. Familiar with the difficulties and high cost of following an offline–online strategy such as CyberPowWow's, Maskegon-Iskwew envisioned a tool, the tipiwiki, which could be appropriated and modified by other members of the community. The strategy followed by Drumbytes.org was ambitious: It presented itself in the more traditional forms of database and space while providing the community with a tool that allowed the modification and extension of that space in a way in which CyberPowWow never did.

If Drumbytes.org's appropriation of the open source model does not explicitly resist the cyberlibertarian and anarcho-utopian elements of the open source discourse, it introduces tensions within it. The appeal to the Aboriginal arts community's self-regulatory nature, together with the fact that the open source model was strategically incorporated into a community media project, distances the project from the laissez faire typical of the open source model. It also introduces a definition of community that challenges the individualism of the "creative commons."

Coda: The Imagination of Community as a Strategy of Translation

The two projects discussed in this chapter illustrate different translations of the Internet's technological and cultural features in an attempt to develop a Native voice online. This chapter has traced this translation at the discursive level— that is, as is manifested in the works.

The analysis of CyberPowWow and Drumbytes .org showed that a crucial aspect of these

Aboriginal Internet art projects is to imagine community online, which requires an active engagement with a series of images and tropes that emphasize the Internet's virtuality and represent the new medium as an autonomous social space. However, as I demonstrated in these pages, these appropriations do not leave these tropes untouched.

Notes

1. The second wave of cyberculture studies chronologically coincides with the Drum Beats to Drum Bytes gathering. This second generation defines cyberspace "as a site of empowerment, an online space reserved for construction, creativity and community" (Silver, 2006, p. 66).

2. New communalism is a counterculture movement that originated in the 1960s, primarily in the United States, and that sought to withdraw from mainstream society to form communes (Turner, 2006).

3. Winner (1997) defines cyberlibertarianism as a "collection of ideas that links ecstatic enthusiasm for electronically mediated forms of living with radical, right-wing libertarian ideas about the proper definition of freedom, social life, economics, and politics" (¶ 4).

References

Abbate, J. (1999). *Inventing the Internet*. Cambridge: MIT Press.

Aboriginal Arts Program. (n.d.). *Organizational profile*. Banff, Alberta, Canada: Banff Centre.

Barlow, J. P. (1996). *A declaration of the independence of cyberspace*. Retrieved November 6, 2007, from http://w2.eff.org/Misc/Publications/John_Perry_Barlow/?f=barlow_0296.declaration.txt

Benedikt, M. (1991). *Cyberspace: First steps*. Cambridge: MIT Press.

Bradley, D. (2005). The divergent anarcho-utopian discourses of the open source movement. *Canadian Journal of Communication, 30*, 585–611.

Coleman, G. (2004). The political agnosticism of free and open source software and the inadvertent politics of contrast. *Anthropological Quarterly, 77*, 507–519.

Crompton, S. (2004). Off-reserve Aboriginal Internet users. *Canadian Social Trends, 75,* 8–14.

Dyson, E., Gilder, G., Keyworth, G., & Toffler, A. (1996). Cyberspace and the American dream: A magna carta for the knowledge age. *The Information Society, 12,* 295–308.

Fragnito, S. (2001). Distribution: Skawennati Tricia Fragnito. *CRUMB Seminars: Presentations.* Retrieved January 24, 2008, from www.crumbweb .org/getPresentation.php?presID=17&op=4&subl ink=&fromSearch=1

Gibson, W. (1984). *Neuromancer.* New York: Ace Books.

Greene, R. (2004). *Internet art.* London: Thames & Hudson.

Jones, S. G. (1997). *Virtual culture: Identity and communication in cybersociety.* London: Sage.

Lévy, P. (1997). *Collective intelligence: Mankind's emerging world in cyberspace.* New York: Plenum Trade.

Lewis, J. E. (2004). *Terra nullius, terra incognito.* Retrieved November 7, 2007, from www.cyberpowwow .net/cpw04_text.html

L'Hirondelle, C. (2004). Aboriginal story in digital media. *Horizon 0, 17.* Retrieved November 7, 2007, from www.horizonzero.ca/textsite/tell.php?is=17&file=0 &tlang=0

Ljungberg, J. (2000). Open source movements as a model for organizing. *European Journal of Information Systems, 9,* 208–216.

Maskegon-Iskwew, A. (2004). *Rationale: Drumbytes, wiki and free hosting.* Retrieved November 7, 2007, from http://drumbytes.org/xoops/modules.news

Mosco, V. (2004). *The digital sublime: Myth, power, and cyberspace.* Cambridge: MIT Press.

Pechawis, A. (2001). *Not so much a land claim.* Retrieved November 7, 2007, from www.cyberpowwow .net/archerweb/index.html

Putnam, R. (2000). *Bowling alone: The collapse and revival of American community.* New York: Simon & Schuster.

Raymond, E. (1999). *The cathedral and the bazaar: Musings on Linux and open source by an accidental revolutionary.* Sebastopol, CA: O'Reilly.

Rheingold, H. (1993). *The virtual community: Homesteading at the electronic frontier.* Reading, MA: Addison-Wesley.

Rickard, J. (1999). *First nation territory in cyber space declared: No treaties needed.* Retrieved November 7, 2007, from www.cyberpowwow.net/nation2nation/ jolenework.html

Ross, A. (2000). Hacking away at the counter culture. In D. Bell & B. M. Kennedy (Eds.), *The cybercultures reader* (pp. 254–267). New York: Routledge.

Silver, D. (2006). Looking backwards, looking forwards: Cyberculture studies 1990–2000. In D. Bell (Ed.), *Cybercultures: Critical concepts in media and cultural studies* (pp. 61–79). London: Routledge.

Todd, L. (1996). Aboriginal narratives in cyberspace. In M. A. Moser & D. McLeod (Eds.), *Immersed in technology: Art and virtual environments* (pp. 179–194). Cambridge: MIT Press.

Tribe, M., & Jana, R. (2006). *New media art.* Cologne, Germany: Taschen.

Turkle, S. (1995). *Life on the screen: Identity in the age of the Internet.* New York: Touchstone.

Turner, F. (2006). *From counterculture to cyberculture: Stewart Brand, the Whole Earth Network, and the rise of digital utopianism.* Chicago: University of Chicago Press.

Whittle, D. B. (1997). *Cyberspace: The human dimension.* New York: Freeman.

Winner, L. (1997). *Cyberlibertarian myths and the prospects for community.* Retrieved October 30, 2008, from www.rpi.edu/~winner/cyberlib2 .html

Zittrain, J. (2008). *The future of the Internet and how to stop it.* New Haven, CT: Yale University Press.

CHAPTER 12

Media Interventions in Racialized Communities

Tanja Dreher

This chapter examines community-based media projects that have attempted to shift racialized discourse and improve the representation of Muslim and Arab communities in mainstream Australian news media since 2001. By seeking to intervene in mainstream media, community news interventions test the boundaries and reveal the limits to changing media representations.

The Racialized News Frame

While Arab and Muslim communities in North America and Europe have been the focus of increased media attention since September 11, 2001, in Sydney, Australia, this public scrutiny began in mid-2001 with the escalation of an "ethnic crime debate" after a series of vicious group sexual assaults in Sydney's southwestern suburbs were labeled a "new race crime" in news reporting (Kidman, 2001, pp. 1, 4–5). At the height of this public debate, the MV *Tampa* appeared off the Australian coast, having rescued 438, mainly Afghani, asylum seekers. Citing "border protection," the federal government

during an election campaign refused the asylum seekers permission to land on Australian soil and then deployed SAS (Special Air Service) troops to transfer the group to a hastily prepared detention center on the tiny Pacific island of Nauru. Less than 2 weeks later, the September 11 attacks on the World Trade Center and the Pentagon in the United States led to Australia's immediate support for the "war on terrorism." In each of these front-page news stories, the themes of "race," difference, immigration, ethnicity, security, multiculturalism, religion, crime, tolerance, the "clash of civilizations," and national identity were central concerns. A range of commentators, politicians, community representatives, talkback callers, and letter writers debated the benefits of immigration and cultural diversity, Australia's international reputation as a tolerant and pluralistic society, and links between ethnicity, religion, and crime.

The discursive linking of local, national, and global news stories produced a "spiral of signification" (Hall, Crichter, Jefferson, Clarke, & Roberts, 1978) in which events were linked in media discourse through the involvement of people categorized as "Middle Eastern," "Muslim" or "Arab" (Anti-Discrimination Board of NSW [ADB], 2003; Poynting, Noble, Tabar, & Collins, 2004). At each level of news reporting, the meanings associated with these categories were amplified. Several researchers have argued that the naming and framing of these events in news reporting has contributed to "the emergence of the 'Arab Other' as the pre-eminent 'folk devil' of our time" (Poynting et al., 2004, p. 3) and the production of refugees, Arab, and Muslim Australians as "The New 'Others'" (Green, 2003). The signification spiral that developed in 2001 can be understood as a "spiral of racialization" linking local, national, and global events through frames of "race," culture, and religion.

The accumulation and convergence of racialized reporting served to position whole cultures as threatening, criminal, foreign, even barbaric, amplifying the scrutiny of Arab, Muslim, and refugee communities. Complex events were explained in terms of essentialized Arab or Muslim "cultures." Racialized news reporting not only contributed to the discursive linking of these events but also privileged a moral frame of explanation rather than a focus on social causes (Poynting et al., 2004). Research has also found that racialized news reporting in 2001 to 2002 contributed to heightened intercommunal tensions and an increase in racist violence, discrimination, and harassment (ADB, 2003; Human Rights and Equal Opportunity Commission [HREOC], 2004; Poynting, 2002).

Community Media Interventions

I use the term *community media interventions* to refer to activities and projects developed by communities subjected to media racism in order to alter or speak back to mainstream news media. The term *intervention* is intended to highlight the change orientation of these activities—they aim not merely for visibility or public relations but rather to expand, diversify, or contest the range and types of representations available in mainstream media. These activities do not address "ethnic communities" or ethnic media in particular—although this is not to argue that community media are unimportant. Many people involved in mainstream news interventions also access and produce media addressed at specialized audiences. Participants in news interventions target mainstream news to influence news agendas and representations that are seen to influence audiences and interactions between communities. Thus, people involved in news interventions seek to change the ways in which communities, identities, and differences are imagined and understood through the news. In addressing the mainstream news media, people working with racialized communities cross the categories of "community," transgressing the boundary that keeps ethnic "others" confined to community media or specialist programming.

Focusing on community-based projects that address the mainstream media highlights activities that have been largely neglected in academic research. Much existing research about "ethnic communities" and journalism involves textual analyses, often identifying media racism (e.g., Jakubowicz et al., 1994; Van Dijk, 1991). A few studies have examined the experiences of "ethnic minority" media producers in mainstream institutions (Cottle, 1997; Gray, 2000; Jakubowicz et al., 1994). Research on diasporic audiences indicates the importance of news media in negotiations of identity (Barker, 1997, 1999; Cunningham & Sinclair, 2000; Gillespie, 1995). Recent work on media and racism acknowledges that "minorities engage in representation battles" (Dunn, 2003, p. 153) and recommends funding and training for community media projects (ADB, 2003, p. 115; Dunn, 2003, p. 163). None of this research makes visible the considerable efforts and the emotional investment of people living and working in culturally diverse communities who attempt to intervene in the mainstream news media and what their achievements might be.

The following sections present specific examples of community media interventions developed in response to racialized news reporting in the Australian news media after 2001. The discussion moves from reactive to proactive strategies, beginning with those activities that serve largely to reproduce the boundaries of journalism, moving on to those that challenge and then contest news conventions and discourses of "culture" and "community," and finally evaluating activities that seek to work outside or to reimagine news conventions and dominant discourses altogether. While the discussion here emphasizes differences between the activities to analyze the range of strategies adopted, in fact most ongoing projects incorporate a variety of activities, and the strategies discussed below are frequently interlinked or overlapping rather than discrete.

Checking the Performance of News

The media intervention strategy of "checking the performance of news" involves monitoring mainstream news media and talkback radio to identify examples for complaint (racial vilification or irresponsible reporting) or reward (fair, balanced, or positive coverage). Arab Council Australia managed a project for "Rating the Media" through its Web site, in which readers were encouraged to send information on media content requiring "attention" that the Council would use "in addressing the misrepresentation and misinformation in the media as well as recognizing the positive and balanced portrayal of the community." The project had low levels of participation and sustainability.

Monitoring and complaints strategies are primarily reactive, responding to problems that have already arisen and occurring only after publication. Complaint processes usually "presume that racism occurs in isolated incidents" and do not require attention to institutional racism (ADB, 2003, p. 101). Responses also largely rely on standards set by media institutions or journalism professional standards—in this regard they police and reproduce the conventions of news rather than necessarily challenging those conventions or developing new possibilities. Racial vilification procedures and formal complaints *are* important mechanisms for voicing community concerns and ensuring a minimum level of accountability in the reporting of cultural diversity. Unfortunately, adjudications are often complex, and there are few serious consequences to act as a deterrent (Eggerking & Plater, 1992; Jakubowicz et al., 1994). However, media monitoring can provide important resources for other strategies of news intervention, enabling activities that contest news conventions and media power.

Learning the Game

Interventions for "learning the game" involve learning media skills and the conventions of news to achieve greater news visibility for community representatives and the issues affecting the communities that they represent. Developing source skills enacts a politics of inclusion and of being heard, aiming to expand the boundaries of who speaks in the news. Many organizations have adopted strategies for developing media skills and media advocacy, and my research is based on experiences in facilitating more than a dozen media workshops for community organizations.

The United Muslim Women's Association (UMWA), based in Sydney, has an ongoing commitment to media intervention, having organized a media skills workshop for young Muslim women within 2 months of the September 11, 2001, attacks in the United States. Over the years, UMWA members have taken part in workshops on writing for the print media, responding to newspaper reporting, and developing media management skills. They have visited radio studios and participated in mock interviews, practicing techniques for adversarial interviews, and developed skills in investigative journalism and talkback radio through all-day workshops. Having developed an interest in dealing more proactively with the news media, UMWA organizers began to adopt strategies of media advocacy—monitoring the media to identify journalists producing fair and balanced reporting, developing news agendas, promoting alternative or untold stories, and developing ongoing professional relationships with journalists. Several participants in UMWA media workshops have since become experienced news sources, and many others have been involved in media production through the production of a magazine, *Reflections* (available online), short films, and community radio broadcasts.

Despite the considerable successes in skilling and empowering young Muslim women to become both news sources and community media producers, UMWA organizers and participants remain frustrated at the difficulty of achieving wider shifts in news framing and news agendas. While community media advocacy work has contributed to the diversification of voices representing Muslim Australians within the mainstream news media, many of those news sources continue to find it difficult to challenge story agendas rather than merely responding to journalists' predetermined questions and storylines. Analyzing news reporting in 2001–2002, the ADB (2003) found that

> when heard in the media, the voices of Arab and Muslim community leaders were perceived as less credible sources in shaping media stories, and were called on to defend their communities rather than to identify the agenda for addressing the impact of the criminalisation of their communities. (p. 78)

Representatives of "ethnic communities" appear in news and current affairs reporting primarily in response to issues and agendas set by media professionals or institutional sources (Van Dijk, 1991) and are routinely framed as representing "special interests" (Loo, 1998). Indeed, learning media skills and conventional news values can be seen as a process whereby racialized communities learn the many ways in which their perspectives and priorities simply do not count as newsworthy (see Dreher & Simmons, 2006).

Building Networks

The Muslim Women's National Network of Australia (MWNNA) developed a media intervention strategy focused on educating journalism students and building networks with professional journalists, aiming for long-term change in the news media by working with students who had not yet been socialized into the mainstream newsroom. The project coordinator developed training modules and online resources that were delivered in seminars at a number of universities throughout Australia. An extensive contact list was developed to encourage budding journalists to expand their range of sources in Muslim communities. The journalism students were also invited to participate in activities such as making a visit to an Arabian horse stud farm and attending an Iftar meal during Ramadan.

The curriculum materials were developed with input from journalism educators, who were also instrumental in persuading their universities to schedule seminars. Nevertheless, intervening in journalism education is no simple task—few universities chose to make the seminars compulsory or to integrate them into the general curriculum. Feedback on early versions of the seminars included complaints that the training presented only the "positives" of Islam; some students felt that they were being proselytized. During the 2 years of the project, the seminars were reworked to address the questions that students wanted to ask—typically on controversial topics such as the hijab and Islam and terrorism. The seminars became framed as a way to assist journalism students in working through these difficult issues.

Talking Back to News Media

In August 2005, the UMWA organized a conference called Jihad: Terrorism or a Muslim's Highest

Aspiration? The name of the conference was deliberately provocative. The strategy was that journalists would ask why the organizers had chosen the title and that the UMWA would have an opportunity to challenge the media's use of the word jihad.

> The word jihad is misused; that was the whole point of us having the forum. The media like to equate jihad with holy war, terrorism and extremism. To us jihad means a struggle and that can be a struggle on numerous levels. The way the media uses it is completely incorrect. (Maha Abdo, UMWA, interview with Frances Simmons, Sydney, August 15, 2005)

Attendance exceeded the organizers' expectations: about 250 people, including media representatives from a range of media organizations. The organizers went to considerable lengths to ensure accurate reporting—speakers were required to read written scripts, and transcripts were distributed to journalists and posted on the Web site. Young women from the UMWA with handheld cameras rolling asked journalists what they expected to get out of the evening. Speakers spoke on a range of topics from misconceptions about jihad to Islamic law and the radicalization of Muslim youth. All three spoke of the media's role in demonizing and isolating Muslim Australians.

Despite a strong media presence at the conference, it received little coverage. An article in the major daily newspaper, *The Australian*, was headlined "Get out of ghettos, young Muslims told." The report focused on one speaker's statement that young Muslims are in danger of being alienated but ignored the speaker's analysis of the causes of this alienation, including perceived Western foreign policy double standards, Islamophobia, and anti-Muslim rhetoric as well as the lack of Muslim representation in media and government. The experience of the UMWA in organizing the Jihad: Terrorism or a Muslim's Highest Aspiration? conference illustrates the difficulty of intervening in the media to not only tell new stories but also challenge the language in which those stories are told.

Outside the News

One response to the difficulties of shifting news agendas is to develop projects that work outside the conventions of news. These projects respond to news media reporting but do not seek news publication outcomes, appropriating familiar media images to different ends and aiming to address wider publics rather than news professionals or institutions. One such project, Radio ArtStart was developed for young Muslim Australians to tell their stories and to develop skills that might see them take up careers in radio. The project involved scriptwriting workshops and radio production based at a community radio station. The young people developed a series of radio plays that were primarily humorous, deploying irony to satirize talkback radio and mainstream news media. Young Muslim Australians played parts, including talkback hosts, callers, journalists, and interviewees in a series of mock reports and radio dialogues. The tone was playful, and themes ranged from addressing stereotypes about Muslims to chatting about football, barbecues, and school. The radio plays explored issues of identity and belonging that are of particular concern to young people of culturally and linguistically diverse backgrounds (see Butcher & Thomas, 2003) and showcased the hybrid lives and popular culture of young people who feel targeted and constrained by rigid labels such as "Muslim," "Arab," or "Middle Eastern." While participants gave highly positive evaluations of the project, none are known to have fulfilled the project's wider and more long-term aim of encouraging young Muslim Australians to explore careers in media.

The project did not seek to develop news "stories," nor do the outcomes fit any conventional definition of journalism. However, it does suggest some of the voices, images, and interests that are excluded by those conventional definitions. The criteria of journalism such as the need for community "spokespeople," clear storylines involving news values such as conflict, and the focus on threat and deviance do not provide opportunities for the "stories" that some "ordinary people" in racialized communities want to tell. News interventions outside the boundaries of news highlight the limits of news—the institution that presents itself as reflecting social reality and communicating the most important events and issues also excludes many issues that are important for people working with racialized communities.

Possibilities and Limits of News Interventions: The Dilemma of Inclusion

Dominant discourses of "culture" and "community" provide both possibilities and limitations for community media interventions into racialized news reporting. Gerd Baumann (1996) analyzes the dominant discourse of "culture" in England as a discourse in which community, culture, homeland, tradition, language, and folklore are almost seamlessly linked, reifying the various categories, creating an emphasis on bounded communities and a focus on tradition. A similar discourse is evident in Australia, positioning "ethnic communities" as homogeneous, essentialized, and bounded entities defined by visible markers of "cultural difference." The discourse of "culture" fixes identities rather than allowing for fluidity and cultural exchange. Cultures and communities remain separated, eliding commonalities across "cultures" and the differences within "communities." As in England, the discourse of "culture" is both dominant and naturalized in Australia, forming the basis of state policies of multiculturalism.

This discourse of "community" raises a particular difficulty for community media interventions as it produces the position of ethnic community leader or ethnic community spokesperson. For those working to diversify the news, the easiest voice to access is that of the "ethnic community leader," yet

in accessing that voice, journalists also reproduce many of the exclusions that underpin the position. These include exclusions around gender, age, sexuality, language, generation, belief, and lifestyle as well as the many diversities within communities. The dominant conception of "culture" and "community" means that "ethnic community leaders" have an interest in mobilizing essentializing and rigid definitions of community, culture, faith, and tradition to legitimate their own voice and position. "Ethnic community leaders" can engage in boundary-policing and doctrinal rigidity to construct the very community for whom they claim to speak. Spokespeople for religious groups or "cultures" are often male and conservative (see also Vasta, 1996). Ethnic leaders are caught between the state and the "community" they claim to represent and actually depend on both to ensure their legitimacy (Collins, Noble, Poynting, & Tabar, 2000; Tabar, Noble, & Poynting, 2003). Acknowledging diversity or division within the "community" undermines the position of "ethnic community leader."

The five community media intervention strategies identified in this chapter are summarized in Table 12.1. The table presents the activities typical of each strategy, the way in which participants in these activities are positioned, the stories mobilized, and the relationship to the conventions of news with the dominant discourse of "community." Reading from left to right, the strategies begin with a politics of complaint; the majority of strategies then adopt a politics of inclusion or adaptation, while strategies of talking back and working beyond the boundaries of news incorporate a politics of representation. These positions are broadly analogous to those identified in research on "ethnic community" politics in the United States and Australia, which has identified a range of strategies adopted by ethnic community representatives, from accommodation to contestation (Tabar et al., 2003). Similarly, Manning (2001) describes four source strategies "in a hostile media environment": lobbying for changes in regulation, bypass involving independent or alternative production, media pressure politics that make news content and allegations of "bias" political issues in their own right, and accommodative strategies (p. 174).

This overview suggests that those strategies that achieve most news media visibility are also those that work within the conventions of news, often reproducing the symbolic hierarchy of media power and mobilizing the dominant discourse of "ethnic communities." Conversely, those strategies that develop alternative discourses and seek to problematize news values and the politics of representation are also the strategies least likely to achieve conventional news publication outcomes. The impact and value of strategies that do not achieve news publication outcomes is most evident in their ability to make alternative stories visible and to suggest possibilities for innovation in news conventions.

Table 12.1   News Intervention Strategies

	Checking News Performance	Learning the Game	Building Networks	Talking Back	Outside the News
Activities (examples)	Media monitoring, formal and informal complaints	Skills training, workshops, source activities	Forums, workshops, meetings	Media events, media critique	Cultural production
Position of participants	Consumers, complainants, victims	Community spokespeople responding to news requests and requirements	Proto-professionals promoting access to valuable story resources	Critics oppositional interests	Media producers
News conventions	Policing, identifying breaches	Work within, politics of inclusion	Both reproduce and widen—exploit the conventions	Use, name and critique, address media institutions	Reappropriate, develop alternatives, politics of representation, address wider publics
Different narratives	Victim narratives	Diversify range of "representative" voices	Shifting frames and alternative stories highest priority	Victim narratives, political demands, story of media, naming racialization	Irony, appropriate familiar media images to different ends
Discourse of community	Reproduce	Reproduce	Diversify angles and voices	Response to racialization in the name of "community"	Develop alternative discourses, cultural exchange, and hybridity

References

Anti-Discrimination Board of NSW. (2003). *Race for the headlines: Racism and media discourse.* Sydney, New South Wales, Australia: Author.

Barker, C. (1997). *Global television: An introduction.* Oxford, UK: Blackwell.

Barker, C. (1999). *Television, globalization and cultural identities.* Philadelphia: Open University Press.

Baumann, G. (1996). *Contesting culture: Discourses of identity in multi-ethnic London.* Cambridge, UK: Cambridge University Press.

Butcher, M., & Thomas, M. (Eds.). (2003). *Ingenious: Emerging youth cultures in urban Australia.* Sydney, New South Wales, Australia: Pluto Press.

Collins, J., Noble, G., Poynting, S., & Tabar, P. (2000). *Kebabs, kids, cops and crime: Youth ethnicity and crime.* Annandale, New South Wales, Australia: Pluto Press.

Cottle, S. (1997). *Television and ethnic minorities: Producers' perspectives.* Aldershot, UK: Avebury.

Cunningham, S., & Sinclair, J. (2000). *Floating lives: The media and Asian diasporas.* St. Lucia, Queensland, Australia: University of Queensland Press.

Dreher, T., & Simmons, F. (2006). Australian Muslim women's media interventions. *Feminist Media Studies, 6*(1), 117–120.

Dunn, K. (2003). Using cultural geography to engage contested constructions of ethnicity and citizenship in Sydney. *Social and Cultural Geography, 4*(2), 153–165.

Eggerking, K., & Plater, D. (Eds.). (1992). *Signposts: A guide to reporting Aboriginal, Torres Strait Islander and ethnic affairs.* Sydney, New South Wales, Australia: Australian Centre for Independent Journalism, University of Technology, Sydney.

Gillespie, M. (1995). *Television, ethnicity and cultural change.* London: Routledge.

Gray, H. (2000). Black representation in the post network, post civil rights world of global media. In S. Cottle (Ed.), *Ethnic minorities and the media* (pp. 118–129). Buckingham, UK: Open University Press.

Green, L. (2003, November). The new "others": Media and society post-September 11. *Media International Australia Incorporating Culture and Policy, 109,* 7–13.

Hall, S., Crichter, C., Jefferson, T., Clarke, J., & Roberts, B. (1978). *Policing the crisis: Mugging, the state and law and order.* London: Macmillan.

Human Rights and Equal Opportunity Commission. (2004). *Isma—listen: National consultations on eliminating prejudice against Arab and Muslim Australians.* Sydney, New South Wales, Australia: Author.

Jakubowicz, A., Goodall, H., Martin, J., Mitchell, T., Randall, L., & Seneviratne, K. (1994). *Racism, ethnicity and the media.* Sydney, New South Wales, Australia: Allen & Unwin.

Kidman, J. (2001, July 29). 70 girls attacked by rape gangs. *Sun-Herald,* pp. 1, 4–5.

Loo, E. (1998). Journalistic representations of ethnicity. In M. Breen (Ed.), *Journalism: Theory and ctice* (pp. 220–237). Sydney, New South Wales, Australia: Macleay Press.

Manning, P. (2001). *News and news sources: A critical introduction.* London: Sage.

Poynting, S. (2002, July). "Bin Laden in the suburbs": Attacks on Arab and Muslim Australians before and after 11 September. *Current Issues in Criminal Justice, 14*(1), 43–64.

Poynting, S., Noble, G., Tabar, P., & Collins, J. (2004). *Bin Laden in the suburbs: Criminalising the Arab Other.* Sydney, New South Wales, Australia: Sydney Institute of Criminology.

Tabar, P., Noble, G., & Poynting, S. (2003). The rise and falter of the field of ethnic politics in Australia: The case of Lebanese community leadership. *Journal of Intercultural Studies, 24*(3), 267–287.

Van Dijk, T. (1991). *Racism and the press.* London: Routledge.

Vasta, E. (1996). Dialectics of domination: Racism and multiculturalism. In E. Vasta & S. Castles (Eds.), *The teeth are smiling: The persistence of racism in multicultural Australia* (pp. 46–72). St. Leonards, New South Wales, Australia: Allen & Unwin.

CHAPTER 13

Community Collaboration in Media and Arts Activism

A Case Study

Lynette Bondarchuk

Ondine Park

The Edmonton Small Press Association (ESPA) celebrates its 10th anniversary this year. As we do this, we are reflecting on a decade of working actively to demonstrate both within our local community (Edmonton, Alberta, Canada) and to the broader global community that the community arts that we promote are legitimate and viable and increasingly important to cultural democracy and equal representation. *Community arts* is a process whereby arts practitioners based in a community develop strategies and processes with which to engage that community in delivering a wide range of cultural programs to target populations. In Canada, the practice of community arts is not yet well established as compared with, for example, the United States, where community arts practitioners have been at work for more than three decades.

This chapter is an overview of ESPA's work and documents some of the challenges and successes we've experienced over the past decade. It addresses the ESPA's development, highlighting our collective efforts in fulfilling our mission, and argues that ESPA's work and methodologies are at least as important as the established "high cultural" organizations under the shadows of which we continue to operate. This has often proved difficult, as we struggle to survive within a political environment that we experience as hostile to the

Author's Note: This chapter (submitted in 2008) emerged as a collaborative effort, and the authors would like to acknowledge this process. Throughout this chapter, the "we" of the ESPA is one that does not always include each of the "we" who collaborated on this chapter and in more ways is more inclusive than this limited "we." Rather, the configuration of "we" has been contingent and shifting. A sincere thanks to Owen Melsness, Paula E. Kirman, and others at the ESPA and to Kevin Howley and the anonymous reviewer who provided insightful comments and provocations on earlier drafts.

arts in general and particularly to independent and politically engaged art. Specifically, we are located in Alberta, a province of Canada that, in the experience of the ESPA, is notorious for fostering corporate-friendly media and promoting socially punitive government policy.

Primary Activities and Philosophies

The ESPA is a registered, nonprofit arts society with a mission to foster the development of, and increase awareness about, independent small press initiatives. As independent media and arts activists working under a community cultural development disposition, our activities are intended to cultivate active citizenship and community building. (ESPA, n.d.)

For 10 years, the ESPA has been a resource network of independent art producers that "recognizes no cultural or professional boundaries and fosters the 'D.I.Y. or Die' philosophy" (ESPA, n.d.). That is, we believe that both individuals and communities can "do it yourself" (and together) in order to be self-sustaining, not allowing themselves to be de-skilled by increasingly ubiquitous capitalist provisioning. Our mottos are "become the media" and "people before profits, collaboration before competition." Our activities promote "the notion that small press initiatives are viable artistic expressions and valuable tools for positive social change" (ESPA, n.d.). Although the term *small press* usually applies only to projects of a printed or "self-published" nature, the ESPA defines it as almost any independent creative venture that may include a wide variety of approaches to arts, documentation, performance, and media. We encourage and support this multidisciplinary approach because we recognize that *small press* encompasses most works "published" (including performed) by underrepresented or independent artists in any medium and therefore remains a valuable asset to cultural diversity (ESPA, n.d.). In our practice, we stress the importance of collaborative, grassroots networking in strengthening a creative commons and engaging in reciprocal

learning, and we put this priority into action by working with several other groups year-round both locally and further afield in addressing a wide range of social justice issues. These issues include, but are not limited to, media literacy and reform, poverty and economic discrimination, corporate globalization, fair trade, food security and genetically modified organisms, peace building versus the military-industrial complex, consumer resistance, aboriginal reparations, environmental stewardship, racial and gender discrimination, prison and judicial reform, and more. In addition to our own projects, we provide creative services to many other activist organizations in an effort to further our community cultural development initiatives. We are interested in exploring how the arts can be used as a tool for social development and personal empowerment and can communicate information on a variety of misrepresented and underrepresented issues.

Our interests and knowledge are constantly evolving and being enriched as we investigate, participate in, and learn from new material, other arts and social justice groups, events, and people. Recognizing both the strengths and limitations of our own knowledge base, we take the perspective that we must continually and actively engage with new expressions, groups, causes, and communities, and intentionally work through collaborative and active processes of learning. Moreover, part of our work is to produce creative programming that educates diverse audiences; the bonus in educating others is that we ourselves are educated in the development stages and through this community engagement.

A foundational belief of the ESPA is that everything is political and, furthermore, that "the media" and politics are inseparable. By our definition, the media (and thus small press) are much more than "journalism." Rather, and more important for us, media also include any expression of community-based creative resistance that rises above the status quo to challenge it head on. This expression may be in the form of zines and other print media, film and video documentation, controversial visual arts installations, street theater and other forms of culture jamming, and any of the many other forms of delivery. *Zines,* a term that evolved from "fanzines," are an excellent example of media that can be tools for social justice and change. Originally, fanzines were small, self-published fan magazines—for example, about a favorite obscure band. Today, zines are produced in an enormous variety of formats on a vast array of topics. They are typically distributed by independent distributors, also known as "distros" or "infoshops." We regard zines as important sources of information on marginalized and underreported issues that often receive little sensitivity, let alone mainstream media attention. We believe that community media can become a tool for peaceful social revolution when collaboration occurs between groups and individuals united in a common cause.

To that end, ESPA engages in a number of diverse activities, directly putting our philosophy into practice. We maintain an extensive small press library and archive that currently represents more than 700 member artists and collectives from 33 countries. The archive is an ever-expanding collection, and the effort to include each item in our online catalog is an ongoing project (www.edmontonsmallpress.ca/catalogue/index .php). We also distribute some of this material and operate an infoshop, selling a wide variety of zines, underground comix, literary chapbooks, activist and anarchist literature, socialist calendars, politically rhetorical T-shirts, patches, buttons, magnets, novelty toilet paper, and other creative ephemera in an effort to disseminate our (fairly diverse) political ideologies.

All proceeds from distro sales support ESPA's nonprofit activities and are funneled back into special projects and ongoing operations. Among these, we produce several events year-round in an effort to gain exposure for our mission, including annual small press and Fair Trade fairs and "edutaining" film and video screenings. In September 2003, we produced our first North of Nowhere Expo—a multidisciplinary festival of independent media and underground art. (Currently, we produce the Expo biennially but, subject to adequate funding support, we aim to make it an annual festival.) We also frequently collaborate with other social justice advocates in producing other active

citizenship projects involving nonviolent civil disobedience and agitprop such as peaceful marches and demonstrations. In addition, ESPA does select in-house publishing projects—most notably, *Our Voice,* a street newspaper that we adopted in November 2006 and that is produced in collaboration with and sold by low-income and homeless people (see below).

For 2 years (2000–2002), ESPA ran the Free Store & Much More. The Free Store & Much More was a community reuse program that we operated out of the garage of our then home-based headquarters and was much like a garage or yard sale, except that everything was free. We encouraged people to take stock of and donate or exchange their underused items in an effort to discourage unnecessary consumerism and promote recycling and resource sustainability. The Free Store was not meant to be a "service to the needy" per se but was shut down by the City of Edmonton after they received complaints claiming that the Free Store was attracting "riffraff," was in violation of city zoning bylaws, and was operating without a business license—even though nothing was being "sold" and the Store was not a business, as such. The Free Store remains on hiatus until a better, permanent space can be secured, but it is a project we hope to resurrect at some point in the future.

We do all this and more with a strong sense of humor and determination, given the political climate and relative geographic isolation in which we operate.

Edmonton, Alberta: Our Local Context

Over the past decade and a half, Alberta's Conservative government (particularly under former premier Ralph Klein) has been privatizing many social services and has slashed budgets for other key social programs such as health care and education.

Alberta was founded as a Liberal-led province in 1905 when Canada's then national government was giving away large tracts of land to European settlers to prevent the United States

Photo 13.1 Photo Representing a Small Portion of the Thousands of Zines and Mail Art in ESPA's Library and Archive

from claiming the territory. Alberta soon turned against eastern Canadian nation-building, however, and all succeeding governments—United Farmers' Association (1921–1935), Social Credit Party of Alberta (1935–1971), and Progressive Conservative Party (1971 to the present)—have gained majority power and ruled on the basis of the popular appeal of their politically, socially, and economically conservative values and strong focus on Alberta's economic and political self-interest. For example, in 1980, amid growing financial problems born of the energy crises of the previous decade, the federal (Liberal) government introduced the National Energy Program, intended to

decrease national dependence on foreign oil and ownership of the oil industry. Significant reserves of oil had been discovered in Alberta in 1947 and had transformed this "poor" province into one of Canada's richest. Officially and popularly, Alberta vigorously opposed the federal energy program. Alberta's renowned resistance to federal influence and its Conservative disposition were assured for decades to come.

The election of Progressive Conservative Ralph Klein as premier in 1992 moved the party sharply to the right, emphasizing fiscal conservatism and high moral authority grounded in so-called family values. Klein's administration was marked by wide-scale corporate privatization and corporate welfare at the expense of vital social programs. These policies continue to negatively affect a significant—and drastically increasing—portion of Alberta's population.

Located within this conservative context, the City of Edmonton (tellingly) has promoted itself quasi-officially as the City of Champions for a number of years, referring, in particular in the popular imagination, to several years of success by our professional sports teams. Unofficially, Edmonton is also referred to as "Redmonton" because, in the face of provincial Conservative government rule, there continues to be significant left-wing activism in our city. Yet, Edmonton is also disparaged as "Deadmonton" by some, perhaps because it seems that no amount of progressive activity and population growth can dig us out of the cultural stagnation of so-called small-town values that include a myopic view of what creative expression can be. From the perspective of ESPA, "culture" has tended to be defined fairly narrowly in this environment, along elitist, corporatist, and mainstream lines, and as a result, innovative and otherwise unique approaches and media cannot often achieve widespread or sustained success.

We have seen many extremely talented artists move on to larger and more cosmopolitan cities or give up entirely (promising careers becoming "hobbies"). Artists struggle here. But marginalized artists with unpopular political ideals struggle much more. In this context, we see the urgency of ESPA's work and the role for community arts organizations in helping challenge the boundaries of culture and push Edmonton toward being a vibrant, expressive, livable, and inclusive community. Since, from our perspective, the government and its funding agencies don't adequately support this aspect of community, our DIY approach has a lot to offer Edmonton. Ironically, less hostile environments may at times diminish the urgency of the artistic message. It should be noted that ever since we began writing this chapter, we have seen some promising steps toward making Edmonton a city that fosters and nurtures arts and culture. However, there is still a long way to go, and it will take time to see how sustained these initiatives turn out to be.

Challenging Financial Barriers

While ESPA has always rejected the elitist commodification of art, we also reject the notion that we must assume the role of "starving artists" for our passion and commitment to be taken seriously. When ESPA incorporated in 1998, we decided to take advantage of public funding opportunities, despite the belief by some of our more anarchist members at the time that we were "selling out" and the cries of hypocrisy being levied at us by more conservative members within grant-making agencies. That said, even as self-described underground art punks at the time, we were still unprepared for the almost total lack of public institutional support: It seemed clear that zine culture was not something the Alberta arts establishment was willing to support.

The first annual operating grant ESPA received (in 1999) by the Edmonton Arts Council (EAC) was the grand sum of $200. That's not a typo. In subsequent years, we were awarded increasingly more, and our annual allocation, as of 2007, is $9,000. While this obviously demonstrates a substantial increase over the course of 8 years, it still leaves us with a pittance to pay rent for our office and production facilities. Certainly, it is not adequate to fund programming or projects appropriately, let alone to pay our currently unpaid staff and coordinators (whose labor amounts to at least a few full-time staff positions for the ESPA). On top of the difficulty of securing sufficient public monies is the difficulty of gaining other sources of financial support. Small press and community arts continue to be largely metropolitan art forms and are still a relatively new idea to our northern Alberta audience: This relative geographical isolation among audiences who largely do not yet "get" small press, combined with ESPA's unapologetically anticorporate philosophy and vocal disdain for the Alberta oil industry, means that it is extremely difficult to receive support or donations from the business community, since the oil industry is the driving economic force here.

Nevertheless, despite this lack of funding, we do not seek to raise funds through higher admission charges at any ESPA event. To be as inclusive as possible, ESPA provides sliding-scale or free admission to all our events—no one will ever be turned away from one of our events for lack of funds. We see this not only as promoting community but as our obligation: Since our provincial and municipal arts funding is provided by the taxpaying public, we believe that they are entitled to attend our events free of charge if they cannot afford otherwise. Unfortunately, this sentiment is not shared by others in our "free market" ideology–driven capitalist economy: On the one hand, the flagship arts institutions in the city—which receive the disproportionately vast share of public funding—charge fairly substantial attendance fees, excluding much of the public. On the other hand, ironically, without large admission fees attached to our events, many people view them simply as having "no value." While this remains one of the most frustrating aspects of ESPA's experience, it has given us an opportunity to explore our resourcefulness.

For the 2005 North of Nowhere Expo, ESPA received our first Seed Festival funding. We planned the festival to be 2 weeks of full programming, including multiple film screenings, workshops, and art displays at multiple sites, as well as art activist actions, salons, and an arts, crafts, and social justice fair. Of the approximately $14,000 for which we applied, we received only $4,000. Although deeply disappointed, we took the opportunity to kick our DIY ethic into high gear to try to pull off this full-program festival successfully despite the limited budget. To accomplish this, we first decided that we would indeed proceed with the project and mobilized a dedicated corps of volunteers who provided all the vast amount of labor that the festival required. For the film screenings, we concentrated on titles by other independent and activist producers to determine our programming. Included among these, we showed films from the National Film Board of Canada (NFB). While not "small press" or "indie," the NFB is a public institution and therefore allows its films to

be presented free of licensing or even permission, provided the screening event remains nonprofit. In addition, ESPA bought other films by indie-friendly producers who actively encourage activists to present their films in an effort to spread the word about their content. Regarding the visual installations, we vastly reduced the number of pieces of original art we chose to feature and instead took advantage of the global activist network for content. We downloaded, reformatted, printed, and self-mounted more than 300 pieces of Internet-archived copyleft antiwar posters. This meant that we didn't have to worry about shipping, insurance, framing, and artist honoraria for original pieces to exhibit. The result was successful in engaging the viewing public and was satisfying for us. The extra bonus was that if anything was damaged, lost, or stolen (and many eventually were) we could fairly easily reproduce them, at minimal cost and at no loss to the artists. Artists did not receive honoraria but, at minimum, they could take satisfaction in having their work shown in Canada at no extra cost or effort on their parts (Figure 13.1).

Operating this way is not our ideal. ESPA wants the ability to present originals and to compensate participating artists reasonably, but given the constraints, that experience was a confident demonstration of our resourcefulness and affirms that ESPA can achieve substantial results despite our still ongoing dependence on volunteer labor. Again, this is a good example of ESPA's DIY ethic and commitment to community arts. And the success of the event—even just being able to pull it off—illustrates what a committed and passionate collaboration of people can do. Collaboration is about building relationships to the mutual benefit of the parties involved, and we will continue to engage others in addressing the issues of resource disparity and lack of institutional capacity building for as long as we operate.

Making a Place for Ourselves

Despite our best efforts and many successes in practicing community arts—that is, arts and/as activism—the ESPA faces ongoing contestation

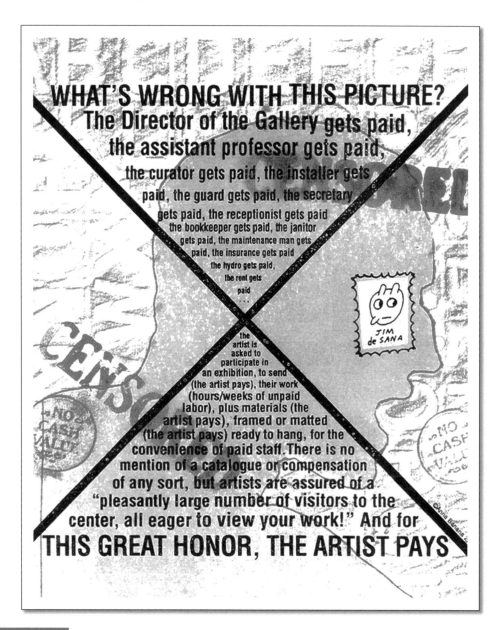

Figure 13.1   "Artist Pays, Variation #10/26, Print #2/2, June 2000"

Note: This stencil/sprayed ink, typeset text mail-art collage by "living legend" mail artist Anna Banana (British Columbia, Canada) sums up one of ESPA's primary criticisms of how community artists remain undersupported by institutional funders.

Source: Used with permission.

of our legitimacy as authentic artists and as genuine activists. In addition to the elitism and struggles for recognition that divides what should be mutual goals of the arts community, our activist community is often equally divided.

Where the arts community rejects the ESPA for being "too political," many in the activist community regard us as being "just artists" who have no demonstrable skills to contribute to "serious" political activism (and ultimately, real social change). Despite our best efforts, the ESPA just doesn't seem to fit in anywhere.

What we continue to argue is that we can and should be (respectfully) exploited to bridge the gap between casual arts patronage and active citizenship. We see that artists' work, including ESPA's, is often undervalued, perceived as frivolous and unworthy of government funding amid more immediate issues such as health care or everyday worries such as feeding and sheltering one's family. And it does seem to be the case that many artists simply are not politically active, themselves caught up in pressing daily and career-related struggles. Yet, from ESPA's understanding and practice of collectively organizing from the ground up, it is apparent that, in many cases, it is a matter of breaking down or bridging perceived and false (sometimes nonexistent) boundaries between art and activism, and sometimes it is a matter of each complementing the other. The ESPA neither seeks nor is mandated to get involved in each and every political struggle at all levels. Rather, our logic is let us do a film screening or art exhibit relating to the issue, and maybe our delivery methods will help raise awareness and encourage increased public action—even if we can't provide measurable results, any effort to inform people who might otherwise be apathetic or uninformed can't be a bad thing. Thus, artists and the larger community can be mobilized toward political participation and work together with activists when common goals can be understood and identified. The key to grassroots networking is to organize collectively where each participant has the opportunity, knowledge, and ability to contribute to determining the processes and outcome of a particular campaign or movement.

Learning to Learn Lessons

Ten years of working toward fulfilling our mission while struggling for recognition has taught us some important lessons about collaboration and picking our battles. In some cases, ESPA reluctantly admits that we can't work with others. While collaboration allows for pooling resources and avoiding a duplication of efforts, occasionally we must respectfully give preference to a fierce DIY ethic countered against our ideal of collaboration, working autonomously to develop our members and ESPA as an organization.

In working toward grassroots networking, we are mindful of the dangers of misidentifying "Astroturf" organizations (of which we have found there to be many) as legitimate grassroots efforts. Astroturf organizations are industry-generated "citizens" groups—that is, fake grassroots groups—that lobby the government and often command mainstream media support. They promote their activities as democratic, with broad-based support, but are really front groups with predetermined agendas that use savvy public relations methods to maintain the status quo. (The original application of the term to refer to organizations is uncertain but might be attributed to Stauber & Rampton, 1995.) We also are becoming increasingly savvy in working with nongovernmental organizations (NGOs) that fall somewhere between the grassroots and the Astroturf. While not front groups of well-oiled public relations machines, many NGOs remain seriously out of touch with their constituent populations on the ground. And again, while many NGOs promote their activities as democratic and having broad-based support, they often operate in a top-down hierarchy with agendas determined at the higher levels. That said, we have collaborated and do collaborate with NGOs on various projects, but as there has not tended to be a great deal of reciprocity in our experience, these projects are limited.

No doubt echoing the experience of other organizations and individuals, we have found that we must exercise care in determining how and with whom the ESPA will collaborate, whether working with artists, activist groups, NGOs, or others. Among the many successes we proudly recollect in our history, the ESPA must also lick its wounds, remembering some disastrous collaborations: occasions on which we were misled, expected to simply provide with no reciprocity, and, in several cases, simply exploited (and not respectfully!). There have been several instances where ESPA has collaborated on a specific event or project with no reciprocal credit for our work or return on our financial or labor investment. A lesson to learn: Things won't improve for us as long as we willingly allow ourselves to be taken for granted. Unfortunately, the result is that we may wind up duplicating efforts and lose opportunities for collaboration. Another (bitter) lesson we're learning: We're considering that to undertake large-scale projects with others, we may have to begin drafting legal contracts—something to which we are generally averse. But without clearly outlining budgets, expectations, and an equitable distribution of donations raised to help offset overhead costs, it's just not worth the investment anymore—emotionally or otherwise.

Increasingly, we have had to step back and revisit our methods of offering support to other projects. We are learning to recognize and honor the limit of the ESPA's resources and what this limit means for what we are able to do. We are an underfunded, understaffed, and undervalued organization and a collection of human beings with our own limits. We are coming to understand that DIY doesn't mean "do it ALL yourself"! The lessons from these experiences are ones we are still in the process of learning and of learning how to learn.

Keeping Our Eyes on the Prize

The following are some particularly good examples of our biggest successes and long-running collaborations: In December 2006, the ESPA adopted the street newspaper *Our Voice: Edmonton's Street Magazine* after the nonprofit society that had been running the paper dissolved. Two of the ESPA's board members were already involved with *Our Voice* (one as a contributor, the other as an editor), which facilitated the transition of operations. *Our Voice* is primarily intended to be a source of earned income for vendors who are people marginalized by poverty,

homelessness, and other challenges. These vendors pay cost for the magazines and sell them for donations. Since ESPA adopted the publication, in addition to being a source of income, *Our Voice* has become a community media outlet for discussion of social justice issues and advocating for community art.

For several years, the Edmonton Public Library and Metro Cinema, a local repertory cinema, have cosponsored ESPA events by reducing or waiving rental fees, which not only saves us money but also saves them time and effort by allowing us to program events in their spaces. Likewise, like-minded organizations actively participate in ESPA activities through in-kind and reciprocal support: For example, at public events, it is not uncommon for us to share space, volunteers, or other resources or even to represent other organizations if they are unable to attend physically, and vice versa. We've had long-running, long-distance relationships with several other national and global independent distros with whom we exchange copyleft zines and other material for cross-distribution in our respective communities (e.g., Revolution Now in Saskatoon, Apoplectic Press in Ottawa, Slingshot in Berkeley, and Peace Not War in the United Kingdom). We also continue to form productive new relationships: In the past 2 years, we've formed great alliances with groups such as Just Seeds Visual Resistance and the Beehive Collective (both based in the United States), whose artwork we purchase at a reduced rate to exhibit but can then keep in our permanent collection for future use.

Our member artists, many who have been with us since the beginning, continue to support the development of the ESPA library and archive by donating their projects and encouraging others to do the same. In turn, we've tried to prioritize the creation of a searchable online catalog that will eventually contain a listing for every item in our library and archive. It doesn't help them in terms of financial support, but at least they know that someone cares enough about their projects to put extra effort into cataloging them for others to access online.

Our volunteers, some also with us since the early years, continue to donate their time and skills despite our tedious development. And many of us actively volunteer with other groups and can represent each other's groups at meetings. Fortunately, we can say the same regarding several other groups with which we continue to work, however large or small the capacity.

Where Do We Go From Here?

In taking this opportunity to look back on ESPA's history thus far, our hope has been in part to prepare other community media groups for inevitable roadblocks and disappointments, but more important, we have seen this as a chance to encourage others to use bad experiences to develop better strategies. Collaboration doesn't always work as planned (or at all, sometimes) but shouldn't be seen as a useless endeavor, either.

Despite our struggles, we feel that we can safely say that sticking to our principles is slowly resulting in the change we want to see. We didn't expect to change people's perceptions overnight, and we know that we still have a lot of work ahead of us. ESPA's best strategy for the time being is to continue to operate as a filter for community media and arts activism and pass on the most promising initiatives we run across to others in our community. That we still exist despite the odds speaks volumes and indicates to us that our people and our underlying values are worth advocating for.

Fortunately, we have had a few outstanding successes that continue to provide hope that mutually beneficial collaborations do exist. In many ways, we have globalization to thank for our development. Without the positive aspects of globalization—for example, our ability to communicate efficiently and affordably with others across the global landscape—the ESPA would not have our diversity or number of members.

This is a good example of the *dot commune,* a term coined by Guerrilla News Network founder Anthony Lappé that describes the paradigm shift of Internet-savvy "average citizens" becoming Internet-enabled activists (Sullivan, 2001/2002).

While we recognize that our development has been uncommon, with more international support over local, we know that to be of any value to the global community we need to backtrack and work harder on building a foundation for our local activities, because it's the only way we will remain sustainable. Yet, without our global membership, we would have a hard time convincing anyone local that others elsewhere are, in fact, interested and supportive of our activities.

As we've increased our presence in the global arts arena, we expect that recognition of community media as a culturally relevant form of expression will increase locally, along with increased organizational legitimacy and funding support. More support will allow us to maintain our ongoing commitment to public presentations and community activism in general and, more important, increase our capacity to deliver programs and services of interest to the larger population. Taking the opportunity to reflect on our successes and failures makes us better activists and stronger advocates for communicative democracy in the long run.

References

ESPA. (n.d.). *About us.* Retrieved 20 November 20, 2007, from the Edmonton Small Press Association Web site: www.edmontonsmallpress.ca/aboutespa.html

Stauber, J., & Rampton, S. (1995). *Toxic sludge is good for you: Lies, damn lies and the public relations industry.* Monroe, ME: Common Courage Press.

Sullivan, A. (2001 December/2002 January). Guerrilla newsworthy: The *Satya* interview with Anthony Lappé. *Satya.* Retrieved November 20, 2007, from www.satyamag.com/dec01/lappe.html

CHAPTER 14

Examining the Successes and Struggles of New Zealand's Māori TV

Rita L. Rahoi-Gilchrest

M any researchers over the past 20 years have commented on the disenfranchisement of indigenous voices by media and the dominant groups that control such media. This has, until recently, been true of the mediated coverage and inclusion of New Zealand's Māori population (comprising 12.5% of New Zealand's 4 million citizens, according to the BBC News Service, "NZ Launches," 2004). To offer a better understanding of the greater significance of New Zealand's struggles to represent and include indigenous voices, this chapter first presents a brief history of global indigenous broadcasting, then moves on to the specific details of the struggle for representation in New Zealand and the television broadcast service designed to address these issues. The chapter concludes with a review of the current strengths and remaining challenges characterizing Māori Television Service's (MTS) first decade of existence.

MTS in Context: Reviewing the History of Indigenous Broadcasting

The relationship between indigenous groups and modern media, particularly television broadcasting, has been a contentious one. Most often, as John Gardiner-Garden pointed out in a 2003 e-brief to the Parliament of Australia, the concern has been that indigenous cultures are misrepresented by the mainstream media in portrayals that are "at best inappropriate, and at worst racist" (Meadows, 1995, quoted in Gardiner-Garden, 2003). Even when there is recognition that indigenous people need to have some control over the representation of themselves and their interests, conflicts remain over the funding and support mechanisms established to sustain indigenous broadcasting ventures. And, as Browne (1996) has observed, the increasing exportation of television entertainment from

America, the United Kingdom, and other industrialized nations leaves even less room for something other than a "North-dominated picture of world events" (p. 10). Despite the odds, however, we can trace progress in the development and support of indigenous broadcasting.

Globally, for instance, Native American radio stations came on air in Alaska and North Carolina in 1971 and have developed into a network of 53 affiliated stations throughout the United States (Gardiner-Garden, 2003). Inuit-language broadcasts were available in Canada much earlier, in the 1960s, and the Canada Northern Broadcasting Policy set forth in 1983 further supported Northern native-produced broadcast programming and the formation of the Aboriginal People's Television Network (APTN) in September, 1999 (Browne, 1996; Gardiner-Garden, 2003; see also Lundberg, 1999). Indigenous broadcasting began with community radio programming in the early 1970s in Australia, and both the Broadcasting for Remote Aboriginal Communities Scheme and the 1992 Broadcasting Services Act were passed to ensure maintenance and development of public, community, and indigenous broadcasting (Gibson, cited in Gardiner-Garden, 2003).

By far, one of the key texts in understanding the history of indigenous broadcasting is Donald Browne's 1996 review of electronic media and indigenous peoples. In his historical review, besides the initiatives previously mentioned, Browne takes note of much earlier movements such as the BBC's initiatives for outreach to Scotland, Northern Ireland, and Wales during the 1930s and 1940s, the Lapp programs offered by Norsk Rikskringskasting (NRK) in the 1930s and 1940s, and Iraq's Kurdish language service, introduced in 1939. France introduced radio licensing for Provencal, Breton, Basque, and other regional languages; regional services have also been a part of broadcast tradition in Mexico (in the late 1970s), India, and Nigeria (see Browne, 1996, for a very detailed discussion of international indigenous broadcast history).

Browne's (1996) specific interest in the unique development of Asia-Pacific indigenous broadcasting is well established. In fact, an entire chapter of his 1996 book is devoted to the development of Māori electronic media (primarily radio and the "third" channel of New Zealand Television, or NZTV), which is where the story of Māori Television—the first truly indigenous television broadcasting station in New Zealand—continues. Browne views the unique progression of Māori broadcasting as a journey beginning with white-dominated efforts on "behalf" of indigenous Māori interests and then moving to the addition of Māori-produced programs to the mainstream television services. As we consider the progress of indigenous broadcasting in New Zealand, however, a new chapter can be added—the struggle to develop a television service that is a true production of indigenous talents.

Struggling for Recognition: Māori History and Indigenous Broadcasting

The initial reasons for the lack of indigenous broadcasting in New Zealand prior to the passage of the Māori Television Service Act in 2003 have been attributed by some critics to biased or minimal coverage of Māori-related issues. For instance, Barclay (2003) has typified the "voice" afforded to Māori in the media as more consistent with minority status in a multicultural community than with the status of "equal partners" mandated by New Zealand's 1840 civil agreement, the Treaty of Waitangi. Certainly, a second contributing factor to this indigenous group's past lack of media inclusiveness could be the decline in the use of Māori language and lack of attention to Māori culture itself. As a July 2007 editorial in the Wellington *Dominion Post* reminded its readers,[1] predictions in the 1970s were that there would soon be no more native speakers of Māori, and even in the 1980s, less than 20% of the Māori community knew enough *te reo* (a Māori term for native language) to be considered fluent speakers ("A Revitalized te reo," 2007). This cultural decline in the formal use of Māori language could be exacerbated by pressure from New Zealand employers as Māori people seek to enter the mainstream workforce in greater numbers (see "Battle to Keep," 2006). As recently as 1984, New Zealand telephone operator Naida Glavish was demoted by management because she refused to stop greeting callers with the Māori phrase *Kia ora,* a common way of offering greetings or hello ("Battle to Keep," 2006).

Whatever the causes of the distancing of the Māori by New Zealand's mainstream media, such disenfranchisement of indigenous groups is not unique. What is unique in this circumstance has been the attempt to create an organization—Māori Television—to help redress deeply embedded social issues resulting from the civil wars that characterized New Zealand's early history and the 1840 Treaty of Waitangi (Lean, 1999).[2] Beginning with the Waitangi Tribunal in 1975, the New Zealand government has attempted to enact legislation that seeks to reverse early government policies focused on assimilating, rather than recognizing and preserving, Māori culture.

The impetus for more indigenous involvement in broadcasting began with passage of the Māori Television Service Act 2003 (*Te Aratuku Whakaata Irrangi Māori*), providing the basis for the foundation of MTS, which went on air in 2004 (Russ, 2005). This initiative dated back to 2001, when the Labour government first began movement to create the service (Horomia, 2001). Similar to other indigenous media, MTS clearly has been directly developed "at least in part as a response to the exclusions and misrepresentations of the national public sphere" (see Couldry & Dreher's, 2007, discussion of the development of indigenous media in Australia, p. 83). Unlike other indigenous media, however, MTS's existence is due to a clear legal mandate. To understand the outcome of that mandate, in the next session of this chapter, we review the successes that MTS has achieved in its brief on-air history.

Truly a Medium for Everyone? The Mission and Successes of MTS

MTS, according to independent television producer and former MTS employee Joanna Paul, is unique in that it has its own legislation (the Māori Television Service Act) and a board selected by both the government and an electoral college that is charged with representing the interests of the Māori (Paul, 2005). MTS's specific company mission statement is "to provide an independent, secure and successful MTS channel broadcasting programmes that make a significant contribution to the revitalization of te reo and tikanga Māori" (Māori Television, n.d.-b, ¶13). MTS's mission to become "a world-class indigenous broadcaster" is embedded in the values expressed in its marketing slogan, "*Mā ātou, mā mātou, mā koutou, mā tātou,*" translated approximately as "for those who have gone before, for Māori, for you whoever you are/wherever you are located, for everyone" (Māori Television, n.d.-b, ¶ 15).

Public support and outreach have been significant in the short time since the station went live on air; 100% of New Zealanders have access to the channel through digital satellite, with 83% also able to view it via UHF (ultra high frequency). Research conducted in 2009 reported that 84% of the general population of New Zealand supported permanent broadcaster status for the company. The research also indicated that MTS reaches more than 1.5 million New Zealanders monthly, that 83% of Māori and more than half of all New Zealanders appreciate the positive views of this indigenous group presented on MTS, and that 73% of Māori and 46% of general populations surveyed agreed that MTS makes a valuable contribution to the sense of nationhood New Zealanders feel (all statistics drawn from Māori Television, 2009a).

Results from late 2006 indicated that MTS had a gain of 20% in its audience share within just 1 year and reached more than 580,000 unique viewers in October 2006 (Nicol Reed, 2006), which rose to 1.5 million viewers per month by 2009 (Māori Television, 2009a). Public support for its efforts has encouraged MTS to release plans for a second channel, broadcasting exclusively in *te reo* Māori from 7:30 to 10:30 P.M. with no advertising and a budget request of $23.1 million allocated over 4 years. This second 100% Māori-language channel was launched on air in 2008, with a live broadcast from the Auckland-hosted World Indigenous Television Broadcasting Conference providing even more tribal-specific programming aimed at older audience members more fluent in Māori or those viewers wanting full-immersion broadcasting (Horan, 2008c; see also www.tereo.tv/).

One of the keys to MTS's programming success can be found in the extensive line of media research on entertainment-education programs. The use of entertainment-education as a prosocial model for change has been defined by the media scholars Everett Rogers and Arvind Singhal as "the process of purposely designing and implementing a media message to both entertain and educate, in order to increase audience members' knowledge about an educational issue, create favorable attitudes, shift social norms, and change overt behavior" (quoted in Papa, Singhal, & Papa, 2006, p. 168).

Entertainment-education programs have been studied in a wide variety of international contexts and among various audiences (e.g., Pant, Singhal, & Bhasin, 2002; Singhal, Cody, Rogers, & Sabido, 2004; Vaughan, Rogers, Singhal, & Swalehe, 2000). Like other entertainment-education soap operas or telenovelas such as *Simplemente Maria* in Mexico (Sabido, 2004) and *Oshin* in Japan (Singhal, Svenkerud, & Rahoi-Gilchrest, 1998), one popular program on MTS, *Kōrero Mai,* combined likable, relatable characters with prosocial messages about current cultural and social issues. *Kōrero Mai,* which translates roughly as "Come talk with me," was originally designed as a Māori language education series.

Embedded within a narrative framework introducing and explaining the words of the week, however, is an ongoing soap opera titled *Akina* that focused on friends and flatmates at the mythical address of 3 Reka Street. The words introduced in the conventional lessons hosted by commentator Piripi Taylor were featured in each episode of *Akina,* but, more important for viewers, the storylines enacted by bilingual cast members featured issues such as unplanned pregnancy, drug and alcohol abuse, career struggles, gambling, and relationship problems. The program was been a critical as well as popular success, receiving the award for Best Māori Programme at the Qantas Television Awards in 2005 (Māori Television, n.d.-a). Since its inception, the number of cast members of the soap opera *Akina* was increased from five to eight, and in its fifth season, the program was being broadcast three times weekly, on Monday, Tuesday, and Wednesday evenings, with rebroadcasts another 3 days each week on Thursday, Friday, and Saturday (Māori Television, 2007).

This combination of entertainment and education has proved as compelling in New Zealand as it has in other countries and cultural settings. CEO Mather observed, "It's entertaining but it's also educational. I think shows like Korero Mai normalise [*sic*] the language. When you hear te reo being spoken regularly, it becomes a more accepted part of everyday life" (quoted in Tahana, 2006). The program continues to emphasize its dual focus to the present time and has added learning units on *waiata* (songs), *tikanga* (Māori culture), and colloquial phrases to its initial basic lessons on counting, colors, and the days of the week (Māori Television, n.d.-a).

As MTS Manager of Acquisitions and Commissioning Manutai Schuster has commented, this program introduced "a very important genre—a Māori language learning programme specifically designed to meet the language learning requirements of Māori Television legislation. This has resulted in a loyal audience for Korero Mai including a high percentage of non-Māori" (Māori

Television, 2005b). The kinds of parasocial relationships that researcher Miguel Sabido claimed audience members engage in with program characters who model socially desirable behavior (as discussed in Papa et al., 2006) are evident given the program's loyal following.

The entertainment-education approach has been extended to other program offerings as well. MTS's 2006 season introduced a segment called "Wai's Word" on *Code,* its sports show, which features New Zealand Warriors player Wairangi Koopu introducing Māori league vocabulary and modeling the kind of bilingual Māori/English fluency that underlies the MTS mission (Tahana, 2006). In adopting the entertainment-education format, however, MTS appears to have been careful to follow the unique expectations established by its founding legislation. CEO Mather noted, "There's a unique Māoriness to our programmes. I think it's very Kiwi but in the same way we don't want to be a brown version of mainstream" (quoted in Tahana, 2006). As "Auntie" Ella Henry, hostess of the popular talk show, *Ask Your Auntie,* said of her folksy, gossipy, all-female-hosted program, "It's a window into our world for non-Māori too, in a way that is safe and entertaining" (quoted in Nicol Reed, 2006). Based on its programming appeal and outreach, MTS appears to be another success story to add to entertainment-education media studies.

MTS's success also might be due in part to its close affiliation with, and leadership of, other indigenous television broadcasters through the creation of the World Indigenous Television Broadcasters Network (WITBN). After MTS hosted the inaugural World Indigenous Television Broadcasting Conference in Auckland in March 2008 (Dykes, 2007), the WITBN was founded; it now has Council membership from nine countries[3] as well as associate members (http://witbc.org/witbn.htm). While the global impact of this newly formed coalition remains to be seen, these community-building efforts among indigenous media reinforce MTS's goal of retaining indigenous language and cultural knowledge while simultaneously taking the cause far beyond the borders of Aotearoa (New Zealand).

Most important, given the mission of MTS, Māori leaders within the country appear to have been satisfied with this initiative; 1 year after MTS began broadcasting, academic Huirangi Waikerepuru was quoted in the online publication *NZ Edge* as saying that "the launch of Māori television is yet another milestone for us and our language" ("Te reo on Air," 2004). More recently, Māori Affairs Minister Parekura Horomia agreed that the launch of MTS has been key to the continuing revitalization of the Māori language (Easton, 2007). Even given these considerable successes, however, MTS is still beset by challenges unique to its status as an indigenous community medium—challenges identified and explained in the following section of this chapter.

Challenges That Remain: Forecasting the Future of MTS

Despite MTS's early successes, recent societal and company events pose new challenges for the continuation and growth of MTS. This list includes the issue of race debate as a keynote of the 2005–2007 elections, *Pakeha*[4] hostility over government-funded Māori rights programs, the challenge of developing sustainable funding strategies for the free-to-air station in the face of public controversy, and the call for the increased use of English subtitles in news and popular programming.

What makes garnering support for MTS even more difficult is that the mainstream media continue to raise and debate many of these issues in print form, leaving the more orally oriented Māori out of the discussion. Māori author Alan Duff made this point in commenting on the recent attempts by Don Brash and the National Party to stop funding for race-based programs, noting, "This race debate is taking place mainly in the print media and so Māori don't know what is being said. We need to be participating in discussions about our own fate and destiny" (quoted in "SCOPE: New Zealand Fired Up," 2004). And clearly, *Pakeha* who oppose the continued funding of MTS are unlikely to seek voluntary exposure to its programming so that they can make an informed decision on the value of initiatives such as bilingual subtitling.

In discussing the challenges of MTS in more specific detail, we can first consider the challenge of subtitling programming for greater outreach—and whether those efforts are congruent with a truly indigenous broadcast television service. MTS CEO Jim Mather has stated publicly that the organization is committed to inclusiveness in its broadcasting, and the most recent effort to be so has been to deliver the Māori news broadcasts with English subtitles. As Mather commented, "The sub-titling of our flagship news programme, Te Kaea, reinforces our commitment to ensuring that 100 per cent [*sic*] of our prime time programming is accessible to non-Māori speakers and those learning the language" (Māori Television, 2005a, ¶ 7).

This issue, however, has engendered debate over the true purpose and representative nature of MTS. Some Māori have opposed this decision on the basis that it means that the "Māori theme has been diluted" (Drinnan, 2007); non-Māori criticize it as an overt attempt to gain advertising dollars from the wealthier *Pakeha* sections of the viewing audience. Both sides, incidentally, seem to miss the point that since many Māori are still essentially monolingual in English (Bell, 1999), subtitling benefits Māori as well as *Pakeha* communities.

This dialectical tension is typical of debates over indigenous issues in New Zealand. Sibley and Liu (2004) conducted two studies of *Pakeha* attitudes toward biculturalism, finding that although support is strong for general discussions of biculturalism (53% supportive, 3% opposed), resource-specific biculturalism (such as the governmental support of MTS) receives far less support (3% supportive, 76% opposed), regardless of level of social dominance orientation. Producer

Joanna Paul (2005) explains that this level of political controversy creates a need to

> deliver a much broader range of genres without the support of years of experience . . . [and establishes] an expectation that we must be able to do it all and NOW or we are wasting public funds and people's precious time. (p. 44)

This feat, as Paul observes, becomes even more difficult because MTS remains committed to empowering indigenous people by placing them within the industry (as producers, directors, hosts, and writers) as well as by broadcasting the programs that are produced.

Given the politicization of these and many other issues, some groups that initially supported MTS's permanent broadcast status are opposing continued funding for the channel and the development of new initiatives such as subtitling (which requires a new three-person bilingual team just to cover the nightly newscast; see Māori Television, 2005a). MTS's most recent response to this controversy had been to suggest, through chief executive Mather, that the proposed new second channel would complement the first channel, so that there would be a 100% Māori-language–only lineup throughout the afternoon on the main channel, with *te reo*-only[5] broadcasting continuing on the second channel after 7:30 P.M. starting in March, 2008 ("Māori TV Launches," 2007).

The problem of whether or not to sustain government funding also renews questions about the cultural politics of indigenous broadcasting. Avril Bell has commented on the specific political issues of the New Zealand's government "cultural subsidy" approach. She found it ironic that an otherwise neoliberal government would claim on the one hand to sustain national identity through programming subsidies yet simultaneously try to manipulate public opinion by using that support to prevent public protests over cultural politics (see Debrett, 2004). In other words, government support of MTS could certainly be viewed as a kind of "branding" that encourages commodification of local programming over the global broadcasting options offered New Zealand viewers by their SKY TV subscriptions. There is certainly reason, as Horrocks (2004) observed, to believe that TVNZ's experience of "dumbing down" its content with much more entertainment than education to further justify its funding support with increased viewership could be repeated with MTS (see also Comrie & Fountaine, 2005, on the past history of TVNZ).

A final challenge to be met is increasing the inclusiveness of indigenous people in MTS's staffing, programming, and operations. A number of programs are produced by Māori directors and writers, with more than 90% of the programming on Te Reo planned to be locally produced (Māori Television, 2009b). New Zealand as a whole, however, suffers from a mass exodus of many young, talented people who could not only support but also contribute to this work; as *NZEdge* writer Paul Ward (n.d.) has explained, "For whatever reason (earning power, opportunity, the Kiwi wanderlust gene) this population is increasing by the day. Young New Zealanders make up the majority of the exodus (one in 20 leaving permanently every year)" (¶ 3). With so many young New Zealanders leaving, there are even fewer young indigenous people available to be employed by MTS, and as recently as early March 2008, the company was promoting new scholarships for New Zealand tertiary students to attend the first ever World Indigenous Television Broadcasting Conference in the hope of increasing interest in fulltime professional employment in the field (Horan, 2008b).

It is also clear that increasing awareness of indigenous cultures and languages is not the same as empowering indigenous people to overcome social and economic injustices. In the case of MTS, this point was effectively made by Wharehuia Milroy, a former academic at Waikato University. Milroy observed that for those Māori who are still economically and socially deprived, language itself has little currency; as he has stated, "It's not the language you can go and purchase things with down at the shops. If you've got empty cupboards and stomachs, learning Māori is not important—what's important is being able to survive" (quoted in Tahana, 2006, p. 7). So the effectiveness or success of the MTS initiative cannot be easily equated with effective, successful social change.

As if these challenges were not daunting enough, there are technical issues still to be overcome as well. In early 2007, a change by TVNZ and MTS to newer horizontal signal transponders threatened to make programming invisible to customers of the pay-per-view service, SKY TV (Pullar-Strecker, 2007). Although the issue appears likely to be resolved, it is another reminder of the complex environment within which MTS is a relatively new and inexperienced player. Having identified the struggles as well as the successes of MTS's efforts to establish itself as a successful indigenous media initiative, we come to the question, "What is the future of truly indigenous broadcasting in the form of initiatives such as Māori TV?"

Looking Ahead: The Future and Sustainability of MTS

Despite the challenges faced by the staff and supporters of MTS, it seems clear from its equally considerable list of strengths that the momentum of this and other such media reform efforts will continue. And although there are undoubtedly those who would take a critical perspective and argue that the emphasis in MTS's entertainment-education efforts is on the wrong half of the equation, its approach seems to be reaching not only within but also outside its targeted indigenous audience. At its most praiseworthy, as one 2007 editorial observed, a dedicated indigenous broadcasting service such as MTS is "the only way to get a proper, thoroughgoing and constant Māori perspective in the media; ethnic minorities will only ever be a minor part of a commercial TV channel aimed at the majority" ("Give TVNZ a Break," 2007).

If we look to make a completely compelling case for the success of MTS in the present day, we cannot overlook the issues of sustainability, public support, and inclusiveness that remain. Perhaps, a more useful approach is to consider the work of this indigenous television broadcast service in light of its much humbler beginnings (Browne, 1996) or to evaluate it in comparison with the many other international venues where successes have been even more difficult to come by and government support has been much less forthcoming (Gardiner-Garden, 2003). Such an approach speaks to the issues Howley (2005) has raised with the prevailing "dependency on so-called 'objective and reliable empirical evidence' for measuring and assessing diversity and localism" (p. 103). Additionally, Dunleavy (2008) believes that New Zealand's past struggles with public service and government support have led to greater clarification of the roles that all of New Zealand's broadcast media have in facilitating commercial television programming in both commercially and culturally "vulnerable areas" (p. 809). Despite its critics and challenges, then, the case study of MTS is of great value to us, not only in terms of broadening our view of the kinds of organizations that we study but also in developing the paradigms and models used to understand how best to serve the struggle for communicative democracy.

Notes

1. Documentation of these issues is drawn from popular editorials as well as from scholarly sources to further emphasize the very public priorities and discussion they elicit among New Zealand's citizens.

2. The Treaty of Waitangi established agreements between the British crown and Māori chiefs in three areas. In the English version, the negotiated agreements were that

Māori ceded the sovereignty of New Zealand to Britain; Māori gave the Crown an exclusive right to buy lands they wished to sell, and, in return, they were guaranteed full rights of ownership of their lands, forests, fisheries and other possessions; and that Māori would have the rights and privileges of British subjects. (Ministry for Culture and Heritage, 2008)

The treaty was neglected and forgotten for much of the 19th century as white expansionism took hold, and rights intended to be protected and preserved for the Māori were not revisited until many years later (Browne, 1996).

3. The WITBN Council foundation members are APTN (Canada); BBC Alba (Scotland); MTS (Aotearoa, New Zealand); NITV (Australia); NRK Sami Radio and Television (Samiland, Norway); TG4 (Ireland); TITV/PTS (Taiwan); S4C (Wales); and SABC (South Africa), according to the WITBN Web site (http://witbc.org/witbn.htm).

4. The term *Pakeha*, a Māori word used to define non-Māori people, refers to New Zealanders of European (primarily British) descent (defined by Bell, 1999).

5. *Te reo* means literally "the language" (Horan, 2008a).

References

Barclay, K. (2003, June). Who gets voice? (Re)presentation of bicultural relations in New Zealand print media. *New Zealand Journal of Psychology, 32*(1), 3–12. Retrieved September 26, 2005, from http://findarticles.com/p/articles/mi_qa3848/is_ 200306/ai_n9266397?tag=content;c011

Battle to keep language alive. (2006, July 26). *Nelson Mail,* p. 18.

BBC News Service. (2004, March 28). *NZ launches first Māori TV station.* Retrieved September 16, 2006, from the BBC News Web site: http://news.bbc.co .uk/2/hi/asia-pacific/3576039.stm

Bell, A. (1999). Styling the other to define the self: A study in New Zealand identity making. *Journal of Sociolinguistics, 3*(4), 523–541.

Browne, D. R. (1996). *Electronic media and indigenous peoples: A voice of our own?* Ames: Iowa State University Press.

Comrie, M., & Fountaine, S. (2005). Retrieving public service broadcasting: Treading a fine line at TVNZ. *Media, Culture & Society, 27*(1), 101–118.

Couldry, N., & Dreher, T. (2007). Globalization and the public sphere: Exploring the space of community media in Sydney. *Global Media and Communication,* *3*(1), 79–100.

Debrett, M. (2004). Branding documentary: New Zealand's minimalist solution to cultural subsidy. *Media, Culture & Society, 26*(1), 5–23.

Drinnan, J. (2007, July 27). Media: Calling the Maori TV shots. *New Zealand Herald.* Retrieved March 24, 2009, from www.nzherald.co.nz/te-reo-maori/news/article.cfm?c_id=336&objectid=10454059

Dunleavy, T. (2008). New Zealand television and the struggle for "public service." *Media, Culture & Society, 30*(6), 795–811.

Dykes, M. (2007, July 30). Māori TV to host world-first conference. *Manawatu Standard,* p. 4.

Easton, P. (2007, July 28). From ka mate to ka ora. *Dominion Post,* p. A9.

Gardiner-Garden, J. (2003, November 27). *Indigenous broadcasting* [e-brief]. Retrieved February 18, 2008, from the *Current Issues* page of the Parliament of Australia Parliamentary Library Web site: www.aph.gov.au/library/intguide/SP/Indigenous_broadcasting.htm

Give TVNZ a break: Watch Māori TV instead. (2007, May 27). *Sunday Star-Times,* p. A11.

Horan, V. (2008a, March 9). *Latest news:* Māori *Television unveils new Reo* Māori *channel name.* Retrieved March 31, 2008, from the Māori Television Web site: http://media.maoritelevision.com/default.aspx?tabid=198&pid=362

Horan, V. (2008b, March 5). *Latest news: Scholarships launched for indigenous television conference.* Retrieved March 31, 2008, from the Māori Television Web site: http://media.maoritelevision.com/default.aspx?tabid=198&pid=365

Horan, V. (2008c, February 24). *Māori Television launches 100% Māori language channel.* Retrieved November 3, 2008, from http://media.maoritelevision.com/default.aspx?tabid=198&pid=367

Horomia, P. (2001, July 24). *New Māori TV service an exciting new era in NZ broadcasting.* Retrieved September 9, 2005, from the New Zealand Cabinet Web site: www.executive.govt.nz/minister/horomia/tv/pr.htm

Horrocks, R. (2004). Turbulent television: The New Zealand experiment. *Television & New Media, 5*(1), 55–68.

Howley, K. (2005). Diversity, localism and the public interest: The politics of assessing media performance. *International Journal of Media and Cultural Politics, 1*(1), 103–106.

Lean, M. (1999). Getting the government to say sorry. *For a Change, 12*(5), 1–3. Retrieved September 26, 2005, from http://findarticles.com/p/articles/mi_m0KZH/is_5_12/ai_30217693

Lundberg, M. (1999, September 17). *The birth of APTN.* Retrieved January 16, 2008, from the Explore North Web site: http://explorenorth.com/library/weekly/aa091799.htm

Māori Television. (2005a, August 15). *Māori Television delivers Māori news with English sub-titles.* Retrieved September 16, 2006, from the Māori Television Web site at www.Māori television.com/newsletter/issue75/index.htm

Māori Television. (2005b, November 15). *MTS best Māori language programme.* Retrieved September 8, 2006, from Scoop Web site: www.scoop.co.nz/stories/CU0511/S00125.htm

Māori Television. (2007, March 10). *Korero Mai: Te reo soap opera on Māori TV.* Retrieved August 8, 2007, from the Throng Web site: www.throng.co.nz/korero-mai/korero-mai-te-reo-soap-opera-on-Māori-tv

Māori Television. (2009a). *Maori Television marks fifth on-air anniversary.* Retrieved April 13, 2009, from the Māori Television Web site: http://media.maoritelevision.com/Default.aspx?tabid=198&pid=1599

Māori Television. (2009b). *Māori Television: New channel announcement media Q and A.* Retrieved April 13, 2009, from the Māori Television Web site: http://media.maoritelevision.com/default.aspx?tabid=198&pid=387

Māori Television. (n.d.-a). *Korero mai.* Retrieved November 8, 2006, from the Māori Television Web site: www.Māoritelevision.com/programmes/tereo/korero_mai.htm

Māori Television. (n.d.-b). *Māori Television corporate information.* Retrieved September 16, 2005, from the Māori Television Web site: http://corporate.Maoritelevision.com/

Māori TV launches Māori-only channel. (2007, July 26). Retrieved August 8, 2007, from the NZCity Web site: http://home.nzcity.co.nz/news/default.aspx?id=75281

Ministry for Culture and Heritage. (2008, January 24). *The treaty in brief.* Retrieved March 3, 2008, from the New Zealand History Online Web site: www.nzhistory.net.nz/politics/treaty/the-treaty-in-brief

Nicol Reed, M. (2006, November 19). The little channel that could. *Sunday Star-Times,* p. C3.

Pant, S., Singhal, A., & Bhasin, U. (2002). Using radio drama to entertain and educate: India's experience with the production, reception, and transcreation of "Dehleez." *Journal of Development Communication, 13*(2), 52–66.

Papa, M. J., Singhal, A., & Papa, W. H. (2006). *Organizing for social change: A dialectic journey of theory and praxis.* Thousand Oaks, CA: Sage.

Paul, J. (2005). Challenges lie ahead for MTS in the Aotearoa public sphere. *Pacific Journalism Review, 11*(1), 42–46.

Pullar-Strecker, T. (2007, February 19). Māori TV: Sky pauses. *Dominion Post,* p. C13.

A revitalized te reo. (2007, July 23). *Dominion Post,* p. B6.

Russ, B. N. (2005, May 1). New Zealand's Māori Television. *Broadcast Engineering.* Retrieved September 26, 2005, from http://broadcast engineering.com/newsrooms/broadcasting_new _zealands_maori/

Sabido, M. (2004). The origins of entertainment-education. In A. Singhal, M. Cody, E. M. Rogers, & M. Sabido (Eds.), *Entertainment-education and social change: History, research and practice* (pp. 61–74). Mahwah, NJ: Lawrence Erlbaum.

SCOPE: New Zealand fired up by race debate. (2004, April 19). *Asian Economic News,* 1–3. Retrieved September 26, 2005, from http://findarticles.com/p/articles/ mi_m0WDP/is_2004_April_19/ai_115506393/ print

Sibley, C. G., & Liu, J. H. (2004, July). Attitudes towards biculturalism in New Zealand: Social dominance and Pakeha attitudes towards the general principles and resource-specific aspects of bicultural policy. *New Zealand Journal of Psychology, 33*(2), 88–99. Retrieved September 26, 2005, from http://findarticles.com/p/articles/mi_qa3848/is_ 200407

Singhal, A., Cody, M., Rogers, E. M., & Sabido, M. (Eds.). (2004). *Entertainment-education worldwide: History, research, and practice.* Mahwah, NJ: Lawrence Erlbaum.

Singhal, A., Svenkerud, P. J., & Rahoi-Gilchrest, R. L. (1998). Cultural transcendence as an alternative to cultural imperialism: Role of pro-social entertainment television programs in developing countries. In S. Melkote, P. Shields, & B. Agrawal (Eds.), *International satellite broadcasting in South Asia: Political, economic, and cultural implications* (pp. 249–271). New York: University Press of America.

Tahana, Y. (2006, July 26). Channelling te reo to masses. *Waikato Times,* p. 7.

Te reo on air. (2004, March 26). Retrieved September 9, 2005, from www.nzedge.com/media/index_live/ index_June04.html

Vaughan, P. W., Rogers, E. M., Singhal, A., & Swalehe, R. M. (2000). Entertainment-education and HIV/AIDS prevention: A field experiment in Tanzania. *Journal of Health Communication, 5,* 81–100.

Ward, P. (n.d.). *Brain exchange: Creating the Kiwi diaspora.* Retrieved March 30, 2008, from the *New Zealand Edge* Web site: www.nzedge.com/ features/ar-brainexchange.html

World Indigenous Television Broadcasters Network. (2008). *Aotearoa 08/WITBC.* Retrieved November 3, 2008, from http://witbc.org/witbn.htm

CHAPTER 15

Itche Kadoozy, Orthodox Representation, and the Internet as Community Media

Matt Sienkiewicz

On May 6, 2007, the Chabad community of Crown Heights (Brooklyn, New York) celebrated the holiday of Lag B'Omer by hosting its annual parade through the streets of their predominantly Orthodox Jewish neighborhood. In accordance with community custom, the procession was geared largely toward children's entertainment, featuring a well-beloved, oversized puppet as one of its main attractions. In the past, characters featured at the Lag B'Omer parade represented two categories. On the one hand, there have been externally produced creations such as Fred Flintstone. While recognizable to a broad audience, this character would seem to be at odds with the values of a community that, according to journalist Sue Fishkoff (2003), "scorn(s) popular media" (p. 27). On the other hand, there have been characters drawn from Orthodox-produced children's literature, including images taken from the magazine *Shaloh*. Created within the Orthodox community and geared toward Orthodox children, these characters are often popular within the Chabad

world but fail to resonate with more secular Jewish children. In 2007, however, there was something unique about the parade's leading character. The star of the show was none other than Rabbi Itche Kadoozy, the titular head of Chabad.org's popular Internet video series, *The Itche Kadoozy Show (IKS)*. While this program is produced in Crown Heights and enjoys enormous popularity among Chabad children, it also garners a significant non-Orthodox audience. For the first time in history, the Chabad community had at its disposal a homegrown character that could serve as a bridge to the rest of the Jewish world.

Like many of the ideas and entities to be described in this chapter, *IKS* defies categorization. A series of Torah-themed mock news reports, interactive Web games, and 5- to 7-minute serialized specials, *IKS*'s irreverent puppetry and animation have become a marquee attraction on Chabad.org, a well-trafficked Web site that plays a major role in Chabad's outreach efforts. The show stars Rabbi Itche Kadoozy, his secular friend Jono, the rascally Gefilte P. Fish (a talking piece of gefilte fish), and a series of other human and nonhuman (but all Jewish) friends.[1] *IKS*'s stories tend to have an ironic edge and an abundance of pop-culture references. However, they invariably stress the lessons of the Torah and the importance of mitzvoth (commandments required of all Jews), thus reinforcing the values that Chabad holds so dear.

In discussing the concept of community media, the scholar Kevin Howley (2005) suggests that community-produced programming is a rich site to consider the ways in which global media engage with specific localities, providing "a site of interpenetration between local and global actors, forces and conditions: one of the many 'heterogeneous dialogues' associated with globalization" (p. 33). The appearance of Rabbi Kadoozy at the Lag B'Omer parade described above is particularly interesting in light of Howley's observation. On the one hand, Itche is without question of and by the Chabad community. His distinctive beard and traditional clothing very clearly mark him as

a member of the community, providing Chabad children with a fictional representation that looks like their fathers, brothers, and local leaders. Itche's co-creator and head producer, Rabbi Dovid Taub, is himself a member of the community, who can often be seen walking down Brooklyn's Eastern Parkway to Shul on Shabbat along with thousands of other Chabad men dressed in fedoras and black coats (Figure 15.1).

However, Itche also belongs to and is heavily influenced by global culture. While his homepage on Chabad.org is perhaps most frequently visited by Chabad children, the message boards attached to each episode make it clear that Itche is, in fact, known and enjoyed by non-Orthodox and even secular Jews across the world. Furthermore, Itche and his cohorts owe their storylines and sensibilities to the world of popular culture. While *IKS* is always, as Taub puts it, "Torah-oriented," it also features images from *King Kong*, plot structures borrowed from *Arrested Development*, and various other markers that complicate an understanding of the local and the global.

Figure 15.1   *The Itche Kadoozy Show* Co-creator Dovid Taub With Star Rabbi Itche Kadoozy

Source: © Dovid Zaklikowski/Chabad.org.

The aim of this chapter is to further interrogate what scholarly understandings of community media have to teach us about *IKS* and to consider how *IKS* brings to light elements of community media sometimes overlooked in scholarly accounts of the subject. Ultimately, I argue that while *IKS* certainly serves as a landmark in Orthodox representation and a fine example of community media, it should not be understood merely as the product of competing local and global forces. Instead, I point to the enabling function played by Chabad.org, an entity that receives partial funding from outside sources and is aimed at outreach, not exclusively community expression.[2] I contend that for a group as small as Chabad, even the production and distribution of inexpensive media require elements of outward-looking, institutional support to find success. The case of *IKS* serves to underscore the fact that, even in the age of the Internet, the global and the local may be farther apart than scholarly accounts of community media suggest.

Chabad

The Chabad community is, at first glance, an utter paradox. On the one hand, members maintain tightly knit familial networks, observe a set of religio-ethical rules that demand a separation from secular society, and, for the most part, live in just a few, densely populated areas. But at the same time, Chabad is often characterized as nonstop outreach. Despite its heavy focus on family, the community devotes enormous financial resources and considerable manpower to educating millions of globally dispersed Jews, many of whom have little or no understanding of traditional Judaism (Fishkoff, 2003, p. 11). In addition to outreach efforts such as Chabad.org, thousands of Chabad families move to cities across the world, from Lima to Beijing to Boise, setting up "Chabad Houses" where they offer kosher meals, classes on Judaism, and other services. However, the noteworthiness of Chabad's outreach mission can potentially serve to obscure the centrality of its community status. Popular discussions of Chabad have a tendency to describe it less as a community and more in terms of an idea or an approach to teaching Jewish tradition. Chabad's institutional elements, in fact, often emphasize this perspective, perhaps obscuring the fact that Chabad's outreach specialists live enormously different lives from those whom they are teaching. For instance, Chabad.org's "about Chabad-Lubavitch" page fails to mention the word "community" at any point. Furthermore, while it references the nearly 4,000 Chabad emissary families working across the world, it says nothing of the many thousands of Chabad families living in close proximity in cities such as New York and Jerusalem. While Chabad may find outside donors and make headlines by publicizing its unique approach to outreach, the community is, at its core, a group of individuals bound together through common values, understandings of history, religious rituals, and social customs ("About Chabad-Lubavitch," n.d.).

In order to begin to understand the Chabad community and its relationship to media, one must take into account the tremendous influence of Rabbi Menachem Mendel Schneerson, a man more commonly known in the Jewish world simply as "The Rebbe." As is traditional in Chasidic communities, Chabad members define their approach to Judaism not only by their adherence to *halacha* (Jewish Law) but also through their profound respect for the words of their leader or *rebbe.* Fishkoff (2003) identifies a rebbe as a "perfectly righteous man," whose "holiness, piety, and devotion to Jewish Law give him tremendous powers, notably the ability to 'move in spheres not understood by ordinary men'" (p. 75). This description certainly applies in the case of Schneerson. Chabad members, however, have a particularly complex relationship with this aspect of their religious and community lives. Schneerson died in June 1994 and has not been replaced, as would be in accordance with Chabad's tradition over the past few centuries. The reasoning behind this decision is too complex to be treated here. However, it must be understood that members of the Chabad community take Schneerson's words very seriously, with some individuals taking the position that Schneerson was and remains, *King Moshiach,* the redeemer of the Jewish people and the world at large.[3] A prodigious writer, Schneerson left behind a seemingly endless series of letters, essays, and speeches, many of which relate either directly or indirectly to media.

While the scope of this chapter does not allow for a full treatment of Chabad's historical approach to media, a brief overview of this evolution is helpful in understanding *IKS*'s place within the Chabad community. This is particularly important in view of the misleading fashion in which journalists have tended to portray and simplify Chabad's complex history with mass communication. For example, in 1983, the *New York Times* stated that "using satellite (television) technology poses no theological problems for Orthodox Jews," specifically referencing Chabad and Schneerson ("Rabbi Using," 1983, p. 39). Twenty years later, *Wired* reported "Rabbi [Schneerson] embraced technology early on" (Kamber, 2000, ¶ 5). On their own site, Chabad.org states that in 1960, the Rebbe took strong exception to "those who felt that radio and television were 'evil' things" ("1960 Technology," n.d., ¶ 3).

While these statements serve to underscore the extent to which Chabad has ultimately come to accept and celebrate the power of mass media, they ignore a strand of discourse that helps explain why many in the community remain ambivalent about a program such as *IKS* to this day. The Rebbe did not, in fact, embrace all media technology from the start. In fact, in a 1954 public letter, he describes television (or at least the totality of television programming) as "an unparalleled departure from Torah morality," decrying its "destructive influence on youth" and claiming that it could induce a total loss of Jewishness. He argues that there can be no such thing as "Kosher television" and describes the defense of TV as the "lowest depths of depravity!" (Schneerson, 1990, p. 461). While both Schneerson and Chabad as a whole eventually came to embrace media as a way to spread its message and keep Chabad families across the world in contact, there persists a strand of thought that radically opposes anything that is associated with television. As recently as 2002, the *N'Shei Chabad Newsletter* published an article in which the impact of television programming is described as the "systematic destruction of Judaism and Jewish culture in America" (Schilder, 2002, p. 58).

According to Chabad.org media director, Rabbi Dovid Zaklikowski (personal communication, May 14, 2007), the Internet had a considerably easier time gaining acceptance within the Chabad community, allowing for *IKS* to emerge despite its surface-level similarities to television content. While it is impossible to know just why this occurred, Zaklikowski suggests the Internet's original text-only content and value as a work tool as partial explanations. After a series of e-newsletters and temporary sites found success within the community, Chabad.org was created in 2001. Conceived as a weekly online magazine, the site eventually began including multimedia components, such as how-to videos instructing (presumably non-Orthodox) viewers on the proper techniques for performing religious rituals. It was not until the arrival of *IKS,* however, that the thin line between television and the Internet was made so apparent on the site.

The Itche Kadoozy Show

In the summer of 2003, Dovid Taub purchased a video camera and some basic editing software and began making video puppet shows heavily influenced by both his newly found faith in the Chabad approach to traditional Judaism and his childhood experience watching *Perfect Strangers* and other secular television. Collaborating closely with his non-Orthodox friend, Jonathon Goorvich, Taub structured the show around the relationship between a deeply intellectual Chabad rabbi, Itche Kadoozy, and Jono, a Jewish 20-something who identifies largely with secular culture. In Taub's own words, these early programs were "extremely esoteric and really not very good." Taub posted the videos to www.ItcheKadoozy.com with the hope of selling them to community members on video CDs.[4] The Web site garnered modest interest from within the community, attracting 100 to 300 hits per week but very little in the way of sales. In an attempt to boost the show's profile online, Taub and Goorvich began producing a weekly program in which Itche would answer viewer mail. Additionally, Taub began incorporating a more striking Web design that employed flash animation.

It was this eye-catching Web design of ItcheKadoozy.com that garnered the attention of Chabad.org, by then well established in its approach to Jewish outreach. Taub (personal communication, May 10, 2007) recounts the following as the terms of his hiring in 2004:

> They said, "we like your menus and the animation and we'd like you to come here and help us create a kids site." But they were also very clear that they weren't interested in my content. They said "don't do Itche Kadoozy, 'cause it's not our style." They just didn't have any interest in this *obviously* Chabad Rabbi talking about Kabbalah, shoving it down your throat. "Don't do that," they said, "no one will like it."

Ultimately, however, the people working on Chabad.org's children's section came to realize that flashy menus and clever graphics were of little use without interesting content to link to. Taub and Goorvich were advised to give *IKS* another shot but to make it more "mainstream" to ensure that the Web site would not limit its appeal to merely the Chabad community. According to Chabad.org's Zaklikowski (personal communication, May 14, 2007), the site's administrators began to see Itche as a continuation of Chabad's decades-old use of "the rabbi as an outreach icon" and a potential update of the "Dancing Rabbi" ad campaign that the community produced in the 1970s. To adjust the show's appeal away from the Chabad community and toward the broader Jewish world that Chabad.org wished to target, significant changes had to be made. Most strikingly, the site's administrators demanded a change in the

question-and-answer vignettes. According to Taub (personal communication, May 10, 2007), "They said to make sure the names of the kids writing in are English names. They said 'you can have Hebrew names every once in a while, but don't make it all a bunch of Mendis and Mushkis.'" As the show grew in popularity and garnered a larger profile within the Chabad.org Web site, Taub worked with Goorvich to develop longer, serialized narratives. Taub also began to "re-embrace his TV-addict past," working in references to mass culture in an attempt to "pair Jewish concepts with the parts of people's brains that get excited by pop culture."

IKS and Community Media

Broadly speaking, scholars have offered two major ways in which to consider the connection between community and media. On the one hand, a media text or event can aid in the formation of a community by virtue of the ways in which individuals relate to it. This is an approach often employed in fandom studies and rests on the assumption that real-life bonds analogous to those of traditional community can be forged through such mediated relationships. On the other hand, a preexisting community can produce media that reflect itself while perhaps affecting the community's structure in the process. It is my contention that *IKS* can be appropriately and profitably interrogated from both of these perspectives, particularly if one includes the message boards that supplement each episode as part of the show's text.

Henry Jenkins (1992) employs the work of Michel de Certeau to dispel the notion that media consumption must be "indifferent" and thereby a passive process incapable of forging true ties between users. By turning to the complex, creative, and sometimes rather intense manners in which viewers have engaged with shows such as *Star Trek* and *Twin Peaks,* Jenkins argues that fans create communities in a true sense (p. 54) *IKS,* I argue, plays a similar role and one that is of particular interest given its unique place in the history of Orthodox media representation.

IKS is one of the first media texts in which members of the Chabad community would be likely to engage in "fan" activities alongside less observant Jews. Furthermore, *IKS*'s place on Chabad.org, as well as its themes and titular character, encourage Chabad viewers to consider the show as a landmark event in their own representation. As a result, the message boards attached to the episodes encourage viewers to debate not only the show's plot points and cliffhangers but also the proper way to make meaning out of what one might consider a "Chabad text."

In discussing the formation of fan communities, Jenkins (1992) writes that "fan reading . . . is a social process through which individual interpretations are shaped and reinforced through ongoing discussions with other readers" (p. 45). On a basic level, such activity takes place on the message boards for *IKS* in the form of debates on the narrative implications of the show. For example, on the board for Chapter 3 of the miniseries, *The Quest for Fish*, user "Mendel" from Hungary questions whether a character in the story "is a CIA, Mossad or terrorist agent?" A few posts later a user named "I have a hunch" puts forth his or her theories on the matter, making references to previous episodes. The debate continues on intermittently for dozens of posts and certainly can be seen as a means by which viewers come to influence the ways in which one another come to experience the show ("Obstacles," 2007).

However, there is another, more specific sense in which viewer interactions influence interpretation. The first few episodes of *IKS* feature the secular character of Jono in his trademark flannel shirt and glasses, playing his typical role as a rascally foil to Itche's wisdom and good sense. His head is uncovered. In the context of a mass-oriented television series such as *Curb Your Enthusiasm*, for example, this situation would create little difficulty in terms of audience comprehension. Larry's famously bare head in no way calls into question his Jewishness. However, after viewing the episode,

"Matzah; What's Up With It?," user "Yosef Shidler" of Denver, Colorado, questions, "Is Jono JEW-ISH???? WHERE IS HIS YARMULKA. WHAT KIND OF EXAMPLE IS HE???" ("Matzah," 2007).

It is unclear, of course, whether Jono's lack of headgear sincerely confused the viewer. What is certain, however, is that there exists a legitimate concern as to whether a show could simultaneously be "Jewish" in a Chabad context and also feature Jews with bare heads. Other viewers echoed Yosef's concern, and for the past few years, Jono has been wearing a baseball cap, an item that is both religiously acceptable and in keeping with his role as the secular side of the odd-couple pairing of Itche and Jono (Figure 15.2).

Similarly, the message boards provide sites on which viewers debate about which aspects of the show should be considered "Jewish." For example,

Figure 15.2 Jono Weinsteinstein Wearing His Much-Discussed Baseball Cap and Holding a Tray of Kosher Donuts

Source: © Dovid Zaklikowski/Chabad.org.

while Taub insists that *IKS*'s mode of storytelling is not itself religiously specific, viewers often use the message board to show the program's inherent Jewishness, thus doing the sort of active work that Jenkins associates with fan-communal activity. For example, the final episode of the *IKS Chanukah Mini-Series* does not conform to traditional expectations for narrative logic generally associated with quality screen media. As a friend and Chabad Rabbi warned me, "It just doesn't make any sense." As a result, the message board for the show uncharacteristically features a series of posts imploring help in understanding what happened and how the story's many loose ends could potentially be tied up. An anonymous poster from Chicago, however, labeled the show "Genius," suggesting that its plot brought home the "clear message of not defending Torah life thru logic (even if/when also logically appealing)" ("Chanukah Mini Series," 2007). This post and others like it speak to the ways in which the social process of media reception and criticism of the show can potentially result in shifting levels of meaning within a viewing community. Other episodes have prompted viewers to consider *IKS*'s employment of "Jewish suspense" (where, according to posters, nonviolence is key) and to debate whether or not the inclusion of popular culture images and references detracts from the "Jewishness" of a media text. Non-Orthodox viewers contribute to this process as well, providing insights informed by the popular culture that the show invokes alongside its religious messages. By providing Torah-oriented stories that have appeal in the secular world, *IKS* creates the potential for a unique community in which individuals with vastly different approaches to media can come together and influence one another's perspectives.

Kevin Howley (2005) stresses the peril in attempting to pin down the essence of community in a simple, concise definition. Howley, therefore, turns to the work of Stuart Hall, employing his notion of articulation as it relates to theories of both personal and communal identity. Eschewing the establishment of binaries or the employment of out-groups as constitutive

others, this approach instead considers "community as a unity of differences; a unity forged through symbol, ritual, language and discursive practices" (p. 6). As such, it is unfair to characterize Howley's work as presupposing the existence of fully formed communities waiting to be expressed in community media. Instead, in this view, such media are seen as one of many elements that constitute the ever-shifting content of a given community.

This said, the members of the Chabad movement have for centuries now considered themselves part of a community that, while certainly not immune to change, holds a very firm grasp on the ways in which symbol, ritual, and language shape their sense of togetherness. Because members hold so many texts as authoritative and perform so many rituals with regularity, it is useful to consider Chabad as a community that exists rather coherently apart from *IKS* but may ultimately come to be affected by it. Furthermore, by considering community media as a site that intermediates between the local and the global, Howley (2005) himself points to a gap that suggests it is fruitful to consider community as something that can be separated from its surroundings, at least as a conceptual tool.

By looking at *IKS* as an expression of a distinct community engaging in one of its first public debates over self-representation, it becomes possible to conceive of the show as just the sort of "participatory communication" that Howley (2005) suggests characterizes community media. While the program does not follow a traditional community access model, it is coproduced by a Chabad member who, without Chabad.org, would be unable to widely disseminate his work without severely adjusting the worldview that it represents. Furthermore, the message boards allow individual community members to engage in media discourse and, as in the case of Jono's baseball cap, influence concrete textual changes to the program. Such community participation in a production viewed so widely outside the Chabad community as well as within it is unprecedented.

Additionally, Howley (2005) points to the ways in which community media can serve to offset "historical amnesia" engendered by nationalist, state-run, and commercially supported media industries (p. 34). As Taub proudly notes when describing his program, *IKS* counteracts the sparse media images of Hasidic Jews that have existed up to now, providing a representation that indicates, "Orthodox Jews are not just Martians walking around with long Peyas and hats in their little neighborhoods in Brooklyn." Furthermore, the intense cultural specificity of the show also works to counter the mostly paper-thin representations of Jewish life that have prevailed in American mass media. From the character Gefilte P. Fish's ethnic food humor to Jono's jokes about playing tricks on classmates through the careful reassembly of empty Chanukah gelt wrappers, *IKS* plays a part in countering the effacement of the depth of Jewish culture in mass media—a process that has been chronicled in media histories outlined by Neil Gabler's (1989) *An Empire of Their Own*, Rabbi Elliot Gertel's (2003) *Over the Top Judaism*, and David Zurawik's (2003) *The Jews of Prime Time*.

Conclusion

The above discussion has aimed to outline the many forces that have brought about tangible effects on the production of and reception of *IKS*. For instance, there is Dovid Taub's personal history with media consumption, his collaboration with the non-Orthodox Goorvich, and his intimate relationship with the Chabad community. By taking pieces of popular culture and infusing them with traditional Jewish messages, Taub and Goorvich very much seem to be playing the intermediary role that Howley (2005) attributes to community media producers who "glean bits and pieces of media culture and invest this material with their own social experience in attempts to make sense of their lives" (p. 34). *IKS*, therefore, can be seen as representing the merging of two factors, the global and the local. Also

along these lines, there is the influence of viewers from both within the Chabad community and outside who make their own suggestions for and demands on the show's content.

However, as useful as Howley's global-local meeting point model is, a close look at *IKS*'s history of production suggests that, at least in this instance, more emphasis must be placed on the mediating institutions that allow for the global and local to commingle. On the most basic level, *IKS* is influenced by the religious standards that have been set by Jewish law and Schneerson's writings. While in some sense, these guidelines emerge from the Chabad community, the specificity of restrictions that derive from these sources should be noted. For instance, on "The Quest for Fish," message board, users complain about a new Rabbi Itche puppet that no longer features its trademark enormous nose ("Detours," 2007, chap. 4). Chabad.org media director Rabbi Dovid Zaklikowski (personal communication, May 14, 2007) suggests that the individuals working within the Chabad.org office may have considered the following fragment of The Rebbe's writing before the change was made:

> It isn't proper to draw people specifically abnormal (**very** fat, **very** long noses, etc.), although this has become the norm in the comic world. My opinion is that this is a serious educational error, because when dealing with children, the more simple **and normal**, the better the effect. (In my opinion the same applies concerning adults.)

Again, while the Chabad community is presumably in support of taking on Schneerson's words as community standards, this admittedly irregular influencing factor brings to the forefront the extent to which community restrictions may reside outside the purview of individual community members.

Furthermore, it should be noted that when *IKS* was produced entirely without institutional support, it was in some sense more authentic in its approach to community. The emphasis on religious philosophy and the Hebrew names of the viewers featured in Itche's question-and-answer segments attest to this fact. However, while the show may have been true to many of the values its community celebrates, it still had poor viewership and became financially insolvent. Taub's choice to move *IKS* away from his original intentions and become more "mainstream" can be viewed as a movement away from Chabad community influence but not necessarily toward mass culture. To keep making *IKS*, Taub and Goorvich did not need to surrender their work to global influences, as the media imperialist thesis might suggest, nor was it sufficient to merely employ the show as a site of resistance to and interplay with major media, as Howley's discussion of community media details. Instead, they had to find an institution with a vested interest in exploring the space that opens up between the global and the local or, as Chabad.org is more likely to see it, the secular and the traditional. Without Chabad.org's cachet and resources, *IKS*'s producers would have struggled for both the financial support and positive feedback necessary to justify the significant level of labor that media production requires.

The Itche Kadoozy Show can be understood as the culmination of a centuries-long shift within the Chabad community from separation from the secular world to an eventual acceptance of its influences. The result, a proponent of community media might argue, is a set of media texts that serve to mediate between these two extremes, illustrating their inevitable interdependence and giving voice to a previously underrepresented minority. However, it is crucial to note that such a situation was only able to arise when a well-funded institution chose to actively work toward this goal. On their own, Chabad community members likely could not successfully support programs featuring a "bunch of Mendis and Mushkis" or focusing on Kabbalistic principles, even though these elements are central to Chabad life. It is Chabad.org's interest in pulling together the local with the global that allows for *IKS* to serve as a site of negotiation, not the mere will of local producers or the democracy of distribution engendered by new media. While

IKS nicely illustrates the ways in which locally produced media can show the connections and tensions between its community and the world at large, it also draws attention to what elements may be effaced in the service of finding the breadth of audience that will justify the participation of funding sources. For example, while it is impossible to gauge the interest of other Chasidic groups in representing themselves via something similar to *IKS*, it is no coincidence that Chabad, with its many outreach-oriented institutions, first succeeded in breaking through this barrier. While the global–local model of understanding contemporary community certainly rings true, the case of *IKS* underscores the fact that, in certain instances at least, an intermediary institution is necessary to provide the common ground on which the community and mass culture are able to meet.

Notes

1. Gefilte fish is a processed food made of trout, pike, and other white fish. An anecdote that perhaps sheds some light on the cultural significance of *IKS*: A Chabad friend of mine had his nephew over for Shabbat dinner. Before serving him a piece of this traditional Ashkenazi food, he asked his nephew, "Do you like gefilte fish?" "Yes," the child responded in earnest, "but I think Rabbi Itche is funnier."

2. In this chapter, I will be distinguishing between Chabad.org and the Chabad community, even though the former emerges from the latter. This is for two reasons. First, Chabad.org is described by those who work for it as an outreach tool, so while it is probably visited most often by Chabad members, it is not intended for them in many cases. Second, while data are not available on this, Chabad.org's administrators admit that the site is funded, in large part, by non-Orthodox Jews.

3. This subject is treated throughout David Berger's (2001) *The Rebbe, the Messiah, and the Scandal of Orthodox Indifference.*

4. It does bear mentioning that Yaakov Horowitz, a Chabad community member based in Crown Heights, created the Small Wonder Puppet Theater in the 1980s and made available tapes of his performances via mail order.

References

1960 Technology: A timeline biography of the Rebbe. (n.d.). Retrieved May 10, 2007, from www.chabad .org/therebbe/timeline.asp?AID=62171

About Chabad-Lubavitch. (n.d.). Retrieved May 10, 2007, from http://www.chabad.org/global/about/ article_cdo/aid/36226/jewish/Overview.htm

Berger, D. (2001). *The Rebbe, the Messiah, and the scandal of Orthodox indifference.* London: Littman Library of Jewish Civilization.

Chanukah mini-series. (2007). Retrieved May 10, 2007, from www.chabad.org/kids/article.asp?AID=455798 &ShowFeedback=true#continue

Detours. (2007). Retrieved May 10, 2007, from www.chabad.org/kids/article.asp?AID=508038& ShowFeedback=true#continue

Fishkoff, S. (2003). *The Rebbe's army.* New York: Schocken.

Gabler, N. (1989). *An empire of their own: How the Jews invented Hollywood.* New York: Anchor.

Gertel, E. (2003). *Over the top Judaism.* Lanham, MD: University Press of America.

Howley, K. (2005). *Community media: People, places and communication technologies.* Cambridge, UK: Cambridge University Press.

Jenkins, H. (1992). *Textual poachers.* London: Routledge.

Kamber, M. (2000). *Ban the Web? Not Lubavitch Jews.* Retrieved May 19, 2007, from www.wired.com/ culture/lifestyle/news/2000/01/33626

Matzah: What's up with it? (2007). Retrieved May 10, 2007, from www.chabad.org/multimedia/media .asp?AID=269486&ShowFeedback=true

Obstacles. (2007). Retrieved May 10, 2007, from www.chabad.org/kids/article_cdo/aid/508038/ jewish/Chapter-4-Detours.htm#comments

Rabbi using modern medium in call for traditional values. (1983, January 23). *The New York Times,* p. 39.

Schilder, R. C. (2002, December). Napoleon's last stand. *N'shei Chabad Newslettter,* p. 58.

Schneerson, Rabbi M. M. (1990). *Likuttei Sichos* (Vol. 18). Brooklyn, NY: Kehot.

Zurawik, D. (2003). *The Jews of prime time.* Waltham, MA: Brandeis University Press.

PART IV

Community Development

In this section, contributors explore the relationship between communication and community building and maintenance. We begin with a few insights gleaned from the field of *development communication:* a subdiscipline of communication studies that has enormous relevance for community media studies. Briefly stated, development communication seeks to transform existing living conditions through communication strategies, practices, and technologies. In the aftermath of the Second World War, development communication emerged as a strategy for addressing a host of development issues—poverty reduction, literacy and basic education, disease prevention and control, and reproductive health care—and otherwise improving the quality of life for people of the so-called underdeveloped world. Following the recessions of the 1970s and 1980s, and the subsequent economic restructuring of the past two decades, community development initiatives have become commonplace in postindustrial societies as well.

Over the past 60 years, the language, practices, and objectives of development communication have changed in response to the diffusion of information and communication technologies (ICTs) and as a reflection of worldwide interest in economic regeneration, social inclusion, and community capacity-building initiatives (Craig, 2007; Fernback, 2005). As a result, the field of development communication is marked by contentious debates over the goals, methods, and efficacy of development programs. While the particulars of these debates lie outside the scope of this volume, this extensive literature addresses a number of conceptual issues—principally the theory and practice of *participatory communication*—that have had a profound influence on the study of alternative, citizens,' and community media. In the chapters that follow, contributors demonstrate the ways in which community media's participatory ethos contributes to the formation of vibrant, inclusive, and sustainable communities.

Development Communication

Development communication was initially conceived as part of a broader strategy taken up by the United States and other industrialized societies intended to promote the political and economic autonomy of newly independent states across the global South. Tracing the rise and intellectual development of the field, the communication scholar Jan Servaes (1991) observes,

> During the late 1940s, the 1950s, and the early 1960s, most development thinkers stated that the problem of "underdevelopment" or "backwardness" could be solved by a more or less mechanical application of the economic and political system in the West to countries in the Third World. (p. 55)

This observation reveals a great deal about the orientation of Western governments, aid agencies, and charitable organizations toward "developing societies" during the post-Colonial period. What's more, it highlights the shortcomings of an instrumentalist approach to community communication.

For development practitioners of that era, development was synonymous with modernization and the wholesale adoption of "modern lifestyles" by people living in "traditional societies." The trappings associated with modern living—the scientific management of agricultural and industrial sectors of the economy, the rise of consumer culture, and, significantly, the construction of systems of mass communication—were all viewed as indicators of modernization. However, this approach belied a paternalistic attitude toward developing societies and traditional ways of living. Based on questionable assumptions that developing societies were somehow "lacking" or "deficient," development workers were largely indifferent to local knowledge and tradition and all but ignored the utility that local cultural forms and practices might have for achieving development aims.

Equally important, this early approach to development communication was deeply influenced by a "transmission" model of communication that places a premium on social control, persuasion, and behavior modification. With its emphasis on message design, production, and distribution, and relative neglect of audience feedback and response, this linear model of communication privileges the sender over the receiver of a message. In this model, meanings are imposed on members of an audience rather than interpreted and constructed by members of a community. Put another way, this top-down model of communication fails to recognize the dialogic character of communication that is central to community building and maintenance.

Throughout the 1960s and 1970s, two distinct groups offered incisive critiques of development communication. The first group consisted of communication researchers and development practitioners. These critics suggested that the focus on large-scale and nationwide media campaigns overlooked a chief failing of this approach—namely, national media systems, controlled by coercive, sometimes repressive, state authorities, had limited credibility with local audiences. The perceived illegitimacy of development messages produced and distributed by centralized state authorities seriously compromised the efficacy of development campaigns.

On a more conceptual level, Everett Rogers (1974) suggested that development projects needed to recognize the value of traditional media—song and dance, storytelling, and street theater, as well as interpersonal channels of communication—in development communication. Rogers argued that development messages that combined traditional modes of communication with modern electronic and print media could help overcome resistance to development projects at the local level. This critique helped reorient development programs away from large-scale, national media and toward more localized, participatory approaches to development communication.

A second group, consisting of leftist intellectuals and cultural critics from across the global South, especially Latin America, challenged development communication on ideological grounds (Huesca, 2003). These critics argued that development projects focused on the symptoms rather than the root causes of uneven development. Furthermore, these critics charged that in the absence of substantive efforts to address the ways in which political-economic structures and arrangements perpetuate inequalities between industrial and so-called developing societies, development projects served only to increase and deepen the Third World's dependency on developed nations (Bessette, 1996). From this perspective, development communication amounted to a form of neocolonialism that used mass media as a mechanism for domination and ideological manipulation rather than as a means of liberation and empowerment.

One of the most forceful and influential critics to articulate this perspective was the Brazilian educator Paulo Freire. Freire's (1970/2006) critique focused attention on the dominant paradigm's approach to identifying and addressing development problems. Specifically, Freire questioned the efficacy of development communication projects that identified problems and offered solutions based on the observations and recommendations of outside experts. Freire's criticism underscores the problem with vertical or top-down approaches to communication that emphasize information transfer instead of local knowledge construction. In other words, Freire held that the dominant approach to development communication was dismissive of local populations and underestimated the community's potential to alter its own circumstances in an independent and autonomous fashion.

Instead, Freire (1970/2006) argued that development projects must promote dialogue, cultivate critical thinking, and stimulate self-reflexive action (*praxis*). Doing so raises the community's awareness of the wider social conditions and relations that lead to and exacerbate local development problems. Through a process of *conscientization*, communities would learn to analyze their situation, identify their needs, acquire the skills to address these issues, and organize themselves to effectively deal with these problems. In this way, Freire believed, communities would come to realize their potential to transform their everyday lives and experience.

Freire's (1970/2006) approach yields two important insights for community media studies. First, Freire recognized the value of grassroots

media for empowering marginalized individuals and groups within a local community. Grassroots and community-based media provided the resources and skills for oppressed people to not only comprehend their marginal status but also challenge and alter the circumstances of their oppression. Second, Freire's analysis foregrounds the contested character of community relations. Rather than view communities as homogeneous social entities, Freire's educational practice sought to illuminate social, economic, and cultural differences within the community.

Thus, Freire (1970/2006) sought to "politicize" community relations as a means for identifying the sources of conflict that divide interest groups and inhibit collaboration efforts. Only through the recognition and negotiation of these differences, Freire contended, could local groups work together and effectively address common interests and concerns. As the chapters in this section demonstrate, this emphasis on individual and group empowerment, the politicization of community relations, and the value and importance of participation in collective efforts continues to guide the work of community media initiatives around the world.

Participatory Communication and Community Building

The critiques outlined above provoked "a wide range of theoretical responses" that acknowledged, to one degree or another, the value of participatory approaches to development communication (Huesca, 2003, p. 213). These new perspectives held that participatory communication has distinct advantages over the "transmission" model long associated with development communication. Over time, this emphasis on participation would change the ways in which national governments, international aid agencies, and nongovernmental organizations approached development communication (Rogers, 1976). Equally important, the insights and innovations associated with participatory approaches to development communication would have enormous implications for community media theory and practice.

For instance, substantive and sustained participatory practices were deemed impractical on a large scale. Grassroots media, on the other hand, represented an effective means of amplifying and enhancing existing channels of horizontal communication within a particular region or locality. As this insight gained currency, a range of initiatives predicated on the twin pillars of *access* to communication systems and *participation* in media planning, production, and management, began to coalesce around the use of community-based media in development communication (Berrigan, 1979).

Likewise, participatory approaches proved invaluable to the production of development messages that were culturally relevant and appropriate within a specific social setting. This technique was useful for overcoming resistance to development messages that either ignored or were insensitive to local cultural values, forms, and practices. Moreover, by incorporating indigenous knowledge and traditions into development projects, development workers helped "level the playing field" between outside experts and local communities. In this way, participatory approaches to development communication "bestows the same status to indigenous knowledge as is given to 'expert or scientific' knowledge" (Protz, 1991, p. 33).

Furthermore, participatory communication provides local communities with a sense of agency and ownership of development projects. Rather than view themselves as somehow deficient or lacking in their ability to effect social change, communities could, through participatory methods, reassert and reclaim their capacity to transform their daily lives. Empowered in this fashion, local communities direct development processes on their own terms, and do so in a relevant, accountable, and sustainable fashion (e.g., Harris, 2004; Paranjape, 2007). In short, participatory communication "enables people to go from being recipients of external development to generators of their own development" (Bessette, 1996, p. 1).

Finally, participatory communication underscores the importance of "process" over "product" in the context of community communication (Higgins, 1999; Lewis & Jones, 2006). That is to say, the product—say, a documentary about a job-training program for young people—is secondary to the process that unfolds as community members work collaboratively to produce this message. In this light, the goal of participatory communication is twofold. First, participatory communication raises the community's awareness of its own resources and talents as well as its capacity to alter or transform some aspect of daily life. Second, participatory communication encourages communities to act in concert and to do so in a deliberate, conscious, and self-perpetuating fashion that builds and maintains social relations over time.

Here, we should note the similarity between a process view of communication, one that values dialogue and promotes horizontal communication within a particular location or culture, and James Carey's (1988) ritual model of communication. In contrast to the transmission model of communication, which views communication as a linear, hierarchical method of information transfer across space, a ritual model understands communication as a collective activity in which participants (re)produce knowledge, (re)create meaning, and (re)construct communal relations and collective identity over time. In sum, the emphasis on "process" associated with participatory communication underscores the fundamental and decisive relationship between communication and community.

From a theoretical perspective, then, participatory communication promotes greater participation in public life, stimulates creative problem solving, and fosters a sense of community cohesion that acknowledges difference—difference that can be overcome, but not necessarily erased, through shared decision making and collective action. In local settings, however, participatory communication is a far more complex sociocultural process: one that demands critical scrutiny of actual practices.

For instance, one of the most perplexing issues confronting advocates of participatory communication centers on the level of participation in media planning, design, production, and management afforded by community media organizations (Gumucio Dagron, 2001a). Early efforts to promote local participation in development communication were limited to the use of audience surveys and focus groups. While this approach helped development workers create more relevant and effective development messages, it served a largely administrative function that, in the end, reinforced rather than dismantled the hierarchical division between media producers and media audiences. Other approaches to participation use community members as the subjects of news reports and documentaries or occasionally feature locals as talent in fictional or entertainment-style programs while leaving the design, production, and distribution of media messages to "communication professionals."

More ambitious approaches to participatory communication put the tools of media production—microphones, audio and video recorders, computers, and the like—into the hands of community members (e.g., Manyozo, 2007; White, 2003). Typically, this approach incorporates an intensive media-training component that provides nonprofessional media makers with basic production skills. One noteworthy example of this approach is *The Palestinian Diaries:* a television program that aired throughout the Middle East and portions of western Europe in the early 1990s (Kuttab, 1994). A collaborative project supervised by Al Quds Television Production (ATP), the documentary featured footage shot by residents of the Palestinian-occupied territories during the first intifada (popular uprising) from 1987 through 1993.

At yet another level, participatory communication includes instances in which community members have a role in the management and decision-making processes of grassroots media outlets. Thus, participatory communication also refers to community owned and operated media outlets established for the explicit purpose of facilitating community communication and promoting local development initiatives. For instance, the "participatory radios" of El Salvador are self-organized media outlets that have proved highly effective in bringing new social actors into the public sphere in the aftermath of that nation's long civil war (Agosta, 2007).

All this is to suggest that constructing an adequate, let alone comprehensive, definition of "participation" can prove to be a daunting, if elusive, task (Carpentier & De Cleen, 2008; Gumucio Dagron, 2001b). Instead of trying to develop hard-and-fast rules for what constitutes "genuine" or "authentic" forms of participation, development practitioners, communication scholars, and media workers are better served by conceptualizing participation along a *continuum.* In doing so, we can explore the levels and degree of participation afforded by a particular media organization within a specific geographic location. Herein lies the heuristic value of community media: They are sites for empirically grounded analyses of participatory communication in a variety of sociocultural settings.

In other words, instead of applying a generic definition of participation across disparate cases, this tack focuses our energies and attention on the structural, economic, political, and cultural factors that enable and constrain participatory communication within a particular place (e.g., Daley & James, 1992; Williamson, 1991). Indeed, attending to these factors, at the level of the local community, allows us to critically evaluate the character and quality of participatory communication in the era of global communication. And by refusing to give in to the temptation of "fixing" a standard definition of participation on the limitless variety of community media initiatives found across the globe, we avoid the grievous error of excluding "many interesting communication processes" that do not adhere to "the blueprint definition [of participatory communication]" (Gumucio Dagron, 2001a, p. 4).

In the chapters that follow, contributors demonstrate how community media's participatory ethos promotes a more inclusive and representative local media culture. Likewise, the following chapters illustrate how, through the use of participatory communication practices and techniques, community media create spaces in which diverse, sometimes competing interests can work collaboratively to achieve common ends. As we shall see, despite the geographic and cultural diversity of the initiatives discussed below, we can detect in each the value of community media for achieving a number of development aims: education, economic regeneration, social inclusion, and problem solving.

Chapter 16 maps out important distinctions in the goals and objectives of media education programs available through community media organizations across the United Kingdom. Taking a practitioner's perspective, Shawn Sobers argues that in an era of digitization, convergence technologies, and user-generated content, policy makers, educators, and media access organizations must reconceptualize the relationship between community media and media education. In light of the new technologies, cultural forms, and practices associated with Web 2.0, Sobers wonders if "community media" remains a useful framework for thinking about perennial issues of media access, ownership, and control. Sobers' tentative conclusion is that community media's emphasis on participatory communication holds the key for ensuring the future relevance and viability of the community media sector.

In Chapter 17, Sourayan Mookerjea describes the creative output and organizational culture of a women's video collective, the Community Media Trust, in rural India. Drawing on insights from participatory communication, subaltern studies, and autonomous media practice, Mookerjea argues that the video work produced and distributed by Dalit women farmers—a historically marginalized group within Indian society—is inextricably bound up in the women's wider struggles for social-political-economic autonomy. Throughout, Mookerjea highlights the distinct character of the women's video practice: a work culture that leverages the women's local knowledge and oral traditions with the expressive and communicative potential of grassroots video production.

Our next selection (Chapter 18) considers the efficacy of using ICTs for purposes of economic regeneration in a postindustrial setting. Specifically, Philip Denning assesses the impact of new media technologies on the working class, coalfield community of Craigmillar in Edinburgh, Scotland. Drawing on Paulo Freire's insights on development communication strategies and practices, Denning calls for a more culturally and contextually sensitive approach to community development in the information age. Throughout, Denning contends that residents of Craigmillar are using new media technologies to ensure that neighborhood redevelopment schemes reflect working-class values, interests, and culture.

The final chapter in this section (Chapter 19) details the participatory processes used in the production of disease prevention and control messages in Accra, the capital city of the West African nation of Ghana. Aku Kwamie observes the shortcomings of HIV/AIDS prevention messages predicated on behavior modification. Throughout, Kwamie calls our attention to various levels of community participation that proved most effective in the production of social change messages designed to overcome the stigma of HIV/AIDS. As with the previous chapters, Kwamie finds that participatory approaches to development communication yield important insights into the relationship between communicative forms and practices and community building and maintenance.

References

Agosta, D. (2007). Constructing civil society, supporting local development: A case study of community radio in postwar El Salvador. *Democratic Communiqué, 21*(1), 4–26.

Berrigan, F. (1979). *Community communications: The role of community media in development.* Paris: UNESCO.

Bessette, G. (1996). *Development communication in West and Central Africa: Toward a research and intervention agenda.* Retrieved November 3, 2007, from http://idl-bnc.idrc.ca/dspace/handle/123456789/21110

Carey, J. (1988). *Communication as culture: Essays on media and society.* New York: Routledge.

Carpentier, N., & De Cleen, B. (Eds.). (2008). *Participation and media production: Critical reflections on content creation.* Cambridge, UK: Cambridge Scholars.

Craig, G. (2007). Community capacity-building: Something old, something new . . . ? *Critical Social Policy, 27*(3), 335–359.

Daley, P. J., & James, B. (1992). Ethnic broadcasting in Alaska: The failure of a participatory model. In S. Riggins (Ed.), *Ethnic minority media: An international perspective* (pp. 23–43). Newbury Park, CA: Sage.

Fernback, J. (2005). Information technology, networks and community voices: Social inclusion for urban regeneration. *Information, Communication & Society, 8*(4), 482–502.

Freire, P. (2006). *Pedagogy of the oppressed.* New York: Continuum Books. (Original work published 1970)

Gumucio Dagron, A. (2001a, May). *Call me impure: Myths and paradigms of participatory communication.* Paper presented at the International Communication Association Preconference on Alternative Media, Washington, DC.

Gumucio Dagron, A. (2001b). *Making waves: Stories of participatory communication for social change.* New York: Rockefeller Foundation.

Harris, U. S. (2004). From coconut wireless to the global knowledge society: Internet development in Fiji. *Convergence: The International Journal of Research Into New Media Technologies, 10,* 106–113.

Higgins, J. W. (1999). Community TV and the vision of media literacy, social action and empowerment. *Journal of Broadcasting and Electronic Media, 43*(4), 625–644.

Huesca, R. (2003). Participatory approaches to communication for development. In B. Mody (Ed.), *International and development communication:* *A 21st century perspective* (pp. 209–226). Thousand Oaks, CA: Sage.

Kuttab, D. (1994). Palestinian diaries: Grassroots TV production in the occupied territories. In T. Dowmunt (Ed.), *Channels of Resistance: Global Television and Local Empowerment* (pp. 138–145). London: British Film Institute.

Lewis, P. M., & Jones, S. (Eds.). (2006). *From the margins to the cutting edge: Community media and empowerment.* Cresskill, NJ: Hampton Press.

Manyozo, L. (2007). Method and practice in participatory radio: Rural radio forums in Malawi. *African Journalism Studies, 28*(1/2), 11–29.

Paranjape, N. (2007). Community media: Local is focal. *Community Development Journal, 42*(4), 459–469.

Protz, M. (1991). Distinguishing between "alternative" and "participatory" models of video production. In N. Thede & A. Ambrosi (Eds.), *Video the changing world* (pp. 31–39). Montreal, Quebec, Canada: Black Rose.

Rogers, E. M. (1974). Communication in development. *Annals of the American Academy of Political and Social Science, 412,* 44–54.

Rogers, E. M. (1976). Communication and development: The passing of a dominant paradigm. *Communication Research, 3,* 213–240.

Servaes, J. (1991). Toward a new perspective for communication and development. In F. L. Casmir (Ed.), *Communication in development* (pp. 51–85). Norwood, NJ: Ablex.

White, S. (2003). Participatory video: A process that transforms the self and other. In S. White (Ed.), *Participatory video: Images that transform and empower* (pp. 63–101). Thousand Oaks, CA: Sage.

Williamson, H. A. (1991). The Fogo Process: Development support communications in Canada and the developing world. In F. L. Casmir (Ed.), *Communication in development* (pp. 270–287). Norwood, NJ: Ablex.

CHAPTER 16

Positioning Education Within Community Media

Shawn Sobers

Finding an Identity

Outside formal educational institutions, driving forward the agenda of how media technologies are creatively applied in the learning process are the film makers, artists, youth workers, producers, and other facilitators working on educational projects in the sector loosely known as community media. Existing writing and research on community media activity seldom, if ever, acknowledge the differences in motivations and aims between broadcast activities such as community radio and television initiatives, and more direct educational activities such as creative workshops, media clubs, and training schemes. They often combine the two together with general talk of "media democracy" and "access." I feel that it is necessary, however, to treat the broadcast and educational elements of community media as distinct in order to get a more accurate insight into the nature of the sector and to understand what it can achieve as a whole. This is especially true in the current climate, where new technologies have allowed community media activities to grow widespread and become increasingly varied in their approach and motivation.

In the context of *the personal is political,* there is no ideological distinction between the concepts of having the right to vote, the right to own your own home, the right to equality in the workplace, and the right to be in control of your own representation in the media (Nigg & Wade, 1980, p. 7). In practice, however, when dealing with the range of community media activities on a wider scale, it soon becomes clear that the political agenda of much of this activity is not always worn as clearly on the sleeve as it is often stated in academic analysis. The principles of media *democracy, access,* and *inclusion* underlie the majority, if not all, of the work happening in the sector, but in some cases, they are more overt than others (Downing, 2003; Harding, 2005; Miskelly, Cater, Fleuriot, Williams, & Wood, 2005, p. 5).

Based on my own observations of activities happening under the "community media" banner, the following diagram is a map of the sector based on the notion of the balances between overt and subtle intention. This positioning forms the overriding structural framework of the sector, with its various activities categorized into two main areas: *communication platforms* and *educational activity.* Each of those sections is subdivided into two further areas:

community broadcast and *media democracy,* and *media education* and *media literacy,* respectively (Table 16.1).

A more detailed description of the main areas of emphasis within the community media sector follows.

Communication Platforms

This area of emphasis is concerned with broadcasting messages (productions, text) from those who may have been otherwise voiceless with no access to mainstream media outlets.

- *Community broadcast:* structures and activities within the community media sector that most directly emulate the traditional media industry platforms, albeit with a different "voice" (e.g., community radio and television stations and neighborhood newspapers; community versions of mainstream media broadcast

Table 16.1   Community Media Activity Framework

Community Media Sector (main areas of emphasis)			
Communication Platforms		**Educational Activity**	
Community broadcast (Community versions of industry structures and models)	Media democracy (Overt ideological use of media tools)	Media education (Activities with direct primary aim of feeding media industries)	Media literacy (media in education) (Activities with primary aim of enhancing transferable skills)
Types Community radio Internet radio Community TV Wireless broadcasting Pirate radio Community newspapers	Types Political blogs Underground investigative filming Campaigns (alternative voices) Antiglobalization journalism Political opposition radio and press Indymedia	Types Training Media workshops Young people film festivals Traineeships Targeted recruitment of identified groups Short film projects Skill development	Types Summer schools in creative media production Youth projects with marginalized communities Widening participation, social exclusion, social regeneration activities Citizenship (i.e., using media as a tool to find out about social issue) Using video as a consultation tool (filmed by the participants of the consultation) Projects with schools (using media across the curriculum)

◄──────── MEDIA LITERACY ────────►

structures) (Howley, 2005, pp. 4, 83; Rennie, 2006, pp. 22, 51).

- *Media democracy:* structures that have been established to consciously undermine traditional media, to redress the balance between the reporters and the reported. Media democracy is the most overtly political of the two areas in communication platforms and is also the work most accurately described by the term *alternative media* (Rennie, 2006, p. 9). Media democracy also includes activists who film anticapitalism campaigns, environmental protests, and so on and publish pamphlets highlighting specific political and multinational controversial business practices, and so on (Gillmor, 2004, p. 144; Steven, 2003, pp. 71, 127).

It is work carried out on these *communication platforms* that most commonly gets identified as community media in general discussions of the topic and in academic analysis of the sector.

Educational Activity

This area of emphasis is concerned with the pedagogic or sociological process of the learning involved when making media messages.

- *Media education:* educational activity carried out with the direct motivation of aiming to inspire the participants to become aspiring creative media practitioners. It aims to give participants skills at operating media equipment to give them confidence in making their own productions and also to boost skills to raise the participants' potential to enter careers in media (e.g., practical video and animation workshops for young people, media clubs at schools, short film production summer schools). It includes activities that look to raise awareness about media production in the hope that a new generation of media producers/writers, actors, and so on, are being inspired.

- *Media literacy (media in education):* in many cases, these activities can seem to an external observer to be exactly the same as media education, but, vitally, the aims and objectives are different. Rather than trying to inspire the participants about media for media's sake, *media literacy* aims to encourage participants to use media tools as a means of raising the levels of other areas of their development (often by stealth), such as communication skills, literacy, confidence, decision making, knowledge of subject, and so on (Goldfarb, 2002). Any interest on the part of a participant to work in the media industry as a result of that activity would be a fortunate and welcome by-product rather than a priority target result. A project example: working with a group of young people from "challenging" and "disenfranchised" inner-city neighborhoods to make a short documentary or drama about their area or issues that they feel are important in their lives. In the process, participants in the project work as a team, thinking creatively about themselves and their surroundings; they look for the positive elements of their neighborhood and analyze the negatives. The aims of such a video project would be to empower the young people to open their eyes to their surroundings from a questioning perspective rather than passively living, unaware, without making informed choices using media as the tool of that empowerment and agent of advocacy.

Across the community media sector as a whole, community broadcast and educational activities alike, the aim for participants to begin to think less like consumers and more like producers is to embrace the core principles of media literacy: "the ability to access, understand and create communications in a variety of contexts" (Ofcom, 2006). Rapid advancements in media technology have seen *traditional literacy* and media literacy become so entwined that they are inseparable (Bazalgette, 2005). In fact, what is thought to be traditional literacy is actually media literacy that was defined in a past age and is as important as it has ever been (Sobers, 2005). To resist the fact that texts are now as much time-based as they are literary is a denial that can only last so long. Revolutions of any kind are rarely fast, and educational revolutions take place at snail's pace.

This assessment of the community media sector in relation to its main areas of emphasis has led me to construct and work with the following definition that, I feel, embraces the distinct elements of the related areas of activity.

> A loose structure of independent agencies and individuals working on media-related broadcast, transmission, and educational activities at a community level. The work happening in the community media sector can generally be divided into *communication platforms* and *educational activities,* with the former being primarily concerned with providing access to broadcast/transmission platforms and the latter with access to production equipment, skills, and promoting the educational potential of the participant group.

In the terms of this overview, community media activity is not a closed seal, and it is acknowledged that there are crossover and individual nuances in every case. But still, it is the prime motivating factors behind activities that have informed the framework of this mapping structure. From this definition, the main area that I will be concentrating on in this chapter for analysis will be the work coming under the banner of *educational activities.*

The Potentials of Impact

Measuring levels of impact of any given creative endeavor is a problematic and complex task (Buckingham, Fraser, & Sefton-Green, 2000), though it is a common pedagogic understanding that "to fail to assess is to fail to teach" (Best, 1992, p. 75). For facilitators to accurately get a sense of the appropriateness of the activity they are running, there needs to be an understanding of the motivations of the participants involved. There is a stark difference in usefulness, however, between generating information about the participants to please the agendas of funding organizations and having the actual facilitators themselves conduct some *soft* analysis in the early stages of a project to inform the appropriate levels of project delivery.

Table 16.2 contains data collected on the first day of a 1-week *media literacy* project I co-ran called Channel Zer0 during the school summer holidays of 2003.[2] The aim of the project was to engage local young people in journalistic video and radio production as a means of connecting them with local stories and the concerns of their community and also (maybe more important) to give them something meaningful to do during their school holiday. The project was funded by the city council and a local educational organization, and it had in-kind support from the BBC (British Broadcasting Corporation). Table 16.2 highlights the motivations that brought the young people onto Channel Zer0 in the first place.[3]

With only 38% of participants interested in gaining skills to enter the media industry, a balance needed to be struck in the delivery between specialist industry training and the wider set of looser interests that would appeal to the majority. Furthermore, breakdowns showing ages, gender, ethnicity, academic achievements, parents' employment and economic status, and so on would highlight other statistics that may or may not be of use to the facilitators, though these data are commonly used by funders to justify investing in such activities. At the end of each financial year, these statistics are fed into the number-crunching machines of funding bodies, presented in the annual reports, and used as evidence of the positive impact that their funding allocations have had on

Table 16.2   Motivations of Participants

Aspirations to Work in Media Production as a Future Career	Fun Holiday Activity (could as easily have been sports, etc.)	Came With Friend or Family Member With No Particular Agenda	Was Interested in Local Community Issues and Had Aspirations in Non-Media-Related Careers
Participant A	Participant G	Participant L	Participant P
Participant B	Participant H	Participant M	
Participant C	Participant I	Participant N	
Participant D	Participant J	Participant O	
Participant E	Participant K		
Participant F			

the community. Meanwhile, the small community media outfits with no core funding are forever trying to stay financially afloat, looking for the next pot of funding for the next project, and the work piles up while the capacity shrinks, again knocking on the door of the funding body. Such fragmented working landscapes are all too common in this sector, and the cry for sustainability is a loud and frustrated one. This frustration is not surprising for a sector that has to operate in a hand-to-mouth manner, counter to the sustainable development and regeneration it seeks to address. Working within these stifling constraints, each project in its own right therefore needs to have built-in structures that attempt to maximize sustainability for the participants to elongate moments of impact of positive experience (even if behind the scenes the organizations themselves are simultaneously barricading up the business structures for their own survival). Working within this turbulent climate, the project model is key (see Figure 16.1, Stage 1). After the participants of Channel Zer0 worked through the preproduction idea development phase (represented here as a mind map), the productions began and the work was screened. The arrow from the projector back to the mind map represents how, in many cases, this is the end of a project. The work gets screened to friends and

family, all applaud, the project ends. The participants go back to their lives and the facilitators go on to the next project with different funding. After the work is (it is hoped) duplicated and sent to the participants, the master edit gathers dust on a shelf. This is a pessimistic but sadly very real assessment of how things often actually are.

Now look at Stage 2. The audience are now considered. Who are they and how can they help increase the impact? In the case of Channel Zer0, the audience consisted of not only friends and family but also council members, teachers, police officers, and anybody else in the neighborhood who could affect change. The screening event included a discussion session between the young people and audience members to talk about the ideas contained in the journalistic pieces in more detail. (The series of films and radio pieces included investigations into a wide variety of topics, including tolerance between religious groups, racism in the local media, lack of provision for young people, youth talent and role models, and an exploration into Jamaican "Yardie" culture. All the topics were chosen by the young people themselves.) The studio-style discussions with the audience generated more ideas, which eventually led to more funding, and the cycle continued aiming to decrease the chance of so many "Lost

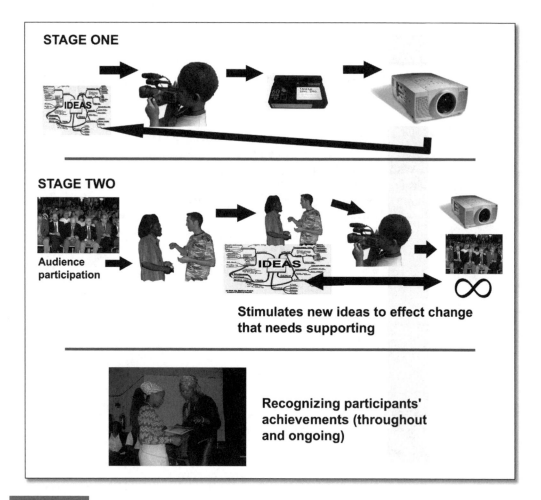

Figure 16.1 Stages of Channel Zer0

Contact" entries as seen in Table 16.3 and increasing the chance of the participants staying engaged and (it is hoped) working toward positive futures, whether media related or not.

To maintain this level of engagement obviously needs much support and commitment, and it bucks the trend of the stop/start tendency that so many fragmented projects have. In classic adventure stories, discrete Pacific islands are generally abandoned and left to ruin. Everyone who works in community work knows (even if they may not like to admit it) that, likewise, participant groups can also be cast away and left to fend for themselves when the funding dries up.

Jumping ahead 5 years, where are the participants of Channel Zer0 now?

In 2007, 5 years after this Channel Zer0 project, I conducted interviews with Participants A and B and also with participants from other projects for my current PhD research. I wanted to gain an insight into how they talked about the experiences and whether they saw these projects as having any impact on their future life choices. Among other things, the interviews highlighted the deep level of ownership participants can have of projects they take part in, and how they make connections with their own personal histories, sense of identity, and values.

Table 16.3   Participants Beyond the Project

Participant	Before the Initial Contact Did the Participant			Since Project A, Has the Participant Been Involved on Any Media Projects With the Same Organization?	What They Are Doing Now
	Work With Organization Before?	Have Any Prior Hands-On Media Experience?	Have Any Prior Community Involvement?		
A	No	No	Yes	Yes	University on media course and also a DJ and steering group member for community radio station
B	No	No	No	Yes	Freelance media work as a presenter and non-media-related part-time employment
C	No	Yes	No	Yes	Youth worker for community music organization
D	Yes	Yes	Yes	No	On a media and music production course at College
E	No	No	No	Yes	Various, including media course at college, youth work, involvement in community radio, non-media-related employment and modeling
F	Yes	No	No	Yes	Drama course at college
G	No	No	No	Yes	Still at school
H	No	No	No	Yes	Still at school
I	No	No	No	Yes	Still at school

| Participant | Before the Initial Contact Did the Participant | | | Since Project A, Has the Participant Been Involved on Any Media Projects With the Same Organization? | What They Are Doing Now |
	Work With Organization Before?	Have Any Prior Hands-On Media Experience?	Have Any Prior Community Involvement?		
J	No	No	No	Yes	Media course at college
K	No	No	No	Yes	Lost contact
L	No	No	No	No	A couple of years after project had a child. Now working part-time in non-media-related employment. Has recently got back in touch with project facilitators seeking media related work
M	No	No	No	No	Lost contact
N	No	No	No	No	Lost contact
O	No	No	No	No	Had a child after completing drama and performance college course
P	Yes	No	No	Yes	Graduated from university in non-media-related subject and now full-time employed in the discipline studied

As stated by Participant B,

Throughout my life I've always had people dictating to me; "You do this" or "do that" or "do it this way," "do it that way." There's always been a way to do it. But with [Channel Zer0] it was my way.

The interviews also showed how participants can think very differently about the idea of sustainability. Responses were more about the relationships they had built up with the facilitators and peers and feeling comfortable to ring us for advice on a school project, popping in the office to use the Internet or to ask for a reference for a job, and so on. It was that sense of ad hoc continuity that participants valued in a sustainable framework, that people were willing to be there when they needed them, and not necessarily the possibility of there being more media activities on the horizon. Another theme that was strong in the interviews was how aware they were of the impact of the transferable skills they had acquired.

As stated by Participant A,

> It helped me with confidence, big time. Because I had to deal with people quite different to me, so it helped a lot when I was going to college to study media, and when I started to work part time as well. Helped with dealing with customers. If I didn't do Channel Zer0 I probably would have given up on media, it's simple. Full stop.

This highlights why, in the city of Bristol, United Kingdom, where this project took place, in approximately the past 6 years there has been a rapidly growing interest in funding these types of activities by mainstream services for purposes such as education and social regeneration and also by support organizations for housing, drugs awareness, and so on. A large vibrant city, Bristol has been troubled in recent years by poor educational achievements. In 2006, the city ranked 141 out of 148 mainland authorities in educational standards for 11- to 16-year-olds in the whole of England. Partly as a result of this, informal educational activities are extremely rife and varied in the city. Social-inclusion agencies, even more than the traditional media-funding bodies, have seen the benefit of using public funds to deliver hands-on media production as the means by which to keep young people actively engaged in constructive activity, away from some of the more destructive temptations on offer to them elsewhere. Community media, of course, cannot be expected to tackle and solve all the ills of society by itself, and building strong working relationships with partner agencies is key. Developments in how digital technologies are

suggested to be used for community engagement, though, are not always moving in the same direction, and this is why community media advocates need a keen sense of "who we are," "what we do," and "why we do it" to reaffirm core values of the practice. In cities across western Europe and North America, increasingly there are doctors' surgeries, council offices, community centers, schools, libraries, and other neighborhood servicesusing online forums, blogs, and other digital means to communicate with the residents about local issues while at the same time cutting costs for actual, real-life personnel. It seems that the building up of digital communities within geographic ones is the way to keep people connected, though at the cost of actual civic participation (De Zengotita, 2005).

Old Dust, New Challenges, New Opportunities

Advances in media and communication technologies have allowed a broader range of access to information than at any other time in history, with many now one step closer to the *means of representation* (albeit at a domestic and not a professional level); the Internet allows even wider access to the means of exhibition and distribution networks. This generalization is, of course, based on the position in North America and west Europe. It is acknowledged, however, that large parts of the world, particularly in Africa, South Asia, and the Arab States are still on the deficit side of the digital divide (Steven, 2003). These technological advancements *for the few* raise more questions for community media than answers.

What is now actually meant by the term *community media* in a time when one can make a video in an afternoon, upload it straight from a camera linked to a computer, and have a global audience within 10 minutes? What does community media mean in a time when your 500 best friends are from all over the globe, and you chose each other as friends based on seemingly common interests and values, even though none of you have ever met in the flesh or heard each other's voices? And what does community media mean in a time when mainstream mass media are attempting to become more localized and tailored by having an even bigger footprint online, trying to look like the same alternative media that were reacting against them.

On the surface, one could assume that community media had achieved its dream of democratization of the media in witnessing an era of media production, exhibition, and distribution moving closer to being controlled by "the people," but in most senses, nothing has changed. It is more a case of a *new mass media* landscape being established on Web 2.0 that has the outward appearance of access, participation, and democratization but in fact is no different from the traditional mass media landscape in terms of its economic power base. In the mid-1990s, the large commercial companies (department stores, etc.) and multinationals began to populate (and arguably take over) cyberspace in the first Internet battle between individuals and corporations. Now, mass media organizations are positioning to have a greater presence on Web 2.0, an eye to capitalizing on the second revolution of Internet ownership, but they may already be too late. In 2005, Rupert Murdoch's News Corporation bought the social networking site MySpace, but the price paid was overshadowed by the price that Google, itself a *dot-com* company, paid on buying YouTube for a record amount. On October 9, 2006, Google acquired YouTube for $1.65 billion in an all-stock transaction. Google is currently reported to be the world's largest media company. Who is David and who is Goliath is no longer so clear.

So where do community media sit within this new media landscape, and why are we still needed by "the community" if they can now do it for themselves? A large number of educational projects are being commissioned by schools, youth clubs, senior citizens' groups, and youth

engagement organizations to carry out facilitated projects with their client groups. The incentives for bringing in external media professionals are numerous, including being able to use new methods of engagement outside the teacher/group leader's capabilities and also to access expertise in participatory media production with high-quality final results that can be enjoyed. Part of what makes us human is our love of the rewards of social interactions with others, and community media and arts are long-serving advocates of harnessing our participative tendencies for positive creative outcomes (Harding, 2005).

The challenges now for community media educationalists are to evidence the value and impact of participative/facilitative approaches of learning and engagement and to convince decision makers to ensure that the sector is not passed over in policy decisions and changes in the political landscape. These are also the challenges faced by the stakeholders of the communication platforms—to avoid being drowned by the sea of individual voices now across the digital airwaves.

There is no doubt that Web 2.0 holds some exciting possibilities for all areas of community media, and the community media sector is best placed to harness its full potential. But, as a word of caution, new technologies can simply put a new face on an old problem. Now, rather than video tapes on the shelves of production companies gathering dust, the new trend is to upload the video onto YouTube for all the world to see and let it sit there online, gathering *Cyber Dust*. Web 2.0 highlights why we who work on a practical level in community media want it both ways in the *process versus product* debate, as our activity was never about just one thing. Participatory processes are, if anything, holistic. Web 2.0 professes to be all about access and democratization but, in reality, is just providing access to platforms in a galaxy of a million and one other platforms. So access to what exactly? Democratization of what really? The claims of Web 2.0 are only relevant if you happen to have a computer with a broadband connection. The majority of people in the world have no such luxury.

The "democratization of media" agenda was about so much more than access to media platforms. It was about not only the opportunity to stand on a soapbox and shout into the wilderness but about to empowering people to know how strategic use of the soapbox placed in the right relation to the right audience can enable one to effect change in one's corner of the world. With access also comes representation, and this cuts two paths. Postcolonial and feminist calls for representation were both about seeing more "authentic" voices and narratives reflected in mainstream media's production output, in parallel with the more crucial representation of different faces in the boardrooms. The *community media project,* therefore, is not only to serve the communication platforms and encourage participation in educational activities but also to agitate mainstream services and encourage participation in civil society and decision making. Web 2.0 provides an effective bag in which to carry ideas, but it is the facilitation of the participatory process that will continue to ensure that critical questioning, participant-centered learning, and pastoral conversation take place in the journey toward filling up the bag, not just marveling at its contents.

As simply stated by Participant B,

[The project] helped me get defined as a person. Your interpersonal skills are grasped and sharpened. Because when you're in there you have to discipline yourself, you have to listen, you have to watch, you have to imagine. Your imagination is something that nobody can ever take away from you. Same as the skills you've learnt. They might be able to take the money and they might be able to take the location but they won't take away what you've learnt. And that's what's important and that's what should be understood definitely.

Absolute definitions of any social or cultural phenomenon are problematic, and with regard the construction of a definition of community media, it is acknowledged that there are some "excellent arguments for avoiding tidy definitions" (Downing, 2003). I feel, however, that the current climate of such swift evolutions of digital technologies highlights the need for hands-on practitioners working in the sector to take a step back, to reassess what we do, why we do it, how we do it, and the impact it can truly have.

Notes

1. An observation rather than criticism of current research. It highlights the need for further research into the pedagogical aspects of the sector.

2. This project was coordinated by Firstborn Creatives, the community media production company I co-run with colleagues Rob Mitchell and Louise Lynas.

3. All data in Table 16.2 (p. 192) were collected verbally during the first hours of the project via informal conversations and were mentally noted. This conversational approach to data collection was preferred to questionnaires as such a "rigid" method would have set up a formal atmosphere that we wanted to avoid.

References

Bazalgette, C. (2005). Media literacy for all? In *Implementing media literacy: Empowerment, participation and responsibility* (pp. 59–61). London: Westminster Media Forum Seminar Series.

Best, D. (1992). *The rationality of feeling: Understanding the arts in education.* London: Falmer Press Library on Aesthetic Education.

Buckingham, D., Fraser, P., & Sefton-Green, J. (2000). Making the grade: Evaluating student production in media studies. In J. Sefton-Green & R. Sinker (Eds.), *Evaluating creativity* (p. 129). London: Routledge.

De Zengotita, T. (2005). *Mediated: How the media shapes your world and the way we live in it.* London: Bloomsbury.

Downing, J. D. H. (2003). Audiences and readers of alternative media: The absent lure of the virtually unknown. *Media, Culture & Society, 25,* 625–645.

Gillmor, D. (2004). *We the media: Grassroots journalism by the people, for the people.* Cambridge, UK: O'Reilly Books.

Goldfarb, B. (2002). *Visual pedagogy: Media cultures in and beyond the classroom.* Durham, NC: Duke University Press.

Harding, A. (2005). *Magic moments: Collaboration between artists and young people.* London: Black Dog.

Howley, K. (2005). *Community media: People, places and communication technologies.* Cambridge, UK: Cambridge University Press.

Miskelly, C., Cater, K., Fleuriot, C., Williams, M., & Wood, L. (2005). *Locating story: Collaborative community-based located media production.* Retrieved April 8, 2009, from http://tinyurl.com/ypf9ku

Nigg, H., & Wade, G. (1980). *Community media: Community communication in the UK: Video, local TV, film and photography.* Zurich, Switzerland: Regenbogen-Verlag.

Ofcom. (2006). *Media literacy audit: Report of media literacy amongst young children.* London: Author.

Rennie, E. (2006). *Community media: A global introduction.* Lanham, MD: Rowman & Littlefield.

Sobers, S. (2005). Media literacy in community contexts, and sharing experience with the mainstream. In *Implementing media literacy: Empowerment, participation and responsibility* (pp. 84–86). London: Westminster Media Forum Seminar Series.

Steven, P. (2003). *The no-nonsense guide to global media.* Oxford, UK: Verso.

CHAPTER 17

Dalitbahujan Women's Autonomous Video

Sourayan Mookerjea

This chapter examines the video-based media of a group of Dalit women farmers from Andhra Pradesh, India, who belong to a media cooperative they have named the Community Media Trust (CMT). They have been active as videographers for 7 years now and have made more than 100 videos. Their work is regularly screened in their own communities and in farming villages throughout the district of Medak through an institution of their own creation, the annual traveling biodiversity *jathara*. Their videos circulate nationally and internationally in VCD format through development and environmentalist social movement solidarity networks and have been screened at major Indian congresses bringing together environmental scientists, agricultural policy makers, nongovernmental organizations, and subaltern farmers. All their videos are politically engaged: Agricultural, environmental, and gender issues,

particularly pertaining to biodiversity, seed sovereignty, and subaltern women's empowerment and dignity, are constant themes of their work. The videos these women have made range in genre from point-of-view documentaries, grassroots investigative journalism, and promotional videos showcasing development projects they have been involved in to participatory research videos for some of these projects in collaboration with the Deccan Development Society (DDS) and the network of *sangham* (agricultural cooperatives) to which the women belong.

My account of the CMT's video work is based on participant observation and interviews I carried out with members of the CMT (C. Narsamma, E. Manjula, B. Nagamma, I. Mallamma, Z. Punyamma, and H. Laxmi) and the secretary and founding member of the DDS, P. V. Satheesh, in December 2005. In addition to these interviews, I was able to watch and study almost the CMT's entire catalog of productions.

Author's Note: I wish to express my deepest thanks to the members of the Community Media Trust, to my host and translator, Mr. Murthy, and to all the staff at the Deccan Development Society in both Pastapur and Hyderabad for their gracious assistance and cooperation. I also want to thank Dr. Gail Faurschou, Dr. Stephen Crocker, and Ashok Kumbamu for their assistance with carrying out this research. This research was funded by a research fellowship from the Indo-Canada Shastri Institute and a grant from the Social Sciences and Humanities Research Council of Canada. I thank them also for their support. Responsibility for any missteps remains my own.

Over the years, the women of the CMT have pursued what they understand to be autonomous media. This quest is, however, one part of a larger political-existential project involving their pursuit of a range of autonomies: over food production, access to seeds and other natural resources, markets, and, through all these, autonomy in their livelihoods and for their community's future. Their struggle for autonomous media cannot be understood apart from their struggles for these other autonomies. It is the connections between their experiments with developing an autonomous medium and these various other forms of autonomy that is extraordinary about their media practice; for this reason, it is this aspect of their media that deserves greater critical attention. These connections have led to a media practice that introduces a new dialectic with regard to the distinction between "product video" and "process video." In this regard, the CMT's experiments with autonomous video both negates participatory video (PV) and sublates it into a more complex and radically effective political form. This chapter, then, will describe the key features of this dialectic.

Subaltern Autonomy and Autonomous Media

The Dalit farmers of Medak are among the most marginalized of agricultural communities in a region where farming is generally a precarious way of life beset by numerous unforgiving impediments and subordinated to distant political forces. The domination of Indian agriculture has a long history, but the dependency of the Indian farmer on world-scale politics and globalized markets begins with the transformation of Indian agriculture from being primarily subsistence and regional food production into plantation and cash cropping for imperial export under British rule. In postcolonial times, the situation of Indian agriculture has been more complicated.

As Green Revolution "modernization" of agriculture was pursued in postcolonial India, farmers increasingly became dependent on a national network of agricultural research institutes, public authorities, and private companies as well as the technocratic expertise embodied by this apparatus of agricultural management. This dependency has two crucial aspects to it that are both fronts of struggle in the *sangham* women's quest for autonomy. There is, on the one hand, a dependency based on the access to key farm inputs, especially seeds and fertilizer, as seeds bred by research institutes and private companies displace those that used to be collected and saved by farmers themselves. Along with industrially produced, petrochemical-based fertilizers, seeds and pesticides would also have to be purchased. On the other hand, these new modern components of agriculture now require monopolized instructions on their use that immediately disqualify and render obsolete whatever agroecological knowledge farmers have been traditionally taught across generations. During the 1980s, agribusiness corporations increasingly gained access to markets created by this managerial complex (Patel & Müller, 2004, p. 24). With official liberalization in 1991, U.S.- and European-based multinationals have gained greater control over agricultural policy. These regulatory changes consequently struck at what little autonomy the small farmer retained after the reorganization of agriculture by the first Green Revolution.

The women farmers of Medak have been at the forefront of the battle against multinational corporate domination of agriculture in India. Once Monsanto was granted approval to market its genetically engineered Bt cotton in Andhra Pradesh after controversial and secretive field trials, and local farmers—persuaded by Monsanto's marketing campaign promising a quick path out of debt—began to grow Bt cotton with mixed to disastrous results, the CMT made two point-of-view documentaries that followed the disappointing experience of several farmers with Bt cotton over 3 years, *Why are Warrangal Farmers Angry?* (CMT, 2003) and *Bt Cotton in Andhra Pradesh* (CMT, 2005). Since Monsanto marketed their patented seeds through promotional videos and intensive advertising in all media, the CMT's documentaries were a direct counterstrike in a media struggle over the fate of small farmers. These documentaries are likely the most widely seen work of the CMT. Their ability to draw an audience stems from the intensity of the controversy, locally and internationally, over the dangers of corporate monopoly control and possible environmental damage posed by these new biotechnologies in agriculture.

Moreover, Monsanto introduced Bt cotton in India at a time when the news of farmer suicides could no longer be ignored. Caught in debt and facing crop failure just when social security programs were being withdrawn by the neoliberalized Indian state, thousands of farmers were being driven to suicide across India (Kumbamu, 2006, p. 24; Patel & Müller, 2004, p. 50). As these social and ecological crises began to grow, the Dalit women of Medak began to organize themselves into a network of agricultural cooperatives that they call "the *sangham*" in pursuit of their autonomy. One of the key achievements of the *sangham* women was their construction of their own agrobiodiversity register, which both serves as the foundation for their petroleum-free, organic, and biodiverse agriculture and prevents agribusiness multinationals from monopolizing genetic information.

To consolidate and further their pursuit of autonomies, the *sangham* women resolved to create their own autonomous media. Two conjunctural processes gave special urgency to this resolution. As we have noted, the women were engaged in a "class struggle through the networks" (Hardt & Negri, 2000) against the further subsumption of their agriculture under monopolies managed by the multinational agribusinesses and the leverage these multinationals have with the Indian state. Second, the new satellite and private channel mediascape that emerged in India in 1991 was, as P. V. Satheesh put it, a "media by the urban elite for the elite." Rural issues, problems, and concerns generally receive scant attention in urban Indian media. Ten women thus completed a yearlong training

program organized by the DDS in a series of media workshops led by P. V. Satheesh and another professional media producer in 1998–1999. The DDS also built and maintains a production studio that the women use. The CMT was formalized on International Rural Women's Day (October 15) in 2001 when a board of 11 trustees, including 8 *sangham* women, assumed management of the media cooperative.

Four features of the CMT's ties to the political body of the *sangham* are crucially important for understanding the singularity of the women's media practice. First of all, the network of networks configuration of which the *sangham* is a part not only connects urban spaces to rural ones but, in doing so, also rearticulates an elaborate and historically formed division of labor within the *sangham* and across the convergence of antiglobalization social movements and academic research institutes. Second, in rearticulating this division of labor, this political body both presupposes and demands the invention of a wide array of "powers of cooperation"—cultural traditions, competences, and identifications—without which it could not exist. Third, in constituting itself as a decentralized political body, not only are a whole range of new communication needs created but also an entire *lacework* of molecular public spheres are called into being—from urban lecture halls, classrooms, theaters, laptops, laboratories, and boardrooms to village *panchayats* and, especially, the rural itinerary of the travelling biodiversity *jathara*. Last, this rearticulation of social spaces must communicate across the barriers posed by literacy. To explore the significance of each of these, let us begin by considering the reasons the women of the CMT themselves give for why they chose video for their medium of communication.

In interviews, in DDS publications, and in their own videos, the CMT members identify several key implications of their video practice. Many of them turn on the *sangham* women's control over their self-representation.[1] For example, the women pointed out to me (and they also assert this in their "manifesto" video, *The Sangham Shot;* CMT, n.d.) that when outsiders such as myself come to videotape their activities, we don't know much about their work and lives and often ask them to perform scripted, stereotyped roles. They then worry about being misunderstood. With regard to the silence on their concerns in the elite media, they point out that the regional elite television is broadcast in a dialect of Telegu they sometimes find difficult to follow, and their own dialect is not understood and is scorned by city people. Video also allows them to document meetings, especially when officialdom visits their villages. They are able to keep a record of statements and promises made and hold bureaucrats to their word. Occasionally, they have even set the agenda of a consultation or hearing to which they have been invited by making a video on issues of importance to them. Moreover, as one of the primary tactical weapons of sexism, caste oppression, and class domination is to simply deny the credibility of the subaltern on the ground of her identity, video images provide testimony to their problems and difficulties and so authorize their speech. Indeed, the women frequently emphasize that they place considerable value on being able to communicate with the wider world.

Another related set of reasons for choosing video involves the importance the *sangham* network gives to their responsibilities to teach others (*sangham* members, their children, outsiders) as well as recruit women and help them organize. For example, they explained to me that when outsiders come to them to learn how to practice biodiverse agriculture, videos are helpful in two ways. Seeing helps one understand what one hears. But agriculture also has its own temporality, while visitors can usually stay with them for only a few days. They may need to see crops and fields at different times and seasons to understand how things can be done, and video allows the women to work around these limitations of timing. Another key issue of timing involves communicating the agricultural knowledge and experience the community possesses, especially elders, so that their children can be taught how to work with biodiversity and the various properties of ecological relationships before this knowledge is totally lost. In

this regard, there is the importance of their video profiles of seed savers and other honored women of the *sangham* that, like most of their work, are screened at public meetings convened during the biodiversity *jathara*. Equally important for them is their ability to tape public meetings and *sangham* councils to record community participation and make transparent *sangham* decision-making processes in a timely way. Their videos of public meetings also serve to teach other farmers how to participate and cooperate as *sangham* members. Moreover, women elders of the *sangham* are especially anxious to reach a wider audience with their agricultural and nutritional expertise than they can by attending meetings.

There is one further crucially important aspect to their choice of video. This has to do with video's specific capacity to translate across orality and literacy. Without devaluing literacy programs (which the DDS provides in its schools), the CMT women observe that their videos not only allow them to communicate with literate professionals but also disarm the usual dismissive paternalism thrown in the face of their nonliteracy by literate employers and officials. P. V. Satheesh, moreover, notes that the emphasis usually placed on literacy often has the unintended consequence of undermining the self-confidence of nonliterate adults who no longer have the possibility of catching up with young people. Video has apparently proven to be quite personally empowering in this regard, and, as has been often reported, the gendered and class status ascribed to "advanced" technology seems to play a role in this. Nevertheless, the "deconstruction and reconstruction" of identity, as also noted in the scholarly literature on PV (Bery, 2003; Dudley, 2003; Gadihoke, 2003; Rodriguez, 2001, p. 117), is not exactly the same thing as being able to communicate persuasively across the class divide of language and literacy. Indeed, such "empowerment," in the case of the CMT, is nothing less than their engagement in all out, gendered, class struggle. For such reasons, the women's own accounts of their video praxis are instructive and point to a path beyond the limitations in the theory and practice of participatory community video as it is commonly found today. It is to these lessons that I now turn.

Beyond Participatory Video

Clemencia Rodriguez (2001) argues in the conclusion of her study of three women's video projects in Colombia that PV productions "provoke" processes of identity deconstruction, personal and group empowerment, the demystification of mainstream media, the reversal of power roles, and increasing collective strength (p. 127). However, Rodriguez then qualifies this claim: "In no way do I want to suggest a causal relationship between PV production and these altering forces" (p. 127). It is one thing to search for various mediations between PV production and "these altering forces" instead of asserting some immediate relationship between them. But if there is no causal relationship of any kind, however mediated, then how can video production "provoke" any of the things it is said to provoke? Indeed, what then would be the point of undertaking PV projects or of studying them? Such confusions seem to be symptomatic of many aspects of the scholarship on PV. In her study, Rodriguez tells us that she has tried to articulate her "own bewilderment" at the ways in which these video practices were able to "bring about transformative processes that spread out in a ripple effect through many layers of a community's social fabric" (p. 127). But why should we settle for bewilderment, given our recognition of the political stakes of such media? If we are not to fall prey to a depoliticizing complacency, we then need to develop a mode of scholarly inquiry that studies the processes of video mediation itself. To understand the effective (or even transformative) power of video practices, we need to situate video practices in relation to the many ways in which the events that people live through rise out of and then fall back into large-scale social and historical processes, altering their course either subtly or dramatically. In the sections to follow, I therefore outline some of the lessons that may be learned from the CMT's video

practice for furthering a critical approach to PV studies that can take us beyond the limits of PV.

Narratives of Self-Transformation

One of the commonest tropes in the scholarly literature on participatory community video is the testimonial that asserts video's power to promote self-transformation, self-empowerment, or finding one's voice. Thus, Renuka Bery (2003), reporting on a Bangladeshi woman's video documentation of a politician's election promises, observes that the participatory communication "enables the individual to examine his/her self-identity and build his/her confidence" (p. 107). In fact, Bery places considerable emphasis on PV's capacity to build self-confidence as the foundation of its power to effect change and influence the world (pp. 108–117). Along these lines, Guidi (2003) also argues that involvement in PV processes can enable women to "make the choice to come out of their communities; often they can change their lifestyles" (p. 267). Gomez (2003) goes so far as to argue that the most important outcome of his PV project involving street children is the "increased sense of self-esteem gained by the children." Similarly, Rodriguez's account of a PV project involving a group of urban Colombian women in their efforts to organize day care facilities concludes, "by the time the process ended, those eight women involved in the video project were not the same. Something deep, definitive, and irreversible had happened to them" (p. 115).

The difficulty posed by such claims does not arise out of any doubt regarding their veracity.[2] Indeed, as I noted before, the women of the CMT also made a point of mentioning during our interviews how their self-esteem and self-confidence grew with experience. The difficulty rather has to do with how we interpret the significance of this. In particular, we need to be careful regarding the slippage that often occurs between the welcome psychological effects of growing self-confidence, self-esteem, and so on, and the properly social and political process of empowerment itself. The development of self-confidence may indeed be a step in the process of conscientization, as White (2003, p. 49) outlines in her model of the participatory process. As an effect of a participatory process however, it cannot always be taken to be the political endpoint of PV—as either its ultimate achievement or as the primary analytic-narrative category for understanding processes of video mediation. It may be the case that in North America we have, at least from the radicalization of the 1960s, closely associated empowerment with self-empowerment. But there is no reason to assume that this contingent and conjunctural link is a fundamental or universal characteristic of politicization always and everywhere. In fact, the would-be-empowered self presupposed in such accounts remains historically linked to a specific social and political space of consumption. To be sure, domination gives rise to a wide range of clinical psychopathologies, from neuroses and self-loathing to suicidal depression. But the grounds of subaltern militancy, the assertion of rights and entitlements, the crystallization of class consciousness have much deeper historical roots in the formations of various mass political movements than the encouragement that gaining a new skill or the infectiousness of the researcher's own enthusiasms brings. Our analyses of media empowerment need to study and trace these histories of politicization rather than deploy middle-class, pseudo-therapeutic ideas of self-transformation taken from the self-help manuals as taken-for-granted, natural categories of cultural-political analysis.

In the case of the work of the CMT, we have already noted two crucial politicizing aspects of their media practice. First, the CMT's media practices crucially serve the needs of the network of women's cooperatives or *sangham*. The term *sangham* here derives from the Buddhist conception of an egalitarian cooperative political community as was formed by the Buddhist movement in the 5th century BCE. The term's use in this context needs to be understood in light of the revival of Buddhism in India by Dalit mass conversions to Buddhism in the 20th century. The great Dalit intellectual activist B. R. Ambedkar (1891–1956) converted to Buddhism in 1956 after developing a socialist political theory and praxis based on Buddhism as a cultural strategy against Brahmanical hegemony. More than 10 million Dalits have since followed Ambedkar's example. Moreover, a Dalit caste-class social movement has continued to grow in postcolonial India and, since the 1980s, has been a prominent and enduring protagonist in class struggles in India. There is a prominent statue of Ambedkar in the village near where the CMT is based. In our interview, P. V. Satheesh noted the Buddhist ideas animating the work of the DDS but also stressed the resonances of the concept of *sangham* with Muslim, folk-Hindu, and Christian conceptions of community. In fact, the DDS-CMT alliance is overdetermined, in terms of the historical conditions of possibility of its mode of political self-organization, by the confluence of Gandhian and communist traditions of mass politics with Dalit neo-Buddhism and with insurrective, multifaceted feminisms. "Empowerment," or better, "politicization," here has a determinate significance as articulated by the theory and praxis of *autonomy* invented through and against these subcontinental cultural-political traditions.

Second, we have noted that a crucial feature of the CMT's video work is to construct and sustain a network-of-networks form of mobilization for the *sangham* in which political solidarities with other subaltern farmers, on the one hand, and politicized sections of the technical intelligentsia (environmentalists, agricultural scientists, farmers' union organizers, etc.), on the other, can be maintained on regional, national, and international scales. The CMT's media work is directly involved in political mobilization not only through ideological contestation but even more so through the CMT's video documentation of the *sangham's* political self-management, its meetings and decision-making processes, rendering the cooperative's management transparent and responsible. In this way, the CMT's video work is "empowering" because it is intimately linked to both enabling *cooperation* and extending the range of *collective* autonomy.

My point here is not that building self-confidence, raising self-esteem, or transforming oneself are unimportant and without any political value. They are, of course, crucial if a collective, political body is to be able to cooperate and self-organize itself. My point, rather, is that it is naive, politically regressive, and analytically confusing to assert, as White (1994) does, that

> though empowerment is usually conceptualized as moving out of a condition or sense of deprivation or oppression, it can also be looked at as a positive, holistic outcome of self-discovery, successful human interaction, and the ability to dialogue with people different from one's self. (p. 23)

Although "self-discovery," "dialogue," and so on were the watchwords of the "politics of 1968," what is forgotten here is that the social world has to be politically organized in a particular way for self-discovery to be a social possibility in the first place. The North American experience of personal freedom, in particular, makes large and demanding claims on the lives and labor of the world's multitudes through a global system of violence and inequality. If we reorient the concept of empowerment "positively" away from its connection to a militant struggle against oppression, not only does "empowerment" lose all meaning, but we also have admitted to ourselves only the vaguest conception of the social organization of oppression. No doubt, we have also made the World Bank happy. The work of the CMT, on the other hand, not only makes these limitations of the critical theory of PV apparent but, in connecting its video practice to a politics of collective autonomy, also points out a path of video praxis beyond them.

Through the Looking Glass

Moreover, the narrative of self-transformation in the scholarly accounts of community media is strikingly thin on explaining how video practices

specifically intervene in the process of identity deconstruction. Researchers often observe that video enables people to see themselves in new ways. It is also pointed out that what people then see in the televisual screen is their own objectified or distanced ordinariness rather than the stereotypes of wealthy and powerful elites (and sometimes also stereotypes of the poor) that appear on commercial or state television. Apart from this, however, there are not many precise descriptions of what is new about these mediated self-perceptions, and even in this case the specific effectivity of the televisual screen remains undertheorized. What, then is the relationship between the "reality" that is newly framed and objectified by the participatory community media process and the series of broadcast media stereotypes? Is it a distinction? A difference? A negation? Some other more complex relation? Another step in the formation of class consciousness? Does this relationship mediate everyday practices in any way? Critical approaches that reify media, arbitrarily disconnecting media processes from their broader historical and social context, tend to lean heavily on the "mirror" metaphor and to this extent end up proposing technologically determinist accounts of mediation ("the viewfinder is a mirror," etc.). If we are to gain a deeper understanding of how video intervenes in politicization, then we need to better situate identities in their actual social relations. What then comes to view is a *tactical* political field in which video practices may be deployed.

Video Tactics

The existing scholarly literature itself provides many clues to help us conceptualize how video practices can be mobilized tactically. This is clearly evident, for example, in the case of the Bangladeshi women's video discussed by Bery (2003). These women attempted to monitor politicians campaigning in their village and thus pressure them to keep their promises. The women of the CMT also reported this. For example, the agrobiodiversity conservation plan developed by the women's *sangham* became the national plan adopted by the Government of India and CMT videos on the issue played a prominent role in achieving this. This was also a key tactic of the Fogo Process as it was developed by Fogo islanders, filmmakers from the National Film Board, and Memorial University of Newfoundland researchers in the early 1970s (Crocker, 2003; Wiesner, 1992).

Often cited as the inaugural forerunner of PV community animation processes, one of the key accomplishments of the Fogo project was to reverse the government's decision to relocate the people of Fogo off their islands closer to the provincial capital. Screening films of the islanders' concerns at the ministry in St. John's not only drew the government's attention to Fogo islanders' discontent, persuading them to change course, but also prompted the premier to visit Fogo and make Fogo Island issues a government priority (Gwyn, 1972; Williamson, 1988). This involved the displacement of a vertical command structure of community development with "horizontal dialogue" that White (2003) identifies as one of the crucial features of how PV media can effect positive change. Yet I want to argue that, in both the cases, of Fogo Island and that of the CMT's dealings with government, what is crucial about video's mediation of the politicization of the situation is not just the establishment of a horizontal dialogue but more specifically video's capacity to put reputations at stake through the indeterminacy of its potential to construct a public space.

Governmental power in the modern world must play the game of hegemony. For this reason, the state is always ready to enter into a dialogue, as this is a long-standing tactic of crisis management by which states seek to depoliticize a given situation. Most modern states have consequently developed various infrastructures for "systematically distorting" (Habermas, 1984) the public and political possibilities of dialogue in the depoliticized domain of administration by letting dialogue take place within a space of trustworthy

obedience. Here there is speech, but nothing is said, nor heard. Any and all contradictions may be described, but their contradictoriness will pass unnoticed. If such ploys draw on and exploit speech's capacity to subvert its public address into secrets whispered into the ear, then it is because correlative moves have been invented for writing and print—illiteracy, jargon, legalese, the kinds of euphemistic and obscurantist prose that Orwell famously attacked. The communication theorist Harold Innis (1951) invented a pair of concepts— "monopoly of knowledge" and "bias of communication"—to draw our attention to these historically new forms of structural secrecy in which the collusions between state and private corporate power find room for maneuver. Here, we reach the limits of Nair and White's (1994) model of "participatory message development," which takes properties of dialogue as its normative framework (dialogue is oversimplistically understood to be horizontal exchange rather than top-down command) and thus remains oblivious to communicative distortions of the kind Innis (1951) describes. Video, however, imposes itself into such regularized strategies of management with an unpredictable visibility and intelligibility that is, for the time being, difficult to monopolize and control. Digital video, especially, has greatly accelerated the printed page's nomadism. Who knows where a video file will pitch its tent and unfurl a micro or macro public sphere? Video's indeterminacy with respect to who, when, where, and why it might find an audience puts reputations once more at stake but in a way quite different from the sphere of face-to-face trust, where it is a matter of the immediate relation between "walking one's talk." Or rather, the face-to-face situation is now inextricable from position taking in a public ideological field. Routine promises that were cynically never meant to be kept are thereby suddenly brought back to symbolic life. Video's capacity to break up established monopolies of knowledge in this way enables it to repoliticize communication. This is not to suggest that video is intrinsically beyond policing, only that the control mechanisms for speech and print do not work as well. It remains quite possible that communication scholars will be recruited to invent analogs of legalese for PV communication.

What I am calling here video tactics involve another characteristic feature of the CMT's video practices. Many of their videos are dominated by the aesthetic principle of what they call the *sangham* shot—an eye-level, direct, face-to-face shot that signifies that in the *sangham,* they all are equals. In the important video *Making of an Agricultural Biodiversity Register,* for example, this syntax plays a particularly crucial role, as the video documents extensive community involvement in making up an agrobiodiversity register. Both individual involvement and community cooperation are foregrounded in this way, as are women's leadership and expertise in the process. In its efforts to advocate the making of such biodiversity registers as a seed sovereignty and autonomy strategy, the video explains how the village of Khasimpur made its biodiversity register and presents this as an example for other subaltern farming communities to follow. For the *sangham's* solidarity network of outsiders, this explanation takes the form of English subtitles outlining the steps. But this is the sketchiest of explanations, as it becomes clear from another form of writing that the farmers compose on the grounds of the village assembly out of flour, vegetable colors, and dyes, seeds, plants, and terracotta figures that extensive knowledge of dryland agriculture is presupposed in this account. This, however, allows the video to drive home another key point that it sets out to make. Not only are the assembled farmers experts in biodiverse agriculture, but this expertise also belongs to the community. As the editing cuts back and forth between the colorful register on the ground and the public deliberation between farmers around it, the *sangham* shot's face-to-face immanence serves to show how this expertise is cooperatively sustained. The video concludes with the transcription of the register from the ground to a book and the *Gram Sabha's* (village assembly) certification of the veracity of the book's contents.

This aspect of the CMT's video work, then, crucially involves such tactical subordination to the needs of keeping a political body of cooperation in movement. To meet these needs—especially the key ones of conserving and disseminating knowledge of biodiverse agricultural techniques handed down by farmers of the region or invented in the *sangham*—many of their videos present analyses of various types of embodied movement that make up this kind of agriculture. In this analytical relationship to indigenous knowledge, the work of the CMT goes well beyond the opposition between process video and product video that has structured most discussions of PV. Rooted in various documentary and PV traditions, the *autonomous media* of the CMT nevertheless constitute a singular political breakthrough.

Notes

1. For an extended discussion of the relevant issues, see White, Nair, and Ashcroft (1994), though it must be observed that their claim that the PV process allows the women they have worked with to represent themselves, giving them back their "own voice," is questionable (to say the least), when the participatory process involves shopping around for the right village where prospects for the project seem more promising rather than emerging out of some well-researched and -described communicative need faced by the community.

2. Although I do wonder where and when the stereotype of the timorous and passive subaltern woman underwriting this narrative emerged and how it remains in circulation.

References

Bery, R. (2003). Participatory video that empowers. In S. White (Ed.), *Participatory video: Images that transform and empower* (pp. 102–121). New Delhi, India: Sage.

Community Media Trust. (2003). *Bt cotton in Andhra Pradesh.* Pastapur, Andhra Pradesh, India: Deccan Development Society.

Community Media Trust. (2005). *Why are Warrangal farmers angry?* Pastapur, Andhra Pradesh, India: Deccan Development Society.

Community Media Trust. (n.d.). *The sangham shot.* Pastapur, Andhra Pradesh, India: Deccan Development Society.

Crocker, S. (2003). The Fogo Process: Participatory communication in a globalizing world. In S. White (Ed.), *Participatory video: Images that transform and empower* (pp. 122–144). New Delhi, India: Sage.

Dudley, M. J. (2003). The transformative power of video. In S. White (Ed.), *Participatory video: Images that transform and empower* (pp. 145–156). New Delhi, India Sage.

Gadihoke, S. (2003). The struggle to empower: A woman behind the camera. In S. White (Ed.), *Participatory video: Images that transform and empower* (pp. 271–285). New Delhi, India: Sage.

Gomez, R. (2003). Magic roots: Children explore participatory video. In S. White (Ed.), *Participatory video: Images that transform and empower* (pp. 215–231). New Delhi, India: Sage.

Guidi, P. (2003). Guatemalan Mayan women and visual media. In S. White (Ed.), *Participatory video: Images that transform and empower* (pp. 252–270). New Delhi, India: Sage.

Gwyn, S. (1972). *Cinema as catalyst: Film, video-tape and social change; a report on a seminar.* St. John's, Newfoundland, Canada: Memorial University of Newfoundland.

Habermas, J. (1984). *The theory of communicative action* (Vol. 1; Trans. T. McCarthy). Boston: Beacon.

Hardt, M., & Negri, A. (2000). *Empire.* Cambridge, MA: Harvard University Press.

Innis, H. A. (1951). *The bias of communication.* Toronto, Ontario, Canada: University of Toronto Press.

Kumbamu, A. (2006). Ecological modernization and the "Gene Revolution": The case study of Bt Cotton in India. *Capitalism, Nature, Socialism, 17*(4), 7–31.

Nair, S. K., & White, S. (1994). Participatory message development: A conceptual framework. In S. White, K. S. Nair, & J. Ashcroft (Eds.), *Participatory communication: Working for change and development* (pp. 345–358). New Delhi, India: Sage.

Patel, R., & Müller, A. R. (2004). *Shining India? Economic liberalization and rural poverty in the 1990s* (Policy Brief No. 10). Oakland, CA: Food First/Institute for Food and Development Policy.

Rodriguez, C. (2001). *Fissures in the mediascape: An international study of citizens' media.* Cresskill, NJ: Hampton Press.

White, S. (1994). The concept of participation. In S. White, K. S. Nair, & J. Ashcroft (Eds.), *Participatory communication: Working for change and development* (pp. 15–34). New Delhi, India: Sage.

White, S. (Ed.). (2003). *Participatory video: Images that transform and empower.* New Delhi, India: Sage.

White, S., Nair, K. S., & Ashcroft, J. (Eds.). (1994). *Participatory communication: Working for change and development.* New Delhi, India: Sage.

Wiesner, P. K. (1992). Media for the people: The Canadian experiments with film and video in community development. *American Review of Canadian Studies, 22*(1), 65.

Williamson, T. (1988). *The Fogo Process.* St. John's, Newfoundland, Canada: Memorial University of Newfoundland, Don Snowden Centre for Development Support Communications.

CHAPTER 18

Coketown and Its Alternative Futures

Philip Denning

I n January 2001, the then–U.K. New Labour Prime Minister Tony Blair launched a new policy initiative. This was contained in a document titled *A New Commitment to Neighbourhood Renewal: National Strategy Action Plan* (Office of the Deputy Prime Minister, 2001). The aim of this plan was to transform the nation's most deprived neighborhoods, using external government funds.

The action plan was drawn up following wide consultation and statistical research into deprivation across both government and wider society. Specifically, the action plan was developed from the conclusions of 18 policy action teams and their reports over the period from 1997 to 1999. These action teams looked at what could be learned from previous attempts to regenerate poor neighborhoods across a wide range of interventions—for example, in health, housing, education, and crime. What these action plans ignored, however, was the capacity and experience of neighborhoods to transform themselves.

What was ignored was the role of those communities that existed before the new top-down focus on renewal and regeneration. Instead, a discourse that combines moral, pathological, and

paleological imagery was applied. In the discourse, communities are "forgotten," "left behind," "plagued," "damaged," "relics," or "dinosaurs." The reality of deprived communities in the United Kingdom is much more complex and contradictory than this discourse allows. What was lost was the role of deprived communities in actively making both the present and future and how they could offer alternatives to both discourse and policy development.

In this chapter, I address two main points. First, I argue that, far from being left behind by the modern world, deprived communities are instead key agents of change. They actively engage practically with this change and the underlying theory, but from their own perspectives and for their own aims. I analyze the complexity and contradictions of the discourse through focusing on the ways in which the local urban community of Craigmillar, in Edinburgh, Scotland, has engaged with this discourse, resisted it, and posited alternatives. These include the creative use of information and communication technologies (ICTs).

Second, I argue that if we are to understand the more complex dynamics of social and technological change and community development over time, then linking a cultural planning approach, with an explicit focus on a *place as it changes dynamically through time, which notes its interdependence with other places* to a community development approach that is focused on *local community organizations* is key to a more nuanced, sensitive engagement and relationship between communities and professionals, since, as Paulo Freire (1972) suggests, "The need to think creatively and critically empowers the individual and ultimately the community" (p. 21).

Before this occurs, however, it is necessary to provide the background on the policy context in the United Kingdom for readers who are not familiar with this area. I also wish to outline the needs for a different form of approach to address the complexity of community change and development over time.

Policy Background

The Neighbourhood Renewal Action Plan set out a future vision that according to Blair, "*Within 10 to 20 years, no-one should be seriously disadvantaged by where they live*" (Office of the Deputy Prime Minister, 2001, p. 1).

Its long-term goals are as follows:

- To have lower unemployment, less crime, better health, better skills, and better housing and physical environment in all the poorest neighborhoods

- To narrow the gap on these measures between the most deprived neighborhoods and the rest of the country

This neighborhood renewal project and the policy action teams can be seen to be at one with the modernizing ethos behind New Labour. Tony Blair commented specifically on this on becoming Prime Minister: "We were elected as New Labour, and we will govern as New Labour" (*The Guardian,* May 2, 1997).

The New Labour administrations (of 1997–2001, 2001–2005, and 2005 to the present) have consistently promulgated a discourse on policy that privileges and emphasizes the new via key terms such as *newness, modern, renewal,* and *modernization.*

In turn, these are linked to a broader discourse regarding the position of the United Kingdom within the modern world with the rise of the "information society," information age and digital technologies, and media. A central feature of this discourse is that it appears that the United Kingdom (and the rest of the developed world) is on a path where telecommunications and computers are driving major social and industrial change, just as the internal combustion engine, the assembly line, and factories did during the so-called Fordist era. In this discourse, these are unstoppable megatrends that have not only changed the world on a global level but also affected the local. In this discourse, time moves relentlessly forward; the past has gone and can never be recovered. The role of discourse is central to not only imagining a narrative of "the future" but also closing down alternatives.

This discourse with its focus on the new and rejection of the old is, as Lovering (1997) cautions, an overtly deterministic "simple story" with a stark, brutal moral of "adapt or die" for those who stand in its way, whether these are countries, industries, workforces, or local communities.

To act as a counterpoint to the simple story, I wish to provide an example of an approach that blends cultural planning methodologies with those of community development. It is my contention that such an approach not only posits a counter-discourse to that of the policy action teams but also reflects the complex, multilayered, and creative nature of urban neighborhoods themselves.

Layers of Time

In terms of structuring this paper, I want to adopt an approach that is constructed of layers and, specifically, layers of time. In this, I follow the examples to the study of urban communities to be found in the writings of Kevin Lynch (1960), Richard Sennet (2003), Jonathan Raban (1972), and Doreen Massey (1991). Each of these writers has emphasized the dynamic process of the cultural "layering" of cities, where past and present exist together, and cities, neighborhoods, buildings, and events are "texts" that repay close reading that can be read and reinterpreted.

To aid this process, I use the musical concept of the *motif* (from classical music), *phrase* (from jazz), or *version* (from reggae) in the following pages as a structural tool to facilitate analysis. This will involve the repetition of a short introductory paragraph but will then follow a different trajectory of investigation and analysis.

The rationale underlying this approach is that the process of change occurs for both generations and communities, but its presence is registered in both *catastrophic* (the demolition of housing, factory closure, unsuccessful collective actions) and *mundane* terms that coexist. It is easy to find the evidence of catastrophic events. They can be found in newspaper headlines, empty buildings, and oral histories of working-class communities all over the United Kingdom. The mundane is more difficult to find. All too often, its effects are found through attention to details of traces, symbols, and the forgotten. Here, cultural planning approaches come to the fore. These traces and symbols can also be resources of hope and signal the possibility of alternatives. The cultural planning methodologies that focus on the broad culture of a community and not just its community organizations enable us to pay attention to what appears to be mundane, or part of the everyday, for example, children's play.

This chapter will seek to move beyond the narrow confines of the dominant discourse of the simple story surrounding deprived communities such as Craigmillar and, instead, seek to bring to light other perspectives on these places, since, as Massey (1991) notes,

If it is now recognised [*sic*] that people have multiple identities, then the same point can be made in relation to places. . . . It is from this perspective that it is possible to envisage an alternative interpretation of place. (pp. 27–28)

Craigmillar: Setting the Urban Community Context

Craigmillar is a conurbation of local authority housing estates built after 1930, in a period of industrial relocation and central city slum clearance, and located on the southeast of the city of Edinburgh. It is an area that has steadily been positioned from the late 1950s as existing on the periphery, both geographically and economically.

In this period, the majority of the industries on which the community traditionally depended were coal mining, brick making, agriculture, brewing, and creamery. Craigmillar is a workers' place, a "Coketown" (named after the town in Dickens's 1854 novel *Hard Times*). These industries linked Craigmillar to the then existing forms of local, regional, national, and global economies (e.g., local beer being sent to British imperial troops in India). These were either relocated or closed down completely.

Craigmillar appeared to be bypassed in the last four decades of the 20th century with the introduction of new technology to Edinburgh's major industries in defense and finance. These changes ran alongside the processes of deindustrialization and industrial relocation in the city economy.

The rapid removal of local industry with the loss of more than 10,000 jobs and no subsequent industrial investment in the area gave rise to attendant social distress. As a result, the area of Craigmillar gained an unenviable reputation and a battery of deprivation statistics (City of Edinburgh Council, 1997). The discourse and imagery used to portray and position Craigmillar drew heavily from a bank of long-established national and global images. The area has been consistently projected (and misleadingly in the viewpoint of residents) in the Scottish metropolitan and national media and academic texts as a latter day rookery of Victorian London (in terms of crime) or a Scottish version of urban Calcutta (in terms of urban destitution).

This imagery is somewhat at odds with the reality of local urban development. In the past 5 years (though planned 15 years previously), the southeastern edge of Edinburgh (of which Craigmillar is a part) has witnessed the major expansion of the so-called southeast wedge with the largest postwar investment by the National Health Service (the United Kingdom) in Scotland in the location of the new Royal Infirmary of Edinburgh. This has led to further major investment (and associated positive boosting images) in road improvements, housing, a medical and biotechnology park, and retail parks.

Despite this investment and planning, the standardized negative portrayal of Craigmillar has continued. A BBC (British Broadcasting Corporation) Scotland television op-ed program (August 2001) fronted by Richard Holloway, the Scottish Episcopalian Bishop (and then chair of the City of Edinburgh Commission on Social Exclusion in the city) portrayed Craigmillar as a world away from the booming economy of central Edinburgh when it is only 2 miles in reality. The neighborhood was depicted as "Edinburgh's shadow," a community on the abyss with population dropping to ghost town levels, racked by crime, full of poor and empty housing with a barren environment, child prostitutes, and finally ravaged by HIV/AIDS following the (unexamined) investment by a modern global industry, the drugs industry, in the city.

As Short (1999) stresses, this "shadow" is a key part of a distinct discourse of urban representation whereby some issues and groups are either silenced or presented as dangerous and beyond the confines of debate. Furthermore, as Short notes, these representations are "not politically neutral, neither are they devoid of social

implications . . . the dominant representations play down equality, social justice, and an inclusive definition of the good city" (pp. 40–41). Just what issues and groups were being silenced will now be explored by examining the many versions of Craigmillar that exist.

Urban Alternatives Version 1: The Gentle Giant That Shares and Cares

Craigmillar is a conurbation of local authority housing estates built after 1930, in a period of industrial relocation and central city slum clearance, and located on the southeast of the city of Edinburgh. The area has steadily been positioned from the late 1950s as existing on the periphery, both geographically and economically.

Despite being positioned as an area of socioeconomic deprivation, there is at the same time a strong tradition of progressive community action on which many groups have built themselves. For over four decades, the community of Craigmillar, through the work of the Craigmillar Festival Society (CFS), have pioneered the use of creative cultural projects as catalysts to explore the possibilities for community development and empowerment to "let the people sing" (Crummy, 1992) and posit an alternative to accepted trajectories for local residents into low-paid, low-value jobs and lives.

The CFS instead explored key issues for the neighborhoods of Craigmillar using art forms such as drama, carnival, festival, poetry, visual art, sculpture, and musical theater. These drew on play, creativity, and performance and in doing so achieved involvement and ownership of these processes by the local communities. These approaches are perhaps difficult for modern practitioners to comprehend given the dominance of politician-led strategies for urban renewal with business-marketing approaches such as focus groups, "expert" panels, invite-only conferences, and other present-day consultation and visioning techniques.

An example of how radically different this approach was can be found in the Gulliver statue. In 1976, the CFS worked with sculptor Jimmy Boyle while he was still a prisoner in the Special Unit in Barlinnie Prison in Glasgow. At the time, Boyle was by his own admission, one of the most intractable and violent prisoners in the U.K. prison system. He was considered a man beyond redemption by the public media, judiciary, and politicians. Working with the CFS, Boyle conceived and designed a 100-foot long land sculpture of Gulliver as the center of an adventure playground for local children. The actual concrete sculpture was constructed by unemployed adults and youth with voluntary advice from professionals.

The Gentle Giant Gulliver symbolizes both Boyle and the community's long journey of regeneration from "hard man"/hard place to "gentle giant." This art for a playground then fed into the development of local action planning by the community itself. Moving then from playground to policy, Craigmillar was the first urban community in Europe to obtain funding directly from the then European Economic Community (now the European Union). As a result, in 1978 the CFS produced a major report with 400 recommendations on how to improve life in the community. The majority of these recommendations were achieved. The title of the report, "The Gentle Giant," referred to Gulliver caring and sharing in a vision that simultaneously looked back to the imagery associated with the founding of the postwar Welfare State in the United Kingdom and forward to a vision that many people worldwide would share of how a society should be.

This approach grew from the traditions and ongoing activities of what Denning (1998) terms the *movement cultures* of the area from across a number of social groupings such as trade unions, the labor movement, the mining community, traveling people, and church-based social activity.

These actions have been notable in their consistent determination to move beyond traditional

Photo 18.1 The Gulliver Sculpture

community development approaches that focus only on the local area and a limited perspective. Instead, the CFS sought to link Craigmillar to the local, national, and global economies and events past and present. As the Gulliver's story has shown, there were also literally concrete attempts to imagine alternative futures and radical transformations. This approach has brought national and international acclaim and links with community leaders and workers, academics, professionals, artists, musicians, and actors from all corners of the globe.

The Craigmillar community is notable both in its consistent application of cultural politics, aligning itself alongside urban working class and labor movements both within Scotland and beyond. The activities of the Festival Society gave the community the opportunity to explore the cultural field and apparatus through the above art forms.

While many of the techniques were pioneered in Craigmillar, it is possible to argue, drawing on the analysis of cultural formations developed by Williams (1989, pp. 174–175), that the community actions were part of a much wider cultural formation by the working class within urban Scotland during this period. An exhibition/review of his own work by the artist Richard De Marco (2001) at Edinburgh's City Art Centre in 2001 was notable for the placing of the activities of the CFS within an artistic and social context of the past 60 years. Richard De Marco also explicitly linked the work of the CFS to the concept of "social sculpture" developed by German artist Joseph Beuys, who visited Craigmillar in 1970.

For Beuys, Social Sculpture refers to an interdisciplinary participatory process in which thought, speech and discussion are core "materials." All human beings are seen as "artists" responsible for the shaping of a democratic, sustainable social order. This lifts the aesthetic from its confines within a specific art media, relocating it within a collective, imaginative work-space in which we can see,

re-think and reshape our lives in tune with our creative potential. (De Marco quoted in Beuys & De Marco, 2001, pp. 22–23)

Further research is required to place these distinct artistic forms of resistance and alignment within their wider social formation.

At the same time, the silencing of the community continues in other ways. A key problem facing any researcher is collating and analyzing the primary material. Despite one of the founders of the CFS, Helen Crummy, archiving the posters, plays, music, songs, film, video, minutes, books, and photography of the organization within her house, there has been no attempt to include this material in the mainstream Scottish cultural research archives or libraries. The nature of culturally focused community development work is based on short events as much as physical art works. There was the distinct possibility that this work would be lost to posterity, unless other means of storage were found. However, the creativity and innovation of the community has again been applied, but this time using ICT.

Urban Alternatives Version 2: Using ICT to Make a World for Sharing and Caring

Craigmillar is a conurbation of local authority housing estates built after 1930, in a period of industrial relocation and central city slum clearance, and located on the southeast of the city of Edinburgh. It is an area that has steadily been positioned from the late 1950s as existing on the periphery, both geographically and economically.

Craigmillar has engaged with ICT through Craigmillar Community Information Services (CCIS), a community project that has accessed funding from European Union and Scottish Executive sources. CCIS is part of Craigmillar's tradition of community development, and the project emerged from other cultural projects relating to film and radio developed by the CFS. However, CCIS has a distinctive focus on empowering local people by providing access to ICT.

Set up in January 1994, at a time when more than 80% of those living in the area were on some form of welfare benefit, CCIS is an explicitly *community-based* Internet service, access, and training provider. Since then, the project has developed digitally inclusive programs of activity for those groups and individuals who would not otherwise be afforded the opportunity to help define, reflect on, and share in the prosperity of the global "information society." Examples of these programs are work with low-income parents and children, the elderly, former drug and substance users, and new immigrants to the area. These programs were among the first in Scotland and the United Kingdom and publicly opened up alternative community uses of ICT beyond academia and business.

From its inception, CCIS has attempted to define Craigmillar as an "alternative space" in cyberspace by being explicit in terms of its values and ethos. CCIS is exploring the potential of a community developing its sense of place and structures of feeling in cyberspace.

This is achieved, as will be seen below, by the purposeful development of schemes, programs, and initiatives specifically designed to bridge the "digital divide" and usher the otherwise digitally excluded across the threshold of the information society. This approach called into question the deterministic discourses regarding the information society itself by the deliberate decision taken by CCIS to revisit, reuse, and reposition the thoughts of one of the prophets of that society, Marshall McLuhan.

Marshall McLuhan was one of the earliest academics to explore the implications of mass media for modern life. His insights into the changing role of technology and its impact made him one of the most celebrated thinkers of the 1960s. With his memorable aphorisms and concepts such as "the global village," "the global theatre," the "medium as message," the "medium as *massage*," the "rearview

mirror society," and his articulation of the "center and periphery," McLuhan provided profound "probes" for readers to grapple with.

In short, his style is poetic and therefore reasonably open to creative interpretation and license. This is something community activists have not been slow to grasp in Craigmillar but with a unique interpretation. Likewise, ICT as a cultural field and apparatus is "open" and as such open to poetic and creative interpretation and license using play, performance, and creativity. CCIS explores this dimension and "road tests" such ideas via practical activities and projects. One of the key ways CCIS have addressed the potential of ICT to offer deprived urban communities viable alternatives is via an exploration of the concept of the global village.

McLuhan was among the first to see that the feudal village with its town crier supplying public information had been replaced by a reconstituted village at the global level with a new "tribal" electronic consciousness replacing individual consciousness.

The CCIS Teleport project fundamentally recognized from the outset that Craigmillar had both the potential and the right to be a player and a place in the global village and that by harnessing ICT for community advantage, local people could act "locally" and "be global."

From 1994, when access to the Internet in the United Kingdom was largely restricted to academic institutions and businesses, CCIS deployed a "computer outreach worker" who worked with local groups in their premises, getting them online to the global village. At CCIS, the initial engagement with ICT was about not only enabling broader access to the information sources but also providing participants with the confidence and competence to generate user knowledge of the media so that they can use these tools for their own ends and purposes to allow them to develop really useful knowledge (Johnson, 1979).

Additionally, community activists were encouraged to come along to CCIS's offices and surf the Net free on 20 public access terminals. In the process, Craigmillar was successfully internetworked with the rest of the global village by continually reforging links and repositioning Craigmillar with Edinburgh, Scotland, the United Kingdom, Europe, and the rest of the world. In this way, the project has raised questions over concepts such as center/periphery and included/excluded.

One of the key features of ICTs is that they offer the potential for urban areas such as Craigmillar that have been externally defined as excluded and peripheral to be at the center of the online phenomenon. This is linked to a central tenet of McLuhan's thinking—that with electronic communication, any marginal area can become center and marginal experiences can be held at any center.

Communication media such as the Internet can, within the context of the developing global networks, make urban communities more powerful, for they can become centers of interesting ICT activity. The Internet is not only creating a global village but also presenting an opportunity for disadvantaged urban communities to reconstruct themselves as "intelligent" constructs on their own terms. Craigmillar as a community has followed this opportunity in two ways.

First, Craigmillar in 1996 became the European superhub for an international BBS freenet called OneNet. Thousands of users in Europe were linked to the United States via CCIS servers in Craigmillar, with millions of e-mail messages passing between countries every day. Thanks to the proactive stewardship of OneNet by CCIS, Craigmillar began to successfully network with other agencies and individuals where hitherto there had been no contact.

Second, Craigmillar has presented these concepts within the places of power where dominant discourses are formed. For example, in October 1997, to commemorate the Commonwealth Heads of State visit to Edinburgh, CCIS developed and hosted an international conference titled Connecting Commonwealth Communities Digitally:

Fast Forward Through the Rear View Mirror? Potential and Problems for the Millennium. The linkage of McLuhan with the work of the project was made explicit in the title of the conference and its associated documents.

The conference, attended by delegates from all over the Commonwealth, included videoconferencing links to Canada, the United States (MIT), and South Africa. Contributors included community futurists, leading academics from MIT, as well as local cyber grannies who gave an account of their work. Overwhelmingly, the view of the conference was that local communities such as Craigmillar could become centers of ICT activity within the ambit of the global village and that ICTs are socially shaped and constructed as opposed to being predetermined. The fact that elderly, working-class women can also shape ICT as much as prestigious academic institutions was made explicit at this event. The exact shaping of ICT by and for communities can be found if we analyze the work of the project. This can broadly be split into four main areas.

Initially, local groups invariably had a cause to pursue related to combating social exclusion and fighting for social justice: saving the environment, training the unemployed for work, supporting care in the community, engaging the poor in the arts, combating racism, promoting women's rights, facilitating community education, supplying child care, running credit unions, and publishing community newspapers.

However, as groups became more familiar with the medium, they began to explore the possibilities of ICT by originally developing an IT-based "living archive," the Timelines project (a cross-generational computer-mediated communications project), and a radio station. The tag line throughout is that "the kettle is bilin [boiling]" (all are made welcome—food and drink are shared) as opposed to the traditional Edinburgh bourgeoisie welcome of "you'll have had your tea" (a grudging welcome with food and drink jealously guarded).

Second, local groups have also used ICT for advocacy purposes (using e-mail campaigns). A recent successful example was brought to the attention of Historic Scotland, a 1934 mural of children at play within a local school by the Scottish artist, John Maxwell. This mural had been painted to celebrate both the opening of the school and the new community. This mural shows that when the community was built, it was seen as a place of sunlight, hope, possibility, and play, a welcome escape from the dark, gray slums of central Edinburgh. The mural was painted over and forgotten except for the photographs, and the school was scheduled for demolition, but public pressure through campaigning resulted in both reopening the school as an art studio and gallery and also fully restoring a work of public art that celebrated a different version of the community for posterity. The postrestoration photograph of the mural is reprinted here.

Local people have used the facility as a mechanism for learning new ICT skills to gain access to the wider urban labor markets. CCIS was at the forefront of this aspect and was recognized as a Department of Trade and Industry (DTI) retraining "center" in 1995. Staff from local businesses used the facility to learn new ICT skills for office administration and to advertise their business online. This area of work was central to CCIS combating the view of the community as the home of the permanently unemployed and unemployable as well as being an enterprise-free zone.

CCIS staff and users have served on a number of policy committees that have addressed the issue of bringing ICT to low-income communities. This includes serving on the Scottish Executive's Digital Reference Group, the Scottish National Grid for Learning Communities Working Party, and as board members of U.K. Communities Online. CCIS has also been the starting point for a number of similar versions of community-based ICT across Edinburgh through

Photo 18.2 John Maxwell Mural

the development and movement of staff and activists. The CCIS project in Craigmillar has posited one urban alternative.

As an example of how the community has developed and built on this work, the Craigmillar Communiversity site (www.communiversity .org.uk/) contains the archive, documents, publications, films, a Flickr photo site, and directions to the public art trail that now exists in the community. The community has further developed McLuhan's concept of the global village to create an online World Community Arts Day every year on February 17. Starting locally in 2007, the aim is to create not only a Craigmillar Festival Society but also a World Festival Society. World Community Arts Day in 2008 revisited the theme of sharing and caring from the Gulliver's statue and featured involvement by community groups from Europe, the United States, Latin America, India, and Australia.

Conclusion

I hope that this chapter and its layering techniques will lay the groundwork for new research into social and cultural histories of working-class communities in Scotland and beyond. I would suggest that the focus is broadened to include new means of expression. I have outlined the potential of new means of production such as ICT. Rather than just being Web sites and bulletin boards, these new media and communication forms are also cultural texts that will repay decoding and close analysis by cultural planners and community development practitioners.

Craigmillar is still stereotypically depicted as an awful place, bereft of talent, positive energy, and ability. This focus only on the deficits of the area is all too often allowed to go unchallenged by community development practitioners. This highlights that it is crucially important for professionals to look at their own representation of Craigmillar as a "community." Other perspectives uncovered by adding cultural planning and layering

approaches to community development techniques, I hope to have shown, suggest that the area is in reality full of culture, intelligence, humor, and skills if you "let the people sing." The area also has its share of beautiful buildings and high-quality public art. The difficulties that people in the area presently face lies in their exclusion from the "social sculptures" of power, business, finance, and influence. Unlike many other urban communities both within Edinburgh and elsewhere in the United Kingdom (but very like the mining communities in the United Kingdom), when faced with this exclusion, the people of Craigmillar have challenged these processes.

The concept of "let the people sing" pertained to local people expressing and communicating their beliefs, feelings, and ideas through both individual and collective artistic means of production. It is also indicative of the fact that the "culture" of Craigmillar and its people is ongoing and broad based. It refers to a culture that is historically rich, a culture that harks back to the lived lives and various traditions of working people, and a culture that is still largely ignored in the "social sculptures" of national action plans, books, contemporary media, archives, and journals that focus on regeneration, renewal, community development, and empowerment.

At present, the bulldozers and demolition squads are at work, erasing the past of the community. The builders are also at work, physically imposing another "urban alternative" via another reconstruction of Craigmillar. If this is allowed to occur uncontested, then Craigmillar will indeed become a "ghost town," a "nonplace," devoid of historical context and stripped of the memories of collective action.

In this chapter, I have argued that both the work of the CFS and of CCIS within artistic and electronic media attempt to provide a counterpoint and a challenge to such actions. I would hope that fellow practitioners will recognize the links to their own work and that we will see greater research on this area of practice in the future. As Joseph Beuys said, "*We go this way.*"

References

Beuys, J., & De Marco, R. (2001). The road to Meikle Seggie. In *Retrospective exhibition catalogue.* Edinburgh, UK: City Art Centre.

City of Edinburgh Council. (1997). *Closing the gap: Social exclusion in Edinburgh.* Edinburgh, UK: Author.

Crummy, H. (1992). *Let the people sing.* Edinburgh, UK: Mainstream.

Denning, M. (1998). *The cultural front.* New York: Verso.

Dickens, C. (1854). *Hard times.* London: Chapman & Hall.

Freire, P. (1972). *Pedagogy of the oppressed.* London: Penguin Books.

Johnson, R. (1979). "Really useful knowledge": Radical education and working class culture, 1790–1848. In J. Clarke, C. Crichter, & R. Johnson (Eds.), *Working-class culture: Studies in history and theory* (pp. 75–102). London: Hutchison.

Lovering, J. (1997). Global restructuring and local impact. In M. Pacione (Ed.), *Britain's cities: Geographies of division in urban Britain* (pp. 63–88). London: Routledge.

Lynch, K. (1960). *The image of the city.* Boston: MIT Press.

Massey, D. (1991, June 28). A global sense of place. *Marxism Today,* June, 24–29.

Office of the Deputy Prime Minister. (2001). *A new commitment to neighbourhood renewal: National strategy action plan.* London: HMSO.

Raban, J. (1972). *Soft city.* London: Collins Harvill.

Sennet, R. (2003). *Flesh and stone: The body and the city in Western civilization.* London: Penguin Books.

Short, J. (1999). Urban imagineers: Boosterism and the representation of cities. In A. Jonas & D. Wilson (Eds.), *The urban growth machine: Critical perspectives two decades later* (pp. 37–54). Albany: State University of New York Press.

Williams, R. (1989). *Resources of hope: Culture, democracy, socialism.* London: Verso.

CHAPTER 19

Addressing Stigma and Discrimination Through Participatory Media Planning

Aku Kwamie

HIV/AIDS in Ghana, as in many other parts of the world, is at a critical junction. The estimated number of adults (ages 15+) living with HIV is 250,000—a statistic that has been increasing in recent years. HIV prevalence in Ghana is low by comparison with other countries in the region (UNAIDS, 2008). There remains, however, much work to do to prevent HIV/AIDS from becoming a generalized epidemic. The country's HIV profile is characterized by a higher prevalence rate among at-risk groups. Sixty-three percent of all HIV-positive persons are women (Ghana AIDS Commission, 2003).

In 2000, the Ghana AIDS Commission (GAC) was established to coordinate the national HIV/AIDS strategic framework and oversee implementation of the national response. GAC has published several guidelines on HIV/AIDS control and management. Although GAC supports 16 ministries, departments, and agencies; 133 nongovernmental organizations; and 3,600 community-based organizations across the country (GAC, 2003); it is interesting to note that visible national-level HIV/AIDS civil society organizations are lacking. The result has been that though, importantly, there are small local groups to serve their constituents' needs, few are able to bring their voices to the HIV/AIDS policy table.

HIV Prevention in Ghana Through Behavior Change

In Ghana, HIV/AIDS efforts are focused on prevention rather than treatment. To illustrate, a 2004 grant from the Global Fund to fight AIDS,

Author's Note: The views expressed herein are of the author only. This work was supported by Canadian Crossroads International (CCI) and the Canadian International Development Agency. CCI is an international development organization focused on promoting women's rights, community economic development, and combating HIV/AIDS. CCI celebrated 50 years of South-North collaboration in 2008.

tuberculosis, and malaria provided for antiretroviral therapy to treat HIV to become available in Ghana. While a step in the right direction, the grant only provided access to 1% of people who needed it, keeping treatment inaccessible from many (Ghana Ministry of Health Country Coordination Mechanism, 2002). Currently, treatment is available to 15% of people who need it (UNAIDS, 2008). Information, education, and communication (IEC) materials and behavior change communications (BCC) are the most frequent modes of HIV communications. Most of these appear as billboards and as television and radio broadcasts.

The earliest national prevention strategy was the mass media campaign, "Stop AIDS Love Life," launched in 2000 collaboratively between the Ministry of Health, Ministry of Information, GAC, Ghana Social Marketing Foundation (a private, not-for-profit organization funded by the U.S. Agency for International Development [USAID]), and the Johns Hopkins University Bloomberg School of Public Health Center for

Communication Programs (Center for Communication Programs 2003). The campaign adhered to the focus endorsed by international donors on *a*bstinence, *b*eing faithful to one partner, and *c*ondom use (ABC). ABC remains the key message of most donor-driven HIV communications. A limitation of these social marketing methods is that they are very often presented in English, with minimal translation into the local languages. The result is messaging that is targeted to literate, English-speaking people, denying information access to vulnerable socioeconomic groups. The continued focus on promoting condom use, abstinence, and fidelity also neglects the fact that sources of HIV risk exist outside the context of stable relationships (Benefo, 2004), negates considerations of power, and further implies that HIV is transmitted through immoral sexuality. Despite these mass-media campaigns, gaps in HIV knowledge remain, leading to myths and misconceptions about transmission, treatment, and the "type" of people who become HIV

Photo 19.1 A BCC Billboard Outside Accra

Source: Aku Kwamie.

positive. HIV-related stigma in Ghana remains high and continues to be felt by people living with HIV.

Stigma and HIV

Stigma has been described as "an undesirable attribute that one possesses" (Brown, Trujillo, & MacIntyre, 2001; Goffman, 1963) and can either be perceived (real or imagined) or enacted (experienced). Stigma is most often enacted by family, friends, and the local community, factors important within the Ghanaian social context. Stigma can also negatively affect health behaviors, for example, by discouraging people from getting tested for HIV or seeking care postdiagnosis. Stigma also creates psychosocial stress that can worsen health outcomes. People living with HIV in Ghana frequently experience stigma in myriad ways: sacking from the family home, loss of work, substandard health care, compromised educational and economic capacity, isolation, blame, and abuse. Evidence from Botswana shows that lack of access to antiretroviral therapy may also be a factor in HIV-related stigma (Wolfe et al., 2006). In the case of Ghana, where the number of people with access to treatment is so low, alternate modes of addressing stigma are needed.

In 2005, the West Africa AIDS Foundation (WAAF) in Accra sought to establish a community development program with the aim of using participatory media to address HIV/AIDS-related stigma and discrimination. WAAF's specific objectives were to reach out to the local community, to reduce stigma felt by HIV-positive people, and to increase the community's capacity to address and provide its own solutions to the problem of stigma as it manifests itself within that community.

The Question of Participatory Communication and HIV

Communication in development has a long history, where development communication initially promoted peoples' involvement in the development process (UNFPA, 2002). Participatory approaches in development communication (participatory communication) first appeared in the early 1970s in evolution to the vertical approaches of "transmission of information" employed by international development partners. They highlighted planning processes and sought to use communication resources to bring about change with the involvement of people in the change efforts (Boafo, 2002). Early participatory communication efforts, however, were only partially participatory: Beneficiary communities may have been called on to participate in implementation or evaluation but were rarely involved at the decision-making phase (Yoon, 1996). Increasingly, questions are being asked about traditionally accepted modes of communication and their specific applicability to the realm of HIV communications (Airhihenbuwa, Makinwa, & Obregon, 2000; Airhihenbuwa & Obregon, 2000). The univocal messages being sent to communities are slowly being replaced by community networks that are asking their own questions (FAO, 2005). As HIV communications have developed into a specialized area, the field has been dominated by three main forms of communication: BCC, social change communication (SCC), and advocacy communication (AC) (UNFPA, 2002). BCC is intended to permit individuals to increase their knowledge, thus changing their attitudes and practices (UNFPA, 2002). SCC seeks collective action and emphasizes the process of dialogue by which people can remove barriers and build on their existing structures to achieve self-identified goals (UNFPA, 2002). It is premised on the notion that social change is more likely to be sustained if affected communities own the "process and content" of communication.

HIV communications based on the rationale that knowledge equals behavior have been widely ineffective. For the most part, they have been driven by international donors and have failed to adequately represent affected communities in decision making (Scalway, 2002). The shift to SCC has been encouraged by the Rockefeller

Foundation's Communication for Social Change network (Grey-Felder & Deane, 1999) and the Joint United Nations Program on HIV/AIDS (UNAIDS, 1999). The UNAIDS Framework for HIV/AIDS Communication has adopted an SCC perspective, acknowledging that HIV/AIDS is embedded within complex social dynamics and that individual responses are dictated by societal norms, gender, and socioeconomic status, thus requiring broader social support in transformation coupled to longer-term changes in attitude (Scalway, 2002). Therefore, to be effective, the communications response must be equally socially ordered.

In applying participatory techniques to HIV communications, the emphasis shifts from being solely the transmission of information to the "organisational value of communication and the role of communicative efforts" in empowering people—that is, how can communities use information to mobilize themselves? (Krishnatray, Melkote, & Krishnatray, 2006). It moves beyond the view that community problems stem from ignorance and acknowledges the fact that problems arise from lack of access to and availability of resources. Participatory communication in health is two-way learning between the community and the facilitator, based on the principle that community members have the capacity to create knowledge, and takes a problem-solving approach (Krishnatray et al., 2006). In the specific case of addressing HIV-related stigma, participatory communication is practical because it facilitates community empowerment to deal with social stigmas. Participatory communication seeks to establish a dialogic process with the community to elicit knowledge from the community, emphasize local capabilities, and identify appropriate solutions.

More and more frequently, community-based media or alternative media are being used in HIV communications. Interesting examples are DramAidE and SoulCity in South Africa (Botha & Durden, 2004; Goldstein, Usdin, Scheeper, & Japhet, 2005). In Ghana, media structures have been described as elitist and undemocratic

(Boafo, 1987), further underscoring the need for innovations in communications at the community level.

The Participatory Media Planning Process at WAAF

WAAF was established in 1998 and is a recognized member of the Ghanaian Network of HIV/AIDS-based nongovernmental agencies (GHANET). In 2005, WAAF had well-diversified services oriented around HIV/AIDS prevention, care, and support. They included hospice services, home visits, free voluntary counseling and testing (VCT), condom distribution, a food assistance program, links to training and apprenticeship programs, and transportation to the local teaching hospital for access to antiretroviral therapy. The clinic was staffed by one doctor, one nurse, a pharmacy technician, and two ward assistants who live on the premises to provide care for patients in the 10-bed ward. WAAF had pioneered a successful secondary school peer education program. It also ran various social programs, including a Positive Living Association (PLA) that met biweekly and focused on peer support and socialization. Twice as many women as men used the services at WAAF.

Although WAAF had been successfully operating since 1998 despite the challenges inherent in resource-constrained settings, the organization did not have a detailed strategy for engaging with its local community. WAAF is located in central Accra and as such serves an urban population, though people travel to WAAF from every region of the country. WAAF is not far from Nima, a poor, densely populated community, historically made up of migrants from northern Ghana. The particularities of the community, predominantly Muslim and Hausa-speaking, make it a minority area in the capital, not reflected in mass-media campaigns. Nima residents have little access to clean water or proper health care and little voice outside the community. The health-seeking behavior of the community is not known, nor is the HIV prevalence, though it is believed to be higher than the general population, exacerbated by poverty. In 2005, a Nima-based youth group had approached WAAF to help them build HIV/AIDS awareness in the community. WAAF felt that it was important to work with the community to develop a strategy to begin addressing some of the issues they faced, in particular, issues of HIV-related stigma and discrimination.

The planning process took place between September 2005 and March 2006. The first and most important step was for WAAF to develop its communication strategy. In this case, the idea was for WAAF to develop its own organizational capacity to offer its services to the particular needs of Nima residents. WAAF follows a participation model of colearning and interactive participation and describes its community development goals as such:

> The role of the community is as equal partner, and WAAF as facilitator. The community will participate in the creation of an action plan and the analysis of solutions in order to construct new local structures or reinforce existing ones to deal with HIV-related stigma and discrimination at the community level. The community and WAAF will share their respective knowledge, combining a familiarity of local information with an expertise in HIV treatment, prevention and advocacy to establish a new community vision, and to work in collaboration to develop an appropriate action plan. (WAAF, 2006a)

Given the proactivity demonstrated by Nima community members, the communication strategy had to serve two functions: It had to be educative, with the goal of making information known and sharing knowledge, and it had to be facilitative, with the goal of providing a platform for participation and dialogue (Ramirez & Quarry, 2004). There was a clear need to exchange perspectives and explore new ideas around building this new program.

The communication strategy had to be participatory in Nima because the communication modes traditionally used and trusted within the community are such. Community members in Nima source their information in a variety of manners, the main forms building on the oral culture through faith-based institutions and cultural meetings. Personal problems are often solved by the executive boards of various social support clubs and trade associations. Money is collected on a regular basis to support the efforts of community members—women have such groups to assist with marriages and older men support the young to go abroad. Thus, the approach identified by WAAF sought to support local communication structures.

WAAF wanted to build on its expertise in peer education and, having recently acquired digital video equipment, sought ways to incorporate the two resources. Examples WAAF drew on of participatory media with video included the pioneering Fogo Process (Williamson, 1991) and Maneno Mengi in Tanzania (Gumucio Dagron, 2001), both of which used the camera as a community "mirror" to address pertinent issues. In this method, community members are integral in community diagnostics, planning and producing a short video, and subsequently facilitating community action planning based on what is captured on video. In this way, the process is as important, if not more so, than the product.

WAAF assembled a multidisciplinary, multilingual, and multifaith team of staff members to work with the Nima group. This team consisted of the school outreach program leader, the IT officer, the president of the PLA, and the community development specialist. The group received training in participatory media methods[1] and developed a program to combine participatory media with the resources of peer educators skilled in antistigma training and community action planning.

Eight peer educators were recruited, four from WAAF's PLA and four from Nima—disclosure of HIV status was not required. The peer educator team had an equal number of Christians and Muslims and of women and men. In the case of the HIV-positive members of the team, each was at a different stage of her or his personal healing after the HIV-positive diagnosis. This design ensured that throughout the process of dialogue, different perspectives were engaged—the community is not homogeneous, and multiple inputs for broad-based participation were key.

The rationale of *vidéo-mirroir*[2] as the method is referred to here is that if an individual sees her reflection in the mirror, she can admire herself, but she can also work to adjust the flaws she sees. Similarly, video can be used to reflect the community, being used in consultation and close observance; the camera becomes an active participant in community action planning to develop community-based interventions. Five steps are outlined in Figure 19.1.

Participatory diagnostics is the first step of an ongoing iterative process. Meetings were held with community leaders to discuss the problems of the community, to learn, to build a trusting relationship, and to obtain permission to enter the community. Once entry to the community was granted, in-depth consultations were held with groups of women, men, and youth in the community to obtain their perspectives on what the problems were and also to allow them to exercise their voice.

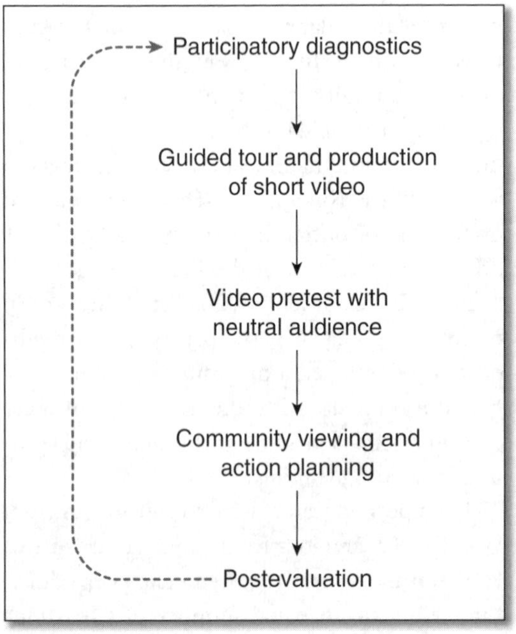

Key informants from Nima indicated that there was a sense that problems existed within the community but were not being addressed. There was ignorance about HIV—people did not undergo VCT, though it was not clear whether this was due to nonbelief in at-risk behaviors, lacking access to services, or fear. Quick burials without known cause of death, according to custom, compounded myths and misconceptions, resulting in a near invisibility of people living with HIV within the community: "People are dying silently and no action is being taken. We know of [the] Ghana AIDS Commission, but we do not know what it is doing for the community" (Key informant, Nima).

The consultations presented WAAF with the opportunity to further learn the environment and the particular norms and power dynamics of the community, and WAAF prepared the community for further steps. Peer educators trained in basic video skills (WAAF, 2006b) were given a guided tour of the locale and used the camera to draw a community map of where and how stigma happens. Furthermore, confidential interviews from community members about their views and perspectives were captured.

Building Antistigma Capacity

The recruitment process for the peer educators was designed to elicit information from those who were interested—why did they want to be peer educators, what was their experience with community outreach, and what were their thoughts on stigma? The selected group was highly qualified; several of the PLA members had been peer educators in the past, attending international conferences such as the 14th International Conference on AIDS and STIs in Africa (ICASA).[3] One was a journalist from Liberia. Several of them had a good understanding of stigma, expressed by what they themselves had experienced, simply

Participatory diagnostics

↓

Guided tour and production
of short video

↓

Video pretest with
neutral audience

↓

Community viewing and
action planning

↓

Postevaluation

Figure 19.1 Five Stages of Vidéo-Mirroir

described as "the pointing, the gossiping and the lack of love" that happens when people discover someone is HIV positive. Compassion was the only response given as the answer to stigma. Fewer participants had an understanding of what community participation was or had opinions on whether media had the ability to affect the way people thought.

Two separate training curricula were developed by the WAAF team, the first focused on participatory antistigma training and the second on video skills training. They were set up as train-the-trainer modules to further build the capacity of WAAF to continue running these training sessions in the future and also to increase the peer educators' capacity to facilitate such sessions within the community. In the case of the antistigma training, the goal was to provide accurate information, sensitize and raise awareness, and assist in community discussions and skills development. The training workshops were each 1-week long, with the antistigma training taking place first, followed by the video skills training.

The workshops were conducted in Twi, Ga, Hausa, and English and took place in the shade of the almond tree in the WAAF front yard.

Participants first reviewed basic HIV facts—transmission, prevention, care, and myths and misconceptions. The second training module focused on stigma and on learning to identify stigma: How does stigma manifest itself in different locales within the community, for instance at the market, in the mosque, at school, at the health center, or at a funeral? Participants might suggest an image of a family sharing a meal from a single bowl, with one member isolated and eating from his own bowl of food. Problem-tree techniques were used to address the social root causes and common attitudes and their effects, the prevailing myths and misconceptions that promote stigma, and concrete methods of addressing stigma at the household and community level.[4] The third module dealt with participation, the elements and principles of planning, working, and problem solving in a participatory manner, and the overall goals of community

Photo 19.2 Peer Educator's Training Workshop

Source: Aku Kwamie.

development. Forms of stigma as they occur in the community and building support for HIV-affected households were addressed, as were learning effective responses to stigmatizing statements, learning how to assess community barriers and channels, and learning how to plan action-oriented activities as a community. Discussions topics included organizing community meetings, providing neutral people to mediate conflicts pertaining to HIV-status disclosure, home visits, house repairs and going to market for households in need, watching children, and providing work for out-of-work community members where possible.

The video skills training was a beginner-level course and focused on basics of camera operation (lighting, sound, image composition, and perspective), practice on filming and planning shoots, use of video to reflect the community and as an antistigma tool, and how to interview sensitive subjects.

The Diagnostic Process and the Beginning of Dialogue

By the time the participatory diagnostics were underway, the peer educators group had practiced their video skills extensively and had made very good progress in a short period of time. After earlier consultations with the chief of Nima, the team was invited to have sequential meetings with faith leaders and with women's, men's, and youth groups in Nima to learn their ideas about HIV/AIDS.

The Challenges of HIV-Related Stigma

In addressing aspects of stigma, the degree of self-stigma expressed by HIV-positive team members was surprising. During the recruitment interviews when asked to speak about themselves, several candidates began by describing how they first found out their HIV status, as though this was the origin of their present

selves. This was especially profound in the Ghanaian context, where answers to questions of self or place are almost always rooted in where people, and by extension their parents, come from. It is also interesting to note that the HIV-positive team members were more likely to make comments that were more stigmatizing and less sensitive than other workshop participants. A memorable discussion was on the notion of *innocent* people living with HIV versus those who were *guilty* in their acquisition of the virus, a view shared by many of the workshop participants and not altogether useful to the stigma discourse. One of the most animated exchanges was about "blame," a powerful exercise that sought to evaluate the attribution of particular characteristics to the likelihood of becoming HIV positive. After rigorous investigations about the roots of stigma and about learning how to identify and address it, participants were amazing in their convictions about who was "most likely" or "least likely" to become HIV positive. Examples such as the male physician, the young wheelchair-bound girl, and the elderly seamstress would be on the "least likely" end of the spectrum, while the scantily clad woman, the fat businessman, and the shoeless drunk would appear on the "most likely" end of the spectrum. Participants eagerly shouted out comments such as "prostitute" and "sugar-daddy," but after the banter and explanations underlying the reasoning ("Madam is holding a mobile phone—most likely"; "look at him with his cap backwards—most likely!") the workshop participants were surprised that their comments, which came so easily and seemingly made sense ("but just *look* at him") were acts of stigma and could still occur despite a newly developed understanding of what stigma was. By drawing attention to the symbols that characterize a particular position in the social order, here denoted by age, education, gender, money, and power, this example powerfully exhibits how much stigma is socially linked, how stigmatized HIV is, and how deeply those perceptions are held. This example supports the conceptual framework for addressing HIV-related stigma and discrimination posited by Parker and Aggleton (2003), which rejects the notion of stigma as static to individual traits or characteristics but rather understands stigma and discrimination as social processes. Thus, HIV-related stigma can be resisted and challenged through social action (Parker & Aggleton, 2003). The framework also leans on "concepts of symbolic violence and hegemony" to explain that those who feel stigmatization often accept and, in turn, internalize stigma (Parker & Aggleton, 2003). As such,

> The processes of symbolic violence and hegemony convince the dominated to accept existing hierarchies and allow social hierarchies to persist over generations, without generating conscious recognition from those who are dominated. In addition, these processes limit the ability of oppressed and stigmatised groups and individuals to resist the forces that discriminate against them. (p. 18)

Shame, punishment, and otherness over time develop such legitimacy that those who find themselves stigmatized against, regardless of their position in society, perpetuate the cycle through self-stigma and stigmatizing others. Given this, how can didactic BCC methods adequately address HIV-related stigma?

Also surprisingly, stigma was addressed head on during community consultations—community members recognized it and called it by name. During one particularly telling consultation with a group of elderly women, the discussion turned to the incidence of people falling ill without the community's knowledge of the cause. The women knew that they consciously stigmatized against others. As it was stated, "We know stigma is bad, but the disease is worse, and so stigma helps us to protect our youth" (Key informant, Nima).

This example further illustrates how the "production" and use of stigma helps maintain societal order (Parker & Aggleton, 2003). In this case, stigma becomes a tool, a prevention strategy in itself.

According to Ramirez and Quarry (2004) information is either adopted or rejected knowledgably when a communication strategy has successfully achieved its goals. What the WAAF experience in participatory media planning demonstrated was that combining peer education with *vidéo-mirroir* techniques was a valid and effective way of addressing HIV-related stigma in this context. Moving beyond BCC, WAAF was able to facilitate dialogue in a manner relevant to the community about stigma, create fora for safe discussion about taboos, and support the community in identifying actionable change. In this case, the process was of greater import than the product.

Further Considerations

WAAF's planning process raised some interesting questions regarding participatory media as it is applied to HIV communications in Ghana. Social change works over the long term, often taking years before any tangible outcomes are observed. While this is no different in the case of WAAF, some short-term positive results have already been witnessed: The community has requested WAAF to bring it VCT. Not a panacea in itself, it is evidence that the community has claimed some ownership over its action plan and ultimately desires change. For WAAF, evaluation over the long term will have to include understanding attitude changes, structural changes, and power shifts within the community as well as improved quality of life for HIV-positive community members and those who care for them.

Intriguingly, there appeared two levels of community that were in operation during the planning process. First and most obvious, there was the Nima community. Recognized only through the process of building capacity and dialogue was the PLA, a smaller group within the WAAF dynamic. What was observed during the course of the planning process was that, as PLA members engaged in community participation and developed new skills, they became more confident and more aware of their own voices. Eventual change in the leadership of the PLA may have been as a result of this process. Formerly dominated by men, the PLA executive subsequently better reflected its constituents by including more women. The development had also been noticed by WAAF management, who have since employed a gender specialist to assist the organization to apply a gender lens to its operations. To a degree, WAAF had to get its own house in order for it to improve its external services, and this new form of dialogue may have led to such empowerment. There is no accurate way to measure the causal link between the two. However, it suggests that the process of participation and dialogue at many levels within the community and within WAAF may have been as important for WAAF on an organizational level as it can potentially be for Nima at a community level. In Nima, the long-term changes, if any, will take much more time to become apparent.

Conclusion

HIV-related stigma exacerbates preexisting sensitivities that are held about sexuality, death, gender, race, and class. HIV-related stigma is driven by lack of awareness, misconceptions about transmission, and values linking HIV-positive people with perceived immoral behavior (Nyblade & Carr, 2006). These "drivers" are what makes HIV-related stigma nearly impossible to communicate through nonneutral ABC messaging. The WAAF experience, while formative, supports a growing body of knowledge that indicates that interventions need to address more than the effects of stigma by investigating stigma's root causes (Nyblade & Carr, 2006). Such a thing is difficult to accomplish through billboards and radio broadcasts alone and rather requires sensitive facilitation in safe and participatory spaces, as the WAAF experience with participatory media planning revealed. If stigma is reconceptualized as a social process, then it follows that it requires a social process to address it. BCC methods, because they rely on the individual as the unit of change, are simply insufficient in this regard. Neither video nor community-mirror techniques are themselves a silver-bullet solution for communities—both the community and its facilitator must understand their own definitions of partnership and participation. Equally, both must be prepared for what comes out of dialogue. Nevertheless, HIV-related stigma and discrimination is an area where greater understanding and action is required. Participatory media offer a dialogic process that can help to fill the gaps left by traditional HIV communications and can better support communities in the process.

Notes

1. In November 2005, members of the WAAF team attended a weeklong workshop in participatory media methods in Kpalimé, Togo, with regional partners to investigate the use of community participation and media in HIV communication.

2. G. Ahialegbedzi (2005). ONG Vivre-Mieux. Discussion during design workshop with partners in Kpalimé, Togo, November 2005.

3. The 14th ICASA conference was held in Abuja, Nigeria, in December 2005. A community village forum promoted discussion about community-based and psychosocial care and support among delegates from youth and women's organizations, people living with HIV, faith-based organizations, traditional healers, and media groups.

4. In 2002, the International Centre for Research on Women and the CHANGE Project (1998–2005) undertook a three-country study of the causes, dynamics, and consequences of HIV-related stigma. The output of this work was a manual for community organizations to raise awareness and promote community-based action.

Understanding and Challenging HIV Stigma—Toolkit for Action (Kidd & Clay, 2003) was adapted and applied to the WAAF and Nima context.

References

Airhihenbuwa, C. O., Makinwa, B., & Obregon, R. (2000). Toward a new communication framework for HIV/AIDS. *Journals of Health Communication, 5*(Suppl.), 101–111.

Airhihenbuwa, C. O., & Obregon, R. (2000). A critical assessment of theories/models used in health communication for HIV/AIDS. *Journal of Health Communication, 5*(Suppl.), 5–15.

Benefo, K. R. (2004, May 5). The mass media and HIV/AIDS prevention in Ghana. *Journal of Health Population in Developing Countries.* Retrieved April 9, 2009, from www.longwoods .com/view.php?aid=17642&cat=396

Boafo, S. T. K. (1987). Democratizing media systems in African societies: The case of Ghana. *African Media Review, 2*(1), 24–37.

Boafo, S. T. K. (2002). Participatory development communication: An African perspective. In G. Bessette (Ed.), *People, land and water* (pp. 41–50). Ottawa, Ontario, Canada: IDRC.

Botha, P., & Durden, E. (2004, March). *Using participatory media to explore gender relations and HIV/AIDS amongst South African youth: The example of DramAidE.* Paper prepared for the UNESCO Institute for Education International Workshop/Seminar, Learning and Empowerment: Key Issues in Strategies for HIV/AIDS Prevention, Chiangmai, Thailand.

Brown, L., Trujillo, L., & MacIntyre, L. (2001). *Interventions to reduce HIV/AIDS stigma: What have we learned?* New York: Population Council.

Center for Communication Programs, Bloomberg School of Public Health, Johns Hopkins University. (2003, February). Stop AIDS Love Life in Ghana "shatters the silence." *Communication Impact, 15.*

FAO. (2005). *Communication for development roundtable report: Focus on sustainable development.* Rome: Author.

Ghana AIDS Commission. (2003). *National report on monitoring: Follow up to the declaration of commitment on HIV/AIDS.* Accra, Ghana: Author.

Ghana Ministry of Health Country Coordinating Mechanism. (2002). *Accelerating access to prevention, care, support and treatment for all persons affected by AIDS, tuberculosis and malaria.* Accra, Ministry of Health of the Republic of Ghana.

Goffman, E. (1963). *Stigma: Notes on the management of a spoiled identity.* New York: Simon & Schuster.

Goldstein, S., Usdin, S., Scheeper, E., & Japhet, G. (2005). Communicating HIV and AIDS, what works? A report on the impact evaluation of Soul City's fourth series. *Journal of Health Communication, 10,* 465–483.

Grey-Felder, D., & Deane, J. (1999). *Communication for social change: A position paper and conference report.* Cape Town, South Africa: Rockefeller Foundation.

Gumucio Dagron, A. (2001). *Making waves: Stories of participatory communication for social change.* New York: Rockefeller Foundation.

Kidd, R., & Clay, S. (2003). *Understanding and challenging HIV stigma: Toolkit for action.* Washington, DC: CHANGE Project.

Krishnatray, P., Melkote, S. R., & Krishnatray, S. (2006). Providing care to persons with stigmatised illnesses: Implications for participatory communication. *Journal of Health Management, 8*(1), 51–63.

Nyblade, L., & Carr, D. (2006). *Towards a stronger response to HIV and AIDS: Challenging stigma.* London: Department for International Development.

Parker, R., & Aggleton, P. (2003). *HIV/AIDS-related stigma and discrimination: A conceptual framework and an agenda for action.* Washington, DC: Horizons Program.

Ramirez, R., & Quarry, W. (2004). *Communication strategies in the age of decentralization and privatization of rural services: Lessons from two African experiences.* Agricultural Research and Extension Network Paper No. 136. London: Overseas Development Institute.

Scalway, T. (2002). *Critical challenges in HIV communication. A perspective paper.* London: Panos Institute.

UNAIDS. (1999). *Communications framework for HIV/AIDS: A new direction.* Geneva, Switzerland: Author.

UNAIDS. (2008). Ghana: 2008 update. *Epidemiological fact sheet on HIV and AIDS—Core data on epidemiology and response.* Geneva, Switzerland: Author.

UNFPA. (2002). *Communication for development roundtable report: Focus on HIV/AIDS communication and evaluation.* New York: Author.

West Africa AIDS Foundation. (2006a). *Community development communication strategy.* Accra, Ghana: Author.

West Africa AIDS Foundation. (2006b). *Tackling HIV-stigma and discrimination through participatory media for community development: Video skills training program manual.* Accra, Ghana: Author.

Williamson, H. A. (1991). The Fogo Process: Development support communications in Canada and the developing world. In F. L. Casmir (Ed.), *Communication in development* (pp. 270–287). Norwood, NJ: Ablex.

Wolfe, W., Weiser, S., Leiter, K., Steward, W., Percy-de Korte, F., Phaladze, N., et al. (2006). *Impact of universal access to antiretroviral therapy on HIV stigma in Botswana.* Paper presented at the 16th Annual Conference of the International AIDS Society, Toronto, Ontario, Canada.

Yoon, C. S. (1996). Participatory communication for development. In G. Bessette & C. V. Rajasunderam (Eds.), *Participatory development communication: A West African agenda* (pp. 37–61.). Ottawa, Ontario, Canada: IDRC.

PART V

Community Media and Social Movements

The chapters in this section explore the relationship between community media and collective action aimed at social transformation. Drawing on work in sociology, communication, political science, and social movement studies, contributors illuminate the role that grassroots and community-based media play in producing and legitimating oppositional discourse, creating a shared identity among movement participants, and sustaining and enlarging social movements over time.

We begin with a brief discussion of the complex interaction between social movements and dominant media organizations. This line of inquiry maintains that news production and distribution constitute a "critical arena" of struggle for activists and community organizers (Ryan, Carragee, & Schwerner, 1998). Following this, we observe the importance of cultural expression and place-based institutions to movement organizing, mobilization, and cohesion. Throughout, we consider mainstream media coverage of social movements as well as the communicative forms and practices generated within and through movements themselves. In so doing, we can better understand and appreciate the strategic value of

communication within social movements and between movement actors and wider publics. Furthermore, these insights reveal the potential that community media studies hold for interrogating the communicative dimensions of social movements.

A Critical Arena

In an influential article, Gamson and Wolfsfeld (1993) identify the structural and cultural dimensions of the interaction between news media and social movements. Briefly stated, analyses concerned with the structural aspects of this relationship examine the power imbalances between social movement organizations (SMOs) on the one hand and news organizations on the other (e.g., Carroll & Ratner, 1999). Typically, structural analyses emphasize the unequal but mutually dependent relationship between media and movements.

According to Gamson and Wolfsfeld (1993), "Movements need the news media for three major purposes: mobilization, validation, and scope enlargement" (p. 116). That is to say, press coverage is instrumental in communicating the movement's goals, status, and activities to its core constituency and beyond. In this way, media coverage can legitimate the change agenda being advanced by social movements. Moreover, favorable press coverage can help movement participants forge alliances with other groups and constituencies, thereby increasing the movement's ranks and enhancing the movement's potential to influence public opinion and affect public policy. In short, movements need media coverage to promote, legitimate, and publicize social change messages in the public sphere.

But, as Gamson and Wolfsfeld (1993) observe, news media depend on social movements as well. Journalists cover social movements because they "often make good copy for media. They provide drama, conflict, and action: colorful copy; and photo opportunities" (pp. 116–117). In contemporary journalistic practice, the importance of compelling visuals of the sort associated with social movements—mass rallies, public demonstrations, and the like—cannot be overstated. What's more, an emphasis on drama and conflict is a central feature of the narrative structures and techniques employed by news workers. All this is to say that reporters and editors find social movements useful insofar as they often provide dramatic and visually arresting raw material for press reports.

Of course, negative press coverage can undermine the credibility of social movements by marginalizing movement participants and otherwise trivializing social change issues and demands (e.g., Solomon, 2000). The difficulty confronting social movements, therefore, lies in getting accurate, ongoing, and, if possible, sympathetic press coverage (Ryan, 1991). The point here is that the relationship between movements and news media is based on *asymmetrical dependencies*. Put another way, movements require press coverage far more than the press needs social movements.

Not surprisingly, this condition "translates into greater power for the media in the transaction" (Gamson & Wolfsfeld, 1993, p. 117). This power differential is, perhaps, most obvious in terms of journalists' newsgathering routines: a preference for the pithy sound bite over nuanced argumentation, an uncritical reliance on "official sources," and an attendant skepticism toward issue advocates. In short, professional news values and practices represent formidable obstacles for activists, community organizers, and SMOs working to influence public opinion and effect social change (Hackett & Zhao, 1996).

More critically, in light of the institutional arrangements between dominant media organizations and powerful corporate, financial, and political interests, it seems unlikely that progressive social movements could receive fair, accurate, and ongoing press coverage in mainstream media (Howley, 2008). As Scott Uzelman (2005) observes,

> The very structure, institutional interests, and routines of mainstream, corporate media effectively act as blockades to dissenting opinion. . . . Media corporations have little reason to give sustained coverage to voices critical of the conditions in which such entities thrive. (p. 19)

Herein we can detect community media's significance to social movements.

As nonprofit, self-managed media organizations, community media are insulated from the structural arrangements and institutional interests associated with corporate and public service media. By providing movement actors and participants with resources for media production and distribution—microphones, recorders, cameras, transmitters, and such—community media circumvent the structural barriers to communication for social change associated with dominant media. In this way, community media provide a forum for dissent and a vehicle for cultural resistance and oppositional politics (e.g., Kellner, 1992; Land, 1999). And in the absence of substantive, let alone sympathetic press coverage from mainstream media outlets, social movements rely on grassroots, independent, and alternative media organizations to mobilize movement participants, publicize their concerns to wider constituencies, and sustain collective identities over time (Downing, 2001; Streitmatter, 2001).

In contrast to the structural dimension of the interaction between dominant media and SMOs, a cultural analysis focuses our attention on the struggle over meaning that takes place between social movements and news workers. Analyses in this vein start from the assumption that journalists and movement actors alike actively interpret social reality: an insight that highlights the constructed (and contested) character of news production (Tuchman, 1978). As Gamson and Wolfsfeld (1993) observe, "Events do not speak for themselves but must be *woven into some larger story line or frame* [italics added]: they take on their meaning from the frame in which they are embedded" (p. 117). In other words, news workers and movement participants engage in a struggle over meaning when they assert different, often-competing frames on news events and issues (e.g., Gitlin, 1980). The implications of this struggle come into focus when we consider the relationship between social movements, news frames, and the formation of public opinion (Entman, 2004; Gamson & Modigliani, 1989).

Once again, grassroots and community-based media serve as a vital resource for social movements, this time by taking up the struggle over meaning between mainstream news outlets and SMOs. For instance, in her study of the controversy surrounding plans to build a new runway at Boston's Logan International Airport, Regina Marchi (2005) identifies two competing news frames. The first, employed by various constituencies who would benefit from runway expansion, framed the issue in terms of "economic progress." Meanwhile, a second group, a coalition of community activists from the neighborhoods surrounding the airport, opposed to the project framed the issue in terms of "environmental justice."

Marchi's (2005) study reveals how community organizers made effective use of new technologies and grassroots communication strategies to challenge the dominant "economic progress" frame employed by the city's political and economic elites—a frame that was uncritically replicated and amplified by the city's daily newspapers. Through community organizing and savvy media practices, the coalition opposed to runway expansion publicized its concerns throughout Boston and educated journalists, politicians, and city residents about the environmental implications of the new runway. In doing so, this grassroots media campaign successfully reframed the news story to reflect the issue of environmental justice and helped generate public support for people living in the affected neighborhoods.

Place, Culture, and Collective Action

In contrast to earlier social movements that were predicated on the redistribution of wealth or the attainment of formal political recognition (e.g., the right to collective bargaining, voting rights), the so-called new social movements are defined by their focus on issues of identity and values. These new forms of collective action—such as feminism, gay and lesbian activism, as well as the peace, environmental, youth, and global justice movements—have challenged traditional political-economic and sociological explanations of social movements (Melucci, 1980). Analysts have since focused their attention on the everyday social interactions and cultural practices that shape collective consciousness: the shared identities, perspectives, and sensibilities that provide the basis for collective action. Accordingly, the "cultural turn" in social movement studies explores "the intersection of culture, practice (collective and everyday) and politics" (Escobar, 1992, p. 396).

This emphasis on everyday practices and social relations highlights the importance of place in understanding the dynamics of social movements. For instance, Stolle-McAllister (2007) found that mobilizing collective affection for place is an effective strategy of popular resistance: one that helps individuals and groups overcome feelings of alienation and powerlessness, provides a basis for the construction and an affirmation of collective identities, and encourages community members to assume considerable risk to their lives and livelihoods. Environmental movements, in particular, offer a compelling illustration of the affective and strategic importance of place in popular forms of resistance. When local communities deem development projects to be unsustainable or when environmental degradation threatens public health and local ecosystems, communities reaffirm place-based identities as the basis for collective action, including popular as well as radical forms of resistance (e.g., Taylor, 1995).

All this is to suggest that place, far from being irrelevant in a global era, figures prominently in the emergence of contemporary social movements. Indeed, the forces and conditions associated with globalization—especially the unsettling effects of global capital on local communities—often prefigure the emergence of collective action. As economic geographer Byron Miller (1992) puts it, "Resistance movements frequently arise in response to colonization and disruption of social life in particular places" (p. 37).

These insights have prompted analysts to interrogate the role played by grassroots and community-based organizations—especially those that facilitate interaction between community members—in movement building. For instance, Evans and Boyte (2000) argue that "the historical evidence now suggests that popular movements with enduring power and depth always find their strength in community-based associations" (p. 259). Indeed, local institutions such as union halls, churches, coffeehouses, university campuses, and the like were instrumental in supporting a variety of movements, including the labor, civil rights, and anti-war movements of the past century.

Introducing the concept of "free spaces," Evans and Boyte (2000) highlight the role that place-based institutions play in supporting social movements that challenge institutional racism, gender inequity, and economic disparity within (and beyond) local communities. Acting as repositories of collective memory and resources for the revitalization of affective relations of solidarity, community-based institutions, such as grassroots media organizations, constitute "free spaces" inasmuch as these institutions, operating

independently of either the state or the marketplace and rooted in the everyday lived experience of local communities, "are the foundation and wellspring for any sustained challenge" to the status quo (p. 268).

Significantly, Evans and Boyte (2000) call our attention to the ways in which these "free spaces" encourage community groups to "rework ideas and themes from the dominant culture in ways which bring forth hidden and potentially subversive elements" (p. 260). This insight is instructive inasmuch as it underscores the complex relationship between culture and politics. On the one hand, cultural texts and practices often work to reinforce and legitimate relations of domination and subordination. On the other hand, cultural expression can be emancipatory, even transformative, inasmuch as poetry, narrative, song, and visual arts offer a glimpse of alternative ways of being in the world.

Furthermore, cultural activity enables movement actors to construct relations of solidarity and affinity within and through collective visions of resistance and transformation. For example, James Lewes (2001) argues that the articles, editorials, and cartoons that appeared in the GI underground press during the Vietnam War reveal how enlisted men "expressed and, thus, produced their relation to other social formations" (p. 137). Lewes focuses our attention on the discursive construction of GI activist identity vis-à-vis the military brass, politicians, and business leaders who supported the war effort. Significantly, the antiwar sentiments expressed in the GI press drew heavily on military culture to articulate collective identities of resistance to the Vietnam War and, more generally, to a military apparatus that denied enlisted men the very rights and liberties it claimed to be fighting for. Accordingly, Lewes contends, "the visions and representations published in the GI press . . . [served] to centre and focus the [antiwar] movement" among enlisted men (p. 138).

These insights reflect a growing awareness of, and appreciation for, the relationship between collective action and cultural expression. And yet, despite the recognition that culture matters to social movements, there is relatively little work that examines the "cultural forms generated within movements" (Reed, 2005, p. xx). This seems at odds with the emphasis Melucci and other proponents of new social movement theory have placed on *symbolic challenges*—communicative strategies and tactics designed to reveal and resist the way in which systems of domination and oppression are legitimated and reinforced through language, discourse, and cultural expression. Indeed, these symbolic challenges are essential for projects aimed at social transformation inasmuch as they provide a "different way of perceiving and naming the world" (Melucci, quoted in Escobar, 1992, p. 407).

Intuitively, then, activists and scholars recognize the significance of Brecht's observation regarding the relationship between cultural expression and social transformation: "Art is not a mirror held up to reality, but a hammer with which to shape it" (quoted in Askew, 2002, p. 1). Still, as Reed (2005) argues, few analysts have looked at social movements as sites of cultural production and reception in their own right. Through a comparative analysis of progressive social movements of the late 20th century, Reed calls our attention to two distinct, but related, facets of contemporary social movements: the importance of "dramatic public actions" and "the rather undramatic, mundane daily acts of preparation" that produce these public displays (p. xv). Here, Reed's analysis foregrounds the importance of public forms of communication, the time and effort required to produce this work, and ways in which movement participants understand and make meaning from public performances, collaborative work practices, and the cultural forms produced by movement actors. If we apply these insights to community-based media, we can begin to appreciate the critical role independent, alternative, and grassroots media play in facilitating cultural expression within and through social movements.

Having said this, it would be a mistake to think that cultural expression aimed at social change is necessarily or inevitably progressive. There are times when collective action, mobilized by grassroots media, becomes repressive, hostile, and violent. Indeed, as Jolyon Mitchell (2007) reminds us,

> Some of the most chilling broadcasts in the history of radio emerged from Rwanda in the 1990s. Radio-TELEvision Libre des Mille Collines (RTLM), One Thousand Hills Free Radio, is frequently blamed for inciting the genocide that claimed over eight hundred thousand lives during a hundred days in 1994. (¶ 7)

This is but one dramatic and horrific instance, in which community-based media was used to mobilize people's fears, inflame ethnic hatred, and organize mass slaughter.

To summarize, then, this emphasis on place, culture, and collective action is especially relevant to community media studies. If, as new social movement theory suggests, collective action emerges out of everyday social interactions, then place becomes a strategic site for identity formation and movement building. Through the production, distribution, and reception of cultural texts embedded with oppositional discourse and resistant politics, community media reveal the importance of cultural expression to social movements.

In the chapters that follow, contributors explore the use of grassroots and community-based media in various social, cultural, and political struggles. As we shall see, grassroots media facilitate community organizing and are instrumental in mobilizing local people and resources. By the same token, community media are, in and of themselves, valuable resources that help nurture and support social, political, and aesthetic expressions of popular resistance. Although each chapter considers community activism in a distinct geographic and cultural setting, taken together they highlight the innovative uses of grassroots and community-based media to achieve political aims and support the struggle for social justice.

In Chapter 20, Mario Murillo argues that the indigenous movement in Colombia is at the vanguard of national struggles for social and economic justice. Drawing on in-depth interviews with movement leaders and participants, Murillo finds that indigenous radio serves two critical functions. First, radio is an invaluable resource for organizing and mobilizing indigenous peoples. Second, radio has proved to be an effective means of forging alliances between the indigenous movement and broader constituencies across Colombia. Murillo is quick to point out that the success of indigenous radio takes place against a background of armed conflict and political intimidation. Not unlike other forms of alternative media throughout the world, then, indigenous radio in Colombia supports democratic communication in an otherwise hostile sociopolitical climate.

Dandan Liu's contribution (Chapter 21) presents an intriguing case study of community activism and ethnic minority media. Specifically, Liu examines the interaction between community activists and local Chinese language media in a campaign to defeat a plan to build a new baseball stadium in Philadelphia's Chinatown. Liu's analysis reveals the complexity of urban politics and economic redevelopment schemes in a multicultural metropolis. Throughout, Liu observes the troubled relationship among minority groups, elected representatives, business interests, and local news organizations. Liu concludes that the campaign to stop the stadium did more than preserve Chinatown's physical and cultural integrity—it helped transform the image of this immigrant community throughout the entire city.

The next two chapters consider the relationship between grassroots media collectives and social movements. Claudia Magallanes-Blanco's contribution (Chapter 22) examines the history and practice of Colectivo Perfil Urban—a video collective based in Mexico City. Magallanes-Blanco's analysis underscores the relationship between the collective and the Popular Urban Movement that emerged in the aftermath of the earthquakes that struck Mexico City in 1985.

Magallanes-Blanco focuses her discussion on the production of *Los Más Pequeños,* a video featuring the voices and perspectives of members of the Popular Urban Movement. Throughout, Magallanes-Blanco illustrates the interaction between social movements and local forms of cultural expression.

Brian Woodman's (Chapter 23) historical case study of guerrilla video in the Twin Cities of Minneapolis and St. Paul, Minnesota, considers the use of what was then a new technology—portable video—to support feminist causes and principles. Woodman traces the development of Iris video, a short-lived and little-known women's video collective. By recovering the history of Iris Video, Woodman examines the relationship between feminist video practice and the wider feminist movement. Woodman's analysis of the collective's organizational structure and philosophy reveals the interplay between culture, aesthetics, and movement politics. In the end, Woodman's contribution highlights the important, but largely overlooked, contributions women have made to alternative, grassroots, and community-based video practice.

References

Askew, K. M. (2002). *Performing the nation: Swahili music and cultural politics in Tanzania.* Chicago: University of Chicago Press.

Carroll, W. K., & Ratner, R. S. (1999). Media strategies and political projects: A comparative study of social movements. *Canadian Journal of Sociology, 24*(1), 1–34.

Downing, J. (2001). *Radical media: Rebellious communication and social movements.* Thousand Oaks, CA: Sage.

Entman, R. M. (2004). *Projections of power: Framing news, public opinion, and U.S. foreign policy.* Chicago: University of Chicago Press.

Escobar, A. (1992). Culture, practice and politics: Anthropology and the study of social movements. *Critique of Anthropology, 12*(4), 395–432.

Evans, S., & Boyte, H. (2000). Free spaces: The sources of democratic change in America. In V. A. Hodgkinson & M. W. Foley (Eds.), *The civil society reader* (pp. 255–269). Hanover, NH: University Press of New England. (Original work published 1986)

Gamson, W. A., & Modigliani, A. (1989). Media discourse and public opinion on nuclear power. *American Journal of Sociology, 95,* 1–37.

Gamson, W. A., & Wolfsfeld, G. (1993). Movements and media as interacting systems. *The Annals of the American Academy of Political and Social Science, 528,* 114–125.

Gitlin, T. (1980). *The whole world is watching: Mass media and the making and unmaking of the new left.* Berkeley: University of California Press.

Hackett, R., & Zhao, Y. (1996). Journalistic objectivity and social change. *Peace Review, 8*(1), 5–11.

Howley, K. (2008). Democracy Now! Decolonizing US news media. *Transformations, 16.* Retrieved November 3, 2008, from http://transformations journal.org/journal/issue_16/article_05.shtml

Kellner, D. (1992). Public access television and the struggle for democracy. In J. Wasko & V. Mosco (Eds.), *Democratic communications in the information age* (pp. 100–113). Toronto, Ontario, Canada: Garamond Press.

Land, J. (1999). *Active radio: Pacifica's brash experiment.* Minneapolis: University of Minnesota Press.

Lewes, J. (2001). Envisioning resistance: The GI underground press during the Vietnam War. *Media History, 7*(2), 137–150.

Marchi, R. M. (2005). Reframing the runway: A case study of the impact of community organizing on news and politics, *Journalism, 6*(4), 465–485.

Melucci, A. (1980). The new social movements: A theoretical approach. *Social Science Information, 19*(2), 199–226.

Miller, B. (1992). Collective action and rational choice: Place, community and the limits of individual self-interest. *Economic Geography, 68*(1), 22–42.

Mitchell, J. (2007). Remembering the Rwandan genocide: Reconsidering the role of local and global media. *Global Media Journal* (Article 4), *6*(11).

Reed, T. V. (2005). *The art of protest: Culture and activism from the civil rights movement to the streets of Seattle.* Minneapolis: University of Minnesota Press.

Ryan, C. (1991). *Prime time activism: Media strategies for grassroots organizing.* Boston: South End Press.

Ryan, C., Carragee, K. M., & Schwerner, C. (1998). Media, movements, and the quest for social justice. *Journal of Applied Communication Research, 26,* 165–181.

Solomon, W. S. (2000, May). More form than substance: Press coverage of the WTO protests in Seattle. *Monthly Review, 52*(1), 12–20.

Stolle-McAllister, J. (2007). Local social movements and Mesoamerican cultural resistance and adaptation. *Social Movement Studies, 6*(2), 161–175.

Streitmatter, R. (2001). *Voices of revolution: The dissident press in America.* New York: Columbia University Press.

Taylor, B. R. (Ed.). (1995). *Ecological resistance movements: The global emergence of radical and popular environmentalism.* Albany: State University of New York Press.

Tuchman, G. (1978). *Making news: A study in the construction of reality.* New York: Free Press.

Uzelman, S. (2005). Hard work in the bamboo garden. In A. Langlois & F. Dubois (Eds.), *Autonomous media: Activating resistance and dissent* (pp. 17–29). Montreal, Quebec, Canada: Cumulus Press.

CHAPTER 20

Indigenous Community Radio and the Struggle for Social Justice in Colombia

Mario Alfonso Murillo

The indigenous movement in Colombia is at the forefront of the national struggle for political, social, and economic justice. For almost 40 years, despite being targeted directly by Colombian state security forces, right-wing paramilitary groups, left-wing guerrillas, and drug traffickers, indigenous communities have resisted militarism, economic exploitation, and cultural annihilation. Although its members represent a small percentage of the population, the indigenous movement has been successful at influencing public opinion by inserting itself into the national dialogue through its broad-based political organization, high-profile mobilizations, and dynamic and charismatic leadership.

Indigenous communication includes the ongoing dialogue with the natural world of all that is living and the spiritual world of the ancestors. It also includes the traditional assemblies, working congresses, and mobilizations of the communities, the *minga*, ranging from the small, internal committees dealing with issues such as health and education, to the local councils of the traditional authorities, to the regional and national gatherings where tens of thousands of people unite to deliberate and debate, resulting in what can be described as bottom-up consensus on a broad range of issues. And it includes communication through the media, whether newspapers, magazines, radio, television, or the Internet (Dorado, 2004; Wilches-Chaux, 2005).

This chapter explores the role of indigenous radio within the context of Colombia's armed conflict and its closed mass media system. In particular, the text focuses on the region of the country where the contemporary indigenous movement initially emerged in the early 1970s, the southwestern department of Cauca. By examining the community radio stations established in the northern part of the department, I argue that, because of the manner in which they emerged organically from a broad-based grassroots movement with a long tradition of social activism and citizen participation, and notwithstanding the many challenges facing them, the communication projects described here serve as a model for alternative, community media.

This assessment is based on the broad consensus that community media should serve as democratic spaces that foster an open and pluralistic public sphere; that they should be participatory in that they facilitate a culture of citizen involvement, grassroots participation, and direct action; that they should be locally generated and distributed to allow their constituents to hold local officials and institutions accountable to the community's primary needs; and that they should be accessible to all with no insurmountable barriers to entry. We can add to these community media objectives the more specific goal of promoting a culture of dialogue and tolerance that may eventually lead to social change on the local, national, and even global levels (Fairchild, 2001). In projecting the communication project of the Nasa indigenous community of northern Cauca as a case study of a contemporary public sphere within the context of an internal armed conflict, I argue that it serves as a powerful example of independent, accountable, and responsive community media.

Background on the Indigenous Movement in Colombia

The Nasa are among the largest of Colombia's more than 90 indigenous nationalities or tribes, with a presence in several of the country's departments (provinces). For decades, the Nasa have been at the forefront of Colombia's contemporary indigenous movement. Out of the 90 recognized tribes, 65 have maintained their native, non-European language, the Nasa being one of them, although the statistics vary as to what percentage of the total Nasa population still speaks Nasa Uwe (Rappaport, 2005).

Colombia's indigenous people continue to be threatened almost daily by the violence of the decades-long internal conflict (Murillo, 2004; Villa & Houghton, 2005). A recent independent, international commission organized by the National Indigenous Council for Peace in cooperation with the United Nations Special Rapporteur on Human Rights reported that indigenous communities are victims of "violations of fundamental human rights and crimes against humanity . . . committed by armed actors in the context of the internal armed conflict," noting further threats facing indigenous communities due to "large-scale development projects . . . in indigenous territories without respect for the consultation process" established by both national and international agreements and norms (Consejo Nacional Indígena de Paz, 2006). Among the five regions of the country the International Commission visited in producing its report was the northern region of Cauca, where the Association of Indigenous Councils of Northern Cauca (ACIN) has been mobilizing its constituents for years.

The contemporary indigenous movement in Colombia dates back to the late 1960s and early 1970s in northern Cauca, when the indigenous leadership, as a way to recuperate territory lost after years of colonialism and displacement, launched a series of land occupations in areas controlled by cattle ranchers, the church, and other wealthy landowners. The dramatic confrontations that accompanied the land recuperation process galvanized indigenous communities throughout Colombia. The leadership in northern Cauca always envisioned itself as part of a much larger social movement that would have a departmentwide and indeed national scope, incorporating not only the Nasa people but also other local indigenous groups, Afro-Colombians, and mestizos in the region.

The indigenous social movement's broad-based organizing efforts within the country's many native communities culminated in the 1991 Constituent Assembly, where the antiquated Constitution of 1886 was rewritten with the direct participation of indigenous leaders. For the first time in Colombia's history, indigenous people were recognized as equal partners in the makeup of the nation, as opposed to the minor—or less than adult—status they had been greeted with for generations.

However, as is the case with many of Colombia's laws, most of those relating to indigenous rights have not been fully implemented, and in many respects, conditions have worsened over the last 18 years. The internal armed conflict pitting left-wing guerrilla groups against government security forces and right-wing paramilitary militias has in some regions escalated, directly affecting indigenous communities (Caldón, 2005; Consejo Nacional Indígena de Paz, 2006). The National Indigenous Organization of Colombia (ONIC) estimates that from 2000 to 2008, more than 1,200 indigenous people have been killed, while more than 400,000 have been displaced from their territories. Furthermore, legislative measures initiated by the government of President Alvaro Uribe Vélez in 2002 and 2003 such as the Forestry Law and the new National Mining Code were seen as deliberate attempts to roll back many of the gains made by the indigenous community in the 1991 constitution relating to their territory (Mondragón, 2005). These counterreform measures, as well as the ongoing violence and human rights violations, provided the basis for the movement's large-scale mobilizations that took center stage in late 2008, not only in Cauca but also throughout the country, protests that received considerable attention in the mainstream, corporate media of Colombia, albeit through the prism of the government's perspective.

The indigenous communities in northern Cauca, led by ACIN, have developed a comprehensive communication strategy to advance their agenda and counteract what they see as deliberate misrepresentation of their communities in the major media. Community radio serves as one of its most important tools for organizing internally, as a space for deliberation and discussion, and externally, directed to the broader public, as a vehicle for denunciation and resistance.

Indigenous Community Radio

Radio—as well as video production and the Internet—is a contemporary manifestation of a long tradition of grassroots communication that is the basis of indigenous organization. The case of Radio Payu'mat and its two sibling stations,

Radio Nasa and Voces de Nuestra Tierra, are extraordinary examples of participatory, community media, precisely because of the operational mandate they receive from the *cabildos*, the autonomous indigenous authorities in the communities of northern Cauca. It should be pointed out that there are many other rich experiences of indigenous radio throughout Colombia. Even within the department of Cauca itself, there exists a diverse cross section of community and public interest radio stations serving distinct constituencies confronting a wide range of social conditions.

Radio Payu'mat and the other components of ACIN's communication project have evolved into truly alternative media that confront on a daily basis the faulty conceptions of nationhood, development, and security that are embraced by the mass commercial media and, in turn, the dominant society. This latter assessment is based on the capacity of ACIN and its allies in the indigenous movement nationwide to mobilize masses of people to protest both private and state-sponsored abuses on a regular basis. For years, ACIN has used its media to serve the interests of the community. Today, their radio stations are models for the entire country, where grassroots, citizens' media experiences have been flourishing since the mid-1990s despite the ongoing challenges of the internal conflict. In 2007, for example, Radio Payu'mat was awarded the National Prize for the Best Community Media Project by *Semana*, one of the country's most important newsweeklies, while in 2008, the entire communication network of ACIN made the list of the "Top 25 People Making Colombia a Better Place," an annual honor put out by *CAMBIO* magazine, another important, national newsweekly.

Radio Payu'mat and ACIN's "Communication Quilt"

The complex social order of the Nasa people, the underlying philosophical principles that form the basis of the Nasa "life plan," and the important function of the community assembly in their daily life are outlined in great detail by Rappaport

(2005), Wilches-Chaux (2005), and Dorado (2004). Tied to these issues is the anthropological/social and spiritual/theological understanding of what is communication for the Nasa people. An understanding of this philosophy is essential in recognizing how all the community's efforts—including their media projects—are extensions of an organizational process that has been evolving for decades within the community and is the foundation for the movement. Nevertheless, here the focus is more on the practical developments that led to the emergence of Radio Payu'mat and ACIN's other communication media.

Radio Payu'mat came about as a result of the Programa Comunidad Señal de Cultura y Diversidad, or "community program for culture and diversity," launched by the Ministry of Communications and Ministry of Culture in 2000, although there were other low-power community stations already operating in different parts of the region, including Radio Nasa, in the indigenous resguardo, or reserve, of Toribio, and Voces de Nuestro Pueblo (Voices of Our People), located in the resguardo of Jambaló, both in northern Cauca.

To strengthen the communication program that was started with these low-power community stations, the *cabildo* of Jambaló established the "School of Communication" in 1999, a 3-year program designed to train and expand the capacity of the members of the community who were charged with working in communication. The school eventually trained 75 people in radio, video, and print media, as well as in other areas relating to the Nasa communication philosophy and to the current political situation facing the country and the communities. Consciousness-raising and political formation are key ingredients of their broader media training efforts.

The general objective of Programa Comunidad Señal de Cultura y Diversidad, was to facilitate internal communication for the indigenous communities within their specific territories and in neighboring regions and to support their "life plans." The ultimate goal was to support the communication strategies of the communities, provide the basic infrastructure for radio transmissions, and initiate training programs that would be spearheaded and directed by the indigenous communities themselves according to their cultural traditions and their community needs. The autonomy of indigenous communities participating in the program would be guaranteed through a comprehensive process of direct consultations with the indigenous organizations and traditional authorities (De Greiff & Ramos, 2000; Unidad de Radio del Ministerio de Cultura, 2000). The Programa Comunidad was a direct response to years of activism within both the indigenous and the popular movements around cultural and civil rights on the one hand, and within the media reform movement about opening up democratic communication spaces for marginalized communities on the other. The latter was a struggle spearheaded by academics, independent journalists, grassroots media practitioners, and social activists throughout the country.

The consultation process to get the indigenous radio stations off the ground was intense and deliberative, with the Ministry of Communication working directly with the indigenous authorities to see what kind of radio (if any at all) they each wanted to establish for their respective communities. Some communities rejected the idea of starting a radio station out of hand as counter to traditional practices and beliefs (Unidad de Radio del Ministerio de Cultura, 2000).

Radio Payu'mat was first established during the administration of President Andres Pastrana in 2000. At the time, President Pastrana was conducting controversial peace negotiations with left-wing rebels of the Revolutionary Armed Forces of Colombia (FARC). Some indigenous activists perceived the radio project as a way for the government to curry favor with popular movements in the countryside, especially those not so comfortable with the direction of those peace talks and the exclusion of civil society from the negotiating table (Dorado, 2004). The last thing the indigenous leadership wanted was to be granted these radio station licenses with considerable political strings attached (Dorado, 2004).

Eventually, after intense consultation with the community and deliberation among the many *cabildos* of the region, ACIN decided to accept the license and committed itself to starting up the radio station.

The initial support for equipment and basic infrastructure came from the government, but the first major wave of funding came to the community after the Nasa life plan was awarded the UNESCO Peace Prize recognizing it as one of the most significant community development programs in the world in 2002. The prize brought the Nasa Project an instant influx of cash: 25 million Colombian pesos (more than US$10,000), more than half of which was directed to the station.

Maintaining the station's ongoing operating expenses remains one of the principal challenges of the organization. At times, staff members of the station and the entire communication team would go several months without receiving any remuneration due to the limited resources of the *cabildos*.

Indigenous Community Radio as an Alternative Public Sphere

Radio Payu'mat and its sibling stations, as well as the other media projects of ACIN, including its elaborate Web site and video productions, all demonstrate an unabashed independence from the state, while providing a space for the community to discuss important issues that affect them directly. Over the years, on a consistent basis, they have not hesitated to be extremely critical on many levels of government policy vis-à-vis indigenous communities and the nation as a whole.

In August 2005, for example, ACIN and other local indigenous groups held a massive protest to denounce controversial statements made by a local army commander who accused the indigenous leadership of collaborating with FARC guerrillas. The Commander of the Army's Third Brigade, General Hernando Pérez Molina, stationed in Cali, stated unequivocally that "in that area of northern Cauca, there existed a co-government where the FARC used resources from the European Union that was directed to the Nasa Project for the guerrillas' own benefit" (Murillo, 2006, pp. 258–259).

The Nasa Project General Pérez Molina was referring to is the multifaceted community development project started by the Nasa people in 1980 in the *resguardo* of Toribio, the same one that won the UNESCO Peace Prize in 2002. According to representatives of the Nasa Project, by linking their organization with FARC, General Pérez Molina was unilaterally discrediting its autonomy, thus opening up its leaders to reprisals from the state and eventually, as in other parts of Colombia, even paramilitary operations. These statements were seen by ACIN as highly irresponsible, given the history of violent backlash directed at anybody accused of collaborating with the left-wing rebels.

The all-day protest rally was held in the town square of Santander de Quilichao, the bustling municipality that serves as the home of Radio Payu'mat. The protest was broadcast live, with a long list of speakers who had very strong words of criticism for the army commander as well as for the government of President Alvaro Uribe. One speaker, Luís Acosta, the director of the Guardia Indígena, or Indigenous Guard, a civilian, unarmed security patrol with some 10,000 members, accused the president himself of having a "co-government" with right-wing paramilitaries. It was one of the first radio broadcasts in the nation that openly made such charges against the president, about a year before the mainstream media in Colombia began reporting on the links between high-level members of Uribe's government and the United Self-Defense Forces of Colombia, AUC, the paramilitary umbrella organization that is on the U.S. State Department's list of terrorist organizations. Numerous associates as well as Congressional allies of President Uribe were arrested in the scandal and faced charges for links to paramilitaries in 2007 and 2008. Nevertheless, after the controversial broadcast of ACIN's rally in 2005, staff members of Radio Payu'mat expressed concern that they would begin to feel pressure from the government because of the harsh tone of the public discourse that emanated in the broadcast.

There are other examples of bold independence taken by the station and its management and programmers. When a public, nonbinding referendum about the U.S.-Colombia Free Trade Agreement was organized by the indigenous communities in March 2005, government officials were invited on the air to debate with ACIN's leadership about the merits and drawbacks of free trade and its potential impact on the countryside. Indigenous communities throughout Colombia have been at the forefront of the national popular resistance to the Free Trade Agreement because of their concerns that it will open up their territories to foreign multinationals, thereby restricting their constitutionally protected rights of territorial autonomy. The U.S.-Colombia Free Trade Agreement was also seen as a direct threat to Colombia's agricultural sector.

The nonbinding referendum results later showed that 95% of the indigenous and peasant population in the southwestern region of Colombia opposed the free trade accords, leading one government minister to charge that the people's vote was manipulated by "dark forces," meaning, once again, the guerrillas. And once again, the station was used as a megaphone to denounce these government accusations. These and other instances over the first several years of operation demonstrate clearly that, notwithstanding the government's role in providing the community with the license to operate the radio station, Radio Payu'mat was acting independently and broadcasting first and foremost with ACIN's activist, community-oriented mission in mind.

Given the very volatile nature of Colombia's conflict and the impact this conflict has had on indigenous communities, there are no guarantees that ACIN will continue to be able to sustain this level of critique without eventually paying for it, whether the retaliation comes in the form of regulatory mechanisms or, as is often the case in Colombia, through violent, repressive means. In December 2008, during a period of increasing tensions in the territory, the station's transmitter

was severely damaged by an act of sabotage by unknown sources, taking Radio Payu'mat off the air for several months. This was seen as a major blow to the organization's ability to inform the community about special events and other developments in Cauca. In the end, the level of independence of the radio stations will always correspond to the strength of the organization controlling the stations and the visibility of the leadership, both of which have up to now favored ACIN's communication team.

Radio Payu'mat's independent, critical approach to content in service of the community is in a sense unique when compared with other community media experiences in Colombia, which is probably why it has been recognized so often for its outstanding work. In many regions of the country, including in Cauca, community radio practitioners have deliberately accepted principles of commercial radio to maintain their financial independence and remain economically viable. Community radio licensees are forced to engage in a never-ending struggle to produce relevant public affairs and cultural programming and still maintain a viable listening audience to compete with the mass-scale commercial broadcasters whose signals reach the farthest corners of Colombia (Murillo, 2003). In many cases, the commercial mission has won the battle, resulting in broadcasters duplicating the formats and sounds heard on popular music stations, despite holding "community" licenses. This is clearly not the case with the three radio stations of ACIN, where commercial principles are systematically rejected.

Today, when it is not off the air due to acts of sabotage, Radio Payu'mat transmits news, interviews, music, and community announcements from 7:00 A.M. to 8:00 P.M. from their studios just across the street from the headquarters of ACIN in Santander de Quilichao. The public affairs programs they produce are often recorded onto a memory card, minidisc or CD and then circulated among the other stations run by ACIN, a type of informal network that distributes the message from the regional station to the local ones. Licensed to broadcast at 2,000 watts, Payu'mat's signal reaches the many small towns that pepper the mountainous terrain of the region, and on some days it can be heard as far north as Cali, the third largest city in Colombia. The station regularly schedules live broadcasts of special events in the community, from local assemblies to national congresses, where all sorts of issues are discussed, an *electronic* manifestation of *actual* public spheres. The station also broadcasts local concerts and, as mentioned above, protest rallies. Its news programs combine comprehensive local coverage that places economic, political, and social issues in a national and indeed global context. Guests range from local youth groups to national political leaders, from human rights activists to international visitors from places such as Mexico and Guatemala. In ACIN's communication mission, commercialism has been explicitly rejected, as they see themselves as providing an alternative in every sense of the word.

However, it would be shortsighted to think that the pressures don't exist, given the prevalence of commercial popular culture even within very traditional indigenous communities. It's a struggle that Dorado (2004) recognizes as one of the fundamental challenges of the entire indigenous movement in Colombia as it navigates between cultural tradition and political autonomy, on the one hand, and the influences of "Western thinking" and all its representative byproducts, on the other. I'll never forget my lengthy conversation with one Nasa activist, Gustavo Ulcué, who edits ACIN's Web site and is a vital member of its communication team. He described in great detail his deep fascination with the *Lord of the Rings* trilogy and his desire to one day translate it in its entirety into Nasa Uwe in order to share the mythological tales of the Tolkien texts with the older people in the community who don't understand Spanish. Here, we see a mass, globalized, highly commercial media product having a direct relevance within a very traditional, localized context.

The question of commercialism inevitably returns us to what some scholars have described as Habermas's (2000) failure to accept "playful aspects

of communicative action" as a possible link to citizen participation (Garnham, 1992). The indigenous stations in northern Cauca are well aware of this challenge and balance it by avoiding popular, commercial music on their play lists, such as salsa or merengue hits, filling the airwaves instead with songs by local artists who play mostly Andean folk music, very often with protest themes, music that is very popular among the many communities they serve. So they deliberately target audiences with their own popular music, bringing in listeners through cultural products that by their nature incorporate citizen participation. As Emilio Bastos, the Nasa programmer and host of the station's popular morning show once told me, "We have to give the people what they like, otherwise they won't listen."

The public sphere role of the stations can also be measured by the overall level of community participation within them. The programming and administrative staff of Radio Payu'mat is small, with only 8 to 10 people working there at any one time, and many of them carrying out nonradio functions related to the Web site, video production, or any of their other media projects. One of the major challenges the directors consistently face is getting more people involved, particularly younger Nasa activists who have an interest in media production. The long travel distances, complicated security situation in the area, and limited economic resources of the potential volunteers make it very difficult to get more people to work as production staff or news reporters, or in a technical or administrative capacity. For example, to get from the highland town of Toribio to Santander de Quilichao takes about 1 hour, *if* you have your own motorcycle, which is not so easy to come by. Otherwise, one must take a local bus, a *chiva*, which could extend the trip to almost 2 hours, if the road is not backed up by a mudslide or there are not too many military checkpoints along the way. Furthermore, when the station started, the staff was much younger, ranging in age between 17 and 22. Add 6 or 7 years to this median age, and you get people in their mid- to late 20s, now with children and other family commitments that ultimately limit the amount of time that can be dedicated to the station.

The staffing concerns are directly tied to the lack of technical resources and basic equipment. All three stations have enough equipment just to get by, but because it is extremely limited, potential newcomers are not so easily enthused about working at the station. One young member of the staff at Radio Nasa told me, "If they can't hold the microphones and tape recorders, they're not going to feel like they're doing radio, which is discouraging to many." It's a practical reality that occurs in community radio around the world, including in the United States. In essence, it is a vicious circle that starts with a lack of financial, then technical resources, meaning less people will get involved, making it more difficult to get people trained and eventually adjust from their older routines of working in the countryside into the newer world of working in community media.

The challenge of getting more community participation in the station is a reflection of the more complex dialogue that has been going on between indigenous people from the community and nonindigenous people who have collaborated with the movement for years. There are a number of nonindigenous, mestizo professionals who have played key roles in getting the station and the other media programs to the level where they are today, conducting workshops in programming, audio and video production, and community journalism throughout the northern Cauca region. While the strategy has always been to train Nasa youth to do the work themselves and duplicate the training, because of all the above-mentioned problems—security, travel distances, cost—this strategy has not always been successful, and the turnover has been great.

The difficulties they face in developing newer personnel has expanded into the video and Internet components of ACIN's media work, all of which is integrally linked to the radio project. ACIN is now producing videos about various aspects of their struggle to share with local communities throughout the countryside, and they use the radio stations to promote the public screenings and community meetings—their *cineforos*—that they organize throughout the region. ACIN also has a comprehensive Web site (www.nasaacin.org) that maintains links to national and international social and media organizations, regularly posting sound from their radio programs so that audiences outside the signal area can listen in. In short, there is a dynamic team of dedicated, talented producers, designers, journalists, technicians, and activists working together in the spirit of collaboration, although not all of them are directly from the indigenous community.

Does the fact that some of the staff of ACIN's communication team are not indigenous diminish the community mission of their radio stations and other media projects? Does it call into question the criteria mentioned earlier about open access, barriers to entry, and true community participation? Some purists might say it does. However, if we consider the Nasa communication philosophy, we see that it is designed to constantly expand the outreach of the community to include other sectors. It is not meant to be exclusionary in nature. Indeed, the history of the indigenous movement, especially in Cauca, demonstrates that outsiders who are committed to the struggle of autonomy are in many ways considered part of the community process. The evolution of the communication strategy reflects this reality.

The point is that indigenous radio is clearly a response to demands from the indigenous community for its own space in an undemocratic and exclusionary national media environment. That Radio Payu'mat was established with some basic support from the state doesn't necessarily negate its independence from the state. In a conflict-ridden society like Colombia, there are pressures coming from many different directions, including nonstate actors, such as guerrillas, paramilitaries, and narco-traffickers, all of whom have a considerable degree of influence in the northern Cauca region. In this regard, the challenge confronting the radio stations of ACIN in terms of independence are even greater than in other parts of the world, making the debate over commercial pressures on community radio seem all the more quaint and almost irrelevant.

Radio Payu'mat and its sibling stations maintain an alternative mission to the commercial marketplace. That it is still influenced by the market in some ways is more a reflection of the much larger and more complex negotiation that goes on constantly within the indigenous community as it struggles to maintain its traditions against the backdrop of a highly mediated popular mass culture. None of these traits diminish its role within the community as a type of public sphere or as a tool for broader resistance.

To measure the actual impact these three stations, the Internet site, and their video production work are having on the community would involve a much more thorough analysis of the audiences that are receiving their respective media products. There is no question, however, based on numerous visits to the area and conversations with countless people in the communities served by the stations, that people are tuning in and see the stations as true alternatives to the other, larger commercial stations in the area. It is not uncommon to hear people express strong feelings that the stations "belong to them"—*nuestra emisora*—or that "those kids are good"—*esos muchachos son buenos*, referring to the mostly young members of each station. Indeed, it is evident that there is a tremendous sense of proprietary interest in all three of the stations. This embrace was especially evident during the massive mobilization and weeks-long protest against the government, spearheaded by the indigenous movement, in October 2008. Radio Payu'mat's coverage of the mobilization was seen as a lifeline for the people who could not attend and remained back home, as government forces confronted the protesters violently, resulting in 1 death and more than 120 wounded. While the government used the major commercial media to once again accuse the movement of being infiltrated by "terrorists of the FARC," Radio Payu'mat and ACIN's other media outlets consistently rejected the charges, broadcasting the voices of the protesters and the leadership as the dramatic events were unfolding.

Unquestionably, these media outlets are seen as the space of the community, where they can announce public events, celebrate birthdays, or alert people about the death of an elder. Little children regularly come into the studios of all three stations to send greetings out to their families and friends. And the *cabildos* that make up ACIN recognize, after several years of operation, that there is no better way to get the word out about a mobilization than through the use of the radio airwaves they now have at their disposal. It allows them to communicate to the community directly, as well as to the outside world, about their generational struggle.

References

Caldón, J. D. (2005). Los indígenas y el conflicto armado en Colombia: A propósito de las acciones bélicas del as FARC en Toribío, Caldono y Jambaló [Indigenous people and the armed conflict in Colombia: The impact of the Belicose Actions by FARC in Toribio, Caldono and Jambaló]. *Etnias y Política, July*(1), 26–34.

Consejo Nacional Indígena de Paz. (2006, September 21–26). *Memoria de la Misión Internacional de Verificación a la Situación Humanitaria y de Derechos Humanos de los Pueblos Indígenas de Colombia (MIV)*. Bogotá, Colombia: Ediciones Antropos.

De Greiff, M., & Ramos, C. S. (2000). *Regimen Jurídico de Radio y Televisión en Colombia* [Legal regime of radio and television in Colombia]. Bogotá, Colombia: Legis Editores, S.A.

Dorado, M. (2004). *Radio Payu'mat: Una Experiencia de Comunicacion en la Zona Norte del Cauca* [Radio Payu'mat: An experience in communication in the northern Cauca zone). Unpublished dissertation, Universidad Pontificia Bolivariana, Anthropology Institute, Medellín, Colombia.

Fairchild, C. (2001). *Community radio and public culture*. Cresskill, NJ: Hampton Press.

Garnham, N. (1992). The media and the public sphere. In C. Calhoun (Ed.), *Habermas and the public sphere* (pp. 359–376). Cambridge: MIT Press.

Habermas, J. (2000). *The structural transformation of the public sphere: An inquiry into a category of bourgeois society.* Cambridge: MIT Press.

Mondragón, H. (2005). Disuasión y corrosión: La política del gobierno de Alvaro Uribe Vélez para los pueblos indígenas [Reversals and corrosion: Alvaro Uribe's policies for indigenous peoples]. *Etnias y Política, July*(1), 15–26.

Murillo, M. A. (2003, June). Community radio in Colombia: Civil conflict, popular media and the construction of a Public sphere. *Journal for Radio Studies, 10*(1), 120–140.

Murillo, M. A., (2004). *Colombia and the United States: War, unrest, and destabilization.* New York: Seven Stories Press.

Murillo, M. A. (2006). Beset by violence, Colombia's indigenous resist. In T. Ballve & V. Prashad (Eds.), *Dispatches from Latin America* (pp. 257–266). Boston: South End Press.

Rappaport, J. (2005). *Intercultural utopias: Public intellectuals, cultural experimentation, and ethnic pluralism in Colombia.* Durham, NC: Duke University Press.

Unidad de Radio del Ministerio de Cultura. (2000) *Memorias: Radios y pueblos indígenas—Encuentro Internacional de Radios Indígenas de America* [Memories: Radio and indigenous peoples—international encounter of indigenous radio in the Americas]. Bogotá, Colombia: Ministro de Cultura.

Villa, W., & Houghton, J. (2005). *Violencia política contra los pueblos indígenas en Colombia: 1974–2004* [Political violence against indigenous people in Colombia: 1974–2004]. Bogotá, Colombia: CECOIN.

Wilches-Chaux, G. (2005). *Proyecto Nasa: La Construcción del Plan de Vida de un Pueblo Que Suena* [Project Nasa: The construction of a life plan of a people who dream]. Bogotá, Colombia: UNDP.

CHAPTER 21

Ethnic Community Media and Social Change

A Case in the United States

Dandan Liu

In the year 2000, the city government of Philadelphia proposed to build a baseball stadium beside what was commonly accepted as the border of the Chinatown community at 12th and Vine Streets. The Chinatown community strongly opposed this proposal. Beginning in April 2000, the Chinatown community, together with other neighborhood advocates, organized to defeat the proposal. In November 2000, the mayor announced that the baseball stadium would be located in South Philadelphia instead, acknowledging that "his preferred site, 12th and Vine, was simply too expensive and too complicated to work" (Benson, 2000, p. A01).

For the mayor, the final decision on the baseball stadium site reflected a failed attempt at building a Center City ballpark. For Chinatown activists, however, the stadium issue represented a successful battle in terms of the protection of the community and the transformation of the image of Chinese immigrants in the mainstream

news media. The Chinese community in the United States has been perceived as a "model minority," hardworking but always inactive in the political environment. However, with the menace of a ballpark in the community, Philadelphia's Chinatown organized sufficiently to keep the stadium out of the neighborhood. The mainstream news media also started to call community activists "tough, battle-tested veterans of urban developments wars" (Boldt, 2000, p. 6). With the involvement of the Chinese American activists and their use of the Chinese language media, the stadium issue becomes an example that illuminates the interaction between ethnic community media and social change groups.

Media and Movements

The success of the community's organizing efforts led a reporter from the *Daily News*—one of the city's major daily newspapers—to note the role of media strategy in the campaign: "As lenses click and cameras roll, Chinatown residents have made their position known loud and clear on Mayor Street's preferred site for a Phillies ballpark at 12th and Vine Street: 'No Stadium in Chinatown'" (Einhorn, 2000, p. 6).

The reporter credited the activists' media campaign as an effective source of frustration to the advocates of the 12th and Vine site. The comment implies that the media had played an indispensable role and were powerful enough to affect official opinion on the stadium issue. Such a view underscores the assumption of most media-movement literature—that is, media are both the means and the end in the process of either initiating or resisting social change. In other words, social movement groups have always strived to put their messages onto the media agenda for the purpose of either seeking or obstructing changes. Activists have expected the media to be the agents for disseminating the ideas and, at the same time, for legitimizing their action.

Looking first at the role of media in social change, one finds an extensive body of research. In contrast to the rare examples of news media as the agent of social change (Cook, 1972), the social control model in the field of mass media has been dominant since the 1960s (Demers & Viswanath, 1999). Scholars in the critical tradition doubt the role of media as agents of social change and have claimed the relationship between news media and social movement to be "hegemonic": that is, the media either represent the movement in a completely positive way by diminishing its transformative goal, or they marginalize the movement with negative coverage (Bradley, 2004; Gitlin, 1980). On the other hand, researchers with an applied approach have started to develop strategies to interact with the media in order to put the activists' messages onto the media agenda as well as the public agenda (Barker-Plummer, 1995). The rationale for this approach—that media framing is a dynamic process, and certain frames may win or lose their prominence in the news media—opens out the possibilities for social movement activists seeking change (Ryan, Carragee, & Meinhofer, 2001; Ryan, Carragee, & Schwerner, 1998).

While research on the media-movement relationship has been extensive and fruitful, it leaves out the role of the foreign-language media that have grown significantly in the United States. The lack of research on media other than mainstream media suggests researchers' underlying assumption that only the mainstream media can help achieve the goals of the movements.

This focus on mainstream media cannot explain today's media-movement interaction because both media and movements have changed. During the past three decades, the composition of the American population has experienced a huge change, due to the influx of immigrants from all over the world. In some immigrant communities, English is not even the major language. When issues come up in such areas, how the activists communicate within and beyond their communities or organizations has become a critical question. Therefore, it is essential to reassess the role of mass media and, beyond that, the role of other factors, such as diverse cultures and foreign-language media, which have significantly contributed to the success or failure of social movements.

This case study contributes to the existing media-movement literature in several ways. It is one of the few studies that examine activism of the ethnic Chinese community in the United States in a media frame. It also adds to the body of knowledge that addresses social change activism in the nation's foreign-language ethnic community media.

The study starts with an introduction to the activist tradition in Philadelphia's Chinatown and to the stadium deal in the city. Then Chinese immigrant community media activism in the historical context is reviewed, followed by the analysis of the role of Chinese community media in the stadium issue.

The Stadium Case: Background

Philadelphia's Chinatown has over a hundred years of history. Like most of the Chinatown communities across the United States, it started as a neighborhood for bachelor sojourners and then served as a space for immigrant families for social and economic development (Kung, 1962). Chiu (1984) argues that "the history of the Chinese in Philadelphia, as elsewhere, has been one of cultural conflicts, economic hardship, political alienation, and social injustice" (p. 12).

In 1966, to join the wave of massive urban renewal projects sweeping the country, the Pennsylvania State Highway Department announced plans to convert Vine Street into an expressway, a plan that called for the demolition of all the properties along Vine Street, including the Holy Redeemer Catholic Church—one of the most important institutions in Chinatown. In response to the direct threat to the survival of the community, the first town meeting was initiated, in 1968, and the Committee for the Preservation of the Chinatown Community was formed and was incorporated into the Philadelphia Chinatown Development Corporation (PCDC) in 1969. Since then, PCDC has maintained "consistent leadership" (Chiu, 1984, p. 10) and represented Chinatown in addressing many issues. PCDC put particular energy into developing strategies. The goal was twofold: to fight for justice as well as to work with government agencies to develop the community for the long term. It took the community almost 20 years to eventually win the negotiation and have a scaled-down expressway built in 1987.

The Vine Expressway fight was crucial in the history of Chinatown activism. Its significance is visible from several perspectives. First, it created several "firsts," establishing the "root" of making social change in the face of injustice and setting the basic tone of activism for future battles. It was the first time that the community ever said "No" to the city government. It was the first time Chinese ever testified in a Philadelphia City Council hearing. Second, this fight provided precious experiences in social activism for this minority group, particularly in terms of using media for social change and in identifying critical issues to frame the messages. In the activists' own words, "the media is fully exploited by PCDC. Newspaper editorials, letters to the editor, almost daily TV news coverage and TV editorials focus the attention of Philadelphia on Chinatown."[1]

There have been a series of fights against urban renewal projects such as the Convention Center and the Gallery shopping mall. The community didn't win all the battles. However, the essence of activism remains fresh: Never hesitate to say no to gain social justice. In 2000, Chinatown confronted another crisis for the community when a baseball stadium was proposed to be built in the area called "Chinatown North" by community developers.

The new stadium for both the baseball (Phillies) and football (Eagles) teams had been on the agenda of the city of Philadelphia and Pennsylvania state government since 1995. Similar to Pittsburgh's fear of losing the Pirates and Steelers, the city of Philadelphia wanted to keep the Phillies and Eagles with new facilities after the end of their lease on Veteran's Stadium in 2011. At the beginning of 2000, Mayor John Street initiated a media campaign to reopen the site selection process, hosting city hearings and Town Hall meetings, touring potential sites, and even showing his presence in an online chat room. All these efforts at collecting public opinions, however, did not make a difference in the Mayor's decision to choose a downtown site at 12th and Vine streets for the baseball stadium, even though this was not the council's choice, was strongly opposed by the Chinatown community, and was even disliked by the team managers.

Impressive as the initial public relations campaign was, the performance of the mayor in the later stage of the issue frustrated the media, the city council, the teams, and other relevant constituents.

After the mayor announced the proposed baseball stadium site at 12th and Vine, he also self-imposed several deadlines to complete the stadium agreement. The mayor claimed that by June 30, the city should have developed a conceptual agreement with the teams. By September 8, the mayor was expected to submit stadium bills to the City Council for approval. None of the deadlines was met. Eventually the site selection issue was settled on November 13, when the mayor abandoned the 12th and Vine site and chose instead to locate the baseball stadium in South Philadelphia.

The Role of Chinese Community Media

The stadium issue gained extensive coverage, both in the mainstream and Chinese community media. In this case, Chinese community media refers to Chinese language newspapers, a type of foreign-language ethnic media that serve the Chinese immigrant community in the United States.[2] The role of the Chinese newspapers in the stadium issue was tied to both the activists' media strategies and the news values indicated by the coverage.

Chinese Immigrants' Media Activism

Park (1922) recognized that the existence of the foreign-language press sought to satisfy the immigrants' need to stay close to their native language and culture, as well as to help them adapt to the environment more easily. Historically, ethnic minority media activism has been embodied in three formats: (1) recruitment of minority journalists in the mainstream media; (2) growth of ethnic community media; and (3) strategic influence on mainstream media coverage (Wilson & Gutierrez, 1985). While the activists in the stadium case have been applauded for their campaign to influence mainstream media coverage, their use of Chinese community media should be acknowledged as another format of media activism.

The first Chinese immigrant newspaper, the *Golden Hills' News,* was exactly an example of media activism via the establishment of the immigrants' own media. It was originated "in a period when the mainstream media were playing an active role in ridiculing and disparaging members of that group [Chinese immigrants]" (Wilson & Gutierrez, 1985, p. 192). Researchers have seen the situation for Chinese immigrants in that period as a "crisis of unusual stress or pain that was not being experienced by the majority population" and described the newspaper as a channel for telling the immigrants' own stories and sending out pleads for the fair treatment of Chinese (p. 192).

The Chinese immigrant press has maintained the function of speaking for its community in severe situations (Huntzicker, 1995; Lai, 1987). Besides voicing the concerns of the community, early Chinese American newspapers followed the partisan pattern of early-19th-century American newspapers (Huntzicker, 1995). Supported by missionaries and businessmen, the early Chinese press in America became a forum for different political agendas. It has remained so in the history of Chinese Americans. Researchers in Chinese American studies have started to relate journalism history to the social history of Chinese Americans. Lo and Lai (1977) documented that each of the major political factions in China published its own newspaper in the United States in the early 20th century. Zhao (2002) illustrated community power structure through a history of the community press before and after World War II. In his study of Chinese American newspapers in the 1980s, Chang (1983) showed that these newspapers retained a stronger connection with the homeland culture than with the Chinatowns in America, and therefore served as a link between the contemporary immigrants and their roots in the past. Similarly, Lum (1997) claimed that regionalism exists among current Chinese American newspapers. Still, both party- and nonparty-affiliated Chinese newspapers in the United States have been involved in activism in Chinese immigrant communities in history (Lai, 1987).

The earliest use of the Chinese newspapers in activism in Philadelphia's Chinatown was related to a radical social change group, Yellow Seeds. The group published their own newspaper, *Yellow Seeds* (1972–1977), during their "Save Chinatown" movement in the early 1970s. It was in this same period that PCDC was leading the fight against the Vine Expressway. However, Yellow Seeds and PCDC didn't agree with each other on the approach to the fight. One issue of *Yellow Seeds* particularly criticized PCDC for not being "militant" and employed rather leftist remarks to mobilize the community: "WORKING CLASS TAKE THE LEAD—THE RULING CLASS WE WILL DEFEAT!" ("We Want Homes," n.d.). Despite the discrepancy in the media leadership in Chinatown, the Vine Expressway fight ended as a victory for the community.

The Chinese newspapers in Philadelphia's Chinatown didn't establish a solid presence until the 1980s. The newspaper owners were a mixture of local businesspersons and news publishers from China. The Chinese newspapers in Philadelphia shared the partisan and regional features of their counterparts in other major markets for the Chinese immigrant press such as San Francisco, New York, and Los Angeles. They also shared the business visions of mainstream newspapers, relying on advertising as the major source of revenue. The national dailies, such as *Sing Tao Jih Pao* and *World Journal*, generally had a higher quality of news articles than the weeklies, due to the journalistic background of their reporters. They turned out to be the agenda setters for the rest of the community newspapers (L. Liu, personal communication, October 26, 2004). The readership of those Chinese newspapers includes residents within and beyond Chinatown. Specifically, Tseng's study found that 90% of Chinatown residents read the Chinese newspapers (as cited in Yin, 1998).

In regard to the stadium issue, both activists and Chinese newspaper reporters recognized the importance of the Chinese newspapers in the community. When asked about the reasons why the community won the battle, most of the activists cited the "united opposition of the community" as one of the most important reasons that kept the stadium away from their neighborhood. United opposition required organizing and mobilizing the community. The role of Chinese newspapers in influencing public opinion in the English-speaking mainstream society might not be vital. But it was one of the driving forces behind the united front of the community, which rendered the Chinese newspapers one of the necessary conditions for the success of the stadium battle.

News Values in the Chinese Newspapers

This study identified four major themes in the Chinese immigrant newspapers.[3] Those themes were interrelated, and they evolved along with the stadium issue.

Community Mobilization. Stories within this theme reflected the activists' efforts to mobilize and organize the *Asian American community*. *Members* in *organizations* formed *coalitions* and *support*ed each other in the *baseball* stadium issue.[4]

Community Opposition. The stadium was in direct conflict with the *plan* the *Chinese people* had for the area to the North of Vine Street. Stories showed the two major players in the conflict—*Chinese people* versus the *mayor*—and clearly showed the theme of *protest*.

Community Life. Another focus of Chinese news coverage was on depicting life in Chinatown. Community *meetings* were part of daily life in Chinatown as people communicated with each other through meetings in their respective *associations*. Meanwhile, part of the activists' vision for the community was related to *schools* for young children.

Community Development. Stories within this theme contained several key words about the community's vision for the area called Chinatown North, such as *north, government,* and *future.* For years, the community was boxed in by urban renewal projects, with the Gallery mall to its south, the Convention Center to its west, and the Metropolitan Hospital to its east. The only direction it could develop in was north. Feeling a threat to the future of development was the main reason for the opposition to the proposed stadium construction. It was a major *issue* for the community. In *June,* the opposition went full length before the public, with the march, the strike, and the hearing.

An examination of the themes of the Chinese news coverage and the change of themes along the timeline of the stadium issue indicated several functions of the Chinese news media. First, the Chinese newspapers served as effective resources to notify the Chinatown community and the Chinese living in the Greater Philadelphia area of the evolving issue and the latest events, especially those who were non-English-speaking Chinese immigrants. The factual information included the mayor's decisions and the time and dates for the community protests. Chinese newspapers, together with community leaders, were considered as the most important channels of communication to help the information flow within the community (X. D. Liang, personal communication, March 26, 2002). One reporter further explained the role of Chinese newspapers:

> It transits in between the mainstream society and the community. Yes, it informs the community. More importantly it creates an atmosphere. When every newspaper is reporting the same issue, it will cause attention from the community. The words from the leadership are not enough to inform the whole community. Without the reports from the Chinese newspapers, there wouldn't be so many people show up in the marches. In a pluralistic society, English mainstream news media wouldn't pay attention to the Chinese immigrants. It is not discrimination. Just that their audiences are white people and the content is always audience-driven. In this sense, the

Chinese newspapers serve as a make-up medium. (B. S. Zhu, personal communication, November 18, 2004)

Second, the Chinese newspapers functioned as a "watchdog" for the community. When issues perceived as potentially harming the community emerged, the newspapers sent a warning signal to the readers. In the stadium case, the coverage in the first few weeks indicated such a function. The theme of community life in the Chinese news coverage was strong at the beginning of the issue. When the site selection issue intensified, the theme of community opposition gained more weight than other themes, as both actions and emotions in the community rose to their peak. Then the major reason for opposition—community development—emerged as the key theme after the city council hearing on June 20. For example, one article explained the rationale for community as opposition to "racial discrimination, environmental discrimination, choking Chinese culture, and destroying the development of Chinatown" (Guan, 2000, p. 6).[5] This rationale served to warn the community what kinds of harm the stadium issue was bringing to people's life in Chinatown.

Third, the Chinese newspapers empowered the community with descriptions of direct actions and the responses from the mainstream society. The empowerment was reflected by reassurances about the righteousness of the opposition. The coverage was positive and supportive all the time. One article commented on the protest being "extremely successful and putting a lot of pressure on the city government" ("Philadelphia Chinese," 2000, p. A16).

Such comments brought confidence to the community and reinforced its determination to fight against the proposed baseball stadium.

The general tone of the original writing in the Chinese newspapers was encouraging to the whole community, clearly indicating the stance of the newspaper as community advocate. Inclusive language such as "we Chinese people . . ." and "please join us . . ." appeared often in the reporting. The second march on June 8, together with the strike by Chinatown businesses, was extensively covered to highlight the unified spirit in the community. According to one of the articles, "Chinese Americans have realized that we have to play this democratic game in the pluralistic American society, i.e., protecting our own benefits by continuous fighting" ("No Stadium," 2000, p. 4). Such a tone of coverage would not be likely to appear in the mainstream media. The Chinese newspapers, therefore, sought to empower the community in the mother tongue and critically contributed to the success of the activist groups.

The fourth function of the Chinese newspapers was closely related to the previous ones. Mobilizing the community was based on distributing information, warning the community, and empowering the people. The Chinese newspapers published notices to mobilize the residents to attend the protests and explain why the people should fight. The coverage indicated the self-consciousness with which the Chinese community viewed itself. For instance, one article reported the community leaders' claims about the weak political representation of Chinatown in mainstream society and how "Chinese people are neglected and treated unfairly" ("Statement," 2000, p. 5). This perception of the Chinese people in the United States served as an appeal to mobilize community residents as well as adjusting the focus of opposition to the stadium issue. There were also statements to mobilize the community from the mainstream perspective, alluding to their eagerness to merge with the mainstream culture.

Last but not least, the Chinese newspapers functioned as a forum for individual opinions. The newspapers were both a weapon to attack others and a healing tool for the community to seek unity. The internal conflict over the leadership role in Chinatown exploded during the stadium issue. One community leader published a call for action notice on the newspaper, which was deemed as illegitimate by leaders in other associations. Who should represent Chinatown became a heated topic in the Chinese newspapers in the format of statements denigrating the opposite side. Those statements were published as paid advertisements. When the attack advertisements became too aggressive, however, the newspapers declined to publish them and claimed "it was too much" and "lack of taste" (B. S. Zhu, personal communication, November 18, 2004).

The flame of the internal conflict was eventually put down by the values shared by most of the community members: unity and peace. The message in the Chinese newspaper editorials was that the *Chinese people* in *Philadelphia's Chinatown* should be *united* in *opposition* against the *stadium* as one *coalition* and abide by *democratic principles in America.*[6]

This message indeed indicated the performance of all the Chinese newspapers as well. While serving as the forums for public debate and representing different regional and partisan interests, all the Chinese newspapers in Philadelphia's Chinatown presented a united tone in the stadium case and acted as a pivotal force within the community.

Conclusion

The media-movement literature has proliferated since the 1960s. The role of the news media in social change movements has been likened to a two-edged sword in the hands of different constituents (Bradley, 2004). Though not entirely considering the news media as the agent of social change, both researchers and activist groups have found it possible to successfully achieve the goals of social activism through working with the news media. Despite the rich literature about the role of news media in social movements, the discussion of the foreign-language news media has been scarce in social change issues that involved ethnic minorities. In the stadium case, Chinatown activists adopted a series of communication strategies to oppose the building of the baseball stadium in their community. This study has examined Chinese immigrant community media activism, using the Chinese newspapers to further illustrate the interaction between news media and social change movements.

The stadium case indicates that the success of ethnic minority social change groups is tied to self-empowerment aided by the foreign-language immigrant news media. The author believes that due to the fact that limited numbers of people speak English while the majority of residents read Chinese newspapers in Chinatown, Chinese newspapers become the primary source of information. In times of mobilizing the residents, a Chinese notice in the newspapers may elicit the mass force needed for the movements. Meanwhile, the positive tone of coverage in the Chinese community media can empower the community. The values of activism, democracy, and freedom of speech, as indicated in the Chinese community media coverage of the baseball stadium issue, serve as the rationale to mobilize and empower.

Future research in the media-movement interaction may look into more cases with the involvement of the ethnic media, especially the foreign-language media. The recent development of the ethnic media challenged the dominant role of the mainstream media in social protests and called for scholars' attention. Wynar (1982) credited the ethnic press as "one of the major instruments that maintain the "spirit" of an ethnic way of life" (p. 41). One cannot afford losing the insights from such an instrument.

Notes

1. PCDC Annual Report in 1973.

2. Two daily Chinese newspapers (*Sing Tao Jih Pao* and *World Journal*) and four weeklies (*China News, China Times, China-Vietnews,* and *China-America News*) were in operation during the stadium case. *China Times* was out of business in Philadelphia in Spring 2003.

3. Two types of media coverage were analyzed with the Centering Resonance Analysis approach (www.crawdadtech.com), including 246 items in English and 45 items in Chinese. All types of articles in the print media were collected for analysis, such as stories by journalists, columnists, editorials, letters to editors, and announcements. Details of analysis are available on request.

4. The themes were based on the interpretation of the relations among the italicized words, which were identified as key words in the computer-assisted qualitative network analysis.

5. All the Chinese newspaper articles cited in this study were translated from the original articles.

6. The italicized words were key words generated in the analysis of the Chinese newspapers editorials.

References

Barker-Plummer, B. (1995). News as a political resource: Media strategies and political identity in the U.S. women's movement, 1966–1975. *Critical Studies in Media Communication, 12*(3), 305–330.

Benson, C. (2000, November 14). Ballpark won't be downtown, Street says the mayor unveiled a plan for 2 south Philadelphia Stadiums. *The Philadelphia Inquirer,* p. A01.

Boldt, D. (2000, April 14). Stadium site a defining moment in the life-or death-Philly. *The Daily News,* p. 6.

Bradley, P. (2004). *Mass media and the shaping of American feminism, 1963–1975.* Jackson: University Press of Mississippi.

Chang, T. K. (1983, August). *The Chinese press in U.S.: A linkage to the past.* Paper presented at the annual meeting of the Association for Education in Journalism and Mass Communication, Corvallis, OR.

Chiu, S. M. (1984). The changing face of Philadelphia's Chinatown. *Bulletin of the Chinese Historical Society of America, 19*(1), 6–14.

Cook, F. J. (1972). *The muckrakers: Crusading journalists who changed America.* Garden City, NY: Doubleday.

Demers, D., & Viswanath, K. (Eds.). (1999). *Mass media, social control, and social change: A macrosocial perspective.* Ames: Iowa State University Press.

Einhorn, E. (2000, June 20). Rally for stadium: Union, tourist & hotel groups push for 12th and Vine. *The Daily News,* p. 6.

Gitlin, T. (1980). *The whole world is watching: Mass media in the making and unmaking of the New Left.* Berkeley: University of California Press.

Guan, B. H. (2000, June 30 to July 6). Urgent call for all the Chinese American Commerce Associations. *China Times,* p. 6.

Huntzicker, W. E. (1995). Chinese-American newspapers. In F. Hutton & B. S. Reed (Eds.), *Outsiders in 19th-century press history: Multicultural perspectives* (pp. 71–92). Bowling Green, OH: Bowling Green State University Popular Press.

Kung, S. W. (1962). *Chinese in American life.* Seattle: University of Washington Press.

Lai, H. M. (1987). The Chinese-American press. In S. M. Miller (Ed.), *The ethnic press in the United States: A historical analysis and handbook* (pp. 27–43). New York: Greenwood Press.

Lo, K., & Lai, H. M. (1977). *Chinese newspapers published in North America, 1854–1975.* Washington, DC: Association of Research Libraries, Center for Chinese Research Materials.

Lum, C. M. K. (1997). Regionalism and communication; Exploring Chinese immigrant perspectives. In A. Gonzelez, M. Houston, & V. Chen (Eds.), *Our voices: Essays in culture, ethnicity, and communication* (pp. 203–214). Los Angeles: Roxbury.

No stadium! Save Chinatown! Philadelphia Chinese protest again. (2000, June 16–22). *China Times,* p. 4.

Park, R. E. (1922). *The immigrant press and its control.* New York: Harper.

Philadelphia Chinese united more than ever. (2000, June 15). *China Viet-News,* p. A16.

Ryan, C., Carragee, K. M., & Meinhofer, W. (2001). Theory into practice: Framing, the news media, and collective action [Electronic version]. *Journal of Broadcasting & Electronic Media, 45*(1), 175–182.

Retrieved April 20, 2002, from Temple University Web of Science Database.

Ryan, C., Carragee, K. M., & Schwerner, C. (1998). Media, movements, and the quest for social justice [Electronic version]. *Journal of Applied Communication Research, 26*(2), 165–181. Retrieved April 20, 2002, from Temple University Web of Science Database.

Statement for the current situation in opposition to the baseball stadium. (2000, July 26). *China-America News,* p. 5.

We want homes not highways. (n.d.). *Yellow seeds.* Retrieved October 16, 2008, from Balch Institute for Ethnic Studies Web site: www2.hsp.org/exhibits/Balch%20exhibits/chinatown/broadside.html

Wilson, C. C., & Gutierrez, F. (1985). *Minorities and media: Diversity and the end of mass communication.* Beverly Hills, CA: Sage.

Wynar, L. R. (1982). Ethnic newspapers and periodicals in the United States: Present status and problems on bibliographic control. *Ethnic Forum: Bulletin of Ethnic Studies and Ethnic Bibliography, 2*(2), 40–51.

Yin, X. H. (1998). Worlds of difference: Lin Yutang, Lao She, and the significance of Chinese writing in America. In W. Sollors (Ed.), *Multilingual America: Transnationalism, ethnicity, and the languages of American literature* (pp. 176–188). New York: New York University Press.

Zhao, X. J. (2002). *Remaking Chinese America: Immigration, family, and community, 1940–1965.* New Brunswick, NJ: Rutgers University Press.

CHAPTER 22

A Participatory Model of Video Making

The Case of Colectivo Perfil Urbano

Claudia Magallanes-Blanco

In this chapter, I take a close look at the grassroots media collective Colectivo Perfil Urbano (CPU) as a communication project based on a participatory model[1] that empowers individuals, strengthens the community, and democratizes communication. Based on interviews with members of the media collective, I analyze the production/distribution process and make a close reading of a video. I discuss how the link between CPU and the Movimiento Popular Urbano (Popular Urban Movement or PUM) sets the basis for the participatory model used by the media collective to produce and distribute their work. I also focus on a video production on the Zapatistas that exemplifies the participatory model of communication of CPU and the way they are democratizing communication by multiplying the channels to obtain information; incorporating the opinions, interests, ideals, and information needs of their intended audiences into their video productions; taking into account the subjects of their productions; and using innovative distribution channels.

Colectivo Perfil Urbano, a Participatory Model of Communication

CPU was formed in 1985 by José Luis Contreras and other students who joined the PUM[2] after the earthquakes that hit Mexico City. The grassroots media collective was created "with the idea to help social organizations [members of the PUM], to be able to provide them with photographic, communication and silk screening services. Later on we were able to get video equipment" (J. L. Contreras, personal communication, July 13, 2001). Currently,

Author's Note: Parts of this work are included in my doctoral thesis on participatory video projects in Mexico.

José Luis Contreras and Carmen Ortiz are the two full-time members of the media collective.[3] They consider themselves militant and committed with the PUM. They identify themselves as members of the unprivileged working class who are part of a popular movement for the recognition of their rights to better living conditions.

When CPU decided to start producing videos, they learned how to do it for and with their *compañeros* from the PUM using dialogue and discussion, a key element of participatory media projects (Gumucio-Dagron, 2001b; Lunch, 2007; White, 2003) as well as of the PUM (Eckstein, 2001; Monsiváis, 2005; "Movimiento Urbano Popular," 2007). It was people from the movement who taught them how to make videos. José Luis Contreras asserts,

> At first, when we screened a video people did not clap, did not say anything. So, we knew people did not like it. When they started to clap, when there were two or three claps, when they laughed or got excited we thought "we are finally learning something." (personal communication, July 13, 2001)

CPU videorecorded the things that were important for the members of the different associations and organizations of the PUM, such as meetings, marches, and issues of relevance to them. Contreras and Ortiz say that they learned from the PUM that the people they recorded had to be able to tell their own stories in order to make these stories appealing and to allow people to identify with them. They decided that in their video productions, they had to

> give people a chance to say, in their own words, [out of their] misery, richness or poverty, how have they come to this or what they are fighting for. Why did they stop the traffic on the street or why did they rise up in arms. (J. L. Contreras, personal communication, July 13, 2001)

When in 1994 the indigenous Zapatista uprising started, Carmen Ortiz and José Luis Contreras identified with the indigenous rebels and their struggle and felt the need to go to Chiapas. Thus, CPU went to the place where the rebellion was happening to respond to the needs and interests of the members of the PUM who wanted to know more about the rebellion and to let the Zapatistas know that the PUM supported their struggle, which they understood as similar to theirs in Mexico City.

Bringing the Indigenous Zapatista Rebellion and the Popular Urban Movement Close Through Participatory Video Making

In early 1994, the sources of information about the insurgency in Chiapas were the mainstream media, and their reports were, as Trejo Delabre (1994) points out, confusing, incomplete, and in some cases even discrepant. For example, there were inconsistencies on the numbers of cities taken over by the rebels or on the number of rebels, ranging from 200 to more than 3,000. Many reports in the mainstream media referred to unconfirmed versions, hearsay, and accounts from alleged witnesses (Trejo Delabre, 1994).

Although the Zapatista rebels were aware of the importance of making their voice public, at the beginning of the struggle the EZLN (Ejército Zapatista de Liberación Nacional) relied on outside media to let people know about its rebellion. In 1994, they favored some media[4] to enter the occupied territories to report on the situation of the conflict in its different stages (Magallanes-Blanco, 1998). It was not until 1998 that the indigenous rebels began their own participatory video-making project, and in 2005, they started their insurgent radio that broadcasts on short wave radio and over the Internet.

In January 1994, when the indigenous rebellion started, Carmen Ortiz and José Luis Contreras wanted to go to Chiapas to film what was happening, but they did not have any money or functional equipment.[5] However, with the aid of the Christian movement *Cristinanos Comprometidos con las*

Luchas Populares, Carmen Ortiz was able to get a ticket to Chiapas. At the time, José Luis Contreras was teaching at a high school and was able to borrow a video camera from the principal. Carmen Ortiz took with her the videotapes from a "sweet sixteen" party they had filmed under commission.[6]

Because of his work as high school teacher, José Luis Contreras was unable to travel to Chiapas; thus, he stayed in Mexico City filming (with an old and faulty camera) the rallies and protests organized by civil society in support of the indigenous rebels. Meanwhile, Carmen Ortiz became "the official correspondent of CPU in Chiapas" (J. L. Contreras, personal communication, July 13, 2001). In January 1994, Carmen Ortiz traveled to the rebel zone for the first time; several other visits followed.

For CPU, approaching the Zapatista rebellion through the video camera was a way to bring into dialogues the interests and realities of the members of the PUM in Mexico City and the indigenous rebels in Chiapas. Contreras and Ortiz say that their work as video makers links geographically separated people who are joined by common interests and a common cause. CPU engaged in a participatory model of video making, acting, in their words, as bridges to bring the stories and images of the indigenous rebels and of the members of the PUM closer. They used the video camera as an instrument to promote dialogue and discussion (Jain, 1991; Lunch, 2007; White, 2003) between the rebels in Chiapas and the members of the PUM in Mexico City. For example, early on in the rebellion, they took the audiovisual testimony of supporters from the PUM in Mexico City to Chiapas.[7] They wanted the indigenous rebels to experience the impact of their fight outside Chiapas and the extent of the movement they had initiated. In response, the Zapatistas sent, with Carmen Ortiz, video greetings and messages to members of the PUM. Following the solidarity ties established between the PUM and the indigenous rebels, the Zapatistas met with members of the PUM during their journeys to Mexico City in 2001 and 2006. Likewise, members of the PUM have gone to

Zapatista territories for diverse encounters convoked by the indigenous rebels.

In January 1994, Carmen Ortiz began to approach the Zapatistas "with the order [from the PUM] to make contact and to ask them permission [to film their story]" (J. L. Contreras, personal communication, July 13, 2001). Carmen Ortiz says that she earned the trust of the indigenous rebels because she demonstrated that she "spoke with the truth," as she returned to Chiapas every time she said she would, and she gave the rebels photos of themselves and of the supporters they had in Mexico City and the video messages they exchanged with members of the PUM (C. Ortiz, personal communication, July 13, 2001). By June 1994, some rebel soldiers knew and trusted Carmen Ortiz and helped her get close to Subcomandante Marcos so she could ask permission to get into a Zapatista community. According to Carmen Ortiz, it was not hard to get permission from Marcos as he was familiar with the work of CPU and was grateful that she had given them the photographs she took in Chiapas and the ones José Luis Contreras took in Mexico City in support of the Zapatistas, as well as the video *De la Ciudad al Campo* (see Note 7).

Because of the trust the Zapatistas had in CPU, they allowed Carmen Ortiz and José Luis Contreras to film the everyday life of the insurgents in a community, which was highly unusual, as the rebels considered the privacy of the community to be a security issue. For this trip, Carmen Ortiz and José Luis Contreras traveled together to Chiapas, and for 2 weeks they lived in a Zapatista community. According to them, being active members of the PUM had told them that people have to work together in solidarity at all times. Thus, being at the indigenous community, they worked hand in hand with the rebels in all sorts of activities, such as washing dishes or making security rounds. Carmen Ortiz says that at first the Zapatistas at the village "did not trust us much or talk much to us"; however, after she and José Luis Contreras skinned a cow and prepared the meat so that the whole population could eat, they proved that they were reliable and earned the trust of the community, becoming their friends (C. Ortiz, personal communication, July 13, 2001). The friendship allowed them to film sites off-limits to non-Zapatistas, such as the kitchen.

According to José Luis Contreras and Carmen Ortiz, the experience of living in a Zapatista community "deeply moved them" to the point that once they were back in Mexico City, they had to let the material "rest" for a while so they could process the extent of their experience. The result of their stay at the Zapatista community is captured in the video recording *Los Más Pequeños*.

Los Más Pequeños

Los Más Pequeños is a concrete example of the participatory approach to video making José Luis Contreras and Carmen Ortiz (1994) have. Its editing process is an account of participatory communication that incorporates into the content the ideas and points of views of the members of the PUM. It also incorporates elements of the cultural and historical background of the video makers who approach video technology as a tool that has social and political uses. It brings the rebels close to the audience through images and testimonies of everyday life. The video is the result of a series of dialogues between the authors and their experiences with the people from the PUM and with the Zapatista rebels. Both its production process and its content respond to the needs and curiosity of the *compañeros* as well as those of the video makers.

While making the video production, Contreras and Ortiz created a style and conveyed a message, including the opinions and interests of members of the PUM, developing a particular way of producing that they have kept on practicing. The participatory style of video making they have developed can be understood as a democratic approach to communication that is embedded in the video productions of CPU. I focus on one concrete scene from *Los Más Pequeños* to exemplify this approach. This scene is an interview with Subcomandante Marcos, in which there is an extreme close up of his eyes. I have chosen it because it is representative of the work Contreras and Ortiz undertake while making a video.

The close up of Subcomandante Marcos' eyes in *Los Más Pequeños* is a shot that can be described as what Mikhail Bakhtin (see Holquist, 2002) calls heteroglot. It embodies the voices of different sectors of Mexican society. It includes the voice of the Zapatista rebels, who speak through their spokesperson; the voice of the people from the PUM, who prompted the inclusion of a particular shot becoming part of the video-making process; the voice of the Mexican government disseminated through television networks; and the voice of the video makers who authored the film (Magallanes-Blanco, 2008).

In an interview, the authors of *Los Más Pequeños* explained their reasons for including the shot of Marcos' eyes. *Los Más Pequeños* answers many questions that people from the organizations of the PUM were asking Carmen Ortiz and José Luis Contreras about the indigenous rebels. Contreras remembers,

> People [from the organizations of the PUM] were asking us if Marcos had green or blue eyes, and they asked us: "Next time you go [to Chiapas], take a shot of Marcos' eyes." So, we took some close-ups of [Marcos'] eyes. . . . That was our logic [for making the videos], to give the people what they wanted. "Here are Marcos' eyes so you can see them." (personal communication, July 13, 2001)

The interest that people from the PUM had in knowing the real color of Subcomandante Marcos's eyes was in response to official reports broadcast on television networks in early 1994 that stated that the indigenous population had been influenced and manipulated by foreigners and that the leader of the rebel group was a tall blond man with green eyes who spoke four different languages (Magallanes-Blanco, 1998). Audiences of mainstream media, such as the members of the PUM, wanted to know what was the real color of Marcos' eyes, as this seemed to be the key to his nationality and to the veracity of the arguments from mainstream media that asserted that the rebellion was not indeed indigenous but only a skirmish caused by some Indians who had been manipulated by foreigners (Magallanes-Blanco, 1998, 2008). Alternative sources of information were needed, and CPU acted as one. Not every person who sees *Los Más Pequeños* is aware of the networks reports about the alleged foreign nature of the leader of the guerrillas. Neither are they aware of the explicit request made by people from the PUM who wanted to see the real color of Marcos's eyes. Nevertheless, the close-up is part of the video with or without this knowledge, and is one of its unique characteristics. The shot is an example of the video-making style of CPU, a style that responds to the information needs and interests of the community, in this case of the members of the PUM. It also demonstrates the approach of Carmen Ortiz and José Luis Contreras to the subjects of their videos not only as objects of interest but also as individuals (Magallanes-Blanco, 2008).

The human dimension of the rebels is highlighted in the interview with Subcomandante Marcos. The direct cut in the middle of the interview from a medium shot to an extreme close up feels drastic and even upsetting, despite the unbroken flow of the audio track maintaining the narrative. However, the close up brings Marcos's eyes, the only visible aspect of his masked face, close to the audience—to the members of the PUM who were interested in knowing more about the rebels, who they were, and how they lived (Magallanes-Blanco, 2008).

The close-up of Subcomandante Marcos's eyes allow us to identify certain elements in the video-making style of CPU. Members of the PUM are the intended audiences of the productions, and they are brought into the video-making process also by considering their opinions while postproducing the video. José Luis Contreras and Carmen Ortiz recall editing *Los Más Pequeños* in a room with open doors at the meeting place of the PUM. Contreras remembers how he and Ortiz asked *compañeros* from different organizations of the movement to join them as they were editing and

asked for their opinions. "Our censors were always the people," says Ortiz (personal communication, July 13, 2001), who relates how the *compañeros* told them if a scene was too long or too boring or too slow or if it looked good. While editing, Contreras and Ortiz (1994) listened to what their audience had to say and included their suggestions. Therefore, it is not only the content of the video that represents the views of the people from the urban movement. Their views have also influenced the editing process, the length of shots, and the use of colors and effects, as well as the ways to distribute videos made by the media collective (Magallanes-Blanco, 2008).

When distributing their video productions, CPU has also taken into account their experience as members of the PUM. Ortiz and Contreras have put into practice innovative forms of distribution. They have followed a model of "information for action" (Atton, 2001), or what Carmen Ortiz calls "distribution-communication," producing materials geared toward mobilizing people through dialogue, discussion, and debate to participate in marches, protests, or campaigns.[8]

The organizations and associations of the PUM have been "natural" outlets for the distribution of the videos made by CPU, as they have been made for its members. José Luis Contreras and Carmen Ortiz share what they are working on with their *compañeros,* who expect to see the video once it is finished. The videos produced by Contreras and Ortiz are much sought after at the PUM meetings, marches, and demonstrations, where members of the organizations collaborate in the distribution and sale of the video productions. CPU also relies on screenings as moments for dialogue (Magallanes-Blanco, 2008) and sale of their video productions. They organize screenings at churches, unions, schools, universities, and the different meeting places and assemblies of the organizations of the PUM. The screenings usually include a dialogue or debate with Carmen Ortiz and José Luis Contreras and on occasions with guests, who may be journalists, activists, or people involved with the PUM. The screenings are announced on radio shows and in newspapers, in flyers handed out at meetings of the organizations of the PUM, and through word of mouth (J. L. Contreras, personal communication, July 13, 2001). Another distribution outlet for the videos of CPU is the shop of the Frente Zapatista de Liberación Nacional, or Zapatista National Liberation Front (FZLN), in Mexico City.[9] The national newspaper *La Jornada* printed three reviews of videos made by CPU, which helped them to become known and sought for among audiences not connected with the PUM. The videos are also distributed at union shops, Zapatista solidarity committees, and networks around the world, at video and film festivals, and through the Internet, although these extended distribution outlets are not always reached directly by José Luis Contreras and Carmen Ortiz but by people who copy and circulate the videos on their own.

Los Más Pequeños is the most successful video production made by CPU. It has been successful in terms of distribution, with more than 500 copies sold in the first month of its release and 12,000 copies sold between 1994 and 1997 (J. L. Contreras, personal communication, July 13, 2001), which is unusually high for an independent community media collective production. It has also been successful in terms of its circulation. Carmen Ortiz and José Luis Contreras assert that they were surprised to find pirate copies of *Los Más Pequeños* in the main square of Mexico City and to know of pirate copies of the video being circulated outside Mexico. They have records of their video being translated and shown in several languages. For example, they say that Federico Mariani, from the Italian organization Monos Blancos (white monkeys), which supports the Zapatistas, invited José Luis Contreras and Carmen Ortiz to go to Italy to present the video. Contreras asserts that when they arrived in Italy, they found that several copies of their video had already been translated into Italian. Carmen Ortiz also travelled to Paris to present the video. They both went to a video forum organized in Berlin by Autofocus, a German organization. At the video forum, they met people from Medium Backstar, who also presented *Los Más Pequeños* in the United States. The video has also been broadcast in free-to-air television in some countries in South America. In 2001, an Ecuadorian free-to-air television channel broadcast the video on the invitation of an indigenous group. José Luis Contreras and Carmen Ortiz say that they constantly receive e-mails from people from around the world congratulating them for their videos. Most of the time, they do not know how these people got hold of the videos they made. During our interview, I informed them of copies of their production that had been screened at places they were unaware the video had been seen in, such as Buenos Aires, Argentina, and Texas Christian University in the United States.[10]

Carmen Ortiz explains that CPU wants their videos to reach more people outside the PUM both within Mexico and abroad to increase awareness and to enable the voice of the Zapatistas to be heard. Carmen Ortiz traveled several times to Chiapas to capture video testimonies that would help people relate to the indigenous rebels as fellow human beings. While filming the videos, Carmen Ortiz became close to the Zapatistas at a personal level as she experienced the same situations as the indigenous rebels. For example, she endured the harassment of the rebels by the military and paramilitary groups or the state police. Because of her involvement with the rebels, she was invited to stay in Chiapas and join the Zapatista army. According to Ortiz, she was "willing to leave behind everything she knew and to exchange her video camera for a machine gun. . . . In the end Carmen did not join the rebel army" (Magallanes-Blanco, 2008, p. 242). After Carmen Ortiz decided not to become a member of the indigenous rebel army, she decided that her mission in life was to use the video camera as a weapon to fight for social justice and to inspire others to learn about the Zapatistas and their struggle (Magallanes-Blanco, 2008).

Since CPU wanted to have its videos out on the market almost immediately to act as catalysts for consciousness-raising and action (Magallanes-Blanco, 2008), they decided to broaden the scope of their distribution. Facing economic challenges and difficulties in independently distributing videos, they tried a new distribution-communication approach. Since they found that pirated copies of their videos were shown on TV sets at the street vendors' market while being sold, they decided to organize a screening of one of their video productions at the main square in Mexico City (*Zócalo*). According to Ortiz, there were many members of the state security forces dressed up as civilians watching over her and José Luis Contreras at the public screening. Unaware of them, people stayed for the duration of the film, while others passed by and glanced at the video or stayed for only a few minutes (C. Ortiz, personal communication, July 13, 2001). The screening at the *Zócalo* is an example of the communication-distribution model of CPU that uses the streets as "fields of action" (Boido, 2003).

Conclusion

CPU has contributed to the democratization of information by acting as an alternative channel of information, incorporating the opinions, interests, ideas, and information needs of audiences into the making of a video production, taking into account the subjects of the productions, and using distribution channels that challenge the traditional commercial circulation circuits.

The way CPU produces videos is linked to the affiliation and active involvement of Contreras and Ortiz with the PUM. The media collective is part of the social movement, and it has helped the members of the movement and its struggles by providing communication technologies, skills, and products that inform, strengthen, and empower the PUM. The different points of view embedded in the videos produced by CPU demonstrate that José Luis Contreras and Carmen Ortiz are not professional filmmakers but participatory video makers who grant the same value to their own opinions as producers as those of the members of the PUM with whom they share interests and the experience of video making.

The different viewpoints presented in productions such as *Los Más Pequeños* reflect the input of Carmen Ortiz and José Luis Contreras as well as that of many of their *compañeros* in both the process of making the video production and the content of the final product. José Luis Contreras and Carmen Ortiz assert that *Los Más Pequeños* has been useful for people to resolve doubts they had about the Zapatistas and to overcome prejudices about indigenous peoples. Carmen Ortiz (personal communication, July 13, 2001) says, "This is what we had to do. If somebody values it, bravo! If not, well . . . we did it because we wanted to."

Not only through the content of the videos but also through the participatory process of video making, CPU puts into practice the characteristics of participatory communication identified by Alfonso Gumucio-Dagron (2001b). Contreras and Ortiz give power to the people from the PUM by placing decision-making processes in their hands while reinforcing the identity of the community and its movement contributing to build self-esteem and pride. By letting people tell their stories in their own words, CPU also strengthens the community's organizations and protects traditions and cultural values.

Nevertheless, the democratic, political, and social potential of the work of CPU has yet to be explored. It constitutes material for future research projects. These projects could take into account how audiences within the PUM and elsewhere react to, relate with, reappropriate, and transform the contents of the videos to make them part of their everyday life and their specific struggles.

Notes

1. For information about participatory communication, see Bery (2003), Gumucio-Dagron (2001a, 2001b, 2003), Rodriguez (2001), and White (2003).

2. According to Carlos Monsiváis (2005), in the mid-1970s, with the increasing growth of urban areas and in the aftermath of the social mobilization linked with the students' movement of 1968, the inhabitants

of many neighborhoods decided to independently get organized in the PUM, a group of left-oriented social organizations that continue to be active and organized. For current information on the PUM see http://mx .geocites.com/movimiento_urbano_popular/ (retrieved November 9, 2008).

3. They are the producers, directors, editors, and distributors of all their videos and of all media products elaborated by the collective (photographs, printing materials, etc.).

4. The EZLN favored media they considered to be "good" or impartial. Specifically, they invited "small," independent media, as well as the Mexican newspapers *La Jornada, El Financiero, El Tiempo*, and *El Norte*; the international publications *The New York Times, The Washington Post, The Los Angles Times, Le Monde*, and *The Houston Chronicle*. They also included the Mexican newsmagazines *Proceso, Siempre!*, and *Mira* and the independent video production company Canal 6 de Julio; the Mexican television stations Multivisión and Canal 11; and the international network CNN. The news agencies AP, UPI, AFP, Reuters, and Prensa Latina were also invited. The list also included the Mexican radio stations Radio Educación, WM, XEVA, Radio Red, and Grupo Acir. For details see Magallanes-Blanco (1998).

5. The video camera they used for filming had been stolen a few months before.

6. In the 1980s, when CPU started, they obtained funds from selling photographs, making T-shirts, or printing business cards, invitations, or flyers for members of the PUM. Since then, other ways of getting funds have been through commissioned work (photos or videos) or through the sales of the videos they produce. They make copies of the videos (50 or a 100) and sell them to NGOs, to organizations that are members of the PUM, or to audiences at the rallies or meetings of the PUM. Their group is not a business, to the point that José Luis Contreras asserts, "As we recover the money [we invest on producing a video] we eat it." Additionally, CPU coproduced the video *Del Dolor a la Esperanza* with the organization Movimiento por la Paz con Justicia y Dignidad, which invested the money while CPU provided the equipment and was in charge of the production, postproduction, and distribution of the video.

7. The video is titled *De la Ciudad al Campo*, and it shows the mobilizations that took place in Mexico City in support of the Zapatistas in January 1994. It shows people putting balaclavas or bandanas over their faces and saying "we are all indigenous peoples." In the video, women and children from the different organizations of the PUM greet the indigenous Zapatista women and children from Chiapas. A caravan of support was organized by members of the PUM to deliver the video, school notebooks, and *piñatas* to celebrate children's day in the indigenous communities. The video was intended for the Zapatistas and not for general audiences or members of the PUM.

8. The strategies that CPU uses for the distribution of its videos resemble the strategies the PUM uses for its diverse mobilizations. The PUM was created with the idea of collective action in mind. People organized to get housing and to face local and federal governments in pressing their claims for better living conditions.

9. The FZLN was created on September 16, 1997, as the civil branch of the EZLN in Mexico City (see www.ezln.org and www.fzln.org).

10. During our interview, I did not explore with Carmen Ortiz and José Luis Contreras the reactions to their videos of audiences who were not members of the PUM.

References

Atton, C. (2001, May). *Approaching alternative media: Theory and methodology*. Paper presented at the ICA Preconference on Alternative Media Our Media, Not Theirs, Washington, DC.

Bery, R. (2003). Participatory video that empowers. In S. White (Ed.), *Participatory video: Images that transform and empower* (pp. 102–121). New Delhi, India: Sage.

Boido, P. (2003, May). *Indymedia, Argentina*. Paper presented at the OURMedia III Conference, Barranquilla, Colombia.

Contreras, J. L., & Ortiz, C. (Directors). (1994). *Los Más Pequeños* [The smallest of them all] [Video]. México D.F., Mexico: Colectivo Perfil Urbano.

Eckstein, S. (2001). La Gente Pobre Contra el Estado y el Capital. Anatomía de una Movilización Comunitaria Fructífera en la Demanda de Vivienda en la Ciudad de México [Poor people versus the state and capital: Anatomy of a successful community mobilization for housing in

Mexico City]. In S. Eckstein (Coordinator), *Poder y protesta popular. Movimientos sociales Latinoamericanos* [Power and popular protest: Latin American social movements] (pp. 214–236). México D.F., Mexico: Siglo XXI.

Gumucio-Dagron, A. (2001a, May). *Call me impure: Myths and paradigms of participatory communication.* Paper presented at the ICA Preconference on Alternative Media Our Media, Not Theirs. Washington, DC.

Gumucio-Dagron, A. (2001b). *Haciendo olas. Historias de comunicación participativa para el cambio social* [Making waves: Stories of participatory communication for social change]. New York: Rockefeller Foundation.

Gumucio-Dagron, A. (2003, May). *Arte de equilibristas: La sostenibilidad de los medios de comunicación comunitarios* [The art of the balancer: The sustainability of community media]. Paper presented at the OURMedia III Conference. Barranquilla, Colombia.

Holquist, M. (2002). *Dialogism. Bakhtin and his world* (2nd ed.). London: Routledge.

Jain, R. (1991). Video: For, by, and with the people. In N. Thede & A. Ambrosi (Eds.), *Video the changing world* (pp. 40–47). Montreal, Quebec, Canada: Black Rose Books.

Lunch, C. (2007, June). The most significant change: Using participatory video for monitoring and evaluation [Electronic version]. *Participatory Learning and Action, 56,* 28–32. Retrieved January, 2009, from www.insightshare.org/pdfs/ PLA%20PV%20ARTICLE%2007.pdf

Magallanes-Blanco, C. (1998). *Mediated revolution: The Ejército Zapatista de Liberación Nacional and its use of media for de-colonization.* Unpublished MS thesis, Texas Christian University, Fort Worth.

Magallanes-Blanco, C. (2008). *The use of video for political consciousness-raising in Mexico. An analysis of independent videos about the Zapatistas.* Lewiston, NY: Edwin Mellen Press.

Monsiváis, C. (2005). *"No sin nosotros" Los días del terremoto 1985–2005* [Not without us. The days of the earthquake 1985–2000]. México D. F., Mexico: Bolsillo Era.

Movimiento Urbano Popular. (2007). Retrieved November 9, 2008, from http://mx.geocites.com/ movimiento_urbano_popular/

Rodriguez, C. (2001). *Fissures in the mediascape: An international study of citizen's media.* Cresskill, NJ: Hampton Press.

Trejo Delabre, R. (1994). *Chiapas: La comunicación enmascarada. Los medios y el Pasamontañas* [Chiapas: The masked communication. The media and the Balaclava]. México D. F., Mexico: Diana.

White, S. (2003). Participatory video: A process that transforms. In S. White (Ed.), *Participatory video: Images that transform and empower* (pp. 63–101). New Delhi, India: Sage.

CHAPTER 23

Feminist Guerrilla Video in the Twin Cities

Brian J. Woodman

In the early years of alternative video, video makers joined together in collectives dedicated to using video as a tool for social change. These organizations, founded on the ideals of the counterculture and the leftist politics of the 1960s, valued video making as a process that could empower individuals and communities. As described by Deidre Boyle (1997) in *Subject to Change: Guerrilla Television Revisited,* these "guerrilla" video makers were interested in creating an alternative to mainstream TV that was democratic, decentralized, and expressed ideas absent on the networks. Specifically, they used portable video to make projects that were shot on the streets or in the crowds, making the video makers part of the events around them. Their video style often was handheld, used in-camera editing, avoided voiceovers, and often aimed for "on the street" interviews. However, as Boyle points out, although these early alternative video groups were committed to an inclusive, democratic vision of video, vestigial sexism often prevented women from being treated as equals to the men within these organizations. According to Boyle (1997), in these groups, "Women were allowed to serve the tea and granola bars but were asked to give up their chairs to the 'guys' when seating ran short" (p. 11).

Although sexism was a powerful presence in the male-dominated alternative video scene, many women versed in leftist activism and the emerging feminist movement became significant players in alternative video in the Twin Cities of Minneapolis and St. Paul, Minnesota. Inspired by the video activism of the gender-heterogeneous organization, University Community Video (UCV), and the strength of the diverse feminist movement in the Twin Cities, one organization in particular, Iris Video, combined elements of video and feminism in effective ways. Iris Video applied the ideals of alternative video to the exploration of women's empowerment and women's issues, creating a distinctly feminist alternative to the male-dominated video scene. Merging liberal feminism's proactive pursuit of equality with an interest in radical, women-focused participatory communalism, Iris Video created a safe place for women to explore the possibilities of the young video medium.

This chapter focuses on Iris Video and its place within the Twin Cities alternative video scene, which largely has been ignored in contemporary scholarship. This little-known collective increased women's access to the tools of video production for the purpose of self-expression. In what follows, I outline Iris Video's origins in, and relationship to, Minneapolis' best-known alternative video production collective, UCV. I explain the philosophy of Iris Video, its operating structure, and the ways in which it engaged the larger community of women activists and video makers in the Twin Cities. I also explore Iris's communal video-making process, focusing on the ways its members functioned both as media makers and as members of the feminist movement. Hopefully, this chapter illuminates the work of this important video organization while also helping shine a light on the often-ignored role of women in early alternative video.

The Godmother of Iris Video: University Community Video

The Twin Cities of the 1960s and 1970s was an area where progressive politics flourished. The presence of the University of Minnesota nourished the area's activist community with a steady stream of students who had been immersed in the politics of the New Left and the counterculture. Just as social protests had broken out on campuses across the United States, students and faculty at the University demonstrated on a variety of issues (Lehmberg & Pflaum, 2000).

Many activists at the University of Minnesota tuned into issues such as feminism and Native American rights. By the end of the 1960s, the Twin Cities' feminists were meeting in consciousness-raising groups, around town, to share their common experiences and find ways to unite against gender discrimination. In 1968, Native American activists founded the American Indian Movement (AIM), headquartered in Minneapolis, to demand the protection of treaty rights and encourage self-determination for all American Indian peoples. Given the sizable presence of social and political activism around the Twin Cities during the late

1960s and early 1970s, it almost seems inevitable that such activities would begin to influence media makers in Minneapolis and St. Paul and help create an environment that would be conducive to the establishment of UCV.

UCV was a University of Minnesota–funded video access center that provided training and equipment to students and community members. UCV also supplied multiple distribution and exhibition outlets for its own producers and for community video makers, including catalog distribution, screenings at community group meetings, and exhibitions through their Minnesota Independent Film and Video Festival. For a number of years, UCV produced two shows that aired on the Twin Cities' public television station, KTCA (Boyle, 1997).

UCV, unlike Iris Video, was not an all-woman video collective; nor was it solely devoted to women's issues. However, UCV's broad mission was to provide an alternative to mainstream television that allowed often-ignored individuals and communities to express themselves. According to UCV's Management Statement (1975–1976), existing media had omitted "programming produced by and for students, women, and other interests that get labeled as minority" (p. 1). To combat this, UCV hoped "to provide a voice through the mediums of television and video tape to those groups who have previously been denied such a voice" (p. 1). Thus, although UCV was not an all-woman collective, its philosophy was one of openness and access that explicitly included women and, consistent with the ideals of liberal feminism, attempted to promote gender equality in both equipment training and programming topics through the cooperation of men and women.

From its early days, women were central to UCV's activities. UCV trained groups, such as the League of Women Voters, the Minnesota Women's Center, and the Twin Cities Women's Film Collective, in Sony Portapak use (UCV Project Fall & Winter, 1973–1974). The UCV staff also cooperated with some of these women's groups in producing tapes. For instance, UCV helped the feminist theater collective, Circle of the Witch, produce tapes of their plays for funding and feedback purposes (UCV Student and Community Projects, 1975–1976). UCV producers also created and disseminated various video projects with feminist themes, through their catalog and television shows, including *Women and Media Collectives, Midwifery: The Rebirth of an Old Art,* a piece on International Women's Day, and various others (Video Documentaries, 1976). One tape, *Rape and the Law* (Mulligan, 1973), was made by UCV user-turned-employee Jim Mulligan after his friend was forced to navigate the complex and sometimes cruel justice system following a rape. In the tape, Mulligan declared, "Some women are raped twice—once by a man and once by the system of rape justice" (J. Mulligan, personal communication, June 27, 2005). Although UCV was not a women's collective, they clearly considered women's concerns as integral to their mission of alternative expression.

Female members of UCV made many important contributions to the organization. Female UCV staff taught video classes, worked with community organizations, and produced their own video projects, often with a pronounced feminist focus. Cara DeVito produced and coproduced *Look Good, Feel Great,* (DeVito, 1974) an exploration of women training to become models; *Elan* (DeVito & Hyker, 1977), which focused on women in prison; and *Ama L'uomo Tuo* (Devito, 1975), about an elderly Italian American widow living alone in New York City. Another UCV employee, Ellen Anthony, produced the well-received documentary *Stay with Me* (Anthony, 1982), about the campaign and election of grassroots feminist Karen Clark to the Minnesota House of Representatives. During her tenure at UCV from its beginnings through 1975, Ellen O'Neill worked as the staff advisor on many tapes, including a video by the Minnesota Women's Center, titled *A Woman Is* (O'Neill, 1974), which analyzed distorted representations of women in television commercials. The tape also provided an opportunity for the individuals from the Women's Center to learn from O'Neill about how to operate the video equipment themselves (UCV Project Form, 1973–1974). In addition, O'Neill taught an all-woman, all-inclusive weekend video workshop to help them gain access to the tools of production (UCV Staff Meeting Notes, 1975–1976).

Women-only workshops were later resurrected by UCV employees Kathy Seltzer and Ann Follett, two important figures in the founding of Iris Video. The classes were necessary because, although UCV attracted women to its regular production classes, most would not stay past the first day. According to Follett, the problem was a combination of women feeling intimidated by the male-dominated medium and the overuse of technical talk. To combat these problems, Seltzer and Follett worked with fellow UCV employee David Brown to revamp UCV's teaching methods to demystify video technology for women new to the field. Their all-women weekend workshops de-emphasized technical talk and instead put the equipment into the hands of women as quickly as possible. According to Follett (personal communication, July 13, 2005), these classes were very helpful for new female students

> because you're not going say to the man in your group, "Why don't you do the camera?" You know, somebody's going to have to pick up the camera. Somebody's going to have to figure out how to hook up the plugs.

Seltzer and Follett encouraged experimentation with the equipment, allowing their students to play with camera height, angles, and points of view. They also let students attempt different shooting styles, and they pushed students to omit voices of authority and narrators from pieces. All this was done to break down preconceived notions of video production so that the students could find their own voice (A. Follett, personal communication, July 13, 2005). Eventually, Seltzer added a women's editing workshop (UCV Winter Education Schedule, 1984–1985).

Female employees like Follett found UCV to be a wonderful training ground to hone their own video skills, as well. In fact, Follett came to UCV with little previous training. Despite being a video novice, UCV hired her as a public service announcement producer for community non-profit organizations, as part of an effort to increase gender equity at UCV. They found her to be an attractive candidate because she had previous organizing experience in leftist and feminist movements from her days as a student in Madison, Wisconsin. According to Follett, "They decided it was easier to teach someone video skills than it was to teach them community organizing skills." Follett, in turn, was attracted to UCV because

> I was really interested in what UCV was able to provide to people as a communication tool; a social change tool. . . . I really wanted to focus a lot on helping women communicate issues that were important to them. (personal communication, July 13, 2005)

Such work seemed especially important to her given that, at that time, there were still few women involved in video. In such a field where traditionally "men were the technicians," Follett felt it was essential to find a way to begin including women's voices (A. Follett, personal communication, July 13, 2005). At UCV, she learned quickly from the men and women already on staff.

During her time at UCV, Follett felt relatively insulated from much of the sexism that women experienced in the field of video. Follett partly credits the executive directors that she worked with at UCV, Sallie Fischer and Tom Borrup, who were very devoted to gender parity and the education of women. She also believes that, for the most part, her fellow producers were extremely supportive and helpful, particularly Ellen Anthony and Cris Anderson. Follett became a much better video maker by crewing her fellow producers' projects and by listening to their constructive critiques of her work (A. Follett, personal communication, July 13, 2005). Given the amount of sexism that was present in many early video groups, UCV seems to have been a supportive environment for women video makers.

The Founding and Philosophy of Iris Video

Partially inspired by the video advocacy work of UCV, Iris Video created a specifically feminist, women-focused substitute for male-dominated video. This all-woman video collective trained women with little or no previous production experience and provided them with opportunities to use their new video skills in feminist activist video pieces. Most of these projects were accomplished with the assistance of UCV equipment and video distribution. However, Iris Video began creeping away from UCV's liberal feminism, with its focus on gender equity achieved from within the system. Instead, Iris Video incorporated some of the ideas of radical feminism that were percolating throughout the feminist movement, such as the desire to create a separate space for women media makers that operated outside the mainstream patriarchy. For several years, the members of Iris Video made an invaluable contribution not only to alternative video but also to the women's rights movement throughout the region.

Iris Video's direct political catalyst was the violence against women movement of the late 1970s. In 1979, a Minneapolis group called Women Against Violence Against Women (WAVAW) organized the Twin Cities' first Women Take Back the Night march. The August 4th event, which attracted 5000 marchers, began with a gathering in Minneapolis' Loring Park, where crowds of women and men listened to speakers, rape and abuse survivors, and singers and poets, all of whom shared their feelings about the issue of violence against women. The event also included opportunities for women to learn self-defense techniques. That night, the crowd then marched down downtown Minneapolis' main artery, Hennepin Avenue, chanting and carrying signs that raised awareness about violence against women. WAVAW saw the event as an important first step in eradicating women's fear of violence in everyday life.

To document the preparation and execution of the march, WAVAW assigned some of its members to act as a video task force. As organizing began, Kathy Seltzer, the equipment manager at UCV, offered assistance to the fledgling group. Seltzer, who was highly skilled in production, guided the inexperienced task force through UCV's video production workshops to prepare them to document the march ("Iris Video: Women Videomakers," 1982, p. 1). This group of women, which included Seltzer, Fran Belvin, Mary Dorland, and Patty Gille, eventually became known as Iris Video. By the time of the march, Iris Video saw the addition of Denise Mayotte, a woman with previous video training from UCV who had a passion for leftist activism and women's folk art. Later additions to the group included Seltzer's fellow employee at UCV, Ann Follett.

For Follett, "The mission of Iris Video was specifically to put the communication tool of video into the hands of women" (A. Follett, personal communication, July 13, 2005). Seltzer summarized Iris Video's purpose as documenting women and their lives from a woman's point of view, "something the commercial media often fails to do" ("Iris Video: Women Videomakers," 1982, p. 1). According to Follett, the name Iris Video was chosen because the word *iris* evoked many aspects of their mission: The iris as a flower represented women, the iris as a part of the eye suggested seeing things from a different point of view, and the iris as part of a camera called to mind the means through which the women documented this new vision (A. Follett, personal communication, July 13, 2005).

From its earliest stages, Iris Video operated as a loose, collective entity. In fact, Iris Video didn't even become an organization with legal nonprofit status until it had already completed three videos. When organizing a project, Mayotte recalls, "We had a lot

of meetings. We'd try to come to consensus on important decisions. . . . There was an effort to make sure that people had experience with every aspect of the production" (D. Mayotte, personal communication, July 18, 2005). This collective organizational structure was a natural outgrowth of the group's origins in activism. According to Follett, "we had a march for everything and a meeting for everything." Likewise,

> at that time, there was really the thinking . . . that you did things collectively and that everybody did everything. So it didn't matter if you weren't very good at one thing or another; you got the opportunity to do it. (A. Follett, personal communication, July 13, 2005)

Generally, at the Iris weekly meetings, the members would set the agenda for the current project, see what work needed to be done, see who wanted to do it, and then move on. When it came to the actual video shoots, much of the members' learning was on the job (A. Follett, personal communication, July 13, 2005). In an effort to be democratic during video shoots, sometimes the camera would be passed from one member to another. At other times, different members would be in charge of videotaping different segments of a project, which would then be combined into a whole, in the editing process. Although every member learned all aspects of video making and the group made most decisions collectively, people's natural inclinations eventually created a division of labor. As Mayotte explains, "People kind of gravitated toward things that they were better at." For instance, Seltzer was an excellent cameraperson. Mayotte, on the other hand, was a natural interviewer, relationship builder, and fund-raiser. She never felt like a great camera operator, but she felt "that was all right because the other skills I had helped to balance that" (D. Mayotte, personal communication, July 18, 2005). Editing was always a tricky collective endeavor, as it is difficult to have everyone's hands at the knobs. In this case, usually the people with the most editing proficiency would sit at the controls while other members of the collective would observe and give comments about what they liked and didn't like. At the end of the project, members shared the production credits (A. Follett, personal communication, July 13, 2005).

This collective process proved to be valuable to many of these women as it helped them learn to use video in a nonjudgmental, nonsexist environment. According to Follett, when the members of Iris came together, "We'd been facing a lot of issues of sexism in trying to do things in the leftist community that came out of the Vietnam War" (A. Follett, personal communication, July 13, 2005). This sexism also translated into video. For instance, while Follett was a member of Iris, she did some freelance work to help pay the bills. The process of doing commercial video was an eye-opener:

> It was like walking onto a construction site or something [where you think] "Oh my God. They're not going to let me pick up a hammer." . . . I would get challenged constantly: "what kind of video camera is that? What kind of tube is that?" People would ask me just to see if I knew what I was talking about, or just to be mean, or to let me know they didn't want me to be there. (A. Follett, personal communication, July 13, 2005)

Given the sexism in many leftist organizations and in the mainstream video production world, the collective was the perfect way for women to become familiar with video technology. In the end, Follett found "the supportive learning process as important as the final product" ("Iris Video: Women Videomakers," 1982, p. 1).

This emphasis on process was important to the work of the collective. Members didn't simply see themselves as video makers while creating *Women Take Back the Night* (Iris Video, 1980); they saw themselves as participants in the activist events around them. According to Mayotte, "When you're shooting, you're part of it. We figured the making of the tape was part of the event. . . . We weren't documenting a movement; we felt we were part of the

movement" (D. Mayotte, personal communication, July 18, 2005). This feeling comes through in the videotape, which includes handheld camerawork, no artificial lighting, and many "on the street" interviews with participants. Although the piece uses brief narration to set up the videotape, most information is conveyed by organizers and participants. The soundtrack is dominated by the songs and chants of the marchers. Iris's focus on process also extended to editing, as the collective showed the tape to organizers and participants during various stages of editing to solicit comments and critique (Larson, 1980).

The collective's best known piece, *The Fear That Binds Us: Violence Against Women* (Iris Video, 1981), further explored some of the themes first highlighted in *Women Take Back the Night* (Iris Video, 1980). The video included interviews with an incest victim, a marital-rape victim, a domestic-abuse victim, and an ex-prostitute, as well as with male perpetrators. The project grew out of the collective's desire to delve deeper into the causes and effects of violence against women. The tape, which was funded by a grant from the Minnesota Humanities Commission, was shown nationally and, in 1982, it was the most-watched program on KTCA (Ellis, 1985).

As an all-woman alternative video collective, Iris Video often had to struggle for money and resources. For many years, the collective had no equipment of its own. They would borrow UCV's equipment for video shoots, a simple task given that Seltzer and Follett were UCV employees. Sometimes, however, they had to be more resourceful. For instance, at the Women Take Back the Night march, Mayotte remembers running alongside the marchers, pushing a shopping cart that they had turned into a makeshift dolly (D. Mayotte, personal communication, July 18, 2005). On occasion, Iris Video would engage in creative wheeling and dealing. For instance, to finish editing their third video, *Living Traditions* (1982), the collective made a deal with the public television station in Bemidji, Minnesota, that allowed them to use the station's superior equipment in return for free, unlimited broadcast of the piece.

The organization also obtained money through grants. Grants, however, could have drawbacks. To receive funding from the Minnesota Humanities Commission, Iris Video had to use academic experts in their video, or, as Mayotte joked, "people with letters after their names." Despite their discomfort with using voices of authority, the collective navigated the problem by finding people that reflected their values and interests. Instead of the traditional white, male voices of authority, their experts included, among others, a Chicana poet and activist, a black female employee at a local women's shelter, and a woman from the Minnesota Department of Corrections. Another grant requirement was that the organization must have "humanist" speakers at community screenings to help justify their video as a "humanities" project. Once again, the members of Iris simply tried to find like-minded speakers who could enhance their video (D. Mayotte, personal communication, July 18, 2005). According to Follett, "the Humanities Commission started using *The Fear that Binds Us* as an example of what they shouldn't have funded" because the video was really "a grassroots project of women talking about their own views" (A. Follett, personal communication, July 13, 2005). It was a social change project, not a humanities project.

Iris Video also worked to connect itself to the larger community of women film and video makers in the Twin Cities. Out of Iris grew Women in Film and Video, a group that would meet every month or so to talk about problems they experienced in the production world. Members would screen works for each other and share advice. The group also was a useful place for women to make contacts with other women or gender-equitable men in the industry. The informal group became quite popular through word of mouth. At its height, around 60 women would show up for a given meeting (A. Follett, personal communication, July 13, 2005). Members of Iris Video helped crew many of these women's projects and also provided video services to many community nonprofit organizations. Iris even organized the first women's film and video festival in the Twin Cities (A. Follett, personal communication, July 13, 2005). What had begun as a small task force intended to document a single feminist demonstration had become the Twin Cities' locus of feminist video activism.

Connecting to Native American Women

Iris Video combined its collectivist vision of feminist video with an interest in Native American artistry in *Living Traditions: Five Indian Women Artists* (1982). Although Iris Video was founded to explore issues of violence against women, their feminist vision widened to encompass additional feminist issues with the joining of Denise Mayotte. Mayotte had been employed through a Comprehensive Employment and Training Act (CETA) grant by Womanswork, a Minneapolis-based women's art collective that promoted traditional arts, such as weaving, embroidering, and quilting (D. Mayotte, personal communication, July 18, 2005).

As part of Iris Video, Mayotte decided that she wanted to make a video in conjunction with Womanswork about the different art forms that came out of Native American culture, such as beading and quilting (A. Follett, personal communication, July 13, 2005). She hoped to document the words and works of these often-ignored women artists. For Mayotte,

> We just really felt like this was part of our work as feminists to [acknowledge] that women may not have had access to art school, especially women with more disadvantaged economic means or from a different cultural tradition. . . . We knew that these women were really talented, significant artists, and we wanted them to get that recognition. (D. Mayotte, personal communication, July 18, 2005)

Through her activist coworker at Womanswork, Juanita Espinosa, as well as through connections with Professor Kent Smith at Bemidji State University, Mayotte contacted several Native American women artists, such as Josie Ryan. Mayotte and a small group of Iris members made the trip to rural Minnesota to begin work on the documentary. The experience proved to be a useful exercise in not only documenting Native American artists and art traditions but also building bridges between cultures.

After pitching the project to the artists, Iris Video initially received ambivalent responses. According to Mayotte, the artists feared that the project might be another example of "these white people coming here to rip us off again. . . . It was a delicate situation coming into a community that's not your own, and especially a community that's undergone such trauma." Recognizing the need for relationship building, the Iris crew spent weeks getting to know their interviewees and their communities. According to Mayotte, "[You] had to spend a lot of time talking with them beforehand before you really felt like they would be comfortable talking with you on camera. Establishing relationships. I think that was the bottom line" (D. Mayotte, personal communication, July 18, 2005).

Mayotte is realistic that she and the other members of Iris may not always have dealt perfectly with this new community and culture, despite their best intentions. For Mayotte,

> We were so passionate about trying to make those cultural connections that we probably glossed over a lot of the difference. I mean I sometimes think that our subjects probably had a really different view of the situation than we did at the time. But again, it was in the context of being involved in the political work of solidarity with native communities. (D. Mayotte, personal communication, July 18, 2005)

Mayotte is certain that at times they sounded insensitive, but "I think that people respected the fact that we were making the effort: 'You're trying. You're here'" (D. Mayotte, personal communication, July 18, 2005).

Over time, the members of Iris and the artists' communities began forging strong connections, especially once it was clear that Mayotte and her companions truly respected them. It also helped that they included community members in the planning stages of the video shoots, talking to them about important issues and asking for help in formulating interview questions. Iris members did not want to promote a "white man's burden" attitude and were certain to make sure that community members felt like they also had ownership of the tapes.

Mayotte became particularly close with the quilter Edith Saginaw at the Red Lake reservation. She still fondly remembers the many days outside taping and spending time with her new friend, who, in a gesture of reciprocal respect, taught Mayotte how to make her own star quilt, a quilt that Mayotte has kept on her bed to this day.

Although the process of taping did generally succeed in bridging cultural gaps and forging new friendships, not everything ran smoothly. The biggest miscommunication occurred when Iris Video, which had no editing equipment to call its own, struck a deal with Bemidji's public television [station] granting broadcast rights in return for access to editing equipment. Since the members of Iris believed in the democratic tenets of public access, giving the tape away in return for much needed resources seemed fair. After all, they did not care about making money on the project; they just wanted to finish and air the video. However, some members of the Native American community did not understand that Iris was not paid for screening the tape. Having felt cheated so many times in the past by seemingly well-meaning outsiders, some Native Americans believed that Iris was receiving checks for the airings and not sharing the money with the reservation. Iris had hoped that its completed project was a respectful celebration of American Indian artistic traditions, but for some, it smacked of white exploitation of Native American culture and values, a misunderstanding that Mayotte regrets to this day.

This brief conflict, however, did not negate the overall importance of the project for Mayotte, a project that had a profound influence on her. According to Mayotte,

"I am a changed person because of the time I spent in that community. I continue to do work that is about trying to build bridges, and I think that was one of my first experiences of trying to do it." Although she sees the potential for misunderstandings, she also feels like the only way to build understanding is to take risks and possibly make mistakes. (D. Mayotte, personal communication, July 18, 2005)

The Lasting Value of Iris Video

By the mid-1980s, Iris Video, for all effective purposes, was no more. After the first few videos had been completed, most of the original members moved on. Kathy Seltzer and Ann Follett tried to keep the organization alive by incorporating it as a nonprofit. They continued to do work for both volunteer and for hire and even managed to complete another project, *Weight of a Woman's Shadow*, an examination of women's body images. Seltzer eventually moved away to Massachusetts. Although she and Follett continued to try to make projects from afar, they soon found that long-distance production did not work well. Iris Video became dormant.

The organization only existed for a little over half a decade, but in that brief time Iris Video had a major impact on the Twin Cities video scene, not only through its collectively produced videos, which are still available for viewing, but also as a safe place for women to come together and develop their production skills in a supportive, sexism-free environment. Through the video trainings provided by Iris Video and UCV, hundreds of women became adept in video production, training that only has become more valuable in our media-saturated present. Some of the biggest effects, however, were on the members of Iris Video themselves. For Mayotte, who

continues to work in the nonprofit sector, "It was a wonderful experience. It was so great working with all the women. I learned from all of them. I felt like everybody was so generous in sharing their talents" (D. Mayotte, personal communication, July 18, 2005). Follett, who has continued her interest in documentary production, also has nothing but warm feelings for her time with Iris Video. According to Follett, "I look back now at some of the things that were made and some of the things that were put on television and I just think, 'it's sort of amazing'" (A. Follett, personal communication, July 13, 2005).

Since Iris Video's demise, the diverse realm of feminist thinking has continued to expand and, in some cases, question the ideas of liberal feminism and radical feminist communalism that characterized the video collective. Today, as always, the women's movement is a rich panoply of ideologies that, in addition to liberal and radical feminism, now includes postcolonial feminism, postmodern feminism, and ecofeminism. Because of the continuing metamorphosis and spread of feminist thought, it is easy to overlook the accomplishments of small, grassroots feminist groups of the past. However, the activist spirit of early feminist video collectives, such as Iris Video, still can be seen in the continuing efforts of organizations such as Women Make Movies, who remain dedicated to ensuring that women's voices are heard. The passion of such collectives is also evident in the spread of grassroots feminist videos, whether produced by satirical guerrilla groups, such as the Barbie Liberation Organization, or by individuals who have invaded popular culture through postings on online sites, such as YouTube. Iris Video, although not well-known, is proof of the power that video can have when wielded not by media professionals but by passionate and dedicated members of the grassroots community. Iris Video, with the support of groups, such as UCV, helped keep the feminist alternative video scene alive and well in the Twin Cities.

References

Anthony, E. (Producer). (1982). *Stay with me* [VHS]. (Available in the Intermedia Arts Minnesota Video Collection at the Minnesota History Center in St. Paul, Minnesota)

Boyle, D. (1997). *Subject to change: Guerrilla television revisited.* New York: Oxford University Press.

DeVito, C. (Producer). (1974). *Look good, feel great* [VHS]. (Available in the Intermedia Arts Minnesota Video Collection at the Minnesota History Center in St. Paul, Minnesota)

DeVito, C. (Producer). (1975). *Ama l'uomo tuo* [VHS]. (Available in the Intermedia Arts Minnesota Video Collection at the Minnesota History Center in St. Paul, Minnesota)

DeVito, C., & Hyker, E. (Producers). (1977). *Elan* [VHS]. (Available in the Intermedia Arts Minnesota Video Collection at the Minnesota History Center in St. Paul, Minnesota)

Ellis, V. (1985, November/December). Women's eating disorders: Topic of new videotape. *Changing Channels* [Newsletter], p. 5.

Iris Video (Producer). (1980). *Women take back the night* [VHS]. (Available in the Intermedia Arts Minnesota Video Collection at the Minnesota History Center in St. Paul, Minnesota)

Iris Video (Producer). (1981). *The fear that binds us: Violence against women* [VHS]. (Available in the Intermedia Arts Minnesota Video Collection at the Minnesota History Center in St. Paul, Minnesota)

Iris Video (Producer). (1982). *Living traditions: Five Indian women artists* [VHS]. (Available in the Intermedia Arts Minnesota Video Collection at the Minnesota History Center in St. Paul, Minnesota)

Iris Video: Women videomakers, women's issues. (1982, Winter). *Changing Channels* [Newsletter], p. 1.

Larson, S. (1980, July 25). Reflecting the march. *Minnesota Daily,* p. 4(AE).

Lehmberg, S., & Pflaum, A. M. (2000). *The University of Minnesota, 1945–2000.* Minneapolis: University of Minnesota Press.

Mulligan, J. (Producer). (1973). *Rape and the Law* [VHS]. (Available in the Intermedia Arts Minnesota Video Collection at the Minnesota History Center in St. Paul, Minnesota)

O'Neill, E. (Producer). (1974). *A woman is* [VHS]. (Available in the Intermedia Arts Minnesota Video Collection at the Minnesota History Center in St. Paul, Minnesota)

UCV Management Statement of University Community Video Center. (1975–1976). Minnesota History Center Manuscripts Collection, Intermedia Arts Minnesota Corporate Records, 1971–1993, Box 2. Folder: Staff Meetings, 1975–1976.

UCV Project Fall & Winter. (1973–1974). Minnesota History Center Manuscripts Collection, Intermedia Arts Minnesota Corporate Records, 1971–1993, Box 1. Folder: University Community Video Briefing Book, 1976.

UCV Project Form submitted by Etta Magnuson of the Minnesota Women's Center. (1973–1974). Minnesota History Center Manuscripts Collection, Intermedia Arts Minnesota Corporate Records, 1971–1993, Box 4. Folder: Center Projects, 1973–1974.

UCV Staff Meeting Notes. (1975–1976). Minnesota History Center Manuscripts Collection, Intermedia Arts Minnesota Corporate Records, 1971–1993, Box 2. Folder: Staff Meetings, 1975–1976.

UCV Student and Community Projects. (1975–1976). Minnesota History Center Manuscripts Collection, Intermedia Arts Minnesota Corporate Records, 1971–1993, Box 1. Folder: University Community Video Briefing Book, 1976.

UCV Winter Education Schedule. (1984–1985). Minnesota History Center Manuscripts Collection, Intermedia Arts Minnesota Corporate Records, 1971–1993, Box 6. Folder: NEA—MAC '84–'85.

Video Documentaries from University Community [Video] catalogue. (1976). Minnesota History Center Manuscripts Collection, Intermedia Arts Minnesota Corporate Records, 1971–1993, Box 1. Folder: University Community Video Briefing Book, p. 19.

PART VI

Communication Politics

In the previous section, we considered the relationship between grassroots media and movements committed to sociopolitical change. As we have seen, community media have played a pivotal role in collective efforts to create more just and equitable societies. Scholars refer to this process as "democratization *through* the media." In this section, we look at the flipside of this equation—what has been described as "democratization *of* the media" (Carroll & Hackett, 2006; Wasco & Mosco, 1992).

Specifically, we explore community media's role in the struggle to create a more accountable, responsible, and representative media culture. To that end, this part demonstrates community media's significance to local, national, and increasingly transnational efforts to reform and remake contemporary media systems. In the chapters that follow, contributors underscore how communication policies and regulatory bodies enable or constrain community communication. Throughout, contributors emphasize the need to enhance public participation in communication policy debates.

We begin with a discussion of the connection between communication policies and the structures, technologies, and institutional logics of media systems. Throughout, we highlight the fact that media systems develop as the result of conscious, deliberate, and often contentious decisions about how and to what ends technologies can and might be used—a dynamic usefully described as "communication politics." Following this, we situate community media in relation to broader media reform campaigns that challenge the structures, behaviors, and performance of dominant media. Doing so reveals the unique strategic position community media occupy in collective efforts to remake the media.

Communication Policy and Policy Making

The introduction of new communication technologies inspires two contrasting feelings: hope and fear (Marvin, 1988). On the one hand, we hope that these new technologies will usher in an egalitarian era of understanding and enlightenment. On the other hand, we fear that new technologies will become instruments of repression and control. This ambivalence is perfectly understandable. After all, new communication technologies often present a challenge to the prevailing social, political, and economic order.

However, these cultural attitudes also reveal a particular way of thinking about technological innovation—what scholars refer to as "technological determinism"—which suggests that technologies are inherently good or bad, useful or destructive, democratic or authoritarian. In short, this line of thinking holds that the uses, impacts, and effects of technological innovation are predetermined and inevitable.

But as historian Kenneth Hacker (1996) reminds us, technologies are far more malleable than we might at first imagine. What's more, Hacker observes that the effects of new communication technologies, while never certain, can be directed to meet specific needs and interests. "A detailed examination of new communication technologies within the context of history and communication theory indicates that the effects of new forms of communication are dependent upon social-political policies for the directions of their impacts" (p. 213).

Hacker's emphasis on "social-political policies" is instructive insofar as it highlights the *constructed and contested* character of media systems. In other words, rather than view these systems as the natural or inevitable outgrowth of any given technology, this perspective illuminates the social, political, economic, and cultural dynamics involved in creating a media system. Robert McChesney (2004) frames this process in terms of a problematic to be resolved in the formation of any system of public communication.

> Media systems do not fall from the sky. The policies, structures, subsidies, and institutions that are created to control, direct, and regulate the media will be responsible for the logic and nature of the media system. Whether their content is good, bad, or a combination, the media therefore present a political problem for any society, and an unavoidable one at that. (p. 16)

This line of thinking highlights the decisive role communication policy and policy-making processes play in addressing what McChesney refers to as "the problem of the media."

For instance, radio broadcasting operates in terms of a hierarchical, one-way flow of information between media producers and media audiences. This centralized form of message production and distribution positions audiences as relatively passive consumers of media messages. And yet, there is nothing inherent in broadcast technology that precludes decentralized communication between message producers and receivers. Indeed, in its early days, radio was a vibrant, participatory, and decidedly two-way medium of popular communication (Douglas, 1987). Terrestrial radio broadcasting, as we know it today, developed as a result of explicit policies—rules and regulations covering every aspect of broadcasting, from technical specifications governing spectrum allocation and transmission power, to the conditions for licensing, ownership, and financial support mechanisms—that favored well-financed private ownership or some form of state sponsorship and control.

Throughout the 1920s and 1930s, regulatory bodies were established at the national and international levels to ensure that broadcasters operated in accordance with specific legal, institutional, and technical frameworks. However, as media and cultural historians remind us, the policies and structures that set the terms of broadcasting in the first half of the past century were the result of a series of negotiations and bitter disputes over how broadcasting would be organized, regulated, and paid for (e.g., Bailey, 2007; Smulyan, 1994). Critically, the level of public participation in these deliberations was constrained by a number of social, economic, and political conditions. As a result, powerful economic and political forces, representing a narrow range of interests, prevailed and established the foundation for present-day broadcast structures and regulations (McChesney, 1994).

These insights enhance our understanding of the limits, as well as the possibilities, of communication technologies. For instance, Torsten Hagerstrand (1986) observes that while radio broadcasting was one of the great "centralizing forces" in Sweden, as in most industrialized societies throughout the 20th century, there is nothing inherent about radio that made this a natural or inevitable application of the technology. Introducing the concept of "possibility space," Hagerstrand demonstrates that radio is uniquely suited to enhance social communication on the local and regional levels.

Viewed in this light, radio's "possibility space" is defined as much by government-enforced policies and regulatory mechanisms as by the limits or potential of the technology itself. And yet, despite radio's unique potential to promote lively and vibrant community communication, the historical record indicates that, more often than not, national and transnational policies and regulatory authorities have stifled the medium's potential to enhance social communication on the local level.

Academic and activist analysts offer several explanations for the inability, or to be more precise, unwillingness of policy makers to uphold and support the principles of democratic communication—participation, viewpoint and ownership diversity, civic engagement, and media pluralism—in policy deliberations. Hackett and Carroll (2006) suggest that this situation is the result of "an elitist process of communication policymaking" (p. 9). This process routinely involves representatives from business and government but effectively bars the public from participating. With little or no direct representation in policy debates, the public's ability to influence communication policy is severely constrained.

Insufficient press coverage also leads to a lack of public involvement in communication policy debates. Reviewing past policy deliberations in the United States and the United Kingdom, Hackett and Carroll (2006) note that public awareness of these debates was, at best, minimal. This lack of news coverage further inhibits public participation in communication policy making. In the absence of thorough and informative reporting, the general public is unaware of the terms of the debate, let alone cognizant of the consequences of policy deliberations that are conducted by powerful economic and political interests behind closed doors.

Of course, the media industries have a vested interest in maintaining a news blackout of communication policy making; doing so is an effective strategy for keeping public involvement in communication policy making to a minimum (McChesney, 2004). Left to their own devices, the media industries pursue policy objectives that give them enormous latitude to pursue their own self-interest, often to the detriment of the public interest. Clearly, this situation is at odds with the basic principles of democratic self-governance. Indeed, the purposeful exclusion of public participation in communication policy debates is decidedly antidemocratic.

Taking this critique a step further, some critics contend that the policy-making process has been thoroughly corrupted by corporate influence peddling. For instance, Jeff Chester (2007) of the Center for Digital Democracy, a U.S.-based public interest group that monitors telecommunications policy making, puts it bluntly: "In Congress and at the FCC, the economic welfare of the owners of media and telecommunications outlets regularly trumps the interest of citizens" (p. 27). This assessment of U.S. communication policy making is a useful reminder of the industry's penchant for increased spending on lobbying efforts and political campaign contributions any time it seeks favorable legislation.

As it happens, the telecommunications giants are currently seeking just such legislation in regard to Internet communication. Specifically, the cable television and telephone industries are lobbying for legislation that would allow them to privilege their own content over that of their competitors. Furthermore, the telecommunications industry wants to be able to charge content providers for access to an Internet "fast lane." Critics contend that permitting Internet service providers (ISPs) to discriminate between content providers based on their ability to pay would, in effect, create a tiered system of Internet access, thereby compromising the Internet's democratic potential.

Large corporations would thus be at an advantage when paying premiums for top-tier loading speeds. The question we must then ask is: Where does that leave bloggers? Small search engines? Independent news outlets? Other small-business websites? It leaves them in the lower tier, without the scale or capital needed to load as fast as their corporate competitors. This is a new variation of the digital divide. (Barrat & Shade, 2007, p. 299)

With enormous profits at stake, it comes as no surprise that the telecommunications industry is dead set against policies and regulations that support the principle of *network neutrality*—the practice of antidiscriminatory access to online communication that has made the Internet a boon to democratic communication and a fertile site of entrepreneurialism, self-expression, and technological innovation (Mowshowitz & Kumar, 2007; Wu, 2003).

At first, these developments may seem unfortunate but ultimately inconsequential outside of the United States. But in the era of media globalization, the United States has been a "trendsetter" in policy-making circles. As a result, market-based regulatory schemes have become increasingly common the world over, putting community media advocates in the uncomfortable position of negotiating in an increasingly unreceptive, often contradictory regulatory environment (Riddle, 2006).

For instance, a report produced by the European Union (EU; European Parliament, 2007) reveals the inconsistency of policy making vis-à-vis community media. On the one hand, EU policies and initiatives support nondiscriminatory use of the airwaves, media pluralism and diversity, freedom of speech, local cultural production, and civic engagement—all hallmarks of community-based media and essential elements of a democratic media culture. On the other hand, the EU report notes that there is "little information . . . available regarding the [community media] sector's scope, its potential and on the status of CM [community media] organizations in different Member States" (p. iii).

Likewise, the report suggests that the digital switchover could be a boon to the community media sector by making use of increased bandwidth and frequency space afforded by digital broadcasting. And yet the report finds that the digital transition plans of most member states "fail to take CM into account" (p. iv).

These incongruities support the conclusion reached by Vinod Pavarala and Kanchan Kumar (2004) in their comparative analysis of national broadcasting policy. They write, "A major hurdle for fostering community media all over the world seems to be the lack of a coherent, appropriate public policy framework to support non-profit access to broadcasting and public communications" (p. 6). Borrowing John Thompson's notion of "the principle of regulated pluralism," Pavarala and Kumar conclude that policy making in support of democratic communication would create a framework that accommodates an array of approaches to the "problem of the media," including provisions for private ownership, public service, and other forms of state-sponsored media, as well as a viable community media sector.

Democratic Media Activism

Community media are but one aspect of a field of democratic media activism that encompasses a range of actors and activities, including media reform and public interest advocacy groups, cultural interventions (popularly known as "culture jamming"), professional and trade organizations, and media literacy programs, as well as news and media "watchdog" groups (Carroll & Hackett, 2006). While it is unclear whether these disparate activities constitute a coherent social movement (Napoli, 2007), it is plain to see that there is growing, worldwide discontent with media structures, practices, and performance. Still, the specific issues and concerns taken up by democratic media activism can vary dramatically.

For instance, in societies making the transition from authoritarian rule to liberal democracy across Eastern Europe and the global South, media democratization often means removing direct and indirect forms of political censorship, opening up the media system to private ownership, and adopting Western models of journalism and entertainment formats. But, as has been well documented, democratic media activism in established democracies is also on the rise. In the United States, Canada, and the United Kingdom, for example, citizens' movements directed against commercialization, repeated press failures, and government and corporate misinformation campaigns as well as media consolidation are increasingly commonplace.

Media activist Scott Uzelman (2005) succinctly captures these varied activities under the banner of "communication-centered struggles." Uzelman makes a distinction between activists who want to reform mainstream media and those seeking to bypass dominant media altogether through the establishment of independent, so-called autonomous media. This distinction is useful insofar as it emphasizes different strategies and tactics taken up by activist projects aimed at overcoming what Carroll and Hackett (2006) describe as media's "democratic deficit."

Notwithstanding their geographic, strategic, and tactical variation, efforts to democratize the media demonstrate

> an impressive degree of convergence around the goals of expanding the range of voices accessed through the media, building an egalitarian public sphere, promoting the values and practices of sustainable democracy, and offsetting or counteracting political and economic inequalities found elsewhere in the social system. (Hackett, 2000, ¶ 14)

Herein lies the significance of community media to democratic media activism. On the one hand, community media compensate for the structural inequalities associated with the dominant media system. In doing so, community media prefigure the sort of media system advocated by "autonomous media" advocates, who believe that the current system is beyond repair and the only

viable solution is to embrace the DIY (Do-It-Yourself) ethic associated with alternative and radical media.

On the other hand, community media provide a forum for oppositional voices and perspectives, including substantive critiques aimed at dominant media structures and practices. In this way, community media support media reform efforts that receive scant attention in the mainstream press. Moreover, in a regulatory climate that diminishes the value and importance of public service broadcasting, community media help restore a public service ethos to an increasingly privatized, profit-obsessed media system. In short, community media represent local sites of resistance to the democratic deficit of dominant media institutions.

The South Korean experience with democratic media activism is both instructive and inspiring in this regard. In the late 1980s, the prodemocracy movement in South Korea emerged as a force for dramatic social, political, and cultural change. Significantly, media reform was high atop the change agenda promoted by various constituencies, including students, trade unions, and independent media makers. In relatively short order, media activists and others successfully pressured lawmakers to enact major structural reforms in the South Korean media system, reforms aimed at enhancing democratic communication. As media activist Myoungjoon Kim (2006) observes, "Korea has become a very rare example of a country where public access to terrestrial, cable and satellite channels has become a reality. This commitment also includes a funding mechanism for access programming" (p. 33).

All this is to emphasize the synergistic relationship between community media and broader media reform efforts. To that end, this section features description and analysis of a range of community media initiatives aimed at democratizing the media. In the chapters that follow, contributors focus on questions of communication policy; the regulation of traditional, new, and emerging technologies; and the prospects for media democracy in the 21st century. In doing so, they offer us a vivid reminder that "another media is possible."

Rosalind Bresnahan (Chapter 24) opens this section with an overview of community radio and video in Chile. Bresnahan calls our attention to the critical role grassroots media played in promoting and sustaining Chilean prodemocracy movements during the 17-year Pinochet dictatorship. As Chile began its transition to democracy, the future looked bright for the community media sector. However, Bresnahan's analysis reveals the tensions between an emerging democratic culture and the government's embrace of neoliberal policies that have led to the privatization of Chilean media. Bresnahan argues that the Chilean government's "limited conception" of democracy undermines social activism and threatens the prospects for a vibrant community media sector.

Chapter 25 explores the uneven development of community radio in Hungary. Gergely Gosztonyi links the rise of the community radio movement to Hungary's transition from authoritarian rule to liberal democracy in the early 1990s. Gosztonyi observes that in the absence of federal legislation effectively challenging the state broadcaster's monopoly, community-oriented broadcasters initially took to the airwaves as unlicensed, so-called pirate radio operators. Despite passage of favorable legislation, however, the Hungarian community radio sector languished in the early part of the new century. The emergence of low-power broadcasting appears to have resuscitated the community radio movement. Nevertheless, Gosztonyi reminds us, renewed popular interest in community broadcasting is no guarantee of the sector's long-term viability in an increasingly market-oriented regulatory environment.

Chapter 26 takes up the question of popular participation in communication policy making at the transnational level. Stefania Milan blends policy analysis with insights taken from social movement studies to examine the impact activists have on media policy debates in contemporary Europe. Specifically, Milan explores the strategies and tactics employed by the Community Media Forum Europe (CMFE)—a "loose network" of community media organizations and advocates—in their effort to gain access to transnational policy arenas and promote a legislative agenda that supports the establishment of a viable community media sector across Europe. Milan concludes by identifying some of the lessons activists took away from their lobbying efforts and offers some useful suggestions for future policy interventions.

The next two chapters return our attention to the struggle for democratic media in the United States. In Chapter 27, Bernadette Barker-Plummer and Dorothy Kidd consider the impact of media conglomeration and restructuring on democratic communication in the San Francisco Bay Area. Drawing on interviews with Bay Area activists and community organizers, Barker-Plummer and Kidd reveal how social change groups are counteracting local closures to democratic communication through innovative applications of Web-based technologies. Barker-Plummer and Kidd conclude that while media restructuring has interrupted established communication flows within and among activist groups, the Internet and related technologies have the potential to open up new discursive spaces. This optimism is tempered, however, by the fact that these new tools are not "equally accessible or equally useful" to socially and economically marginalized communities.

Chapter 28 looks at the potential of next-generation computing applications, devices, and infrastructures to promote democratic communication. Sascha Meinrath and Victor Pickard consider the use of intranets—digital communication networks serving a specific geographic area—to enhance community communication. As Meinrath and Pickard demonstrate, intranets provide unrivaled connectivity to a range of programs and services for local communities. Using case studies to illustrate their insights, Meinrath and Pickard argue that intranets create exciting new opportunities for civic engagement, participatory communication, and community journalism. Nevertheless, Meinrath and Pickard are mindful of the pivotal role communication policy making will play in enabling or constraining the democratic potential of intranets. They introduce the notion of "open versus closed technologies" to reveal the significance that policy making can have in either promoting or inhibiting community communication through intranets.

References

Bailey, M. (2007). Rethinking public service broadcasting: The historical limits of publicness. In R. Butsch (Ed.). *Media and public spheres* (pp. 96–108). New York: Palgrave Macmillan.

Barratt, N., & Shade, L. (2007). Net neutrality: Telecom policy and the public interest. *Canadian Journal of Communication, 32,* 295–305.

Carroll, W., & Hackett, R. (2006). Democratic media activism through the lens of social movement theory. *Media, Culture & Society, 28*(1), 83–104.

Chester, J. (2007). Net neutrality and the supermedia monopolies. *Extra! The newsletter of FAIR, 20*(2), 26–30.

Douglas, S. (1987). *Inventing American broadcasting: 1899–1922.* Baltimore: Johns Hopkins University Press.

European Parliament. (2007). *The state of community media in the European Union.* Brussels, Belgium: Author.

Hacker, K. L. (1996). Missing links in the evolution of electronic democratization. *Media, Culture & Society, 18,* 213–232.

Hackett, R. (2000). Taking back the media: Notes on the potential for a communicative democracy movement. *Studies in Political Economy, 63,* 61–86.

Hackett, R., & Carroll, W. (2006). *Remaking media: The struggle to democratize public communication.* New York: Routledge.

Hagerstrand, T. (1986). Decentralization and radio broadcasting: On the "possibility space" of a communication technology. *European Journal of Communication, 1,* 7–26.

Kim, M. (2006). Expanding public media space and media activism in Korea. *Community Media Review, Winter,* 32–34.

Marvin, C. (1988). *When old technologies were new: Thinking about electric communication in the late nineteenth century.* New York: Oxford University Press.

McChesney, R. (1994). *Telecommunications, mass media, and democracy: The battle for control of US broadcasting.* New York: Oxford University Press.

McChesney, R. (2004). *The problem of the media: Communication politics in the 21st century.* New York: Monthly Review Press.

Mowshowitz, A., & Kumar, N. (2007). Public vs. private interest on the Internet. *Communications of the ACM, 50*(7), 23–25.

Napoli, P. (2007). *Public interest media activism and advocacy as a social movement: A review of the literature.* Report prepared for the Media, Arts and Culture Unit of the Ford Foundation.

Pavarala, V., & Kumar, K. (2004). Enabling community radio: Case studies in national broadcasting policy. *MICA Communications Review, 1*(3), 5–23.

Riddle, A. (2006). What is WSIS? *Community Media Review, 29*(4), 10–11.

Smulyan, S. (1994). *Selling radio: The commercialization of American broadcasting.* Washington, DC: Smithsonian Institution Press.

Uzelman, S. (2005). Hard work in the bamboo garden. In A. Langlois & F. Dubois (Eds.), *Autonomous media: Activating resistance and dissent* (pp. 17–29). Montreal, Quebec, Canada: Cumulus Press.

Wasco, J., & Mosco, V. (Eds.). (1992). *Democratic communication in the information age.* Toronto, Ontario, Canada: Garamond Press.

Wu, T. (2003). Network neutrality, broadband discrimination. *Journal of Telecommunications and High Technology Law, 2,* 141–179.

CHAPTER 24

Community Radio and Video, Social Activism, and Neoliberal Public Policy in Chile During the Transition to Democracy

Rosalind Bresnahan

As Chile entered the 21st century, it was still undergoing the prolonged process of transition to democracy[1] that began in January 1990 when Chileans celebrated the end of the 17-year Pinochet dictatorship and the inauguration of the first democratically elected president since Salvador Allende nearly 20 years earlier. In examining the initial upsurge and subsequent decline of community radio and video during the crucial first decade of the transition, this chapter highlights two interrelated influences: government policy and the vitality of social movements. New community media emerged very strongly at the start of Chile's transition as an outgrowth of the mass movement for democracy and the development of participatory grassroots media during the struggle against the dictatorship. The producers of these new media were inspired by a sense of social purpose and imbued with optimism that a democracy won through mass mobilization would provide fertile terrain for continued activism. However, public policies were hostile to alternative media, including community radio and video, and undercut the grassroots mobilization that provided the impetus for socially engaged community media. I argue that these structural factors—adverse public policies and waning social activism—affected the community radio and video movements as a whole and are more significant for explaining their development during this period than the individual characteristics of specific production groups. Although community radio and, to a lesser extent, community video did become established, their early flourishing was sharply curtailed and their later development was very different from what it would have been in a policy environment that encouraged both grassroots media and social activism.

This chapter draws on the author's interviews with Chilean community media activists in 1998 and 2000 and cites documents from their files.[2]

Community Media and the Struggle for Democracy

The bloody military coup of September 11, 1973, aborted Chile's unique experiment in democratic socialism, extinguished its vibrant multiparty democracy, and unleashed unprecedented repression, including torture and "disappearance" of its opponents. Despite this state violence, a broad network of grassroots organizations gradually emerged in response to hunger, homelessness, human rights violations, and other hardships of military rule, uniting in a mass movement to restore democracy. To a much greater extent than before the coup, grassroots political and social action arose from the base rather than being initiated from above by hierarchical political parties or other national organizations. Thus, the dictatorship's repression paradoxically promoted grassroots autonomy and democratization of social activism.

The struggle against the dictatorship also transformed relations of media production, distribution, and reception for prodemocracy activists as alternative media became a vital terrain of opposition activity (see Bresnahan, 2003b, 2009). Community-based activists took on the empowering task of analyzing their reality and voicing their demands in what Chileans call micromedia such as leaflets and newsletters. They also formed active relationships with newly created prodemocracy mass media, for example, by collectively reading and discussing articles from opposition magazines and circulating photocopied clandestine editions when the magazines were closed during states of siege (J. P. Cárdenas, personal communication,

August 30, 2000; S. Marras, personal communication, September 9, 1998).

Radio and video were also important components of the media infrastructure of the democratic movement. As is detailed later, the participatory relations they established with their listeners and viewers created the foundation for the upsurge of community radio and video that followed the defeat of the dictatorship.

The Concertación, Neoliberal Democratization, and Social Demobilization

The mass democratic movement improbably defeated Pinochet in a 1988 plebiscite offering only a Yes or No vote on his continued rule. This forced a multicandidate presidential election and brought to power the coalition of center-left parties known as the *Concertación* that has governed Chile since 1990.

The Concertación did not rely only on mass support to cement its victory. To obtain military acceptance of the election outcome, the Concertación pledged not to prosecute most human rights abuses and to maintain Pinochet's neoliberal economic model, which included deregulation of business, privatization of state enterprises, drastic reduction of state budgets, free trade, and the opening of the economy to transnational capital.[3] Among its consequences were severe curtailment of social services, low wages to attract investment and stimulate low-priced exports, and disregard of the environmental degradation resulting from exploitation of natural resources. Thus, the Concertación took power with a limited agenda that conflicted with the expectations of its most mobilized supporters, who sought accountability for human rights violations, rapid reduction of the staggering inequality generated during the dictatorship, and action on the pent-up demands of women, indigenous groups, environmentalists, and other grassroots activists (see Bresnahan, 2003a).

Since the terms of the pacted transition allowed only limited reforms, Concertación leaders viewed grassroots organizing for more far-reaching changes as dangerous and counterproductive. Demobilization of social movements became a key component of the Concertación's strategy to maintain control over the direction and pace of the transition. For much of the prodemocracy movement, grassroots activism subsided, to be replaced by political alienation.[4] The credibility of parties and other political institutions eroded and, despite mandatory voting requirements, even that limited political activity declined, especially among young people. The arrest of Pinochet in London in 1998 and the legal proceedings in Chile 2 years later that stripped him of immunity from prosecution[5] reinvigorated the human rights movement, but broad-based activism challenging the social consequences of neoliberalism never recaptured the momentum of 1990.

Media Democratization Versus Neoliberal Media Policies

Communication theorists of transitions to democracy argue that media democratization is an essential component of full political democratization (O'Neil, 1998) and that during transitions "the design of communication processes is as crucial as the design of political, economic, and social institutions" (Bennett, 1998, p. 206). Public policy should promote a vigorous public sphere that empowers civil society by providing the social space where all sectors can exchange information and opinions and express their needs and demands (Sparks & Reading, 1995; Vreg, 1995). As the primary arena of the public sphere, the media constitute a critical democratic site that must be protected from concentrated economic power as much as from state control (Waisbord, 1998). Thus, an incoming democratic government should foster independent media whose primary purpose is what Jakubowicz (1995) terms *civic* rather than commercial. He distinguishes between freedom of speech and the right to communicate and argues that only public policy can guarantee the latter "by assisting, supporting, or subsidizing" the civic sector that allows social groups with limited economic resources "to speak with their own voice" (p. 132). Policies to sustain media diversity should also encourage decentralization and participatory *citizens'* media such as community radio and video (Rodriguez, 2001). The link between participatory media and democracy is also emphasized by Chilean community media organizations cited later in this chapter.

However, as I have argued elsewhere (Bresnahan, 2003b), for Chilean media, the transition has been a "democratic promise unfulfilled," as Concertación neoliberal media policies equated media democratization with unrestricted market forces, thereby making advertiser support the determinant of media viability. Chile's major advertisers strongly identify with the right and have traditionally wielded their economic power on behalf of their political interests, making the advertising marketplace highly unfavorable for socially critical media. Instead of valuing the existing alternative media as democratic resources to be sustained and expanded, Concertación media policymakers criticized them as too "ideological" for the new political environment[6] and approvingly noted their "slim chance for survival" (Tironi, cited in Otano, 1991, p. 19).

Concertación media policy reflected not only adherence to neoliberal doctrine but also the government's political interest in muting potential critics on the left. Thus, in addition to rejecting meaningful limits on media concentration and foreign ownership, it overwhelmingly invested both state and party advertising resources in the commercial media, which were dominated by economic groups that had supported Pinochet and, in one case, the government influenced a foreign donor to withdraw proposed grants to alternative mass media (J. P. Cárdenas, personal communication,

August 30, 2000).[7] Not only did the independent media disappear as predicted, but newly authorized commercial television fell under the control of existing right-wing national media conglomerates and economic groups, often in partnership with politically conservative Latin American media giants, and commercial radio became increasingly homogenized as transnational investors constructed national networks repeating a few standard formats (see Bresnahan, 2003b, 2007). The adverse Concertación policies toward community media that are discussed in this chapter should be understood in this broader context.

Community Radio

Radio During the Dictatorship

Elsewhere (Bresnahan, 2002), I have described the crucial role of mass audience, church-related radio in building the prodemocracy movement. Although community radio had not yet emerged as a significant medium during the dictatorship, of particular relevance for its subsequent development was the Methodist Church's Santiago station Radio Umbral (Threshold), which, in the final years of military rule, broke new ground in creating participatory relations with its audience. Among other innovations, it created community correspondents who reported live from their neighborhoods and organized concerts as public acts of cultural resistance. Activists who relied on prodemocracy radio became aware of the mobilizing and empowering potential of the medium and saw in Umbral a preview of what might be accomplished by community-based "*Umbralitos*" or mini-Umbrals.

ANARAP: The National Association of Grassroots Radio Stations

Following the victory of the Concertación, communication activists moved quickly to tap the potential of radio for grassroots democratic expression and community organizing. In January 1990, they formed the National Organization of Grassroots[8] Radio Stations (Agrupación Nacional de Radio Popular or ANARAP) to promote community radio by training local groups, especially in the shantytowns, and assisting them in obtaining and setting up equipment (Bertín, 1991, p. 3).

ANARAP (1992) envisioned a network of stations operated by "unions, community groups, ethnic groups, youth, women, cultural centers, nongovernmental organizations (NGOs) and all entities who seek to democratize radio for the benefit of average people" that would allow them "to express themselves, raise their voices and become protagonists of their own history in actions and in words, thereby reaching higher levels of human dignity" (p. 68). It stressed the need for autonomy from "the state, political parties, international organisms, churches or other entities" that might limit the stations' independent voice (p. 69).

ANARAP's founders saw this "absolutely horizontal" and "participatory" community radio as contributing to a participatory democracy based on "the action of every one of the inhabitants of a country, region, province, borough, neighborhood, to overcome our difficulties" (Villalobos, 1992, pp. 15–16). For the grassroots democratic movement, participatory communication was "not a mere instrument to make known its programs and demands. **Communication is precisely the axis of organization** so that it can achieve its objectives and fulfill its purpose" (Bertín, 1991, p. 11).

ANARAP advocated legislation legalizing community radio since there was no provision for it in Chilean law. However, the enthusiasm of grassroots radio groups outpaced the legalization process, creating stations that existed in a legal limbo, neither authorized nor prohibited. The first stations emerged in neighborhoods that had been centers of grassroots resistance to the dictatorship. On April 1, 1990, five activists in Santiago's militant Villa Francia shantytown launched the first ANARAP station, transmitting within a 10-block radius for 4 hours a day on weekends. By the time the network held its first National Congress in May 1991, its membership included 38 stations on the air and others in development (Bertín, 1991, p. 9; Yañez & Aguilera, 2000, p. 44).

Controversy, Legislation, and Decline

However, just 2 months later, this promising start for social activist community radio was interrupted by a backlash that led to the stations' closure. Right-wing parties and commercial broadcasters denounced the stations as illegal and dangerous and demanded that they be shut down. ANARAP countered by advocating that two national FM frequencies be designated exclusively for community radio use (ANARAP, 1992, p. 69), that applicants for licenses be sponsored by three community social organizations (Bertín, 1991, p. 9), and that new state-supported funding sources be created (Gallegos, 1992, p. 42; Richards, 1992, p. 34). Despite initial receptivity, the government retreated in the face of political pressure. It persuaded the ANARAP stations to voluntarily suspend broadcasting in return for the promise of prompt legalization, and they went off the air on July 21, 1991.

With the community stations silenced, the government then capitulated to demands from the right and divided the promised legislation into two separate components. Penalties for unauthorized broadcasts were quickly approved in November 1991, with violators subject to fines, jail terms, and confiscation of equipment (Secretaría de Comunicación y Cultura, 1994, p. 320). However, it took an additional 2 years to pass authorizing legislation, which differed significantly from ANARAP's proposal. Station power was limited to 1 watt (W), instead of 20 W. Grassroots community groups received no preference; licenses were awarded solely on technical merit, and the activist groups often lacked the financial ability to meet the requirement for

an engineering report or to match the proposals of wealthier competitors such as local governments or churches. The law also prohibited advertising, even for neighborhood businesses, which limited licensed stations' ability to fund operations (Yañez & Aguilera, 2000, p. 48). Furthermore, unlike 25-year terms for commercial licenses, low-power licenses were awarded for only 3 years, forcing even successful grassroots applicants to undergo the expensive application process repeatedly. Slow implementation of the new law also inhibited community radio development. The first seven successful applicants awarded licenses in 1994 were forced to wait for almost 2 years to begin broadcasting because of government delay in signing the official decrees that authorized them to go on the air (Villalobos, 1996, p. 13). After 2.5 years, the 24 licenses awarded fell short of the 38 stations that had emerged in less than half that time during ANARAP's explosive first wave (Yañez & Aguilera, 2000, p. 53).

In addition to the adverse effects of delay and restrictive legislation, the changed political climate sapped the grassroots energy that had animated the initial movement for community radio. ANARAP had been formed at the height of the political optimism generated by the defeat of the dictatorship. By the time community radio was finally legalized, the impetus for it had dissipated as grassroots activism faded, and most of the original ANARAP radio groups never reconstituted themselves.[9] By 2000, approximately 100 low-power stations were on the air, approximately half of them operated by local governments, churches, and even individuals with no community ties (Yañez & Aguilera, 2000, p. 13). In 2001, ANARAP changed its name to the National Network of Community Radio Stations (Red Nacional de Radios Comunitarios) or RENARCOM. Dropping the word "popular," with its activist and class connotations, from the organization's name was an accurate reflection of the less political character of the majority of the new stations.

A study of community radio in 2000 identified lack of funding as a major problem for grassroots stations, limiting their ability to maintain equipment, purchase computers, and obtain Internet access (Yañez & Aguilera, 2000, p. 39) and called on the government to offer competitive grants and lift the ban on advertising (pp. 53–54). It also advocated legislative reform to increase station power and license terms.[10]

Community Video

Video During the Dictatorship

During the dictatorship, television was the most tightly controlled medium, with military officers heading the management of the four national channels.[11] The introduction of portable video technology offered the opposition a new option for contesting the regime's control of social imagery and opened up new participatory media-movement relationships. When the well-known theater group ICTUS first began to produce video dramas and documentaries in 1980 for screening in shantytowns, they had to go door to door to persuade fearful residents to attend (B. Quintenal de Salas, personal communication, July 24, 1998). After mass protests began in 1983, additional production groups formed[12] and video screenings became commonplace as churches and other community-based organizations accumulated video collections. The producers designed screenings as participatory events with trained discussion leaders to encourage viewers' active reflection on the relevance of the content to their own lives and to the ongoing struggle for democracy. Viewer feedback also influenced future production. Distribution was also participatory, as video makers relied on grassroots groups to copy and circulate their tapes. It was common for 1,000 copies of a tape to circulate through grassroots networks and through repeated showings to reach a cumulative audience of 100,000 or more.

New Community Video Initiatives: Growth, Obstacles, and Decline

As the transition began, parallel to the upsurge of community radio, independent video production groups emerged at the local level, especially in the shantytowns that had been most combative during the dictatorship and that had the greatest unmet social needs. Young people who had grown up viewing the grassroots videos circulated by the democratic movement took advantage of the changed political circumstances to become producers of alternative imagery. A member of the first group to produce community video[13] stressed its importance in countering mass media images that portrayed shantytowns as nothing more than "dangerous places and cradles of drug addicts or thieves" and in challenging Concertación priorities that treated them as "Chile's backyard" (A. Quezada, personal communication, August 30, 1998).

Many of these young video makers had participated in workshops offered by the main prodemocracy video production groups, university professors, and NGOs. Others gained access to equipment and began experimenting on their own. They produced community news, documentaries, original dramas, and music videos dealing with social issues, including human rights, the environment, and the growing problem of drug addiction among alienated youth.

An outdoor screening known as a *pantallazo* (big screen) became the primary outlet for these programs, with the image projected onto a screen, sheet, or wall in a public area to attract a neighborhood audience. The video groups also sought other community outlets such as screenings in schools and cultural centers.

One of the satisfactions for community video makers was their ability to stimulate discussion of the social basis for Chile's extreme social inequalities and to help audiences see through "the myth of neoliberalism" to "conclude that it was the economic system" (A. Leal, personal communication, August 17, 1998).

Despite positive community response and even artistic recognition, video groups were frequently short lived. Interviews with members of seven video groups revealed two primary frustrations— lack of resources and limited opportunities to show completed work. Members used their own funds for production costs and were dependent on borrowed equipment for the screenings. A community news program that took 3 months to make might be shown only on 1 weekend because of the need to borrow a projector for the *pantallazo*. One group disbanded after spending almost 6 months making an award-winning video because "we can go 4 or 5 months without being able to show it and all the effort seems almost wasted. There were times when the circuit of distribution was almost imaginary" (A. Leal, personal communication, August 17, 1998).

Grassroots producers also cited the disadvantages they faced in competing for government arts funding, since there was no separate category for community video makers, who were rarely successful in competing against professionals for the limited funds available.

Grassroots Video Network

The growth of community video led to the formation of the National Network of Grassroots Video and Community TV (Red Nacional de Video Popular y TV Comunitaria) in October 1994, uniting 27 grassroots groups and 10 individual independent producers (*Red Nacional*, 1995a, p. 8). Echoing ANARAP's emphasis on grassroots empowerment, the Network's (Red Nacional, 1995b) Declaration of Principles highlighted

> the need of broad social sectors, especially at the grass roots, to express themselves on their own, to seek and develop their own forms of communication, autonomous, independent, without intermediaries [in order to] project images for social, political, economic and cultural change [and to] share the struggles

and desires for justice, a clean environment, and the overcoming of discrimination and oppression. (p. 1)

The Network attempted to resolve problems such as lack of equipment and financing for production and insufficient opportunities to show completed work. Initial steps to address these problems included organizing local screenings, creating a national Grassroots Video Festival, and setting up a video library. Network founder, community media activist, and professional video maker Javier Bertín made cameras and editing equipment available to community producers, and his production office served as a central node for grassroots video activity. He noted that a decline in requests reflected the waning of community video production. When the network was founded in 1994, requests exceeded equipment availability; by 2000 the opposite was true (J. Bertín, personal communication, September 6, 2000). Workshops at the Network's national assembly in January 2000 concluded that the decline reflected the negative impact of 10 years of Concertación government on community organizing and social movements. According to Bertín, a further consequence was the lack of a new generation of leadership to follow the example of dictatorship-era video activists in inspiring and mentoring young people to become community video producers.

Cable Television and Community Video

Cable television was introduced in 1994 and might have partially met the need for increased diffusion of community video. However, Concertación policymakers chose not to impose public access requirements on Chilean cable companies, despite recognizing that this was the norm in the United States and Europe (Secretaría de Comunicación y Cultura, 1997, pp. 15–18). This decision thwarted two promising initiatives for community video distribution via cable.

Ñuñoa Community Cable Television. In 1994, the Humanist Party[14] mayor of Ñuñoa, a middle-class Santiago borough with relatively high levels of cable subscribers, initiated a municipal cable television channel as a vehicle for public access rather than as an outlet for the municipal government itself. The project provided equipment and training to community residents, including teenagers, housewives, and senior citizens in a series of 2-week training sessions (C. Messina, personal communication, August 17, 1998).

As more community residents became involved, programming increased from 1 to 9 hours per day. However, the cable company, Metropolis Intercom, unilaterally removed the channel after it aired a program on human rights abuses during the dictatorship. Even though the program dealt with the cases of Ñuñoa residents, Metropolis Intercom claimed that the program violated the agreement to show "community" programming. The channel remained off the air for more than 2 months, and this experience demonstrated the vulnerability created by the lack of a community access requirement.

The Ñuñoa case also demonstrated the potential and limitations of local government support for community video. No commercials were allowed, which meant that the channel was subject to the municipal council's financial control. For several months, the few paid staff had to work without pay when the council failed to provide funding. Ultimately, the experiment ended when the Humanist mayor was defeated in the subsequent election. The new, politically conservative mayor closed down the cable project and locked up the equipment for more than 2 years before finally turning it over to the Ministry of Education.

Canelo TV. In 1996, shortly before the demise of the Ñuñoa channel, a more ambitious cable television project, *Canelo* (Cinnamon Tree) TV, reached the stage of a technical trial before its contract was unilaterally terminated by Chile's other primary cable company, VTR Cablexpress. Initiated by the environmental NGO Canelo de

Nos, the proposed channel was intended as an "ecological, citizen and cultural" channel offering a range of socially conscious programming, including the work of Chilean independent and grassroots producers along with programs from the University of Chile, the Chilean national commissions on the environment and AIDS, UNICEF, Greenpeace, and Amnesty International. However, the test run was abruptly cancelled by the cable company. Although the company justified its action as reflecting its preference for imported programming, channel director Hernán Dinamarca (personal communication, August 6, 1998) contends that the reason was political discomfort with program content.

The cancellation led to demands by an ad hoc group of independent and community video producers for new legislation requiring cable operators to provide "local and citizen TV channels" to ensure "pluralism and freedom of expression" ("*Legislación en TV Cable*," n.d.). They proposed that the channels be operated by nonprofit corporations and financed by a mix of government arts funding, support from international agencies, and advertising (p. 6). Despite support from journalists and university communication departments, the government rejected the proposal, and public access remains a privilege controlled by the cable companies rather than being a right guaranteed by law.

Conclusion

The Chilean case clearly demonstrates the interacting impacts on community media of public policy and the level of grassroots social activism. The initial impetus for community radio and video came from social activists who sought a participatory democracy that went beyond the restoration of formal democratic institutions and sought to turn the existing social mobilization to broader ends that recaptured the dynamic of profound social transformation that had been interrupted by the 1973 coup. They considered community media and social activism to be interdependent and mutually reinforcing elements of the new democracy to be constructed. However, the founders' aspirations for community radio and video foundered in the hostile environment of Chile's neoliberal transition. Community media suffered serious setbacks during the first decade of democratization, as public policy choices worked against media diversity and decentralization. The illegalization of community radio for two crucial years just as it reached critical mass prevented its consolidation as an activist medium, and the legislation that was eventually adopted fundamentally transformed its character. Regulatory policy deprived community video of guaranteed public access outlets that would have removed one of the primary impediments to its development. Both radio and video suffered from the Concertación's failure to support grassroots media with public funds.

The indirect effects of Concertación neoliberal policy were at least as devastating. By privileging its relations with the military, the United States, and transnational capital, the Concertación defined the parameters of social and economic reform so narrowly that it felt compelled to discourage independent grassroots activism for a broader agenda. Those most disadvantaged by government social policies were the same groups that the founders of community radio and video sought to involve in the new social struggles of the transition. But after the long years of sacrifices in time, energy, and blood to bring the Concertación to power, dissatisfaction with its performance generated alienation and withdrawal from politics more than renewed commitment to activism. The resulting collapse of social movements cut off the social oxygen that had animated the nascent community media movement.

Nonetheless, as community radio and video continue to evolve in this challenging environment, a dedicated core of activists persist in their media work to advance social justice, empower the communities they serve, and bring grassroots perspectives, concerns, and demands to a public sphere that has been impoverished by the dominant consumerist and entertainment model favored by the Concertación.

Notes

1. The transition refers to the process of political and constitutional reform that gradually eliminated authoritarian institutions established by the dictatorship. As of 2008, an unusual two-member district congressional election system that has consistently given the political right disproportionate legislative representation remained unreformed.

2. Translations are by the author.

3. This commitment also reassured the United States, transnational capital, international financial institutions, and major domestic economic interests.

4. Disillusionment alone does not explain demobilization. Significant sectors of the democratic movement were satisfied with the return of electoral democracy and supported the Concertación program.

5. Pinochet was not prosecuted after being declared mentally impaired.

6. Eugenio Tironi, one of the chief architects of Concertación media policy, elaborates this argument in Tironi and Sunkel (1993).

7. This allegation is denied by the government.

8. In Spanish, "popular" has a strong class connotation, referring to average working or poor people, and "popular" organizations and movements imply class-based activism. To avoid confusion with English usage, I will use "grassroots" as the closest English equivalent.

9. Pioneering station Radio Villa Francia was an exception. After a short shutdown, it returned to the air illegally, and after several unsuccessful applications, it eventually received a license.

10. In October 2007, the government finally responded to persistent pressure from the community radio association, now known as the *Asociación Nacional de Radios Ciudadanos y Comunitarios de Chile* (National Association of Citizen and Community Radio Stations of Chile, or ANARCICH), and sent Congress a proposal to increase station power to a maximum of 25 W, to

increase license terms to 15 years, and to allow limited local advertising. As of January 2009, the proposed legislation had been referred to a special joint committee of Congress for review.

11. Three of the channels remained nominally university based. The fourth was the national public station. There was no privately owned television in Chile until 1990.

12. The *Proceso* and *Teleanálisis* groups had the most consistent production and political impact.

13. The *Canal 3* (Channel 3) group in *La Victoria* shantytown.

14. The Humanist Party was a small progressive party to the left of the Concertación.

References

ANARAP. (1992). Proyecto radiofónico presentado por la ANARAP a la Subsecretaria de Telecomunicaciones [Radio Project presented by ANARAP to the Subsecretariat of Telecommunications]. In *Proceedings of the seminar on La Radio Popular en Chile* [Grassroots radio in Chile] (Appendix 1, pp. 66–69). Santiago, Chile: Ediciones Sonoradio Producciones.

Bennett, L. (1998). The media and democratic development: The social basis of political communication. In P. H. O'Neil (Ed.), *Communicating democracy: The media and political transitions* (pp. 195–207). Boulder, CO: Lynne Rienner.

Bertín, J. (1991). *Radio popular en Chile: Desarrollo y perspectivas* [Grassroots radio in Chile: Development and prospects]. Santiago, Chile: Producciones Radiofónicas Populares/ECO/PROMESA.

Bresnahan, R. (2002). Radio and the democratic movement in Chile 1973–1990: Independent and grassroots voices during the Pinochet dictatorship. *Journal of Radio Studies, 9*(1), 161–181.

Bresnahan, R. (2003a). Chile since 1990: The contradictions of neoliberal democratization. *Latin American Perspectives, 30*(5), 3–15.

Bresnahan, R. (2003b). The media and the neoliberal transition in Chile: Democratic promise unfulfilled. *Latin American Perspectives, 30*(6), 39–68.

Bresnahan, R. (2007). Community radio and social activism in Chile 1990–2007: Challenges for grassroots voices during the transition to democracy. *Journal of Radio Studies, 14*(2), 212–233.

Bresnahan, R. (2009). Reclaiming the public sphere in Chile under dictatorship and neoliberal democracy. In D. Kidd, C. Rodriguez, & L. Stein (Eds.), *Mapping our media: Global initiatives toward a democratic public sphere* (pp. 271–292). Cresskill, NJ: Hampton Press.

Gallegos, L. (1992). Situación actual de la radio popular en Chile y sus perspectivas [The current situation of grassroots radio in Chile and its prospects]. In *Proceedings of the seminar on La Radio Popular en Chile* [Grassroots radio in Chile] (pp. 40–45). Santiago, Chile: Ediciones Sonoradio Producciones.

Jakubowicz, K. (1995). Poland. In D. Paletz, K. Jakubowicz, & P. Novosel (Eds.), *Glasnost and after: Media and change in Central and Eastern Europe* (pp. 129–148). Cresskill, NJ: Hampton Press.

Legislación en TV cable: A crear canales de TV locales y ciudadanos [Cable TV legislation: For the creation of local and citizen TV channels]. (n.d.). Unpublished statement, Santiago, Chile.

O'Neil, P. H. (1998). Democratization and mass communication: What is the link? In P. H. O'Neil (Ed.), *Communicating democracy: The media and political transitions* (pp. 1–20). Boulder, CO: Lynne Rienner.

Otano, R. (1991). Jacque al pluralismo: la venta de *La Epoca* [Pluralism in check: The sale of *La Epoca*]. *APSI, 401,* 15–19.

Red Nacional de Video Popular y TV Comunitaria. (1995a). *Pantallazo* [Big screen]. Talagante, Chile: Author.

Red Nacional de Video Popular y TV Comunitaria. (1995b). *Declaración de fines* [Statement of principles]. Talagante, Chile: Author.

Richards, J. A. (1992). Radios comunitarias y ejercicio de la libertad de expresión [Community radio stations and freedom of expression]. In *Proceedings of the seminar on La Radio Popular en Chile* [Grassroots radio in Chile] (pp. 33–35). Santiago, Chile: Ediciones Sonoradio Producciones.

Rodriguez, C. (2001). *Fissures in the mediascape: An international study of citizens' media.* Cresskill, NJ: Hampton Press.

Secretaría de Comunicación y Cultura. (1994). *Tendencias y desarrollo de los medios de comunicación en Chile* [Tendencies and development of the communications media in Chile]. Santiago, Chile: Ministerio Secretaría General de Gobierno.

Secretaría de Comunicación y Cultura. (1997). Reseña de medios [Media review] No. 33: *TV local a través del cable* [Local TV via cable]. Santiago, Chile: Ministerio Secretaría General de Gobierno.

Sparks, C., & Reading, A. (1995). Re-regulating television after communism: A comparative analysis of Poland, Hungary, and the Czech Republic. In F. Corcoran & P. Preston (Eds.), *Democracy and communication in the new Europe: Change and continuity in East and West* (pp. 31–50). Cresskill, NJ: Hampton Press.

Tironi, E., & Sunkel, G. (1993). Modernización de las comunicaciones y democratización de la política [Modernization of communications and democratization of politics]. *Estudios Públicos, 52,* 215–246.

Villalobos, M. (1992). Rol de los medios de comunicación comunitarios en el momento actual [The role of community media at the present time]. In *Proceedings of the seminar on La Radio Popular en Chile* [Grassroots radio in Chile] (pp. 13–17). Santiago, Chile: Ediciones Sonoradio Producciones.

Villalobos, M. (1996). Radio comunitaria: Recorrido y perspectivas [Community radio: History and prospects]. In *Proceedings of the seminar on Radios comunitarias en Chile: Un aporte al desarrollo* [Community radio stations in Chile: A contribution to development] (pp. 13–17). Santiago, Chile: ECO.

Vreg, F. (1995). Political, national, and media crises. In D. Paletz, K. Jakubowicz, & P. Novosel (Eds.), *Glasnost and after: Media and change in Central and Eastern Europe* (pp. 49–61). Cresskill, NJ: Hampton Press.

Waisbord, S. (1998). The unfinished project of media democratization in Argentina. In P. H. O'Neil (Ed.), *Communicating democracy: The media and political transitions* (pp. 41–62). Boulder, CO: Lynne Rienner.

Yañez, L., & Aguilera, O. (2000). *Radios comunitarias y de mínima cobertura: Diagnóstico estado de situación en las radios comunitarias chilenas* [Community and low power radio stations in Chile: Diagnostic of the status of Chilean community radio stations]. Santiago, Chile: ECO.

CHAPTER 25

Past, Present, and Future of the Hungarian Community Radio Movement

Gergely Gosztonyi

The Community Radio Movement in Hungary

Immediately after the fall of the Iron Curtain, as democratic reforms swept across Eastern Europe, the Hungarian media landscape remained remarkably unchanged. Despite popular support for media democratization, it took several years—and a newly elected Socialist government—before legislators addressed the problem of the media in Hungary. On December 21, 1995, Act I of 1996 on Radio and Television Broadcasting (the "Media Act"; Parliament of the Republic of Hungary, 1996) was enacted. The Act put an end to a moratorium on frequency allocations that had stifled efforts to "open up" the airwaves and that signaled the beginning of a tripartite media system (public service, commercial, and noncommercial broadcasting) in Hungary. While debates over media policy persisted, one thing was certain: The Media Act codified community broadcasting as part of the Hungarian media system and guaranteed parity between community radio stations and their commercial and public service counterparts.

The Media Act refers to these community-oriented stations as "non-profit broadcasters," but this label is inadequate inasmuch as it describes these broadcasters rather narrowly, from a financial perspective, thereby failing to capture the organizational philosophy and operational practices of community broadcasting in Hungary. Nevertheless, the Media Act's formal definition of nonprofit broadcasters reflects the idea that community broadcasting is best understood as a social practice. Thus, a nonprofit broadcaster

> agrees to serve national, ethnic or other minority goals, cultural aims or a disadvantaged group, or intends to serve as the public life forum of a community, provided it uses the financial profit generated by the broadcasting, as recorded separately, solely for the maintenance and development of the broadcasting. (Act I of 1996, Article 2)

The Media Act regulates nonprofit broadcasters as follows: They can only broadcast 3 minutes of advertisements in any given rolling hour (the rule allows 12 minutes for commercial and 6 minutes for public service broadcasters, respectively); they are not obliged to pay any broadcasting fees; and 0.5% to 1% of the annual revenues of the Broadcasting Fund shall be used for the repayable or nonrepayable subsidization of the non-profit-oriented broadcasters (Act I of 1996, Article 78).

The Broadcasting Fund is a segregated state monetary fund, which is supposed to support public service broadcasters and non-profit-oriented broadcasters so that they might preserve and further develop culture, improve the multicolored nature of broadcasts, and fulfill other duties defined in the Media Act. The manager of the Fund is the National Radio and Television Board. The Fund is a legal entity, and its account is managed by the Hungarian State Treasury. Every year, that means approximately US$850,000 to US$1,700,000 for the sector in Hungary. This calculation was made by the author based on the budget of the Broadcasting Fund in 2007. It will be approximately the same amount in 2008. To obtain money from the Fund every year, four main types of application are invited from community radio stations:

- Application for yearly running costs

- Application for technical development (studio equipment)

- Application for starting or developing the broadcast diffusion

- Application for creating news, sport, or magazine programs

There is a fifth type of application, referred to as a "unique application," but as it is not offered on a regular basis, it should not be considered as part of the supporting system. Radio stations may submit a "unique application" at any time; they may apply once a year in response to any of the other calls for applications. The amount of self-financing required for different applications may range from 15% to 50%, which in general may be high enough to intimidate community broadcasters, so despite the relatively high budget, only part of this allocation is used to support the sector. Figures indicate that approximately 15% to 25% of the

yearly budget has not been spent in the past few years. Both parties, the Broadcasting Fund and the community radio stations themselves, share the blame for this situation. For its part, the Broadcasting Fund's bureaucracy presents a formidable obstacle to community broadcasters. And the rather steep self-financing requirements prevent some stations from even bothering to submit an application to the fund. In some instances, station personnel were unable or unwilling to complete funding applications. In other instances, station personnel were simply unaware of these funding opportunities. Others felt that the chances of succeeding in a competitive application process were too slim to bother.

This period (1995–2002) was the infancy of Hungarian community radio. While the stations constitute a legally sanctioned section of Hungarian broadcasting, their unique and sometimes unconventional approach to broadcasting has made them the stepchildren of the Hungarian media system.

Community broadcasting has a long and storied history in Western Europe. But in Eastern Europe, community radio is still something of a novelty. Not surprisingly, given the region's experience with totalitarianism, governments view community radio's commitment to freedom of speech with great suspicion. No doubt, this helps explain the tension between community radio and the Hungarian media authority, Országos Rádió és Televízió Testület (ORTT), over the limited number of frequencies available for nonprofit, community-oriented broadcasting.

For example, three of the best known community radio stations—Civil Rádió, Fiksz Rádió, and Tilos Rádió—all based in Budapest, shared a single frequency (FM98).[1] Notwithstanding the growing popularity of this approach to broadcasting, there were only about 10 to 15 community radio stations throughout the entire country in 1997. That was the time when the media authority established specific criteria for nonprofit stations (213/1997, ORTT resolution amended with 652/2001 and 1069/2001, ORTT resolutions). Since its ruling went into effect, stations have been required to apply to ORTT to obtain nonprofit status. In addition, at least 50% of their daily broadcasting time must serve the chosen aim (according to Article 2, as quoted above). Furthermore, a station's nonprofit status can be revoked if the broadcaster breaches this requirement or other regulations of the Media Act.

Despite the fact that relatively few community radio stations broadcast in Hungary, they demonstrated the viability of alternative approaches to both commercial and public service broadcasting. Community radio offered listeners a distinct approach to broadcasting—an approach that provided opportunities for volunteers, including minorities and other marginalized groups, to produce local news and cultural programs, to exercise genuine editorial control over broadcast form and content, and to otherwise promote the right to communicate.

In these early days, community radio stations played a significant role in the development of Hungarian civil society. And while these nonprofit stations (popularly known as "free radio") were relatively small in number, they were fearless advocates of communicative democracy. In its founding article, the Hungarian Federation of Free Radios defines this approach to community broadcasting as follows:

> Free radios are unlike public and commercial radios in that: they function independently from political and government bodies, local governments and profit interested economic groups; they serve the interests of clearly defined (local, ethnic, religious, cultural or lifestyle directed) communities (or minorities); always striving for their greater participation in making the radio programmes; decisions are taken democratically; no more than three minutes of advertisement is broadcast every hour; the earnings of a free radio are not distributed, but reinvested in the operation of the radio and its upkeep (the non-profit character); it is operated in greater part by volunteers; and no more than 50% of its earnings stem from the advertising business related to radio broadcasting. (Hungarian Federation of Free Radios, 1992)

Years passed, free radio took to the airwaves, but the situation got worse after certain decisions of the media authority: Many stations, such as Szóköz Rádió in Szombathely and Szóla Rádió in Debrecen, lost their frequencies during the renewal process. At the same time, the media authority began to look favorably on commercial licensees and others who were uninterested in nonprofit or community-oriented radio. These decisions produced fierce debates over the future direction of Hungarian media policy. For community radio advocates and their allies, the media authority's rulings and licensing decisions were becoming politicized.[2] At this time, community broadcasting was losing support among policy makers at the media authority. For community radio supporters, it seemed that it was just a matter of time before the last community radio station would close down. The future of the community radio sector was not looking very bright. The map below illustrates the number and location of community radio stations across Hungary at this time (Figure 25.1).

A New Possibility: Small Community Radio Stations

In 2002, the community broadcasting sector experienced a period of renewal and revival. Following a long period of negotiating and lobbying between the media authority and community radio supporters, an entirely new way of nonprofit broadcasting was born: small community radio stations (1218/2002, ORTT resolution). Small community radio stations are very similar to "microbroadcasters": They operate with minimal regulatory oversight and are relatively cheap and easy to operate. As a result, almost anyone could set up his or her own radio station with little technical knowledge or financial support.

Not surprisingly, commercial stations objected to the media authority's decision on the grounds that they would lose market share, advertising

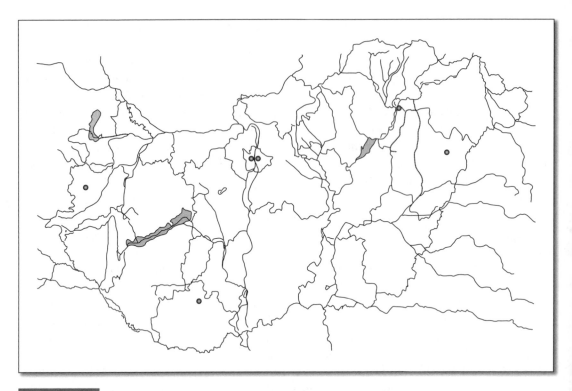

Figure 25.1   Community Radio in Hungary, 2002

revenue, and profits to these small community radio stations. Commercial broadcasters failed to recognize the fact that community broadcasting is not concerned with profit. Nevertheless, commercial broadcasters feared competition from, and the growing popularity of, small community radio stations. The following illustration, based on data from January 2007, illustrates the dramatic growth of small community radio across Hungary (Figure 25.2).

In the intervening years, it has become clear that the fears of commercial broadcasters were unfounded. Small community radio stations have not made significant inroads into the advertising market. In fact, most of these stations are reluctant to run advertisements. We can better understand small community radio's uneasy relationship with advertising by taking a closer look at their distinct approach to broadcasting practice.

Every year, there are two deadlines (March 1 and September 1) for applying for a small community frequency. Typically, there are approximately 30 to 40 applicants each year. The application is much simpler than for a "normal" frequency because great care was taken to make the application process as simple as possible (in general, 60% to 70% of the applicants are awarded frequencies). These frequencies were designed for places where a "usual" local radio station would not be able to sustain itself. They were specifically designed for small local communities such as schools, prisons, hospitals, small villages, festivals, housing estates, universities, local libraries, and neighborhoods. Furthermore, the media authority established obligations for small community radio stations designed to meet the specific and particular needs of these communities.

For instance, the minimum airtime is 14 hours per week, so communities that are small indeed could run their radio stations, too; they receive

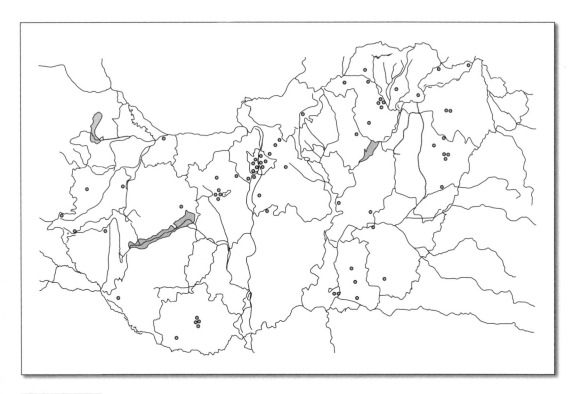

Figure 25.2 Community Radio in Hungary, 2007

the frequency for 3 years with the possibility to renew it for another 5 years (other types of radio broadcasters got the frequency for 7 plus 5 years), and there are frequencies reserved only for non-profit broadcasters. Their legal obligations and rights are the same as those of other community radio stations (those referred to as "normal radio stations," above).

The pioneers of small community radio had a difficult time securing broadcast licenses. Typically, applicants would wait for 2 years or more before they could even begin broadcasting. Today, new applicants can start broadcasting in less than 1 year after winning the application.[3] In Hungary, it is technically possible for all small communities to have their own radio stations simultaneously, because the frequencies do not disturb each other. Theoretically, there is no limit to the number of this kind of small community radio station. What then is the basic difference between old community radio stations

and new-born small community radio stations? De jure there is no difference, because both types are community, nonprofit radio stations, but de facto, they have very different areas of reception.

Although the climate for small community radio has improved dramatically since 2002, several problems persist. First and foremost is the restricted area of reception for these radio stations: Small community radio stations in stereo may only broadcast within a maximum radius of 1 km or with a maximum of 10 watt (W) power or reaching a maximum of 10,000 inhabitants. The problem is that the authorities often make their decisions with no regard to the unique characteristics of these small local radio stations, and the above rules seem to be applied in a way that leaves these radio stations with small audiences.

If we accept the original idea of small community broadcasting (to work for small local communities) then these rules serve fine, but in actual practice, there are small community radio stations broadcasting with only 0.5 W. The frequencies are planned in the offices of the media authority with little regard to the real needs and characteristics of the communities the stations are meant to serve.

For instance, Remete Rádió in Pécs-Istenkút is a small community radio operating in a rural area where the studio and the transmitter are located in a narrow valley. Because of the surrounding hills, however, the station is unable to broadcast beyond the valley. During the application process, representatives from the media authority didn't assess the technical and topographical characteristics of the community and the implications these might have on the station's ability to serve the surrounding community. It seems clear that application procedures and documentation do not accommodate successful planning. This sort of problem might be alleviated if representatives from the media authority worked more closely with potential applicants and visited the sites to evaluate the needs and characteristics of local communities.

The other main problem is financial in nature. Although the average yearly running costs of these radio stations is quite modest (US$7,000 to US$17,000 per year, depending on local circumstances), they have enormous difficulty in applying for funding. Many of these stations cannot apply to the Broadcasting Fund for annual operating costs because the required percentage of self-financing is too high. These funding difficulties are compounded by the lack of private donations from local civic groups and the like. This is not to suggest that civil society is unsupportive of community radio in Hungary. Rather, it is to say that after only 17 years since the change of regime, Hungarian civil society is not as vigorous or well developed as its Western European counterparts. And because of their limited reception area, small community radio stations get precious little in the way of local commercial support. Of course, some local governments provide modest financial support for small community

radio, but this is the exception to the rule. Finally, as the number of small community radio stations increases, there is greater competition for limited financial support from the Broadcasting Fund.

Since 2004, when the pioneer stations got their licenses, 56 small community radio stations signed their contracts (National Radio and Television Board, n.d.) with the media authority. Taken together with other community radio stations, there are currently 68 community radio stations across the country, making the Hungarian community media sector the largest and most robust in all of Eastern Europe.

The present situation can be summed up as follows: There is the possibility to broadcast with "usual" community frequencies, as older radio stations do, but there are almost no new frequencies for this kind of broadcasting. However, there is the possibility to run a small community radio with all the restrictions seen above. If we compare the above figures with the total number of radio stations operating in Hungary, we might think that our work has been completed. There are approximately 240 radio stations in Hungary (community, public service, and commercial stations), which means that 28% of Hungarian radio stations are community radio stations. But this comparison conceals more than it reveals. If we have a look at the number of community radio stations whose reception area is higher than that of small community radio stations, we find that only 12 stations, or about 5% of the total number of radio stations, meet this criterion.

Table 25.1 illustrates the differences between commercial, community, and small community radio stations' transmission power and the number of potential listeners that each station could reach.

Despite the difficulties outlined above, small community radio stations play a significant role in the social, cultural, and political lives of local communities. Small community radio stations help residents participate in civil society and strengthen democracy across Hungary. These stations provide local news in a more timely and efficient fashion than the local press, which generally publish only

Table 25.1	Transmission Power and Reception Areas for Hungarian Radio Stations					
	Commercial		**Community**		**Small Community**	
	Regional	**Local**	**Regional**	**Local**	**Local**	**Local**
	Infó Rádió	**Mediterrán Rádió**	**Civil Rádió**	**Rádió Aktív**	**Füzes Rádió**	**Remete Rádió**
Transmission power (kW)	1.7380	0.2510	0.0407	0.2288	0.00014	0.0006
Reception area (number of potential listeners)	2,699,000	130,000	770,000	164,000	5,300	1,100

Note: The chosen radio stations' numbers are only samples, not averages.

Source: Hungarian National Radio and Television Board (n.d.) and the National Communications Authority (n.d.).

once a week in small communities. Moreover, small community radio stations amplify the voices of marginalized groups within Hungarian society.

Whether they organize local concerts and exhibitions or broadcast local government hearings, these broadcasters share a similar goal: to help inhabitants exercise their rights and to create new channels of communication for the expression of these rights. There are civil groups in almost every small town (in those in which local traditions are protected) that would not be heard in mass media at all. For them, community radio is the best way to express themselves—to make programs about themselves—so that they can create a new public sphere. Those radio programs are made for and by local people belonging to these small communities, creating a more just and democratic culture.

The Past of the Community Radio Movement: "Beware— Pirates on the Air!"

The success of community broadcasting did not come easy. The community radio movement in Hungary started shortly after the fall of the Iron Curtain in the early 1990s. Before the change of regime, only the public service broadcaster (Magyar Rádió—Hungarian Radio) had the right to broadcast. Despite formal statements about freedom of speech in the old era, no other broadcasters had the right to exist. As the Press Act (Act II of 1986 on the Press) states, "Only the Hungarian Radio and Hungarian Television has the right to make and broadcast radio and television programmes" (Article 9).[4]

Other factors limited democratic communication in Hungary. For instance, on July 3, 1989, the Hungarian government, led by Miklós Németh, declared a moratorium on frequency allocations,[5] which meant that no new broadcasters were granted broadcast licenses until the passage of the aforementioned Media Act of 1996. No one imagined that the moratorium would last nearly 7 years. Nevertheless, the political motivation behind the moratorium was quite clear: The communists, who had been ruling Hungary for almost 50 years, didn't want any new political power to have the opportunity of broadcasting on the eve of the nation's first free elections. Fortunately, the communists were mistaken. The change of regime could not be stopped by banning new radio and television stations, and new parties got into the Hungarian Parliament and soon began work on the Media Act. The problem was that the Hungarian Constitution (see Act XX of 1949 of the Constitution of the Republic of Hungary, modified in the autumn of 1989, at http://net .jogtar.hu/jr/gen/getdoc.cgi?docid=94900020.tv &dbnum=62, accessed May 5, 2009) states, "A majority of two-thirds of the votes of the Members of Parliament present is required to pass the law on the public access to information of public interest and the law on the freedom of the press" (Article 61). At that time, no political party had enough representation to successfully pass a new media law on its own.

As the new media act stalled, new kinds of radio appeared out of the blue. This early community radio did not have a historical background in Hungary; nonetheless, the new stations made a significant contribution to the creation of a more democratic media system. They celebrated free speech and opened up discursive spaces for opposition and dissent where few had existed before. These stations operated illegally, as so-called pirate radio stations.

For instance, Tilos Rádió (Forbidden Radio) was the first of the pirate operations when it went on the air on 21 August 1991. Soon thereafter, a host of stations—ZÖM Rádió in Kaposvár, Szubjektív Rádió in Pécs, and Szóköz Rádió, among others, began broadcasting as well. Despite differences between these pirate stations, they shared the same goal: They wanted to break the moratorium, and they wanted to use the airwaves to serve their local communities. In short, they wanted to broadcast freely.

Their programming was free as well. That is to say, they didn't concern themselves with "professional" standards or production values, they played music that couldn't be heard on any of the public stations (alternative, electronic, etc.), and they had talk shows in which people spoke their minds without fear of repercussions from the government or commercial interests. The titles of

some of these old programs—for example, Tilos Rádió's *Radio Stupidity, This Is the Future, Eat It!*, and *Third Ear*—highlight the irreverent and innovative approach to broadcasting practiced by the pirate stations. They produced programming by, for, and about people from all walks of life. Typically, pirate operators worked with a cross section of interest groups, such as environmentalists, feminists, and people with disabilities. In so doing, pirate broadcasters contributed to the development of Hungarian civil society.

As one of the representatives of Tilos Rádió said in an interview, "We are not afraid of the police, because we are right. Everything we do is just a gesture, it is about what will be" ("It's About What Will Be," 1991). But despite their efforts to democratize the airwaves, in the eyes of the authorities, they were operating illegally. Pirate broadcasters were subjected to police investigations and inquiries from the Frequency Allocation Institute. And yet, they were never caught. This raises an important question that remains unanswered to this day: Was this simply a matter of good luck? Evidence suggests that Hungarian civil society supported the efforts of the illegal broadcasters, and this may account for the inability of the police to successfully track down and stop the pirates from broadcasting.

The situation at that time was rather unique: The country was a newborn democracy, but the media landscape was still mainly ruled by the public service broadcasters. Drafts of the Media Act contained proposals for a dualistic media landscape (public service broadcasters and commercial broadcasters), but in these proposals, community broadcasting was marginalized. Even worse, the political parties were engaged in what has been dubbed the first Hungarian media war. Despite their constitutional obligation to pass the Media Act, it seemed that there would be a long fight.[6]

In May 1992, community radio stations set up the Hungarian Federation of Free Radios (HFFR; www.szabadradio.hu) which was—and still is—the nationwide pressure group for community radio.[7] The members of the federation fought very hard and used their limited political and social capital to help pass the Media Act. Although the moratorium on frequencies was still in force, legal loopholes provided opportunities for the nascent community radio sector to emerge.

For instance, through the 110/1993 statutory order, the Ministry of Education and Communication had the right to establish local noncommercial radio and television *studios* (not stations). As a result, lots of radio and television stations found their way onto the air. Lack of enforcement and bureaucratic bungling enabled not only commercial broadcasters but also a handful of genuine, noncommercial, community-oriented radio stations to take advantage of legal loopholes and begin broadcasting. Viewed in this light, the statutory order proved decisive in putting an end to the moratorium on broadcast licensing—and ushered in a new era of communicative democracy in Hungary.

New Challenges, Dark Future?

As we have seen, the present state of Hungarian community radio is mixed. On the one hand, a growing number of radio stations[8] are having a huge impact on the lives of local communities. What's more, these stations are beginning to function collectively as a formidable nationwide pressure group that works nationally and internationally at the European level as well.[9] On the other hand, financial difficulties and persistent transmission problems constrain the development of the community radio sector. And there are new dangers looming on the horizon.

For instance, one of the new drafts of the Media Act—which was made by experts at the request of the National Radio and Television Board in October 2006 (Törvényelőkészítő Szakértői Bizottság, 2006)—makes no mention of community (or non-profit-oriented) broadcasters. Only commercial and public service broadcasters are discussed in this draft legislation. All this indicates how little policymakers know of, or care about, the field of community broadcasting. Fortunately, it is just a draft, and there is considerable opposition to it. Still, if this draft legislation were enacted, it would represent a major setback to the struggle for communicative democracy in Hungary.

This is not the only warning sign. Planning for possible multiplexes in the digitalized media field has just started in Hungary. In this proposed multiplex model, Hungarian community stations will only appear in the local "must-offer" package, as they won't have enough money or power to convince the owners of the multiplexes to broadcast their programs on regional and national levels. The so-called Digital Act (Parliament of the Republic of Hungary, 2007) represents a new set of challenges that the Hungarian community media sector must negotiate if it is to survive into the next decade.

There are new financial threats as well. Up until 2006, 1% of the annual revenues of the Broadcasting Fund was given to the community media sector as the maximum amount stated in the Media Act (see Act I of 1996, Article 78, above), but at the end of 2006, the media authority decided, for no apparent reason, to reduce this amount to 5% of the annual revenues from 2007 on. While it is certainly within the ORTT's authority to do so, the wisdom of this decision is questionable.[10] As more broadcasters take to the air, there is greater competition for limited funds. In the first months of 2007, the community radio sector received less support from the Broadcasting Fund than it had in previous years. It remains to be seen whether or not community broadcasting can survive in the current climate.

Community radio definitely has a bright past in Hungary. Almost 16 years have passed since community broadcasters first took to the air, and there is much to be proud of. Relative to the history of community broadcasting in Western Europe, Australia, and North America, the Hungarian experience may seem inconsequential. But in the context of Eastern Europe, Hungarian community broadcasters have taken up a heroic fight. Hungarian community radio stations fought valiantly for freedom of speech and were instrumental in establishing a tripartite media system. In doing so, community radio played a decisive role in the growth and development of Hungarian civil society.

Community radio also has a bright present in Hungary. The growth of the sector illustrates the degree of popular interest and participation in democratic communication. Moreover, Hungarian community radio has established strong connections across all of Europe. Representatives from the Hungarian community radio sector regularly attend and help organize international conferences on community media and democratic communication. Furthermore, Hungarian community broadcasters have shared their hard-won knowledge and experiences with others across Eastern Europe.

But the future of community radio in Hungary is uncertain. Financial cuts and restrictions, short-sighted legal drafts, and new fights with the media authority and the Hungarian state lie ahead for community radio. It is unclear whether community radio will survive these new challenges and preserve its capacity to serve local communities with innovative, participatory approaches to broadcasting. Let's hope that this is not the end of the story.

Notes

1. The main reason behind sharing was that in Budapest there was only one frequency reserved for this kind of broadcasting. During the renewal process in 2000, Tilos Rádió decided to apply alone for the same frequency, competing against the other two nonprofit radio stations, which applied together. Tilos Rádió lost the application, so Civil Rádió and Fiksz Rádió had the possibility to continue broadcasting on FM98. Tilos broadcast on the Internet until 2003, when it got the FM90.3 frequency. In 2006, Fiksz Rádió became an Internet radio, so Civil Rádió is broadcasting alone 24/7 on the oldest nonprofit frequency in Budapest.

2. There are no proofs of this, but a warning sign could be that Szóköz Rádió won a suit against the media authority in the lower court in 2007.

3. In the Hungarian licensing system for small community radio stations, one first wins only the possibility to broadcast. Then, during the licensing procedure, the frequency itself is assigned, and as the last step, one can sign the final contract with the National Radio and Television Board.

4. There have been some exceptions in the commercial radio field since 1986 when the first commercial radios (e.g., Danubius and Calypso) started broadcasting, but none in the community media field.

5. It was interesting from a legal point of view because this resolution of the government (No. 1008/10, July 3, 1989) was never officially published.

6. The first Hungarian media war took place between 1990 and 1994. The main goal of political parties was to "control" the public service broadcasters (radio and television). We must not forget that at that time, these two were the main media in Hungary and that controlling them meant being able to reach almost the whole population.

7. There have been ongoing debates since 2006 in the Federation about including community television stations as well, because they do not have any nationwide pressure group.

8. There were 15 new applicants on March 1, 2007, and 21 on September 1, 2007.

9. The Hungarian Federation of Free Radios has regular board members in AMARC (World Association of Community Radio Broadcasters) and CMFE (Community Media Forum Europe).

10. The annual budget of the Broadcasting Fund for 2007 (US$167,067,844) was just a little bit less than for 2006 (US$170,522,621), so this was not a justified reason for the cut.

References

Hungarian Federation of Free Radios. (1992). *Founding article*. Retrieved September 11, 2007, from www.szabadradio.hu/hu/alapszabaly

It's about what will be. (1991, September 24). *Journal Magyar Hirlap.* Retrieved May 5, 2009, from http://tilos.hu/index.php?page_id=kronika_sajt01991

National Communications Authority. (n.d). *Registers.* Retrieved May 5, 2009, from www.nhh.hu/index.php?id=menu&mid=679

National Radio and Television Board. (n.d.). *Registry.* Retrieved September 24, 2007, from http://ortt.hu/nyilvantartasok/1190616176kiskozossegi_20070924.xls

Parliament of the Republic of Hungary. (1996). *Act I of 1996 on radio and television broadcasting.* Retrieved September 24, 2007, from http://net.jogtar.hu/jr/gen/getdoc.cgi?docid=99600001.tv&dbnum=62

Parliament of the Republic of Hungary. (2007). Act LXXIV of 2007 on the rules of broadcasting and digital switchover. Retrieved September 27, 2007, from www.meh.hu/misc/letoltheto/eng_2007_74_tv_das.pdf

Törvényelőkészítő Szakértői Bizottság. (2006, October 27). Az elektronikus médiaszolgáltatásokról szóló törvény tervezete [Draft of the Act about Electronic Media]. Retrieved March 14, 2007, from www.akti.hu/mediatorveny/dok/torveny0610.pdf

CHAPTER 26

Community Media Activists in Transnational Policy Arenas

Stefania Milan

How can community media activists—traditionally small, local groups with limited resources—influence the agenda of major policy arenas? What are the challenges, strategies, and shortcomings of getting involved in policy making and what can we learn from past experiences? How could theory help activists to comprehend such complex processes and plan effective intervention?

This chapter explores the challenges and strategies of community media practitioners engaged in policy advocacy at the transnational level. The perspective is that of an engaged scholar who aims at providing a "how-to" guide to community media advocates.

Over the past few years, we have observed among community media activists a growing awareness of policy-making processes across territorial boundaries. Ever since the United Nations' World Summit on the Information Society (Geneva, 2003, and Tunis, 2005), community media have increasingly tried to make their voices

heard in major transnational policy arenas, including the European Union (EU) and the Council of Europe (COE). The World Association of Community Broadcasters (Association Mondiale des Radiodiffuseurs Communautaires [AMARC]) became an interlocutor of transnational institutions, and other networks, such as the Community Media Forum Europe (CMFE), were formed to respond to opportunities in policy-making processes. Created in 2004 as a loose network of community media, CMFE was later institutionalized as a nongovernmental organization (NGO) with the aim of unifying lobbying efforts at European institutions.

Community media's attempts to influence policy makers can be considered as part of the current mobilization for communications justice. Specifically, community media activists ground their advocacy interventions in their daily practices of grassroots communication and derive legitimacy as social actors in policy arenas from their "applied" expertise.

However, community media face some challenges when seeking access to policy arenas: (a) procedural problems of admission and accreditation, (b) financial obstacles to participation in official meetings, since no funding is provided by institutions (Hintz, 2006), and (c) lack of knowhow to be effective in such highly professional environments.

This chapter applies concepts from social movements research and instruments of public policy analysis to investigate an empirical case: the CMFE's lobbying at the Council of Europe's Seventh Ministerial Conference on Mass Media Policy, which took place in Kiev, Ukraine, in March 2005. Looking at the Kiev process provides some "lessons learned" for future involvement and a few suggestions on how to best use the limited resources available to grassroots organizations.

When Theory Can Help Activists: Key Concepts in Policy-Making Processes

Recent developments in the field of global governance have seen the inclusion in decision making of previously marginalized groups of organized civil society.[1] They have been invited to take part in consultations and in some cases to participate in negotiations as stakeholders with rights equal to those of governments. Nevertheless, the power of government delegates often outweighs that of civil society representatives, and the role of the latter in supranational policy making is still fairly limited. However, the chance to get involved is usually received positively by civil society organizations. Drawing from studies on policy making and theories of collective action, this section of the chapter sheds light on the phases of problem definition and agenda setting in which, I believe, activists can potentially intervene and suggests under which conditions policy change is possible.

Problem definition, or "the strategic representation of situation" (Stone, 1988, p. 106), deals with the way a particular issue is "sold" on the policy market. Policy problems are usually constructed through negotiations: The labeling of a problem (issue naming) is crucial for the issue to gain a potential for action (issue recognition: when the issue has entered the policy makers' agenda). Problem definition is particularly complex in the case of community media, for two reasons: First, the assorted mixture of experiences labeled as "community media" and the diverse discourses and features of the groups involved can jeopardize dialogue and consensus; second, community media are not (yet) a shared concept in policy arenas and are not (yet) recognized as a policy problem. Theory suggests that a shared definition of what community media are and do should be the first objective for advocates: It could advance the understanding of the policy problem by policy makers, opening doors for recognition.[2] Besides, it could facilitate identification among kindred groups, fostering coalitions[3] that may result in a stronger agenda.

Once the problem has been defined in a coherent way, the issue has to enter the agenda of policymakers. This process is called agenda setting and is defined as "the politics of selecting issues for active consideration" (Cobb & Ross, 1997, p. 3). When actors succeed in including their issue in the official agenda, the issue gains institutional attention, and thus there is potential for action. However, legitimizing an issue and granting access to the agenda does not mean legitimizing the related demands: Issues can be initially taken into consideration by policy makers but can later be dropped, or the policy outcomes might not be the expected ones. Agenda access is not a goal but a means to advance causes (Dery, 2000).

Under which conditions do social actors have some chance to bring about change? Theory suggests that this is possible when there is a shift in the "political opportunity structure," or an open window to influence policy making. Social movements scholars talk about "political opportunity structure" to describe the context in which social actors interact with institutions and policy stakeholders: A change in this structure might provide social actors with an occasion for action. Political opportunities are defined as the exogenous dimensions of the political context that might foster people's action (Tarrow, 1998). Threats to interests and values can also encourage political action. In both cases, it is crucial that social actors be able to identify the opportunity and act accordingly.

Public policy scholars also argue that possibilities for policy change are influenced by structural conditions. According to John Kingdon (1984), the institutional agenda can be influenced when there is a "policy window," defined as an occasion for political participation. By establishing priorities, an open window affects the institutional agenda, which could result in a favorable position on the issue list for the activists' demands. Since a policy window is a temporary option for action, social actors must be able to recognize it and be ready to "jump in" when the window opens. It might open because of a change in the institutional settings, and it closes when action has been taken or other issues gain relevance.

Possibilities for policy change also come along with changes in the balance of political power within "policy monopolies": "networks of groups and individuals operating inside and outside of government, linked by mutual recognition as legitimate actors concerned with a particular set of policies" (Meyer, 2005, p. 7). A policy monopoly is (potentially) broken when civil society joins previously restricted policy arenas: In Kiev, community media advocates have gained a possibility to break the monopoly and push toward a policy change.

Getting Organized for Policy Advocacy: The Community Media Forum Europe

The CMFE was founded in Halle, Germany, in November 2004, to be "the missing link between community media and EU institutions" (H. Peissl, personal communication, May 16, 2006).

It serves as an umbrella organization to foster the recognition, promotion, and support of community media in Europe and to strengthen their participation in policy-making processes. Its members are not-for-profit media serving local communities, national federations, and networks from EU member states and beyond. They define themselves as "third-sector media," alongside public service media and commercial broadcasters, and share some core principles and features such as not-for-profit status.[4]

In July 2006, the CMFE organized its first members meeting in Brussels at the European Parliament. Some 40 community media representatives from 15 European countries took part in the 4-day debate organized in collaboration with AMARC. They discussed the role of community media in Europe with representatives of EU institutions and demanded full recognition of the third-media sector (also as a policy stakeholder), the reservation of frequencies for community media, the establishment of a European Community Media Fund, and support for community media correspondents at EU institutions (CMFE, 2006).

In November 2006, the CMFE was set up as a nonprofit association under Belgian law with headquarters in Brussels,[5] and a new board was elected in November 2007.

The CMFE is "a flexible structure connecting experts for quick intervention," as CMFE member Thomas Kupfer (personal communication, May 17, 2006) put it. Analytically, it can be seen as a flexible "transnational advocacy coalition": a network of actors connected by shared values and characterized by the production, exchange, and strategic use of information (Keck & Sikkink, 1998). Advocacy coalitions work for norm change and seek "not only to influence policy outcomes, but to transform the terms and nature of the debate." They act as "a communicative structure for political exchange" that multiplies the channels of access to international arenas for its members, and they "bring new ideas, norms, and discourses into policy debates" (pp. 2–8).

As its first public initiative, the CMFE contributed to the public consultation on media policy held by the Council of Europe in 2005. Later, it participated in the EU open consultations on the digital divide (also in 2005), on the review of the EU's 2005 "Television Without Frontiers" Directive, and on the White Paper on a European Communication Policy, in 2006, always trying to raise awareness of community media needs and to transform the nature of the debate.

The Council of Europe as a Political Opportunity Structure

The Council of Europe (COE), founded in 1949 and based in Strasbourg (France), is the only political organization with a Pan-European width and comprises 47 member states, including 22 countries from Eastern and Central Europe. It aims at defending human rights and democracy, promoting standardization of legal practices at the European level, supporting awareness of a continentwide European identity, and protecting cultural diversity. Its role is limited to drafting international instruments approved by consensus among its members. It is perceived to be a progressive environment in areas such as human rights, local democracy, and culture. It has no implementation mechanisms and only limited financial resources.

Article 10 of the European Convention on Human Rights, which provides for the right to freedom of expression, informs the COE activities in the field of media policy. Media are of interest to the Council for their role in promoting a democratic society.[6] The Council supports media pluralism and diversity, freedom of expression, and related rights such as privacy and aims at developing Pan-European policy measures. Several references to community media can be found in COE documents,[7] making the COE a potentially supportive environment for community media advocates. The first chance for the CMFE to have an impact arose in 2005, when civil society was invited to participate in the COE media policy conference.

The "Policy Window": The Seventh Ministerial Conference on Mass Media Policy

Every 5 years, the COE Media Division calls for a ministerial conference on media policy. The Seventh European Ministerial Conference on Mass Media Policy took place in Kiev during March 10 to 11, 2005. For the first time in such a conference, civil society, defined as a nonstate and nonbusiness actor and represented by NGOs as well as thematic networks, was requested to contribute. The conference can thus be considered a policy window, that is to say an opportunity for action for new actors such as the CMFE.

A public consultation was launched by the COE in June 2004, encouraging the citizenry of the EU to submit policy proposals. An NGO forum was held parallel to the official summit; it was attended by 50 civil society organizations, which agreed on the amendments to be presented on behalf of civil society and appointed three spokespersons to address the governmental delegates. Some of their proposals were incorporated in the final documents.

The conference featured three main sessions, each addressing a subtheme: (1) freedom of expression and information, (2) cultural diversity and media diversity, and (3) human rights and regulation of the media and new communication services. The final text, titled *Integration and Diversity: The New Frontiers of European Media and Communications Policy,*[8] comprised a political declaration, a resolution for each subtheme, and an action plan. It set guidelines for COE actions on communications policy for the next 3 years.

Civil society participation was regarded as "positive": According to participant Jim McDonnell from the NGO SIGNIS, "there was a sense that the presence of NGOs was well accepted by governments." Civil society, McDonnell says, had "some influence," and outcomes were "more favourable to the NGO input than many of us believed was possible."[9] Amendments on human rights minimum standards, editorial independence, and transparency were accepted. However, the same cannot be said about community media issues.

Community Media Go to Kiev: Negotiating the Agenda

The CMFE brought to Kiev a detailed document asking for the following: (1) recognition of the role of community media as the "third audiovisual sector" and as "a basic public service"; (2) financial support by national governments and European institutions through the creation of a Community Media Fund; (3) consideration of the radio-frequency spectrum as a "natural resource belonging to all humanity"; (4) support for media providing means of expression for minority languages; (5) a commitment to reduce the "digital and communications divide," as a precondition for development of community media, and free access to Internet services; (6) support for community media, especially in countries where freedom of speech is under threat.

The adopted documents do not mention community media directly and only refer to "minority community media." Thus, although all three NGO addresses to the plenary assembly mentioned the value of community media, these did not succeed in influencing the Kiev agenda. However, this should not be considered a failure. CMFE regarded the achievements in Kiev as "positive," highlighting the novelty of its participation. Which obstacles then prevented the CMFE issues from being included? The following sections focus on the negotiation phases, achievements, and shortcomings of CMFE advocacy and suggest some keys for interpretation of the Kiev official documents.

Changing the Terms of the Debate? The "Relabeling Strategy"

The CMFE strategy consisted of an attempt at renaming the issue "community communication"

within a public interest frame; other demands stemmed from this first one. As Diasio put it, "When we acknowledge there is a public interest in community media, we open doors to a certain number of related requests, legitimizing them" (Diasio & Milan, 2005). This is in line with what theory on policy making suggests: Once a problem is acknowledged to merit public intervention, new demands are legitimate and requests for access to scarce resources such as airwaves or public funding gain legitimacy. But norm change is a long process, and CMFE only managed to have two of their six points included in the official documents, namely the relevance of community media for migrant communities[10] and the provision of free universal access to new technologies.[11] However, minority media and universal public service are not new to the COE: The CMFE could count on previous familiarity of the delegates with these issues.

Coalition Building and Institutional Support

In the months preceding the conference, the CMFE tried to build support around its demands, but the lack of financial resources and time to devote to networking jeopardized the coalition-building efforts. Surprisingly, the CMFE gained the support of the European Broadcasting Union (EBU), a professional association of national public service broadcasters. The EBU provided logistic assistance by hosting a civil society preconference meeting in its Geneva headquarters and participated in a working group with civil society, thus recognizing community media as legitimate stakeholders. But the collaboration with the EBU did not go very far, as the EBU wanted to reserve the prerogatives of public service, such as state funding, to its own members and thus opposed the recognition of a public service character to community media.

In Kiev, the CMFE had to share the limited time resources (for addressing the plenary sessions) with other organizations. However, it was able to create a small but significant coalition around some of its issues. For what concerns the institution, the CMFE gathered limited support from the COE itself, and a COE official referred to community media in the opening speech. But, on the other hand, the CMFE had some problems at the internal level with other NGO delegates from Eastern Europe. According to Diasio,

> They could not understand the very same concept of community media, because of their countries' peculiar history. They moved from a state monopoly in the media sector to a jungle of privatisations, and never experienced the community dimension of communication. (Diasio & Milan, 2005)

Airwaves: Analytical Definition Versus Normative Definition

The attempt at relabeling the issue of the "airwaves" did not succeed. The CMFE asked the COE to consider the radio-frequency spectrum as a "natural resource belonging to all humanity" that "should be managed in the public interest as a publicly owned asset through transparent and accountable regulatory frameworks." Analytically, airwaves can be considered a "club good," characterized by rival consumption and limited access—access is regulated by national public authorities, and broadcasters compete for frequency allocation. The CMFE proposed to redefine airwaves as a "global public good," characterized by no exclusion and no rivalry: If airwaves are a public good, they should be equally enjoyed by citizens and not reserved only to public or commercial broadcasting. CMFE attempted to shift a merely technical issue into a "valence" issue, that is to say, an issue able to provoke emotional responses (Nelson & Lindenfeld, 1978).

Why did the CMFE not succeed in relabeling the airwaves issue? Despite the frequency spectrum being indeed a scarce resource, civil society delegates in Kiev considered the spectrum issue to be too complicated and risky. They privileged established and consensual issues, such as media ownership, to be discussed in the short time slots allocated to civil society. As McDonnell (2005) explained,

> The amendments [to the Action Plan related to community media] were never presented because time for discussion in the CDMM [Steering Committee on the Mass Media] was short and it was thought that they would have little chance of being accepted without a long debate. (See Note 9)

How Can Collective Action Foster Policy Change? Lessons Learned

The CMFE's attempt to relabel its issues under the social justice flag did not succeed: Community media advocates were not able to convince the other stakeholders of the legitimacy of their requests or did not get the chance to do so. This section of the chapter discusses the possible explanations for the failure of this "relabeling strategy," namely the complexity and high value of the issues at stake, the inefficiency of labeling, the scarcity of resources, and the difficulties in building support. It summarizes the lessons to be learned for future involvement.

Complexity of the Issues at Stake, Invisibility, and the Complexity of Framing. Media policy is a highly specialized ground, requiring technical skills and familiarity with the policy arena and its rules. Moreover, community media have scarce financial resources and market value and operate mainly at a grassroots level almost "invisible" to policy makers. For all these reasons, community media issues are (not yet) shared concepts in policy arenas. Besides, their issues are difficult to frame for mobilization, and it is hard to get the citizenry engaged.

High Value of Issues, Both at a Symbolic and Commercial Level. CMFE requests clashed with some core principles of the current media system. (a) Symbolically, the long tradition of public service broadcasting in Europe is an obstacle for new actors that seek the label of public service. If community media provided a recognized public service, they could claim public funding, which is a scarce resource. Moreover, the journalistic tradition connected to public service media would clash with the horizontal production principles of many community media. (b) At the commercial level, airwaves are a state-owned economic good: Commercial broadcasters pay for access and use, and competition is fierce. Earmarking some frequencies to community media could result in revenue losses for governments and fewer spectrum resources for commercial media.

Inefficiency of Labeling. "Community media" and "third sector media" have not proven to be the best labels for a very diverse category, resulting in a blurred identity and confusion among other stakeholders about what community media is all about. If this is true at the civil society level (the concept created some misunderstandings and some internal opposition), it might be even more problematic at the governmental level: In case policymakers do not recognize the identity and features of an actor, they will not understand and accept/legitimize its demands. I believe the best label in such a context would have been "public interest media," but the concept still needs a consistent theoretical framework before entering policy arenas.

Time Is a Scarce Resource. Time slots allocated to civil society were limited in number and short in duration, so that highly consensual "valence" issues prevailed in the civil society selection of the issues to be introduced to delegates. Civil society actors privileged consensual issues with a "history" and higher probability of getting accepted for inclusion and left behind issues requiring a longer and complex debate with uncertain outcomes.

Scarce Internal (Civil Society) Support. The "historical" differences in the backgrounds of civil society organizations resulted in poor civil support for the CMFE: NGOs from Eastern Europe (present in a good number in Kiev due to its

proximity) did not fully recognize the CMFE as a legitimate stakeholder because of their minimal acquaintance with community media. On the thematic level, more established and consensual issues such as ownership transparency and freedom of expression, were put forward by a higher number of actors and ended up prevailing over the issue supported by weaker groups (such as the newly founded CMFE).

Scarce Cross-Sector (or External) Support. The CMFE was not able to gather consistent support from other governmental or media stakeholders due to lack of time and financial resources to promote preconference exchanges. In the case of the EBU, the initial support later clashed with the competition for scarce resources (public funding).

Problem Definition and Policy Niches

The Kiev final documents mentioned only migrant media, a (tiny) sector of community media, but did not go further in legitimizing other demands. However, there are provisions that can be connected to CMFE lobbying and that represent what I call "policy niches": *provisions regarding other issues, to which community media demands can be related and so indirectly legitimated.* They refer to issues that can be linked to community media features or activities, and are valid for them, legitimizing their requests. I have singled out four policy niches in the Kiev documents: (1) cultural diversity, (2) media pluralism, (3) media literacy, and (4) social cohesion provisions that can apply to community media.

1. *Cultural diversity niche:* Community media represent a channel to preserve and transmit cultural identities. Their activities encourage content diversity by providing citizens with direct access to production. In Resolution No. 2, "Cultural diversity and media pluralism in times

of globalization," the Ministers "recognize, preserve and promote cultural diversity as a common heritage of humanity . . . stressing the importance of cultural diversity for the realisation of fundamental rights and freedoms" (Article 2, Resolution No. 2).

2. *Media pluralism niche:* In a pluralistic *mediascape,* there can be a place for community media alongside commercial and public service broadcasters. Community media also promote the diversification of media content by broadcasting many voices that are usually not heard. Resolution No. 2 calls for "the adoption of sector-specific rules designed to safeguard plurality and diversity in the media," which "may be important in addition to general competition law" (Article 7, Resolution No. 2); for "encourag[ing] the production and distribution of diversified content" (Article 14, Resolution No. 2); and for "promot[ion of] media pluralism at the national, regional and local levels" (Article16, Resolution No. 2).[12]

3. *Media literacy niche:* Community media often promote training sessions to empower people in "horizontal" communication. As a means of firsthand access to media production, they provide citizens with the possibility to learn how media work. Provisions on media literacy favor these activities and could thus legitimize community media and potentially open doors to public funding. Article 14, Resolution No. 3, talks about "efforts to ensure an effective and equitable access for all individuals to the new communication services, skills and knowledge . . . as well as to encourage media education for the general public" Action Plan Subtheme 3 of Article 20 supports "steps to promote, at all stages of education and as part of ongoing learning, media literacy which involves active and critical use of all the media."

4. *Social cohesion niche:* Community media often promote dialogue between people living in the same area, promoting exchange and tolerance: They work for community cohesion and dialogue. Resolution No. 1 reads, "When the

media promote understanding and tolerance, they can help prevent crisis situations from occurring." Action Plan Subtheme 1 speaks of "the media's contribution to intercultural and inter-religious dialogue" (Article 6), and Article 17 Subtheme 2 highlights the importance of "access to the media by persons belonging to national minorities in order to promote tolerance and enhance cultural pluralism."

Referring to such niches in their advocacy interventions, community media advocates can find potential fertile ground to legitimate their demands within institutional arenas. These niches constitute "soft spots" of institutions—in this case, the COE—that can be used as "anchors" or "Trojan horses" linking community media demands to the institutional mission and helping translate what community media are about and want into a language that institutions can understand. The "policy niches strategy" could be considered as a first step in the (long) process of norm change and in the attempt to transform the terms of the media policy debate in Europe.

The Way Forward: The Post-Kiev Agenda

How can advocates tackle these obstacles? The Kiev process showed that the most urgent step is the elaboration of an appropriate umbrella term to effectively "sell" the issue "community communication" on the policy market and to gather consistent support across the community media sector and civil society at large. Such a definition could highlight from time to time some of the community media features in accordance with the policy window (and the institutional agenda) at stake. Researchers could effectively help practitioners to elaborate a consistent vision by connecting community media to the notion of "public interest." The relabeling of the airwaves issue should follow, alongside the elaboration of appropriate policy demands: The label "global public good" has barely any chance to be acknowledged, and with the forthcoming digital switchover the problem is likely to reemerge. Both labeling exercises—community communication and scarce resources—should be part of a coherent agenda for policy intervention on which to start building consensus amongst kindred actors and allies. In the long run, community media should aim at changing the terms of the debate around communication and media policy in their countries and within supranational institutions. In the short run, the "policy niches strategy" provides provisional help, legitimizing through other more established issues some of the community media demands and bypassing in this way the phase of full acceptance of the community media realm by institutions. Nevertheless, the latter should be the final aim of any community media advocate.

Notes

1. *Civil society* here means the realm of nonstate and nonbusiness actors.

2. Hadl and Hintz (2009) proposed the concept of "Civil Society Media" as an umbrella term capable of including different identities.

3. In social movement research, networking with kindred groups is based on sharing the same core values ("collective action frame"). Considering community media networks as an embryonic social movement, we can see that an appropriate framing (a shared definition of community media, to start with) could be inclusive toward kindred actors and foster the emergence of vast lobbying networks.

4. There are nine principles in the CMFE statutes: (1) community access to communication means, (2) freedom of speech and media plurality, (3) free access to information, (4) public- and gender-balanced access, (5) encouragement of local participation, (6) cultural diversity and respect for minorities, (7) orientation toward participatory structures and self-determination, (8) editorial independence, and (9) not-for-profit status.

5. It is not a membership organization. The call for members read, "CMFE is not and will not be a member-organisation in the sense that it claims to represent the whole European "third-media sector," or "community media." Rather it shall be a small and flexible entity able to react quickly to current political developments, to focus on specifically selected issues and to cooperate with affiliated bodies (e.g., AMARC, International Network for Cultural Diversity) on the international level" (Thomas Kreiseder, personal communication to potential members, October 30, 2006).

6. For an overview of COE activities in the field, visit www.coe.int/T/E/Com/About_Coe/media.asp (retrieved November 10, 2008).

7. The following aspects were addressed: (a) local radio in Europe (1991), (b) universal community service (1997, 1999), (c) media pluralism (1999), (d) cultural diversity (2000), and (e) migrant communities (1995, 1997).

8. www.coe.int/T/E/Com/Files/Ministerial-Conferences/2005-kiev/texte_adopte.asp (retrieved November 10, 2008).

9. See http://advocacynews.blogspot.com/2005/03/ngos-have-some-influence-on-kiev.html for McDonnell's report on the Kiev process from the point of view of civil society (accessed November 10, 2008).

10. Article 5, Resolution No. 2: "Cultural diversity and media pluralism in times of globalisation." Yet, migrant media are only a tiny sector of the community media realm.

11. Article 17, Action Plan Subtheme 3: "Human rights and regulation of the media and new communication services in the Information Society" (universal community service). Resolution No. 2 talks about "essential public interest" in access to technologies. The CMFE advocated for the inclusion of a reference to community media in this article on "essential public service" but did not succeed. Resolution No. 3 condemns "the attempts to limit public access to communication networks and their content" (Article 7) and reiterates the "commitment to create conditions for equitable access to new communication services by all individuals in their countries in order to promote their participation in public life" (Article 8).

12. In addition, Action Plan Subtheme 2 refers to "any legal or other initiatives which it may consider

necessary to preserve media pluralism" (Article 9) and asks for the revision of Recommendation No. R (94) 1 on media pluralism (Article 10; the Recommendation sets some basic provisions for minority media).

References

Cobb, R. W., & Ross, M. H. (Eds.). (1997). *Cultural strategies of agenda denial*. Lawrence: University Press of Kansas.

Dery, D. (2000). Agenda setting and problem definition. *Policy Studies, 21*(1), 37–47.

Diasio, F., & Milan, S. (2005, December 9). *Community media goes to Europe* [Motion picture]. Interview with Francesco Diasio, Rome. Presented at the Re-Thinking Communications Policy for Civil Society workshop, Stanhope Center for Communications Policy Research, London.

Hadl, G., & Hintz, A. (2009). Framing our media for transnational policy: The world summit on the information society and beyond. In D. Kidd, C. Rodriguez, & L. Stein (Eds.), *Making our media: Mapping global initiatives toward a democratic public sphere*. Cresskill, NJ: Hampton Press.

Hintz, A. (2006). Civil society media at the WSIS: A new actor in global communications governance? In N. Cammaerts & N. Carpentier (Eds.), *Reclaiming the media: Communication rights and democratic media roles* (pp. 243–264). Chicago: Intellect.

Keck, M. E., & Sikkink, K. (1998). *Activists beyond borders: Advocacy networks in international politics*. Ithaca, NY: Cornell University Press.

Kingdon, J. W. (1984). *Agendas, alternatives, and public policies*. Boston: Little, Brown.

Meyer, D. S. (2005). Social movements and public policy: Eggs, chicken, and theory. In D. S. Meyer, V. Jenness, & H. Ingram (Eds.), *Routing the opposition: Social movements, public policy, and democracy* (pp. 1–26). Minneapolis: University of Minnesota Press.

Nelson, B. J., & Lindenfeld, T. (1978). Setting the public agenda: The case of child abuse. In J. V. May & A. B. Wildavsky (Eds.), *The policy cycle* (pp. 17–39). London: Sage.

Stone, D. A. (1988). *Policy, paradox and political reason*. New York: HarperCollins.

Tarrow, S. (1998). *Power in movement: Social movements and contentious politics*. Cambridge, UK: Cambridge University Press.

CHAPTER 27

Closings and Openings

Media Restructuring and the Public Sphere

Bernadette Barker-Plummer

Dorothy Kidd

What I would really love is to cut out the middle-man. I would love for us to have access to a platform to communicate with the public and not be moderated by a television station that is doing their story so they can make a profit, . . . to have even ten minutes just to say what we think is important.

—Andrea Buffa, Code Pink, San Francisco
(personal communication, March 18, 2005)

The general threat to the public sphere associated with increasing privatization, commercialization, and conglomeration of media systems has been well articulated (e.g., Bagdikian, 2002; Kidd, McGee, & Fairbairn, 2005; McChesney, Waterman, & Nichols, 2002; Underwood, 2001).[1] Less attention has been paid, though, to the ramifications of dominant media restructuring for counterpublic spheres—those spaces in society where emergent groups or "critical communities" form and articulate their concerns and identities before (or instead of) engaging with dominant institutions and discourses (Fraser, 1992; Rochon, 1998). How, for example, have media conglomeration and restructuring efforts affected local democratic communication? How are social change groups responding to this restructuring of the local public sphere? Commercial media have always been critical, but problematic, resources for social change groups (Barker-Plummer, 1995, 2002; Ryan, 1991; Ryan, Anastario, & Jeffreys, 2005). Are these structural changes making that relationship even more difficult? Are groups still able to negotiate any access to local news spheres? Or are they counteracting local closures by taking advantage of Web technologies of communication? Is independent, alternative, or community media filling the void of local commercial news for these groups? How exactly is the deregulated local mediascape affecting grassroots communication efforts and with what consequences for democratic communication more generally?

Though the dynamics of dominant and counterpublic spheres are just beginning to be usefully theorized, clearly media systems play a central role in the process of democracy in modern, mediated societies (Couldry, 2003; Fraser, 1992; McLaughlin, 2004; Rochon, 1998). As Garnham (1992, cited in McLaughlin, 2004) has noted, the concept of the public sphere itself is so useful because it makes clear this "indissoluble link between the institutions and practices of mass public communication and the institutions and practices of democratic politics" (p. 157). Changes in media structure, then, are likely to have consequences for democratic processes.

In this chapter, we discuss some of the changes in the Bay Area mediascape and investigate how these changes are affecting local democratic communications. Drawing on a political economic analysis of changes in Bay Area media ownership and format structures, and on interviews with a sample of 26 local groups, we ask how local groups are negotiating the shrinking public sphere.[2] Our groups include women's groups, immigrant rights and environmental groups, housing advocates and bicycle coalitions, media activists and digital rights groups, peace groups, prison reform advocates, youth organizations, and children's advocacy groups. We asked them about their communication goals, strategies, and technologies and about their experiences of recent changes in the local media environment.[3]

Overall, we found an environment in which old communication flows are breaking down, and new ones, though they offer unprecedented freedom in some ways, may also come with new limitations. For example, coverage in local newspapers, radio, and TV is decreasing or becoming more expensive or difficult for all these social change groups. But that closure is accompanied by increasing use of Web communication, which promises the possibility of reaching *around* local news nets to global reach in some cases. However, these net resources are not equally accessible or equally useful to all groups. Nor do they necessarily deliver the audiences, or audience relationships, that social change groups seek. In particular, groups representing the poor or immigrant communities were closed out of English language commercial media *and* unconnected to Web communications. For these low-resourced groups, for whom urban news has often served as an entry point into the democratic communication system, local closures may be especially critical.

For some very successful advocacy groups—such as the Electronic Frontier Foundation (EFF), a locally based, but globally accessed Web "hub" for digital policy and rights information—the Web is a critical resource, providing a site of influence that flows back into the dominant spheres. For other groups (e.g., Global Exchange, Ella Baker Center), the Web is a more mixed resource, connected to conventional media in more complex ways.

Alongside the increase in Web communication, some social change groups are increasing their own independent production (e.g., *POOR News* and *Street Sheet*). Self-published newsletters, papers, and videos are part of the communicative efforts of many groups, as is an increasing use of other independent media outlets (from the *Bay Guardian* to IndyMedia sites). But, as with Web-based knowledge building, the connections between these outlets and more dominant spheres of debate and resource allocation (e.g., city government) were unclear to our respondents.

Generally, then, we see a shifting landscape of social change communication in the Bay Area in which commercial closures are taking place alongside openings created by alternative media and Web technologies, but in which the flows from these alternative sources back to dominant spheres of debate and allocation are less clear than in the case of traditional media.

The Shifting Bay Area Mediascape

The Bay Area is an important location for this kind of study because it offers what may be a best case analysis. Although the area has been subject to many of the same forces of conglomeration and restructuring of the communications industries as other locations, it is also notable for its strong traditions of independent media and vibrant grassroots politics.

Independent media have a long history in the Bay Area. The Pacifica Radio flagship, KPFA-FM, for example, began in Berkeley, and several community and public radio stations, and four Public Broadcasting Service (PBS) television stations, continue to serve the region, as does the San Francisco *Bay Guardian,* one of the oldest alternative weeklies. The Spanish-speaking, African American, and Asian American communities have also developed media organizations, including newspapers, broadcast services, and film festivals, for their communities. More recently, the global Indy Media Center (IMC) has started open-publishing news services, supplemented by the irregular alternative newspaper, *Faultlines.* In addition, the region also hosts several independent film organizations and more than 40 independent film festivals. The Bay Area is also at the forefront in the development of progressive public relations.

However, as in much of the United States, there has been a marked increase in corporate concentration of commercial media ownership in the San Francisco Bay Area. The majority of newspapers, broadcast radio, TV, and cable stations are operated by national chains or transnational conglomerates. Local production of all kinds has been cut, especially extended news coverage and investigative reporting and coverage reflecting the interests of the Spanish-speaking, African American, Asian, and Native American communities. This concentration of ownership has had dire consequences for the newspaper and radio industries especially. Within the past decade, San Francisco has become a one-paper town, with the *San Francisco Chronicle* owned by the New York–based Hearst Company. The Denver-based chain, the Media News Group, controls most of the other dailies and weeklies in the region, including the *Oakland Tribune,* the first major metropolitan paper owned by an African American. The only independently owned alternative weekly is the San Francisco *Bay Guardian,* as the Phoenix-based New Times operates both the so-called alternative *SF Weekly* and *East Bay Express.* As a result of these mergers, hundreds of journalists have been laid off,[4] and there is a marked reduction in editorial diversity and the coverage of local issues. The majority of stories now come from national and international news syndicates (AP) rather than local correspondents.

These patterns continue in the radio industry. Two U.S.-based transnational conglomerates, Clear Channel and Viacom's Infinity, dominate in the Bay area, with 18 radio stations between them and the lion's share of the advertising market, as well as the related billboard industry. Clear Channel also controls the parallel music industry with its ownership of music promotion and concert venues.

The layoffs of staff as well as the automation of content production and broadcasting have led to the elimination of much locally produced news and public affairs. Programs in which there would be opportunities for a wide range of publics to engage in discussion about local issues have been all but removed. A study by the local media advocacy group, the Youth Media Council (2002), demonstrates how little programming is devoted to local social issues of youth, urban poverty, and race, and particularly to the representation of youth in the discussion.

The consequence for local public service programming is particularly marked if we consider factors of race and language. Clear Channel purchased many of the urban radio stations that served African American communities as well as many Spanish language stations (Kidd et al.,

2005). In 2001, NBC purchased Telemundo, the second-largest Spanish-language TV service. Rather than producing better news programming as they had promised, in 2006 they cut news production entirely at the Spanish language KSTS-TV in San Jose, replacing it with a regional newscast from Fort Worth, Texas.

These changes in Bay Area media ownership and formats have clearly already changed the media sphere, expanding the reach of conglomerated media and undermining local, community-oriented media. But how have these changes affected local democracy more generally? How are macrostructural shifts affecting democratic communications? We addressed these questions to Bay Area social change groups.

Negotiating Access in the Wake of Media Restructuring

Just take a look at the sections of the paper. . . . I think that there needs to be an Environmental section. I think there needs to be a Social Justice section of the papers. I think that we really need to look at what we've come to accept as news. I just don't think that sports is an important enough thing to merit having a section and, you know, environmental destruction is not.

—Rainforest Action Network (personal communication, November 19, 2004)

When Gavin Newsom gets on a bike, they'll cover that.

—SF Bike Coalition (personal communication, November 18, 2004)

Community groups in the Bay Area are experiencing media restructuring as a closure of local media space. For low-resourced or non-English-speaking groups especially—groups whose visibility has always been tokenistic—the situation has gotten much worse and reporters "never come around" anymore (Mujeres Unidas). More professionalized groups are still able to get their voices into the public sphere through local and national news media, but they are having to dedicate more resources and staff to compete for that shrinking space, and they encounter constraints regarding some issues (such as media deregulation) that news media routinely ignore.

Children Now is an example of a relatively well-resourced group, and it is one of the most successful Bay Area groups at accessing news media. It does so through continuous production of information subsidies (studies, surveys, policy analyses, quote pages) and by targeting that information quite narrowly to specific reporters. Being an advocate for children's issues also help, of course. Even the most cynical journalist hesitates to present children as "special interests." Children Now's media strategies are well developed because media are key targets for its work. Its mission involves "reaching decision makers" with information about children's issues, and its organizational activities are knowledge production and communication based. It also has as staff ex-journalists and writers. It is not surprising then, that the group does well in interaction with news media.

There are critical limits, however, even to Children Now's access. Although the group's studies and publications on children's education and health issues are usually well received, its critiques of deregulation in media and the consequences for children's TV are ignored. Media reform is a key children's issue for the group, but, until recently, it seldom made it through the news filter.

Besides these issue limits, the cost of media access in organizational resources and time is very high. Global Exchange's spokesperson highlighted this when he noted that 90% of the media coverage of the group and its issues is the direct result of the group's proactive strategies. Other groups—Ella Baker Center, Latino Issues Forum and Justice Now, for example—reinforced this sense of media visibility as a resource that needs to be continually recreated. In fact, Code Pink's media strategist described building visibility as an exhausting and sometimes dispiriting process in which even well-organized groups working on critical issues have to "twist themselves into pretzels" to make it happen. As she notes in our opening quote, many social movement groups dream of the possibility of simply talking to the public without having to jump through the hoops—material and symbolic—created by commercial media.

Sometimes a social change group can become recognized as the "expert" in a particular area, and journalists will come to the group at least on that issue. Global Exchange, for example, for whom fair trade and international labor equity are core goals, has become known to media as the expert on Nike and sweatshop issues, and it receives calls and questions from journalists about Nike without having to proactively seek them out. Ella Baker Center is similarly recognized as a local expert on youth incarceration and prison issues. For some exceptionally successful advocacy groups such as EFF, this expertise covers a whole policy area such as the Internet and digital policy. According to an EFF spokesperson, for example, EFF gets *1.6 million* hits to its Web site a week, and the group seldom pitches reporters anymore but simply responds to questions.

For lower-resourced groups, and groups representing communities of color, immigrants, or poor people, commercial media closures are being experienced more dramatically. These groups said they were much less likely to be able to gain mainstream news media access. Partly, this is a result of their lack of resources to produce the knowledge packages that journalists respond to, and partly, it is the outcome of a passive media strategy in which they wait for media to come to them. But without the authority of dominant sources or the expertise of the well-resourced groups, these groups—despite

newsworthy concerns—are not able to attract media to them except in crisis situations or in tokenistic ways.

Mujeres Unidas and Day Laborers, for example, are groups that represent immigrant Latino/a communities. Their representatives told us that they have little or no contact with English-language media. Several other respondents also talked about the long history of commercial media exclusion and racism in treating minority communities. The Ella Baker Center's spokesperson, for example, explained that one of the group's current challenges is to work in the context of "an audience which has a bias because of 20 or 30 years of racist coverage and racist storytelling."

Groups advocating for housing (e.g., Coalition on Homelessness and the SF Tenants Union) face an additional, political hurdle. By advocating for affordable housing and policy solutions to homelessness, they often find themselves on the other side of local business interests—including that of the local newspaper. The Coalition on Homelessness's representative, for example, talked about the difficulty of sustaining debate on affordable housing issues when the media are underwritten each week by real estate advertising.

This sense of media as part of the establishment was reinforced by a spokesperson for the SF Bike Coalition, who noted how the local press simplifies its issues and presents bicyclists as naive, while carrying large amounts of auto advertising. Rainforest Action Network experiences the mainstream media as lacking any serious interest or space for social justice issues. As the group's spokesperson notes in our section header quote, there is always a sports section in news but no environmental section.

For all our respondent groups, accessing local news is problematic. Even the most successful groups have found that sustaining media access is increasing in cost as commercial media shrink their local news space due to staff layoffs and reformats from news to entertainment. For poorer groups, the commercial news sphere seems to have already closed.

The Web: Another Door Opens?

> We know that we are not going to able to get our message out perfectly through any kind of radio, TV or press interview, . . . and so the idea is really to get the organization's name out in earned media and that will drive people to the website where can say exactly what we want to say, however we want to say it, with a virtually unlimited amount of space.
>
> —Global Exchange (personal communication, March 21, 2005)

There has been a marked increase in the social movement groups' sophistication in, and use of, Internet and Web communication technologies. From the most Web-savvy groups, such as EFF, Code Pink, and Global Exchange, that routinely use the net for international communication and discussion, to local immigrant groups, the Web has changed the ways in which social movement groups work. Global Exchange, for example, according to its spokesperson, attributes a rapid increase in its visibility of the group and issues to their net presence. Its own site has increased its hits by 10-fold (90,000 to a million) in a few years as sweatshop issues have also risen to public attention. Other groups, which came to Web communications later—such as the Ella Baker Center and Latino Issues Forum—have now also revolutionized their organizing and fund-raising through e-mail.

Web communication offers social change groups the chance to reach more people more efficiently and economically and to control their communications content. As Global Exchange's spokesperson explained, Web sites designed by movement members present issues in the way that movements would like to communicate them rather than filtered through news media routines and logics. The general lack of restrictions on Web space also allows groups to go into much more depth on their issues than they could in media reports, encouraging some groups to see their Web presence as the real public message about them and their appearances in mainstream (or earned) media as simply the "driver" of audiences to the Web site.

Web technology has also been used by groups to organize events quickly (by fax blasts and e-mail alerts), to raise money, and to generate large volumes of mail to pivotal policymakers at appropriate moments. The SF Bike Coalition, for example, was a fan of fax blast, which allows the easy generation of mass mailings—with each letter coming from an individual—to key decision makers.

Forest Ethics, an environmental group focused on changing corporate practices, uses just the *threat* of net organizing power in its work with corporations. Its success in generating buzz and discussion about particular companies, in traditional media and net spaces, often persuades companies to make a deal in advance of the publicity. After threatening Staples with concurrent protests at 100 of its stores around the country, for example, Forest Ethics found itself in negotiations with top administrators there about recycled paper.

The net also allows groups to set up independent knowledge bases. Educational and service-based groups such as Asian Pacific Islander Wellness Center (APIWC), use their Web sites as knowledge portals to specialized research and information, as APIWC does for HIV positive Asian/Pacific Islanders, for example. Other groups use net communications to organize petitions and phone banks and to raise money directly. Code Pink, for example, used an e-mail alert in 2004 to raise $100,000 for supplies for refugees from Fallujah.

In Bay Area immigrant communities, groups are also increasing their use of Internet communication, though not necessarily to communicate with their constituents, who do not always have the technology, but to stay connected to allies and to learn about policy issues.[5]

Overall, groups reported an increasing use of Internet resources—and the accompanying death of transition technologies such as paper fax machines—in all aspects of their work. They used the Internet for recruiting; for communicating with members, publics, policy makers, politicians, and corporations; and for fund-raising, event organizing, and tactical interventions. Perhaps, the biggest benefit of Web technologies for movement groups, though, has been the ability to build their own Web sites and communicate freely through them about their issues. Although the audiences for these sites are uncertain, for anyone seeking it, a new interconnected knowledge base on a wide range of social issues, built by social change organizations, is emerging on the Web.

Alternative Routes: Ethnic, Public, and Independent Media Roles

> It's two totally different worlds. Whereas the Spanish speaking press covers all the same things that the English speaking press covers and then sometimes does community based stuff, the English speaking press doesn't try and come into the Latino community.
>
> —Mujeres Unidas y Activas, San Francisco (personal communication, March 4, 2005)

There is also a growing space in new media spheres for independent, autonomous, and ethnic media. Ethnic media are increasingly important to non-English-speaking groups. Faced with exclusion from the dominant media, and supported by cheaper and more accessible technologies

of desktop publishing and Internet distribution, groups are also creating their own communications and subcontracting with independent producers.

The Coalition on Homelessness, for example, produced the *Street Sheet* in direct response to a lack of serious coverage in the local commercial media. POOR News Network and Third World Majority not only produce their own stories, they also include media production and media literacy training for members. The Ella Baker Center also produces documentaries. Most recently, the group produced and distributed a 30-minute documentary about the California Youth Authority that was picked up by local media. APIWC also produces informational videos and films and distributes them to clients and community groups. Several groups—for example, Media Alliance and Film Arts Foundation—have as one of their core activities the support and promotion of alternative media production.

More established alternative media are also playing a central role in the Bay Area counterpublic spheres. For example, *The Bay Guardian*, San Francisco's independently owned alternative weekly, was mentioned many times by respondents as a sympathetic and accurate outlet for social movement communication, much more so than the city's mainstream daily, the *San Francisco Chronicle*. The San Francisco Tenants Union, for example, finds the *Guardian* more sympathetic, while the spokesperson for the Coalition on Homelessness, which is shut out of the mainstream media debate, noted that the *Guardian* respects the group as the local expert on issues of homelessness and housing. Spokespersons for Global Exchange and Latino Issues Forum also noted that the *Guardian* is a useful ally in local policy debates.

National Public Radio (NPR) and Pacifica Radio—a public and an independent radio station—are also seen as generally having more space for social change communication. However, a decision by NPR not to cover "routine" protests concerned the spokesperson for Day Laborers; for this group, street protests are one of the few ways that its members can be heard.

For some, though, *alternative media* still tends to mean Anglo media. As the Latino Issues Forum spokesperson noted, "Most of what is called 'alternative' still does not deal with ethnic communities." Spokespersons for other Latino groups reported that they are more likely to read and try to access the commercial Spanish-language press than alternative media in English. They were also more likely to have their issues and communities covered by national or international Spanish-language networks—for example Univision—than the local English-language press. Although they make some important distinctions between channels—the Latino Issues Forum spokesperson, for example, pointed out that commercial Spanish channels can also be problematic—the Latino groups generally orient themselves toward Spanish-language media.[6] As a Mujeres Unidas spokesperson noted, the Spanish press relate more to the lives of Latino communities and pay attention to what is going on in these communities. The Day Laborers representative noted the limits of English language media for all immigrant communities, as ethnic media, especially Spanish, Chinese and Filipino, know their communities. The APIWC spokesperson, in turn, noted the importance of coverage by the Japanese and Chinese-language (Mandarin) publications.

Overall, movement groups that cannot easily access mainstream media are turning to alternative and ethnic media outlets.

Closures and Openings

> The fight for media justice is central to all struggles for all organizers who are working in communities and confronting crises today.
>
> —Third World Majority,
> San Francisco (personal
> communication,
> March 1, 2005)

Commercial media seem to be functioning even less democratically in the wake of deregulation and downsizing. But this closure is affecting some groups more than others. The best-resourced and more professionalized groups are continuing to interact successfully with mainstream news media, though it is costing them more to do so. Other poorer, grassroots groups find the commercial sphere closed or closing to their voices and are turning more to native language or ethnic media sources. Similarly, it is the most-resourced groups—in terms of education, knowledge, media literacies, and material resources—that are best positioned to take advantage of the possibilities of net communications. For the most tech savvy and resourced groups, in fact, the Web may offer a new form of influence.

Alongside an increase in Web use, social change groups are also increasing their self-publishing efforts and connecting with existing alternative media. This increase in self-publishing and in Web use has been accompanied in many cases, though, by a sense of unease about whether these communications reach the right *audiences.* In particular, groups are concerned about how their social change communications will make it into dominant spheres of decision making and resource allocation—in short, how their messages will get to leaders and publics outside the counterpublic spheres. In this regard, our respondents share a question of central importance with many observers of contemporary communications systems and social change—how will new sites of communication, such as social change Web sites, blogs, online art, or video upload sites, connect to existing democratic communication flows? This is a critical question shared by many in contemporary media studies (Kidd & Barker-Plummer, 2001; Van de Donk, Loader, Nixon, & Rucht, 2004) and one that we have only begun to investigate in this project. We have traced the communication efforts of these groups. The *reception* of social change communications remains a critically important question (Downing, 2003).

The Bay Area is one particular location, with its own dynamics, of course, and this sample of groups, though we tried to have as wide a range of groups as possible, cannot stand in for all groups. However, these dynamics seem to us to present some important questions for the future of democratic communications: For example, how will the concerns of local, low-resourced, grassroots, and especially immigrant, communities, which used to be covered by local news but are now closed out, be heard at all in the new conglomerated public sphere? How will Web technologies and Web spheres that allow so many more groups to *speak* also result in these voices being *heard* by representatives and policymakers? And what can we learn from successful Web mobilizers (such as EFF) about opening up and sustaining new flows of communication and influence *from* the counter-sphere to the dominant, allocative public sphere? These are questions that go beyond the Bay Area media spheres to questions about the future role of local, democratic communication in larger processes of democracy.

Latino Issues Forum, League of Women Voters, Media Alliance, Mujeres Unidas y Activas, National Alliance for Media Arts and Culture (NAMAC), POOR News, Prison Radio, Prostitutes Education Network, Rainforest Action Network, SF Bike Coalition, SF Tenants Union, Third World Majority, and Youth Speaks. They range from organizations with no paid staff to groups with budgets more than $1 million and up to 40 full- and part-time staff. Most organizational funding is a mixture of foundation support, private donations, and membership fees.

4. According to the Pew Center for Excellence in Journalism, newspapers had 2,200 fewer full-time employees in 2004 than in 1990.

5. The Pew Internet and American Life Project reported in March 2007 that Latinos constitute 14% of the U.S. adult population and that about half of this growing group (56%) goes online. By comparison, 71% of non-Hispanic whites and 60% of non-Hispanic blacks use the Internet.

6. This finding is in line with a recent report that a quarter of Bay Area residents rely on Spanish-language media.

Notes

1. Some of these issues include the political and economic consequences of small numbers of corporate owners of media; the loss of genuinely local coverage; problems with diversity in ownership, staffing, and content; and the political consequences of integration between media and nonmedia companies.

2. We thank the University of San Francisco McCarthy Center for the Public Interest and the Common Good for their support of this project and the USF students who were our research partners in this endeavor, including Francisco McGee, Kathleen Emma, Sam Sharkey, Stephanie Bolton, Kendra Kennedy, Maria Savage, Aliza Parpia, Michelle Sanchez, and Kat Amano.

3. The groups interviewed were Asian Pacific Islanders Wellness Center, Berkeley Liberation Radio, Coalition on Homelessness, Children Now, Code Pink, Day Laborers, Electronic Frontier Foundation, Ella Baker Center, Film Arts Foundation, Forest Ethics, Global Exchange, Death Penalty Focus, Justice Now,

References

Bagdikian, B. (2002). *The media monopoly* (6th ed.). Boston: Beacon Press.

Barker-Plummer, B. (1995). News as a political resource: Media strategies and political identity in the US women's movement. *Critical Studies in Mass Communication, 12*(3), 306–324.

Barker-Plummer, B. (2002). Producing public voice: Resource mobilization and media access in the National Organization for Women. *Journalism and Mass Communication Quarterly, 79*(1), 188–205.

Couldry, N. (2003). Beyond the hall of mirrors? Some theoretical reflections on the global contestation of media power. In N. Couldry & J. Curran (Eds.), *Contesting media power: Alternative media in a networked world* (pp. 39–54). Oxford, UK: Rowman & Littlefield.

Downing, J. (2003). Audiences and readers of alternative media: The absent lure of the virtually unknown. *Media, Culture & Society, 25*(5), 625–645.

Fraser, N. (1992). Rethinking the public sphere: A contribution to the critique of actually existing democracy. In C. Calhoun (Ed.), *Habermas and the public sphere* (pp. 109–132). Cambridge: MIT Press.

Kidd, D., & Barker-Plummer, B. (Eds.). (2001, Fall). Social justice movements and the Internet [Special issue]. *Peace Review, 13*(3).

Kidd, D., McGee, F., & Fairbairn, D. (2005). Clear Channel: The poster child for everything that's wrong with consolidation. In D. Skinner, M. Gasher, & J. Compton (Eds.), *Converging media, diverging politics: A political economy of media in the United States and Canada* (pp. 77–100). Lanham, MD: Lexington Books.

McChesney, R., Waterman, R., & Nichols, J. (2002). *Our media, not theirs: The democratic struggle against corporate media.* New York: Seven Stories Press.

McLaughlin, L. (2004). Feminism and the political economy of transnational public space. In N. Crossley & J. Roberts (Eds.), *After Habermas: New perspectives on the public sphere* (pp. 156–175). Oxford: Blackwell.

Rochon, T. (1998). *Culture moves: Ideas, activism and changing values.* Princeton, NJ: Princeton University Press.

Ryan, C. (1991). *Prime-time activism: Media strategies for grassroots organizing.* Boston: South End Press.

Ryan, C., Anastario, M., & Jeffreys, K. (2005). Start small, build big: Negotiating opportunities in media markets. *Mobilization: An International Journal, 10*(1), 111–128.

Underwood, D. (2001). Reporting and the push for market-oriented journalism: Media organizations as businesses. In W. L. Bennett & R. Entman (Eds.), *Mediated politics: Communication in the future of democracy* (pp. 99–116). New York: Oxford University Press.

Van de Donk, W., Loader, B., Nixon, P., & Rucht, D. (2004). *Cyberprotest: New media, citizens and social movements.* London: Routledge.

Youth Media Council. (2002). *Is KMEL the people's station: A community assessment of 106.1 KMEL.* Retrieved February 1, 2008, from the Youth Media Council Web site: www.youthmediacouncil.org

CHAPTER 28

The Rise of the Intranet Era

Sascha D. Meinrath

Victor W. Pickard

No starter pistol announces the beginning of a new technological era. There are no cannon blasts or tower bells ringing forth the end of the old and dawn of the new. And yet, if the previous 10 years were "The Internet Decade," then the next decade may be dubbed the "Age of the *Intranet.*" Intranets are digital communication networks linking devices such as computers or handheld mobile phones and PDAs to each other and to network-based applications and services, often within a specific geographical location. Much as the global Internet has interconnected computer networks, Intranets provide local connectivity, services, and applications to their users. Intranets are often home or office networks used to interconnect computers. In this chapter, we explore the notion of a "community Intranet"—an expanded network of networks spanning a neighborhood, municipality, or geographic region. By amplifying community interconnectedness, Intranets promise to enable new forms of political and democratic engagement that expand on present

day networks and models of cooperation. Intranets are often decentralized and ad hoc, with no one entity owning the entire infrastructure or controlling the expansion of or access to the infrastructure. These arrangements create new challenges for surveillance, command, and control as well as new opportunities for participatory media and information dissemination.

Intranet systems supplant old notions of networking geographic places by allowing people to be both networked and an integral part of the infrastructure—the creation of "device-as-infrastructure networks." These peer-to-peer communications systems provide unprecedented opportunities, as well as serious concerns, for the future of community organizing, political activism, media production, and communication research. Even as evidence accumulates demonstrating how these technologies encourage civic engagement, their social trajectory is far from determined, and the possibility for a more dystopian outcome cannot be dismissed (Brock, 2003; Castells, 2001). While drawing from real-world

---

Author's Note: A version of this chapter is available at www.newamerica.net/publications/policy/rise_intranet_era.

case studies, including community and municipal wireless networks, indymedia, the iPhone, geolocational applications and services, and next-generation wireless devices, this chapter documents the emergence of Intranet technologies, discusses their implications for research (cf. Meinrath & claffy, 2007), and explores policy implications at this critical juncture in telecommunications development and policy making.

The Intranet Potential

Intranet-enabled communications have the potential to accelerate fundamental changes begun in the 1980s with the advent of widespread public use of pagers and cell phones. Like these cellular systems, Intranets are often fully functioning communications networks, connecting participants to one another and to locally run services and applications within homes and offices at the local, state, regional, and even national levels. Similar to businesses connecting computers to share Internet connectivity, printer and file server access via a Local Area Network (LAN), community Intranets connect devices to form a communitywide LAN. Intranet technologies create new possibilities for how information is produced, disseminated, and archived by creating a peer-to-peer infrastructure that parallels the rise of peer-to-peer technologies, services, and applications. Sharing media, educational content, and public services via local telecommunications systems, Intranets provide Web resources for their respective communities, ranging from the mundane, such as e-mail, Web hosting, and file sharing, to the more innovative, such as streaming microbroadcasting, video chat rooms, temporary device-hosted LANs, and audio and video telephony. While some Intranets are geographically bounded, others are regional or even global in nature. Often, Intranets rely on darknets and friend-to-friend networking clients (i.e., peer-to-peer file-sharing networks predicated on social networking and trust)—one example embraced by the open source community is Nullsoft's

WASTE, a decentralized file sharing and instant messaging (IM) program—but increasingly they are focused on providing useful services, applications, and media to local communities (Biddle, England, Peinado, & Willman, 2002).

Using local Intranets, communities can set up forums for political debate, artistic display, and educational fare. Streaming video and audio from local events—from town council and PTA meetings to annual music festivals—have created entirely new media services and information-sharing options for residents. Intranets enhance local government, education, and civic organizations services, allowing services such as online voter registration and real-time directions to polling stations, bill payment and live tax advice, access to school homework and teacher lesson plans, public service announcements, online newspapers and radio, and instant Web casting of emergency alerts.

Public safety and social service groups, local schools, churches, and municipalities are already beginning to embrace the potentials of these technologies; recent shifts in municipal wireless business models have just begun to tap Intranets' potentials. And, as municipal networking business models continue to evolve, Intranet services and applications will increase in importance, becoming meaningful differentiators among different implementation options.

Schools can set up a local wireless network and broadcast a student-produced news program or a theatrical play; a housing project can establish an online media forum to feature local artists, upcoming events, job listings, or educational opportunities; social workers out in the field and municipal workers can dynamically update their caseload files and task lists as they travel around town; religious organizations can Web cast services to residents whose health prevents them from attending; electrical, water, gas, and parking meters can be remotely read; and automated congestion pricing of vehicles and optimal traffic light configurations can be ascertained in real time.

Perhaps one of the most exciting prospects of Intranet-enabled communications is an enhanced potential for community journalism. As national media outlets increasingly omit local news, Intranets may facilitate a municipal service that provides a daily digital community news bulletin, replete with local beat reporting and investigative news. Community news, most likely delivered via a municipal or community wireless network offering ubiquitous high-speed broadband, could be treated as a public utility, provided each morning in the form of an informational service and supported by local tax revenues. As local broadcast and print news continue to be eviscerated by national market pressures, the potential for Intranets to provide local journalism will be increasingly valuable.

Many of the projects already using Intranet technologies aim to change the cultural economy of the Internet by creating resources for people to democratize media distribution and information dissemination, often via existing infrastructures and off-the-shelf networking hardware. Unlike the Internet, which disproportionately favors capitalized publishers, such as the NYTimes.com and CNN.com, Intranets reliance on local networks allow low capital users to host Web sites, e-mail lists and accounts, stream audio and video programs, and create dynamic media for local consumption—creating an integrated system that provides affordable access to everyone from independent musicians and journalists to teachers and civic officials (Meinrath, 2004–2005).

The remainder of this chapter provides a glimpse of community Intranets' implications for reconceptualizing the theory and study of emergent communications technologies, with the goal of not just providing a thought piece of what might be but also showing how these technologies are already being used and studied.

Community Intranet Case Studies

Champaign-Urbana Wireless Network

An exemplar of Intranet technology is the Champaign-Urbana Wireless Network (CUWiN; see http://cuwin.net), launched by a coalition of wireless developers in 2000 with a mission to "connect more people to Internet and broadband services; develop open-source hardware and software for use by wireless projects worldwide; and, build and support community-owned, not-for-profit broadband networks in cities and towns around the globe" (http://cuwin.net). Although the CUWiN Foundation is a nonprofit organization headquartered in the small town of Urbana, Illinois, it has received considerable national and international attention during its years of successful open-source development. Through the ongoing support of the Acorn Active Media Foundation (see acornactivemedia.com), CUWiN has integrated the wireless network with a host of different services.

In spring 2000, a group of software programmers, radio techies, system administrators, and community activists began discussing ways to set up a community-operated wireless network using widely available, off-the-shelf hardware. After 2 years of intensive work, CUWiN's software development allowed the first multi-hop, bandwidth sharing, wireless cloud to become operational, creating shared access to the Internet from multiple locations. This milestone marked the first time a single Internet connection (in this case, donated by the Urbana-Champaign Independent Media Center Foundation; see ucimc.org) was used from houses located a half kilometer away from one another, with traffic routed *through* an intermediary wireless node. This technology later became known as "mesh" wireless networking (Figure 28.1).

CUWiN went on to deploy additional wireless routers (often called "nodes") in the community and develop the system software to deal with real-world conditions. This initial deployment brought CUWiN's first major press coverage and created opportunities for over two dozen new organizations to partner with the project. Realizing that scaling up the system would require major upgrades, CUWiN received an exploratory grant in 2003 from the Threshold Foundation to buy much-needed additional equipment as a proof-of-concept for deployment in impoverished communities. Henceforth, CUWiN has been building a

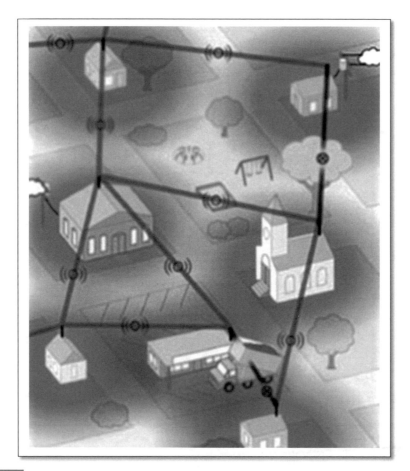

Figure 28.1 Illustration of a Mesh Network

new generation of hardware chosen for its durability, price, and suitability for this application. The initial exploratory grant allowed CUWiN to double the number of nodes in the test bed network to try out software improvements under in vivo conditions. Continuing collaborations with the Acorn Active Media Foundation have led to the development of lower-cost equipment and the implementation of free public Internet access in areas throughout downtown Urbana.

In 2004, CUWiN received a $200,000 grant from the Information Program of the Open Society Institute to develop networking software as a model case for transfer to other communities. That same year the Center for Neighborhood Technology began using CUWiN's software in the economically disadvantaged, minority Chicago suburb, North Lawndale, to help bridge their digital divide by

bringing broadband connectivity to many residents for the first time. Over 50 different communities are considering using CUWiN's software worldwide, and key facets of CUWiN's technology have been integrated into many open-source wireless technologies. As these open-source technologies have continued to stabilize, the number of organizations and communities looking to use them for Internet service and Intranet applications in their neighborhoods has increased dramatically (Figure 28.2).

Today, the CUWiN foundation project has more than 200 members and 100 developers and has deployed systems in multiple locations around Illinois, across the United States, and internationally. In CUWiN's local community, there is a long waiting list to join the network, and the City of Urbana has allocated funding to build additional nodes and added them to

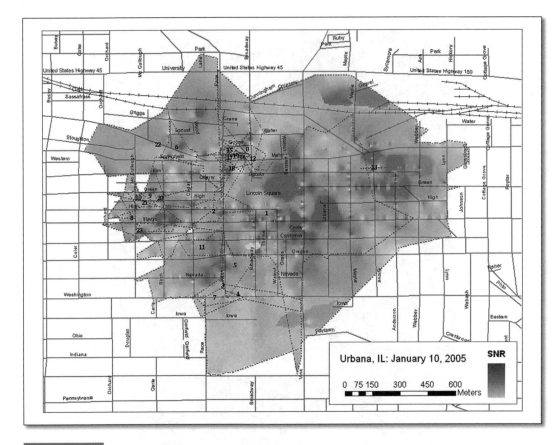

Figure 28.2 CUWiN Coverage Map

extend the CUWiN network in the downtown region. This may represent the first time that a municipality has actively deployed an open-source, open-architecture wireless solution, thus helping to further advance these technologies. As isolated wireless "clouds" grow within the City of Urbana, distinct areas will merge, creating a single transneighborhood, interconnected wireless community. This process of conglomerization of distinct wireless clouds creates a community Intranet capable of providing multimedia services to network users, as described in more detail in the next section. CUWiN has also formed numerous partnerships with university research laboratories to develop next-generation wireless technologies and is now working with a diverse array of groups,

from the Council for Scientific and Industrial Research in South Africa to the University of Illinois at Urbana-Champaign (UIUC) in its own backyard.

Chambana.net

Community Intranets are as diverse as the constituencies they serve. In Urbana-Champaign, Illinois, the Chambana.net project is a proving ground for next-generation Intranet services and applications. Chambana.net is built and maintained by the Acorn Active Media Foundation and creates a community LAN that interconnects the local-mesh wireless network with multimedia resources located at the Urbana-Champaign Independent Media Center (UCIMC). Chambana.net hosts scores of Web sites for local organizations as well as Web portal capabilities and hundreds of e-mail lists; it serves tens of thousands of users, integrates an Internet Relay Chat (IRC) server and file storage capabilities, streams audio and video, provides telephony capabilities, and is a platform for darknet participants and local information technology (IT) developers. By directly integrating the local low-power FM radio station, WRFU 104.5 FM (Radio Free Urbana), the project allows such innovations as the streaming of live shows from the performance venue, which are also simulcast through the radio station and the Internet. By harnessing the Intranet capabilities of this system, this community Intranet allows local and global participants to communicate via the chat servers with audience members, sound engineers, and so on. The project allows Intranet participants to access video files they have been editing at the UCIMC's production center from their laptop computer at a local cafe. Soon, social networking and geolocation-multimedia Web portal functionality will allow media producers to upload their work to local wireless hotspots and comment on each other's work (Figure 28.3).

The power of Intranets lies in their potential for supporting new forms of communication. As the functionality of mobile devices increases, Intranet usage will expand as well. Together, CUWiN and the Chambana.net project provide a natural laboratory for Intranet services and applications. By integrating media production and information dissemination, they support a return to localism—the potential to blend participatory media production (cf. Howley, 2005) with the reach of regional networking. Intranets represent a clear shift away from the broadcast model enabling a two-way flow of information, community and shared ownership of communications infrastructure, and more services and applications than the existing telecommunications systems (De Bernabé, 2004). In Urbana, the Independent Media Center, CUWiN,

Chambana.net, Acorn Active Media Foundation, UCIMC, WRFU 104.5 FM (see wrfu.net), and a host of allied organizations are using these new technologies to advance democratic communications.

Community Informatics

In response to these emergent digital communications, vibrant new strands of communications theory have begun to coalesce, while traditional barriers between participatory action, policy, and regulatory debate and technological innovation are breaking down. Feedback loops among developers, implementers, policy reformers, and community organizers are placing pressure on decision makers in Washington, D.C., to substantially reform our telecommunications policies to better match on-the-ground realities. Telecommunications reforms in 2008 are set to extend Intranet capabilities from the margins of "techno geekery" into the mainstream.

Current battles over access to the television white spaces (unused frequencies between existing broadcast channels; see Meinrath & Calabrese, 2007) have pitted public interest groups (who want to foster more democratic communications) and hi-tech firms (who want to sell next-generation wireless equipment) against the National Association of Broadcasters and its allies (who want to protect their current business models and prevent competition). The 700 MHz spectrum auction that was concluded in March 2008 created, for the first time, an "open platform" band that requires the license holder (in this case, Verizon) to open its network to all compatible devices. With Google's Android phone and the continuing work of the Open Handset Alliance (a coalition of over 30 corporations working on next-generation open-cellular hardware), community Intranets are poised to become an everyday part of normal life. And with the increasing functionality of next-generation handheld

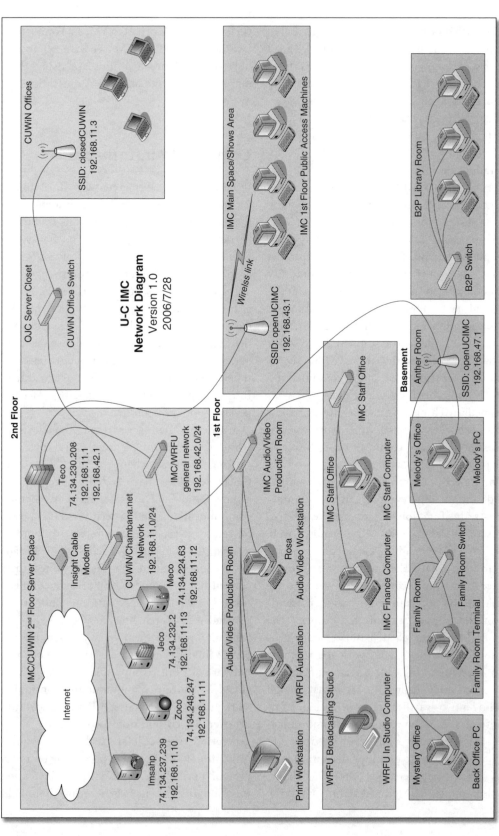

Figure 28.3 The Chambana.net Infrastructure and Community Intranet

computers, device-as-infrastructure networking is rapidly becoming an everyday reality.

Meanwhile, contemporary researchers are increasingly drawing from current telecommunications and regulatory deliberations, familiarizing themselves with new and emergent technologies, and immersing themselves in the communities they study. A promising development in communications theory since the late 1990s is the emergence of the field of community informatics (CI), which is particularly well suited to address issues raised by Intranet technologies and digital media production practices. Howard Rheingold underscores the importance of formulating a new field as a potential starting point for new communications theories that is "based on actual findings by people who have tried to use online media in service of community, then reported on their results." He notes that "in the absence of such systematic observation and reporting by serious practitioners, public discussion will continue to oscillate between ideological extremes, in a never-ending battle of anecdotal evidence and theoretical rhetoric" (quoted in Keeble & Loader, 2002, p. xx). Emphasizing the cross-disciplinary and emergent aspects of CI, Keeble and Loader define CI as a multidisciplinary field for the investigation and development of the social and cultural factors shaping the development and diffusion of new ICTs and its effects upon community development, regeneration and sustainability. It thereby combines an interest in the potentially transforming qualities of new media with an analysis of the importance of community social relations for human interaction. (Keeble & Loader, p. 3)

CI draws from a wide range of source material and expertise based on the understanding that new and emergent technologies often fall outside traditional disciplinary boundaries. Therefore, expertise concerning their use, impacts, and diffusion are found through a participatory action research methodology (Meinrath, 2004). Similarly, since CI is, first and foremost, involved in the systematic study of contemporary technologies and social phenomena, it relies on the work of "community activists, Web masters and Internet enthusiasts, policy-makers, digital artists, science-fiction writers, media commentators, [and] a wide variety of academics, including sociologists, computer scientists, communications theorists, information systems analysts, political scientists, psychologists, and many more" (Keeble & Loader, 2002, p. 3). Beyond media research, these new technologies also have a profound impact on the formation and nature of communities. One of the most overlooked facets for determining whether technological innovation is empowering to its users is whether it is open and how that openness is operationalized.

Open Versus Closed Technologies and Network Architectures

At its heart, one of the most significant barriers to the potential of Intranet comes down to the differences between *closed* and *open* technologies. These notions often bring to mind issues related to open-source and proprietary software (e.g., Linux versus Windows), but the distinction is more encompassing. Stolterman (2002) defines the important attributes thus:

A closed technology is one that does not allow the user to change anything after it has been designed and manufactured. The structure, functionality and appearance of the artifact are permanent. . . . The technology is a relatively stable variable in social settings. . . . An open technology allows the user to continue changing the technology's specific characteristics, and to adjust, and or change its functionality. When it comes to an open technology, changes in functionality pose a question not only of change in the way the existing functionality is used or understood but also of a real change in the artifact's internal manifestation. (p. 45)

The Internet, generally speaking, was conceived as and remains an open and designable technology. One can "add, embed, contain or surround the artifact with other technology in a way that radically changes it" (Stolterman, 2002, p. 45). This aspect has contributed to the successes of the so-called Web 2.0 applications. Unfortunately, this openness is also under attack, as moves by Comcast to block Bittorrent communications, the blocking of prochoice text messaging by Verizon, and the editing of a live Pearl Jam concert by AT&T all exemplify. Unfortunately, the "gentlemen's agreements" that have been sold as "solutions" (assurances that these corporations will not engage in these practices again) do nothing to prevent these sorts of anticompetitive, antifree speech, and antidemocratic actions from being repeated at a later date. Thus, a growing list of public interest organizations have grown increasingly worried that by abdicating their responsibility to prevent this sort of corporate malfeasance, the Federal Communications Commission (FCC) and other regulatory agencies are all but guaranteeing that these sorts of behaviors will continue.

In fact, without the advent of the landmark Carterphone decision to allow interconnection of "foreign attachments" to the AT&T telephone network, wireline communications may well have taken a different turn—even preventing the emergence of the Internet in its present form. Prior to Carterphone, the FCC tariff governing interconnecting devices stated, "No equipment, apparatus, circuit or device not furnished by the telephone company shall be attached to or connected with the facilities furnished by the telephone company, whether physically, by induction or otherwise" (FCC, 1968). The growth and successes of the Internet are predicated on an open architecture (Cooper, 2004; Kahin & Keller, 1997) that facilitates the interconnection of a variety of different devices and technologies (Benkler, 2006; Louis, 2000; Meinrath, 2005). While AT&T may have wanted end-to-end control over every part of their network, the FCC wisely concluded that the best interest of the general public would be achieved by ensuring that innovation could not be stifled

by AT&T and that end users could decide for themselves which devices and technologies they wanted to attach to the telephone network.

In fact, the Internet stands as a remarkable reminder of the potential power (and problems) of network effects (Hiller & Cohen, 2002; Nuechterlein & Weiser, 2007) and the promise that this new "networked information economy" (Benkler, 2003) makes possible. As Benkler sums up,

> For over 150 years, new communications technologies have tended to concentrate and commercialize the production and exchange of information, while extending the geographic and social reach of information distribution networks. . . . The Internet presents the possibility of a radical reversal of this long trend. It is the first modern communications medium that expands its reach by decentralizing the distribution function. Much of the physical capital that embeds the intelligence in the network is diffused and owned by end users. (p. 1249)

While thus far true for much of the wireline communications infrastructure, this analysis breaks down within the wireless realm (Meinrath & Pickard, 2008). Wireless communications are a particularly interesting case study, since the transport medium—the public airwaves—is not only publicly owned but also, for data communications in particular, often unlicensed (Meinrath et al., 2005). Yet, the wireless systems that an increasing number of Internet participants use to connect to the Internet remain closed technologies (Nuechterlein & Weiser, 2007).

The 2007 deal inked by Apple and AT&T is a classic example of the problems with this approach. Apple's iPhone was only available to be used on AT&T's network, even though it could be used on any cellular network. Likewise, AT&T only allows certain services and applications to run on the iPhone, even though the iPhone could run many additional programs that would be useful for end users. Innovative iPhone owners and entrepreneurs have already found ways to unlock the device, and consumer groups have launched campaigns to get iPhone limitations removed (see, e.g., freetheiphone.com), but the extra work and cost are borne by end users as a result of anticompetitive business practices. By comparison, the superiority of open architectures is immediately apparent:

> An open architecture means fewer technological restrictions and, thus, the ability to explore more options. In an open architecture, there is no list of elements and protocols. Both are allowed to grow and change in response to changing needs and technology innovation. ... With an open architecture you are not making bets on a specific direction the technology will take in the future. You are not tied to a specific design or a particular vendor or consortium roadmap, so you can evaluate and select the best solution from a broad and energetic competitive field. Competition facilitates innovation and reduces equipment and implementation costs. (Waclawsky, 2004, p. 61)

With data communication networks, the costs of closed architectures are particularly devastating because they affect almost every communications medium (Waclawsky, 2005). As Tim Wu (2007) documents, wireless cellular carriers may be the worst purveyors of closed technologies:

> The wireless industry, over the past decade, has succeeded in bringing wireless telephony at competitive prices to the American public. Yet at the same time, we also find the wireless carriers aggressively controlling product design and innovation in the equipment and application markets, to the detriment of consumers. In the wired world, their policies would, in some cases, be considered simply misguided, and in other cases be considered outrageous and perhaps illegal. (p. 1)

Luckily, open-architecture cellular devices are just around the corner. Projects such as OpenMoko.org are working to develop "the world's first integrated open source mobile communications platform" and the Open Handset

Alliance is committed to creating a cellular platform that supports innovation (though how open this hardware platform will be is still to be determined). In fact, the superiority of these open systems is so strong that both Verizon and AT&T have declared their intention to run open networks (though the details of their "openness" have yet to be released as of this writing and Verizon only released a few key facets in April 2009). Yet, even these approximations of openness are only steps away from a fully proprietary infrastructure and far from a more open, interoperable, and innovation-supporting one.

Within the data communications realm, today, most municipal and enterprise 802.11 (WiFi/WiMAX) wireless networks are entirely proprietary. For example, a Motorola 802.11 system will not interoperate directly with a Tropos system, which will not interoperate directly with a Meru system, which will not interoperate directly with a Meraki system, and so on. In fact, most consumers have no idea that the links they rely on to access Internet and Intranet services lock geographical areas into path dependencies with specific vendors (and their specific capabilities and limitations). Disconcertingly, in an era when interoperability of applications, services, and communications is assumed and the communities that people participate in are geographically dispersed, the immediate and long-term ramifications of this geospatial lock in remain almost entirely unexplored. Closed technologies have the potential to constrain the positive potentials of Intranets if their widespread adoption stems more from an emphasis on corporate profits than on maximizing wireless networks' public benefits.

Unlike the Internet, these wireless "last-mile" links can *disallow* users from extending the network (e.g., using bridges and routers), adding applications (e.g., VoIP [Voice over Internet Protocol], P2P [peer-to-peer], IRC, IM), interconnecting additional services (e.g., streaming servers, distributed file storage, local Web hosting), or connecting directly with one another. The wireless medium is a de facto throwback to an era paralleling AT&T's control over which devices could be connected to their network and thus could control which technologies would be developed. For unsuspecting communities and decision makers, the long-term effects of wireless lock-in may be more detrimental than any policy previously witnessed in telecommunications history.

Thus far, regulatory bodies and decision makers remain unwilling to address these fundamental concerns, even though, as Nuechterlein and Weiser (2007) document, telecommunications history is rife with cautionary tales of regulatory inaction. Within this context, communications researchers, in particular, have an opportunity to both study and positively effect the future of U.S. telecommunications. By facilitating interventions in telecommunications policy, engaging with community-media activists, and emphasizing how the democratic potentials of new technologies are dependent on sound public policies, the praxis of contemporary academics can help shift the trajectory of global communications and shake the foundations of current and future Intranet practices.

The Challenges of the Intranet Era

The opportunities of Intranet technologies hold much promise but also require meaningful changes to how we study communication and render media policy as we implement these new telecommunications systems. Communications departments are increasingly adding new-media strands to study emergent technologies and are beginning to support more research addressing issues such as privacy and surveillance; Intranet versus Internet services and applications; social networking; wired- and wireless-network neutrality; technology convergence, empowerment, and independence; digital divides and inclusion efforts; digital rights management; and current and pending telecommunications proceedings (Lessig, 2001, 2006; Meinrath & Pickard, 2008; Schejter, 2009; Wu, 2007).

The emergent roles of Intranets enabled by the Internet, digital television, cell phones, personal digital assistants (PDAs), and other digital media are providing a powerful set of tools which challenge and shift social and economic behavior (claffy, Bradner, & Meinrath, 2007). While it is easy to slip into a perspective where we see these changes as a positive *global* phenomenon, the vast majority of humanity—more than 5 billion people as of 2008—do not have Internet access and are not directly participating in this "information revolution"; and these divides have implications that have only just begun to be studied.

Today, computer-mediated communication is, according to OECD (Organisation for Economic Co-operation and Development), ITU (International Telecommunication Union), PEW Center, FCC and other sources of statistics, far more prevalent among the affluent and highly educated. Meanwhile, the rural–urban divide in Internet connectivity, contrary to rosy press reports, may actually be worsening in the United States. While we often look to emergent technologies and new media for their "potential of being used as a liberatory and empowering tool by many people and . . . for the disadvantaged and excluded to 'challenge entrenched positions and structures'" (Keeble & Loader, 2002, p. 5), these new communications media are actually little understood and grossly underused (Anderson, 2005; Cooper, 2003, 2006; Pickard, 2008). Media activists have played a pivotal role in deploying these technologies and opening up and shaping policy debates regarding community Intranets and other forms of Internet-enabled communication (Pickard, 2006a, 2006b). As they expand the boundaries of what is possible with new technologies, increasingly they engage with policy debates, including spectrum ownership, network neutrality, and open-access issues of the Internet, privacy, surveillance, and intellectual property law.

Likewise, the political and regulatory battles of the next few years will determine the trajectory of communications development for generations to come. Nonprofit organizations, such as the New America Foundation, Free Press, Public

Knowledge, and the Media Access Project are often on the front lines of debates that will affect the lives of all U.S. residents and reverberate around the globe. These groups are often battling against telco incumbents with orders of magnitude more funding than they receive, as well as hundreds of lobbyists, and enormous PR (public relations) war chests. Top-down telecommunications reforms are critically important to the creation of a more just society, but given the systematic under-resourcing of public interest organizations, grassroots implementation of next-generation communications infrastructures is useful and a much-needed strategy for illustrating the potential benefits that national reforms could facilitate.

In summary, community Intranets hold great promise, but the onus is on researchers and their allies to document the positive effects of these new technologies for civic engagement and democratized communications. Attentiveness to the issues discussed in this chapter will help scientists, activists, decision makers, and practitioners better understand the intersections among the technologies, uses, and policies of Intranet-enabled communications. Communications research strives to shed light on changes in how we interact and communicate. As observers and participants during this time of rapid change, we have a responsibility to the global community to develop sound public policy dedicated to social justice. Keeping up with the rapidity of change is certainly a challenge, but while many outcomes of these shifts in communications are still to be determined, the opportunity to help shape the technologies and policies of next-generation communications and positively impact the day-to-day lives of millions of people has never been greater.

References

Anderson, J. (2005). *Imagining the Internet.* Lanham, MD: Rowman & Littlefield.

Benkler, Y. (2003). Freedom in the commons: Toward a political economy of information. *Duke Law Journal, 52,* 1245–1249.

Benkler, Y. (2006). *The wealth of networks.* New Haven, CT: Yale University Press.

Biddle, P., England, P., Peinado, M., & Willman, B. (2002). The darknet and the future of content distribution. Retrieved May 5, 2009, from www.google.com/url?sa=t&source=web&ct=res&cd=1&url=http%3A%2F%2Fcrypto.stanford.edu%2FDRM2002%2Fdarknet5.doc&ei=SYkASvCYJpeMtgfE8piIBw&usg=AFQjCNHZkIYjxy6LnWvUSt6kGrZ3SYLMZQ

Brock, G. (2003). *The second information revolution.* Cambridge, MA: Harvard University Press.

Castells, M. (2001). *The Internet galaxy.* Oxford, UK: Oxford University Press.

claffy, kc., Bradner, S., & Meinrath, S. (2007, May/June). The (un)economic Internet? *IEEE Internet Computing, 11*(3), 53–58.

Cooper, M. (2003). *Media ownership and democracy in the digital information age.* Washington, DC: Consumer Federation of America.

Cooper, M. (2004). *Open architecture as communications policy.* Stanford, CA: Center for Internet and Society.

Cooper, M. (2006). *The case against media consolidation.* New York: Donald McGannon Center for Communications Research.

De Bernabé, F. G. (2004). *Connected homes.* London: Premium.

Federal Communications Commission. (1968, June 26). In the matter of use of the Carterphone device in message toll telephone service (FCC Release No. 68–661). Retrieved June 20, 2007, from www.uiowa.edu/~cyberlaw/FCCOps/1968/13F2–420.html

Hiller, J., & Cohen, R. (2002). *Internet law & policy.* Englewood Cliffs, NJ: Prentice Hall.

Howley, K. (2005). *Community media.* Cambridge, UK: Cambridge University Press.

Kahin, B., & Keller, J. (1997). *Coordinating the Internet.* Cambridge: MIT Press.

Keeble, L., & Loader, B. (Eds.). (2002). *Community informatics: Shaping computer-mediated social relations.* New York: Routledge.

Lessig, L. (2001). *The future of ideas.* New York: Random House.

Lessig, L. (2006). *Code: Version 2.0.* New York: Basic Books.

Louis, P. (2000). *Telecommunications internetworking.* New York: McGraw-Hill.

Meinrath, S. (2004). *Reactions to contemporary activist-scholars and the Midwestern mystique: A case study for utilizing an evolving methodology in contentious contexts.* Unpublished master's thesis, University of Illinois, Urbana-Champaign.

Meinrath, S. (2004–2005, Winter). The Champaign-Urbana wireless network. *Community Technology Review.* Retrieved August 17, 2009 from http://www .comtechreview.org/winter-2004-2005/000259 .html

Meinrath, S. (2005). Wirelessing the world: The battle over (community) wireless networks. In R. W. McChesney, R. Newman, & B. Scott (Eds.), *The future of media: Resistance and reform in the 21st century* (pp. 219–242). New York: Seven Stories Press.

Meinrath, S., Bahl, V., Carter, K., Cooper, M., Scott, B., & Westervelt, M. (2005, May). Openness and the public airwaves. In *Proceedings of the 6th ACM International Symposium on Mobile Ad Hoc Networking and Computing.* Retrieved May 5, 2009, from http://portal.acm.org/ft_gateway.cfm?id= 1062718&type=pdf&coll=GUIDE&dl=GUIDE& CFID=33362015&CFTOKEN=48694739

Meinrath, S., & Calabrese, M. (2007, December). *Unlicensed broadband device technologies: White space device. Operations on the TV Band and the Myth of Harmful Interference* (Policy Backgrounder). Washington, DC: New America Foundation.

Meinrath, S., & claffy, kc. (2007, September) *The commons initiative: Cooperative measurement and modeling of open networked systems.* Paper presented at the Telecommunications Policy and Research Conference, Washington, DC.

Meinrath, S. D., & Pickard, V. W. (2008). The new network neutrality: Criteria for Internet freedom. *International Journal of Communication Law and Policy, 12,* 225–243.

Nuechterlein, E. J., & Weiser, P. (2007). *Digital crossroads.* Cambridge: MIT Press.

Pickard, V. W. (2006a). Assessing the radical democracy of indymedia: Discursive, technical and institutional constructions. *Critical Studies in Media Communication, 23*(1), 19–38.

Pickard, V. W. (2006b). United yet autonomous: Indymedia and the struggle to sustain a radical democratic network. *Media, Culture & Society, 28*(3), 315–336.

Pickard, V. W. (2008). Cooptation and cooperation: Institutional exemplars of democratic Internet technology. *New Media and Society, 10*(4), 625–645.

Stolterman, E. (2002). Creating community in conspiracy with the enemy. In L. Keeble & B. Loader (Eds.), *Community informatics: Shaping computer-mediated social relations* (pp. 43–52). New York: Routledge.

Schejter, A. (Ed.). (2009). *. . . And communications for all: A policy agenda for a new administration.* Lanham, MD: Lexington Books.

Waclawsky, J. C. (2004, October). Closed systems, closed architectures, and closed minds. *Business Communications Review, 34*(10), 57–64.

Waclawsky, J. C. (2005, March). Where do system standards go from here? *Business Communications Review, 35*(3), 38–45.

Wu, T. (2007, February). *Wireless net neutrality: Cellular Carterfone and consumer choice in mobile broadband* (Working Paper No. 17). Washington, DC: New America Foundation, Wireless Future Program.

PART VII

Local Media, Global Struggles

In this, our final section, we consider the role community media play in creating opportunities for collective action across national borders and in nurturing alternative visions for a more just and equitable global order. We begin with a discussion of the concept of "globalization-from-below" (Falk, 1999). This line of thinking foregrounds the work of grassroots organizations and advocacy groups, including nongovernmental organizations (NGOs) and social movements, in challenging the dominant vision of globalization associated with neoliberalism. This discussion illuminates community media's relationship to transnational mobilization—variously described as the "antiglobalization," "global justice," or "counterglobalization" movement—against the economic and political logics of "globalization-from-above."

Throughout this discussion, we draw on academic and activist insights related to the emergence of global civil society. Doing so allows us to consider community media's relationship to this new social formation and to assess community media's status as a tool for international solidarity building. In the chapters that follow, contributors demonstrate the value of community media in articulating relations of solidarity and significance in local-global struggles for self-determination, social justice, and communicative democracy.

Globalization-From-Below

In public statements, political and economic elites affiliated with the institutions of global capitalism—the International Monetary Fund (IMF), the World Trade Organization (WTO), and the World Bank—invariably extol the benefits of free markets and an integrated global economy. These advocates of globalization-from-above maintain that the restructuring of social, economic, and political relations associated with global capitalism is an unambiguously beneficial process. Furthermore, promoters of neoliberal economics contend that globalization provides unparalleled opportunities for the attainment of individual liberty and collective prosperity. Typically, there is an air of inevitability to these assertions; the complex and contradictory processes associated with globalization—its varied causes and consequences, let alone its contested meanings—are rarely acknowledged or addressed.

Over the course of the past decade, new social actors and forces have emerged to challenge the hegemonic discourse of globalization. Critics argue that globalization-from-above marginalizes whole populations, thereby inhibiting democratic participation in policy-making processes and precluding the development of alternative systems that might promote a more just social, political, and economic order. Furthermore, these critics contend that the global restructuring of local, regional, and national markets enhances neither the personal freedom nor the economic fortunes of the vast majority of the world's people. Opponents of globalization-from-above maintain that global capitalism undermines political autonomy, exacerbates economic inequalities, destroys local ecosystems, and otherwise threatens the social fabric of local and national communities alike.

Not surprisingly, these conditions have sparked popular opposition to "elite globalization" (Korten, Perlas, & Shiva, 2002). As political scientist E. Osei Kwadwo Prempeh (2004) observes, "The widening reach and uneven nature of globalization has provoked resistance and political countermovements aimed at challenging its exclusionary practices, its silencing of the voices of the people, and its undemocratic or even anti-democratic tendencies" (p. 581). The varied and widespread forms of resistance to global capitalism that have emerged from civil society in recent years—from the formation of transnational coalitions and the organization of countersummits to the establishment of alternative news and information services—are but a few instances of globalization-from-below.

Mass demonstrations, such as the "Battle of Seattle" in November 1999; the protests surrounding the G-8 summit in Genoa, Italy, in July 2001; or the worldwide rallies against the U.S.-led invasion of Iraq on February 15, 2003, are the most visible and dramatic manifestations of globalization-from-below. These transnational mobilizations are noteworthy insofar as they are tangible expressions of popular frustration with the political and economic agenda of globalization-from-above. However, the global justice movement is a far more dynamic process than even these massive demonstrations would suggest.

That is to say, globalization-from-below is "a movement of movements" that seeks to harness the creative energy, collective wisdom, and nascent political power of global civil society. The movement's strength, and therefore its potential to produce substantive change, lies not only in its sensitivity to the specificity of local struggles but also in its capacity to forge connections between these and broader struggles for peace and justice. To that end, the counter globalization movement has successfully employed some of the techniques associated with earlier transnational movements, such as the anti-Apartheid and antinuclear movements of the 1980s (Kaldor, 1995; Thorn, 2007). Indeed, one of the distinguishing features of counterglobalization is the sheer diversity of actors, action repertoires, and concerns taken up by advocates of globalization-from-below (Della Porta, Andretta, Mosca, & Reiter, 2006).

For instance, in the global South, concerns regarding access to water, land, and food have mobilized rural farmers, women, and indigenous peoples to challenge the corporate consolidation of these essential resources. In industrialized societies, labor unions protest trade agreements that make it easier for corporations to move their operations to locations where a living wage is virtually unheard of and workers' rights are negligible. Likewise, family farmers in the First World and subsistence farmers in the Third World have found common cause in the struggle against the anticompetitive practices of transnational agribusiness. Finally, environmentalists across the globe have raised public awareness of the threats posed by deforestation, strip mining, acid rain, and global warming (Brecher, Costello, & Smith, 2000; Steward, 2004). In short, globalization-from-below links a constellation of grassroots efforts aimed at mitigating the adverse effects of globalization and ensuring popular participation in debates over (g)local issues.

What unites these disparate constituencies, then, is not a flat-out rejection of globalization; far from it. Rather, globalization-from-below articulates a vision of global civil society that empowers people at the local, national, and international level. It is a vision of, as well as a demand for, a more inclusive, participatory political culture, one in which local communities play a decisive role in shaping the terms and conditions of globalization. As several analysts put it, "Participants in the movement for globalization-from-below have varied agendas, but the movement's unifying mission is to bring about sufficient democratic control over states, markets and corporations to insure a viable future for people and the planet" (Brecher et al., 2000). In other words, the global justice movement promotes a progressive vision of globalization by heightening public awareness of the interdependent and interconnected character of human relations.

Accordingly, globalization-from-below embraces strategies and tools that are irrevocably bound up in the process of globalization. Thus, while globalization often pits communities one against the other in an effort to attract global capital with the promise of cheap labor markets and lax environmental regulations—a dynamic aptly described as a "race to the bottom"— globalization also presents opportunities, made possible in large measure through the decentralized, horizontal channels of communication engendered by the Internet and related technologies, to forge alliances between distant communities who confront common problems: declining standards of living, environmental degradation, militarism, forced migration, and human rights abuses, to name but a few (Fenton, 2006).

This realization has enormous implications for activists, organizers, NGOs, and others interested in nurturing global civil society. The cultural theorist Arjun Appadurai (2000) puts it plainly, "The idea of an international civil society will have no future outside of the success of these efforts to globalize from below" (p. 3). In other words, the growth and development of global civil society depends on the strength and vitality of local civic organizations and initiatives. Likewise, global civil society is virtually inconceivable without a critical communication infrastructure that promotes participation, engagement, and informed decision making on the local as well as the national and international levels (O'Siochrú, 2005). All this supports geographer David Harvey's contention that "a global strategy of resistance has to begin with the realities of place and community" (quoted in Miller, 1992, p. 23).

With this in mind, we can begin to discern community media's significance to global civil society. For instance, community media plays a vital, although largely unacknowledged role in "calling positive attention" (Falk, 1999, p. 2) to a host of civic initiatives associated with the movement for globalization-from-below. Here, then, community media's ability to provide a counterweight to corporate media's shoddy coverage of the global justice movement should not be underestimated. As we have noted throughout this volume, social movements depend heavily on press reports to create awareness of their activities and objectives. Moreover, media are instrumental in mobilizing support for collective action. Without accurate, ongoing, and substantive news coverage of the sort provided by independent, grassroots, and community-based media, resistance movements are hard-pressed to move from the margins to the mainstream of public discourse.

Equally important, community media are uniquely suited to examine the impact and consequences of globalization as local communities come to understand and experience it. In contrast to dominant media, then, community media open up discursive spaces for marginalized groups and individuals to register and articulate their hopes and fears regarding globalization. What's more, community media amplify these voices within and beyond their respective communities, thereby disseminating these perspectives to local, national, and increasingly international publics. Finally, as several of our contributors demonstrate, activist community media are especially adept at creating information networks that support and stimulate globalization-from-below (e.g., Carpentier, 2007). In doing so, community media are fast becoming an integral part of a "new architecture for producing and sharing knowledge about globalization" (Appadurai, 2000, p. 18).

Apart from the publicity that community media generate for resistance movements, and the increasingly important role grassroots and independent media play in coordinating transnational mobilization, community media also provide an institutional basis for the growth and development of global civil society. Academic and activist thinking on the subject of global civil society emphasizes the strategic value of autonomous spaces—self-organized institutions that operate independently of both the state and the market—for promoting popular participation in matters of public interest, creating a relatively safe environment for citizens to challenge government and corporate power, and linking local resistance movements with like-minded efforts around the world (Kaldor, 2003). In this way, autonomous spaces, such as those constituted through alternative and community media, are instrumental in opening up new realms of political action outside of formal political structures and practices (Downing, 1988; Langlois & Dubois, 2005).

Significantly, this new approach to politics is not about acquiring power through party politics, let alone armed struggle. Rather, the goal is "to contest power by working through civil society to push for modification of the existing political system, and push it to the limits to achieve necessary change and restructuring" (Vanden, 2003, p. 324). This movement away from traditional politics is significant inasmuch as it rejects elite models of democracy, with the attendant "division of labor" between political classes and civil society that tends to engender apathy and indifference among the citizenry (Cohen & Arato, 2000). Rather, this new form of political participation, which has been cultivated, in part, by

alternative and community media, has proven to be an effective mechanism for closing the gap between formal rights and the full exercise of those rights—especially the right to communicate.

Herein, we can detect community media's significance to what Carroll and Hackett (2006) refer to as "the politics of connections." That is, community media facilitate communication and engender new relations of solidarity between disparate constituencies involved in the global justice movement. And in an era when the global political economy is marked by a democratic deficit that inhibits participatory decision making, community media provide a forum for "substantive participation" (Sane, 1993) in debates over matters of global concern. Thus, community media serve as a mechanism for people the world over to speak as well as listen, to realize the strategic value of cooperation and reciprocity, and, finally, to seek out commonalities while also respecting differences. In short, with its commitment to participatory communication and social change, community media is uniquely suited to construct alliances between different communities working together in the pursuit of a range of common interests.

Community Media and International Solidarity Building

In the face of growing resistance to elite globalization, champions of globalization-from-above contend that "There is no alternative." Global civil society replies with a defiant and far more affirmative declaration: "Another world is possible." Realizing this vision is as much an act of imagination as it is the result of cooperation and reciprocity between distant people and places.

By way of illustrating this point, consider the work of the Global Action Project (GAP), based in New York City. For nearly 20 years, GAP has sought to enhance international solidarity among young people around the world through community-based media training and production. GAP's cultural exchange programs are premised on the fact that

> young people in the US rarely have the chance to hear the perspectives of their peers, especially those in other countries [to that end] G.A.P. created programs that supported youth producing meaningful work that linked local issues to global realities. (Dukes, 2006, p. 38)

In recent years, GAP producers have traveled to counterglobalization summits, such as the 2005 World Social Forum in Porto Alegre, Brazil, for purposes of documenting these events and producing videotapes that illuminate the interdependent and interconnected character of global relations for young people. Like other projects produced through GAP, these tapes are made available to local residents and shared with global audiences through various distribution schemes, including public screenings and film festivals. Significantly, there is a conspicuous educational component to these screenings. Audiences are invited to discuss and debate the issues raised by GAP projects, to consider the global implications of the issues raised by these videos, and finally, to get involved in collective efforts designed to address these problems.

Equally important, GAP aims to create long-term relationships between video makers and the communities they visit around the world. To that end, GAP promotes international exchange and cultivates collaborative work practices between local students and their peers around the world. Like other forms of activist community media, then, GAP supports the global justice movement by amplifying the voices of people working on the frontlines of local struggles for peace and justice. In doing so, GAP illustrates how community media can serve as an important tool of international solidarity building.

GAP is but one example of the modest but increasingly important contribution that community media can make to the growth and development of global civil society. By enhancing our awareness of the crucial and decisive relationships

spread out across the globe, community media promote feelings of solidarity and affinity that are vital to any effort to create a more just and equitable global order. Equally important, by linking the local and global in this way, community media alert us to a profound and inescapable feature of human communities in an era of global communication:

> The bonds and concerns of community . . . need not be totalizing and exclusionary. Indeed, most of us belong to, and identify with, a multiplicity of communities and collectivities ranging from partners and friends to, perhaps, the human species. It is these bonds with distant others— both literally and metaphorically—that need to be developed and strengthened, while always recognizing and respecting difference. (Miller, 1992, p. 39)

With this in mind, then, we move on to our final selection of chapters. The initiatives discussed below demonstrate the progressive possibilities of globalization: the provision of structures and practices, like those associated with community media, that are transparent and accountable to local populations; the critical importance of reciprocity in supporting and sustaining efforts to protect human rights; and, finally, the deep commitment of community organizers, media activists, independent journalists, and other segments of global civil society for promoting and defending human dignity.

Chapter 29 examines the Zapatista movement's innovative approach to building local, national, and international support for its campaign for social and economic justice in Chiapas, Mexico. Specifically, Fiona Jeffries analyzes the Zapatista's "revolution in speaking and listening"— arguably the defining feature of the movement's engagement with the neoliberal project of economic globalization. Throughout, Jeffries challenges the media-centric perspective that has characterized previous analyses of the Zapatista's communication strategies. Instead, Jeffries focuses our attention on the community-building dimensions of the Zapatista's practice of radical democratic communication. Introducing the concept of "communicational insurgency" Jeffries contends that the movement has successfully opened up political space for resistance, struggle, and solidarity among civil society actors around the world.

In Chapter 30, Elvira Truglia describes a global experiment in community radio, *Voices Without Frontiers,* produced by the World Association of Community Broadcasters. The yearly broadcast features the work of activists, journalists, and others involved in the migrant rights movement. Truglia contends that community radio is one of the few venues in which migrants can express their opinions and perspectives on immigration policies that effectively deny them basic legal and human rights. Writing from a practitioner's perspective, Truglia describes the technical and logistical facets of the 2004 broadcast, which featured programming in 9 languages aired on over 200 community radio stations worldwide. Truglia emphasizes the collaborative and participatory potential of global community media projects and concludes that such broadcasts hold enormous potential for building international solidarity around this and other human rights issues.

Chapter 31 considers activist community media in relation to mainstream media performance and behaviors. Noting mainstream media's problematic coverage of the global justice movement (GJM), Anne Marie Todd surveys the work of two leading media activist organizations, Protest.Net and Indymedia, and their efforts to provide fair, accurate, and ongoing coverage of the GJM. Todd observes the critical role new communication technologies have played in building and sustaining the GJM and in countering corporate media's efforts to discredit the movement. Throughout, Todd highlights independent and community-based media's capacity to enhance public awareness of the movement and mobilize popular resistance to economic globalization. Todd concludes that activist community media hold enormous potential for democratizing the global mediascape.

Our final chapter assesses indymedia in relation to academic and activist thinking on alternative media. Acknowledging the social, cultural, and political impact of alternative media in local settings, Carlos Fontes (Chapter 32) argues that, until recently, these initiatives have been unable to create a broader democratic media system. Fontes proceeds with an analysis of what he describes as the "global turn" in the alternative media movement. Drawing on his experience as an academic and a media activist, Fontes suggests that we reconceptualize alternative media in light of the limits and possibilities afforded by the technologies, organizing principles, and communicative structures and practices associated with indymedia. In doing so, Fontes revisits some of the key concepts and debates surrounding alternative, citizens,' and community media taken up throughout this volume.

References

Appadurai, A. (2000). Grassroots globalization and the research imagination. *Public Culture, 12*(1), 1–19.

Brecher, J., Costello, T., & Smith, B. (2000). Globalization from below. *Third World Traveler.* Retrieved March 17, 2008, from www.thirdworldtraveler.com/Globalization/Globalization_Below.html

Carpentier, N. (2007). The on-line community media database RadioSwap as a translocal tool to broaden the communicative rhizome. *Observatorio Journal, 1,* 1–26.

Carroll, W., & Hackett, R. (2006). Democratic media activism through the lens of social movement theory. *Media, Culture & Society, 28*(1), 83–104.

Cohen, J., & Arato, A. (2000). Civil society and political theory. In V. A. Hodgkison & M. W. Foley (Eds.), *The civil society reader* (pp. 270–291). Lebanon, NH: University Press of New England. (Original work published 1992)

Della Porta, D., Andretta, M., Mosca, L., & Reiter, H. (2006). *Globalization from below: Transnational activists and protest networks.* Minneapolis: University of Minnesota Press.

Downing, J. (1988). The alternative public realm: The Organization of the 1980s anti-nuclear press in West Germany and Britain. *Media, Culture & Society, 10,* 163–181.

Dukes, D. (2006). Global voices: Making another world possible. *Community Media Review, 29*(4), 38–39.

Falk, R. (1999). *Predatory globalization: A critique.* Cambridge, UK: Polity Press.

Fenton, N. (2006). Contesting global capital, new media, solidarity, and the role of the social imaginary. In B. Cammaerts & N. Carpentier (Eds.), *Reclaiming the media: Communication rights and democratic media roles* (pp. 225–242). Edinburgh, UK: Intellect.

Kaldor, M. (1995, July/August). Who killed the Cold War? *Bulletin of Atomic Scientists,* 57–60.

Kaldor, M. (2003). Civil society and accountability. *Journal of Human Development, 4*(1), 5–27.

Korten, D. C., Perlas, N., & Shiva, V. (2002). *Global civil society: The path ahead.* Retrieved March 17, 2008, from www.pcdf.org/civilsociety/path.htm

Langlois, A., & Dubois, F. (Eds.). (2005). *Autonomous media: Activating resistance and dissent.* Montreal, Quebec, Canada: Cumulus Press.

Miller, B. (1992). Collective action and rational choice: Place, community, and the limits of individual self-interest. *Economic Geography, 68*(1), 22–42.

O'Siochrú, S. (2005). Finding a frame: Toward a transnational advocacy campaign to democratize communication. In R. Hackett & Y. Zhao (Eds.), *Democratizing global media: One world, many struggles* (pp. 289–311). Lanham, MD: Rowman & Littlefield.

Prempeh, E. (2004). Anti-globalization forces, the politics of resistance, and Africa: Promises and perils. *Journal of Black Studies, 34*(4), 580–598.

Sane, P. (1993, December 20). Human rights: An agenda for action. *West Africa, 3978,* 2294.

Steward, C. (2004). Globalization from below: Why resource rights matter. *Grassroots International.* Retrieved April 17, 2009, from www.grassrootsonline .org/node/543

Thorn, H. (2007). Social movements, the media and the emergence of a global public sphere: From anti-apartheid to global justice. *Current Sociology, 55*(6), 896–918.

Vanden, H. E. (2003). Globalization in a time of neoliberalism: Politicized social movements and the Latin American response. *Journal of Developing Societies, 19*(2/3), 308–333.

CHAPTER 29

"Asking We Walk"

The Zapatista Revolution of Speaking and Listening

Fiona Jeffries

In the first hours of January 1, 1994—the day NAFTA (the North American Free Trade Agreement) officially went into effect—a group calling itself the Zapatista Army of National Liberation (EZLN) surged out of Chiapas' Lacandon jungle and entered the world stage with a lucid pronouncement: "Ya Basta!" (Enough Already!) The rebels wore ski masks or scarves around their faces. Most were indigenous, and a notable number among them were women. Some carried arms and others carried only sticks carved and painted into the shape of a weapon. The Zapatistas released political prisoners, occupied municipal buildings and town centers, commandeered radio stations, held press conferences, distributed public declarations, and conversed with astonished crowds. Spectacularly, the rebels "sin rostro" (without a face) leaped onto television and computer screens and the front pages of newspapers around the world. Their remarkable articulation of common problems was cathartic. In the days following the uprising, while the military descended on Chiapas and financial markets grumbled, hundreds of thousands of protestors packed Mexico City's massive public plaza shouting, "We are all Zapatistas!" Demonstrations supporting the rebels and denouncing neoliberalism took place around the world. Activists and journalists flocked to Chiapas to witness what some commentators labeled the "first revolution of the 21st century" (Lorenzano, 1998).

The EZLN's widely circulated analysis of neoliberal capitalism provoked a renaissance in radical thought and action in Mexico and internationally (Holloway & Peláez, 1998). Communicational politics have been central to its remarkable influence on debates and practices of the global anticapitalist movements that came to prominence in the uprising's wake. Much of the analysis of the Zapatistas' philosophical and tactical impact has focused on the rebels' savvy "media strategy" and the revolutionary possibilities hidden in the harnessing of new information technologies. But in this chapter, I endeavor to challenge the media-centric view of Zapatismo and to show that the celebrated "information revolution" is not constitutive of the movement but a complementary aspect of what makes the

Zapatistas so significant, namely the radically democratic communicational basis of their organizing. This organizing has taken shape simultaneously through the formation of the political communities of the autonomous municipalities developed over the past decade and through the Zapatistas' relationship with the broader political scene across Mexico and internationally. This has involved a continuous process of movement elaboration, turning the once isolated political organization of the Zapatistas into a locally situated and globally articulated movement known as Zapatismo.

In this chapter, I explore the Zapatistas' communicational insurgency to situate their project as a "revolution in speaking and listening" (Lorenzano, 1998). Drawing on Jesus Martín Barbero's (1993) insistence that we challenge the dominant instrumental approach that reduces communication processes to technological considerations and the circulation of information, this discussion of the Zapatista communicational insurgency engages with the project of overcoming the media-centrism that has dominated the field of communication studies (Barbero, 1993). I argue that the community-building significance of the Zapatista communicational insurgency poses a challenge to the instrumental conception of both politics and communication that has informed many influential analyses of the post–cold war "Information Society." I seek to show that the Zapatistas' elaboration of radical democratic communication has opened the terrain of political struggle, evidenced in the fact that the contest between the insurgents and the state has been primarily communicational, not military. "As they say in these mountains, the Zapatistas have a very powerful and indestructible weapon: the word," explained Zapatista spokesperson Marcos in the days following the uprising. "It is not our arms that make us radical," he wrote in a letter addressed to "civil society" in 1996.

> It is the new political practice which we propose and in which we are immersed with thousands of men and women in Mexico and the world: the construction of a political practice which does not seek the taking of power but the organization of society. (p. 1)

The Zapatista communicational insurgency as a practice of antipower is the most important contribution the movement makes to a crucial renovation of revolutionary thought, discourse, and action.

In a suggestive departure from 20th century political movements, the Zapatistas do not claim to represent a social base. Rather, the movement seeks to remain inseparable from the social base. According to Zapatista testimonies, the shape of this political project emerged out of an encounter between the historical left and a culture of resistance elaborated over five centuries of indigenous resistance. Out of this dynamic emerged the central Zapatista principle and communicational practice of *mandar obedeciendo* (to lead by following), which governs life in the Zapatista political commune. As I show, this communicational insurgency inverts conventional political practices, of both left and right, through the radically democratic principle of leading by following. This is organized concretely around a politics of *visibility* and *encounter*.

Communicating Zapatismo

How did the once anonymous Zapatistas make this stealth journey from the relative isolation of the information-poor Lacandon jungle to the center of the debate on neoliberal globalization? The symbolic date of the uprising was instrumental in catapulting the Zapatistas to the forefront of world politics because it provided an aperture through which they could enter the debate. But the rebels' own labor of communication provided the catalyst. While the rebels descended on six towns of Chiapas clutching their founding documents, they also quickly set to work contacting sympathetic media to have the first word. After 3 days of fighting with government forces, the

Zapatistas melted back into their jungle, a vast dense rainforest with the sparsest of infrastructure. This geographical isolation became central to the contest over the public imagination between the Zapatistas and the government and progovernment media. The state responded militarily and through a campaign of demonization—labeling the rebels "transgressors of the law," "foreigners," and "professionals of violence"—designed to contain, isolate, and destroy the movement. But it was too late. By that point, the relatively novel cyberspaces of the Internet whirred with communiqués, reportage, and firsthand accounts of witnesses that were quickly translated, circulated, and reproduced in other media around Mexico and internationally. Within a few days, almost 1,000 journalists had descended on Chiapas, and the Zapatistas invited select Mexican and international media to the jungle to witness and conduct interviews.

The enormous media attention the Zapatistas garnered, the important role that the Internet played in the movement's remarkable dissemination, and the historical collision of the uprising at the waxing of the celebrated "information revolution," rendered the Zapatistas virtually synonymous with "communication." For many commentators, the Zapatistas, with their provocative style and moving, irreverent discourse, appeared as the other face, or mask, of this revolution.

For example, Manuel Castells (1997) labeled the EZLN "the first informational guerrilla movement," basing this claim on the Zapatistas' unique relationship with both traditional and new communication media. In his study on the rise of identity movements in the context of "informational" globalization, he asserts that the EZLN's "ability to communicate with the world, and with Mexican society, and to capture the imagination of people and of intellectuals propelled a local, weak insurgent movement to the forefront of world politics" (p. 79). Intriguingly, the conservative RAND Corporation also conducted a major study (commissioned by U.S. military intelligence) on what the think tank

termed the Zapatistas' *social netwar*. In the section titled "Implications for the U.S. Army and Military Strategy," the authors assert,

> The fight over "information" has made the Zapatista conflict less violent than it might otherwise have been. But is has also made it more public, disruptive and difficult to isolate; it has had more generalized effects than if it had been contained as a localized insurgency. (Ronfeldt & Arquilla, 1998, p. 128)

The authors emphasize that the Zapatistas' surprising success is due to their relationship with a wide range of social movements in Mexico and internationally, achieved through a strategic access to a variety of communication media, especially the Internet.

There is no doubt that the Internet, the most novel among other new and older communication media, played a vital role in the circulation of Zapatismo. In the best of the genre, the radical economist Harry Cleaver (1998), one of the most active and dedicated disseminators of Zapatista-related material on the Internet, supplies an important analysis on the significance of the electronic circulation of Zapatismo. His assessment subordinates the importance of the technology per se to the social uses of it, in this case, the active appropriation of communication media and the new possibilities for horizontal, transnational solidarity networks embodied in the Internet.

But even Cleaver's (1998) analysis can be pushed further, to challenge the often-unquestioned conflation of the Zapatista movement with the technologies associated with the "Information Society." While by now much of the earlier deterministic narratives of the Internet are treated with skepticism, these interpretations point to a central and persistent paradox of communication politics in the context of neoliberal globalization. The role of communication in politics is often conceptualized and assessed in terms of the proliferation and circulation of information, and it seems that the media itself is the privileged space of contemporary politics, as the crisis of the constituted power of representative democracy deepens. The commercial media, as a space of politics, are also an expression of constituted power. The Zapatistas' communicational insurgency, I argue, is an expression of a movement for constituent power that emphasizes a politics of presence, not representation. I return to this distinction later.

Communicational Insurgency: Breaking the Blockade for a "Uniting of Dignities"

The central Zapatista concept of dialogue as political practice is reflected in their phrase "asking we walk," which is integral to everything this political community undertakes: from the creation of Revolutionary Laws, to the 1994 uprising, to the steady stream of widely disseminated communiqués and transcripts of interviews and public addresses flowing out of the Lacandon Jungle, to the innumerable national and international *consultas* (consultations) and *encuentros* (encounters) organized to connect the movement with others across Mexico and internationally. The irreverent March of the People the Color of the Earth in 2001 and the Other Campaign of 2006 are further instances of the Zapatistas' constant moving against the blockade set up to consign the movement to its jungle territory. Through these initiatives, we can see the practices of visibility and encounter at work. By identifying and analyzing them more closely, we can deepen our understanding of the materiality of communication and work toward overcoming the media-centric conception of communication practices. The pairing of visibility and encounter as the locus of Zapatista activities refers to the manner in which the movement has focused the struggle for democracy on the problem of communication, representation, and power. This communicational practice uses, but is not subordinated to,

mediation as a stimulant to forge dialogical spaces for what the Zapatistas call a "uniting of dignities" among groups and individuals seeking radical social transformation. From here, we can populate communication processes to show that it is not a technological matter so much as an experiential and dialogical relation that can be both local and global simultaneously, and with very diffuse effects.

The Zapatista communicational insurgency that takes place both within the local political commune in Chiapas and in the movement's relationship with the broader national and transnational space seeks to make visible the struggles of ordinary people, rendered invisible by the constituted power of representational politics. It seeks to bring the two together in ways that assert the conviction that power does not, or should not, reside somewhere "up there" but is instead dispersed in the terrestrial realm of where people are. Visibility is regarded as the first step to assert the political agency of those "down below" to make encounter possible and enable a process of continuous elaboration as new visibilities emerge and new dialogical spaces are forged.

Visibility as politico-communicational practice is evident in Zapatista activities such as the sudden shock of the uprising or the rebels' startling and persistent covering of their faces—an act symbolizing invisibility and exclusion, which has brought to the movement a remarkable visibility. The centrality of visibility as a way to galvanize a recognition of the presence of the excluded, a prerequisite to begin a process of encounter, is summed up in the insistent affirmation, "Here we are!" that resonates in everything the Zapatistas do, even, or perhaps especially, when they enter periods of silence, a tactic that makes governments nervous and newspapers publicly ponder the goings-on in Chiapas' dense jungle. The politics of encounter that new visibilities provoke involves making spaces for dialogue, regardless of affiliation, identity, or ideology (Callahan, 2004). While the Zapatista political community retains its arms in a defensive posture against the belligerence of the state, dialogue occupies the heart of the Zapatista project to build the world anew. This contradiction, which they have publicly acknowledged, has generated a new round of dialogue and renovation, as I discuss below.

Hence, the Zapatista communicational insurgency is built not on the latest communication technologies or on humble weaponry but on the primacy of dignity and circumstances negated by neoliberal capitalism, coupled with an insistence on democratic practice grounded in the constituent power of ordinary people versus the constituted powers of the state. This alliance of dignity and the consistent repudiation of formal state power are crucial to grasping the radically democratic and innovative nature of the Zapatista proposal. Its legitimacy is rooted in the practice of a direct democratic politics of encounter or *presence* in contradistinction to the limited democracy of *representation* (Esteva, 2006). In practice, this entails the building of networks of autonomous communication that challenge the vanguardism of both the representative neoliberal state and the "seize the state" historical aspirations of 20th-century revolutionary movements.

In an informal speech during the Intercontinental Encounter for Humanity and Against Neoliberalism in 1996, Marcos described the Zapatista conception of antipower, elaborated during preparations for their public appearance in 1994:

> We thought that it was necessary to reconsider the problem of power, to not repeat the formula that in order to change the world it is necessary to take power and then once in power, we will organize everything in a way that is best for the world, that is, the way that it is best for me since I am in power. We thought that if we conceived of a change in the way power is seen, the problem of power, proclaiming that we do not want it—this would produce another way of doing politics and other kind of politics, other human beings that do politics differently from

politicians of the entire political spectrum. (EZLN, 1996, p. 69)

The substance of these practices is reflected in the Zapatistas' numerous communication-infused concepts explicitly geared toward overcoming the problem of top-down decision making: "to lead by following"; "asking while walking"; "everything for everyone, for ourselves nothing"; "for a world where many worlds fit."

While grounded in the specific historical practices of the local movement, this proposal to not take power but to exercise it is, the Zapatistas argue, a form of antipower that is universally applicable because it is a practice that emphasizes diversity and heterogeneity versus the homogeneity and conformity necessary for representational, constituted power (Esteva, 2006). The communicational insurgency is a refusal to be politically confined, and the Zapatistas' communication is peppered with references to conformity and confinement as constant challenges to face. "Do not believe those who offer conformity and fear," implored Marcos in that 1996 letter addressed to the world.

Through their communication insurgency, the Zapatistas constantly penetrate the national and international media landscape and make their way into the geographically distant metropolitan consciousness. On another level, the emphasis on dignity and community establishes "de-territorialized" connections between their struggles and those of others living across the world or in a neighboring town. The Zapatistas' rehabilitation of dignity as a revolutionary concept, John Holloway (1998) argues, becomes a unifying concept that organically links their local proposal to the national and transnational:

> Dignity is not peculiar to the indigenous peoples of the southeast of Mexico: the struggle to convert "dignity and rebellion into freedom and dignity" (an odd but important formulation) is the struggle of (and for) human existence in an oppressive society, as relevant to life in Edinburgh, Athens, Tokyo,

Los Angeles or Johannesburg as it is to the struggles of the peoples of the Lacandon Jungle. (p. 160)

Thus, dignity helps open up the confines hidden within the normative concept of community and thereby generates relevance among those who do not conform to conventional conceptions of the "organized" activist left sectors, those the Zapatistas constantly reference as their constituency. This discourse and practice of dignity, versus a stricter concept of identity, has captured the imagination of the excluded. Now, we turn to two concrete instances of the Zapatista communicational insurgency: the formulation and circulation of the communiqués and the promulgation of the Revolutionary Women's Law. Through these examples, I seek to develop the concept of communicational insurgency as an analytic to problematize the technological conception of communication.

The Communiqués: Reinventing Discourse and the Circulation of Struggle

On January 13, 1994, the first packet of communiqués arrived at the offices of three independent newspapers, one local (*El Tiempo*) and two national (*La Jornada* and *El Financiero*). The documents explained the Zapatistas' position and views on events that had taken place from the time of the military's offensive and the declaration of the ceasefire. This provided a communicative crack into which the Zapatistas entered, turning fire into a frenzy of words. A month later, Marcos (1995) describes the decision to directly contact the press on the first days "when the air smelled like gun powder and blood; the [leadership] of the EZLN called me and said: 'We need to say our word and for others to listen. If we don't do it now, others will take our voices and unwanted lies will come out of our mouths. Find out how our truth can get to those who want to hear it.'" (p. 27)

In the first 31 days, the Zapatistas issued 31 communiqués. In February, that shortest of months, the 41 dispatches were delivered to an increasingly large and eager audience (Ross, 2000). By September 1994, the number had swelled to more than 400 communiqués (Ross, 1995). Comprising letters, declarations, demands, clarifications, explanations, responses, and invitations to dialogue, the communiqués are a mix of stories, allegorical tales, satire, polemics, and historical and popular cultural references and commentaries on local, national, and international events. Their insubordinate, irreverent tone broke with the monologic of conventional political discourse, galvanized imaginations, and attained national and international circulation. "As more and more rebel communiqués were issued," historian Antonio García de León (1995) reflected, "we realized that in reality the revolt came from the depths of ourselves" (p. 10).

Addressed variously to "civil society" (understood not in the influential Hegelian sense that connects civil society with the contractual and representative framework of capitalist liberal democracy, but rather as ordinary people who are *not* necessarily part of any organized grouping, organization, or current), to the national and international press, and sometimes to particular individuals and organizations, the communiqués are the Zapatistas' principal mode of direct communication with the assorted publics outside the jungle. They represent the enormous collective effort entailed in this communicational insurgency. Once the communiqués make the dangerous journey from the jungle to the city, they are reproduced across a variety of media forms and flow across a virtual geographic space. Zapatista documents flowed out of Chiapas, hitting the pavement and the information highway as activists in El Paso, Mexico City, and elsewhere embarked on translating and posting them on the Internet; from there, they were reprinted in independent publications and recirculated in innumerable forms.

How to reconcile the democratic framework of this communicational insurgency with the seemingly protagonist role of Marcos, the most famous Zapatista author? The EZLN insists that the multilingual, urbane Marcos's role is that of a bridge and translator. According to Zapatista testimony, the process of constructing the communiqués materializes a practice of decision making based on the principle of "allowing your true word to meet my true word." Their elaboration and dissemination is guided by the Zapatista decision-making principle of *mandar obedeciendo*. In the early days of the uprising, a communiqué described the two ways that the communiqués come about. The first is where members of the leadership express the need to address a particular issue or concern publicly. The issue is proposed and debated until a consensus is reached. Marcos (1995) is then responsible for drafting the communication in the spirit of the debate and presenting it back to the committee for revision, approval, or rejection. The second mode also clarifies his role in the organization:

> On the arrival of information from far off parts or confronted by a fact that I think merits it, and seeing the value of commenting on it, I propose to the committee that we send out a communiqué. I then write it and present it as a proposal. It is discussed and approved or rejected. Did I say "rejected"? Yes, even though the current circumstances contribute to the appearance that Subcommandante I. Marcos is the "head" or "leader" of the rebellion, and that the [leadership] is just the "scenery," the authority of the committee in the communities is indisputable. It is impossible to sustain a position there without the support of the leadership of this indigenous organization. I have made various proposals for communiqués that were rejected, some for being "too hard," others for being "too soft," and some others because they "confuse things rather than clarifying them." Also, some communiqués were sent out despite my objections. (p. 27)

Elsewhere in his description, Marcos (1995) extols the vital labor of the couriers who are responsible for getting the communiqués out of the jungle: "What you probably cannot understand is the complex and anonymous heroism of the couriers who carried, from our lines to the cities, these white pages with black letters that spoke our thought" (p. 27). The figure of the unknown courier is in many ways the most evocative of this communicational insurgency. The journey from the local to the global begins on a highland footpath and involves evading military checkpoints and paramilitary gangs, cultivating a wide web of contacts, and, finally, arriving in the city to deliver a packet of communiqués. Suddenly unveiled is the profound labor of communication, dialogue, negotiation, and reflection, first revealed in the construction of the documents and again in their perilous journey out of the jungle. In this way, the courier makes a powerful critique of media-centrism and eloquently narrates the complex communication inequality that underwrites it. The ease of downloading a communiqué on the Net is the consequence of the tremendous collective work of thousands of people, engaged in years of struggle.

Perhaps nowhere is this dynamic more sharply demonstrated than in the protagonist role of women. The remarkable and vital activities of women in this protracted, complex, and often-invisible labor of building the movement have been the subject of much incisive commentary. But little explicit attention has been paid to the connection between the horizontal communicational practices associated with the Zapatistas and the women's liberation movement that emerged out of, and gave shape to, the larger movement that came to be known as Zapatismo.

The First Uprising: Revolutionary Women's Law

One third of the Zapatista fighting force comprises women, who are among its most public figures (Ross, 2006). For many women, joining the EZLN represented a life option, an immediate avenue of liberation (Millán, 1998). While the mainstream and independent media eagerly reported on the presence of so many women combatants and leaders in the first days of the uprising, much less attention was paid to the document that they carried with them: the Revolutionary Women's Law. The Law tells a powerful story about the internal, intensive communication processes that produced the conditions for the extension of the movement from the intimate to the global levels. The formation of the Women's Law is an instructive example of how the Zapatistas' dialogic decision-making process has been crucial in more ways than one. Not only is it critical to women attaining formal equality, it also opened new spaces of empowerment through a community-level insurgency of visibility and encounter.

A number of "Revolutionary Laws" govern public life in the Zapatista political commune (Millán, 1998). Covering everything from agriculture policy to education, the laws were elaborated prior to the 1994 uprising along the procedural lines of *mandar obedeciendo*. Zapatista women developed the Women's Law through a process of consultation in the dispersed communities of the emergent political commune. Its content, which reflects a practical critique of the gendered organization of society, illustrates autonomous decision-making practice in action, a concrete expression of a process of gender politicization elaborated through a dialogical network. Formalized in 1993, the Law articulates women's demands to control their own lives free of violence. It establishes a framework of basic rights: to determine maternity, to have choice in marriage, and to have equal access to education, nutrition, and decent work.

The Law reflects the sea change in revolutionary thought and action that occurred within the Zapatista commune prior to the public uprising. It is part of the process of building new social relations of equality "internally," which is then projected outward as a proposal to the wider network of speaking and listening. It is, then, a dialogical

tool and space built around visibility and encounter: the visibility of women, first within the emergent political communities as political actors and then in Mexico and internationally over the years of the uprising. In a letter published in the progressive Mexican daily *La Jornada,* Marcos characterizes the Law's creation as an "internal revolution" enacted through a long process of consultation among the diverse and dispersed Zapatista base communities:

In March 1993 we were discussing what would later be the revolutionary laws. . . . Susana was assigned to visit dozens of communities to talk with women's groups and develop the women's law. . . . Susana read out the proposals that she had gathered from the thinking of thousands of indigenous women. . . . She began to read and as she read, the assembly became more and more disquieted. Murmuring and remarks became audible. . . . Susana did not shrink from her task, but forged ahead against everything and everyone. 'We do not want to be forced to marry anyone we don't want to. We want to have the children we choose to have and are able to care for. We want the right to say our word and be respected. We want the right to study and even be drivers. And she went on like that until she finished. At the end, there was a heavy silence. . . . Suddenly, practically simultaneously, the translators, all women, finished and the compañeras began increasingly to applaud and talk among themselves. Needless to say, the laws on women passed unanimously. One Tzetal representative said, "the good thing is that my wife doesn't speak Spanish. Otherwise . . ." One woman insurgent . . . counterattacked, saying, "Well, now you're fucked because we're going to translate it into all dialects." The compañero lowered his gaze. The women were singing. The men just scratched their heads. . . . That's the truth. The first EZLN uprising was in March 1993 and it was headed by the Zapatista women. There were no casualties and they were victorious. That's how things are in this part of the world. (quoted in Millán, 1998, p. 75)

The Zapatistas' own narrative of the formation of the Women's Law tells a story of communication as an empancipatory practice, the exact opposite of abstract "information" circulation. The Law itself represents an eschewal of decrees imposed from above that are hence external to subjective experience. Rather, it is reached for from far below and, thus, interior to and reflective of the historical experience and struggle of Zapatista women. As a relation of creating power and building on the actually existing plurality within the Zapatista political commune, the Law is considered part of a process of struggle that is always incomplete, a "revolution to make revolution possible." In contrast to the constituted power of the state, this dispersal of power to create a new social reality through dialogue challenges the patriarchal norms of both the state and the local communities within which they were made. In this way, the Law is both a space and a vehicle for a process of social transformation for both men and women. In contrast to the relatively closed space of the legal state, this space remains permanently open not only because the very people subjected to it collectively developed its content, but crucially because it seeks to dissolve the separation between subject and object.

they find themselves connected (Esteva, 2006). But most significantly, this communicational insurgency constitutes an important and audacious refusal of conventional power politics that strikes at the heart of the Zapatista proposal for a new world.

Constructed around the politics of presence versus representation, this communicational insurgency proposes a confrontation with power rather than an aspiration to hold it. As journalist Luis Hernández Navarro (2006) explains, "The Zapatistas and the movement they have created are trying to open a space for millions of people who do not have real political representation" (p. 25). Amid the devastating privatization of all life under neoliberalism, the Zapatistas in Chiapas and the transnational circulation of Zapatismo continuously opens dialogical space and provides public visibility and connection that no single individual organization or project possesses, he argues. By opening up spaces for encounter, the Zapatistas aim to make audible the voices of the voiceless and make the invisible visible. This example injects new possibilities into the relationship between communication, community building, democracy, and revolution today, in a way that gives rise to new spaces of speaking and listening.

Conclusion

If the enormous communications industries can be seen as a space of constituted power, the Zapatista communicational insurgency represents its constituent other. The Zapatistas may very well be revolutionaries with a knack for timing and theatrics uniquely appropriate to the "information age." Their communication practices and emancipatory discourse were certainly pivotal to popularizing the critical language of opposition to neoliberalism and introduced a fresh conception of social revolt that helped galvanize a nascent *alter*-globalization movement. Indeed, resistance to neoliberalism has always bonded the Zapatistas and the divergent national and international social struggles with which

References

Callahan, M. (2004). Zapatismo beyond Chiapas. In D. Solnit (Ed.), *Globalize liberation: How to uproot the system and build a better world* (pp. 217–228). San Francisco: City Lights Books.

Castells, M. (1997). *The rise of the network society: Vol. 3. The information age: Economy society and culture.* Oxford: Blackwell.

Cleaver, H. (1998). The Zapatistas and the electronic fabric of struggle. In J. Holloway & E. Peláez (Eds.), *Zapatistas! Reinventing revolution in Mexico* (pp. 81–103). London: Pluto Press.

Esteva, G. (2006). The "Other Campaign" and the left: Reclaiming an alternative. *Znet.* Retrieved December 17, 2006, from www.zmag.org/content/showarticle.cfm?SectionID=59&ItemID=11652

García de León, A. (1995, July/August). Chiapas and the Mexican crisis. *NACLA: Report on the Americas, 29*(1), 10–13.

Hernández Navarro, L. (2006). El Romper de la Ola [The breaking wave]. In G. Ruggiero (Ed.), *La otra campaña* [The other campaign] (pp. 6–59). San Francisco: City Lights Books.

Holloway, J. (1998). Dignity's revolt." In J. Holloway & E. Peláez (Eds.), *Reinventing revolution in Mexico* (pp. 159–198). London: Pluto Press.

Holloway, J., & Peláez, E. (Eds.). (1998). *Reinventing revolution in Mexico.* London: Pluto Press.

Lorenzano, L. (1998). Zapatismo: Recomposition of labor, radical democracy and revolutionary project. In J. Holloway & E. Peláez (Eds.), *Reinventing revolution in Mexico* (pp. 126–158). London: Pluto Press.

Marcos, S. (1995). Prologue: Subcomandante Marcos introduces himself. In F. Bardacke, L. López, & the Watsonville, California, Human Rights Committee (Eds.), *Shadows of tender fury: The letters and communiqués of Subcomandante Marcos and the Zapatista army of national liberation* (pp. 21–30). New York: Monthly Review Press.

Marcos, S. (1996). *Letter to civil society.* Mexico City: Nuevo Amencer Press.

Martín Barbero, J. (1993). *Communication, culture and hegemony: From the media to mediations.* London: Sage.

Millán, M. (1998). Zapatista indigenous women. In J. Holloway & E. Peláez (Eds.), *Reinventing revolution in Mexico* (pp. 64–80). London: Pluto Press.

Ronfeldt, D., & Arquilla, J. (1998). *The Zapatista "Social Netwar" in Mexico.* Santa Monica, CA: RAND Corporation.

Ross, J. (1995). *Rebellion from the roots: Indian uprising in Chiapas.* Monroe, ME: Common Courage Press.

Ross, J. (2000). *The war against oblivion: The Zapatista chronicles.* Monroe, ME: Common Courage Press.

Ross, J. (2006). *Zapatistas! Making another world possible: Chronicles of resistance 2000–2006.* New York: Nation Books.

Zapatista Army of National Liberation. (1996). *Crónicas Intergalácticas: Primer Encuentro Intercontinental por la Humanidad y contra el Neoliberalismo* [Intergalactic Chronicles: First Encounter for Humanity and Against Neoliberalism]. Mexico City, Mexico: Planeta Tierra.

CHAPTER 30

Radio Voices Without Frontiers Global Antidiscrimination Broadcast

Elvira Truglia

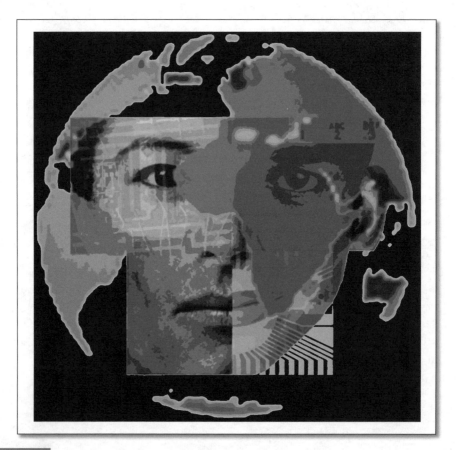

Figure 30.1 RVSF (*Radio Voix Sans Frontières*) Logo

No One Is Illegal![1] This is a manifesto and an example of an expanding community-based migrant rights movement that has taken off in Canada, especially in the aftermath of 9/11. Increasing border controls between Canada and the United States to keep goods flowing but people contained have been creating what some call the new "Fortress North America."[2] It is a familiar refrain, as the term *Fortress Europe* has been used to describe the increasingly restrictive immigration policies (e.g., the Schengen Agreement)[3] designed to keep people of European countries moving freely within their borders but to keep *out* non-Europeans. Meanwhile, the reasons why people from Asia, Africa, and Latin America keep migrating remain compelling—armed violence, ethnic and racial conflict, economic globalization, and environmental degradation are just a few (Taran, 2000, "Causes of Migration," ¶ 5). Migration-receiving countries now commonly characterize undocumented workers as "illegal migrants," rendering them outside the law, with no legal status, no legal identity, and no existence, and effectively denying them any human rights (Taran, 2000, "Ten General Trends," ¶ 7).

One of the spaces where all migrants do have a voice and a status is on community radio. Check your local listings, and chances are that you'll find a broadcast and/or podcast produced by and about migrant communities—refugees, temporary workers, migrants with no legal status, new and established immigrants, and so on. In Canada, chances are you'll find all of the above, including programming by members of the No One is Illegal migrant rights movement mentioned earlier. The beauty of community radio is that it breaks down the traditional divide between broadcaster and listener. With community radio, the listener can become the broadcaster and get engaged in the production of media and in the process of communication. Linked to movements for social change, the strength of community radio is its ability to reflect the concerns of local communities. Yet,

local realities often have global catalysts and global resonance. Migration is one of these areas of global concern. Imagine, not just one program about migrant rights or discrimination issues but dozens of programs on a similar theme being broadcast on the same day, not by circumstance but by direct action, a concerted effort by broadcasters around the world. *That* is Radio Voices Without Frontiers.

Every March 21, through the use of traditional and new communications technologies, journalists from every corner of the globe advocate against racial discrimination during a (typically) 24-hour broadcast. Running for more than a decade, Radio Voices Without Frontiers, also known by its French acronym RVSF—*Radio Voix Sans Frontières*—has become the flagship project of the World Association of Community Radio Broadcasters (AMARC).[4] Relying on an expanding international network of community radio practitioners, RVSF is one of the first community media production and distribution projects to be organized on a global scale.

The project is a testament to the socially inclusive ethos of community radio and to how the local is traced through the global and back again. Although the Voices Without Frontiers Network was started in Europe in 1996, the first broadcast took place in 1997 to commemorate the European Year Against Racism. It remained a regional event until 2000, when North American broadcasters joined the campaign. By 2001, it had become a global broadcast with the participation of broadcasters from all continents.

By 2004, programming in nine languages was broadcast on some 200 community radio stations worldwide. Focusing largely on the 2004 campaign, this chapter will demonstrate how RVSF attempts to develop its potential in using ICTs (information and communication technologies) for development and building international solidarity. It will also share the lessons learned to date and observations about the process of international network building. The lessons and reflections below are drawn from my experience as the coordinator of the RVSF broadcast from 2000 to 2004 (in 2000 as the North American broadcast coordinator; from 2001–2004 as the international broadcast coordinator). This chapter does not dwell on theory but, in many ways, reflects my experience as a practitioner and advocate of media for community development since the early 1990s. RVSF has been an opportunity to test and put into practice the ideals of community radio on a global scale.

An Inspiring Experiment in Community Media

Community media researcher and advocate, Bruce Girard (1992) says that when community radio broadcasts succeed they are marked with passion rarely seen in commercial or large-scale State media. "This passion arises out of a desire to empower listeners by encouraging and enabling their participation, not only in the radio but in the social, cultural and political processes that affect the community," states Girard (p. 3). Almost 20 years later, this observation still holds true. Broadcasters are highly motivated when they advocate for and are part of a social change process. Through its content and structure, the 2004 RVSF broadcast is a testament to the passion and transformational struggle of community radio broadcasters (Figure 30.2).

Programming on March 21, 2004 began with the first-ever broadcast from Asia: The marathon kicks off in Kathmandu, Nepal. Suman of AMARC–Asia Pacific has spent the past 24 hours trying to upload audio to the RVSF server. Finally, at 3:00 A.M. GMT (Greenwich Mean Time), all is ready to go, and he adjusts his audio player to the 3-hour Internet broadcast in Nepali and Arabic. This is the first major contribution to the global broadcast from the Asia-Pacific region, produced in partnership with Radio Sagarmatha, Nepal's first community radio station.

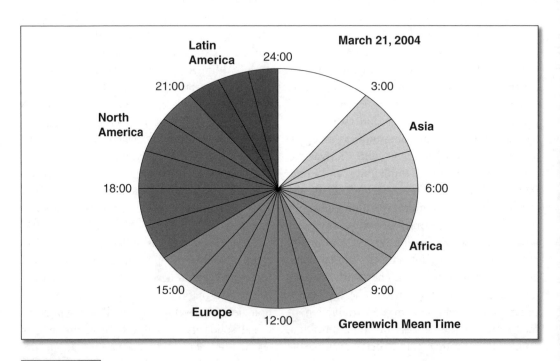

Figure 30.2 The 2004 RVSF Broadcast Time Clock

In the meantime, at close to 6:00 A.M. GMT, Gilles Eric of the Simbani news agency is gearing up for a live broadcast from Johannesburg, South Africa. Journalists from throughout Africa have been assembled in the newly created studios and are about to go on the air, one language team at a time. While a phone call confirms all is going well in the local studios, the constant buffering of the Web stream creates an inaudible Web cast for the first time in the 4-year collaboration with RVSF. Luckily, the French, Portuguese and English programs go off without a hitch on the satellite broadcaster, Channel Africa.

Four hours later, the European team is ready to take the baton. Francesco of AMISnet (Agenzia Multimediale d'Informazione Sociale) in Rome sends a staccato e-mail message—only 10 minutes before going on air. Following tradition, the social information agency has gathered a multicultural crew in the studio. Hosts will take turns announcing in Italian, French, Spanish, and English. Last-minute news that some programming from Africa has fallen through creates a hurried shuffle and gives Europe an extra hour in the global broadcast schedule. The 1-hour Lusophone feed from Radio Universidade Marao in Portugal is matched by a 1-hour feed from 15 community-access stations in the United Kingdom and a contribution from the Palestine News Network. In total, Europe broadcasts globally for 6 hours.

In a home office, the international coordinator is zigzagging time zones to communicate between continents and across hemispheres. Next, the baton is in North American hands. This year, three different broadcast hubs participate. There is French programming from the *Reseau Francophone des Amériques* in Ottawa. Spanish programming is broadcast live from Radio Centre-Ville in Montreal. And a blend of English programs from community radio stations in Canada and the United States are broadcast live from KCSB-FM in Santa Barbara. As the 5 hours of programming come to a close, Elizabeth, KCSB Staff Advisor, denounces the U.S.-led

occupation of Iraq and the closing music fades into Latin beats.

The final 3 hours of the marathon have now begun. This time the baton is in Latin America. Uruguay's Internet radio station, Radio Mundo Real, has spent the past few days putting together the 3-hour feed of programs collected by Chile's Radio Tierra in Santiago. Contributions come from Uruguay, Chile, Argentina, Ecuador, Peru, and Mexico.

With programming in nine languages, the 21-hour broadcast is realized with some 70 community radio stations or production groups and 90 contributors and team members from 29 different countries (Table 30.1). These are the people of Radio Voices Without Frontiers.

Producing and Distributing Through a Global Network

Coordinating the RVSF broadcast from 2000 to 2004 gave me the opportunity to witness the potential created by ICTs as tools for development and network building. It was a time when the potential for building international solidarity through Internet networking was growing momentum. In 1994, the Zapatista Revolution, facilitated by Internet communication, was seen as a turning point in global mobilization. And then, in 1999, the civil society protests in Seattle against the World Trade Organization (also coordinated greatly through the Internet) inspired even more energy and excitement. Today, with the so-called personal media revolution putting a blog, podcast, and vodcast within reach of almost anyone with an Internet connection, the potential of Internet networking as a great democratic force is expanding more boundaries. RVSF was and still is an experiment in testing this potential. The most important characteristics of the broadcast are presented below along with some insights on the challenges of putting it together as well as lessons learned. Specifically, we consider a

Table 30.1 2004 RVSF Broadcast Schedule

Broadcast Hub	KCSB-FM	CINQ-FM	Radio Tierra		AMISnet	Simbani	AMARC Asia-Pacific
Location	Santa Barbara	Montreal	Santiago	START TIME	Rome	Johannesburg	Kathmandu
Time Zone	GMT – 8	GMT – 5	GMT – 4	GMT*	GMT + 1	GMT + 2	GMT +5:45
Asia	19:00–22:00	22:00–1:00	13:00–2:00	3:00–6:00	4:00–7:00	5:00–8:00	8:45–11:45
Africa	22:00–3:00	1:00–6:00	2:00–5:00	6:00–11:00	7:00–12:00	8:00–13:00	11:45–16:45
Europe	3:00–8:00	6:00–11:00	7:00–12:00	11:00–16:00	12:00–17:00	13:00–18:00	16:45–21:45
North America	8:00–13:00	11:00–16:00	12:00–17:00	16:00–21:00	17:00–22:00	18:00–23:00	21:45–3:45
Latin America	13:00–18:00	16:00–19:00	17:00–20:00	21:00–24:00	22:00–1:00	23:00–2:00	3:45–6:45

Note: The Global Broadcast marathon started at 3:00 Greenwich Mean Time (GMT) and ended at 24:00 GMT (see middle column). It moved from Asia, to Africa, to Europe, to North America, and finally to Latin America. The shaded boxes indicate the GMT and corresponding regional time of the live broadcast.

broadcast that mixes new and old technologies, promotes collaborative work practices, fosters international solidarity on discrimination issues through participatory programming, and attempts to build a global network through activism.

A Mix of New and Old Technologies

RVSF is a global broadcast that spreads information in a new way, in particular, through a mix of technologies—satellite, Internet, and broadcast radio. With their multimedia digital platform, ICTs offer a means of producing and distributing content on a local and global level—locally, on radio stations that carry RVSF programming to an audience of thousands and, globally, through

the Internet to a potential audience of millions (Figure 30.3). Here's how it is done.

In 2004, RVSF was not only Web cast on www.rvsf.amarc.org but was also distributed by satellite and picked up by community radio stations around the world. With some 70 participating stations, it is estimated that 200 stations reaching millions of listeners worldwide carried RVSF programming on March 21.

Sometimes RVSF programming is available on regional or global satellite and is picked up by broadcasters "on demand" (this is the case with Italy's Global Radio and Latin America's Asociación Latinoamericana de Educación Radiofonica). It is also available on established program slots of regional satellite networks; for example, "Native America Calling" aired on American Indian Radio on Satellite (AIROS) service.

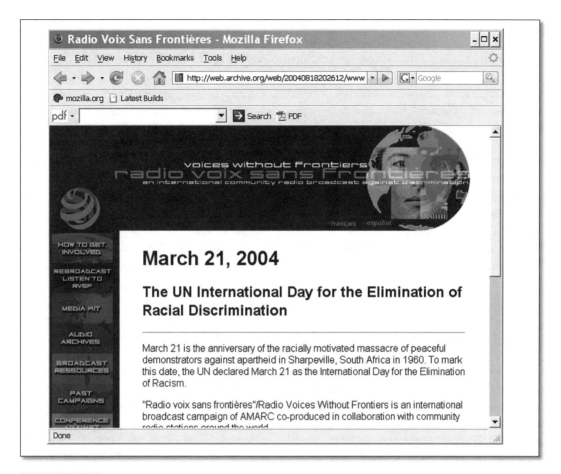

Figure 30.3   Screenshot of RVSF 2004 Web Site

Source: Contributor & AMARC created/permission granted by AMARC.

Programming carried on the *Web* stream is what makes RVSF a global continuous broadcast. In 2004, it was hosted by AMARC's home base in Montreal; in other years, different Internet Service Providers (ISPs) or networks (e.g., the Community Media Association in the United Kingdom) have hosted regional portions of the Web cast.

Despite offering different options for picking up RVSF programming, distribution remains the biggest weakness of the broadcast. Commenting on the RVSF campaign in 2001, AMARC Board member and KCSB Staff Advisor Elizabeth Robinson (2001) said,

It's a process that we don't know very well in the U.S.—a focus day where everybody does the

same thing on the same day. (Usually) we go to our little stations and we do what we do but getting people to commit their programming for one day to a common theme is new to us.

Precisely because it's new, the "build it and they will come" approach does not work for a new-technologies broadcast. "On-demand" satellite distribution and Web casting are forms of narrow-casting, not broadcasting, as they outreach specific rather than general audiences. These specific audiences might indeed tune in but only if they know you exist, so just making programming available via satellite does not mean a broadcaster will carry it. Audiences, in this case community radio stations, need to be actively solicited.

Another important aspect of the broadcast is the RVSF Web site. The Web site is the window to the global campaign; it is the only element that presents the broadcast as a global initiative. As a nongovernmental organization (NGO) based initiative, with the mandate to broker information, this is arguably one of the most important aspects of the international effort.

The Web site platform has gone through many incarnations—it was first published in HTML (Hypertext Markup Language), then it moved to an organizational content management system, and at the time of writing, it is still on a wiki platform. Each move has been made to make the site more accessible and more sustainable.

When using HTML, there is usually just one webmaster responsible for managing Web site content. In contrast, using the open-source platform wiki[5] makes it easier to access and change content. In the case of the RVSF Web site, there is still a webmaster responsible for the overall structure of the site; however, by using a set of simple commands, various individuals can be responsible for managing content.

For RVSF, this means that content can be added and revised in a more timely manner and by different sets of people.

Another ICT used to facilitate working together is File Transfer Protocol, or FTP. It is a relatively simple new technology that is used to connect two computers over the Internet so that the user of one computer can transfer files and perform file commands on the other computer. During a typical RVSF campaign, an FTP site is made available to all regions for posting temporary and permanent audio files to be shared and exchanged.

The audio archives[6] are another important part of the mix. Although the global broadcast is a 1-day campaign, radio stations (and civil society) are encouraged to listen to or download audio archives and broadcast RVSF programs on their local radio stations throughout the year. In general, archives are an important way to preserve the historical memory of community radio

and to keep the spotlight on targeted social issues. At the end of the 2004 broadcast, there were 31 individual archives and 11 complete broadcast hours published on the Web site (Figure 30.4). If you check the site now, you'll only find archives as of 2005. The crash of AMARC's server and a nasty virus invasion resulted in the loss of much information—an anecdote mentioned as a cautionary tale about relying too heavily on computer networks (J.-P. Théberge, AMARC-International, personal communication, November 29, 2006).

This survey of the technological mix used in the broadcast illustrates how ICTs are helping people communicate (although imperfectly) from the many to the many. Yet, ICTs can also reconstruct the same power imbalances that are being redressed. Thanks to different technical and human resource capacities between regions and within regions, the RVSF broadcast sometimes reflects North-South power imbalances but also those that are North-North and South-South. For example, Radio Mundo Real in Uruguay is a fully functioning Internet radio station, while Radio Tierra in Chile barely has a reliable dial-up connection. CJSF in Vancouver may be in the global North, but that didn't help when trying to figure out how to enter a URL in an audio player. It's also worth noting that FTP may be a simple technology, but if you don't have access to a high-speed connection it is very impractical. In Kathmandu, the Asia-Pacific coordinator set up a plan just in case the local Internet connection was unsuccessful; he would ship an audio CD by airmail to New Delhi for upload from there. Also, while digital radio production is now more common, it is still not universal, nor is Internet broadcasting. Therefore, RVSF still accepts audiocassettes and accommodates analog production and broadcasting.

Together, this is undeniable proof that technology is not an end in itself. But it also shows how technology is always adapted on a local level—each of these radio stations found ways to produce and distribute their programs, whether

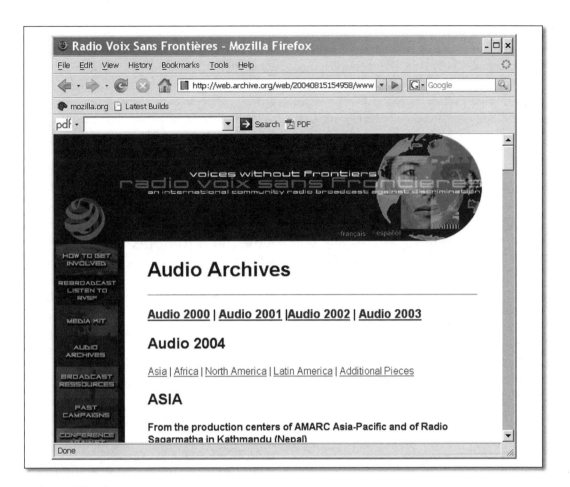

Figure 30.4 Screenshot of 2004 RVSF Archives

Source: Contributor & AMARC created/permission granted by AMARC.

by mailing recorded audiocassettes, uploading digital audio, downloading the Web stream, or broadcasting live on their analog stations. In other words, they were able to participate in the broadcast by using a mix of traditional and new technologies.

The regional coordinator for AMARC Asia-Pacific, Suman Basnet, says that a global campaign cannot be over reliant on the Internet: "Internet is not a reality in most of the communities in the Asia-Pacific" (personal communication, December 10, 2006). Clearly, stations without an Internet connection cannot stream content or download audio files.

To be successful, Basnet says, "global campaigns must also have smaller—community to community—exchanges within them." This is true especially for the Asia-Pacific region because of language constraints. "Most community radios in the region exist in areas where English is not understood. Most of Asia-Pacific's contributions were in local languages/dialects. Therefore programs produced by one community radio could not be used by another," says Basnet (personal communication, December 10, 2006).

This reality is built into the design of the broadcast. Stations can still be part of the global campaign by producing local programming and by exchanging programming with other local or regional stations, even by snail mail.

Yet, as Basnet points out, this means that more lead time is needed for planning and for promotion of the broadcast within the region. In other words, enough effort needs to be placed on preparing, not just on gathering the right technological mix.

New Ways of Working

How does it all come together? General operations are managed using electronic lists, news groups, online workspaces (e.g., FTP), Web sites (Wiki platform), and instant messaging services. RVSF producer María Suárez Toro (Kidd, 2002) of Feminist Internet Radio Endeavor (FIRE) in Costa Rica says, "Too many people think that the technology is the communication" (p. 18). Her production strategy focuses on access and finding creative ways of using technology (Suarez, 2000). In other words, it is the networking opportunity provided by the technology that creates communication not the technology itself (p. 20).

For RVSF, this means going beyond hierarchical relationships and applying new ways of working. As an example, the international coordinator, regional teams, and partners, located in five continents, work together on coordination, mobilization, programming, distribution, and promotion. There are common campaign objectives, timelines, and responsibilities, but these are adapted to each region's priorities, work cultures, and capacities.

A big challenge for RVSF is overcoming language barriers. Group interaction online is difficult because there is no common language. Language divides are often just seen as communication barriers, while the power relations implicated in the use of one language over another are ignored. One of the ways this is addressed is by sending out collective messages in three working languages (English, French, and Spanish). On an operational level, this becomes a time-consuming and challenging task to sustain.

Managing "activist fatigue" is another concern. The whole broadcast relies on the volunteer participation of community radio broadcasters, independent producers, and affinity groups—sometimes voices are from the marginalized communities themselves and sometimes they are from activists who represent them. Because of social inequalities, the communities being targeted may have the least amount of time to contribute to a campaign or project. The challenge is then to be creative and flexible in coming up with ways to involve people while at the same time accepting their limits.

New Technologies Meet Social Activism

But what do you actually hear in the broadcast? The RVSF campaign encourages the analysis of a global issue (racial discrimination) on local levels, and through the sharing of experiences it fosters local, regional, and global solidarity on these issues.

In fact, the linking of global issues on a local level is what community radio does best. Since the inception of the international campaign, programming on March 21 has illustrated how the same global economic and political forces are shaping regressive policies in the North and the South. Neocolonialism, xenophobia, the creation of Continental Fortresses, and the communication divide are regular features of RVSF. Each year, a broadcast theme is chosen, which is linked to a current event. In 2002, the theme was the post-9/11 environment; in 2003, it was the impending Iraq War; in 2004, the theme was communication rights in the context of the World Summit on the Information Society. In general, programming usually reflects three major themes: (1) migration; (2) systemic racism and antiracism work; and (3) identity, difference, and self-determination.

Here are some highlights of the 2004 broadcast—one of the most diverse and dynamic ever:

Asia-Pacific: For the first time, there was a special 3-hour broadcast from Asia with contributions from community radio stations and producers in Nepal, Sri Lanka, India, and the Philippines. Stories covered included the following:

- Caste-based discrimination in Nepal and education as a key to overcoming it

- The case of the *dalits,* who are not allowed to worship in Hindu temples because of their social status as "low caste"

- The history, present situation, and future prospects of the Kumals, a so-called low-caste group from Nepal's Palpa region

- A discriminatory law that makes it difficult for women to acquire citizenship in Nepal

- Discrimination against indigenous people in Nepal and ways to fight it

- The role of mass media in challenging discrimination

Africa: Working with a team of journalists throughout the African continent, RVSF broadcast live from the (no-longer opera- tional) Simbani News Agency of AMARC Africa in Johannesburg, South Africa. There were stories on the following:

- South Africa: farmers rights, xenophobia, human rights, the role of ICTs, youth in the South African education system of the postapartheid era, and HIV/AIDS and antiretroviral drugs

- Gambia: forced marriages, women, and employment

- Ghana: Marginalization of people who practice traditional religions, digital divides

- Tanzania: community radio and AIDS awareness campaigns

- Community radio in Ethiopia

- Media and reconciliation on the Ivory Coast

- Media and conflict resolution

- NGOs and the right to communicate

Europe: Hosted by AMISnet in Rome, one of the unique features of the broadcast was the Link Lusofono, a collaboration between Portuguese speakers from community radio

stations in 12 countries. There were also con- tributions from 15 access radio stations (a new tier of local radio in the United Kingdom with programs for social and educational ben- efit, legalized in July 2004). Stories covered included the following:

- Racial discrimination in Romania

- The living conditions of the Roma people in the Czech and Slovak Republic

- Youth on racial discrimination in Europe

- The Bossi-Fini law and its effects on migrants living in Italy

- The behaviour of the Israeli army and the discrimination between Muslim and Christian Palestinians

- The "administrative genocide" in Slovenia when a number of nonethnic Slovenes were erased from the public registries after Slovenia declared independence from Yugoslavia in 1991

- Multiculturalism and freedom of speech issues in the Netherlands

- An inquiry on the situation of 400 African asylum seekers who live in an occupied building in Rome

- Media and migration issues

North America: For the first time ever, there was a 1-hour national feed in French by the Ottawa- based Reseau Francophone des Amériques and a 1-hour feed in Spanish by Radio Centre-Ville in Montreal. The English broadcast came from KCSB-FM in Santa Barbara, California. Featured stories included the following:

- The impact of U.S. immigration policies on U.S.-Mexico border residents

- Actions against the deportation of refugees in Canada

- Anti-immigration laws around the world

- Racism in sports media

- Poverty, women, and discrimination

- Reparations for victims of discrimination in the United States

- Community media at the World Summit on the Information Society

- Struggles of resistance and self-determination in Haiti, India, and the United States; for example, one story covered a *rapero's* efforts to build Latino cultural consciousness in the United States through music.

- Relations between Anglophones and minority Francophones in Canada

Latin America: From the broadcast centers of Radio Mundo Real in Uruguay, in collaboration with Radio Tierra in Chile, the broadcast featured contributions from community radio stations and producers in Chile, Mexico, Argentina, Uruguay, Peru, and Ecuador. Stories covered were as follows:

- Promoting citizenship, civics, and democratic culture in Latin America

- Migration struggles on the U.S.-Mexico border

- Media and discrimination against women in Mexico

- The Andean communities and their struggle for water in Cochabamba, Bolivia

- The role of women in the Mapuche community in Chile

- Violence against women

- Refugee struggles in Ecuador

- The Peruvian Truth and Reconciliation Commission and its report on discrimination against indigenous peoples, peasants, and women

- Racial discrimination against rural peoples who migrate to urban centers in Peru

- Racism in Argentina

- A public forum for art, politics, and human rights in Argentina

As described above, the concept of participatory communication is well represented in the programming content of the broadcast. According to Bruce Girard (1992), "the role of the radio [community radio] is to respond to the priorities set by the community, to facilitate their discussion, to reinforce them, and to challenge them" (p. 3). In the case of RVSF, this role was bestowed on the broadcast coordinators. As long as contributions were on theme and respected the principles of the broadcast, all contributions were accepted and included in the broadcast according to priorities set by each region.

Nevertheless, RVSF is not just a series of regional broadcasts but is presented as a global broadcast on a common theme. In this respect, there could be more interactivity, including live discussion/commentary between regions during the broadcast. There could also be more joint programming; for example, the lineup could include a cross-continental panel on migration policy. Of course, this is only possible permitting there are adequate technical and financial resources—a common challenge for community radio initiatives. Earlier, the call for more local-to-local exchanges was reported; there is also a need for more region-to-region exchanges; in both cases, the imperative is to raise the bar and increase the chances of making a social impact.

Building a Network on a Day of Hope

RVSF remains a day of hope as it fosters the incorporation of people into a worldwide antidiscrimination community radio network. The International Day for the Elimination of Racial Discrimination commemorates the anniversary of the 1960 Sharpeville massacre, when antiapartheid demonstrators were killed in a South African town. Almost 50 years later, and in a postapartheid South Africa, Sharpeville remains an international symbol of resistance and hope and has become the common reference point across the RVSF antidiscrimination network.

Photo 30.1 RVSF International Broadcast in Johannesburg, South Africa, 2001

Source: Waag Society.

Elizabeth Robinson (2001) has helped coordinate the RVSF broadcast in North America since 2000. Commenting on the importance of the campaign, she refers to the beginning of the 20th century:

> [At the time, it was said that] *the* problem of the 20th century was going to be race and racism. Well, we are now in the 21st century and it remains a problem. So, I think one of the things that we wanted to do in North America when we joined the campaign was to remind people that it was still a problem. But also to educate people about the problem and all of the various sorts of resistance to these human problems that are expanse in the world today.

To address racism issues, many events have been organized under the RVSF banner: conferences and training workshops on content production and mobilization. RVSF teams have also come together for remote broadcasts at events such as the World Social Forum in Brazil, the UN World Summit on Sustainable Development in South Africa, and the UN World Conference Against Racism also in South Africa. The broadcasts have always taken place in parallel with advocacy work at official and counterforums. This kind of advocacy is considered a priority for AMARC and many other international NGOs.

Media studies professor and longtime community media activist Dorothy Kidd (2002) regards attending counterforums of UN conferences and other global meetings as one of the most important networking areas for international NGOs (INGOs)—these meetings become opportunities to influence official organizations. Kidd notes that the most successful NGO strategy has been discursive, in which "knowledge does appear to be power" (p. 7). These forums are opportunities for NGOs to broker alternative information and put a human face on complex social problems by featuring individual testimonies and stories (p. 7).

Yet, Kidd (2002) cautions that sometimes these advocacy efforts result in INGOs losing touch with their activist roots and compromising their goals to a United Nations and government focus (p. 14). In this respect, AMARC is present at most of these international gatherings with both advocacy and broadcaster contingents, so it becomes more difficult to lose focus and easier to keep both the lobbying efforts and activist roots in play. When it comes to RVSF, whether on March 21 or at global forums, more work needs to be done to partner with community and antidiscrimination organizations as well as other affinity groups to ensure that the broadcast network is truly connected to a broad network of social activists.

RVSF is an opportunity to create a dialogue between the institution of community radio and the social movement of community radio. It is a symbolic and therefore discursive initiative, but it is also a vehicle for networking among community radio and social activists who continue the lived social struggle for rights and dignity.

Elizabeth Robinson (2001) says about the RVSF broadcast,

> The possibility of not only linking with other stations in our own region but of linking with people all over the world is irresistible in some ways and I think it points to all the best of what we are; . . . it reminds us of our potential.

Rosario Puga (2004) of Radio Tierra in Chile shares this perspective: "As a global initiative, Voces Sin Fronteras represents the great potential of radio exchange initiatives" (p. 3).

The long-term objective of the RVSF initiative has been to develop a sustainable program of work, incorporating broadcast and training components throughout the year in every region of the world. In a nutshell, RVSF is an opportunity to test and put into practice the many ideals held by the progressive communications community.

Conclusion

While economic globalization continues to push and control the migration of peoples, the themes of migration, discrimination, and racism will remain contemporary for some time to come. This makes RVSF an important expression of international solidarity.

The continuing growth of community radio around the world positions it as a part of a social movement—one where the global forces shaping local contexts are being heard, debated, contested, and repositioned:

> Community radio is a great equalizer. As proponents of community radio, if we do not campaign against racial discrimination then it will be like doctors stopping to provide a cure. It is our primary job to raise our voices against all kinds of discrimination. (S. Basnet, personal communication, December 10, 2006)

For more than a decade, the Radio Voices Without Frontiers broadcast campaign has been raising voices and expanding global and local mediascapes through a mix of new and traditional technologies. It's an experiment still worth pursuing, regardless of the challenges.

At the end of the day each March 21, participants are sustained with their sense of euphoria. A community radio broadcast marathon around the world has been realized, collectively. Imagine what could happen if this year's listeners, social activists, and displaced people became next year's broadcasters? *Another kind of communication is possible:* That is the message and the struggle.

Notes

1. See http://nooneisillegal-montreal.blogspot.com/ and http://solidarityacrossborders.org/en/node as an example of the migrants' rights issues addressed by this community-based activist network.

2. *Fortress Europe* is the term given (usually pejoratively) to the concept of the European Union's efforts to keep non-EU goods, businesses, and nationals out of the Union's 25 member states (Wikipedia at http://en.wikipedia.org/wiki/Fortress_Europe, accessed December 2006). The term *Fortress North America* is sometimes used to make a parallel between EU border policies and the increasingly harmonized border controls between the U.S. and Canada since September 11, 2001.

3. The 1985 Schengen Agreement is an agreement among European states that sets out a common policy on the temporary entry of persons and the integration of external border controls. It is touted as a way to simplify the circulation of people between member states. In practice, it creates a class of non-European "undesireables."

4. See www.amarc.org.

5. See www.wiki.org for more information about Wiki.

6. To see the audio archives, go to www.rvsf.amarc .org. Click on "audio archives" in the main menu and then scroll to see the list of archives by year, as of 2005 (information from previous years is no longer on line).

References

Girard, B. (1992). Introduction. In B. Girard (Ed.), *A passion for radio* (pp. 1–11). Montreal, Quebec, Canada: Black Rose Books.

Kidd, D. (2002, July). *Which would you rather: Seattle or Porto Alegre?* Paper presented at Our Media II Conference, Barcelona, Spain. Retrieved December 1, 2006, from www.ourmedianet.org/papers/om2002/Kidd.om2002.pdf

Puga, R. (2004). *Evaluación América latina y el Caribe– Voces Sin Fronteras 2004.* Santiago, Chile: AMARC-Latin America and the Carribbean.

Robinson, E. (2001). *Audio interview by María Suarez Toro of Feminist Internet Radio Endeavor (FIRE) for the Radio Voices Without Frontiers broadcast campaign.* Retrieved December 4, 2006, from www.fire.or.cr/voicesfrontier.htm

Suarez, M. (2000). FIRE: Popular communication in many forms. *InteRadio* (Journal of AMARC—World Association of Community Radio Broadcasters, Montreal, Quebec, Canada).

Taran, P. (2000). Human rights of migrants: Challenges of the new decade [Electronic version]. *International Migration Quarterly Review* (Special issue 2), *38*(6). Retrieved November 29, 2006, from www.migrantwatch.org/Resources/challeges_new_decade.html

CHAPTER 31

Media Activism for Global Justice

Anne Marie Todd

The movement against corporate globalization is a grassroots globalization effort (Appadurai, 2000; Karliner, 1997) known to activists as the global justice movements (Anderson & Cavanagh, 2001; Starhawk, 2002). The American mainstream media most often refer to this movement as the "antiglobalization movement" (Cockburn, St. Clair, & Sekula, 2000; Danaher & Burbach, 2000).[1] For most Americans, this movement is a series of isolated events that flicker across their television screens every few years. Accounts of sea turtles marching in the streets and violent clashes between police and anarchists have dominated American news stories chronicling the movement. In years since the Battle of Seattle in November 1999, when 50,000 demonstrators protested the World Trade Organization (WTO), we have seen visible massive demonstrations at the meetings of multilateral economic institutions (MEIs) around the world. However, American media coverage of these protests has limited their impact and effect on the general public's awareness of such issues. Clashes between police and protesters dominate the headlines as news coverage of protests focus on violent acts at demonstrations and emphasize the necessity of heavy police presence. Particularly after September 11, 2001, a zero-tolerance attitude for antiestablishment activity has limited the media effects of these protests. Mainstream American media have written off the movement as a passing trend, not a serious critique of the global economy.

This chapter reexamines the failure of the movement as represented in American mainstream media to lay out the role for activist media in framing the movement's actions for both sympathetic and also more general audiences. This chapter first analyzes the American mainstream media narrative of the antiglobalization movement to understand how the movement plays to the general public and to provide a perspective on the prevailing sentiment about the antiglobalization movement. Next, this chapter presents the work of two leaders in media activism from the antiglobalization movement: Protest.Net and Indymedia. This chapter concludes with lessons from the antiglobalization movement for understanding how activist community media have the potential to democratize the global mediascape.

Antiglobalization Demonstrators at It Again: The Dominant Media Narrative

Media presentation is composed of tacit theories about "what matters." Media frames are "persistent patterns of cognition, interpretation, and presentation, of selection, emphasis, and exclusion, by which symbol-handlers routinely organize discourse, whether verbal or visual" (Gitlin, 1980, p. 7). The agenda-setting function of the press is premised on the power of media as a central element to the perceived success of a social movement. "The major communication links between movements and the public or the audience are provided by the mass media" (Ball-Rokeach & Tallman, 1979, p. 84). Media activism's success consists of making democratic communication a "conscious priority . . . articulating different elements of radical democracy" (Carroll & Hackett, 2006, p. 100). The nature and extent of media coverage affects how the public perceives a movement's actions and thus influences the level of movement success.

The Seattle protests in November 1999 were the most successful American demonstrations in years (Ramsey, 2000), launching the antiglobalization movement in the United States and establishing a "congruence between the protesters' goals and the effect on public policy issues" (de Armond, 2000, p. 232). The Seattle protests exploded across the headlines, largely because the sizable turnout was unexpected, and television and other media coverage led to the perception of the protests being marked by clashes between police and protesters. The *Seattle Times* declared the protests to be "chaos" ("Countdown," 1999). On ABC television news, the late Peter Jennings noted that Seattle was a meeting ground for any group in the world with a complaint (Ackerman, 2000). While the protests clearly signaled the emergence of a vocal sector of civil society and were considered successful by activists (Brecher, Costello, & Smith, 2000; Cockburn et al., 2000; Danaher, 2000; Prokosch & Raymond, 2002), the goals and specific demands of this movement remained elusive to the public eye.

While the Seattle protests caught the city and the nation off guard, the next large demonstrations at the IMF/World Bank's April 2000 meetings in Washington, D.C., were met with significant police presence. After the Washington protests, mainstream media coverage remained skeptical: Protesters were merely a marginal curiosity. An Associated Press report described the protesters as having "far-fetched" concerns (Ackerman, 2000). The *Washington Post* reported on the IMF/World Bank demonstrations in the "Style" section, emphasizing hair, nose rings, and body art. This type of coverage portrayed the movement as a popular trend that would dissipate in the momentum of world trade.

The Washington protests were such "a hodge-podge of slogans and causes that, to the casual observer, it was hard to decode the connection between Mumia's incarceration and the fate of the sea turtle" (Klein, 2000, p. 25). The protesters were described as a "kooky crowd" (*Time*), a "circus" (*New York Times* [by the political commentator Thomas Friedman]), a "motley crew" for whom "disparate isn't the word" (*Newsweek*), and a mob of "militant dunces" (*Economist*).[2] Activist concerns were seen as nothing more than platitudes rather than serious gripes with the system and certainly not a vision for an alternative to global capitalism.

The death of an Italian protester, Carlo Giuliani, at the hands of *carabinieri* (Italian police) during the June 2001 G8 Summit meeting in Genoa, Italy, was a defining moment for the antiglobalization movement. His death tragically exposed the increasingly violent clashes between the police and demonstrators and revealed the dramatic conflict emerging between the pillars of the global economy and a growing faction of dissent. However, mainstream media coverage focused exclusively on violent *protesters,* not police. For example, the *New York Times* described protesters as people who "simply come along for the fun of banging heads. When not demonstrating against globalization, they fight at soccer stadiums" (Stanley & Sanger, 2001). The escalation of violence relegated the protesters to a fringe status in the mainstream media and activists were divided on the future of the movement.

Just a few months later, the terrorist attacks of September 11 dramatically changed media coverage of the antiglobalization movement from incoherent anarchists to potential security threats. Protest events lost media coverage in the wake of the terrorist attacks, overshadowed by the "war on terror" in Afghanistan and Iraq and stories of heroism and grief. Furthermore, the antiestablishment rhetoric of such protests stoked public fears amid government security concerns, and economic institutions took measures to contain the type of "militant activity" normally associated with demonstrations (Blustein, 2001).

Protests in Cancun, Mexico, at the WTO's September 2003 meeting marked a new phase of movement growth, with more than 10,000 activists converging, yet the movement remained in the shadow of September 11. Newspapers "ran almost daily warnings of terror. Tens of thousands of Mexican federal police officers were on hand, and navy ships floated off the coast" in case protests became a cause for terrorism (Thompson, 2003). When Lee Kyung Hai, a Korean farmer, wearing a sign that said "WTO kills farmers" stabbed himself fatally in the chest, protests captured headlines: "Bloodshed mars Cancun WTO summit" (Jack, 2003). Media reports focused on the lone event of Lee Kyung Hai's suicide as part of larger "protests, some playful and other deadly serious" (Thompson, 2003). Protesters seemed out of touch, willing to kill themselves in a futile attempt to protest against WTO farming policies.

Two months later at the FTAA's (Free Trade Area of the Americas) November 2003 summit, media reported on the Miami police's clampdown on the protests as necessary standard practice (Getzan, 2004), and the level of institutional control and security fears was reported to have weakened the protesters' momentum (Reel & Fernandez, 2002). Police presence at protest events has continued to escalate: When the G8 held their June 2004 summit in Sea Island,

Georgia, an isolated resort island accessed by a single highway, 20,000 security personnel outnumbered the few hundred activists who marched in the abandoned streets. In contrast to the coverage of the strong showing of Miami's police force, media coverage focused on low turnout: Reuters noted that the G8 protests in Sea Island were particularly small; protesters had expected 5,000 protesters to come out, but barely 300 people marched (Simao, 2004). CNN noted that the "G8 protest draws small crowd" (Walton, 2004), while the *New York Times* emphasized that the police and delegates outnumbered the demonstrators (Hart, 2004). During one protest "several dozen protesters gathered . . . flanked by almost as many members of the media" (Walton, 2004). Without dramatic clashes with police or property destruction to report, mainstream media pointed to the failure of the movement to sustain its protest.

The mainstream media narrative illustrates two ways in which the movement has failed: First, while the movement has helped to put issues of social, economic, and environmental justice on the radar of the public agenda, the specific demands of the protests remain unclear. Stuck with the moniker "antiglobalization," the movement's specific call for action is not understood by the public because they are eclipsed by numerous other causes, which dilute the overall protest message. Mainstream media coverage continuously classified the protests as a fad, not as a tenable movement that might enjoy strong public support. This strategy circumvents the appeal of the protesters' issues, by describing them as periodic crises' in the inevitable processes of economic globalization and free trade. Activists are seen as protesting for the sake of protest, of failing to offer informed solutions.

Second, negative media attention is a major problem facing movement organizers, who strive to keep the cause of global justice from being trivialized as a hodgepodge of issues to keep peaceful protestors from being criminalized due to the conduct of more violent elements within the movement, and to check the heavy-handed police responses. Media coverage of violence and arrests frames the debate around the legitimacy of civil disobedience rather than on the demands of the protests. When the nightly news shows police dragging away protesters who are blocking a city intersection, it is unlikely that the message received by the public is that the World Bank has unjust policies. The television-viewing public may not make those connections, especially when the confrontation is reduced to the spectacle of the physical conflict itself (Lakey, 2000). While the protests have increased the public's awareness of these issues, they have detracted from the issues and causes they represent, and it is questionable whether public awareness is positive or negative regarding their causes. For example, the *Seattle Times* noted that following the protests the WTO will "stand for a mix of issues, images and events. Meetings of government and business officials. Protests of those meetings. Tear gas and pepper spray, curfews and restricted areas" ("Countdown," 1999, p. A6). This exemplifies how protests call attention to issues, but their message is not always coherent when viewed through the lens of mainstream media. In this way, the antiglobalization movement appears to have failed to sustain its push for social change because it never overcame its public relations problem(s).

Activist Media Spin: Protest.Net and Indymedia

Whereas the mass media narrative of the antiglobalization movement portrays the failure of the movement to sustain itself or win popular support, we may tell the movement's story another way: as a success in the democratization of media. Media *produce* the public sphere (Deluca & Peeples, 2002) as democracy is integrated into "individual subjectivities and collective identities" mediated through symbolic practices of protest (Best, 2005, p. 214). Communication technologies have greatly enabled the ability of global justice movements through new, productive coalitions of activists; technologically

enhanced strategies of resource mobilization to coordinate local efforts; and discursive space to resist corporate globalization and become an active component of global civil society (Todd, 2003). The evolution of this movement in the establishment of global communication networks, mobilization of thousands of activists at local demonstrations, and response to unfavorable media coverage demonstrates a success that is useful for theorizing about the nature and future of social movements in a global media market.

In America, mainstream media continue to write the story of the movement. So how do activist groups attempt to combat these media effects? One answer lies in new technologies, which have changed the organization and the action of social movement communities. "The Internet gives today's low-budget activists mobilizing powers that their predecessors could only dream of, providing cheap, easy, and instantaneous communication with and between huge numbers of people all over the world" (Beiser, 2000, p. 13). Technologies such as Web pages, bulletin boards, and e-mails enable activists to create a consortium of organizations with a broader base of people to organize and deploy direct actions.

While many activist groups use the Internet to organize protests and promote their causes, two groups have become "tech-support for the revolution" (E. Henshaw-Plath, personal communication, November 28, 2001). Protest.Net and Indymedia both organize and mobilize new communication technologies in ways that provide broad support for activists. Both Protest.Net and Indymedia are prominent architects of antiglobalization movement's media strategy but fulfill two different and equally important functions. Protest.Net is an online calendar for protest events for the purpose of organizing, while Indymedia is a clearinghouse for news of these protests and other events. As different arms of the movement, they complement each other and demonstrate the importance of an activist media spin not only to counteract the mainstream media narrative but also to build solidarity among activists.

Protest.Net: Solidarity Through Mobilization

Protest.Net is a self-defined "collective of activists who are working together to create our own media" (Protest.Net, 2005a). Protest.Net exemplifies the unifying effects of new technology for activism, because it serves as a central source of information about current issues and upcoming events for myriad protest groups. Speaking about Protest.Net, the *New York Times* describes the power of a "protest portal [that] unites activists under one URL": With Protest.Net's quick access to information, prospective protesters can find out about upcoming local action as well as similar events around the world (Tedeschi, 1998). Protest.Net enables activists to stay informed by having protest and event information condensed onto one Web site, which lists ways to help further the cause and invites visitors to its site to add events, donate money, or join events.

One of the most intriguing parts of Protest.Net is the Web site's *Activist Handbook,* which urges would-be activists that they can act to change their world (Protest.Net, 2005b). The *Handbook* encourages people interested in global justice to get involved because "The work of each individual helps"; "Once you do something, others will join you" (http://protest.net/activists_handbook/join.html); "Helping the world is helping yourself" (http://protest.net/activists_handbook/help.html); "If the system doesn't work, change it"; and "Protest is an effective means of creating change" (Protest.Net, 2005b, see http://protest.net/activists_handbook/change.html). These phrases are quite evocative for the would-be activist and express solidarity with all individuals wanting to push for social change. The *Handbook* urges readers to get involved with their issues, and by doing so they can "indirectly help others . . . it's all interrelated" (Protest.Net, 2005b, see http://protest.net/activists_handbook/interrelated.html)—this is a particularly motivating phrase because it describes different acts of protest as mutually empowering and uses the complexities of globalization processes to tie each specific cause into one coherent need for social change.

Being part of a group helps inspire protesters. Seeing that other individuals share concerns about free trade and corporate exploitation is empowering and makes people more willing to become activists. The founder of Protest.Net explains: "Part of the antiglobalization project is to reconstruct notions of locality and national identity. . . . Today in the antiglobalization movement we're creating a new notion of internationalist localism" (E. Henshaw-Plath, April 22, 2002, personal communication). The antiglobalization movement promotes an ideological unity that begets shared visions, values, and principles that perhaps at some point in the evolution of the movement transcend the previous ideological boundaries and the movement becomes one whole. Decentralized coordination of protests empowers different groups through a common goal. Protesters work together to convey a sense of collective identity, which is integral to the idea of a movement, and also to mobilize in numerous locations a greater number of activists locally who exhibit solidarity across expansive geographical distances. The challenge is to translate this solidarity into a coherent message.

Indymedia: Solidarity Through Awareness

Independent Media Center (Indymedia) is a network of collectively run online media outlets whose mission is the creation of "radical, accurate, and passionate" truth. Established by activists in 1999 for the purpose of providing grassroots coverage of the WTO protests in Seattle, Indymedia is an international organization that acts as a clearinghouse of information, providing journalists with real-time reports, photos, and audio and video footage. Indymedia has no central office: More than 100 local

Independent Media Centers organize themselves through the Web site. While the decentralization of Indymedia makes it difficult to estimate usage, as a whole, Indymedia receives between 500,000 and 2 million page views a day (Indymedia, 2007).

Indymedia uses a democratic, open-publishing system, which allows anyone to post to the Indymedia newswires. Indymedia invites comments on their news stories with the goal of promoting public debate. All original content posted to Indymedia is free for reprint and rebroadcast for noncommercial use. In this way, the mission of Indymedia is to empower activists to create media: "If you want to see more coverage of an issue, post more stories about the issue and encourage other newswire readers to do the same" (Indymedia, 2007). Indymedia offers its services as a way to counteract corporate domination of media stories and to provide "safe space" for telling the story of the movement: "People participating in protests . . . are unlikely to receive honest consideration in the corporate-owned media" (Indymedia, 2007). Indymedia endeavors to "empower people to become the media" and to "present honest, accurate, powerful independent reports." The long-term goal is to "foster and facilitate the development of as much independent media as possible around the world," such as the development of independent national/international television networks and newspapers, to ensure public access to independent news reports (Indymedia, 2007).

The technological capabilities of Protest.Net and Indymedia reveal the importance of activist media in creating solidarity among global justice activists. First, the mass media story of antiglobalization and the countermeasures of Protest.Net and Indymedia reveal new modes of resource mobilization, which change the existing notions of collective action and social movements. That is, the new technologies not only ease information dissemination and thus change the ways that social movements increase public awareness of causes, but also enhance the structure of

movement activity through a more decentralized infrastructure, and thus change the way scholars must evaluate the communication processes of social movements. One of the best ways that global and local movements can attract international attention is to create media buzz through events that are newsworthy, largely because of the numbers of people they attract. Internet technologies help to make local campaigns visible in a global (virtual) forum: Events posted on Protest.Net and covered by Indymedia have more of an impact on a global scale; local activists can distribute information, post reports of campaign progress, and issue press releases online. Through the use of new technologies, movements can increase the number of participants, have greater geographic reach and more flexibility, reduce the time for exchanging information, and make possible immediate action. On the other hand, technology also makes the task movement organizers face harder, as standards for communication and information dissemination go up and the movement's technological infrastructure must expand to support a large mobilized populace.

Second, the movement's claims to accuracy through firsthand accounts of the protests are important for efforts to disseminate information about the protesters and their causes. The protests are thoroughly and extensively documented; for example, the Independent Media Center issued press credentials to hundreds of activists who, due to the affordability of recording equipment, have been able to record nearly every moment of the protests. These firsthand accounts can counteract mainstream media coverage and resist suppression. Once the people are aware of questionable state tactics, it is easier to win favor in the media and the public eye and also force authorities to respond. However, it is important to consider that many visitors to Internet sites are people who are already aware of the movement and its causes. Alternative media need to attract an audience; the antiglobalization movement must expand its audience beyond its choir. Raising awareness of actions is an important function of Protest.Net and Indymedia. Enhanced awareness of the struggle creates solidarity among activists that has sustained the movement's momentum despite mainstream media coverage.

Third, contemporary activists have been shown to be profoundly aware of how their actions are communicated in the media. Activists have developed independent media to counter the dominant interpretations of the press through information dissemination, as well as creating their own media images, and a vision for a more democratic world. The electronic space of the networks of global justice movements changes the power structure of the debate about globalization. Through their online media spin, activists reframe the issues surrounding the global economy in a way that creates a space for an energized civil society. The technological infrastructure of the movement has created activist networks that continue to mobilize campaigns and actions.

In this sense, the legacy of the antiglobalization movement is broader than single policy victories. Ganesh, Zoller, and Cheney (2005) note the need for understanding resistance as a collective to understand its political and ideological significance. What we see in Protest.Net and Indymedia is an energized sector of civil society, one with lasting networks of activists who communicate about issues of social justice and continue to push for social change.

Conclusion: Communicating Through Solidarity

Any analysis of social movement success invariably must address questions of effectiveness. Evaluating the effectiveness of social movements, in general, and activist media, in particular, remains a difficult task. With the paucity of public opinion polls, scholars must rely on inexact measures to assess the impact of protests and other forms of activist communication. One may refer to the number of page views or "hits" for activist Web-sites, or the number of submissions to Protest.Net's calendar or Indymedia's newswire, but these numbers do not tell the whole story of the movement. Perhaps even asking for proof of movement success ignores the redemption and emancipation in the struggle itself. Such focus ignores the continuum of social politics evident in the postings to Protest.Net and Indymedia and transformations that may only be visible in the long term. Nevertheless, a meaningful account of the antiglobalization movement must account for its successes and failures as lessons for social movements. The movement's failures also point to its successes and indicate the potential for activist media to assume an important role in the sustenance of a faltering movement.

Fundamentally, antiglobalization activists have succeeded in enhancing the communication of social justice issues. Protest.Net and Indymedia enabled activists to make their struggle visual and bring the face of the movement to a global audience through the alternative media. This chapter points to future directions for scholars and activists. Scholars must continue to track mainstream media coverage of the global justice movement to evaluate the effectiveness of activist media spin. Global activists must continue to work hard to get their movement's message(s) out to the public—potential supporters as well as the opposition—and thus frame the debate about globalization in a way that gains favorable mainstream media coverage.

Notes

1. Some members of the movement object to the term *antiglobalization* because it portrays activists as against globalization and free trade in general. I use the term *antiglobalization* purposely, to highlight the primary reason that the movement is considered a failure: media framing. In some cases, I use the term *global justice* in reference to the movement's goals and causes.

2. Quoted descriptions taken from McKibben (2000, p. 13).

References

Ackerman, S. (2000, January/February). *Prattle in Seattle: WTO coverage misrepresented issues, protests.* Retrieved March 16, 2009, from www.fair.org/extra/0001/wto-prattle.html

Anderson, S., & Cavanagh, J. (2001, September). *What is the global justice movement? What does it want? Who is in it? What has it won?* Washington, DC: Institute of Policy Studies. Retrieved March 16, 2009, from www.ips-dc.org/projects/global_econ/movement.pdf

Appadurai, A. (2000). Grassroots globalization and the research imagination. *Public Culture, 12*(1), 1–19.

Ball-Rokeach, S. J., & Tallman, I. (1979). Social movements as moral confrontations: With special reference to civil rights. In M. Rokeach (Ed.), *Understanding human values: Individual and societal* (pp. 82–96). New York: Free Press.

Beiser, V. (2000, April 20). Moving toward a movement? *Mother Jones, March/April,* 13.

Best, K. (2005). Rethinking the globalization movement: Toward a cultural theory of contemporary democracy and communication. *Communication & Critical/Cultural Studies, 2*(3), 214–238.

Blustein, P. (2001, November 12). Protest group softens tone at WTO talks. *The Washington Post,* p. A1.

Brecher, J., Costello, T., & Smith, B. (2000). *Globalization from below: The power of solidarity.* Cambridge, MA: South End Press.

Carroll, W. K., & Hackett, R. A. (2006). Democratic media activism through the lens of social movement theory. *Media, Culture & Society, 28*(1), 83–104.

Cockburn, A., St. Clair, J., & Sekula, A. (2000). *Five days that shook the world: Seattle and beyond.* New York: Verso.

Countdown to chaos. (1999, December 5). *Seattle Times,* p. A6.

Danaher, K. (2000, June 26). *Between the lines Q&A.* Retrieved March 21, 2005, from www.btlonline.org/2000/danaher063000.html

Danaher, K., & Burbach, R. (2000). *Globalize this! The battle against the world trade organization and corporate rule.* Monroe, ME: Common Courage Press.

de Armond, P. (2000). Netwar in the emerald city: WTO protest strategy and tactics. In J. Arquilla & D. Ronfeldt (Eds.), *Networks and netwars: The future of terror, crime, and militancy* (pp. 201–238). Santa Monica, CA: RAND Corporation. Retrieved March 16, 2009, from http://nwcitizen.com/publicgood/reports/wto

DeLuca, K., & Peeples, J. (2002). From public sphere to public screen: Democracy, activism, and the "violence" of Seattle. *Critical Studies in Media Communication, 19*(2), 125–152.

Ganesh, S., Zoller, H., & Cheney, G. (2005). Transforming resistance, broadening our boundaries: Critical organizational communication meets globalization from below. *Communication Monographs, 72*(2), 169–192.

Getzan, C. (2004, June 8). Infamous "Miami model" of protest clampdown, coming to a town near you. *New Standard.* Retrieved April 21, 2009, from www.globalpolicy.org/ngos/advocacy/protest/2004/0608infame.htm

Gitlin, T. (1980). *The whole world is watching.* Berkeley: University of California Press.

Hart, A. (2004, June 10). At summit, police and delegations outnumber the demonstrators. *The New York Times,* p. A14.

Indymedia. (2007). About Indymedia. Retrieved January 8, 2007, from www.indymedia.org

Jack, I. (2003, September 11). Bloodshed mars Cancun WTO summit. *Financial Post.* Retrieved April 21, 2009, from http://newsmine.org/content.php?ol=cabal-elite/globalization/wto/sept-2003/bloodshet-mars-cancun-summit.txt

Karliner, J. (1997). *The corporate planet: Ecology and politics in the age of globalization.* San Francisco: Sierra Club Books.

Klein, N. (2000, July 10). The vision thing. *The Nation.* Retrieved April 21, 2009, from www.thenation.com/doc/20000710/klein

Lakey, G. (2000, August). Mass direct action: Options to consider in developing the movement further. Retrieved April 21, 2009, from the Starhawk Web site: www.starhawk.org/activism/lakeyarticle.html

McKibben, B. (2000). Muggles in the ozone. *Mother Jones, March/April,* 13.

Prokosch, M., & Raymond, L. (2002). *The global activist's manual: Local ways to change the world.* New York: Thunder's Mouth Press/Nation Books.

Protest.Net. (2005a). *About Protest.Net.* Retrieved March 16, 2005, from http://protest.net/about_protest_net.html

Protest.Net. (2005b). *Activist's handbook.* Retrieved April 16, 2009, from www.protest.net/activists_handbook/

Ramsey, B. (2000, February 4). WTO protest message had some effect, survey finds. *Seattle Post-Intelligencer Reporter.* Retrieved April 21, 2009, from www.seattlepi.com/business/surv04.shtml

Reel, M., & Fernandez, M. (2002, September 29). Protesters' momentum weakens. *Washington Post,* p. C01.

Simao, P. (2004, June 8). G8 protests make little impact at summit start. Reuters. Retrieved April 21, 2009, www.globalpolicy.org/ngos/advocacy/protest/2004/0608impact.htm

Stanley, A., & Sanger, D. E. (2001). Italian protester is killed by police at Genoa meeting. *The New York Times,* pp. A1, A6.

Starhawk. (2002). *Webs of power: Notes from the global uprising.* Gabriola Island, British Columbia, Canada: New Society.

Tedeschi, B. (1998, September 2). Protest portal unites activists under one URL. *The New York Times.* Retrieved May 7, 2009, from www.nytimes.com/library/tech/98/09/cyber/articles/02protest.html

Thompson, G. (2003, September 14). WTO protests turn violent in Cancun. *The New York Times,* p. A1.

Todd, A. M. (2003). Global justice movement networks: New technology and the mobilization of civil society. *Controversia, 2*(2), 17–38.

Walton, A. (2004, June 9). G8 protest draws small crowd. Retrieved March 20, 2005, from the CNN Web site: http://afwalton.org/resume/g8/index.html

CHAPTER 32

The Global Turn of the Alternative Media Movement

Carlos Fontes

For the past 40 years, media activists throughout the world have produced different viewpoints from those of mainstream media, given voice to progressive civic groups, grassroots organizations, and social movements, forged democratic processes of communication, and organized across national boundaries to form an international alternative media movement. While this movement has had a palpable impact at a local level, where media have been used to educate, inform, and activate small groups and communities around specific issues, it has traditionally been unable to reach larger audiences or create a broader democratic and participatory system of communication.

In this chapter, I argue that Indymedia is a radically democratic network and that it represents a new global stage in the development of the alternative media movement. I start by contextualizing the discussion with a proposal that we conceptualize alternative media as a set of practices with common principles, varying in reach from the level of small groups to the global sphere. I continue with an overview of the precursors and development of Indymedia and then describe the radically democratic characteristics, functioning, and organization of Indymedia based on interviews with Indymedia activists, the analysis of documents, and my own participation in the Independent Media Center (IMC) movement.

Theorizing Alternative Media

Since the late 1960s, the alternative media literature has been marked by the introduction of various terms such as *guerrilla video, pirate TV, tactical media, advocacy video, community media, process video, video product, participatory media, popular video, radical media, citizens' media,* and, of course, *alternative media*. This array of terms—some of which have often been used interchangeably and without agreed-on meanings—emphasize different aspects of alternative media but also betray the difficulty that scholars have had in theorizing the panoply of alternative media practices, its goals, strategies, and impact on diverse sociopolitical contexts.

Traditionally alternative media theorists tend to fall into two main groups. The first group defines alternative media from a macrosocial perspective and focuses on their capacity for counterinformation in a struggle with the mainstream for the hearts and minds of citizenry (Schechter, 1991) as well as their role in building a counterhegemonic project of society. Spa (1979), for example, affirmed that it would be possible for video activists from grassroots organizations to replace the communicational power of the state and the big economic groups, while Getino (1985) argued that alternative media had to be conceptualized by their role in an "historical political project of development" (p. 34). By all historical accounts, alternative media have fallen short of these all-encompassing goals and because of that have been assumed to be a set of communication practices restricted to the level of small groups and communities. The literature on alternative media has an abundance of descriptions of local media experiences working with small groups of women, young people, rural workers, shantytown dwellers, and so on.

The second group of theorists focus their analysis on the way alternative media practices change subjectivities and everyday social relations in community settings and argue that the wider impact of alternative media can be detected cumulatively over time in the strengthening of grassroots organizations and the struggles of local communities. John Downing (2001), for example, asserts that alternative media build grassroots solidarities and contribute to social "eddies and ferments" in a "slow burn" fashion and that sometimes they simply "keep alive the vision of what might be, for a time in history when it might actually be feasible" (p. 9).

In a similar line of reasoning, Rodriguez (2001) invites us to focus on the ways in which the use of media by common citizens can strengthen

democratic forces and proposes that we replace the term *alternative media* with the concept of "citizens'" media:

> Citizens' media implies first that a collectivity is *enacting* its citizenship by actively intervening and transforming the established mediascape; second, that these media are contesting social codes, legitimized identities, and institutionalized social relations; and third, that these communication practices are empowering the community involved, to the point where these transformations and changes are possible. (p. 20)

It is my contention that the exclusive focus on the local level and the analysis of alternative media that is restricted to community contexts eschews a theorization of the forms of organization, modes of operation, and roles that alternative media play in broader national and global contexts. It is not productive to theorize alternative media solely on the basis of their capacity to effect major social changes or challenge, reform, or replace mainstream media, because such analysis lead to defeatist conclusions and overlooks the real tangible impact alternative media practices have on the social, political, and cultural fabric of communities. However, alternative media scholars do need to pay attention to the ways in which alternative media might "challenge, at least implicitly actual concentrations of media power" (Couldry & Curran, 2003, p. 7). The failure to do so will limit the ability of alternative media theory to inform broader media practices in any relevant manner and understand the significance of key events within the context of prospective views of a different media landscape.

I propose that alternative media theory move beyond the micro–macro dichotomy and view alternative media as a broad spectrum of practices with a set of common principles that are expressed to different degrees in small group settings, communities, specific public spheres, social movements, and larger national and global arenas. This view may lead us to overcome the dichotomy of microperspectives and macroperspectives and focus instead on the interrelations, breaks, and continuities between alternative media practices taking place at various levels in a given conjuncture.

Common Principles and Levels of Alternative Media

It is beyond the focus of this paper to discuss these various levels and common principles. I would submit, however, that there is a consensus in the alternative media literature (a) that access to technology and participation in media production are central tenets of alternative media practice; (b) that the pursuit of democratic social relations of media production and decision making regarding its use is, in the majority of cases, as important as the content produced; (c) that alternative media focus on issues and perspectives neglected by the mainstream (Atton, 2002); (d) that, at the core, alternative media practices are steeped in an ethic of social solidarity and resistance to oppression; and (e) that unlike their commercial counterparts, alternative media have a not-for-profit orientation. A number of writers (Kawaja, 1994; Protz, 1991; Rodriguez, 1994) have clearly demonstrated that media are often used in small groups to build individual and collective identities, as a tool of consciousness-raising and as a stepping-stone toward political activism.

From a community lens, alternative media appear as a small scale form of communication operating within the bounds of a small geographical area or as a means of bringing people with similar interests—but dispersed geographically—together in a virtual manner, as in the case of Zines (Duncombe, 1997) and the Internet (Jordan, 2002). One of the key goals of street television all over the world is to build a community by bringing people into public spaces and engaging them in critical discussions about issues. At a community level, alternative media are used to represent the community to itself, to

inform, educate, and organize the community, and to develop common identities and shared purposes. Alternative media are also used strategically to project the message and image of a community outside itself into a specific public sphere as part of a campaign to achieve a predetermined set of goals (Fontes, 1996). Building on Rodriguez's (2001) concept of citizens' media, Rennie (2006) sees community media as a privileged means for the development of citizens' discourse and the civic engagement necessary for the existence of a functioning civil society.

If we shift our analysis to the next social level, we see that media activists within social movements often use media not only to communicate with their constituencies but also to effect the development of the movement as a whole. Atton (2002), in his study of alternative media and the environmental movement in England, found that the environmental press reflected the organizational structure of the environmental movement, "involved individuals and groups in reflexive practice," and "empowered activists in their communities of resistance" (p. 102).

The experience of the group Damned Interfering Video Artists, or Diva TV, is also illustrative of how a social movement can use media to effect its own development. Diva TV emerged in New York City in 1987 as part of ACT UP's (AIDS Coalition to Unleash Power) struggle against AIDS. As G. Borowitz (personal communication, October 20, 1994), one of the original founders, recounted, Diva TV started out by simply recording ACT UP's events for the purpose of documenting and lessening police brutality and creating a video archive of the movement.

As time passed, the core group of roughly 20 video activists inside ACT UP became more highly coordinated and began to use video more purposefully to affect ACT UP's activities, discourses, and mode of organization. After each public event, the still raw or roughly cut video recording would be passed around among the participants and shown at meetings. This, as Borowitz (personal communication, October 20, 1994) noted, made the members of ACT UP take the movement seriously and also led a large group inside the organization to develop a collective sense of self and "self-conscious strategic thinking" that eventually sharpened the organization's identity, goals, and sense of purpose. Media are usually used within a social movement to reflect the social movement back to itself, to identify and develop leadership, as a means of communication between the members of a social movement, and to inform other sectors of society of the movement's goals and activities.

The advent of Indymedia has pushed alternative media beyond the levels of small groups, local communities, and social movements onto a global arena. In the remainder of this chapter, I argue that despite its size and geographical dispersion throughout the world, the Indymedia network is organized according to the fundamental participatory principles of alternative media present in smaller-scale experiences and that Indymedia represents the first global alternative medium.

Indymedia: Overview

The first IMC in Seattle was set up from scratch in a donated space in just a few days, by local techies who in turn were supported by Rob Glaser, a former Microsoft executive who contributed technical expertise and the latest streaming technologies (Kidd, 2003), and also online by Mathew Arnison in Australia. Arnison, along with Gabrielle Kuipper, created Active, the open-code software used to set up the first Indymedia site and many other subsequent sites. According to J. Sands, a longtime Global IMC activist and a member of Indymedia Philadelphia, the creation of Indymedia

> was a coming together of technology, political will and an emerging global movement for social justice inspired by the Zapatista Encuentro. The idea that we could do anything global was new and we had the communications infrastructure that made this

organization possible. So Indymedia emerged as a model of a global organizing network. (personal communication, February 18, 2008)

By November 30, 1999, the Indymedia site was getting 2 million hits and being featured on CNN, America Online, BBC online, and many other sites. According to Norman Stockwell, a longtime Indymedia activist and operations manager for Madison's WORT radio, the reason for this sudden notoriety was that Indymedia reporters were telling stories from the protesters' perspectives and showing the rubber bullets on the streets at the same time that most mainstream media were reporting the official line that no such bullets were being used N. Stockwell (personal communication, July 1, 2003).

Since then, the number of IMCs have grown rapidly and unexpectedly throughout the world—more than 150 at the time of this writing—in close connection with the peace and antiglobalization movements. One of these sites (www.indymedia.org) is the global site of the Indymedia network, and it features articles drawn from IMCs throughout the network. While the biggest concentration of IMC locals is in the United States and Europe, there are a significant number of local centers in Latin America, Africa, the Middle East, Asia, and the Pacific region. There are also regional IMCs, such as those for the United States, Oceania, and Estrecho/Madiaq (for the Spanish and Moroccan areas around the Strait of Gibraltar). The network also has other centers, such as Biotech, Climate, Video, Radio, Publishing, and Satellite, that are organized around a topic and don't reflect a geographical area. Each local center functions autonomously with its own mode of organization and connection with other local or nonlocal affinity groups; but all centers are connected through hyperlinks. While the Satellite Center, for example, is linked with the European NewsREEL, the Video Center is connected to a large number of nonprofit organizations producing and distributing videos throughout the world.

The network as a whole is guided by a philosophy of solidarity and a set of shared principles of unity, affirming nonhierarchical relationships, democratic decision making, inclusion, open access, and participation in the production of content. Each local center is staffed by volunteer grassroots reporters and technicians, who provide the news and maintain the digital infrastructure of each center and the network as a whole. IMC locals with a critical number of activists are usually organized in working subgroups for each medium or function, such as video, print, or tech. Each of these subgroups may have their own listserves and hold their own meetings, but they also participate in the larger meetings and listserves of the local (Halleck, 2002). Some locals have their own physical meeting space (or share space with kindred organizations), while others, such as the Western Massachusetts IMC to which I belong, meet wherever it is possible. Each IMC Web site has variations in color, type of banners, and style, but they all share a common structure that includes the Indymedia network logo, a newswire on the right hand column constituted by self-published articles, and a link to a self-publishing page supporting print, audio, photo, and video files, a center section of news features selected from the newswire postings by volunteer editors, and a left or bottom column with links to all other IMCs in the network and to archived material, discussion lists, and other backstage areas of the Indymedia process. Many sites have sections or links to local organizations and a calendar page publicizing local events. A few local centers also produce their own hard-copy newspapers, wall postings, and radio programs.

Since its inception in 1999, the IMC network has been part of a larger collaborative web of alternative media organizations that exchange programming, resources, and technical expertise. During its first days in Seattle, the IMC produced videos that were shown by Deep Dish TV and Free Speech TV over satellite and Web radio programs that were retransmitted on many low-power and community radio stations (Halleck, 2002). This collaboration has taken different forms over time: "In some places, Indymedia has fostered the emergence of other alternative media, while in other communities it became part of an already established web of alternative radio and newspapers" (N. Stockwell, personal communication, July 1, 2003).

Indymedia: Radical Democracy

At its core, Indymedia is organized as a nonhierarchical, all-channel open network, in which every node or local is able to communicate directly and autonomously with any other node in the network. Each local is itself a smaller network of people connected through face-to-face meetings and also through listserves and Internet Relay Chats (IRC)—real-time text-based discussion rooms in cyberspace. Some IMCs—such as the Brazil IMC and the Italy IMC—are constituted by smaller, independent groups of IMC activists located throughout the country, who post on a common Web site. Some IMCs also form loose regional associations, such as those from Europe, Latin America, and the Southern Cone. The hardware infrastructure of the network is composed of a number of computer servers, each hosting several IMC sites. IMC activists are trying to train more technical people and increase the number of servers to further decentralize the infrastructure.

The network is also bonded by a set of shared principles of unity (https://dev.docs.indymedia.org/Global/PrinciplesOfUnity) adopted in 2001. These principles set forth a common vision based on equality, social diversity, decentralization, local autonomy, open publishing and access to information, use of open-source code, democratic process and consensus decision making, and being not-for-profit. The whole network is coordinated at the local and global levels by a dense but decentralized communication process. This includes between 500 and 600 active listservs addressing a large number of issues, projects, common interests and subgroups within the network, about one million messages exchanged weekly across the network, tens of IRC chat rooms open at any given time bringing together people from throughout the network, face-to-face regional gatherings, and strong interpersonal relationships. The network is also sustained by more than 16 global working groups, at the time of this writing (e.g., video, audio, IMC process, tech, finance, legal, translation), focused on global projects and global issues pertaining to functioning of the network as a whole. These can be seen at https:// dev .docs.indymedia.org/Global/WebHomeWG# Global_Features.

The network is also held together by exchanges of resources and technical expertise between the South and the North, exchanges between sister IMCs, and social relations based on trust, solidarity, inclusion, and open process:

> The commitment to function in a democratic participatory manner is part of the ideological ethic and the very fabric of Indymedia. Ideologically, Indymedia is about open process, democratic process, collective and consultative process. But this is more than an ideological commitment. It is also a commitment that is felt deep down. People do feel that way and respond viscerally to any attempts to redirect from that democratic process. This is the reality factor that keeps the network healthy. (N. Stockwell, personal communication, July 11, 2003)

Radical Democracy at a Global Level

In 2002, Argentina IMC, with the tacit support of other Latin American locals, blocked a decision for the network to accept a grant from the Ford Foundation, which would have enabled Indymedia members from all over the world to come together in an international conference to reflect on the nature of the network and discuss future steps for its development. The inability to reach a consensus around such an important global issue and the fact that the interpretation of

the principles of unity continue to be an object of discussion and have not yet been ratified by the global network as a whole led Pickard (2006) to argue that Indymedia is facing serious difficulties in functioning effectively as a radically democratic organization on a large global scale. Moreover Pickard argues that this breakdown in consensus has set the network into a crisis and casts doubt over the possibility of its long-term survival as a radically democratic organization.

Even though Indymedia has indeed been strained by the lack of consensus on this important issue, this does not necessarily mean that the organization is unable to function in a radically democratic fashion on a large scale. In fact, the continued functioning of Indymedia shows that when it is imperative to deal with practical matters with clear parameters and deadlines, such as organizing new IMCs getting servers back on line, or dealing with legal matters, the global working groups responsible for those areas continue to use the consensus process to make decisions and move things forward. J. Sands notes incisively that, over the years, the network has developed organically and that the failure to reach a consensus on accepting a grant from the Ford Foundation could be seen just as well as a case of consensus decision making working as it should, because "taking the grant and then having the meeting could have pushed the network to make great political decisions at a time when it was not yet ready to do so, and torn it apart" (personal communication, February 18, 2008). The organic unfolding of Indymedia is exemplified historically by the development of the principles of unity. Until 2000, new IMCs approached the global tech group to become a part of the network because the tech group had the expertise to make that happen on a technical level. Realizing that their decisions were affecting the network as a whole, the tech group stopped adding collectives to the network and asked the Indymedia community to create a set of guidelines to direct their own development. This process culminated in the development of the principles of unity.

My own research—based on interviews with a number of long-time Indymedia activists and the analysis of various global and local documents—indicates that Indymedia has a sophisticated participatory structure of decision making that balances agility with shared power on a large scale. This structure is anchored on four participatory processes that articulate local IMCs and global working groups.

The first process consists of working groups empowered by and accountable to local centers. Local centers participate in decisions affecting the whole network by having one or more of their members as liaisons to global meetings, groups, or processes. A liaison is a member of a local center who also participates in a global group, meeting, or process. The function of the liaison is to relay information back and forth between the local IMC and the global group. The liaison takes critical information discussed in a global group back to the local, facilitates discussion and consensus decision making about that issue at the local level, and then relays that decision back to the global level. In this way, global groups are empowered to make decisions based on the collective will generated at the local level. The editorial group charged with working on the editorial policy for the global site is an example of this first form of decision making.

The second process of decision making is put into effect by semiautonomous global groups that also have liaisons but are empowered by the local centers to make some decisions without consultation with the local level. An example of this is the Finance working group, which is allowed to disburse small amounts of money at its own discretion but has to consult the locals for the allocation of larger sums. The semiautonomous groups are accountable for all their actions to the local IMCs.

Some global decisions are also made via a third process by subworking groups that do not have local liaisons but are accountable to larger global working groups with local liaisons. The Donate working group, a subgroup of finance, makes some decisions regarding funds contributed to the network without having to directly consult with the locals. While the Donate group was not empowered to make a networkwide decision in the case of the Ford Foundation grant, it has been empowered in the past to make decisions about less significant contributions.

The fourth process of decision making is through empowered working groups without local liaisons who have the trust of the majority of Indymedia activists to make decisions without consultation with the local level. The tech and new IMC working groups are examples of this last form of decision making. These processes are still evolving and are not perfectly or even consistently implemented, but they constitute a radically democratic structure of decision making on a large scale, which balances widespread participation and consensus at the local level with agile decision making on a global level.

The radically democratic organization of Indymedia is also maintained through transparency, the use of open and free source code, autonomy of each collective, organic development of the democratic process, shared resources, and the use of multiple languages. All the decisions, documents, e-mail discussions, and work proceedings developed throughout the network are archived and open to anybody with access to the Internet. This degree of transparency enables and invites people to participate on an equal footing in any area of the network. Whenever possible, Indymedia activists use open and free source code software, because it can be designed collaboratively, used freely, and tailored to serve the particular needs of each center. Unlike proprietary software, open-source code allows multiple autonomous expressions through its various versions. Local autonomy is a crucial principle of democratic functioning because it maintains decision making at a local level and contradicts any movement toward centralization of the network. Besides the requirement to abide by the principles of unity, each IMC collective has the freedom to organize itself and link up with any other organization as it sees fit.

Resource sharing is also a fundamental tenet of democracy. The idea that asymmetry of resources can lead to asymmetric relations of power has been openly discussed within the network and has led on several occasions to the allocation of money and equipment to centers with the most difficult access to resources and to the free exchange of technical expertise between locals from the South and the North. Indymedia activists engage in these exchanges with an explicit awareness and determination to avoid reproducing colonial relationships and maintain egalitarian power within the network.

Even though English is the dominant language, Indymedia strives to exist as a multilingual environment. The translation working group does simultaneous translations of IRC meetings into the languages of those attending them and also translates some news and important documents into several languages posted on the global site. The effort to communicate in a multilingual environment runs counter to the hegemony of the English language on the planet and reveals a commitment on the part of activists to share power at the various levels of the network.

Indymedia: A Latent Global Alternative Medium

Despite any strains it may be facing as a radical democratic organization, Indymedia continues to be grounded in a nonhierarchical, decentralized infrastructure that allows the news network domain to maintain strict adherence to open publishing and the principles of access and participation at work in alternative media functioning at a smaller scale. This does not mean that there is universal agreement among all locals on how to implement open publishing. The issue of whether editors are empowered to delete certain posts has been an object of perennial discussion in the network. Each local center has its own editorial policy with varying levels of elaboration that guide the procedure to hide or delete spam and other offensive material, such as child pornography or Nazi propaganda. The editorial policy of the

Worcester IMC provides an example of a thoughtful policy that preserves the spirit and the letter of open publishing and maintains the site as a community space, and a safe environment for users, especially the members of disempowered or marginalized groups (http://worcester.indymedia.org/about). In spite of these differences, as J. Sands emphatically asserts,

> there is a basic strong consensus in the network that if there is not an open element in a local site, then it is not an Indymedia site. It could have the IMC logo and be making decisions by consensus, but if you wouldn't have an open publishing component, then it would not be an IMC site. Every site has to have a moment of open publishing. (personal communication, February 18, 2008)

A Latent Global Medium

In recent years, Indymedia has undergone a number of changes. As long-standing activists "have moved on to new media projects" (G. Rodriguez, personal communication, February 3, 2008), some older locals in the United States and Latin America have become inactive or partly dismantled. At the same time, there has also been a resurgence of new locals, such as Kenya, Panama, Lancaster (Pennsylvania), or Estrecho/Madiaq. Indymedia has also seen a decrease of activity focused on maintaining the global network matched by an increase of activism on a local level that has resulted in a process of localization of the network and greater autonomy of local centers. As N. Stockwell notes, "Each local has become more self sustained and there is a lot of things that people now do in the locals without checking in with other people in the network" (personal communication, February 7, 2008). A number of centers, such as Worcester (Massachusetts) and Urbana–Champaign (Illinois), now share physical spaces and work collaboratively with other alternative media groups and progressive organizations toward social justice at a local level.

While these changes can be seen as a sign of crisis of the global network brought about by the difficulty to implement principles of radical democracy on a large scale, they are also most certainly the result of a natural ebb and flow between globalization and localization that is also being felt by the global justice movement as a whole. My conversations with Indymedia activists suggest that the network is in fact going through a period of renewal and a process of weaving connections with other alternative media and social justice groups at a local level. On the one hand, Indymedia activists are "accumulating a substantial organizing experience" on the ground, and on the other they are "refashioning the network infrastructure with new models of social networking functional in a Web 2.0 environment" (J. Sands, personal communication, February 18, 2008). The Alternatives Indymedia site currently being organized is an example of this new approach articulated in its mission statement:

> The goal of the Alternatives Indymedia [working title] is to open a vibrant, inspiring, and multilingual Indymedia site through which users will both share information about current efforts toward creating fundamental change and work collaboratively on projects to make change happen in their communities. (See www.openplans.org/projects/imc-alternatives/project-home)

Indymedia is certainly in a global ebb, but it is also being articulated at a local level with other alternative media organizations and grassroots movements. This expanded web might just be the right type of network to support a new global stride toward social change at the right historical moment in a foreseeable future.

Conclusion

The analysis of the short history of Indymedia shows a surge of activity at peak political moments such as the unfolding of the global antiwar movement. While it is currently undergoing a process of localization, Indymedia continues to exist as a participatory global medium and to maintain a radically democratic global network infrastructure that is partly latent but that can be fully activated by a mobilized social network at a time of historical need. The current level of local activism, the continual rise of new centers, and the maintenance of the global infrastructure as well as the development of an expanded social networking component indicate that Indymedia is in a process of active renewal and that it could in the future redirect its collective energy more effectively to a global purpose.

The emergence of Indymedia as a global, participatory alternative medium urges us to consider old questions from a new global perspective and to pose new questions and challenges to alternative media theory. How do we theorize participatory media practices from a global perspective, and what is the function of these practices in the wider landscapes of alternative and mainstream media? How are alternative media and social movements being articulated? What are the effects of this articulation on a local level and on a global scale? What are, and how can we detect, the interactions between alternative and mainstream media at the local, regional, and global levels? What are, and how can we track, the interactions between alternative media at different levels? What are the interactions between alternative media, the state and transnational entities? What are the frameworks to study the social, political, and cultural effects of alternative media in the short and long term? What forms of alternative media networks are emerging worldwide and how are they changing the concept of network? The global turn in the alternative media movement opens up the possibility for the production of daring scholarship with a prospective engagement with practice.

References

Atton, C. (2002). *Alternative media.* Thousand Oaks, CA: Sage.

Couldry, N., & Curran, J. (2003). The paradox of media power. In N. Couldry & J. Curran (Eds.), *Contesting media power* (pp. 3–16). New York: Rowman & Littlefield.

Downing, J. (2001). *Radical media: Rebellious social movements*. Thousand Oaks, CA: Sage.

Duncombe, S. (1997). *Zines and the politics of alternative culture*. New York: Verso.

Fontes, C. (1996). *Alternative video at crossroads*. Unpublished doctoral dissertation, University of Michigan, Ann Arbor.

Getino, O. (1985). La importancia del video en el desarollo nacional [Video's importance in national development]. In J. Tello (Ed.), *Video, cultural nacional y subdesarollo* [Video, national culture and underdevelopment] (pp. 23–35). Mexico City, Mexico: Filmoteca de la UNAM.

Halleck, D. (2002). *Hand-held visions: The impossible possibilities of community media*. New York: Fordham University Press.

Jordan, T. (2002). *Activism! Direct action, hacktivism, and the future of society*. London: Reaktion Books.

Kawaja, J. (1994). Process video: Self-reference and social change. In P. Riano (Ed.), *Women in grassroots communication* (pp. 131–148). Thousand Oaks, CA: Sage.

Kidd, D. (2003). Indymedia.org: A new communications commons. In M. McCaughey & M. D. Ayers (Eds.), *Cyberactivism* (pp. 47–69). New York: Routledge.

Pickard, V. W. (2006). United yet autonomous: Indymedia and the struggle to sustain a radical democratic network. *Media, Culture & Society, 28*(3), 315–336.

Protz, M. (1991). Distinguishing between alternative and participatory models of video production. In N. Thede & A. Ambrosi (Eds.), *Video the changing world* (pp. 31–39). Montreal, Ontario, Canada: Black Rose Books.

Rennie, E. (2006). *Community media: A global introduction*. Lanham, MD: Rowman & Littlefield.

Rodriguez, C. (1994). A process of identity deconstruction: Latin American women producing video stories. In P. Riano (Ed.), *Women in grassroots communication* (pp. 149–160). Thousand Oaks, CA: Sage.

Rodriguez, C. (2001). *Fissures in the mediascape*. Cresskill, NJ: Hampton Press.

Schechter, D. (1991). Distinguishing between alternative and participatory models of video production. In N. Thede & A. Ambrosi (Eds.), *Video the changing world* (pp. 31–39). Montreal, Ontario, Canada: Black Rose Books.

Spa, M. (1979). El trabajo teórico y la alternatives a los mass media [Theoretical labor and alternatives to the mass media]. In J. Vidal-Beneyto (Ed.), *Alternativas populares a las comunicaciones de masas* [Grassroots alternatives to the mass media] (pp. 63–82). Madrid, Spain: Centro de investigaciones sociológicas.

Index

About the Editor

Kevin Howley is an associate professor of media studies at DePauw University, Indiana. His research and teaching interests include the political economy of communication, cultural politics, and the relationship between media and social movements. He is author of *Community Media: People, Places, and Communication Technologies* (2005). His work has appeared in the *Journal of Radio Studies, Journalism: Theory, Practice, and Criticism, Television and New Media,* the *International Journal of Cultural Studies,* and *Social Movement Studies.* A contributing writer for *The Bloomington Alternative,* he continues to produce program material for community radio and public access television. His latest project, *Hard Times Come Again No More: A Tribute to Russell J. Compton* (2007), was featured on *Sprouts,* Pacifica Radio's weekly news magazine. He received his PhD from the Indiana University in 1997.

About the Contributors

Bernadette Barker-Plummer is an associate professor of media studies at the University of San Francisco, where she also directs the interdisciplinary minor in gender and sexualities studies. Her research interests are in media, social movements, and social change. Some of her work can be found in *Critical Studies in Mass Communication, Journalism and Mass Communication Quarterly, Feminist Media Studies,* and *Peace Review.* Her current research projects include a book-length study of the mediation of transgender politics through popular culture and (with Dorothy Kidd) a book project investigating social movement communication strategies in the context of transforming public spheres. She received her PhD in 1997 from the Annenberg School, University of Pennsylvania.

Rosalind Bresnahan is a coordinating editor of the journal *Latin American Perspectives,* for which she edited a special edition on Chile in 2003. She is retired from the Department of Communication Studies at California State University San Bernardino. Her interest in Chilean media began when she lived in Chile during the first 2 years of the Allende government and observed the key role of media in the political conflict preceding the 1973 military coup. In 1998, she began research on alternative media during the struggle to end the dictatorship and in the post-1990 transition to democracy. She has interviewed more than 100 alternative media producers and distributors from both periods as well as current policy makers. She received her MA in Latin American studies from Stanford University and her PhD in mass media and communication from Temple University.

Lynette Bondarchuk is a professional illustrator and designer and a founding member of the Edmonton Small Press Association (ESPA). She has freelanced in the commercial arts and the nonprofit, community-based arts sectors for many years and is the production editor for *On Spec,* an award-winning speculative fiction magazine. She has several years production, project management, and curatorial experience in both her freelance capacity and as the ESPA's artistic director and programming coordinator. As a community cultural development activist, she believes the arts to be vital tools for positive social change and argues that work initiated through the ESPA is historically vital to Canadian arts and culture. For 3 years, she was a jury member of the Community Investment Grant Review Subcommittee of the City of Edmonton Community Services Advisory Board (CSAB), and she remains an advocate for increased appreciation and funding toward all genres of social and community-based arts.

Philip Denning is one of Her Majesty's Inspectors of Education (HMIE) in Scotland. Prior to joining HMIE 5 years ago, he was CEO of the U.K. national training organization for community learning and development. He has extensive experience of both the strategic development and the practical delivery of education and regeneration programs. He is qualified at the master's level in education and cultural planning and is a director of community organizations and six social enterprises across the United Kingdom.

Tanja Dreher is an ARC (Australian Research Council) postdoctoral fellow in the Transforming Cultures Research Centre at University of Technology, Sydney, Australia. Her research explores news media and community conflict resolution with an emphasis on debates around whiteness, multiculturalism, and listening and around media, gender, and violence. Her previous research has focused on news and cultural diversity, community media interventions in western Sydney, experiences of racism, and the development of community antiracism strategies after September 11, 2001.

Charles Fairchild is a lecturer in popular music at the Sydney Conservatorium of Music, University of Sydney, New South Wales, Australia. He has written widely on the possibilities and realities of democratic media in *Media Culture and Society, Journal of Popular Music Studies, Southern Review, Canadian Journal of Communication,* and *Transformations.* He is the author of *Community Radio and Public Culture* (2001) and *Pop Idols and Pirates* (2008). He received his PhD from the Department of American Studies at the State University of New York at Buffalo.

Carlos Fontes is a professor of communication at Worcester State College, where he founded and now directs its Center for Global Studies. He has published and presented in the United States, Canada, Brazil, and Portugal on the general topic of alternative media. He worked for 3 years as a community media organizer in a social service agency in Western Massachusetts with at risk youth groups and mothers of sexually abused children. He is a longtime member of Western Massachusetts Indymedia and the original organizer of Worcester Indymedia. He is currently working on a documentary with the Sarayacu-a kichwa–speaking people from the Ecuadorian Amazon. He received his PhD from the Department of Communication at the University of Massachusetts Amherst and was a Fulbright Scholar in Portugal in 2003.

Ian Goodwin is currently a lecturer in the School of English and Media Studies, Massey University, Wellington, New Zealand. His research interests include new media studies, media and politics, media policy analysis, and media and community development. He is particularly interested in exploring the social shaping of new media technologies and in examining how virtual spaces interact with "real" places. He completed a PhD in cultural studies at the University of Birmingham, the United Kingdom, in 2003.

Gergely Gosztonyi, is a lawyer and media researcher. He teaches at the Faculty of Law, Eötvös Loránd University (ELTE), Budapest. He studied sociology and political science for 1 year in Finland and media law for a half a year in Denmark. His research field is alternative media and nonprofit broadcasting. Between 2000 and 2004, he was the office coordinator of the Hungarian Federation of Free Radios, and between 2005 and 2006, he was the managing director of Civil Radio. He graduated in 2003 at the Faculty of Law, ELTE Budapest.

María Victoria Guglietti is a part-time lecturer on social research methodologies and communication theory at Mount Royal College in Calgary, Alberta, Canada. She is also a PhD candidate in cultural mediations at the Institute for Comparative Studies in Literature, Art and Culture (ICSLAC), Carleton University. She is currently finalizing her dissertation on community imagination within the field of Canada-based Aboriginal new media art, a project for which she developed an interdisciplinary methodology that combines historical and discursive analysis of artists' works and curators' writings and interviews with Aboriginal new media artists, curators, and Canadian funding bodies. Her areas of interest are visual culture, community media practices, and the interdisciplinary study of cultural production.

Fiona Jeffries's research focuses on contemporary antienclosure movements and the circulation of dissident cultural practices. She is currently a postdoctoral fellow at the Center for Place, Culture and Politics at the City University of New York, where she is researching social movement practices of antifear amid the neoliberal enclosures. She completed her PhD in communication studies at Simon Fraser University in Vancouver, Canada.

Dorothy Kidd is Associate Professor of media studies at the University of San Francisco. Her research interests are in media and social change, political economy of media, and community and alternative media. She has also worked extensively in community radio and video production. Some of her recent research can be found in the *International Journal of Media and Cultural Politics, Development in Practice,* and the *Media Research Hub* of the Social Science Research Council.

Aku Kwamie is a health researcher with the International Development Research Centre in Ottawa, Canada. She has worked in community health settings in Ghana, Nigeria, Lesotho, and Toronto, Canada. She has also worked with the World Health Organization's Department of Chronic Disease and Health Promotion in Geneva, Switzerland. She holds an MSc in Biomedical Science Research from King's College, London.

Dandan Liu is an assistant professor at the University of North Carolina at Pembroke (UNCP), where she teaches public relations courses in the Department of Mass Communication. She served as a volunteer for the Philadelphia Chinatown Development Corporation (PCDC) for more than 3 years, helping with the publication of organizational media and planning community activities. Her research interests include news media and social movements, ethnic media, crisis communication, and instructional communication. She holds a PhD from Temple University.

Claudia Magallanes-Blanco is a professor and full-time researcher at the Universidad Iberoamericana Puebla in Mexico. She is the author of *The Use of Video for Political Consciousness-Raising in Mexico: An Analysis of Independent Videos About the Zapatistas* (2008). She received her PhD from the University of Western Sydney, Australia, where she worked at the Centre for Cultural Research.

George McKay is a professor of cultural studies at the University of Salford, United Kingdom. He is currently working on popular music and cultures

of disability. His books include *Circular Breathing: The Cultural Politics of Jazz in Britain* (2005), *Glastonbury: A Very English Fair* (2000), and *Senseless Acts of Beauty: Cultures of Resistance Since the Sixties* (1996). His edited collections include *Community Music: A Handbook* (with Pete Moser; 2005), *Issues in Americanisation and Culture* (with Neil Campbell and Jude Davies; 2004), and *DiY Culture: Party & Protest in Nineties Britain* (1998). He also coedits *Social Movement Studies: A Journal of Social, Cultural and Political Protest.*

Sascha D. Meinrath is the Director of the New America Foundation's Open Technology Initiative and Research Director of the Foundation's Wireless Future Program. He has been described as a "community Internet pioneer" and an "entrepreneurial visionary" and is a well-known expert on community wireless networks (CWNs), municipal broadband, and telecommunications policy. In 2009, he was named one of Ars Technica's Tech Policy "People to Watch." He is a cofounder of Measurement Lab, a distributed server platform for researchers around the world to deploy Internet measurement tools, advance network research, and empower the public with useful information about their broadband connections. He also coordinates the Open Source Wireless Coalition, a global partnership of open source wireless integrators, researchers, implementers, and companies dedicated to the development of open source, interoperable, and low-cost wireless technologies. He is a regular contributor to Government Technology's Digital Communities, the online portal and comprehensive information resource for the public sector. He has worked with Free Press, the Cooperative Association for Internet Data Analysis (CAIDA), the Acorn Active Media Foundation, the Ethos Group, and the CUWiN Foundation. He serves on the Leadership Committee of the CompTIA Education Foundation as well as the Advisory Councils for both the Knight Center of Digital Excellence and the Knight Commission on the Information Needs of Communities in a Democracy. He blogs regularly at www.saschameinrath.com.

Stefania Milan is a researcher at the European University Institute in Florence, Italy. She wrote her PhD dissertation on emancipatory communication practices seen through the lens of social movement studies. Her research interests include social movements, participatory approaches to public policy and governance, theory and practice of community/alternative/citizens' media, media and communication policy, communication, and information and communication technologies (ICTs) for development and social change. She teaches at the University of Luzern, Switzerland. She is an associate of the London-based Stanhope Centre for Communications Policy Research and a member of the Civil Society Media Policy Research Consortium. As a journalist, she has been working for print and Web-based media.

Sourayan Mookerjea, PhD, teaches sociology at the University of Alberta, Canada. His research addresses contradictions of Canadian cultural politics, immigration, multiculturalism, media and subaltern social movements, and the class politics of globalization. His current projects include *Canadian Cultural Studies: A Reader* (coedited with I. Szeman and G. Faurschou, 2009), *Our Multicultural Times* (forthcoming), and *Kolkata Wonderland: Urbanscapes of Outsourcing* (with G. Faurschou).

Mario Alfonso Murillo is an associate professor in the School of Communication at Hofstra University. An award-winning radio journalist and feature documentary producer, he has worked as a correspondent and producer in commercial, public, and community radio for the past 25 years. Throughout his professional career, he has focused considerable attention on Latin America and the Caribbean, as well as the Latino immigrant experience in the United States. He was a Fulbright Scholar in Colombia in 2008.

Nkosi Martin Ndlela is an associate professor of media studies at Hedmark University College in Norway. He has taught media and communication studies at universities in Zimbabwe and Norway. He has undertaken research on a number of themes relating to the media in Africa, including media and democracy, globalization, popular culture, development, and new technologies. He received his PhD from the University of Oslo, Norway.

Ondine Park is a PhD candidate in the Department of Sociology at the University of Alberta. She is interested in urban and cultural studies and is currently writing a dissertation on representations, desire, and the promise of the suburban good life. She is actively involved in community organizations, including having volunteered with and served on the boards of directors of the Edmonton Small Press Association and of *Our Voice: Edmonton's Street Magazine*. She also continues to be an active volunteer with the Edmonton chapter of Oxfam Canada and a contributing editor of *Take Zine* (a graduate students' zine, based out of the Department of Sociology at the University of Alberta), of both of which she was one of the founding members.

Vanessa Parlette is a doctoral candidate in geography and planning at the University of Toronto, Ontario, Canada. Her research and activism are focused on community mobilization for spatial and social justice in marginalized spaces and populations of the city, with particular emphasis on the suburbanization and racialization of poverty in Toronto's postwar suburbs. She is interested in exploring the potential for grassroots movements to confront negative media stigmatization of "at-risk" populations and to develop participatory democratic practices that facilitate citizen engagement and influence in the decision-making processes of urban planning in response to local and global influences of neoliberal governance.

Victor W. Pickard works on telecommunications policy in Washington, D.C., as a research fellow at the New America Foundation, a public policy think tank. His scholarship explores the intersections of United States and global media activism and politics, media history, democratic theory, and communications policy and has been published in a number of journals, including the *Journal of Communication; Global Media and*

Communication; Media, Culture & Society; New Media and Society; Journal of Communication Inquiry; International Journal of Communication Law and Policy; and *Critical Studies in Media Communication.* Currently he is working on a book on 1940s media policy and media reform. He holds a PhD from the Institute of Communications Research at the University of Illinois.

Mojca Planšak is an assistant director at Maska Institution in Ljubljana, Slovenia. She is also an assistant lecturer on media topics/radio at the University of Maribor, Media and Communication Studies. She is a journalist, media researcher, and received her MA in the area of comparative studies of ideas and cultures in Ljubljana, Slovenia, at the University of Nova Gorica. She is also a foundress and board member of the Community Media Forum Europe (www.cmfe.eu) and a foundress and member of the So0gledi group (http://www.soogledi .blogspot.com/).

Shayna Plaut has worked with human rights issues domestically and internationally for more than 10 years as an educator and activist. She designs and teaches human rights and media courses at Columbia College, Chicago; in addition, she currently serves as the Assistant Director of Employer Relations (focusing on careers in the nonprofit and public sector) at the University of Chicago. In 2003, she received a Fulbright Scholarship to Macedonia, where she focused on Romani media and social change. Most recently, she participated in an Amnesty International research mission (and drafting of the report) to document the human rights abuses and activism regarding Romani women in Macedonia. She has served as AIUSA's Macedonia country specialist since 2004. She received her BA from Antioch College and her MA from the University of Chicago and, in 2009, will begin a doctoral program at the University of British Columbia.

Rita L. Rahoi-Gilchrest started her career in public and commercial broadcasting. She has been a corporate communications consultant and manager,

also teaching at the University of Missouri-St. Louis, Winona State University, Bergen University in Norway and the University of Canterbury in New Zealand. She has published book chapters and journal articles in the areas of organizational communication, image restoration, viral marketing, and entertainment-education, earning numerous teaching awards for her classroom work. She received her PhD from Ohio University.

Matt Sienkiewicz is a graduate student in communication arts at the University of Wisconsin-Madison. His research focuses on independent media in Palestine, community media in the United States, and the representation of religion and ethnicity in popular culture. In addition to his scholarly work, he also works as a screenwriter and documentary producer. He was nominated for an Emmy Award for program writing for his work with Vermont Public Television.

Shawn Sobers is currently undertaking PhD research into community media education at the University of the West of England, Bristol, where he is also a senior lecturer in photography and media. He is a board member of the Community Media Association. He has worked in community media extensively since 1995. His roles have included Media & Community Education Officer for At-Bristol and Production Workshop Leader for ITV West. He cofounded Firstborn Creatives (FbC) in 1999 with Rob Mitchell. He has also directed for television, including *Unfinished Business* (2007, BBC1, FbC), *Under the Bridge* (2000, ITV West, FbC), and *Footsteps of the Emperor* (1999, ITV West) and assistant producer of *Eazy Riders* (1997, Channel 4, Black Pyramid Films). He has a first class BA (Honors) in film and photography from the University of Wales, Newport, and studied for an MA in anthropology of media at the School of Oriental and African Studies (SOAS). He writes about his experiences of working in community media at his blog—www.beyondproject.wordpress.com.

Anne Marie Todd is an associate professor of public communication in the Department of

Communication Studies at San Jose State University. Her published research on activists' use of new media includes articles on technological organization of global justice movements, anticorporate protest tactics, and MoveOn.org's political mobilization. She has also published in the area of environmental communication, including articles on green consumerism and environmental rhetoric in popular culture. She is currently researching climate change and conservation movements' mobilization. She received her PhD from the Annenberg School for Communication at the University of Southern California in 2002.

Otto Leopold Tremetzberger is cofounder and managing director of Free Radio Freistadt, a community radio station in Austria. He cocurated conferences at the Ars Electronica Festival in Linz, Austria, on the topics of freedom of information and communication, with a focus on the question of technology and media development. Currently, he is also a doctoral student at the Arts University of Linz and is working on the creation of a community TV channel together with Matrix e.V., a collective of researchers and media artists. He has published articles and essays on media policy and prose texts in literary journals. He graduated with a degree in theater studies, philosophy, and international arts and media management from the Universities of Vienna and Salzburg.

Elvira Truglia is a journalist and consultant in communication and development. For the past 4 years, she has been Project Director for "A Different World," a print- and Web-based multimedia educational resource on global issues developed for the Social Justice Committee, Montreal, Canada. She worked for the World Association of Community Radio Broadcasters (AMARC) as Public Education Programme Director from 1996 to 2002. She was the international coordinator of Radio Voix Sans Frontières (Radio Voices Without Frontiers) during 2000 to 2004. As a broadcaster, her sound stories have

been heard on CBC Radio (Canada's national public broadcaster) as well as various community and independent media networks. As a print and radio journalist, she has covered global social justice movements in Mexico, Italy, South Africa, and Brazil. She holds an MA in media studies from Concordia University in Montreal, Canada.

Pantelis Vatikiotis is a lecturer in the Department of Sociology at Panteion University of Social and Political Sciences in Athens, Greece. His teaching and research interests are in social theory and media, political communication and culture, sociology of cyberculture, new media, social movements, and alternative, grassroots media practices. He received his PhD in sociology of alternative media from the University of Westminster, London, in 2004.

Zala Volčič is a postdoctoral fellow at the Centre for Critical and Cultural Studies at the University of Queensland, Australia. She is interested in the cultural consequences of nationalism, capitalism, and globalization. She is currently working on a project titled "Mapping Commercial Nationalism." She has published numerous books and articles, including "Yugo-nostalgia: Cultural Memory and Media in the former Yugoslavia," in *Critical Studies of Mass Communication* (2007), "Technological developments in Central-Eastern Europe: A Case-Study of a Computer Literacy Project in Slovenia" (with Karmen Erjavec), in *Information, Communication & Society* (2008), and "Former Yugoslavia on the World Wide Web: Commercialization and Branding of Nation-States," in *International Communication Gazette* (2008).

Brian J. Woodman is currently working as an archivist for the Western Historical Manuscript Collection at the University of Missouri-St. Louis, and he is a collections consultant for the Kinsey Institute Library and Special Collections. He has previously published in the *Journal of Film and Video* and *The Journal of Popular Culture*. He received his PhD in film/media from the Department of Theatre and Film at the University of Kansas.

Supporting researchers for more than 40 years

Research methods have always been at the core of SAGE's publishing program. Founder Sara Miller McCune published SAGE's first methods book, *Public Policy Evaluation*, in 1970. Soon after, she launched the *Quantitative Applications in the Social Sciences* series—affectionately known as the "little green books."

Always at the forefront of developing and supporting new approaches in methods, SAGE published early groundbreaking texts and journals in the fields of qualitative methods and evaluation.

Today, more than 40 years and two million little green books later, SAGE continues to push the boundaries with a growing list of more than 1,200 research methods books, journals, and reference works across the social, behavioral, and health sciences. Its imprints—Pine Forge Press, home of innovative textbooks in sociology, and Corwin, publisher of PreK–12 resources for teachers and administrators—broaden SAGE's range of offerings in methods. SAGE further extended its impact in 2008 when it acquired CQ Press and its best-selling and highly respected political science research methods list.

From qualitative, quantitative, and mixed methods to evaluation, SAGE is the essential resource for academics and practitioners looking for the latest methods by leading scholars.

For more information, visit **www.sagepub.com**.